THE WAR WITH SPAIN
IN 1898

David F. Trask

University of Nebraska Press
Lincoln and London

⊗ The paper in this book meets the minimum requirements of American National Standard for Information Sciences—Permanence of Paper for Printed Library Materials, ANSI Z39.48-1984.

First Bison Books printing: 1996
Most recent printing indicated by the last digit below:
10   9   8   7   6   5   4   3   2

Library of Congress Cataloging-in-Publication Data
Trask, David F.
The war with Spain in 1898 / David F. Trask.
p.   cm.
Originally published: New York: Macmillan; London: Collier Macmillan, c1981.
ISBN 0-8032-9429-8 (pbk.: alk. paper)
1. Spanish-American War, 1898.   I. Title.
E715.T7   1997
973.8'9—dc20
96-21710   CIP

Contents

Maps

Preface

The War with Spain in 1898 has not received as much scholarly attention as most other American struggles. In 1911 Rear Admiral French Ensor Chadwick, veteran of the naval battle off Santiago de Cuba in 1898, published the only important general history of the conflict, a two-volume work entitled *The Spanish-American War*. Chadwick concentrated on military and naval events, but devoted more than passing attention to political developments. More recent treatments, including the well-known book by Walter Millis entitled *The Martial Spirit* (1931), do not add measurably to Chadwick's findings. It is not difficult to divine the reasons for this paucity. The War with Spain lasted for but a few months. It has seemed to offer far less of interest to historians than earlier American wars, such as the Revolution or the Civil War, or later ones, particularly the two world wars.

Those scholars who returned to the 1898 conflict usually chose to examine its causes or consequences rather than its conduct. The reasons why the War with Spain occurred and the changes that took place in its aftermath appeared to be more important than the course of the battles. Scholars interested in the causes of the war debated certain intriguing questions, among them whether the war could have been avoided and whether imperialistic motives had brought it on. Those who examined the war's consequences advanced various interpretations of America's new role in world politics following the victory of 1898.

In recent years, however, historians have begun to evaluate the war anew in all its aspects, including its conduct, seeking improved descriptions and explanations of an event generally recognized as one of the most important turning points in the national experience, a conflict that thrust the United States into the maelstrom of world politics. A place exists now for a new study of the war that gives due attention to its conduct during the spring and summer of 1898. This subject is itself of considerable importance, and those primarily interested in what occurred before and after will benefit from an improved understanding of the conflict itself.

In keeping with the general intent of the Macmillan Wars of the United States series, the present volume offers a modern synthesis of its subject. Although owing much to the pioneering efforts of Admiral Chadwick, it makes use of considerable information not available in 1911, and has benefited from the transformed perspective of eighty years. Two aspects of the presentation deserve mention:

1. It is "international history" because it examines the activities of all the protagonists—Spain, Cuba, Puerto Rico, the Philippines, and the United States, as well as certain concerned neutrals—and strives to avoid national bias.

2. It combines military and political history, and is therefore neither one nor the other: It can be called "military-political history." This approach is a response to the truism that war is a continuation of politics by other means, an attempt to force a given political settlement by the exercise of force rather than peaceful methods. At the very center of the present work is an extensive discussion of the relation between force and diplomacy during the War with Spain. On the military side strategy is emphasized as well as tactics and logistics. On the political side are examined both domestic and foreign influences on the decisions of the contending governments and dependencies.

Certain interpretations herein depart from generally accepted views. For example, the widespread belief that the United States Army performed badly in 1898—a view to which Millis gave spurious currency in *The Martial Spirit*—does not survive a close look. Neither does the thesis that the United States attacked the Philippines in order to acquire it, a legend perpetuated in recent years by a goodly number of historians. President McKinley emerges as a serious strategist who effectively related the use of force to the achievement of larger political goals. The Naval War Board—later dismissed as of little consequence by one of its members, Captain Alfred Thayer Mahan—turns out to have influenced events notably: Among other things it administered an effective intelligence network. A little-known Spanish initiative, the voyage of Admiral Cámara in relief of Manila after Commodore Dewey's victory, exercised considerable influence on American decisions during the summer of 1898. And students of the causes and consequences of the war may be interested in the author's view that President McKinley strove mightily to avoid the break with Spain and was most reluctant to support annexation of the Philippine Islands.

This book is based principally on published sources and authorities and has taken full advantage of numerous recent studies, although unpublished information has been used to illuminate certain subjects not treated fully in extant secondary accounts. Extensive annotations and a "Note on Sources and Authorities" in the back of the book identify these contributions. Of modern authorities the works of greatest utility are those of Graham A. Cosmas, Ernest R. May, and Ronald Spector.

Many friends and colleagues contributed in various ways to this study, among them Robert H. Ferrell, John A. S. Grenville, Milton O. Gustafson, Franklin Knight, Clara Lida, Ernest R. May, David Pletcher, John W. Pratt, Bernard Semmel, Iris Zavala, and the late Louis Morton. I would also like to thank Barbara Chernow and William Martin of The Free Press for helpful editorial advice.

Certain libraries and archives proved most helpful, among them the Library of Congress and the National Archives in Washington, D.C.; the Archivo Histórico Nacional, the Biblioteca Nacional, and the Museo Naval in Madrid; the Public Record Office and the British Museum in London; the Melville Library of the State University of New York at Stony Brook; the Archives of the Naval War College in Newport, Rhode Island; the United States Army Military History Institute at Carlisle Barracks, Pennsylvania; and the New York City Public Library. Special acknowledgement is due to the Research Foundation of the State University of New York and to the State University Center of SUNY at Stony Brook for many forms of assistance. Sandra Perry typed the manuscript expertly. Once again Elizabeth Brooks Trask lent indispensable advice and support.

The author, who alone is responsible for this book's content, wishes to acknowledge the lasting influence of three historians who guided his early studies—Samuel Hugh Brockunier of Wesleyan University, Ernest R. May of Harvard University, and Carl E. Schorske of Princeton University.

DAVID F. TRASK
Washington, D.C.

Introduction

In the early evening of February 15, 1898, the United States Battleship *Maine* lay quietly at anchor in the harbor of Havana, Cuba. Captain Charles D. Sigsbee sat tranquilly in his cabin, writing letters about the experiences of his command in troubled Cuba. A seasoned veteran—he had served during the Civil War at Mobile under Admiral David Farragut—Sigsbee was fully qualified to direct a capital ship assigned hazardous duty, and surely the *Maine* was in a dangerous situation. For three years Cuba had been the scene of an insurrection, and the United States had become deeply interested in the struggle between the Cuban *insurrectos* and the Spanish garrison. The *Maine* had been ordered to Havana late in January, 1898 to protect American citizens in the city after riots there posed the possibility of serious trouble. Then, a fortnight after the *Maine* arrived in Havana, relations between Spain and the United States had suffered a severe blow: An American newspaper had published an indiscreet letter written by the Spanish minister, Enrique Dupuy de Lôme, highly critical of President William McKinley. Sensing danger around him, Sigsbee had prohibited unescorted visitations to his ship, and posted sentries on deck. Boxes of ammunition had been placed near the one- and six-pound guns.[1]

Suddenly, at 9:40 P.M., a massive explosion shook the *Maine*. The blast occurred within the forward section of the ship near the living quarters of the enlisted men. It sank the ship almost immediately. Of the 354 officers and men aboard the *Maine*, 266 were killed and many others suffered grievous injury.

Captain Sigsbee's first command after the explosion had been to prepare to repel boarders. This indicates that he incorrectly construed the explosion as coming from an external source, a tragic error.[2]

What caused the disaster? Captain Sigsbee's initial report counseled suspension of judgment, but most Americans immediately jumped to the conclusion that the Spanish had committed the crime. Soon Sigsbee inclined to the theory that, before the *Maine* had moored in Havana Harbor, a mine had been placed beneath the berth assigned the ship. Secretary of the Navy John D. Long's reaction was to attribute the accident to an internal explosion, but a much more typical view came from Captain Sherman Vanaman, master of a merchantman (the schooner *Philadelphia*), who had been in Havana harbor on the night of the explosion. He was convinced that a torpedo launched against the *Maine*, presumably by the Spanish, had caused the ship to sink. "If the U.S. don't fight over this," he trumpeted, "the whole country ought to be blown up." The Spanish government had immediately expressed shock and sympathy, but nothing sufficed to dissipate the tidal wave of public anger that swept the United States and led overnight to demands for American intervention in Cuba.[3]

Former Secretary of State Richard Olney wrote to ex-President Grover Cleveland only four days after the catastrophe, "The Dupuy episode and the Havana explosion have furnished more material for the inflammation of popular passions against Spain than all that has happened during the past three years." This estimate has withstood the test of time. A careful contemporary student of the American public's outburst, Ernest R. May, notes that when the Cuban insurrection began in 1895 only a few people had concerned themselves with it. It became a consuming issue only after the destruction of the *Maine*. Thereafter "neighborhoods, suburbs, small towns, and rural communities simply caught fire. No section, no type of community, no occupational group was immune." Before February 15, 1898, no great national movement in the United States had materialized in support of Cuban independence, despite the perfervid journalism of certain newspapers; no unified sentiment governed the national constituency. After February 15, popular insistence on immediate action—including, if necessary, war against Spain—became manifest instantly, and it grew by leaps and bounds in succeeding days and weeks. "Yellow journals" only rode the wave of feeling; they did not create it.[4]

Despite the extraordinary outpouring of public emotion, President McKinley reacted in measured terms. He told Senator Charles W. Fairbanks (Republican of Indiana) that he had no intention of being swept off his feet. "My duty is plain," he contended. "We must learn the truth and endeavor, if possible, to fix the responsibility. The country can afford to withhold its judgment and not strike an avenging blow until the truth is known." In the interim he would prepare for possible hostilities while working for peace; the Administration would not be "plunged into war until it is ready for it." A close associate of the President, Charles G. Dawes, reported exactly the same impression of McKinley, noting that he "has withstood all efforts to impede him. He will endeavor in every possible way consistent with honor to avoid war. If war comes, the people will be united behind him."[5]

For the moment the President awaited the report of a naval board of inquiry appointed to ascertain the cause of the disaster. Captain William T. Sampson and his associates on the board had begun their labors on February 21, 1898. If nothing else, the period required for the completion of Captain Sampson's inquiry might cool passions. Spain had proposed a joint investigation, but this suggestion received no support whatever in Washington; the Department of the Navy believed that the inflamed public would not accept the report of such a panel. Spanish historians quite naturally have inclined to the view that the United States opposed a joint investigation because it would have forced acknowledgment that Spain had no hand in the disaster. Whatever the reason, the American position led to separate inquiries.[6]

The destruction of the *Maine* greatly prejudiced attempts to find a peaceful settlement of the Cuban insurrection against Spain, master of the island for some four centuries. It stimulated an American diplomatic campaign to force a grant of independence for Cuba. When, two months later, the Spanish government definitively rejected freedom for Cuba, the United States faced the most excruciating of all political decisions—the choice between peace and war.

☆ ONE ☆

Origins of the War with Spain

On February 25, 1895, a group of dissidents in eastern Cuba uttered the *grito de Baíre* ("cry of Baíre") to signal the start of an armed uprising against Spanish authority. Soon thereafter hostilities commenced, and Spain proved unable to put down the rebellion. As time passed, two Presidents of the United States, the Democrat Grover Cleveland and the Republican William McKinley, became increasingly preoccupied with Cuban matters. Partisans of *Cuba libre* persevered through many months and years of guerrilla warfare, keeping alive the dream of independence, and events ultimately played into their hands.

An earlier rebellion in Cuba, known as the Ten Years' War, had ended in 1878 with acceptance of the Treaty of Zanjón, a settlement that preserved Spain's sovereignty in the island. This agreement provided for reforms intended to benefit disaffected Cubans, but permanent improvements did not materialize, largely because the arrangements did not resolve certain economic problems. Cuba's main product was sugar, and its principal market was the United States. Lying primarily within the trading area of the northern republic rather than that of Spain, the island's economic well-being depended heavily on the terms of trade with its neighbor. In 1894, when the United States Congress levied a tariff of 40 percent on sugar imports, American demand for the product declined, and a notable disruption occurred in the Cuban economy. The economic shock waves helped revitalize the quest for independence from Spain.[1]

1

THE CUBAN INSURRECTION

The *grito de Baíre* issued from partisans of the Cuban poet and patriot José Martí, who for many years had devoted himself to achieving Cuban independence by organizing a revolutionary movement among emigrés in the United States and various Latin American countries. The center of revolutionary sentiment lay in Florida, where Cuban cigar makers formed no less than sixty-one *juntas,* or clubs. Each member was expected to contribute a tenth of his earnings to the cause of independence. Early in 1892 about two thousand Cubans in such organizations became members of the *Partido revolucionario cubano*—the Cuban Revolutionary Party—destined to become the political arm of the movement to achieve independence through armed action. In New York Tomas Estrada Palma, former President of the Cuban Republic during the Ten Years' War and veteran of many years in Spanish jails, coordinated these revolutionary activities. Although the New York *junta* never accumulated much capital or eliminated dissension in its own ranks, it made an important contribution to Cuban independence. It gradually gained considerable support from two influential groups in the United States—labor unions and the press.[2]

Martí labored mightily to correct a major defect that had compromised the Cuban cause during the Ten Years' War—poor coordination between supporters outside Cuba and armed forces within the island. To accomplish this purpose he appointed military commanders to lead revolutionary forces in various locations within Cuba and organized a supportive political network. Martí recruited one of the heroes of the Ten Years' War, the Dominican Máximo Gómez, to serve as Commander-in-Chief of the revolutionary army. He also attracted a fabled black warrior, the intransigent Antonio Maceo, who many years before had refused to accept the Treaty of Zanjón. Hoping to take advantage of the economic crisis, Martí decided early in 1895 to launch his uprising with landings on Cuba at three widely separated places. Maceo, proceeding from Costa Rica, and Gómez, departing from Santo Domingo—each with about two hundred followers—were to coordinate with another force starting from the United States. Its leaders were two other veterans of the Ten Years' War—Serafín Sánchez and Carlos Roloff. Unfortunately for this plan, American officials at Fernandina, Florida, seized the ships on which Sánchez and Roloff were to embark; but, nothing daunted, Martí decided to go ahead, gambling that the other landings would spark a revolutionary conflagration across Cuba. The *grito de Baíre* followed, but a general uprising did not materialize, in part because the Spanish immediately imprisoned the leaders of the movement in the western provinces around Havana. There would be no quick victory for the insurrectionists.[3]

On March 23, 1895, Martí and Gómez issued a manifesto from Montecristi, Santo Domingo, calling their followers to arms and proclaiming the principles of their crusade: They planned to conduct warfare in accordance with accepted practices of civilized nations. They insisted that blacks in Cuba take part in the uprising, a means of frustrating Spanish efforts to divide the revolutionaries along racial lines. Insurrectionists were not to attack noncombatants, and were forbidden to destroy rural wealth unless necessary to accomplish the objects of the revolution. The revolutionary movement announced its intention to reorganize the economy and establish an equitable system of distributing its yield.[4]

After Maceo landed near Baracoa on March 31, 1895, and Gómez—with Martí—came ashore at Playitas on April 11, the two generals developed the strategy that guided Cuban operations throughout the ensuing War of Independence. Martí, however, did not survive to assist in this endeavor; following his landfall with Gómez, he fell victim to an ambush at Dos Ríos. Gómez was convinced that the Ten Years' War had ended in failure because the uprising had been confined to eastern Cuba and affluent Cubans had failed to support it. He wanted to pursue a scorched-earth policy throughout the entire island, aimed particularly at the sugar industry. To obtain relief from the resulting economic catastrophe Cuban supporters of Spain would be forced to accept the revolution. Spain ultimately would concede independence because the cost of maintaining control would exceed the yield of imperialist exploitation. Maceo advocated a somewhat less thoroughgoing approach. He wanted to levy tribute from planters on pain of destroying their crops if they failed to cooperate. After a period of indecision Gómez's views prevailed. His scorched-earth policy produced immediate results. In 1895 Cuba had produced over a million long tons of sugar, valued at about $62 million, but in 1896 volume fell to 220,000 long tons, worth just $13 million.[5]

Late in 1895 Gómez and Maceo launched a coordinated military campaign that established the credibility of their insurgency. From October 22, 1895 to January 22, 1896 the two generals conducted extensive operations in western Cuba. Journalistic accounts of this effort imparted the false impression that the Cuban forces constituted a regular army. Gómez later characterized the western campaign as a "great military movement that insured the triumph of the revolution. The supreme necessity of the uprising was to make itself felt everywhere as decisive, strong, and bold." When this image materialized, it was only "a mat-

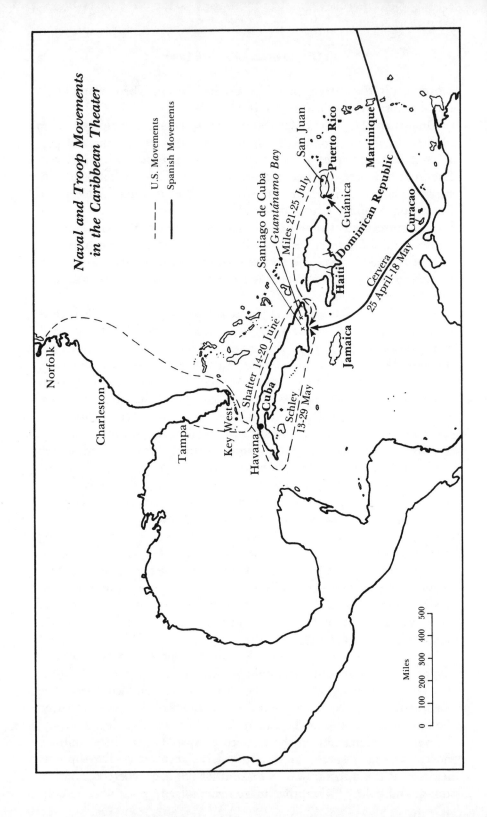

Naval and Troop Movements
in the Caribbean Theater

U.S. Movements
Spanish Movements

Norfolk

Charleston

Tampa

Key West

Havana

Cuba

Schley
13-29 May

Shafter 14-20 June

Santiago de Cuba
Guantánamo Bay

Miles 21-25 July

San Juan

Puerto Rico

Guánica

Haiti

Dominican Republic

Jamaica

Cervera
25 April-18 May

Martinique

Curacao

Miles

0   100   200   300   400   500

ter of time until victory came." The insurrectionists never ventured a comparable offensive again, but none became necessary.[6]

Gómez knew that he could not defeat the enemy in the field, so he made war against the Cuban economy. This brutal campaign plan would ultimately force Cubans to either support him or take refuge in Spanish-controlled towns. He would win by outlasting the opposition; Spain, eventually exhausted, would ultimately give up the struggle. The insurrection turned into a seasonal affair; because the rainy season—lasting from April into October—precluded extensive summer campaigns, most of the fighting took place in winter. Although correspondents reported constant engagements and extensive casualties, pitched battles rarely occurred and few losses resulted from hostile actions. Irregulars sneaked out of the jungle to pillage and burn, departing before the enemy could bring them to battle. No one was more adept at this task than Maceo, the "bronze titan."

The *mambises* (a designation applied to the Cuban guerrillas) subsisted on limited supplies, drawing heavily on the surrounding countryside or captured Spanish material. Little assistance reached them from outside Cuba, despite Spanish propaganda to the contrary. Although the Spanish had sufficient naval power to campaign effectively against gun-runners and filibustering expeditions, they captured only one Cuban vessel. Some seventy-one filibustering expeditions set out for Cuba, but only twenty-seven reached their destinations. The United States intercepted thirty-three of these attempts, the British two, and storms interfered with four others.[7]

Earlier in 1895 the insurrectionists had developed a political structure. The Cuban Republic declared itself independent on July 15, and a constituent assembly met in September at Jimaguayú, in Camagüey, to establish a provisional government. Maceo opposed this course; he argued that a small military *junta* should direct the insurrection—a measure designed to avoid political squabbles like those that had undermined the Cubans during the Ten Years' War. However, he did not prevail; a council of government was created that included a President, Vice-President, four Secretaries of State (for war, the interior, foreign relations, and the treasury), and a General-in-Chief. There was also provision for a judiciary. The army was placed under civilian control, but in practice Gómez and his lieutenants exercised plenary freedom of action. Salvador Cisneros Betancourt was chosen President, but a rival, Bartolomé Masó, replaced him somewhat later. Tomas Estrada Palma, still at the head of the New York *junta,* was designated Delegate Plenipotentiary and Foreign Representative of the Cuban Republic. This provisional structure, half humorously, half scornfully called a "government of the woods," played an inconsequential role. The course of the battle determined the outcome, not the manipulations of politicians.[8]

The Cuban Revolutionary Army never mustered more than from twenty-five to forty thousand troops at any one time. Armed almost exclusively with the rifle and machete, the Cuban guerrillas usually were deployed in small, mobile detachments engaging in hit-and-run operations. Although recruited mainly from the lower classes—plantation workers, lesser tradesmen, and urban laborers—the Cuban army enjoyed good leadership from wealthy planters, businessmen, and middle-class professionals who had left lives of comfort to serve in the field. Gómez divided his forces into two "armies"—one in the east, known as the Liberating Army, and the other in the west, called the Invading Army. Although a formal organization existed—from corps on down through division, brigade, regiment, battalion, and company or squadron—these units rarely took the field as such. After the western incursion late in 1895, only General Calixto García—commanding the Liberating Army—indulged in formal campaigning, but he did so only on rare occasions. Gómez succeeded in retaining the strategic initiative, an outcome that forced dispersion of Spanish forces throughout Cuba to protect vulnerable locations. The *insurrectos* could rely for excellent information on the people of the countryside. Their adversaries controlled only urban centers, and had difficulty divining the intentions of the guerrillas.[9]

SPAIN'S RESPONSE TO THE INSURRECTION

On March 14, 1895, shortly after the *grito be Baíre,* a minor incident in Madrid precipitated a ministerial crisis in the Spanish government that brought to power the Conservative Party and its leader, Antonio Cánovas del Castillo, known as *el monstruo* ("the monster"). In the incident, thirty lieutenants of the Spanish army had stormed the office of a newspaper in Madrid, *El resumen,* to protest its statement that generals and sergeants were prepared to go to Cuba, but not junior officers. Upon taking power Cánovas voiced his intransigent views about Cuba: "The Spanish nation is disposed to sacrifice to the last *peseta* of its treasure and to the last drop of blood of the last Spaniard before consenting that anyone snatch from it even one piece of its sacred territory." He would brook no compromise with the insurrectionists.[10]

To put down the rebellion Cánovas sent back to Cuba a distinguished Spanish general, Arsenio Martínez de Campos, who earlier had brought the Ten Years' War to a victorious conclusion. The old hero showed little optimism as he accepted his new task. When the Queen Regent of Spain, María Cristina of Austria, asked him to return to Cuba, he reportedly remarked to her, "War of the present day is another thing; my heart tells me that it will be the last that Spain has to endure in America." To achieve pacification Martínez de Campos applied the strategic methods that had served him well a generation earlier. He sought to deal with the insurgents by containing them in the province of Oriente—located at the extreme eastern end of Cuba—manning a defensive line called a *"trocha"* running from Morón at the north to Júcaro at the south, near the border between the provinces of Camagüey and Oriente. About two hundred yards wide, this *trocha* extended fifty miles, and included a military railroad and various forts and blockhouses at short intervals as cover for the defenders. To reinforce the army in Cuba about eighty-five hundred troops went out from Spain immediately on the *Reina Mercedes,* a vessel destined to play a role in the campaign of 1898 at Santiago de Cuba. Many good troops followed; by 1898 the force in Cuba had grown from twenty thousand regulars and sixty thousand loyalist Cubans to about one hundred fifty thousand regulars and eighty thousand Cubans.[11]

The essentially passive defensive strategy of Martínez de Campos did not produce an early decision, an outcome that slowly but surely caused a profound decline in the morale of the Spanish army. When the troops first went out they sang gleefully,

> With the beard of Maceo
> We will make brooms
> To sweep the barracks
> Of the Spanish troops.

But the situation gradually changed. A diplomat who somewhat later watched recruits departing from Cádiz for Cuba reported sadly, "A spectacle, truly very doleful, because everyone was persuaded that at least half of those unfortunates, the majority recruits, would not see their homes again, and would perish far from their country, because of the harshness of the war and the fevers." A British observer in Cuba noted that most of the replacements were "boys, to look at, fifteen or sixteen, who have never held a rifle till this moment, and now are almost ignorant which end it fires, good lads—too good to go to such uneven butchery—with cheerful, patriotic, willing faces, but the very antithesis of a soldier." Not many Spaniards perished in combat, but many thousands succumbed to the tropical diseases endemic to Cuba—particularly malaria, dysentery, and yellow fever.[12]

After Gómez and Maceo had demonstrated their ability to move freely through the Cuban countryside during their "invasion" of western Cuba in late 1895 and early 1896, Cánovas withdrew the ambivalent Martínez de Campos and replaced him with General Valeriano Weyler y Nicolau, a stern professional soldier who, it turned out, did not hesitate to use all the military methods deemed necessary to pacify Cuba. A native of Majorca, sprung from German immigrants, the man who became known in America as "Butcher" Weyler took command on February 10, 1896, and immediately expressed confidence in his ability to pacify the Pearl of the Antilles. Announcing that he would treat those insurgents who left the field generously, he threatened condign punishment for those who continued to resist. To demonstrate good will he chose not to oppose reforms for Cuba, although he obviously believed that pacification should precede any political concessions emanating from Madrid.

Less than a week after his advent in Cuba Weyler issued a decree of reconcentration, the act for which he is known to history. All inhabitants of the districts around Sancti Spíritus, Puerto Príncipe, and Santiago de Cuba were ordered to remove themselves to locations near military headquarters; no one was supposed to travel without permission; military commanders were empowered to act summarily against insurgents; and those aiding or abetting the insurrection became subject to military law, a much more drastic code than the civil alternative. Many were the military benefits Weyler believed would derive from reconcentration. Above all, the practice would deprive the insurgents of subsistence and ammunition. It would also restrict their access to accurate intelligence concerning Spanish movements, diminish the effect of their anti-Spanish propaganda, and vitiate efforts to replenish the guerrilla bands. Since reconcentration jeopardized the well-being of civilians, Cubans in the field would worry about loved ones in the zones of reconcentration. Weyler believed that reconcentration also would lower the casualties of his forces.

Responding later (in 1906) to charges that with reconcentration he had violated the laws of civilized warfare, Weyler justified the practice as a legitimate military response to guerrilla tactics, noting that the British had adopted this practice during the Boer War and the Americans had acted similarly in the Philippines during the insurrection of 1899–1902. He mentioned also that during the American Civil War, on August 25, 1863, General Thomas Ewing had issued a decree requiring inhabitants to evacuate a large part of Missouri within fifteen days.[13]

Having adopted reconcentration to deny the insurgents the support of the countryside, Weyler then based his military operations on two *trochas* traversing Cuba from north to south. These fortified roads were intended to deprive the insurgents of free movement, particularly in the more westerly provinces of Cuba. One was the old *trocha* from Morón to Júcaro, isolating the two most easterly provinces, Camagüey and Oriente. The other *trocha* connected Mariel to Majana, separating the most westerly province, Pinar del Río, from all points east. Between the two *trochas* lay the central provinces—Havana, Matanzas, and Santa Clara. Weyler planned to campaign initially in the west against Antonio Maceo in Pinar del Río. Then he would concentrate on the central regions around Havana and Matanzas. Finally he would move from both east and west to the *trocha* between Morón and Júcaro, driving the remaining insurgents upon it and ending all remaining resistance. This sequential strategy revealed Weyler's belief that he lacked sufficient troops to move simultaneously on all fronts. The Spanish army would maintain control of most urban centers but ignore vast districts of the countryside, allowing *insurrectos* to operate freely in these unoccupied areas.[14]

The *trocha* strategy failed miserably. It represented more a modification of Martínez de Campos's essentially defensive methods than a departure from them. Weyler should instead have taken the offensive, leaving the *trochas* behind and pursuing insurgents ruthlessly until they were pushed to the point of total exhaustion; but he dallied, and neither side in Cuba came close to a decision. This outcome favored the Cuban insurrectionists, who sought to deny Spain a victory in the field. Either Spain would weary of fighting, or a third power—probably the United States—would come to the assistance of Cuba, an act that would ensure independence.[15]

Reconcentration caused an immediate outcry, especially in the United States. Because in carrying it out Weyler struck directly at civilians, his approach attracted more criticism than the scorched-earth practices of the Cubans. The fate of the *reconcentrados* gave currency to allegations of Spanish illegality and immorality. Many suffered and died in Weyler's camps. Some estimates indicated that by 1898 over four hundred thousand Cubans—about a fourth of the population—had perished as a result of reconcentration. The correct figure, however, was closer to one hundred thousand, but this total was itself astronomical—certainly sufficient to trouble many a conscience in the United States. Cánovas sought to achieve military victory before the Americans would become sufficiently aroused to intervene in Cuban affairs. According to Weyler's timetable, pacification would be achieved by March or April, 1898.[16]

For many years Spain had embraced a foreign policy of isolation and neutrality. Both her Liberal and Conservative parties generally followed this design, remaining aloof from European entanglements—although between 1887 and 1895 there had been a flirtation with the Triple Alliance, composed of Germany, Austria-Hungary, and Italy. Given its severe domestic problems, Spain lacked sufficient power to contemplate active involvement in European power policies. Cánovas was forever realistic in his course. "It is never good policy," he once said, "whatever excellent intentions one has, to undertake the impossible." In 1883 he formulated his foreign policy cogently: "Everyone knows that I am a declared enemy of all intermeddling of Spain in external affairs; it has enough [trouble] with its internal difficulties." His rival, the Liberal Práxedes Mateo Sagasta, did not differ in fundamentals; pro-French in orientation, the leader of the Liberals opposed connections with enemies of the Third Republic—meaning most of all the German Reich—but he was hardly more activist than his Conservative rival.[17]

In the summer of 1896, however, Cánovas broke with the past, hoping to attract external support for Spain's policy to repression in Cuba, which presumably would discourage interference by other powers, especially the Americans. The Prime Minister authorized his Foreign Minister, the Duke of Tetuán, to prepare a diplomatic message for presentation to the six great powers of Europe—Great Britain, France, Russia, Germany, Austria-Hungary, and Italy. The message consisted principally of objections to certain critical representations made by the United States. Before the American envoy in Madrid, Hannis Taylor, learned of the message's existence, it had been circulated unofficially to Spanish ambassadors in various European countries. Once alerted, Taylor made known to Tetuán that delivery of the statement would be interpreted in Washington as an unfriendly act. This action forced the Foreign Minister to desist from communicating the note formally, but he nevertheless made sure that its contents became known to appropriate governments. Although this initiative provoked nothing more from the powers than noncommittal expressions of sympathy, Tetuán fatuously decided that he had built a foundation for future diplomatic initiatives to deter the United States.[18] This premature enterprise reflected the Foreign Minister's belief that Spain could not rely entirely on its armed forced in order to avoid serious international complications, especially with the United States.

Cánovas had decided on Spain's course. He would quell the Cuban insurrection by force rather than grant independence. To head off damaging interference by outside parties such as the United States, he would undertake various diplomatic measures. And victory over the insurgents would come before international political pressures became unmanageable.

GROVER CLEVELAND AND THE CUBAN INSURRECTION

When the Cuban insurrection began, President Grover Cleveland reacted mildly, adopting a policy of studied inaction. Finally, on June 12, 1895, he issued a proclamation of neutrality that had the effect of recognizing the Cuban insurgency but fell short of granting the Cubans the rights of belligerents under international law. The fact is that Cleveland and his Secretary of State, Richard Olney, never showed special sympathy for the insurgents. Both concentrated on avoiding steps that might eventually lead to war. As the insurrection continued, they leaned more and more toward offering to mediate between the Cubans and Spanish, affirming a position midway between those favoring United States recognition of Cuban belligerency and those wanting the United States to oppose the insurrection actively. As the insurrection continued into 1896, the Administration noted growing public interest in Cuban affairs. It disliked the growing tendency in Congress to favor more active support of Cuban aspirations. On April 6, the House and the Senate passed, by large majorities, a joint resolution calling upon the executive branch to recognize the Cuban revolution and extend the good offices of the United States.[19] William L. Wilson, the Postmaster General, summarized the general reaction of the President and his closest advisers to this uninvited congressional act. "The jingoism in the air is a curious craze," he confided to his diary, "and unaccountable, except on account of the unrest of our people, and the willingness to turn from domestic to foreign affairs, always making the greatest allowance for political maneuvering, and the ridiculousness of conducting foreign affairs by such town meetings as the House and Senate have become." Perhaps Wilson had in mind the public approbation of Secretary Olney's recently manifested defiant attitude towards Great Britain during a dispute about the boundary separating Venezuela and British Guiana. He certainly must have assumed a connection between the "jingoism" of Congress and the nation's reaction to an economic downturn that had begun in 1893 and would persist for several years.[20]

On April 7, 1896, Olney revealed the Administration's determination to avoid a course even remotely conforming to the desires of the Congress. In a note to Spain predated April 4 to dissociate it from the joint congressional resolution, Olney, while asking that Madrid consider certain reforms designed to end the insurrection, tendered the good offices of the United States. In this fashion the Secretary of State implied that the United States would support the Spanish government if Madrid agreed to mediation.

Spain delayed its response for two months; when Tetuán finally replied on June 4, 1896, a thoroughgoing defense of Spanish policy was presented that rejected all of the proposed reforms. This intransigence disturbed Cleveland because it suggested the possibility of further complications. As recorded by an unidentified observer, Cleveland wanted to go far in demanding humanitarian behavior on both sides, but, more important, he felt a need for extreme caution because "the public mind seemed to be an inflammable state, and a spark might kindle a conflagration. . . . There seemed to be an epidemic of insanity in the country just at this time."[21]

Despite the President's alarm, the Cuban question did not become the principal public issue in 1896. In that year the country engaged in one of the most dramatic presidential campaigns in American history—the "battle of the standards" between the Republican William McKinley, advocate *par excellence* of "sound money," and that doughty proponent of silver coinage, William Jennings Bryan, who received the nomination of the Democratic Party. Domestic issues dominated the stirring contest. However, the Republican platform expressed "deep and abiding interest" in the cause of Cuba, holding that the United States government "should actively use its influence and good offices to restore peace and give independence to the island"; the Democrats also referred to Cuba in their platform. Still, neither candidate commented extensively on the Cuban insurrection during the campaign. This foreign issue had little or no effect on the outcome of the contest—McKinley's decisive victory.[22]

During his last months in office Cleveland persisted in the opinions that had shaped his Cuban policy since the beginning of the insurrection. Commenting once again in his annual message of December 7, 1896, he emphasized his opposition to recognition of the revolutionary Cuban government. The President realized that the United States had a legitimate interest in the stability of Cuba; American investments there amounted to between $30 and $50 million and the annual export-import trade reached $100 million. The best solution to the difficulties in Cuba might be a grant of autonomy—a large measure of home rule. His most important pronouncement here, however, was mention of the possibility that the United States might take action at some future point, should Spain fail to resolve the problem in reasonable time. Cleveland thus moved away from the strict neutrality of his earlier offer to mediate, calling now for autonomy and threatening intervention.

Minister Taylor pressed the proposal of Cuban autonomy in Madrid, but Cánovas showed no inclination to respond. Cleveland went so far as to authorize two American planters with interests in Cuba to discuss autonomy privately with insurgent leaders, but nothing came of this ill-conceived initiative. Despite these moves, Cleveland proved as unresponsive as ever to congressional pressure for recognition of Cuban independence. Thus ended his efforts to deal with the Cuban insurrection, an exercise notable for its futility.[23]

What of the incoming President's views? Senator Henry Cabot Lodge (Republican from Massachusetts) reported to Theodore Roosevelt—a friend who was about to become the Assistant Secretary of the Navy—what he had learned about McKinley's views of Cuba: "He very naturally does not want to be obliged to go to war as soon as he comes in, for of course his great ambition is to restore business and bring back good times and he dislikes the idea of such interruption." McKinley actually hoped that the matter would be settled before he would become President. Lodge concluded cheerily, "I was greatly pleased to see how thoroughly he appreciates the momentous character of the question." Roosevelt, who expressed delight at McKinley's position, wanted strong policy, advocating not only independence for Cuba but annexation of the Hawaiian islands. "I do not think a war with Spain would be serious enough to cause much strain on the country, or much interruption to the revival of prosperity," he told Lodge, implying his willingness to fight if necessary; but he too wished that the issue would be settled during the winter.[24]

The night before McKinley took office he had a conversation with Cleveland in which he spoke forebodingly of the Cuban question: "If I can only go out of office at the end of my term with the knowledge that I have done what lay in my power to avert this terrible calamity [—war with Spain—] with the success that has crowned your patience and perseverance," he told the outgoing President, "I shall be the happiest man in the world." At about this time he expressed to another auditor his pacific inclination in the most unmistakable terms: "We want no wars of conquest, [and] we must avoid the temptation of territorial aggression. War should never be entered upon until every agency for peace has failed; peace is preferable to war in almost every contingency." It is impossible to doubt McKinley's sincerity; this view accorded with both his sentiments and interests. His allies within the Republican Party were strongly opposed to war, preferring that the new Administration concentrate on stimulating economic recovery at home. Moreover, it was by no means clear that the great powers of Europe would remain aloof from an American-Spanish conflict.[25]

Cánovas was no more anxious for such a conflict than was McKinley. To preserve his power he had to find ways to maintain firm control over his political associates. At the time he faced challenges from within the Conservative Party, one from a clerical faction headed by Alejandro Pidal and another from dissidents led by Francisco Silvela, who sought electoral reform. Traditionally, the governing party had been able to manipulate elections in its own interest, an aspect of a tacit arrangement between Cánovas and the Liberal leader Sagasta known as the *turno pacífico*—peaceful alternation of the two parties in power. Cánovas, however, was having difficulty controlling one of his principal allies, Francisco Romero Robledo, a notorious manipulator of elections who uncompromisingly opposed concessions to Cuba, and he also had to deal with the intransigence of Governor-General Weyler in Cuba. If Cánovas seemed to lean too strongly towards Romero and Weyler, he might precipitate a coalition of *Silvelistas* and *Pidalistas* capable of ousting him from leadership. There was still another difficulty—the antagonism of the Queen Regent, María Cristina.[26]

In December, 1896, word came to Madrid of a dramatic event in Cuba: Antonio Maceo, the most dashing of the *insurrectos,* had been killed while attempting to cross the western *trocha.* Cánovas exploited this news to repair his political fences. On April 29, 1897, changing course, he announced that reforms would be introduced into the pacified areas of Cuba.[27]

In both the United States and Spain domestic political considerations had great influence on foreign policy. President McKinley hoped to avoid confrontation with Spain because he wanted to concentrate on internal measures designed to end the economic depression following the panic of 1893. Furthermore, the President abhorred the thought of violence and did all he could to avoid it. Cánovas moved haltingly towards reforms that implied home rule for Cuba, hoping by this course to undermine political opposition within his own party and outside it. Spain had no desire to fight the United States; it had enough war on its hands in Cuba. Not until the last weeks of peace did either Washington or Madrid recognize the likelihood of war. What Cánovas—and also Sagasta—never recognized was the possibility that McKinley might be unable to control events in America. What McKinley never fully sensed was the intensity of Spain's attachment to Cuba.

Cánovas summarized the profound Spanish commitment to the Pearl of the Antilles as early as 1865, when the Cortes was debating the sale of Cuba. Asked how he would respond to a very good offer, he cried, "I will not have it. . . . I will not have it, and I will not have it because the conservation of the island of Cuba is in the sentiment, it is in the heart of all Spaniards." Charles Benoist, a sensitive French journalist, understood what Cánovas had in mind: "Cuba—it is the flesh of the flesh of Spain; it is part of the history, the glory, and the grandeur of Spain." However reduced in stature during modern times, all of Spain could call to mind the glorious past. To surrender Cuba was to deny that national heritage. This belief, general in Spain, made it most difficult for Spanish politicians to allow any outside government to participate in decisions about Cuba.[28]

The very legitimacy of Spain was at stake as Cánovas strove to settle the problem of Cuba. Ever since the glorious days of the *Siglo de oro*—the golden age of the overseas empire during the sixteenth century—Spaniards had looked upon their grand domain in the New World and elsewhere as literally a gift of God—an explicit reward for expelling Islam from Europe and preserving Christendom from that greatest of all challenges to its sway in the West. Over time, however, almost all of the Spanish empire had been lost, so that by the late nineteenth century only Cuba and Puerto Rico remained of the American domain, although Spain still held the Philippines and lesser islands in the distant Pacific. During the 1890's no Spanish government could seriously contemplate relinquishing Cuba; to propose such a course would be to risk revolution.

The constitutional regime established in 1875—usually called the Restoration monarchy—continually faced severe challenges from both the left and the right. For many years stubborn reactionaries known as Carlists challenged the Spanish ruling family—the consequence of a dispute over the throne dating from the 1830's in which Ferdinand VII, King of Spain from 1808 to 1833, had willed his crown to an unborn child—Isabella, daughter of his fourth wife, María Cristina of Naples. Opponents believed that Ferdinand's brother, Don Carlos, should have become the ruler rather than Isabella. Carlist sentiment, strong in the Basque provinces of northern Spain, perennially supported a pretender. A short-lived Spanish republic, antimonarchical and liberal, succeeded to power in 1868, but it collapsed in 1875 and the son of Isabella, Alfonso XII, was restored to power. The resuscitated monarchy was no more palatable to the republicans than to the Carlists, and both movements sought to destroy it. The moderates, Cánovas and Sagasta, resolutely avoided policies that might have lead the extremists to unite against the constitutional monarchy or prosper independently. They deemed weakness in colonial questions such a policy. Any sign of a tendency to surrender Cuba would have given enemies of the Restoration an issue around which to consolidate feeling against the established order.

Two other circumstances hindered the Cuban policy of the Restoration; the views of the army and the activity of a pro-Cuban bloc in the Cortes. No Spanish regime could hope to survive without the support of the military. Since the army was fully committed to the retention of the imperial remnant—and in the case of Spanish Morocco to actual expansion of the empire—civilian leaders did not believe themselves free to propose serious Cuban reforms, much less the surrender of the island. The army had traditionally viewed itself as the savior of Spain in periods of political turmoil. In 1868 it had allowed the Republic to establish itself, and later had forced through the Restoration of 1875. It was conceivable that, if challenged on its views about Cuba, the army might lend support to a coalition of Republicans and Carlists seeking to overthrow the Restoration. Besides the army, Cánovas and Sagasta had to consider Cubans who preferred Spanish control to independence. Spanish officials in Cuba had fostered a political organization, known as the *Unión constitucional,* that was closely allied with commercial and industrial interests in Spain, particularly those of Catalonia. This coalition of colonial bureaucrats and Catalan businessmen controlled a parliamentary bloc of sufficient strength to ensure the defeat of either the Conservatives or Liberals should one party or the other show an inclination to dispose of Cuba.[29]

The most important reality in the latter stages of the Cuban crisis was that both Madrid and Washington possessed little freedom of action, while each failed to grasp the other's situation. These circumstances played a most important role in the failure to maintain peace. Spanish leaders naturally found it difficult to understand that public opinion greatly influenced the behavior of the American President, and their American counterparts had all too little appreciation of the profound emotions associated with Spanish sovereignty in Cuba, not to mention the peculiarities of power politics during the Restoration. Ignorance on both sides, much more than design, greatly influenced the tragic outcome.

THE WOODFORD MISSION

Cánovas certainly appreciated the importance of avoiding confrontation with the United States, even if his Cuban policy stemmed primarily from domestic considerations. A Madrid newspaper quoted him as saying to a group of journalists on May 21, 1897, ''If, over and above what exists, we were to add thirty thousand . . . Americans on that island [Cuba], the great fleet, and all the power of that republic, what would be our fate?'' Some action seemed called for, given rising tensions in Spain itself. On the very day Cánovas met the reporters, his Foreign Minister, the Duke of Tetuán, physically assaulted an antagonist from the Liberal Party, Augusto Comas, an indiscretion that posed the possibility of a duel. Although further violence was averted, this episode reflected the heated political atmosphere in Madrid as the Cuban insurrection continued on into the summer of 1897. Some Spanish authorities later maintained that Cánovas entertained at this time the thought of selling Cuba to the United States, but the Marqués de Lema, well-informed on Cánovas's activities, doubted that the Prime Minister ever really contemplated such a course. The historian Gabriel Maura Gamazo noted correctly that any Spanish government proposing the sale of Cuba would have been signing its political death warrant.[30]

While Cánovas deliberated his course, the Liberal Party finally moved openly towards support of autonomy for Cuba, always assuming continued Spanish sovereignty. Segismundo Moret y Prendergast, a leading spokesman for the party of Sagasta, hinted broadly in a much-discussed statement at Zaragosa on July 19, 1897 that the Liberals, if called to power, would immediately adopt a policy of home rule for the troubled island in the Caribbean. "Military force will tear the flesh of Cuba," he declaimed histrionically, "but autonomy will staunch the blood that gushes from wounds opened by the steel."[31]

At this timely juncture McKinley decided to send a new minister to Madrid with instructions to press for an acceptable settlement. He realized that failure to find a diplomatic solution might ultimately require the United States to use armed force, a policy he very much hoped to avoid. The President found it difficult to locate an appointee to Spain. He offered the mission to a number of leading Republicans, including Elihu Root of New York, before finally obtaining the services of General Stewart Lyndon Woodford, a veteran of the Civil War who had enjoyed a successful legal and political career in New York.[32]

Prior to Woodford's departure for Europe, Secretary of State John Sherman sent a formal note to the Cánovas government through the Spanish envoy in Washington, Enrique Dupuy de Lôme, in which McKinley expressed his views clearly for the first time. This communication called for revocation of General Weyler's orders of reconcentration, an early end to hostilities, measures to alleviate suffering in Cuba, and permanent changes in the Spanish-Cuban relationship (presumably some form of home rule). McKinley followed Cleveland's lead by intimating that the United States might have to act unless the situation improved markedly in reasonable time. Madrid delayed its response, and when it came, in August, it gave no ground. McKinley had taken his position in the knowledge that members of Congress were continuing efforts to force American recognition of Cuban belligerency. His instructions to Woodford authorized a solution acceptable to both Spain and Cuba, but also called for pacification according to the laws of war, a not-so-veiled criticism of Weyler and reconcentration.[33]

Before taking up his duties in Madrid, Woodford consulted with several American ministers to various European governments. He came away from these talks with the view that most Europeans would not "resent any action by the United States that would be just, humane and in line with the progressive purposes of modern civilization." The attitude of the great powers was an important consideration; should Spain find friends in Europe, the United States would have to proceed cautiously.[34]

Suddenly, on August 8, 1897, a totally unanticipated development transformed the situation. An Italian anarchist, Miguel Angiolillo, assassinated Antonio Cánovas del Castillo—which event ultimately led to a change of government in Madrid, putting the Liberals in power. An interim cabinet led by the Minister of War, General Marcelo Azcárraga, performed the functions of government while the Queen Regent contemplated her course of action. She could call another Conservative to the leadership or else turn to the opposition party—which meant, of course, to Sagasta. Woodford delayed his advent in Spain because of the assassination, not wishing to give Spanish leaders an excuse to form a united front against American pressure. If left to their own devices, he thought that "they may embarrass themselves very seriously without any effort by us to increase their difficulties."[35]

Woodford could not delay too long, however, and after presenting his credentials to the Queen Regent on September 13, 1897, he called on the Duke of Tetuán, emphasizing the American view that a settlement should come soon. Once again he extended the good offices of the United States. When Tetuán attempted to argue that the insurrection continued only because of American support, Woodford countered with a virtual ultimatum. He suggested that before November the Spanish government should provide "such assurance as would satisfy the United States that early and certain peace can be promptly secured, and that otherwise the United States must consider itself free to take such steps as its Government should deem necessary to procure this result, with due regard to our own interests and the general tranquility." This blunt statement reflected Woodford's conviction that he must apply unremitting pressure. "The least wavering on my part," he informed President McKinley, "and the Spanish Government will rely on its old policy of delay and the Cuban campaign will be prolonged into the Winter and so of necessity run over into next Summer." He had in mind the fact that the dry season in Cuba—from October to April—would permit active campaigning.[36]

At this critical juncture, Queen María Cristina recalled Sagasta to power, a step that foreshadowed a change in policies towards Cuba. In June Sagasta himself had said, "In the [proposed] reforms of Sr. Cánovas, whether considered together or in detail, one sees nothing more than the principles of autonomy. Let us then go on to autonomy." Sagasta could move expeditiously towards Cuban reform at this point because the leaders of right-wing elements within his party—notably Germán Gamazo and Antonio Maura—had refused office in the new ministry. This circumstance placed the progressive Segismundo Moret y Prendergast, a leading exponent of autonomy and the new Minister for the Colonies (*Ministro de ultramar*), in a position to make a new departure. Woodford's reports to Washington nevertheless tended toward pessimism, suggesting that the exaggerated pride of the Spanish people might stand in the way and that Sagasta had assumed power too late to alter the course of events. More to the point was his observation, "The insurrection may have acquired such strength that nothing short of complete independence will induce the insurgents to lay down their arms." Woodford need not have worried about Sagasta's intentions. First the new leader sent General Ramón Blanco y Erenas, formerly Governor-General in the Philippines, to Havana as General Weyler's replacement. Then, late in October, he made his move.[37]

On October 23, Tetuán's replacement at the foreign ministry, Don Pío Gullón Iglesias, delivered a formal diplomatic note to Woodford in which he announced that Spain would grant autonomy to Cuba. A program of "true self-government [would] give to the Cubans their own local government, whereby they shall be at one and the same time the initiators and regulators of their own life, but always forming part of the integral nationality of Spain." The mother country would continue to administer "national requirements or needs"—among them foreign affairs, justice, and the armed forces. Gullón took care to trace the course Spain expected the United States to follow in the future: McKinley should support Spain against the insurgents, at least to the extent of preventing material assistance from reaching them and avoiding actions that implied sympathy for their cause.[38]

Although it appeared that Spain was acting in response to American pressure, Sagasta had also considered other developments: The national treasury was almost empty. Warfare was in progress, not only in Cuba but in the Philippines. Moreover, domestic opponents of the regime—Carlists, Republicans, and even anarchists—appeared active in their efforts to undermine the established order. Sagasta's prime concern was not to meet the demands of the Americans but to preserve the Restoration.[39]

If Sagasta had believed that the insurrectionists would respond favorably, the outcome must have been extremely disappointing. The offer of autonomy only strengthened the insurgents in their aspiration to independence. Tomas Estrada Palma busily communicated the attitude of the New York *junta* to various of his correspondents. It remained firmly behind a policy of "independence or death." Máximo Gómez was even more positive, notifying his army that he would shoot any member who supported autonomy, and that outsiders raising the issue with the insurgents would suffer the same fate. "All proposition of peace will rest necessarily on the independence of Cuba," Gómez trumpeted, "and will be submitted to the government of the Republic." To drive home his policy he actually executed an emissary that General Blanco sent to negotiate with him, Lieutenant-Colonel Joaquín Ruíz. A close observer at the time, Augusto Conte, summarized the failing of Spanish policy thus: "This concession [of autonomy] perhaps would have been sufficient had it been granted in the time of Cánovas," he noted, but it had lost its meaning "because the Cubans relied more each day on the aid of the United States." Fitzhugh Lee, the American Consul General in Havana, reported accurately that the insurgents had no intention of accepting the half-loaf of autonomy, but this reality was not fully grasped in Washington.[40]

American officialdom responded sympathetically to Sagasta's initiative, although maintaining pressure on Madrid to expedite home rule. Responding to Spanish insinuations that Washington was actively supporting the Cuban insurgents, the State Department instructed Woodford to inform Gullón that the United States strictly enforced its own laws and adhered to accepted international practice in dealing with filibusters. At the same time American leaders continued to inveigh against reconcentration, taking note of grim reports emanating from consuls in Cuba. However, overall Woodford had been much pleased with Gullón's note of October 23. Considering that McKinley had won a "great moral victory" because he had forced the Spanish government to recall Weyler and to concede autonomy, Woodford wrote the President that he thought he could "begin to see some reasonable chance of maintaining in honorable ways the peace you so earnestly seek." Beginning to appreciate Sagasta's difficult domestic situation, the American envoy arranged to grant Spain reasonable time to pursue its new course in Cuba. He believed that Spain eventually intended to revoke reconcentration.[41]

Sagasta now matured the policies to which he had committed himself earlier. In Cuba, Blanco gradually modified Weyler's more extreme measures, although pursuing a military strategy quite similar to that of his predecessor, attempting to roll up the guerrillas by campaigning sequentially from the western provinces to eastern Cuba. On November 25 the Liberal ministry in Madrid published a series of decrees that spelled out autonomy for Cuba and Puerto Rico. Two of these documents extended both the political and electoral privileges of Spaniards to inhabitants of the islands, and a third described the autonomic government. Historians still debate the potential impact of these home rule measures, some believing that they represented a considerable break with the past and others emphasizing that they did not after all deprive Spain of control in Cuba. In any event the architect of the plan, Moret, obviously hoped that a combination of military vigor and political concessions would bring about pacification in Cuba before the United States felt compelled to intervene. All this activity convinced Woodford that Spain sought to avoid war and meet the requirements of the United States.[42]

On December 6, 1897, in his first annual message to the Congress, President McKinley dealt at length with the Cuban question. He reviewed several options—recognition of Cuban belligerency, recognition of Cuban independence, and American intervention—rejecting all of them, particularly intervention, arguing that Sagasta should have full opportunity to pacify Cuba. He did add, however, considerable commentary on the evils of reconcentration and the importance of ending inhumane practices in Cuba. Most significant was a quite specific reference to a deadline that Spain must meet in settling affairs in Cuba. McKinley used the phrase "near future," a hint that Spain must accomplish its purposes before the beginning of the rainy season. Despite this ominous warning the note was received with relief in Madrid, where emphasis was placed on McKinley's obvious distaste for recognition or intervention rather than on the deadline. Woodford summarized the state of affairs accurately: "Everything now depends on the success or failure of the Cabinet program in Cuba."[43]

Despite the grant of autonomy the situation in Cuba showed no signs of improvement during December. Consul General Lee's doleful reports from Havana substantiated his earlier assertions that Spain could neither suppress the insurrection by armed action nor pacify Cuba by a grant of autonomy. Noting that about fifty-two thousand out of one hundred one thousand *reconcentrados* had perished in Havana province—not including the city of Havana—he showed that available funds for relief, which amounted to only about seventeen cents per person, could not be expected to help improve the situation. On

December 15 Lee urged that Blanco be granted thirty days in which to relieve this suffering; otherwise the United States should undertake the necessary humanitarian work "in the interest of peace, prosperity and humanity."[44] These messages stimulated energetic efforts in Washington to set up an extensive program of charitable endeavor. On Christmas Eve the State Department announced arrangements to receive contributions, Spain having agreed to permit entry of clothing, food, and medicine into Cuba free of duty; the Red Cross would supervise distribution of relief. McKinley showed special interest in this project. The astute Herbert Croly later wrote that the President wished thus to not only sustain his pressure on Spain but placate public opinion at home.[45]

Probably hoping to help repair the rift with Spain, the State Department encouraged a proposal from Moret to negotiate a commercial treaty. The Minister for the Colonies apparently assumed that economic considerations lay behind Washington's Cuban policy, thinking that the United States would relax its pressure for reforms in Cuba if allowed good terms in the Cuban market. By the end of January arrangements had been made to conduct formal discussions in Washington. Woodford believed that Moret was sincere not only in his desire to further autonomy but in his support for an effective commercial treaty. He was less sure of Gullón, who might have been reflecting the protectionist sentiments traditional among the merchants and manufacturers of Catalonian Barcelona.[46]

When bad military news from Cuba continued to arrive in Madrid, the Queen Regent ventured a highly unorthodox diplomatic enterprise: Late in December, 1897, Woodford suddenly requested permission to visit the United States briefly, mentioning his need to transact some personal business but hinting also that Queen María Cristina might ask him to deliver a secret message for McKinley. Washington did not grant Woodford's request. Nevertheless, on January 17, 1898, the Queen Regent called in Woodford and conveyed thoughts to be transmitted to President McKinley. She wanted him to recognize Spain's conciliatory policy by issuing a proclamation designed to end all American assistance to the Cuban insurgents and break up the *junta* in New York. Presumably this course would force the Cubans to abandon insurgency and accept autonomy. Woodford promised to convey the request to Washington. However, after this interview he learned from Moret that dissident elements in Spain might bring down the Liberal ministry. In this connection the Colonial Minister mentioned the followers of Romero Robledo, Weyler's supporters (the General by this time having returned to Spain), the ultraconservatives, the Carlists, the Socialists, and the Republicans. However, Moret did not think the plot would succeed, because he believed the government's autonomy plan would lead to pacification in Cuba.

In one of his most insightful reports Woodford summarized the considerations he thought lay behind the statements of the Queen Regent and Moret. The Liberal ministry could maintain itself in power only as long as it appeared that its policies would end the Cuban insurrection. If it became evident that autonomy would not work or the United States planned to intervene, "the Queen will have to choose between losing her throne or losing Cuba at the risk of war with us." Sagasta and Moret he deemed both patriotic and pacific, but, if forced to choose between war or the overthrow of the dynasty, they would accept war.[47]

This cogent analysis had no effect in Washington. Despite Woodford's obvious desire that McKinley dispose as the Queen Regent proposed, the President made no move whatever. To have done so would have been to accept the Spanish thesis that the Cuban insurrection continued only because of illegal American encouragement.

The autonomic governments decreed for Cuba and Puerto Rico were inaugurated in January, 1898, but the one for Cuba never attained any discernible success. Reform had come too late. Insurgent leaders interpreted Sagasta's *démarche* as indication that a little more perseverance would ensure independence. Moreover, the autonomy program contained sufficient ambiguities to arouse their suspicions that Spain was not acting in good faith. In his later years Weyler argued that, had Madrid allowed him to continue his military operations, he could have completed the pacification of eastern Cuba, having already suppressed the guerrillas in the western regions. This claim seems far-fetched: By early 1898 there was no longer a solid political or military foundation in Cuba upon which to base the autonomic regime. The Spanish army had not been able to destroy Gómez's forces, and was not likely to accomplish this task in the foreseeable future. Time—which so often in the past had favored Spanish diplomacy—in this instance worked against it.[48]

Whatever the prospects for autonomy, two events of February, 1898, radically transformed the situation and precipitated a great diplomatic crisis between Spain and the United States. One of these was the unauthorized publication of an indiscreet private letter written to a Spanish politician by Enrique Dupuy de Lôme, the Spanish minister in Washington, that castigated President McKinley—by itself an embarrassing but inconsequential affair. The other, incomparably more inflammatory in effect, was the destruction of the battleship *Maine* in Havana harbor.

TO THE SINKING OF THE *MAINE*

In October, 1897, President McKinley became concerned about the protection of American citizens and interests in Havana. Thus began the train of events that culminated in the destruction of the second-class battleship *Maine*. In order that a naval vessel be available for quick deployment to Havana in case of an emergency, the *Maine* was ordered to Port Royal, South Carolina on October 8. It then was sent to the American naval base at Key West, Florida, on December 15, less than one hundred miles from Cuba. Arrangements were made so that it could leave immediately should Consul General Lee request its presence in Cuban waters. Lee did not believe that the *Maine* should come to Havana as yet or that Americans should be evacuated, giving as reasons the absence of a discernible security problem and the tendency of such measures to excite public opinion. Nevertheless, he recommended that at least two naval vessels wait at Key West for possible dispatch to Havana and that other ships move to the Dry Tortugas—just west of Key West—for additional security.[49]

Towards the middle of January, 1898, an outbreak of violence in Havana revealed the bleak prospects of the autonomic government and inaugurated the process that soon brought the *Maine* to the Cuban capital. Officers in charge of Cuban *voluntarios*—the home guards who made up a significant proportion of the forces opposing the insurgents—had become angry at three Havana newspapers that had criticized General Weyler. When the *voluntarios* precipitated a serious riot, Lee at first thought the *Maine* should be called, but the rioting subsided and he then counseled restraint. Washington, however, did not take his advice. On January 24, McKinley acted, informing Lee that the *Maine* would call at Havana in a day or so, ostensibly to resume the customary practice of making regular naval visits to Cuba that was suspended during Cleveland's Administration. In response the Consul General advocated postponement for six or seven days to let tensions relax further. After his advice again had gone unheeded, he reported that authorities in Havana attributed an ulterior purpose to the United States action: The coming of the *Maine* might be intended to undermine the policy of autonomy. Once more Lee's views were dismissed. After Washington cleared the visit with Madrid, the *Maine* set out for Havana.[50]

Secretary of the Navy John D. Long summarized in his personal journal the reasons behind the dispatch of the *Maine*. Cleveland earlier had ordered an end to these naval visits, but McKinley had decided to alter this policy "not only because our vessels ought to be going in and out of it [Havana] like those of any other nation, it being a friendly port, but

[also], in view of the possibility of danger to American life and property, some means of protection should be at hand." Noting the existing arrangements to deploy the *Maine* to Havana should trouble develop, Long criticized them as being risky; it would seem better to send the *Maine* before an emergency developed, rather than afterwards. He thought it wise policy to send the *Maine* "in a friendly way to Havana, to make the usual visit and to resume the usual practice, which exists with all other nations, of free ingress and egress, to exchange courtesies and civilities with the Spanish authorities there, and to emphasize the change and the improved condition of things which have resulted from the new Spanish policy." Some journalists attributed "hidden meaning" to the visit, but Long maintained that it was "purely a friendly matter, and a resumption of customary relations." The Secretary ended his diary entry on a worried note: "There is, of course, the danger that the arrival of the ship may precipitate some crisis or riot; but there is far less danger of this than if the ship went in any other way. I hope, with all my heart, that everything will turn out right." Sadly, he was not to gain his fervent desire.[51]

The *Maine* anchored in Havana harbor on January 25, and the visit began well. Both Captain Charles D. Sigsbee, commanding the battleship, and Consul General Lee reported favorable reactions to the presence of the *Maine*. Sigsbee paid official visits to dignitaries and attended a bullfight and other such events, none of which led to difficulties. On February 1 he reported complacently, "In my opinion the arrival of the *Maine* has caused the United States Government to dominate the situation. It has reduced to absurdity the warnings and implied threats published from Spanish sources previous to the arrival of the vessel." Even if there was evidence of deep antagonism toward Americans, he believed that the presence of the *Maine* tended to discourage demonstrations. And to sustain the moral effect that his visit had produced, he recommended that his relief take the form of a vessel with equal or greater power, perhaps one of the battleships *Texas, Massachusetts,* or *Iowa.*

Lee quickly objected when Secretary Long subsequently suggested withdrawal of the *Maine* from Havana for reasons of sanitation. He anticipated no health problem for the ship until April or May. "Ship or ships should be kept here all the time now," he informed Assistant Secretary of State William R. Day. "We should not relinquish position of peaceful control of situation, or conditions would be worse than if vessel had never been sent." Like Sigsbee, the Consul General believed that a first-class battleship should relieve the *Maine* to serve "as object lesson and to counteract Spanish opinion of our Navy." In a personal letter to Day he expressed himself even more bluntly: If the *Maine* left and were not replaced, "many will claim Spain demanded it should go, and thought it had been here long enough." He preferred the status quo: "We are master of the situation here and I would not disturb or alter it." Whatever McKinley or Long had intended, their representatives in Havana believed that the *Maine's* principal mission was to intimidate the Spanish authorities.[52]

Meanwhile, reports of terrible human suffering continued to come in from Cuba. While the *Maine* remained in Havana, another American man-of-war, the unprotected cruiser *Montgomery*, visited several coastal cities of Cuba. On February 3 it called at Matanzas, and five days later at Santiago de Cuba. The officer in command, Commander George A. Converse, rendered a frightening report on the *reconcentrados*. Most of those at Matanzas were women and children, "all emaciated, sick, and almost beyond relief, unless they could have the benefit of regular treatment in the hospitals." An average of forty-six people died each day. Equally disturbing reports came from Havana. Sigsbee supported Lee's conviction that autonomy could not succeed. This reform, he wrote Long, was acceptable only to Spaniards temporarily located in Cuba who were "irreconcilably in favor of the old order of things."[53]

At the same time Woodford began to report signs of hesitancy in the Spanish government. The delay in developing autonomy for Cuba he attributed to the state of public opinion in Spain. Sagasta was planning an election to return members to the Cortes, and the Ministry (except for Moret) wished to take account of public attitudes and proceed deliberately. A few days later Woodford noted public disappointment in the Liberal government because of its failure to break the will of the Cuban insurgents. It now seemed unlikely that pacification could take place before the rainy season. As February wore on, the American minister once again expressed fear that war would occur because of the failure of autonomy, noting signs that Spain was seriously considering hostilities rather than further concessions. War with the United States might offer the only means of preserving not only the Liberal ministry but the dynasty itself.

The growing suspicions in Madrid that autonomy might not succeed possessed a real basis in fact. Bereft of other options, Sagasta tended more and more to rely simply on delay, hoping that a way out of the crisis would eventually materialize. This sterile policy could not counteract the destabilizing impact of the dramatic incidents that soon took place.[54]

On February 9, 1898, the *New York Journal* published a private letter from Enrique Dupuy de Lôme, the Spanish minister, to José Canalejas, an influential Spanish editor and politician, that contained highly derogatory references to President McKinley. After a sojourn in the United States Canalejas had carried this missive to Havana about the middle of December, 1897. The letter returned to New York in the possession of one Gustavo Escoto, who had managed to steal it in Havana. Escoto immediately delivered his prize to Tomas Estrada Palma. Not wishing to publicize the letter himself, the chief of the *junta* assigned this responsibility to an active supporter, a lawyer named Horatio Rubens, who offered the letter both to William Randolph Hearst's *Journal* and Joseph Pulitzer's *New York World.* When inquiries were made in Washington concerning the letter, Dupuy de Lôme became aware that his candid comments had come into the possession of the *junta.* Realizing that their publication would make his position in Washington untenable, he offered his resignation on February 8. The next day the letter appeared in the *Journal.* Dupuy de Lôme immediately reported this news to Gullón, who accepted his resignation the following day. Rubens took the purloined document to the State Department on the morning of February 9. Alvee A. Adee, an experienced official, at first denied its authenticity, but a comparison of the signature of Rubens's letter with another in the possession of the State Department forced the unwilling official to admit that it was genuine. When Assistant Secretary of State Day raised the matter with Dupuy de Lôme, the Spaniard made no attempt to deny authorship, saying that he had already sent in his resignation to Madrid. Woodford received the same information when he called on Gullón to demand the luckless diplomat's recall. On February 11, Juan du Bosc, a subordinate in the Spanish legation, announced himself as *chargé d'affaires,* and Dupuy de Lôme went off to Spain by way of Canada.[55]

Dupuy de Lôme's letter to Canalejas discussed a number of topics. Reporting that the situation remained stable in Washington, the minister opined that the outcome of the crisis in relations between Spain and America would depend on the results of political and military activity in Cuba. He strongly opposed negotiations with either the insurgents or the autonomists, contending that neither group possessed legal standing. Unless a settlement were achieved, public opinion in the United States—if not overt action by the government itself—would lend encouragement to the insurgent cause. Adverting momentarily to the negotiation of a new commercial treaty, he thought it might be advantageous to send an emissary to discuss the question, particularly with members of the Senate, if only for effect. At another point he inveighed against the "newspaper rabble" of England, maintaining that "England's only object is that the Americans should amuse themselves with us and leave her alone, and if there should be a war, that would the better stave off the conflict which she dreads but which will never come about."

These aspects of the letter, while certainly indiscreet, were not nearly as explosive as a paragraph dealing with President McKinley:

> Besides the ingrained and inevitable bluntness [grosería] with which is repeated [in McKinley's annual message] all that the press and public opinion in Spain have said about Weyler, it once more proves what McKinley is, weak and a bidder for the admiration of the crowd, besides being a would-be politician [*politicastro*] who tries to leave a door open behind himself while keeping on good terms with the jingoes of his party.[56]

Dupuy de Lôme had gained a reputation as a skilled and respected diplomat, but this statement—which, had it come from a partisan orator of the Democratic Party, would have aroused hysterical applause in many quarters—immediately ended his usefulness in Washington.

However scandalous, it seemed likely that the Dupuy de Lôme affair would soon fade from public notice, especially given Madrid's willingness to rectify the blunder. Secretary of the Navy Long summed up the feelings of at least some within the McKinley Administration, referring to Dupuy de Lôme's letter as an "unfortunate occurrence" and and "exceeding folly," especially because the Spanish minister was "a man of a good deal of ability" who had rendered excellent service. For his part the President reacted calmly. He appears to have drafted a note indicating how the Spanish government should respond to the American protest: The apology should contain "expressions of pained surprise and regret at the Minister's reprehensible allusions to the President and the American people, which it is needless to say the Govt. of His Majesty does not share, and promptly disavows." Woodford did not believe that the scandal would affect his activities in Madrid adversely, although he feared that Dupuy de Lôme's slighting reference to the negotiations for a commercial treaty might slow that enterprise. As soon as possible the Spanish government posted a new envoy to Washington—Luis Polo de Bernabé, whose father, an admiral, had once held the same position. Since both Madrid and Washington had acted intelligently, the sensation seemed to decline.[57]

Just six days after the publication of the Dupuy de Lôme letter, the whole situation was revolutionized when the battleship *Maine* exploded in the harbor of Havana. The destruction of the American vessel marked a most important juncture on the road to war. Prior to this catastrophe the problem of Cuba had constituted only one of a number of public issues to which the American people and their leaders gave attention. After February 15, however, Cuban issues consumed the body politic, displacing all other concerns.

In 1897 McKinley had pressed Spain to adopt autonomy for Cuba. Spain, for reasons of its own, followed that course, but it did not lead to the relaxation of tensions devoutly hoped for in both Washington and Madrid, primarily because the Cuban insurgents, sensing victory in the offing, refused to settle for any arrangement short of independence. McKinley had granted to Sagasta what seemed a reasonable period of time in which to pacify Cuba. Now the extraordinary public reaction to the sinking of the *Maine* was forcing the President to consider making new requirements of the Spanish government; he might ultimately have to move beyond his demand for autonomy. For its part, Spain adopted delaying tactics while seeking support from the great powers of Europe to counteract the pressure of the United States.[58]

☆ TWO ☆

The Failure of Diplomacy

Opponents of intervention in Cuba reacted powerfully to the popular clamor for action that followed the sinking of the *Maine*. General Grenville M. Dodge, a leading railroad executive, proclaimed to McKinley that the United States could not afford war and should not fight unless it had to defend its integrity. Like many businessmen, he believed that warfare would engender economic instability. "Other nations would be brought into it," he added, "and then no one could underestimate the great distress and destruction that would come upon our country." A leading journalist, the liberal Edwin L. Godkin of the *Nation*, chastised the principal "yellow journals" of New York City—William Randolph Hearst's *Journal* and Joseph Pulitzer's *World* —thus: "Nothing so disgraceful as the behavior of . . . these newspapers in the past week has ever been known in the history of American journalism." Within the Administration the sensitive Secretary of the Navy, John D. Long, observed that despite a certain surface calm "underneath there is an intense excitement. The slightest spark is liable to result in war with Spain." Unlike the jingoes of the day, he was not absolutely certain of victory. Although the United States would probably prevail, he realized that "the horrors and costs and miseries of war are incalculable; so much, too, especially in naval warfare, now depends upon chance and accident." The armored ships upon which the United States was placing its principal reliance had never been tested in combat. Probably remembering the *Maine*, he characterized modern steel ships as "experiments which have never

30

been tried. . . . In the friction of a fight [they] have almost as much to fear from some disarrangement of their own tremendous armament as from the foe.''[1]

The humanitarian, economic, and prudential arguments against war with Spain obviously influenced McKinley. On February 26 a close observer and confidant of the chief executive, Charles G. Dawes, recorded his impressions: ''While the President stands for peace and conservatism he is prepared to deal with events as they may arise. With such a man as President, war is impossible unless our cause is absolutely just and right.'' Dawes ended with a comment about McKinley's firmness that Theodore Roosevelt and other impetuous proponents of action would have ridiculed: ''When his mind is made up he is inflexible and immovable.'' Nevertheless, the man from Oyster Bay otherwise agreed with Dawes's observations on McKinley's policy. Writing to his brother-in-law at about this time, Roosevelt noted, ''We are certainly drifting towards, and not away from war; but the President will not make war, and will keep out of it if he possibly can.'' Perhaps hopefully, he concluded, ''Nevertheless, with so much loose powder round, a coal may hop into it at any moment.''[2]

No one in the Administration would have entertained the possibility of war, had it not been for the ungovernable uproar throughout the country that followed the destruction of the *Maine*. One of Secretary Long's correspondents, Robert M. Morse, complained bitterly about the public hysteria and saw trouble in it. ''I believe that to-day our greatest danger as a people is in the existence of this braggart and jingo spirit which is ready to insult other governments and nations and to threaten war and perhaps go to war.'' He was grateful that Washington had remained unaffected: ''All the more are we proud and thankful that the national administration is calm and just and that it will not permit such a blot on civilization as a war with Spain would be.'' Another of Long's correspondents, a state legislator in Massachusetts named Walter L. Bouvé, pointed out that many Americans thought McKinley might yield too much for the sake of peace: ''If peace can be obtained without sacrifice, the people desire it, but they are not in a mood to yield much; and there is a general desire to have action taken to free Cuba.'' Within the United States, then, a tug of war was shaping; it would pit the people against William McKinley.[3]

RISING TENSIONS

In Madrid the conscientious Woodford continued to search diligently for a diplomatic opening, but he did not find one during the brief lull following the initial reaction to the sinking of the *Maine*. On February 23 he described to McKinley a discouraging discussion with Queen

María Cristina, who once again brought up the question of the Cuban *junta* in New York. Woodford immediately observed that the Spanish note of February 1 accusing the United States of giving aid and comfort to the Cuban insurgents had been "most unfortunate," but the Queen Regent refused to concede that the *junta*—and thus the Cuban rebels—did not receive American assistance. Whatever the facts, he concluded, "all Spain has been educated to believe that all help to the insurrection comes from us and that the rebellion only lives because of our sympathy and assistance." He doubted that this conviction could be altered or that Spain would make further substantive concessions. Writing to the President again only three days later, he rehearsed his view that, while Moret and his colleagues very much desired peace, they would fight should they decide that war was necessary to avoid revolution and preserve the Restoration of 1875. "They prefer the chances of war, with the certain loss of Cuba, to the overthrow of the Dynasty. They know that we want peace, if we can get such justice for Cuba and such protection of American interests as will make peace permanent and prevent this old Cuban question from continental resurrection." He had informed Moret and Gullón that the Spanish attempt to attribute the continuance of the insurrection to America was "a serious mistake," and that he would advise his principals to delay their response. "Whether our answer should be pleasant or disagreeable must depend entirely on practical results in Cuba."[4]

Spain was playing for time, seeking to avoid further concessions to the Americans and thereby to placate domestic criticism. In these circumstances McKinley had to pin his hopes for a peaceful outcome on the possibility that Cuban autonomy might begin to yield results. On February 26 Sagasta dissolved the Cortes to hold an election that he felt would strengthen his parliamentary support. The new legislature was to convene on April 20. Woodford realized that the rainy season in Cuba—when active military campaigning normally slackened—would have begun before the new Cortes could complete much business, and the Spanish government could then argue that it required additional time to pacify Cuba.[5]

On March 1 McKinley sent Woodford a long instruction as guidance for his minister's efforts to obtain quick action on Cuba. This message—not to be communicated to Gullón—consisted largely of general observations about the situation in Cuba: Information available in Washington indicated "the absence of any substantial success of Spanish arms." Although autonomy had been undertaken in good faith, it had been extended only to a limited region of Cuba; therefore "it may be premature to judge how far it effectively supplies a remedy for the evils under which the Cuban administration has admittedly labored for many years past.'' Neither the Cuban insurgents nor the pro-Spanish elements in Cuba were reconciled to autonomy. Finally, ''the condition of the island in its financial and productive aspects has not changed for the better. It is rather, if anything, worse.'' In this context the President once again brought up the *reconcentrados:* Despite efforts to ameliorate their suffering by distributing private relief through the Red Cross, thousands of Cubans still found themselves in the most grievous circumstances. Although McKinley did not say so, he expected Woodford to employ the four points as counters to the delaying tactics of Madrid. Presumably, if Spain did not correct the situation in Cuba, the United States would have to take action.[6]

The Liberal ministry ventured nothing in the early weeks of March to indicate that it might alter established policy. Far from conceding anything, Moret communicated to Woodford his lack of confidence in Consul General Lee and also his objections to the use of American naval vessels as means of conveying relief to Cuba. The State Department summarily refused to either relieve Lee or deliver aid for the *reconcentrados* in noncombatant vessels. On March 3 Assistant Secretary Day—the *de facto* Secretary of State, given John Sherman's senility—penned a commentary to Woodford on the growth of anti-Spanish sentiment in the United States after the Dupuy de Lôme and *Maine* affairs: ''The policy of starvation, the failure of Spain to take effective measures to suppress this insurrection, the loss of our commerce, the great expense of patrolling our coast (to stop filibustering)—these things, intensified by the insulting and insincere character of the [Dupuy de Lôme] letter, all combine to create a situation that is very grave, and which will require the highest wisdom and greatest prudence on both sides to avoid a crisis.'' This letter, like McKinley's instruction of March 1, was intended to supply Woodford with diplomatic ammunition. Washington obviously believed that it must convey to Sagasta and his colleagues the increasing possibility that the United States would intervene if pacification did not occur in Cuba.[7]

At this point President McKinley engineered a dramatic effort to exert additional pressure on Madrid; he pushed through Congress a law authorizing the expenditure of $50 million for national defense. Working through Representative Joseph G. Cannon (Republican from Illinois) and other members of the House Appropriations Committee, he introduced this legislation on March 7. As Cannon remembered it, McKinley told the congressmen whom he enlisted for this purpose, ''I must have money to get ready for war. I am doing everything possible to prevent war but it must come, and we are not prepared for war.'' He added an ominous reflection: "Who knows where this war will lead us; it may be more than war with Spain." Cannon may have embroidered McKinley's statements. Although McKinley must certainly have recognized by March that war was now much more probable than at any previous time, and that some steps must be taken to prepare the armed forces, it is most likely that the "Fifty-Million-Dollar Bill" was designed primarily to deter Spain from continuing intransigence. It was intended not as the beginning of mobilization but generally as a means of improving the nation's defenses and particularly as a show of strength to impress Spain. Secretary Long interpreted the bill in the latter light, referring to it as a "peace measure" and hoping that it would exert a "mollifying effect" on Spanish opinion. "The Queen Mother, a good woman, mother and ruler, is anxious for peace; a liberal Spanish Ministry is evidently desirous for peace and has made every concession that we have asked, and if we can allay the excitement of the Spanish public, a quiet result is to be hoped for." The Fifty-Million-Dollar Bill became law on March 9, the House approving it by a vote of 311 to 0 and the Senate by 76 to 0. Its key provision allocated $50 million "for the National defense and for each and every purpose connected therewith to be expended at the discretion of the President." This flexible authority gave McKinley almost unprecedented freedom in dispensing the appropriation.[8]

This lightning action of Congress much pleased President McKinley. Charles G. Dawes summarized the views of the White House thus: "The President stands for any course consistent with national honor which will bring peace." The fund would be most useful in the event of war, but, more important, "the fact that it is placed in his hand is a vindication of his policy, and adds to his power to control the situation in the interests of honorable peace." Even William Jennings Bryan, the titular leader of the Democratic Party, lent support to the Administration's course, saying that the Fifty-Million-Dollar Bill would "show the world that Congress and the American people, without regard to political differences, are ready to support the Administration in any action necessary for the protection of the honor and the welfare of the nation."[9]

Woodford immediately reported Madrid's reaction to the bill. "It has not excited the Spaniards—it has stunned them," he chortled. "To appropriate fifty millions out of the money in the Treasury, without borrowing a cent, demonstrates wealth and power." Like Dawes, he noted to the President that the unrestricted scope of the legislative authority and the unanimous vote in Congress showed "absolute confidence in you by all parties. The Ministry and the press are simply stunned." He cautioned, however, that a Spanish acquaintance had told him, "The vote of fifty millions by the American Congress ended all hope of the success of autonomy, as it would certainly encourage the rebels to persevere."[10] Here was an important observation indeed. With each turn of the screw on Spain, the Cuban insurgents were the more emboldened to hold out for independence. McKinley could thus expect no cooperation from Estrada Palma, Gómez, and other insurgent leaders in his efforts to force a satisfactory outcome to the autonomy experiment.

Leaders in both Washington and Madrid realized that the report of the American naval court of inquiry on the *Maine* would have imposing political consequences. Du Bosc, the Spanish chargé d'affaires, reported to Gullón on the "feverish anxiety" with which the finding was awaited: "If it declares that the catastrophe was due to an accident, I believe I can assure your excellency that the present danger will be over, but if, on the contrary, it alleges that it was the work of a criminal hand, then we shall have to face the gravest situation." The most critical question that the naval inquiry would decide was whether the explosion was of external or internal origin. If the naval court found it of external origin, President McKinley would have to take important steps.[11]

Both the United States and Spain conducted investigations. They were completed almost simultaneously, but they were not in agreement. On March 21, 1898, the American court held that a submarine mine, set off outside the *Maine* by persons unknown, had caused the forward magazines of the vessel to explode, the force of which explosion sunk the ship. The very next day the Spanish inquiry predictably came to a different conclusion: The *Maine's* forward magazines had indeed exploded, but from internal causes. In support of this allegation the Spanish report stressed various circumstances: the failure of a geyser of water to shoot up, as normally occurs with an external explosion; the lack of dead fish in the vicinity of the wreck; and the absence of an opportunity for anyone to place a submarine mine near the *Maine's* mooring. It is now almost universally believed that the Spanish view was correct, but the situation in 1898 did not permit a comprehensive and objective inquiry. Because both governments defended their own reports, the investigations accomplished nothing, except to strengthen the conflicting prejudgments that had become general in the two nations.[12]

Although the Sampson report had increased the probability of intervention, McKinley persevered in his search for peace. He decided to submit the report to Congress without appending recommendations. If intervention were to come, Dawes learned from the President, it would be based "on broader grounds than the question of responsibility for the disaster to the *Maine.*"[13] The Administration could hope to resist pressures for intervention only if McKinley's broad natural constituency among the most respected conservative elements in the country did not desert him.

Even before the court of inquiry completed its report on the *Maine,* there had come a most significant indication of concern from McKinley's supporters. On March 17, Senator Redfield Proctor of Vermont—a Republican with impeccable conservative credentials who was known as the "marble king" of his home state—reported to the Senate on a fact-finding visit he had recently made to Cuba. In sober and therefore all the more compelling language, Proctor confirmed tales of vast human suffering. He made no recommendations, but his speech certainly influenced many moderates to adopt a more bellicose view—and they were just those people who hitherto had followed the President's lead in supporting efforts to find a peaceful solution. In his speech the Senator definitely indicated that victory against Spain would come without much effort and would open up opportunities for investment in a desirable region. More important, however, was the emotional appeal inherent in Proctor's comments; he developed a full-blown rationale for intervention based on "undiluted humanitarianism," in which the United States would act as an unselfish representative of the civilized world in behalf of the suffering Cubans, now crushed under the heel of the cruel Spaniard. Proctor timed his effusion well, making his speech at a moment when it was most likely to have maximum impact, particularly on those who had resisted the war fever earlier. One dissent came from Thomas B. Reed (Republican from Maine), Speaker of the House of Representatives and a steadfast opponent of the war, who is alleged to have said of Proctor, owner of marble quarries in Vermont, "Proctor's position might have been expected. A war will make a large market for gravestones." This cynical reaction—apocryphal or not—was characteristic of "Czar" Reed, but what Proctor conveyed to most of his auditors was the belief that intervention was justifiable on the highest grounds of principle.[14]

Even McKinley's most avid partisan, Dawes, began to wonder whether the President would prevail. The situation had grown "more perplexing and ominous. War will be difficult to avoid." In a moment of prophetic insight—possibly in the light of Proctor's speech—he recorded his opinion that should intervention occur "it will be because starvation and suffering in Cuba is such that the United States orders it stopped on grounds of humanity and outraged justice, and that order of intervention is resisted by Spain." Military considerations as well as rising opinion may have affected Dawes: On that day he had heard the bellicose Theodore Roosevelt oppose undue delay in deciding on intervention, because Spanish naval movements, then in progress, might otherwise prejudice American prospects in a contest for command of the sea.[15]

In Spain, the resourceful if credulous Woodford felt moved to propose a new solution of the Cuban question. Despondency appeared general in Madrid; he conceded that no one but Moret still believed that the insurrection might end before the beginning of the rainy season. For this reason Woodford requested permission from Washington to negotiate for the United States to purchase Cuba, with either the Queen Regent or the Minister for the Colonies should one or the other raise the subject. Independence seemed most undesirable to him; it might "turn the Island over to a part of its inhabitants against the judgment of many of its most educated and wealthy residents." On the other hand, he also advanced a compelling argument against advising the Cuban insurgents to accept autonomy: "We may do injustice to men who have fought hard and well for liberty and they may not get justice from the insular government should it once obtain control of the Island." But if intervention should take place, the Americans would have to occupy Cuba and assume control of it. After sending this report to Washington Woodford had a talk with Moret, who wanted to know whether the United States would counsel the insurgents to accept a cease-fire and support autonomy. When Woodford replied in the negative, Moret said, "We must have peace with honor to Spain. Tell me what can be done." Woodford seized this opportunity to suggest the sale of Cuba. The very next day, however, Woodford learned that the Queen Regent was definitively opposed to any such possibility: "She wished to hand over his patrimony unimpaired to her son when he should reach his majority. . . . She would prefer to abdicate her regency and return to her Austrian home rather than be the instrument of ceding or parting with any of Spain's colonies." It appears that both McKinley and María Cristina explored the possibility of purchase, but neither could identify sufficient domestic support for this expedient.[16]

LAST NEGOTIATIONS

Woodford now realized that he must press the Spanish government more firmly than ever before, perhaps finally sensing that, despite the tantalizing gambits of Moret, Spain had no real policy except delay. On March 19 he suggested an ultimatum. He wanted to inform the Spanish government that McKinley required a solution by April 15. Assistant

Secretary Day replied immediately, noting that feeling about the *Maine* remained acute and that the grant of autonomy to the Antilles had not produced results. The situation in Cuba, he said, would force action "unless Spain restores honorable peace which will stop starvation of people and give them an opportunity to take care of themselves, and restore commerce now wholly lost." He deemed April 15 a "none too early date for the accomplishment of these purposes." The report of the naval board of inquiry would state that an external attack had sunk the American ship, and unless Spain took appropriate action the President would lay the whole matter of Cuba before the Congress. When Woodford visited Gullón, the Foreign Minister pleaded for delay until the beginning of the Cuban rainy season, but the American minister rejected this course and delivered his instruction.[17]

The very next day, however, Moret conveyed an unofficial proposal to Woodford that once again sent the American minister down the primrose path. The Minister for the Colonies suggested that the question of peace might be submitted to the legislature established in Cuba as part of the autonomic government, which would meet on May 4 with authority from Spain to work out a settlement. Madrid was prepared to accept an immediate armistice, provided that the United States would arrange for the Cuban insurgents to request it. But what if, asked Woodford, no settlement had come about by September 15? In this event, replied Moret, he would advise Sagasta to join with the United States in compelling Cuba to accept a settlement agreed upon between Washington and Madrid.[18]

A more astute diplomatist might have recognized Moret's proposal as still another delaying tactic; but Woodford rose to the bait. He reported his talk with Moret to Washington in glowing terms, concluding that he had achieved a substantive breakthrough. What was left to do was "largely a question of form." He was soon disabused of this notion. Talking with Gullón on March 25, he found the Foreign Minister interested only in the *Maine,* proposing that McKinley withhold the Sampson report from Congress and negotiate the question. Gullón referred to Moret's proposal only to the extent of indicating that nothing further could be done about the situation until the Cuban autonomic legislature met on May 4. When Woodford asked whether an armistice could be arranged immediately, he received a discouraging answer. Surprised, he sought clarification from Moret. He was told that Gullón's statement covered his proposal and that Spain would accept a request for an armistice emanating from the Cuban insurgents. Woodford still persisted in his own form of optimism, assuming that the autonomic legislature would not settle affairs during an armistice and that the only probable outcome as of September 15 would be cession of Cuba to the United States. Here was an innocent indeed![19]

McKinley could no longer delay certain important decisions. On March 25 he determined how to dispose of the Sampson report, planning to submit the document to Congress after the approaching weekend, without mentioning the Cuban imbroglio. At the same time he would request funds from Congress to provide additional relief for the *reconcentrados*. Obviously he was hoping that the *Maine* affair could be managed quietly, but he did not retreat from his view that Spain was responsible for the sinking of the *Maine*, even though the naval court of inquiry had not identified the instigator of the attack. The President had a message sent to Woodford that stated his view: "The control of the harbor remained in the Spanish Government, which, as the sovereign of the place, was bound to render protection to persons and property there, and especially to the public ship and the sailors of a friendly power." Regardless of what had caused the explosion, he believed that Spain should accept responsibility for the *Maine*'s destruction and make proper indemnification.[20]

Meanwhile, the President rejected the advice of those (including Theodore Roosevelt) who urged that the United States intercept a flotilla of Spanish destroyers supposedly then en route to the Antilles. (Actually they were destined for the Cape Verde islands.) Should he ask Madrid to recall its ships he would be placed under obligations; should his request be accepted and hostilities ensue later on, he would be accused of bad faith. Spain, he noted, had just as much right to send its vessels to Havana as the United States had to concentrate certain of its ships in the vicinity of Cuban ports. In addition, Dawes argued that to intercept the destroyers without first requesting their recall would constitute an act of piracy under international law.[21] Once again McKinley shrank from actions that might commit the country irretrievably to war.

On March 27 Assistant Secretary Day conveyed to Woodford a general statement of American views and a comprehensive proposal. Beginning with a flat statement that the President desired peace, he reviewed events since the Spanish proclamation of autonomy for Cuba, noting the failure of pacification. He dealt summarily—perhaps even a bit unkindly—with Woodford's notions about annexing Cuba: "We do not want the island." Then he stated the President's plan: "If Spain will revoke the reconcentration order and maintain the people until they can support themselves and offer to the Cubans full self-government, with reasonable indemnity, the President will gladly assist

in its consummation." McKinley would mediate to further this arrangement if both the Spanish government and the Cuban insurgents asked
him to act.[22]

When Woodford sought clarification of certain instances of broad
language in this message, he evoked from Day the most important of all
communications sent from Washington to Madrid throughout the final
crisis. What did the terms "self-government" and "full indemnity"
entail? The Secretary of State's answer moved American policy beyond
the earlier requirement that Spain grant Cuba a wide measure of home
rule to the position that Spain must give up the island: "Full self-
government would mean Cuban independence."

The earlier message of March 27 established a scenario for the accomplishment of Cuban independence. Woodford was ordered to present three general propositions:

First. Armistice until October 1. Negotiations meantime looking for
peace between Spain and insurgents through friendly offices of President United States.

Second. Immediate revocation of the reconcentrado order so as to
permit people to return to their farms, and the needy to be relieved
with provisions and supplies from United States cooperating with
authorities so as to afford full relief.

Add, if possible:

Third. If terms of peace not satisfactorily settled by October 1,
President of United States to be final arbiter between Spain and insurgents.

If Spain agrees, President will use friendly offices to get insurgents
to accept plan. Prompt action desirable.

Woodford now had in hand new policy and procedure to present to the
Liberal ministry.[23] Autonomy had not brought pacification; the United
States must either support Cuban independence or withdraw from the
affair. The latter course was impossible, given the state of public opinion
at home, and McKinley, however reluctantly, decided to press onward.

The procedural arrangements proposed on March 27 stemmed from a
meeting of the "peace faction" among Republican Senators—Mark A.
Hanna (Ohio), Charles W. Fairbanks (Indiana), Nelson W. Aldridge
(Rhode Island), Eugene Hale (Maine), John C. Spooner (Wisconsin),
and Orville H. Platt (Connecticut). However, this group was acting on
the assumption that Spain would retain nominal sovereignty of Cuba.
Unbeknownst to his senatorial supporters, McKinley simply added the
requirement of outright independence in other communications to
Woodford.

Therefore, after March 27, the terms upon which Woodford was to insist were: (1) an end to reconcentration; (2) an immediate armistice to last until October 1; and (3) a commitment that Spain accept Cuban independence, should McKinley opt for this course in the role of "final arbiter."[24]

President McKinley took this course because he decided that a less aggressive option might result in disastrous political consequences at home. Those elements in the nation who stood with him against war had lost control of opinion. As the war fever burgeoned everywhere, the historian Ernest R. May notes, "a frightened elite retreated from resistance to acquiescence." Senator Orville H. Platt of Connecticut, an advocate of peace, put McKinley's situation in a nutshell: "I think the President himself believes that the people of the United States will not tolerate much longer the war in Cuba and that, if he cannot end it by negotiations, the people will insist that he shall do so by force." If diplomatic representations did not achieve "absolute independence," Platt thought, "nothing can restrain Congress from declaring for intervention, which is the same thing as declaring war." He and fellow supporters of peace hoped that the terms sent to Woodford on March 27 would gain at least a little additional time in which to test Spain once more. Dawes summarized the President's position thus: If Spain refused the American proposition, McKinley "will use force, and his conscience and the world will justify it. He is making a magnificent fight for peace and God grant he may succeed."[25]

On March 29 Woodford presented the American proposals to Gullón. After informing the Spanish Foreign Minister that the United States did not want Cuba but desired "immediate peace," he reviewed Washington's desire for an armistice, presidential mediation, and revocation of reconcentration. The most interesting thing about Woodford's statement was its failure to make explicit mention of "full self-government." With an eye to sparing the susceptibilities of his Spanish auditor, Woodford chose to avoid the term. In any event he was convinced that negotiations would lead inexorably to some outcome satisfactory to the United States. In reporting the session with Gullón, Woodford informed McKinley, "My judgment grows more strong each day that we shall probably have to accept the ownership and the responsible management of Cuba in order to establish permanent peace in the island." Woodford's failure to state the American position fully—truly a profound dereliction of duty—has caused confusion among historians. Many have not grasped the full range of American demands at this juncture in the final crisis. Independence was indeed the most basic and important of America's requirements; if it could not be obtained, McKinley would probably have to bow to the war-hawks.[26]

Arrangements were made for Spain to respond on March 31 to the President's proposals, amid continuing indications of Washington's desire for the utmost haste. Day warned Woodford that the United States could not wait long: "It is of utmost importance that the conference be not postponed beyond next Thursday [March 31] and definite results achieved. Feeling here is intense." Day also notified Woodford that his report of affairs was "encouraging but vague as to details." He wanted it firmly understood that the United States "can not assist in enforcement of any system of autonomy." Here was another indication that the United States demanded independence for Cuba. To avoid undue provocation at this moment McKinley sent the Sampson report on the *Maine* to Congress without comment. As Charles G. Dawes noted, there was "great indignation among the more radical members of Congress" at the President's restraint. Dawes reflected a growing belief that war might not be avoidable, and even stated the principle on which it should be waged: "We all want Cuban independence, but if we fight it must be for humanity's sake, not from other motives. War is a hideous wrong when used to achieve ends possible by peace."[27]

Congressional pressure on the White House reached its height in late March and early April. Two anecdotes reflect the mood of the House and Senate. In one, an unidentified Senator visited Assistant Secretary Day about this time and expostulated, "Day, by ——, don't your President know where the war-declaring power is lodged? Tell him, by ——, that if he doesn't do something Congress will exercise the power." In the other, when Speaker Thomas Reed, bitterly opposed to a war, was asked why he did not dissuade his colleagues from their bellicose opinions (as a former governor of New York had suggested) he responded, "Dissuade them! . . . He might as well ask me to stand out in the middle of a Kansas waste and dissuade a cyclone." Another instance of the mood of the times demonstrates also how Americans of the time were wont to express their feelings in rather tasteless poetry. One versifier, Frank A. Putnam attacked the President directly in March, 1898, accusing McKinley of nothing less than cowardice and greed, because he did not take up the cause of Cuban independence:

A mighty people, proud and free, await their captain's battle call;
Their captain bends the coward knee; his nerveless hand the sword lets fall.
The heroic deeds that reft our chains arouse in him no answering fire;
Trembling, he schemes for sordid gains and sees a race in rags expire.

This expresses a view, relatively common at the time, that McKinley's policy reflected self-interested economic considerations—an indication of the public realization that the business community generally opposed intervention in Cuba.[28]

As Woodford prepared to receive Spain's response to the American proposals, Day once again described to him the mood in Washington, perhaps to make certain that the American minister fully executed his instructions. Referring to congressional sentiment for intervention as a "profound feeling," Day noted that "the most conservative members" thought a resolution to move into Cuba might pass both houses of Congress. "Only assurance from the President that if he fails in peaceful negotiations he will submit all the facts to Congress at a very early day will prevent immediate action on the part of Congress." Perhaps McKinley had begun to suspect that Moret and Gullón had to some extent succeeded in their efforts to manipulate Woodford, for Day concluded, "The President assumes that whatever may be reached in your negotiations to-morrow will be tentative only, to be submitted as the proposal of Spain. We hope your negotiations will lead to a peace acceptable to the country."[29]

At the same time the new Spanish minister in Washington, Polo de Bernabé, informed the State Department of Spanish efforts to end reconcentration. He had been reporting accurately to Gullón on the situation, noting that strong passions had been aroused because of the *Maine* disaster but also that McKinley was seeking a peaceful settlement. He made every effort to aid the distribution of American relief in Cuba, commenting on improving conditions as reported to him by Governor-General Blanco. On March 31 he eagerly conveyed to Washington the news that orders of reconcentration had been revoked for the more westerly provinces of Cuba—Havana, Matanzas, Santa Clara, and Pinar del Río. (The Spanish army had managed to achieve some degree of control in this area.) Polo was also assiduous in attempting to convince the State Department that the autonomic government had begun to function successfully.[30] These efforts, however, could not be expected to decide the outcome of the crisis. Only Spanish agreement to McKinley's proposals could accomplish that result.

On March 31 Woodford received a disappointing reply from the Liberal ministry. Spain would submit the case of the *Maine* to arbitration and proceed with efforts to end reconcentration, Blanco already having been ordered to revoke the decrees for western Cuba. The Governor-General would receive a large sum to facilitate the return of the *reconcentrados* to their homes. Spain would refer peace negotiations to the Cuban legislature—scheduled to meet on May 4—with the proviso that "the powers reserved by the constitution to the Central Government are not lessened and diminished." Presumably Madrid could repudiate any unpalatable decision reached in Cuba. Finally, Spain would accept a request from the Cuban insurgents that they be granted a truce, but its duration would be left to Blanco. Woodford admitted to Day that certain provisions of this program were unacceptable and that the response generally did not provide for an "immediate or assured peace." And yet, in a cable to McKinley on March 31 he stressed the fact that Spain had now made concessions it could not have considered a month earlier—even if, because of "Spanish pride," Madrid would still not propose an armistice. (The American minister had been confidentially informed that any such action would precipitate a revolution in Spain.) In a letter written the next day Woodford wrote of detecting a decline in the "war spirit" among the middle and lower classes of Spain, although the upper classes remained intransigent, particularly the military. The army, he conceded, was "still the controlling factor in Spanish politics, and the attitude of the army constitutes the real danger to-day." On April 2 he reiterated his earlier view that, provided an armistice could be arranged, negotiations would lead to peace.[31]

Like so many well-intentioned, conscientious, but inexperienced American diplomats before and since, Woodford found it exceedingly difficult to accept failure. He lacked sufficient insight into the history of Spain and its contemporary circumstances to realize that Sagasta's refusal to grant independence was much more than a question of punctilio. Neither Woodford nor any other American leader of 1898 fully comprehended the extent to which the loss of Cuba represented a repudiation of Spain's most pervasive and emotional national myth—the conviction that Cuba and the rest of the great overseas empire had been a gift from God as reward for the *reconquista,* the reconquest of Spain from the Muslims. Nor did Woodford and his superiors understand the workings of the Spanish constitutional system that had functioned since 1875. That delicate structure could not withstand the shock of losing Cuba without a fight, or so believed the leaders of Spain.

On April 3 the guileless Woodford experienced a rebirth of hope; Gullón informed him that Pope Leo XIII, responding to a suggestion of President McKinley, had offered to mediate the conflict between the United States and Spain. The Foreign Minister said that Spain would accept the Pope's proposal if the United States agreed to withdraw its naval forces from the vicinity of Cuba, this action to come after the insurgents had been granted an armistice. Woodford then reported to Washington his continuing belief that, once an armistice took effect, hostilities would not resume and it would become possible to arrange a permanent peace. He wanted the United States to move its naval vessels from Cuban waters, arguing that Spain would proceed as fast and far as it could toward peace. "If conditions at Washington still enable you to give me the necessary time," he concluded, "I am sure that before next October 1 I will get peace in Cuba with justice to Cuba and protection to our great American interests." The Queen Regent, her Cabinet, and the Spanish people desired peace; if given reasonable time and adequate freedom of action, he promised McKinley once again, he would obtain "the peace you desire so much and for which you have labored so hard."[32]

The proposal for papal mediation represented an outcropping of an enterprise that Spain had pursued with considerable vigor during the final crisis, an effort to marshal diplomatic support in Europe as one means of deterring American intervention in Cuba. If the great powers could be persuaded to support Spain in some fashion, the United States would have to calculate the cost of defying not simply Spain but organized international opinion as well.

SPAIN'S QUEST FOR INTERNATIONAL SUPPORT

In September, 1897, when Woodford first pressed Spain to grant autonomy to Cuba, the German Kaiser, Wilhelm II, had expressed violent irritation: "It is high time that we other monarchs . . . agree jointly to offer our help to the Queen," he argued, "in case the American-British Society for International Theft and Warmongering looks as if it seriously intends to snatch Cuba from Spain." In response to this comment Prince Bernhard von Bülow, the German Foreign Minister, urged caution upon the Kaiser. If Germany lent support to Spain, France and England might exploit this action for their own purposes. (He had in mind affairs in the Far East and Africa.) If Germany tied itself to Spain, its rivals might steal a march in their efforts to gain advantage in the imperialist competition of the day. In his memoirs Bülow left no doubt of his purpose: "I strove to convince the Kaiser that we must steadily pursue a strictly neutral course and stand carefully aloof for many reasons, one of them being that the ultimate victory of the Americans was certain."[33]

Bülow's views found an echo in the reactions of Count Mikhail Muraviev, the Russian Foreign Minister. When the French envoy in St. Petersburg inquired about Russia's attitude toward the quarrel between Spain and the United States, Count Muraviev in unmistakably frigid language "declared . . . unhesitatingly that he would regard as inopportune any *démarche* in the United States by the powers." He wanted to neither intervene in American affairs nor allow the United States to participate "in any version of the concert of powers." Obviously Russia would not accept leadership in a campaign to frustrate American desires.[34]

Spain's cause proved more attractive elsewhere, but to no real effect. Gabriel Hanotaux, the Foreign Minister of France, evinced greater interest than Bülow and Muraviev in coming to the assistance of Spain, but he did not enjoy room for maneuver. France's main ally, Russia, opposed any such course, and impending difficulties with Great Britain over African questions—soon to erupt in the incident at Fashoda—also suggested restraint. Austria-Hungary's Foreign Minister, Count Agenor von Goluchowski, might be expected to support Spanish interests because the Queen Regent came from his country, but the Dual Monarchy was in no position to exert prime leadership. It held no overseas colonies, and its trade with the United States was negligible. Ernest R. May points out that if Austria had proposed European intervention in behalf of Spain, it would have been asking others to take risks it would not have had to run itself. "Austria," therefore, "could only act as broker, as go-between for nations with more varied interests at stake." Italy, weakest of the six great powers, never contemplated a vigorous American policy. Rome could promise only to cooperate with the initiatives of others.[35]

Despite irritation with the Americans and sympathy for the Spanish, none of the great powers showed any inclination to act against the United States without assurance of support from all the others. Hannis Taylor, President Cleveland's minister in Madrid, had summarized their situation well: "The interests of Europe are so diverse, and in many respects so mutually hostile, that it would be very difficult to organize a coalition of them against us." Some Americans, however, remained wary. Theodore Roosevelt reflected the tendency to worry more about Wilhelmian Germany than any other power: "With Russia I don't believe we are in any danger," he wrote to a friend, "but with Germany, under the Kaiser, we may at any time have trouble if she seeks to acquire territory in South America." Roosevelt need not have troubled himself. At just this time Bülow was explaining to his ambassador in Austria-Hungary that any suggestion of concerted European action against the United States "made by the Berlin or the Vienna Cabinet would be without result and merely increase the tension existing between America and Spain."[36]

Of greatest concern to the United States was the attitude of Great Britain, because that nation was best equipped to act against American interests. It possessed a great navy, one fully capable of protecting

Spain's possessions in the Caribbean Sea. However, when on March 17, 1898 María Cristina wrote to her relative, Queen Victoria, in search of support, the Marquess of Salisbury, serving in the dual capacity of Prime Minister and Foreign Minister, pointed out the reasons why Great Britain could not take action. He agreed that although María Cristina was in a "lamentable and grievous" position, one that aroused the deepest sympathy, "any communication from this country to the United States, in the way of remonstrances, might arouse susceptible feelings and produce a condition of some danger, without any corresponding advantage." He would not repulse collective action by all the great powers, but he doubted its wisdom because it might strengthen rather than weaken the "war party" in the United States. Obviously, Spain could expect no real aid from London.[37]

María Cristina's letter to Queen Victoria constituted one aspect of a general Spanish effort to acquire European support as a crisis with the United States approached late in March. On March 25 Gullón informed his envoys to the important powers that, should the United States fail to accept Spain's views concerning the *Maine* and other pending matters, they should "ask the counsel of the great powers and, in the last resort, their mediation to adjust the pending differences, which differences, in the near future, may disturb a peace that the Spanish nation desires to preserve as far as its honor and the integrity of its territory will permit, not only on its own account, but because war, once begun, affects all other powers of Europe and America." To its various diplomatic inquiries, Spain received diverse responses from the powers. Most commonly it heard that the government approached would participate in a joint representation—if all the others were in agreement. The unlikely possibility of unanimity disappeared altogether when Salisbury, inquiring of his ambassador in Washington, Sir Julian Pauncefote, about the American attitude, learned that the United States considered European action premature and unacceptable. For a brief moment at the end of March Fernando León y Castillo, the Spanish ambassador in Paris, erroneously reported that all the powers were prepared to make representations to the United States; Sagasta, Moret, and Gullón must have been overjoyed, but they were quickly disabused of their notion. Madrid soon heard that Britain would not act and Germany would also probably refuse to participate.[38]

At this point, much to the surprise of Madrid, it received news of the Pope's offer to mediate its differences with Washington. This papal *démarche* stemmed from a German proposal. After the Vatican made known its support of Catholic Spain, Bülow on March 27 instructed his agent at the Vatican to propose papal assistance. He did not particularly wish to help Spain retain Cuba; instead he wanted to see to it that its loss occurred "in a form which should not threaten the continuance of the present monarchy, or throw the country into the arms of either the Carlists or a republic—or both together, as happened early in the seventies." Berlin thought this proposal opportune because it seemed to provide a means of preserving the Spanish monarchy without running the risk of diplomatic complications with the United States. The Vatican received the impression from Berlin that Madrid was prepared to accept Cuban independence and that Germany was acting for Spain. Cardinal Rampolla, the Vatican's Foreign Minister, then arranged to have the Roman Catholic Archbishop John H. Ireland of Minneapolis, a friend of President McKinley, visit Washington to explore the possibility of papal mediation. Hastening to the nation's capital, Ireland saw McKinley on April 1. He then reported to Rampolla that McKinley desired peace and wanted help to obtain it. Washington would accept either a proposal to purchase Cuba or an armistice leading to Cuban-Spanish negotiations. The President sought authority to dictate a final settlement if negotiations between the principals came to naught.[39]

On the strength of this inaccurate information about McKinley's willingness to accept a purchase or an armistice the Vatican made its proposition of papal arbitration to Spain. Merry del Val, the Spanish representative at the Holy See, cabled Gullón that McKinley appeared "well disposed to accept the offices of the Pope. . . . The latter, wishing to aid us, inquires, first, if the intervention of His Holiness to ask the armistice would save the national honor; second, if such intervention would be acceptable to His Majesty and the Government." Gullón responded immediately that his nation was prepared to accept papal mediation as soon as the United States gave the signal to proceed. The Queen Regent and Moret supported Gullón in this course despite opposition from the Ministers of War and the Marine. Spain would agree to suspend hostilities in Cuba, provided the United States withdrew its naval forces from the Caribbean area, a way of showing that the United States did not support the insurrection. Gullón then communicated Spain's views to Woodford.[40]

However, all this activity led only to an immediate and definitive rejection from Washington. McKinley had not intended to request papal mediation in his conversation with Archbishop Ireland. His purpose had been to exert additional pressure through Ireland for acceptance of the American offer earlier presented to the Liberal ministry. When Washington learned of the Vatican's proposal, Day on April 3 sent Woodford a clear summation of the situation as it appeared to him. The United States had authorized no presentations to Spain except those of March 27. An armistice must stem from voluntary actions on the part of the Spanish authorities and the Cuban insurgents. "The disposition of our fleet must be left to us. An armistice, to be effective, must be immediately proffered [by Spain] and accepted by insurgents." Day then closed with a truly significant question, one that revealed Washington's growing doubts about Woodford's relationship with the Spanish ministry and that group's commitment to Cuban freedom: "Would the peace you are so confident of securing mean the independence of Cuba?" McKinley, he noted, could not withhold a message to Congress concerning intervention in Cuba any longer than until Tuesday, April 5.[41]

Woodford soon clarified the situation in Madrid. He could not claim that his approach would ensure Cuban independence; if an armistice were to be declared, it would lead to either autonomy or cession of Cuba to the United states. Spain's attitude came through clearly in a communication to the State Department from Minister Polo de Bernabé that compared Spain's grant of autonomy to Cuba with that of Britain to Canada. He insisted that "the franchise and liberties accorded to the Cubans are such that no motive or pretext is left for claiming any fuller measure thereof." As for the discussions with Archbishop Ireland, McKinley did not immediately break them off, hoping that their continuance might influence the Spanish government—but nothing came of this course.[42]

McKinley now began to prepare his message to Congress requesting authority to intervene in Cuba. Dawes believed that the President would not recommend recognition of the insurgents, preferring instead to "defend the right to stop the trouble upon the broad grounds of humanity, by force if necessary." Senator Platt guessed that McKinley still had not made up his mind to act. No truly logical basis for a declaration of war had yet been arrived at, Platt thought: "Those who have been most eager for it are casting around for reasons to give for it." Seeking to account for the nation's hazy course, Secretary Long wrote of the toll the situation had taken on McKinley. He had "been robbed of sleep, overworked; and I fancy that I can see that his mind does not work as clearly and directly and as self-reliantly as it otherwise would." The war-hawks discerned a clear drift toward intervention. Theodore Roosevelt, for instance, told a friend: "I am happy to say that I believe the administration has made up its mind that we will have to fight unless Spain makes the only amends possible for the loss of the *Maine* by at once leaving the western world." He was exceedingly scornful of those American interests that shrank from war, complaining bitterly to Elihu Root, "You would be amazed and horrified at the peace-at-any-price telegrams of the most abject description which come in multitudes from New York, Boston, and elsewhere to the President and Senators.'' Fortunately, he informed another correspondent, other views had come to the fore: ''Pressure from the honest men of this country who are not careless of the nation's honor has been such that I believe the President will be forced to intervene. I have preached the doctrine to him in such plain language that he will no longer see me!''[43]

McKinley did not, however, observe his self-imposed deadline of April 5 for submission of the message to Congress. He delayed because Fitzhugh Lee had asked for additional time to arrange the departure of Americans from Havana. He may also have been heeding still another quixotic message from Woodford, who on April 5 cabled to ask whether McKinley would withhold action if the Queen Regent immediately proclaimed an immediate cessation of hostilities in Cuba to endure until October. This truce would allow negotiations between the autonomous government and the insurgents. In support of his plea, Woodford asked that it be considered in the light of all his previous dealings in Madrid. ''I believe that this means peace,'' he maintained, ''which the sober judgment of our people will approve long before next November [when elections would be held], and which must be approved at the bar of final history. I dare not reject this last chance for success. I will show your reply to the Queen in person, and I believe that you will approve this last conscientious effort for peace.'' He had shown the text of this message to the papal nuncio. Clearly the American envoy believed in miracles.[44]

McKinley, forever aspiring to peace, held out some grounds for hope. He had Day inform Woodford that, although his message on intervention would go to Congress the next day, April 6, he would also communicate to Congress information about any armistice that Spain might arrange, but he insisted that nothing short of ''restoration of peace and stable government in Cuba'' would satisfy the United States. He did not intend to extend diplomatic recognition to the Cuban insurgents, but would propose ''measures looking to the cessation of hostilities, the restoration of peace and stability of government in the island in the interests of humanity, and for the safety and tranquillity of our own country.'' Woodford forwarded to Gullón the text of the President's intervention message on April 6, assuming that it would go to Congress that day. Much to his relief, the minister learned that its delivery to Congress had been postponed to April 11. To Day he wrote wishfully, ''I hope that this [delay] will also give the Spanish Government the time in which to issue a frank and effective proclamation of such an armistice as may lead to an early and honorable peace.'' Woodford clearly did not think that the Sagasta government would concede independence. But he still hoped that, when an armistice had been arranged, McKinley would agree that cessation of hostilities must eventually lead to the end of Spanish sovereignty in Cuba.[45]

As Woodford awaited a break in the Spanish position, a diplomatic charade in Washington occurred that revealed the United States did not have to fear European intervention on behalf of Spain. On April 6 the ambassadors of the great powers—Austria-Hungary, France, Germany, Great Britain, Italy, and Russia—called upon President McKinley to present a brief note. This message called for manifestations of "humanity and moderation" in dealing with the Cuban question and expressed the pious hope that further negotiations would lead not only to peace but to guarantees of order in Cuba. It ended lamely, "The Powers do not doubt that the humanitarian and purely disinterested character of this representation will be fully recognized and appreciated by the American nation." McKinley responded in his most kindly fashion, marking the good will of the great powers and expressing hope for an end to the "chronic condition of disturbance" in Cuba. The United States understood the motives of the great powers, he stated; it was "confident that equal appreciation will be shown for its own earnest and unselfish endeavors to fulfill a duty to humanity by ending a situation the indefinite prolongation of which has become insufferable."[46]

Hengervar von Hengelmüller, the Austrian envoy, seems to have led this movement to approach the President. But all this ceremony merely confirmed what had become apparent long before, that the great powers sympathized with Spain but had no intention of provoking the United States, especially since the British government would not agree to challenge the United States directly. Spain could not count on anything but empty tokens of good will from the giants of Europe, preoccupied with matters of far greater import than Spanish problems and desirous of avoiding trouble with the United States. Madrid's policy of abstention from the grand diplomatic combinations of Europe had deprived it of any claim on other capitals. Altruism was not in great supply during the anxious year of 1898, when affairs in East Asia and Africa were commanding the attention of the imperialist nations.[47]

WAR

Because McKinley had been forced to take an inflexible position, the only possibility of a diplomatic breakthrough lay with Madrid, and the Queen Regent did her best to arrange one. On April 9 she had the am-

bassadors of the great powers call at her court, as their counterparts had
called on McKinley at the White House several days earlier. The envoys
delivered a comparable message. Their joint representation forced the
Sagasta government to decide on an armistice in Cuba. Opposition to
this step, which had emanated mainly from the Ministers of War and
the Marine, had declined, because of growing awareness that Spain was
unprepared to fight the United States. Moreover, a Spanish refusal to
offer an armistice would stifle whatever remained of the prospect that
the great powers might ultimately act in behalf of Spain. Gullón immediately notified the powers of the armistice, and on April 10 Blanco
proclaimed it in Cuba. Since the Governor-General had already ended
reconcentration, this meant that two of the American demands had
been met—although not fully, because the armistice as announced in
Madrid did not provide for continuance through the rainy season. Spain
rejected this crucial requirement. Nor did it agree to Cuban independence, the *sine qua non* of peace.[48]

On April 11 President McKinley took the step he had so long
resisted; he sent a message to Congress asking authority to intervene in
Cuba. On April 10 Woodford made one last effort to delay, again
pressing the President to follow the formula urged upon him in
Madrid—negotiations after May 4 in Cuba between the autonomous
government and the insurgents; he remained convinced that this course
would lead to an acceptable outcome—autonomy, independence, or
cession of Cuba to the United States. McKinley's congressional message
summarized the course of prior negotiations in simple terms and stated
the grounds for armed intervention. The United States had suffered
economic injury, and, more important, a "perilous unrest" among the
citizenry stood in the path of "that close devotion to domestic advancement that becomes a self-contained commonwealth whose primal
maxim has been the avoidance of all foreign entanglements." Tensions
had mounted because Spain had been unable to quell the insurrection.
"The war in Cuba is of such a nature," the President continued, "that
short of subjugation or extermination a final victory for either side
seems impracticable." He contended strongly against recognition of
"the so-called Cuban Republic." This step was not required to prepare
for intervention. Furthermore, it might place the United States under
embarrassing obligations. Recognition could occur later, when the
Cuban government demonstrated the ability to function effectively.
The President then offered four reasons for armed intervention: It
would end bloodshed in Cuba; it would afford protection to American
citizens in Cuba; it would preclude further damage to trade and prop-

erty; and it would remove the menace to peace that had proved so disruptive in recent times. Given all this, McKinley asked for the necessary authority and power to intervene with such "military and naval forces of the United States as may be necessary." Here the original text ended, but McKinley appended a brief postscript: he gave notice of Madrid's most recent steps, thus fulfilling his promise to Woodford. Noting the armistice for Cuba, he held that it ought to receive careful attention. "If this measure attains a successful result, then our aspirations as a Christian, peace-loving people will be realized. If it fails, it will be only another justification for our contemplated action."[49]

McKinley asked for authority to intervene in Cuba finally because he no longer felt able to resist the manifold pressures that poured in upon him, especially from representatives of his party in Congress reflecting the passions of their constituents. Jennie Hobart, wife of the Vice-President, recalled a conversation between McKinley and her husband about this time. Garrett Hobart reported, "Mr. President, I can no longer hold back the Senate. They will act without you if you do not act at once." McKinley then asked, "Do you mean that the Senate will declare war on its own motion?" When Hobart replied affirmatively, McKinley exclaimed, "Say no more!" A congressman summarized the setting neatly in a comment to Secretary Long: There was "intense excitement which is hardly suppressed among the members of the House and Senate who, in their turn, are violently pressed by their constituents for some positive action." Long added sardonically, "Just what action, nobody seems to know." Supporters of the President's quest for a peaceful solution now sensed that no time remained to them. Ex-President Cleveland wrote sadly to a friend, "I wish the President would stand fast and persist in following the lead of his own good sense and conscience; but I am afraid he intends to defer and yield to the Congress." Moorfield Storey, a Bostonian who later became a staunch opponent of American expansionism, warned the Massachusetts Reform Club of what might come from war: Victory would be more dangerous than defeat; "in the intoxication of such a success, we should reach out for fresh territory, and to our present difficulties would be added an agitation for the annexation of new regions which, unfit to govern themselves, would govern us." He revealed a frightening vision of the future if the United States intervened in Cuba. "We should be fairly launched upon a policy of military aggression, of territorial expansion, of standing armies and growing navies, which is inconsistent with the continuance of our institutions. God grant that such calamities are not in store for us." Utterances of this sort had no effect. However prescient the opponents of war, their faint voices could not be heard above the tumult of those who screamed for armed action.[50]

McKinley took the least aggressive stance he thought possible in the circumstances. His decision not to recognize the Cuban republic distinguished his position sharply from that of extremist proponents of action. Senator Platt summarized the situation cogently: "The President and those who sustain him do not want a recognition of independence, do not want any haste, but a simple resolution directing the President to take at once such steps as may be necessary to terminate hostilities in Cuba, to form a stable government there, and to this end employ the land and naval forces of the United States." McKinley's opponents, however, sought much more; "Jingoes want independence and intervention." Platt predicted, accurately, that "the contest between the President and his opposers will go along this line." The congressional debate led to further delay.

McKinley did not oppose recognition because he wanted Cuba for the United States; overwhelming evidence points in quite another direction. He followed a moderate line because he deemed it less provocative than any other course, and it preserved a modicum of flexibility. Certain critics claim that he did not give sufficient attention to the Spanish arrangements for an armistice in Cuba. This misconception results from failure to understand that McKinley's basic requirement of Spain was that it grant independence to Cuba. Madrid's revocation of reconcentration and extension of the armistice did not meet the demands of March 27.[51]

After McKinley had asked Congress for authority to intervene in Cuba, Charles G. Dawes decided that "the hope of Spain is a foreign alliance," but despite continuing diplomatic efforts Madrid could not budge the great powers from their settled posture of nonintervention. As if to signal his failure to find support, Gullón circularized the powers on April 18, justifying the prior actions of Spain and condemning those of the United States. In Washington a curious, though ultimately trivial, incident took place: The diplomatic representatives of the great powers there considered submitting individual identic notes of remonstrance to the President. Once again Hengelmüller took a leading role in urging this course, this time with the connivance of the British Ambassador, Sir Julian Pauncefote. No one can tell what might have resulted from such an initiative, because it never came to fruition. Arthur Balfour, acting at the Foreign Office in London for the absent Lord Salisbury, effectively torpedoed it. The Austrian Foreign Minister, Goluchowski, who sympathized strongly with Spain, had to admit that "the European Powers would be playing an undignified and humiliating part in [making] representations which might be taken no notice of and which they were not prepared to follow up by any ulterior measures." In Paris Hanotaux expressed the view that European intervention "would be inopportune at this moment as being likely to cause irritation rather than appeasement." In St. Petersburg the worldly Count Muraviev told the German ambassador that Queen María Cristina, bereft of support from fellow monarchs, faced a choice between evils: "The dynasty can only be saved if the Queen puts herself in the forefront of a chauvinistic agitation and, cost what it will, go to war, even if there is no chance whatever of a happy outcome." However cynical this analysis, it possessed the virtue of verisimilitude.[52]

While Spain fruitlessly sought last-minute help from the powers, Congress debated McKinley's message. Proponents of recognition realized what the President was seeking to accomplish. Theodore Roosevelt saw that the proposed resolution embodying McKinley's request did not necessarily require immediate use of the armed forces. He wanted his friend Senator Lodge to press for recognition. "Otherwise we shall have more delay and more shilly-shallying." Lodge recognized political danger in any other than vigorous action. To an opponent of intervention, Henry Lee Higginson, he cited a cogent consideration: "The course you are advising leads straight to free silver and Bryanism." Those who wished to override the President's advice pushed for adoption of an amendment recognizing the Cuban republic, offered by Senators David Turpie (Democrat from Indiana) and Joseph B. Foraker (Republican from Ohio). The Senate accepted it by a vote of 51 to 37, but it went down in the House narrowly, by 178 to 156. An element of compromise entered into the final outcome: Spain was required to withdraw immediately from Cuba, a proviso that precluded any more than nominal delay. Proponents of recognition wisely decided to accept half a loaf. Senator William E. Chandler (Republican from New Hampshire) summarized their reasons thus: "Having accomplished our object [intervention], we did not think it was wise to go further and delay proceedings and thus play into the hands of the peace men by continuing to insist upon specific recognition."[53]

Meanwhile, without fanfare, Senator Henry M. Teller (Democrat from Colorado) had offered an amendment of great substantive importance, a disclaimer of any purpose to annex Cuba. This self-denying ordinance lent substance to the claim that the United States intended to intervene in Cuba solely on disinterested moral and humanitarian grounds. The Senate approved the Teller amendment without debate or roll-call vote; it did not arouse controversy because it seemed simply

to reiterate the principle inherent in the Foraker-Turpie amendment—that Cuba should receive its independence. At the time some
observers saw trouble ahead arising from intervention. Whitelaw
Reid—later an important member of the American commission that
negotiated peace with Spain in Paris—expressed a view that gained considerable currency during the postwar occupation of Cuba: "I hope
they [the Cubans] prove more orderly and less likely to plunge into civil
strife and brigandage than has been expected." Intervention entailed
practical obligations, but the Teller amendment repudiated them. "If
the result of our efforts is merely to establish a second Hayti nearer our
own coast," Reid worried, "it will be so pitiful an outcome from a great
opportunity as to make Mr. Gladstone's pledge to 'scuttle out of Egypt'
respectable in comparison."[54]

On April 19, 1898, the joint resolution providing for intervention in
Cuba passed the Congress, and McKinley signed it the next day at
11:54 A.M. It called for Cuban independence, immediate Spanish
withdrawal from Cuba, and, if necessary, intervention by the armed
forces of the United States. It disclaimed any American intention to ab-
sorb Cuba.[55]

If McKinley had finally capitulated to the jingoes, he did so at considerable personal cost. One of his secretaries, George M. Cortelyou,
noted his poor appearance. The President was "bearing up under the
great strain, but his haggard face and anxious inquiry of any news which
has in it a token of peace tell of the sense of tremendous responsibility
and of his devotion to the welfare of the people of this country." Cortelyou railed at those critics who charged that McKinley had been
sheltered from opponents of peace. Claiming that at least 90 percent of
the mail coming to the White House had supported the President's
pacific course, he concluded bitterly, "The ranters in Congress, the
blatherskites who do the talking upon the street-corners and at public
meetings, and the scavengers of the sensational press misrepresent
public opinion . . . when they assert that this country is for war except
as a necessity and for the upholding of the national honor." Secretary
Long believed that McKinley could have reached a settlement with
Spain if Congress had nor forced his hand.[56] Contemporary judgments
charging presidential warmongering ignored definitive evidence to the
contrary. By April, McKinley and other advocates of peace constituted a
lonely and debilitated remnant indeed. If ever there was a "popular
war"—one forced upon a reluctant leadership by the people—it was
the war of 1898. The views of the voters—particularly as refracted
through the Congress—found expression in April, 1898 only after President McKinley had unsuccessfully called on all of his political skill to
frustrate them.

In Madrid the Sagasta government had played a game parallel to that of McKinley, but time had run out. Its policy had been delay, hoping against hope that something might ultimately prevent war. Along the way the Liberal ministry made all manner of concessions—except the American *sine qua non*, independence for Cuba. By April fatalistic attitudes prevailed, one American observer in Spain noting, "Everyone here expects war, and the lower classes ardently desire it." The ministry and the "intelligent classes," dreading its prospect, were "willing to do anything they can to avoid it *without revolution,* but will accept it, from their point of view, if it is forced upon them." The Queen Regent's desire to preserve the throne of Spain for her son and the Liberal ministry's determination to preserve the constitutional regime dictated Spain's course. The prospect of victory seemed remote indeed, but armed resistance would maintain Spanish honor—at least enough to preclude a revolutionary conflagration. The same American summarized another consideration very well: The Spanish "could not be worse off with the war than without, as they are about to lose Cuba anyhow; but they can do incalculable damage to our commerce; seriously injure, if not destroy, our Navy; and although they would probably be beaten in the end, they will have taught us a salutary lesson in the meantime." On April 20, when the Cortes met, the Queen's message spoke of the "glorious traditions" of the army and navy, a united nation, and faith in God as Spain faced an obscure future.

The American ultimatum to Spain required that Spain indicate its future course by noon, April 23. Before Woodford could deliver this message, however, Gullón on April 21 ordered Polo de Bernabé to leave the United States and informed the American minister that Spain had broken diplomatic relations with the United States. On April 23, 1898 Spain declared war. In distant Luzon, at Tarlac, when a Spaniard named Carlos Ría-Baja read about the beginning of the war, he felt "cold in my soul."[57]

Meanwhile, the United States had taken action. On April 21, the navy received orders to blockade the north coast of Cuba. On April 25 the President asked Congress to make a formal declaration of war. The House and Senate responded immediately, specifying the beginning of the conflict as April 21, a step "legitimizing" the blockade of Cuba already in effect. Two important public figures left the government, though not in protest: One was the Secretary of State, John Sherman, who was finally asked to resign because of his age and infirmity. Judge William R. Day, the Assistant Secretary of State, who had performed many of Sherman's functions, took his place. At the same time the Navy Department lost its Assistant Secretary, Theodore Roosevelt, who resigned to join the army. Secretary Long, who admired his associate's energy and honesty, could not understand Roosevelt's desire for military service. "He has lost his head to this unutterable folly of deserting a post where he is of the most service and running off to ride a horse and, probably, brush mosquitoes from his neck on the Florida sands." But, Long mused, "how absurd all this will sound, if by some turn of fortune he should accomplish some great things and strike a very high mark." Sherman's departure from government ended an era; Roosevelt's exit began a new one. The struggle ahead was to change everything; America would never be the same as it had been in John Sherman's heyday.[58]

Thus on April 25, 1898 ex-Major William McKinley became a war president. Remembering all too well the Civil War, he had made every effort to get peace, saying on one occasion, "I shall never get into a war until I am sure that God and man approve. I have been through one war; I have seen the dead piled up; and I do not want to see another." Just before the war started, the President exclaimed, "I do not care for the property that will be destroyed, nor the money that will be expended . . . but the thought of human suffering that must enter many households almost overwhelms me." Other motives also stirred him. He had hoped to devote himself to domestic policy, particularly to measures aimed at the return of prosperity. War might preclude this service to the American people, one he felt qualified to perform. If economic influences affected McKinley at all as he made the decision for war, they suggested an entirely different choice. What compelled him to act against his deepest desire for peace was the irresistible popular demand welling up everywhere in America after the destruction of the *Maine*.[59]

What lay behind the great wave of war fever of 1898? The American people went to war convinced that they had embarked upon an entirely selfless mission for humanity. One of the founders of the social gospel, the Reverend Washington Gladden, verbalized this attitude in the flamboyant rhetoric of the day: "To break in pieces the oppressor, to lift from a whole population the heavy hand of the spoiler, to lead in light and liberty, peace and plenty—is there any better work than this for the great nations of the earth?" America would fight "not for territory or empire or national honor, but for the redress of wrongs not our own, for the establishment of peace and justice in the earth. . . . Any foreign war which had not for its central purpose the welfare of humanity would curse this nation with a great curse." True to his social gospel he concluded, "Perhaps this experience may awaken in us that enthusiasm of humanity by which life is purified. In saving others we may save ourselves."[60]

But was there more to it? Richard Hofstadter once argued persuasively that the American people had experienced exceptional frustrations during the 1890's, and that the war provided an outlet for aggressive feelings, feelings that in the special circumstances of 1898 could masquerade as humanitarianism. Hofstadter's views lead naturally to the view that a paradoxical concatenation of irrational impulses may have come to the surface when the *Maine* went to the bottom of Havana harbor. For a humanitarian crusade could serve two purposes: It could help to down the fear of the future many Americans may have experienced as they recognized that an older America was passing at the end of the century. The economic downturn of 1893 raised the "social question" for Americans. Moreover, a humanitarian crusade could serve as a vehicle for the expression of a quite different, emerging aspect of American consciousness, recognition of the indubitable fact that the nation now possessed the capabilities of a great power. Fear and pride may have come together in the early months of 1898, following the sinking of the *Maine,* to produce that extraordinary burst of public opinion to which a struggling President could find no effective antidote. In any event the people, acting out powerful irrational impulses, dictated the decision of April, 1898.[61]

The leaders of Spain were no more able than their American counterparts to find the way to peace. María Cristina, Sagasta, Moret—all sought a diplomatic solution with every means at their command. In the end they accepted war, even though defeat seemed all but certain, because they believed that Spain could be preserved from revolution at home only by waging an honorable war abroad, no matter how disastrous the military outcome. As in the United States, domestic political considerations here controlled the ultimate decision. Had Gullón been able to obtain the diplomatic support of the great powers, Spain might have deterred the United States. His failure to find help in Europe condemned his nation to fight without allies.

Neither side was well prepared for war in April, 1898, in great part because the leadership in both Washington and Madrid had persisted in the belief that they would find a diplomatic solution. After the sinking of the *Maine* war had become much more probable than before, but the two months that passed before the outbreak of fighting gave by no means enough time to gird for modern warfare. Nevertheless, both nations did what they could in this period to prepare their plans and forces, while the political leaders were seeking fruitlessly to arrange a peaceful outcome.

☆ THREE ☆

Spain's Preparations for War

According to Captain Víctor M. Concas, a distinguished Spanish naval officer who served at Santiago de Cuba during 1898, the Spanish government never realized that the only way to avoid war with the United States was to sacrifice Cuba. Spain's armed forces had not prepared extensively for hostilities, even if, as Concas wrote, "the whole world was under the impression that we were frantically getting ready for a struggle to the bitter end." Everyone in Spain had presumed that the diplomatists would arrive at a solution to the Cuban question. Concas bitterly noted that Spain had failed to make necessary repairs to its ships, restore crews to full strength, and provide complete batteries for all of its armored vessels. The nation had already strained its economy in order to finance the operations against insurrectionists in Cuba and the Philippines. Even if war with the United States had appeared imminent, it seems unlikely that Spain could have marshaled sufficient resources to strengthen its forces significantly.[1]

DEFENSE OF CUBA

On October 30, 1897, Admiral Pascual Cervera y Topete took command of the Spanish naval squadron based at Cádiz, succeeding Rear Admiral Segismundo Bermejo (who had taken a place in Sagasta's Liberal ministry as Minister of the Marine), but for several months the new commander managed little improvement in his forces, despite growing alarms in Madrid about the United States. Foreign Minister Pío Gullón expressed concern when he learned that the United States North Atlantic Squadron had moved to Key West for winter exercises, but Dupuy de Lôme informed him on December 16, 1897, that this activity only indicated a resumption of normal practice; it might even be a good thing, he claimed, in that it lessened pressure to send one or two American ships to Havana. On January 25, 1898 to be sure, José Gutiérrez Sobral, the Spanish naval attaché in Washington, reported to Madrid that a meeting had been held the previous day at the Navy Department in which it was decided that Spain could not at once properly defend both Cuba and the Philippine Islands. The Americans therefore had calculated that a menace to the Philippines would force Spain to weaken its naval screen in the Caribbean Sea. "I think, then," Gutiérrez Sobral concluded, "that as soon as war is declared between this country and ours, the Philippines will be one of the objectives on the part of the Pacific squadron." This accurate guess did not receive the attention it deserved in Madrid.[2]

Early in February, 1898, after the *Maine* and *Montgomery* had gone to Cuba, Gullón asked Dupuy de Lôme to gather information about the movements of American vessels, "having recourse not only to your official position, but also to any personal means"—possibly a reference to espionage. He also instructed his minister to express to the Americans "how much surprise has been felt by the European press and public on account of the activity and apparent concentration of naval forces of the United States in waters adjacent to Cuba and Spain." Dupuy de Lôme again responded soothingly; his informants thought that "the movement of the American vessels has no other purpose than for its effect upon the jingoes." As favorable indications he drew attention to the steady stock market and noted the refusal of Congress to appropriate funds for certain defense purposes. Gullón was not satisfied, however, cabling word that the presence of the *Maine* and *Montgomery* in the Antilles and other American naval activity near the Spanish peninsula itself had caused anxiety. It might, "through some mischance, bring about a conflict." Maintaining its public pose of business as usual, Madrid dispatched the armored cruiser *Vizcaya* on a visit to New York—a formal return of the *Maine*'s visit at Havana. The ship anchored in New York harbor on February 19, four days after the sinking of the *Maine*. After the briefest possible stay the *Vizcaya* departed for Havana.[3]

Even before the sinking of the *Maine* Admiral Cervera had developed totally pessimistic views of his prospects in an engagement with the United States Navy. At the end of January, 1898, he saw his country as

trapped "in one of those critical periods which seem to be the beginning of the end." Because of a sluggish building program, Spain had
lost ground to the United States in naval power. Two weeks later he
wrote to Bermejo, observing that he could not help thinking about the
prospect of war and requesting intelligence relating to American vessels'
movements, their bases, and possible combat zones. In the event of
war, what would be his principal objective—the defense of the peninsula and the Balearic Islands, of the Canaries, of Cuba? Or could it be
to attack "the coasts of the United States, which would seem possible
only if we had some possible ally?" He needed this information because
the American fleet was three or four times as strong as the Spanish fleet
and because the insurgents could make fine Cuban harbors available to
Spain's enemy. "The best thing would be to avoid war at any price,"
he concluded, "but . . . it is necessary to put an end to the present
situation, because this nervous strain cannot be borne much longer."[4]

Bermejo responded almost immediately, sending Cervera a general
plan of operation in the event of war with the United States. The admiral was to retain a division of vessels in the vicinity of Cádiz,
presumably to defend the peninsula and nearby possessions. He would
prepare another division for Cuba, consisting of the battleship *Pelayo*
and five armored cruisers—the *Carlos V, Cristóbal Colón, Vizcaya,
Almirante Oquendo,* and *Infanta María Teresa*—with three destroyers
and three torpedo boats as escort. Joining eight vessels then based in
Havana, this squadron would "take up a position to cover the channels
between the Gulf of Mexico and the Atlantic and try and destroy Key
West." If this object were accomplished and the season favorable, then
"the blockade could be extended to the Atlantic coast, so as to cut off
communications and commerce with Europe—all this subject to the
contingencies which may arise from your becoming engaged in battles
in which it will be decided who is to hold empire of the sea." Bermejo
apparently envisaged a decisive naval battle preceding the proposed
operations in the Caribbean Sea and along the Atlantic Coast.[5]

To this fatuous plan Cervera responded in patient but obviously worried accents. He doubted that the *Pelayo* or *Carlos V* would be
available, as well as two lesser vessels, the *Numancia* and *Lepanto*. Ap-
praising the eight vessels at Havana as valueless, he reiterated his
estimate that the American naval forces were three times as strong as
those of Spain. It appeared to him "a dream, almost a feverish fancy, to
think that with this force, attenuated by our long wars, we can establish
the blockade of any port of the United States. A campaign against that
country will have to be, at least for the present, a defensive or a
disastrous one, unless we have some alliances, in which the tables may

be turned." Otherwise all that could be done was to consider making some raids with the fastest Spanish ships. Should a general naval engagement occur, he noted that the Spanish squadron, even if successful, would have no port available in which to repair damages. He would do what was deemed necessary, but he felt compelled to speak realistically rather than entertain "illusions which may bring about terrible disappointments."[6]

After the destruction of the *Maine* Bermejo retained his early optimism, but Cervera became even more pessimistic. The Minister of the Marine held out the prospect of an improving situation by the end of April, although he agreed on the importance of avoiding war until that time. Presumably he meant by this that Spain's navy could be placed in better condition in two or three months. Or perhaps he thought that Spain by then would have gained the support of the European powers. He worried, however, about the "excitable nature" of his country and "the evil of a press which it is impossible to control." To this breezy overall outlook Cervera responded with some hard information about the disparity between his ships and those of the United States. His displacement—assuming availability of vessels then out of repair—amounted to 56,644 tons as against the American displacement of 116,445 tons. His guns totaled less than two-fifths of the American armament. Arguing that the prime purpose of naval operations was to gain command of the sea, obtainable only by defeating the enemy fleet or blockading it in port, he asked, "Can we do this with the United States?" and answered himself starkly, "It is evident to me that we can not." Even if God granted victory in an initial encounter, battle damage would doubtless force most of his ships into inactivity for the rest of the war. "In the meantime the enemy could repair its damages inside of its fine rivers, aided by its powerful industries and enormous resources." He drew the obvious conclusion: If the Americans gained command of the sea, they could use the assistance of the insurgents to establish good bases in Cuba and conduct operations from them on land against the Spanish garrisons. Since Spain could not reinforce its army, the Americans would soon become unchallengeable. On February 26 he sent an impassioned plea to Bermejo:

> Do we not owe to our country not only our life, if necessary, but the exposition of our beliefs? I am very uneasy about this. I ask myself if it is right for me to keep silent, make myself an accomplice in adventures which will surely cause the total ruin of Spain. And for what purpose? To defend an island which was ours, but belongs to us no more, because even if we did not lose it by right in the war we have lost it in fact, and with it all our wealth and an enormous number of

young men, victims of the climate and the bullets, in the defense of what is now no more than a romantic idea.

It is hard to imagine a more forthright admission of weakness.[7]

Despite his entirely candid statements Cervera did not succeed in convincing the Liberal ministry to alter its planned military strategy, much less its foreign policy. Bermejo informed him that Spain would not give up Cuba. Disputing Cervera's calculations, he claimed that the United States could not put all its forces in the Atlantic because of commitments in the Pacific. He also insisted that Spain could make up its naval deficiencies and that its crews were better trained than those of the United States. Cervera, however, did not refrain from further argument. Commenting on the situation in the Pacific, he pointed to Dewey's Asiatic Squadron being a great threat to the Philippine Islands, whereas the Americans had no reason to fear an attack on their western ports. After presenting a mournful catalog of problems he had encountered in attempting to prepare his ships for sea duty, he disputed Bermejo's estimate of sentiment in Spain. He was inclined to believe that "the immense majority of the Spaniards wish for peace above all things," but this majority kept silent and therefore allowed a militant minority to dominate policy. Nothing swayed the Ministry of the Marine, however, and so on March 13 the Spanish Navy began a deployment to effect the Bermejo plan, that is, the establishment of two centers of resistance designed to protect the peninsula and Cuba. Captain Fernando Villaamil sailed from Cádiz to Cuba by way of the Canary Islands with three torpedo boats, three destroyers, and a troop transport. Lieutenant George L. Dyer, the United States naval attaché in Madrid, dutifully noted the departure of Villaamil's flotilla, also reporting activity underway to prepare a second group of vessels. The United States Department of the Navy showed special interest in the progress of repairs to the battleship *Pelayo* and the armored cruiser *Carlos V*. When these vessels would be ready for action, Spain's naval position would improve markedly.[8]

ADMIRAL CERVERA'S FINAL PREPARATIONS

As the diplomatic crisis continued to unfold, Admiral Cervera redoubled his efforts to dissuade the Liberal ministry from war. On March 16 he asked Bermejo to urge third-party mediation or arbitration of the dispute with the United States. Seeking to avoid "a certain and frightful disaster," he discounted the feasibility of bilateral negotiations with the Americans because their "bad faith is notorious."[9] Faced with the undeniable evidence that his ships lacked sufficient strength to challenge the United States Navy on reasonable terms in the Caribbean Sea, Cervera naturally hoped for peace, but his views could not overcome the larger political considerations that controlled the behavior of Sagasta and his colleagues.

Efforts were begun to concentrate the Spanish squadron in the Portuguese Cape Verde Islands, although Cervera continued to protest. On April 1 two armored cruisers, the *Vizcaya* and *Almirante Oquendo*—both at Havana—left that port for San Juan, Puerto Rico. Orders waiting there directed them to the Cape Verdes. Leaving on April 8, the two ships arrived at St. Vincent on April 19. Meanwhile, Minister of War Miguel Correa allowed a statement to be published in the press intended to prepare the Spanish people for early adversity in a war with the United States. On the same day Cervera warned privately that the Spanish forces might, "like Don Quixote, go out to fight windmills and come back with broken heads." If he proceeded to the Caribbean Sea, the Americans would force a battle that Spain could not hope to win. Then the enemy could establish a base in the Canaries, from which it could operate against Spanish commerce and bombard coastal cities. These sensible arguments fell on deaf ears. No doubt the appeal from General Blanco to send naval assistance to Cuba carried more weight in Madrid than Cervera's defeatism.[10]

On April 7 Bermejo ordered Cervera to depart from Cádiz for the Cape Verde Islands, thus triggering the movement that the prudent commander had struggled so desperately to prevent. Off went another despairing message: "The loss of our flotilla and the defeat of our squadron in the Caribbean Sea may entail a great danger for the Canaries and perhaps the bombardment of our coast cities," he wailed. "I do not mention the fate of the island of Cuba, because I have anticipated it long ago." Seeking to dispel any illusions about the strength of the Spanish squadron, he asserted that he had not been a true prophet earlier in that his vessels were in even worse shape than expected. He could not have welcomed the boastful statements in Madrid about the superiority of the Spanish Navy emanating from José María Beránger, a former Minister of the Marine. Captain Víctor M. Concas later claimed that this public stance of confidence reflected the continuing assumption of the Liberal ministry that war somehow could be avoided, even at this late date. Bermejo's response to Cervera's message was to give notice that his probable mission would be to proceed to Caribbean waters, specifically, to defend Puerto Rico. Presumably the Minister of the Marine believed that the United States might make its first move against the island.[11]

Cervera arrived in the Cape Verde Islands on April 14 with two armored cruisers, the *Cristóbal Colón* and *Infanta María Teresa,* to collect his other vessels. Captain Villaamil's flotilla of three torpedo boats and three destroyers was already there. On April 19 the armored cruisers *Vizcaya* and *Almirante Oquendo,* long at sea, arrived from San Juan with foul bottoms. Both were in need of repair. When finally assembled, Cervera's squadron was painfully deficient in important respects. Its most powerful ship, the *Cristóbal Colón,* actually lacked its main batteries of ten-inch guns and machinery required to use the fifteen-centimeter ammunition. The torpedo boats were in various states of disrepair and decrepitude, and the destroyers—designed principally to pursue torpedo boats—could play no useful role in the approaching campaign. Captain William T. Sampson's six armored ships of the United States North Atlantic Squadron, soon to be joined by the *Oregon* notably overmatched the Spanish units. In the *Cristóbal Colón* Spain had a better armored cruiser than either the *Brooklyn* or *New York,* but only with its main batteries aboard. (Displacing 6,840 tons and rated at 20.25 knots, it carried ten 5.2-inch and six 4.7-inch guns.) The three remaining armored cruisers—the *Infanta María Teresa, Almirante Oquendo,* and *Vizcaya*—closely resembled the British *Aurora* class. Rated at 20.25 knots, they displaced 7,000 tons. Each carried two 11-inch guns and ten 5.5-inch rapid-firing guns.[12]

When Cervera discovered that his probable destination would be Puerto Rico, he immediately raised objections and proposed an alternative. Although pleased that the Ministry of the Marine apparently no longer contemplated a voyage to Cuba, he argued, "If Puerto Rico is loyal, it will not be such an easy task for the Yankees; if it is not loyal, it will inevitably follow the fate of Cuba, at least as far as we are concerned." What concerned him were the Canaries and the Philippines, and also an American descent on the Spanish coast—"not unlikely, considering the audacity of the Yankees, and counting, as they do, with four or five vessels of higher speed than our own." On April 20 he recommended that his squadron return to Spanish waters, probably the Canary Islands. In defending this proposal Cervera depended heavily on the well-conceived arguments of Captain Concas. If the Spanish forces were divided—by an expedition to the Caribbean—the American Flying Squadron would immediately raid the Spanish coast, forcing the recall of Cervera from Caribbean waters. In any event it was unwise to send the squadron to the Antilles, because this movement would precipitate an engagement in which the Spanish force would have no chance of victory. Other reasons for not going were the absence of facilities to refit damaged vessels and the lack of an auxiliary fleet. Concas frankly admitted that the American first-class battleships *Indiana,*

Iowa, and *Massachusetts* were each capable of defeating the Spanish squadron without assistance. He claimed that the *Texas, Brooklyn,* and *New York* were superior to any of Cervera's ships, and he had no doubt that the Americans were well prepared for the impending war. In addition to these military considerations, Concas raised a prime political argument against a naval movement west. It was "mad, criminal, and absurd to go out to surrender the country to the mercy of the enemy, for there was no doubt that the . . .[fewer] difficulties the campaign presented to them, the more exorbitant would be their demands."[13]

These arguments failed to convince the Liberal ministry, which had decided that a disastrous war was preferable to supine surrender; a noble defeat would at least preserve the established order at home. On April 21 Cervera reported that he was prepared to depart for the Canaries on the following day, but Bermejo responded with a chilling command: "It is absolutely necessary to go out [to Puerto Rico] as soon as possible." Cervera finally reconciled himself to the outcome. "Though I persist in my opinion, which is also the opinion of the captains of the ships," he informed Bermejo, "I shall do all I can to hasten our departure, disclaiming all responsibility for the consequences."[14]

At long last Cervera's pleas led to a high-level review in Madrid. On April 23, the day that Spain declared war on the United States, Bermejo convened a council of leading naval officers to consider Cervera's orders. Four of those present opposed the sortie, but former Minister of the Marine Beránger supported it, as did Captain Ramón Auñón y Villalón and everyone else in attendance. All that changed was that Cervera was granted wide discretion in executing the order. Captain Joaquín María Lazaga y Garay, one of those who opposed the expedition, arranged for Francisco Silvela, a leading Conservative, to discuss the question with Sagasta, but the Prime Minister did not reverse the decision. He told Silvela, "The instructions to Cervera gave him absolute freedom as to his route; . . . the superior speed of his ships will permit him to elude an encounter if he is not in condition to fight; . . . he can go to Cuba, Puerto Rico, or United States harbors, and can await, for a decisive battle, the ships that will be sent from here to join him." Captain Villaamil, one of Cervera's subordinates and a member of the Chamber of Deputies, also made a direct appeal to Sagasta but without result.[15]

Captain Alfred Thayer Mahan, reviewing the decision to send Cervera to Puerto Rico, noted that it had to be made in haste because of a requirement that the Spanish squadron leave Portuguese St. Vincent within twenty-four hours after a declaration of war. Mahan was astounded that no one in the meeting at the Ministry of the Marine pointed out the dangers of dividing the Spanish fleet. Such a course would allow the United States to prevent any future junction of the entire Spanish force. "If Spain decided to carry on the naval war in the Caribbean—and to decide otherwise was to abandon Cuba in accordance with our demand,—she should have sent all the armored ships she could get together, and have thrown herself frankly, and at whatever cost, upon a more defensive policy for the home waters, relying upon coast defenses—or upon mere luck if need were—for the safety of the ports." Mahan then cited one of his favorite maxims to support this analysis: "War cannot be made without running risks." Cervera should have gone to the Caribbean Sea with all the forces available, Mahan thought, or else taken up a defensive position in the Canary Islands. It was probably political considerations that foreclosed the second course. Madrid's actual decision had nothing to recommend it from the military viewpoint, because Cervera was not given sufficient strength to accomplish anything in Caribbean waters.[16]

Thus, by April 25 Cervera was poised to depart for Puerto Rico, while Admiral Sampson lay off the north coast of Cuba, blockading the principal ports on that shore. At the same time another Spanish squadron, that of Admiral Patricio Montojo, awaited in Manila the advent of Commodore George Dewey's Asiatic Squadron, then making last-minute preparations at Mirs Bay near Hong Kong for the voyage across the South China Sea to the Philippine Islands.

DEFENSE OF THE PHILIPPINES

The Spanish authorities in Manila realized several months before the onset of hostilities that Commodore Dewey was preparing in the event of war to attack the Philippines. Early in March the German consul in Hong Kong informed Berlin that his American counterpart had revealed Dewey's orders to undertake operations against the Philippines. When the Kaiser had this news transmitted to Madrid the Queen Regent asked for German help, but the cautious Bülow refused to cooperate further. On March 3 General Fernando Primo de Rivera, the Governor-General of the Philippine Islands, notified the Minister for the Colonies in Madrid, Segismundo Moret, that informants in Hong Kong had reported Dewey's orders for a move on Manila. Moret's response merely indicated that if Dewey made a peaceful naval call, he was to be received just as were other foreign visitors; should developments in Cuba lead, however, to war, Primo de Rivera was to act according to instructions sent from the Ministry of War. A few days later, on March 12, the Governor-General received an equally vague instruction: If the United States attacked Manila, he was to utilize available means of defense. Presumably no supplies and reinforcements would be sent out from Spain.[17]

The existing plans for the defense of Manila, dating from 1885, called for action based at both the capital city and fortifications at Cavite, a peninsula several miles south of Manila. In 1892 additional elements were incorporated into the plan. An anchorage located a few miles north the entrance to Manila Bay, Subig Bay was to be defended; it commanded the approach from the South China Sea. Also, a location in the interior of Luzon was to be prepared to receive troops withdrawing from Manila, should that city fall to an invader. Studies designed to put these plans into effect were made in 1897, but the improvements had not been completed by March, 1898, although some new fortifications were in place. As an aspect of a campaign against Filipino insurgents in 1897, Primo de Rivera developed a system of fifteen strong points around Manila covering land approaches from the north, east, and south. The defense of the western side of the city, fronting on Manila Bay, fell principally to Admiral Montojo, in command of Spanish naval forces in the Philippines. Dewey would encounter this force should he enter Manila Bay.[18]

On March 15, 1898 Primo de Rivera convened a council of war to plan against a possible American descent. Montojo began proceedings by describing Dewey's forces at Hong Kong. He also reported, incorrectly, that the armored battleship *Oregon* was at Honolulu ready to sail westward. He did not conceal his belief that his squadron could not defeat Dewey's or prevent bombardment of the city. Therefore he proposed to take his ships to Subig Bay. Its narrow eastern entrance could be blocked by the sinking of vessels in it, and artillery could cover the western entrance, a canal. He wished to place his squadron in the bay behind a line of fourteen Mathieson torpedoes, all that he had available. Land batteries to the rear would help repulse the American assault. Primo de Rivera approved this scheme, the best option available to Montojo. The admiral then made arrangements to emplace 5.9-inch (15-centimeter) Ordoñez guns at Subig, and ordered all naval vessels under his command elsewhere in the archipelago to concentrate at Manila.[19]

During the month that remained to him before the declaration of war, Montojo sought desperately to obtain additional forces and supplies from Spain. To such requests Bermejo responded only that local commanders should take whatever precautions they deemed necessary. Montojo persisted in his plan to make a stand at Subig Bay, planning to mount guns and moor mines. Nevertheless, Montojo showed no more optimism at Manila than did his counterpart at Cádiz, Cervera. His defeatism surfaced plainly when on April 11 he informed Bermejo of Dewey's activities. "I am without resources, or time," he complained, to which the Minister of the Marine, as usual, replied that he hoped deficiencies would be made up for by "zeal and activity." Four days later Montojo reported himself able to undertake defensive operations only—although if he had two armored cruisers he could contemplate offensive operations against California. Bermejo's rejoinder was a promise to send out seventy mines—which of course could not possibly arrive for many weeks. Unaccountably, he ordered Montojo at this time to close entrances to important ports by mining their entrances, to which Montojo could only reply, "You know I have no torpedoes. I will do it when I can." When he learned that hostilities were imminent, Montojo held a council of war that reiterated the earlier decision to make the defense at Subig Bay. There the enemy might be taken by surprise and defeated in detail. On April 25 the Spanish squadron straggled out of its anchorage at Manila, bound for Subig.[20]

In making his decision Montojo considered only two options— defense in either Manila Bay or Subig Bay. He gave no thought to any other possibility, although he might have considered a third course: His small, weak, and antiquated vessels could have been dispersed to various locations throughout the Philippine Islands, avoiding their immediate sacrifice and ultimately creating considerable difficulty for Dewey. In his later review of these events the Spanish commander claimed that he did not adopt this design because the ships would ultimately have fallen one by one into American hands. He also argued that he had no orders from his superiors in Madrid to justify such a decision. Moreover, the Governor-General would have vetoed any plan that left Manila without naval defense. As in Cervera's case, political considerations forced Montojo to accept battle with vastly superior American forces in truly disadvantageous circumstances.[21]

The home government lent no real assistance during the months preceding the declaration of war. Minister for the Colonies Moret stubbornly retained his hopes for a diplomatic settlement, but on March 26 Minister of War Miguel Correa had informed Primo de Rivera that war appeared inevitable, and others in Madrid had concurred in this view. On April 9 Moret had cabled, "Situation the same. Question will be resolved before Sunday [April 10]. In case of war American squadron will attack islands immediately." The next day Montojo reported the same information about American intentions to Madrid: Dewey, then at Hong Kong, would move on Manila as soon as war began. At this juncture Primo de Rivera was replaced as Governor-General. Sagasta chose General Don Basilio Augustín as his successor. Primo de Rivera had, however, indicated his willingness to remain, and, just as

Augustín arrived, he received permission to stay. But for unexplained reasons he departed soon thereafter.[22]

Augustín had only a few days to make final preparations. He did what he could, enrolling public officials and Spanish nationals in the military service, creating courts to punish treason with death, establishing military zones in Manila, and making fruitless preparations to defend the port of Cavite (the location of a naval arsenal). On April 23, when it became obvious that war was only hours away, General Augustín set up a "civil commission of defense," a device to organize united local support for Spain during the impending conflict. That same day he informed Madrid of his preparations to defend "the national honor and integrity," but he also mentioned a lack of resources with which to offer basic resistance to Dewey. Moret concluded his prewar correspondence with a reply to the Governor-General that the longer the struggle lasted the more certain the victory of Spain—brave but foolish words, in keeping with his prior fatuous optimism. There was no lack of knowledge in either Madrid or Manila that if war came Commodore Dewey intended to attack the Philippines. What was lacking was the means of frustrating this enterprise. Manila's defenses had long been neglected, and there had been no time to modernize them during the early months of 1898. While the government in Madrid had maintained its hopeful belief that a diplomatic solution would settle the controversy over Cuba, inertia in the Philippines precluded proper disposition of the few available resources. To complete the fiasco, Montojo did not adopt the soundest strategy available to him—dispersion of his ships throughout the archipelago rather than concentration at Manila. This policy would have delayed their destruction and at least postponed American successes. And Madrid might have been spared the political shock that followed the naval battle of Manila.[23]

Neither Cervera nor Montojo received the support both deemed essential to permit successful operations against the United States Navy. The Liberal ministry was unwilling at one and the same time to strengthen its navy and to consider the only political expedient that could have avoided war. Cervera recognized that Spain faced a desperate choice between the loss of Cuba or a humiliating defeat at sea. His superiors turned a deaf ear to his pathetic laments. Montojo received no significant reinforcements, despite the threatening proximity of Dewey's vastly superior squadron at Hong Kong. Like his counterpart in the Atlantic Ocean, he could anticipate nothing but almost certain defeat. Given the circumstances, surely Cervera should not have been ordered to Cuban waters and Montojo should not have attempted to defend Manila.

FOUR

War Plans and Preparations in the United States

In the United States prior to the sinking of the *Maine* neither the navy nor the army had made comprehensive plans and preparations for war with Spain. The Navy Department had bestirred itself to a degree, sending the North Atlantic Squadron to the Gulf of Florida for winter exercises. Warships in other parts of the world were concentrated at specified locations and alerted for possible orders, and squadron commanders were instructed not to release men who completed their enlistments. For its part the War Department did nothing. It was merely a consequence of established routine that it was able later to make use of intelligence collected at this time relating to guerrilla warfare in Cuba. After the *Maine* had gone to the bottom of Havana harbor, however, the United States rapidly accelerated military and naval preparations. The pace of this activity reflected the adverse outcomes of the diplomatic negotiations aimed at achieving a peaceful settlement.[1]

EARLY PLANNING

A relatively well-placed official in the United States government, Assistant Secretary of the Navy Theodore Roosevelt, was among the first to contemplate war with Spain. In this connection he energetically urged a wide range of preparatory activity, but encountered indifference. In June, 1897, Roosevelt complained to one of his regular correspondents, Captain Alfred Thayer Mahan—already known around the world for his works on naval strategy—that Secretary of the Navy John D. Long was showing no interest in adding ships to the fleet, particularly battleships. He wanted Mahan to urge more construction, making the argument that it would contribute to peace. In letters to other correspondents at this time Roosevelt made no secret of his concern about possible external threats—principally from Germany, but also from Japan and Great Britain. He did not hesitate to present this argument to Secretary Long himself. Nothing annoyed Roosevelt more than the low level of public information about the importance of naval expansion: "The bulk of our people are curiously ignorant of military and naval affairs, and full of ignorant self-confidence," he complained nastily, "which is, I hope, the only quality they share with the Chinese." He was temporarily buoyed when he learned that the President planned to "deal thoroughly and well with any difficulty that arises"—with either Spain or Japan—and that the Administration would recommend some new naval construction. To both Secretary Long and his close friend Senator Henry Cabot Lodge (Republican from Massachusetts), he sketched an operations plan to be followed in the event of war with Spain: The main part of the navy would move against Cuba, presumably to blockade it. A flying squadron composed of four fast cruisers would harass the coast of Spain. Finally, the Asiatic Squadron would blockade, and if possible seize, Manila.[2]

In making his recommendations Roosevelt reflected naval contingency planning that had been under way since 1894. In that year several students at the Naval War College in Newport, Rhode Island, took up the question of war with Spain as a training problem. One exercise posited a war with Britain and Spain on one side and France and the United States on the other. It assumed a naval conflict localized in the Caribbean Sea, the South Atlantic, and the Pacific coast of Central America (apparently centered on a Nicaraguan isthmian canal, considered for purposes of the exercise to be in existence). More to the point was Lieutenant Commander Charles J. Train's plan, which assumed a war between Spain and the United States only. The belligerent who managed to establish command of the sea would prevail. Spain could be expected to send an expedition from Cádiz by way of the Canary Islands. Train's recommendations concentrated on repulsing this expedition: American forces would seize Nipe Bay on the northeast coast of Cuba as a rendezvous point, coaling station, and anchorage. While awaiting the Spanish expedition, the navy would blockade the principal ports on the coast of Cuba—Havana, Matanzas, and Sagua la Grande in the north, and Cienfuegos in the south. It would engage the hostile expedition when it approached Cuba. Train considered the possibility that the enemy might enter the Caribbean Sea from the south and proceed to Santiago de Cuba, avoiding American scouts, who would expect an approach from the east via San Juan, Puerto Rico—but thought the southern route unlikely because of logistical problems associated with it. In order for the navy to set up for a move on Havana, Train suggested seizure of Mariel.[3]

Sometime in 1895 the Naval War College developed a somewhat more advanced document entitled "Situation in the Case of War With Spain," sent to the Navy Department early in 1896. It considered three options: The United States might attack Spain itself, although this operation was deemed risky and unduly expensive. Second, the United States could attack Spain's possessions in the Pacific. This activity would be inexpensive and safe, but it would not bring the enemy to terms. Finally, the United States could attack Cuba and Puerto Rico. Success here might not end a war, but it would place the burden of continuing operations on Spain. Moreover, "the strategic relation of Cuba to the Gulf of Mexico is so close and intimate that the value of that island to the United States in a military and naval way is invaluable." The plan of campaign envisioned about thirty days before reinforcements could arrive from Spain. In that period the United States could send land forces to Cuba at Bahía Honda and Cabanas (after a feint at Matanzas) in order to prepare for the seizure of Havana. The eastern half of the island would be left to the Cuban insurgents, who would receive financial assistance. "It is not probable that this section [of Cuba] would be used as a landing place by the Spanish forces, nor in any way as their base." Key West would serve as the advance naval base, rather than the Dry Tortugas. Tampa would be the principal naval base and the port of embarkation for the Cuban expedition. The object of operations would be to seize Havana and other coastal points. To mount the campaign against Havana, the army would have to utilize an advance corps of thirty thousand regulars and two hundred fifty thousand volunteers enlisted for three years. Meanwhile, the navy would prepare to meet the Spanish expedition proceeding from Spain to reinforce Cuba and Puerto Rico.[4] Success would lead either to Cuban autonomy or to an independent republic. As compensation for its efforts, the United States would acquire from Cuba the Isle of Pines, off the south coast.

This early work exercised some influence—how much is impossible to determine—on the first full-scale war plan produced in the Navy Department itself. On June 1, 1896, Lieutenant William Warren Kimball, assigned as Staff Intelligence Officer at the Naval War College from the Office of Naval Intelligence, proposed a document entitled "War With Spain," the first in a series of war plans to materialize during the next year. Kimball's plan, designed to "liberate Cuba from Spanish rule," assumed a strictly naval war, since operations at sea would be least costly, could be conducted during the rainy season, and represented the only practical option in the early stages of the war, when it would be necessary to seize control of the Florida straits and meanwhile prepare a land army. "It would be the quickest way of wounding the prestige of Spain, of crippling her revenues, and of thus bringing her to treat for peace upon reasonable terms." Kimball also pointed to a "diplomatic or sentimental" reason, as against a strategic one, for a purely naval operation. "It would contemplate the establishment of the Cuban Republic through the efforts of its own citizens within its own borders, aided only by the exteriorly applied sea power of the United States, instead of a conquest and invasion of Spanish territory by an organized army of invasion from this country." The main theater of operations would of course be in the Caribbean Sea. If an army campaign were required, it would involve projection of forces ashore for a limited purpose. A landing could take place in the area of Bahía Honda and Matanzas, aimed at the reduction of Havana. Tampa would serve as the base for concentration of the army. Matanzas would be used as the advance base for operations in Cuba because it was the only port of sufficient size. The navy's objective would be to ward off the Spanish fleet by gaining control of the Florida straits to make possible the seizure of Matanzas and the capture of Havana. The fall of Havana would presumably end the war, "because it is the only strong place on the island of strategic importance and the capture of it is practically equal to the conquest of Cuba."

To support the main effort in the Caribbean Sea, Kimball proposed two secondary campaigns. A squadron would be sent to Spanish waters to harass trade, raid coastal points, and hold the Spanish armored vessels in home waters. Another force, the Asiatic Squadron, would reduce and hold Manila, thus controlling the commerce of the Philippine Islands "so that the release of our hold of them may be used as an inducement to Spain to make peace after the liberation of Cuba." Kimball obviously had no thought of the United States annexing the Philippines. He summarized his motives for proposing operations in the Pacific archipelago clearly, if generally: "The ease with which the revenue of the island[s] could at once be attained and the fact that these revenues might be held until a war indemnity were satisfactorily arranged for, both indicate that Manila should be made a serious objective." [5]

During the remainder of 1896 the Naval War College, unhappy with Kimball's plan, considered other options. In the summer it worked out the consequences of a war against the allies Great Britain and Spain: In this situation the United States would wage defensive naval warfare in the Gulf of Mexico. More important was an updated version of Lieutenant Commander Train's plan of 1895 called "Situation in Case of War With Spain" (dated November, 1896), that likewise concentrated on operations at Bahía Honda. Considering an attack on the Philippines, it concluded, "Success there, however, would not be of great value to us, as it would not certainly bring the enemy to terms." Unlike earlier plans it stressed joint army-navy operations. Deemed of vital importance were "vigorous preparations on such a scale that there will be no possibility of a failure. Anything less than this is liable to meet with such a resistance or perhaps such a failure at first as will cause a greater delay in the final settlement." In "Synopsis of the War College Plan for Cuban Campaign in a War With Spain," Captain Henry C. Taylor, the president of the Newport institution, summarized its main points: There should be a supporting demonstration against the Philippines, but the Cuban campaign would have to be ended before any operation took place in Spanish waters. Taylor was convinced that a premature campaign in the eastern Atlantic Ocean had several disadvantages. "Its military effect as a diversion would be inconsiderable, its political effect would be to consolidate Spain's national spirit, and our ships thus employed will be needed in Cuba." Taylor emphasized that the key element in the plan was maximum preparatory effort at the outset. This approach would allow the United States to complete certain operations "before Spain can bring upon the scene her heavy fighting ships, and any large force of troops to add to those already in Cuba." Such operations included use of heavy American ships in attacks on the Cuban coast; blockade of the coast and seizure of Cienfuegos and other points as bases; seizure of Bahía Honda or Matanzas as a base for land operations against Havana to be conducted by a force eventually numbering about sixty thousand troops. All these efforts should be accomplished within thirty days in order to prepare for the arrival of a Spanish expedition.[6]

Presumably because the Navy Department was not satisfied with either the Kimball or the War College plans, it convened an *ad hoc* group that reported a distinct plan of its own on December 17, 1896. The Chief of the Bureau of Navigation, Rear Admiral Francis M. Ramsey—who strongly opposed the activities of the Naval War College—appears to have played an important role in this activity. Assuming a war against Spain alone, the planners emphasized the establishment of a blockade against Cuba and Puerto Rico. They gave much more attention than earlier planners to the role of the land forces that would occupy locations in Cuba taken by the navy and attack the Spanish army there. Greater stress was placed on providing assistance to the Cuban insurgents, who would carry most of the burden ashore. The Asiatic Squadron, instead of conducting operations against the Philippines, was to proceed to European waters, where it would join the European Squadron. This combined force, operating from a base to be seized in the Canary Islands, would engage the enemy in Spanish waters and operate against commerce. Captain Taylor, however, expressed strong opposition to these European operations, maintaining that it would be most difficult to establish a viable base. Calling for concentration of all available naval strength in the Caribbean, he stressed the importance of close cooperation between the army and navy from the outset—a reflection of views expressed in the War College plan.[7]

The Navy Department's new plan was reconsidered in June, 1897. The planning board now had a different membership, with only one officer remaining from the previous group. It revised the plan considerably, restoring the attack on the Philippine Islands. Although it retained the idea of sending a flying squadron to Spanish waters—a means of holding Spanish naval strength in home ports—it dropped the hazardous scheme to seize the Canary Islands. It also provided for early capture of Puerto Rico. The official version of this plan, adopted on June 30, included an observation that Puerto Rico offered ''certain advantages for the rendezvous of Spanish ships of war coming from Europe, for the purpose of breaking and annoying our blockade of Cuba, and reinforcing their navy there.'' A detachment drawn from the land forces operating in Cuba would seize and garrison the second island.

This plan also included a discussion of what to do if the United States found itself at war with Spain and Japan at the same time. It provided for defensive operations to guard the Hawaiian Islands and the American west coast against Japanese fleet action. It made only one change in the operations against Spain, eliminating the attack on the Philippine Islands. The board did not fail to note that ''the completion of an isthmean [sic] canal would be a great advantage to the United States, as it would greatly shorten the distance between her two lines of defense, and enable us to reinforce from one to the other in vastly less time than is now possible.''[8]

The Naval War College drew up still another plan in the summer of 1897, one taking a different tack than any of the others in emphasizing American coastal defense to counter possible Spanish operations against the Delaware and Chesapeake bays. To frustrate a thrust of this nature, American naval forces would be concentrated for operations to intercept various elements of the enemy's assault force before they could unite. The planners were convinced that it would be unwise to scatter the armored ships of the fleet along the east coast to defend various harbors. This plan—along with the others—suggests that the navy had no really settled conception of what it might undertake in the event of war with Spain.[9]

Prewar planning did not contemplate major territorial acquisitions. However, without exception the prewar schemes assumed that if the United States fought Spain, it would be to achieve autonomy or even independence for Cuba. Attacks on Spanish territories such as the Philippines, Puerto Rico, and the Canaries were intended only to support operations against the prime objective—always assumed to be Spain's forces in and around Cuba. The only recommendation for annexation noted in any of the plans was the fugitive reference to the Isle of Pines in the War College plan of 1895, an idea that did not appear in later schemes.

Although these plans contain variations and contradictions, certain elements recur with relative frequency. Among these are a blockade of Cuba and Puerto Rico, a land operation against Havana, occupation of Puerto Rico, a blockade or assault directed at Manila, and naval attacks against objectives in Spanish waters—coastal cities, insular possessions, and commerce. All plans assumed that the navy would bear most of the operational burden, the army restricting its functions to garrisoning coastal locations and perhaps supporting the Cuban insurgents. Most of the plans assumed that the United States possessed sufficient naval power to ensure the liberation of Cuba.

Throughout the period from November, 1897 to February, 1898, Theodore Roosevelt continued to discuss strategy with various correspondents and bewail the nation's failure to prepare for war. In November he rehearsed for Lieutenant Kimball his latest views of a proper campaign against Spain, reflecting the ideas of the second *ad hoc* board formed in the Navy Department. He made no bones about his desire for war, first because of humanitarian reasons and national self-interest—relief for the Cubans and elimination of Spanish influence in the western hemisphere—and, second, because it would benefit both the general public and the armed services. The American people would gain because it would provide them "something to think of which isn't material gain," and the army and navy would have an opportunity to obtain useful practice in warfare, especially in mounting amphibious landings. In December he again wrote to Kimball, worried that "our hopes as to the Spanish business are a dream," but also doubtful of Spain's ability to pacify Cuba—a circumstance that could force eventual American intervention. In his mind the greatest international danger emanated from Wilhelmian Germany. As before, but now with growing vehemence, he berated those who disagreed with his bellicose views. "Oh, how bitterly angry I get at the attitude of some of our public men and some of our publicists!"[10]

One of those with pacific views was Secretary of the Navy John D. Long, Roosevelt's superior, to whom the Assistant Secretary ventilated his case for active war preparations. Such a course would help preserve "life, money, and reputation." Roosevelt wanted to relocate vessels to have them available in the best possible places should war be declared, and he wished to expand available supplies of ammunition and manpower. He also urged that the Navy Department hasten work on vessels under repair and purchase new ones, particularly colliers needed to support combat operations. Roosevelt wished to raid places such as Cádiz and Barcelona on the coast of Spain, using Great Canary Island as an advance base for a flying squadron. This operation, he claimed, would "demoralize the Spaniards [and] keep their fleet in Spanish waters." Summarizing his arguments for these manifold activities anticipating war, Roosevelt asserted, "If we drift into it, if we do not prepare in advance, and suddenly have to go into hostilities without taking the necessary steps beforehand, we may have to encounter one or two bitter humiliations, and we shall certainly be forced to spend the first three or four most important weeks not in striking, but in making those preparations to strike which we should have made long before." Clearly he supported Captain Taylor's emphasis on the importance of early activities before Spain could send an expedition to the Caribbean Sea. Roosevelt did not make much progress in this one-man campaign for preparedness. Secretary Long did not take kindly to his associate's constant advice, confiding his negative opinions to his diary: "He bores me with plans of naval and military movement, and the necessity of having some scheme of attack arranged for instant execution in case of an emergency."[11] Did Long realize that these views were not simply those of Roosevelt, but in fact of a significant group of naval officers, particularly those associated with the Naval War College?

At this time Roosevelt doubted the possibility of pursuing a "consistent foreign policy" that would force every European power out of the western hemisphere. "[Because] our people are not yet up to following out this line of policy," he claimed, "the thing to be done is to get whatever part of it is possible at the moment." Perhaps it would be feasible to annex the strategically located Hawaiian Islands.[12]

As if to practice his own preachment to seize whatever opportunities presented themselves. Roosevelt played a part in the negotiations in Oc-

tober, 1897 that placed Commodore George Dewey in command of the
Asiatic Squadron. When Roosevelt discovered that Senator William E.
Chandler (Republican from New Hampshire) was pressing the nomina-
tion of Commodore John A. Howell to this post, he suggested that
Dewey enlist the support of Senator Redfield Proctor (Republican from
Vermont), an influential legislator from the Commodore's home state.
Dewey took this step, and Proctor lobbied President McKinley—an effort that proved successful. Dewey gained the appointment, with
Howell receiving command of the European Squadron. However, Long
later claimed that the Navy Department had made its decisions about
these appointments well before supporters of the two rivals made their
representations. In any event, Dewey possessed the qualities of leadership that Roosevelt and others of like mind hoped might come into play
during hostilities with Spain.[13]

The lassitude of the Navy Department disappeared immediately
after the destruction of the *Maine*. Roosevelt urged upon Long the importance of immediate action: "It may be held against us for all time to
come, not merely by the men of to-day, but by those who read history
in the future, if we fail to point out what the naval needs of the country
are, and how they should be met." Not content with this effusion, he
bombarded the Secretary with suggestions of various kinds—for example, the need to prepare various types of vessels for action.[14] War with
Spain—only a possibility prior to February 15—now appeared quite
probable, and, although the President continued to seek a diplomatic
solution, the armed forces bestirred themselves to make preparations.

INITIAL NAVAL PREPARATIONS

On February 25, 1898 Roosevelt seized an opportunity to put in motion various enterprises that had been discussed earlier within the navy.
On that day Long left him in charge of the Department—with
unlooked-for consequences, as the Secretary noted in his diary:

> Having the authority for that time of Acting-Secretary, he im-
> mediately began to launch peremptory orders: distributing ships,
> ordering ammunition, which there is no means to move, to places
> where there is no means to store it; sending for Captain Barker to
> come on about the guns of the Vesuvius, which is a matter that
> might have been perfectly arranged by correspondence; sending
> messages to Congress for immediate legislation, authorizing the
> enlistment of an unlimited number of seamen; and ordering guns
> from the Navy Yard at Washington to New York, with a view to
> arming auxiliary cruisers which are now in peaceful commercial pur-
> suit. . . . He has gone at things like a bull in a china shop, and with

the best purposes in the world has really taken what, if he could have thought, he would not for a moment have taken; and that is the one course that is most discourteous to me, because it suggests that there has been a lack of attention which he was applying. It shows how the best fellow in the world—and with splendid capacities—is worse than no use if he lack a cool head and careful discretion.

The Secretary immediately reviewed Roosevelt's orders, cancelling some but allowing others to stand.[15]

One of the orders that remained in force was an important message to Commodore Dewey, then based in Japan:

Secret and confidential. Order the squadron, except *Monocacy* to Hongkong. Keep full of coal. In the event of declaration of war Spain, your duty will be to see that the Spanish squadron does not leave the Asiatic coast, and then offensive operations in Philippine Islands. Keep *Olympia* until further orders.

Many historians have treated this episode as evidence of a plot on the part of Roosevelt and his friend Henry Cabot Lodge to launch an imperialist enterprise—a "large policy" of territorial expansion including annexation of the far-off Philippine Islands. While both men were in favor of overseas expansion—particularly with a view to protecting a projected canal across the Central American isthmus—Roosevelt's order of February 25 was consistent with Department thinking and reflected considerable prior planning. It was no surprise, but rather a logical step at the time. Dewey was simply ordered, should war come, to ensure that the Spanish naval squadron in the Pacific could not be used elsewhere and to put pressure on Manila in the hope that Spain would end the fighting at an early date. This pressure was no conspiracy; it did not involve concealed or unexpected machinations. Roosevelt did not originate the order; he simply decided the timing of its transmission. Operations against Manila had been contemplated long before. Roosevelt, summing up for Lodge what he considered his "chief usefulness" in the Navy Department, reported accurately, "When I was Acting Secretary I did not hesitate to take responsibilities. . . . I have continually meddled in what was not my business, because I was willing to jeopardize my position in a way that a naval officer could not."[16]

Only a few days later the Navy Department initiated another important movement, the first leg of a long voyage that would bring the first-class battleship *Oregon* from the Pacific coast to the Caribbean Sea. On March 7 Long dispatched the vessel from Bremerton, Washington, to

San Francisco. On March 12 it was directed to Callao, Peru, to await further orders; leaving San Francisco on March 19 under the command of Captain Charles Edgar Clark, it reached Callao on April 4. An untutored enlisted man recorded his reaction with pardonable pride: "We have allready made one of the grandest runs on record. Just think of it, a First Class Battle Ship making 4800 miles in just 16 days and used 900 Tons of Coal, That being the longest trip on record for a First Class Battle Ship." On April 6 the *Oregon* was instructed to proceed immediately to Montevideo or Rio de Janeiro. Captain Clark did not report again until April 30, from Rio de Janeiro, where he learned that the United States was already at war with Spain. The odyssey of the *Oregon* stemmed from the Navy Department's desire to concentrate all its modern armored vessels near the island of Cuba, where in case of war American naval strategists expected to encounter the Spanish fleet. The voyage placed enormous demands on the *Oregon*. Nothing could have dramatized the utility of an interoceanic canal through the Central American isthmus so effectively.[17]

When the Navy Department learned that Spain was attempting to purchase warships from other European nations, it launched a similar effort; at about the same time the Department began to seek merchant ships and pleasure boats suitable as auxiliaries. Early in March telegrams went to the American naval attachés in London, Paris, and Rome to locate available warships and destroyers, and very soon Commander Willard H. Brownson went abroad to arrange acquisitions. After the passage of the Fifty-Million-Dollar Bill funds became available for actual purchases. Of the navy's expenditures under this authority— $29,354,827.05—almost $18 million was used to purchase ships at home and abroad. On March 16 Commander Brownson and Lieutenant John C. Colwell, the naval attaché in London, completed arrangements to acquire two protected cruisers being built for Brazil at Elswick, England. One of these vessels, the *Amazonas*—renamed the *New Orleans*—served in Cuban waters later on. The other, the *Almirante Abreu,* was rechristened the *Albany*. Because it did not clear port before the beginning of hostilities, it was held in England until the end of the war. The navy also obtained a gunboat in England and two torpedo boats, one in the United States and the other in Germany. These vessels were renamed the *Topeka,* the *Manly,* and the *Somers;* all of them saw service in 1898. Back in the United States, four fast ocean liners chartered from an American shipping company proved most helpful as scouts, transports, and blockaders. Four other ships obtained from the Pacific Railroad Company were converted into armed auxiliary cruisers. Some private yachts were donated or purchased—for example, that of J. Pierpont Morgan, rechristened the *Gloucester,* which gained fame at Santiago de Cuba.[18]

At this time the Navy Department added personnel to provide crews for the vessels being put into service as part of the mobilization. Before the *Maine* was lost the navy had a roll of 1,232 officers and an authorized enlisted strength of 11,750 men. During the war its manpower more than doubled, rising to 2,088 officers and 24,123 enlisted men. The naval militia made up 2,600 of the additions to the regular service. Another 1,800 militiamen served in the auxiliary service. Because of its early concern in this respect, the navy did not have undue difficulties filling the complements of its ships during the wartime emergency.[19]

FINAL NAVAL PREPARATIONS: CARIBBEAN SEA

On March 15 Theodore Roosevelt met with a group of senior naval officers, apparently an extension of the "board of defense" that had prepared plans in 1897, to consider the American response to news of Spanish naval movements. The board's principal conclusion was that the navy should not be diverted to coast defense, a task it hoped to delegate to the army. Instead, naval forces "should be used to strike at the enemy's fleet, and especially to get and keep the dominance in Cuban waters until Cuba and Porto Rico fall, and from this [they] must not be diverted by the clamorous outcry which is certain to arise from almost every point of the coast as soon as war begins." Already pleas for naval vessels had come from several coastal points. Roosevelt's committee did not think that the Spanish flotilla said to be en route to Cuba should be allowed to reach its destination; there it would threaten the projected American blockade. Any European country would consider itself justified in reacting to such a movement; just as another nation would treat "the mobilizing of an army corps on its borders as a cause for action," the United States should deal energetically with Villaamil's deployment. There was also concern about the progress of repair work on the *Pelayo,* the *Carlos V,* and an old second-class battleship named the *Vitoria.* In recommending a strike against Villaamil before these armored vessels became operational, the American committee came close to proposing preventive war.

A war with Spain would pose no serious problems if the army could successfully defend New York, Boston, and Hampton Roads, Virginia, against raids and keep Spanish naval vessels from reinforcing Cuba and Puerto Rico. Roosevelt realized that he and his fellow planners needed information about the probable date for the anticipated beginning of warfare. He believed that the presentation of the pending reports on the *Maine* would simplify matters. For the moment the planners recommended a series of tentative movements: Four monitors should be placed at Key West for use in the contemplated blockade of Cuba; they would be of little help along the Atlantic seaboard if scattered at widely separated places. In addition, for the moment a division of heavy ships should be located at Hampton Roads to provide interim protection for the coastline, including the armored vessels *Massachusetts, Texas,* and *Brooklyn,* along with two protected cruisers, the *Columbia* and *Minneapolis.* If war began, this division could join the main fleet at Key West or deploy elsewhere.

Although provision had to be made against possible Spanish raids on the Atlantic coast, the planners had no doubt that the main objective of the United States should be Cuba and that the army and navy should cooperate in seizing it. "Our blockade of the island should not be abandoned, no matter what raid is made upon our own coast, for nothing but a raid can be made." If raiders could be intercepted, "well and good. . . . But in any event our grip on Cuba should not be relaxed until the island falls." To accomplish this purpose the army must prepare an expeditionary force. It would not be necessary to conquer the entire island, but "we should have sufficient troops on hand to take places like Santiago or Matanzas." The entire island did not have to be blockaded, because supplies and troops could not be moved by land from east to west. "The western half will have to be blockaded, and all the vessels in the eastern half destroyed, and possibly some town like Santiago captured by the Navy and held by the Army." Roosevelt observed, "Some scheme of cooperation between the military and the naval authorities should be arranged." He wondered whether the United States should have an institution like the English Board of Defense.[20]

On March 17 orders were issued to form a flying squadron at Hampton Roads, a quick response to the recommendation made two days earlier. It was to include the very vessels suggested by the planning group, and its mission was to protect coastal points. Captain Robley D. Evans, commenting later, argued strongly against this decision to divide the fleet: "The Flying Squadron was the badge of democracy," he complained, "the sop to the quaking laymen whose knowledge of strategy derived solely from their terror of a sudden attack by Cervera." Without exception the responsible leaders of the navy wanted to concentrate their ships for use in a blockade of Cuba, but public opinion precluded this course.[21]

On March 23 Secretary Long issued a detailed plan for the Cuban blockade, following the suggestions of Captain Alfred Thayer Mahan.

The blockade would close the western half of Cuba's north coast, particularly the ports of Matanzas and Havana. Outside the latter port the blockade would consist of a close-in screen including torpedo boats and revenue cutters, a second line of protected cruisers, and a third line of armored ships. Rather histrionically, Long made reference to one of the great heroes of the Civil War: "Each man engaged in the work of the inshore squadron [that is, the first line] should have in him the stuff of which to make a possible Cushing: and if the man wins the recognition given him shall be as great as that given to Cushing, so far as the Department may bring this about."[22]

These actions of March decided the pace of naval preparations. The Navy Department worked furiously to complete its purchase of vessels, create a rudimentary intelligence service in Europe, mature coast defenses, establish a board of strategy, and complete plans for operations against Spanish forces in the Caribbean Sea. Secretary Long, in some irritation, described the changing atmosphere in his Department: "Incessant activity, constant conversation, pressure from the reporters, interviews about auxiliary ships, building new ships, passage of the Personnel Bill, and more things than I can remember to mention. Since the war-scare began, my mail is three or four times as great as it was." It included all manner of information—"tenders of services, suggestions of new inventions, songs from patriotic poets, advice as to official administration and even personal conduct." The demands of office had indeed burgeoned well beyond the requirements of peacetime, and the pacific Secretary of the Navy, an unpretentious but conscientious administrator, did his best to respond. He adopted an intelligent *modus operandi*, delegating to his bureau chiefs full authority, but holding them strictly accountable for their actions. He would do all he could to meet the requirements of the navy. This course of action paid dividends. A month after the onset of the war he could claim justly, "Whether we succeed or fail, everything has been done that can be done with the means at our disposal to render the Navy efficient."[23]

Whatever the situation elsewhere in the government, the Navy Department responded efficiently to the challenge of 1898. Long certainly assisted this process by not interfering with his bureau chiefs as they met their responsibilities. Also, there was no division of authority in the Navy Department between the civilian and military heads, contrary to the situation in the War Department. His bureau chiefs could be rotated every four years. "Good men are retained, but . . . changes are always possible if a man does not quite fill the bill, or if there is a call for him elsewhere." Long was fortunate in his assistants. Roosevelt, for all his bumptiousness, was a most energetic subordinate in many respects, and his successor during the war, Charles H. Allen, manifested particularly admirable skills. Long described him as possessing "thorough business training, special aptness for his work, complete system, and that orderly poise which makes the executive administration run like a well-oiled machine."[24]

Between March 16 and August 12, 1898, the Navy acquired 103 vessels, most of them by purchase. It extended $21,431,000 for this purpose, almost all of it from the funds made available through the Fifty-Million-Dollar Bill. In addition to ships of war obtained in Europe and merchant vessels chartered or purchased from various sources, the navy also took control of revenue cutters, lighthouse tenders, and the vessels of the Fish Commission. Altogether 131 new vessels joined the fleet for the war with Spain, making a force of 73 fighting ships and 123 auxiliaries—a total of 196.[25]

The heart of the United States Navy consisted of seven relatively modern armored vessels—four first-class battleships, one second-class battleship, and two armored cruisers, all in operational condition. Only one of these, the aforementioned first-class battleship *Oregon,* was stationed regularly in Pacific waters, but it arrived in the Caribbean Sea in time to play a vital role in the campaign of 1898. The battleships *Indiana, Massachusetts,* and *Oregon* were sister ships. Commissioned in 1893, they displaced 10,288 tons and boasted a rated speed of 16 knots. Built primarily as coast defenders, their design stressed guns and armor rather than speed. Each had two main turrets with four thirteen-inch guns each and four smaller turrets with two eight-inch guns each. There was also a respectable secondary armament of four six-inch guns (rapid-fire), twenty six-pound guns, six one-pound guns, and four Gatling guns. The *Indiana* class had a belt of armor eighteen inches thick that stretched around three-fifths of the ship's length, and a protective steel deck of 2½ inches thick. The other first-class battleship, the *Iowa*—commissioned in 1896—weighed slightly more and made a bit more speed. The oldest battleship, the *Texas,* of the second class, displaced 6,315 tons and was rated at 17.8 knots. Two armored cruisers, the *New York* (1891) and the *Brooklyn* (1895), were used as flagships during the war. They displaced 8,200 and 9,215 tons respectively, with rated speeds of 21.0 and 21.9 knots.

Other vessels of importance included a group of ocean-going monitors and some thirteen protected cruisers, each displacing three thousand tons or more. The six double-turreted monitors were heavily armed but very slow and uncertain at sea (*Puritan, Monterey, Amphitrite, Monadnock, Miantonomah,* and *Terror*). The three largest protected cruisers were the *Columbia* (1892), *Minneapolis* (1893)—

both displacing 7,375 tons—and *Olympia* (1890), flagship of the Asiatic Squadron, displacing 5,800 tons.[26]

By April 15, 1898, the United States Navy was deployed in five operational squadrons prepared for war. In response to unreasoning public concern the Navy Department had organized a Northern Patrol Squadron under Commodore John A. Howell to monitor coastal waters between the Delaware capes and Bar Harbor, Maine. Another command, manned mostly by naval militia—dubbed the United States Auxiliary Naval Forces but usually called the "Mosquito Squadron"— helped with coast defense, protection of mine fields, and quarantine patrol. Two squadrons operated in the Atlantic Ocean. The Flying Squadron under Commodore Winfield S. Schley was based at Hampton Roads, Virginia, with several possible missions. Including the battleships *Texas* and *Massachusetts*, the anchored cruiser *Brooklyn*, and the protected cruisers, *Columbia* and *Minneapolis*, it would cover the east coast, ready to be deployed to the Caribbean Sea or to Spanish waters. The rest of the fleet in Atlantic waters was concentrated at Key West, Florida. Designated the North Atlantic Squadron, under the command of Captain William T. Sampson, it included three armored vessels—the battleships *Iowa* and *Indiana* and the armored cruiser *New York*. The battleship *Oregon* was at this time still en route around South America. Sampson's prime assignment in the event of war was to blockade Cuba and Puerto Rico, operating against whatever enemy vessels might appear in Caribbean waters. From the beginning it was assumed that the Flying Squadron would join the North Atlantic Squadron at an appropriate time, presumably after the Navy Department ascertained the intentions of the enemy. The remaining naval force was the Asiatic Squadron, then based at Hong Kong under Commodore George Dewey. Poised to operate against the Spanish squadron at Manila, it did not include any armored vessels.[27]

The maneuvering of these squadrons depended on accurate information concerning the location and intentions of the enemy fleet; to assist in this enterprise the Navy Department improvised an emergency intelligence service in Europe. For news of the Spanish fleet it relied principally on the American consuls at various foreign stations and the naval attachés in Great Britain and France, Lieutenant John C. Colwell in London and Lieutenant William S. Sims in Paris. The latter two officers organized clandestine operations to supplement the information derived from diplomatic and commercial sources. Sims was particularly assiduous in this respect, assembling a group of informers that included an impoverished French baron, a doctor practicing among the Spanish aristocracy in Madrid, and the mayor of a French town near Paris who doubled as a private investigator for none other than Georges Clemenceau, then a Paris journalist. Since the Navy Department was particularly interested in information about the movements of Spanish ships in European waters, it dispatched two special agents to Europe—Ensigns Henry H. Ward and William H. Buck. Arriving at Liverpool on May 8, 1898, they chartered yachts and sailed to the Mediterranean in the guise of British subjects. Ward went to Gibraltar and thence to the Madeiras and the Caribbean, providing occasional information of some use during the war. Buck remained in the Mediterranean, observing the Spanish squadron under the command of Admiral Manuel de la Cámara. This jerry-built organization was usually able to generate intelligence sufficient to avoid egregious errors by the Navy Department.[28]

Since no entity existed in the Navy Department charged specifically with the direction of strategy or preparation of war plans—although the Navy War College had provided some help in this respect—Secretary Long wisely organized a group that became known as the Naval War Board. It stemmed from the *ad hoc* groups that had developed plans during the period from December, 1896 to March, 1898. When formally organized in March, 1898, it included Assistant Secretary Theodore Roosevelt; Captain Arent S. Crowninshield, the Chief of the Bureau of Navigation; and two other officers, Rear Admiral Montgomery Sicard— just detached as commander of the North Atlantic Station—and Captain Albert S. Barker. Roosevelt left the Department early in May to join the army. Captain Alfred Thayer Mahan, ordered home from Europe, reported for duty on the board on May 9. Captain Barker was soon posted to other duties, so that during most of the war the board consisted of Sicard (chairman), Crowninshield, and Mahan. It served simply as an advisory body to the Secretary of the Navy. It had no executive authority, although it undertook certain administrative duties, particularly supervision of the improvised intelligence apparatus. It did not decide the movements of any force at sea.[29]

Captain Mahan later minimized the role of the Naval War Board in the events of 1898, a perverse tendency on his part that has obscured the group's important services. He believed that a single officer with command authority could perform the functions of the board more efficiently than a committee. Only a day after his arrival at the Navy Department, he wrote Long that professional judgments should come to the Secretary of the Navy "not as the result of majority vote, but with the far weightier sanction of a single competent man, acting under the high sense of high personal responsibility." He was angered when the Secretary ignored his recommendation. Thereafter the choleric strategist made no secret of his distaste for the board. Long observed on May 19, "Captain Mahan is on the rampage again. He is very frank and manly; does not go around Robin Hood's barn, but blurts out his entire dissatisfaction with the entire Naval War Board." In 1900 Mahan described the Board to Admiral Dewey as "simply a meeting of officers whose other . . . duties indicated them to be proper persons for a fruitful consultation and for coordination of the many and speedy steps which had to be taken outside and beyond bureau action. . . . As such steps would need the Secretary's sanction, the Board fell naturally into the position of an advisory body." Given Mahan's views students of the war with Spain have usually assumed that the Naval War Board did not play a significant part in the struggle, but a close look suggests a different conclusion. Exercising considerable influence on naval operations in the Caribbean, the board proved itself a fitting predecessor to the first permanent institution within the Navy Department charged with comparable functions—the General Board founded in 1900.[30]

In March, 1898, the Naval War Board enunciated a principle that governed naval operations throughout the struggle with Spain; following earlier war plans, it recommended that the navy concentrate its attention on the outlying, poorly defended insular possessions of Spain. When war began, Captain Sampson would initiate a close blockade of Cuba, with secondary activity around Puerto Rico. After the enemy's naval force had been defeated in Caribbean waters, operations against Spain might take place. This plan allowed time for the army, ill prepared for large-scale activities at the beginning of the war, to mobilize a large expeditionary force for campaigns in Cuba and Puerto Rico. Meanwhile, in the western Pacific, Commodore Dewey would attack the Spanish ships at Manila, securing a base of operations for the Asiatic Squadron from which it could protect American shipping. No responsible naval leader worried that the Spanish squadron in the Philippines would descend on the Hawaiian Islands or the American west coast. In Admiral Patricio Montojo's modest force at Manila there were but two vessels displacing more than 1,250 tons and capable of carrying more than 250 tons of coal. French Ensor Chadwick justly wrote, "The difficulties of coaling and repairing in the vast stretches of the Pacific were too great to encounter in the face of an active enemy on its own coast, even had Spain been free to send the greater part of all of its naval force."[31]

When, after the war, Mahan assessed the naval struggle, he questioned whether Cuba should have been the initial center of operations, but he strongly endorsed the decision to inaugurate the conflict with a blockade. To his way of thinking, Puerto Rico ought to have been

dealt with before blockading Havana and other Cuban ports. Left undisturbed, Puerto Rico "would be invaluable to the mother country as a
base of supplies and reinforcements for both her fleet and army; . . . if
left in her undisturbed possession, it would enable her, practically, to
enjoy the same advantage of nearness to the great scene of operations
that the United States had in virtue of her geographical position."
More generally he considered Puerto Rico's relation to the projected
United States isthmian canal and the Pacific coast to be as important as
Malta's to the Suez canal and beyond. Mahan had no doubt, however,
that the navy had to establish a close blockade of Cuba before attempting offensive operations. This measure would not only exhaust the
Spanish army in Cuba by depriving it of supplies and reinforcements; it
would force the enemy to relieve the beleaguered garrison with naval
forces. Mahan never deviated from one of his strategic dicta, that the
American fleet must be concentrated for eventual employment against
the enemy fleet. For this reason he criticized proposals to use naval
vessels for bombardment of shore points or patroling the American
coasts. He opposed risk-taking "unless it gave a fair promise of
diminishing the enemy's naval force, and so of deciding the control of
the sea, upon which the issue of the war depended." He was pleased to
note that this "single idea" in fact controlled the Navy Department's
direction of strategy throughout the war.[32]

Despite the obvious prudence of Mahan's view, Captain Sampson
developed a plan to begin the war by bombarding and reducing the
forts protecting Havana harbor. Two of his principal officers, Captains
Robley D. Evans of the *Iowa* and French Ensor Chadwick of the *New
York,* later defended Sampson's scheme on the grounds that an early
and powerful strike on Havana would force a quick end to the war, obviating the need to conduct further operations. Two prime considerations, however, led the Navy Department to veto Sampson's proposal,
so reminiscent of Admiral Farragut's exploits during the Civil War. It
believed, with Mahan, that armored vessels should not be risked against
land batteries or underwater mines and torpedos. The battle fleet
should be kept intact for operations against the enemy's main naval
forces. Also, the United States did not have an army in hand to project
ashore after a bombardment. Even the belligerent Theodore Roosevelt
doubted the advisability of a naval attack on Havana. To Captain Evans
he wrote somewhat apologetically, "I think we could probably whip the
dagoes even with crippled battleships, but I don't want to try; and ten
and twelve-inch guns even in the hands of the Spanish might knock out
one or two of our ships." He admitted the force of Evans's view that

battleships should not be used in blockades. "I hope that we can speed-ily put them to better use," he wrote.[33]

Frustrated in his desire to storm the enemy's defenses at Havana, Sampson devoted most of his energies during the last few weeks of peace to preparing plans for the blockade. Early orders from the Navy Department called for operations concentrating on the northern coast of Cuba at Matanzas and Havana. Some attention was also given to certain ports on the south side of Cuba—Santiago de Cuba, Manzanillo, and Cienfuegos. The Navy Department may have hoped that the blockade by itself would force a Spanish surrender before the end of the rainy season in October. Sampson modified this scheme; he wanted to con-centrate his forces on the northern coast against Mariel, Havana, Matan-zas, and Cárdenas, having in mind a technical consideration that was to influence operations throughout the war. To Secretary Long he ex-plained patiently, "I regard it as impossible on account of the limited coal capacity of many of our ships to begin the blockade of the southern ports until the colliers shall be on the ground to supply the blockading vessels with coal." When on April 21 Sampson received orders to move against the Cuban coast, the Navy Department asked him to include one southern port in the blockade—Cienfuegos—which enjoyed good rail connections with Havana. The Department advanced another reason for avoiding an extensive blockade on the south coast of Cuba; naval vessels would soon be needed to escort army troops to Cuba. To make sure that Sampson did not act rashly, the Department reminded him not to take the offensive: "The Department does not wish the defenses of Havana to be bombarded or attacked by your squadron." As the North Atlantic Squadron prepared to leave for Cuba, Sampson was notified of his promotion to Rear Admiral in Command of United States Naval Forces on the North Atlantic Station, a designation that presumably included the Flying Squadron as well as the force concen-trated at Key West.[34]

FINAL NAVAL PREPARATIONS: WESTERN PACIFIC OCEAN

When Commodore Dewey took command of the Asiatic Squadron at Nagasaki, Japan, on January 3, 1898, it included only four vessels: The protected cruiser *Olympia,* the flagship; a small unprotected cruiser, the *Boston;* the gunboat *Petrel;* and an antique paddle-wheel steamer, the *Monocacy.* Dewey remained in Japan until the unprotected cruiser *Concord* joined his squadron on February 9 with a much-needed supply of ammunition. Then he left immediately for Hong Kong. "My decision to take the squadron to Hong Kong," Dewey later wrote, "was entirely on my own initiative, without any hint whatsoever from the department that hostilities might be expected." It was evident "that in case of emergency Hong Kong was the most advantageous position from which to move to the attack."[35]

After arriving at Hong Kong Dewey busied himself with careful preparations for a descent on Manila, particularly after being ordered to do so late in February. To augment his squadron he purchased the collier *Nanshan* to carry fuel and a steamer, the *Zafiro*, to transport supplies. This step compensated in part for the lack of a base in the area. About the same time he learned that the revenue cutter *McCulloch*, then at Singapore, had been ordered to join his command; it arrived on April 17. His force was completed with the arrival on April 22 of the protected cruisers *Raleigh*, fresh from the Mediterranean, and *Baltimore*, with additional ammunition. However, even with the *Baltimore's* cargo in hand, Dewey's magazines contained only about 60 percent of the squadron's full supply of ammunition.[36]

Dewey early decided that he could make a successful attack on the Spanish squadron in Manila Bay. He was familiar with the Navy Department's plan to either attack or blockade Manila, and he knew that the Philippine port's defending force was much inferior to his own. Information received from Oscar F. Williams, the American consul in Manila, confirmed his view that if he blockaded or captured the Philippine city the rest of the archipelago would then fall into the hands of either the insurgent movement there or the United States. The Naval War Board concurred in this estimate, adopting the view that Dewey had sufficient firepower to reduce the forts guarding Manila bay.[37]

On April 23 the American commander received notice from Major General Wilsone Black, the British administrator of Hong Kong, that a state of war existed between Spain and the United States, and that he must therefore leave port no later than 4:00 P.M. on Monday, April 25. Dewey informed the Navy Department of this requirement and asked for orders, indicating that he awaited the arrival of Consul Williams from Manila with late information. On April 24 Dewey moved his squadron to Mirs Bay, an anchorage in Chinese territorial waters about thirty miles from Hong Kong. That same day orders were sent from Washington directing him to attack. Secretary Long recalled the scene at the White House as McKinley made his decision: "It was a lively, sunny spring day, a bright contrast to the grim business at hand. We sat on a sofa, he thoughtful, his face showing a deep sense of the responsibility of the hour."[38]

Because the attention of the American people had been riveted on military and political developments associated with Cuba, little notice had been taken of events in the western Pacific Ocean; but nevertheless Commodore Dewey's naval operations had been long under consideration. In ordering the attack on the Spanish squadron at Manila the McKinley Administration had in mind no other purpose than the relatively limited desire to exert pressure on Spain at a weakly defended colonial outpost far distant from the Spanish Peninsula. Dewey's military aims were well understood by all involved: He intended to seize a base for future operations of his squadron and ensure that Spain did not pose a threat to American commerce in the Pacific.

No reader relying on Theodore Roosevelt's frenzied correspondence during the last weeks of peace would have believed the United States Navy was reasonably well prepared for war in the Caribbean on the day that Sampson became a Rear Admiral and sailed from Key West for Havana. Roosevelt, writing to Henry White, still maintained that war should have come late in 1897, when the United States enjoyed much greater naval superiority and weather favored operations. He was full of "bitter wrath and humiliation" at the lack of comprehensive war plans. "We have our plans for the Navy," he told a friend, "and beyond that there is absolutely nothing." Even as late as April 18 he was complaining to Benjamin F. Tracy, a former Secretary of the Navy, about lack of progress in various projects, including construction of naval vessels and measures to prevent shipments from United States ports to Cuba. In a show of false modesty he concluded, "With the facts as I know them, all these measures seem indispensable. But there may of course be reasons to the contrary, of which I know nothing." The reason he knew but refused to accept; it was McKinley's last despairing hope that he might yet discover some means of avoiding war.[39]

On April 22 Charles G. Dawes summarized the considerations that must have been influencing the men around the President as naval operations were beginning against Cuba:

> The abnormal moral principle which justifies war (that the end justifies the means) must clearly apply only when war is clearly the least evil as compared with any peaceful settlement of the difficulty. In the pursuance of a peaceful but strong policy our country had forced Spain from one concession after another until she had gained the release of the reconcentrados and the right to feed them, thus enabling her to relieve Cuba from starvation in peace. The destuction of the *Maine* led her to demand that which heretofore she had refrained from demanding only in deference to International precedent—the withdrawal of Spanish government from the un-

happy island so terribly wronged by Spain. And now the war has come. God grant that it may be a step toward better things. We cannot tell.

In these terms, reminiscent of themes in Lincoln's Second Inaugural Address, those who had worked to avoid war girded for the conflict ahead.[40]

FIVE

The Battle of Manila Bay

As we have seen, prewar planning in the United States provided for seizure of the strategic initiative in Cuban and Philippine waters. Commodore Dewey's attack on the Spanish squadron at Manila and Admiral Sampson's blockade of Cuba were intended to prevent Spain from reinforcing and resupplying its vulnerable overseas possessions. The United States was relying initially upon these operations at sea not only for strategic reasons; its army hardly existed, whereas its modest but efficient navy was ready for action. The use of naval power against Spain's colonies was clearly the best means of exerting immediate pressure on Spain to seek peace. President McKinley had been forced into a conflict he had sought desperately to avoid. His aim now was to gain independence for Cuba rather than conquer overseas territories; no annexationist aims were contemplated. Once in the war the President sought victory by the quickest and least expensive means. As soon as command of the sea was established, the United States could conduct whatever additional operations—including the dispatch of expeditionary forces—might be required to force the capitulation of Spain.

For its part the Liberal ministry in Madrid could do little but authorize commanders in Cuba, Puerto Rico, and the Philippines to use local resources in defensive operations against American forces. Efforts had begun to prepare naval forces for dispatch to both the Caribbean and the western Pacific, but these activities were far less promising than those of the United States. Spain failed to shore up its colonial possessions against American attack because Madrid realized too late that war was probable, because land forces had already been deployed to Cuba and Luzon in considerable numbers, and because the long and frustrating insurrection in Cuba had seriously depleted the nation's resources. The energy and confidence of the American preparations in 1898 contrasted markedly with the lassitude and pessimism that characterized prewar activities in Spain. Such was the situation when the war came.

PRELIMINARIES

Commodore Dewey and his little squadron left Hong Kong on April 24–25, moving to Mirs Bay. There he awaited orders from Washington and the advent of Consul Williams, en route from the Philippines with late intelligence. At 12:15 P.M. on Monday, April 25, the American commander received his orders:

> War has commenced between the United States and Spain. Proceed at once, particularly against Spanish fleet. You must capture vessels or destroy. Use utmost endeavors.

These orders came as no surprise; they were perfectly consistent with prior expectations. Consul Williams arrived two days later, during the late morning of Wednesday, April 27, bearing news that Admiral Montojo's squadron intended to make its defense at Subig Bay.[1]

At 2:00 P.M. on that day the American squadron departed for Manila, about 620 miles distant, steaming in column with support craft in the rear. Maintaining eight knots over a smooth sea, Commodore Dewey anticipated a landfall north of the entrance to Manila Bay. No attempt was made to conceal the squadron's course because there was no reason to expect interference. During the voyage the crew took measures to prepare the ships for action, particularly removal of woodwork that might burn if struck by enemy fire. Dewey—that "fit, ruddy little Vermonter of nearly sixty, with frosty hair and mustaches and an authoritarian manner"—was off to his moment in history.[2]

Meanwhile Admiral Patricio Montojo awaited the American squadron. At 11:00 P.M. on Monday, April 25 his bedraggled squadron left its anchorage near Manila for Subig Bay, where he planned to challenge the American invaders. To Minister of the Marine Bermejo he wrote that he would have preferred to fight at the entrance of Manila Bay, basing his defense on a line of mines and on batteries located at various points, including Corregidor Island. He had been forced to decide against this course because he lacked the requisite ordnance. For similar reasons he also rejected a stand based on the naval station in Manila Bay at Cavite, a few miles south of Manila. His mines there were few in number and widely spaced—unlikely to deter an attacker.

When Montojo arrived at Subig Bay on April 26, he discovered that little or no progress had been made in preparing its defenses. None of the four 5.9-inch (15 cm.) guns that were to have been mounted on the little island of Isla Grande were in place. Only five of fourteen available Mathieson mines had been laid in the entrance of the bay, and there was no guarantee that they would function. At this point Montojo could only hope that he would have time to complete the work in Subig Bay; but on Thursday, April 28 the Spanish consul in Hong Kong informed him that Dewey had departed from Mirs Bay for the Philippines.[3]

Montojo then held a council of war with his captains and decided to return to Manila Bay; he now thought it "crazy" to fight at Subig in forty meters of water "since besides the squadron being destroyed, the loss of lives would be great in such depths." The Spanish officers weighed three options: They rejected a fight at Corregidor near Boca Grande—the main entrance to Manila Bay—because at this location the water was very deep, mines were not available, and land batteries located in the area could detain the Americans only briefly. The council of war also turned down a stand by the squadron under the batteries protecting Manila, because this course would subject the people of the city and their property to destructive naval bombardment. Montojo decided to anchor after all in shallow water off Cavite in Cañacao Bay—within Manila Bay—where the guns of the Spanish squadrons would enjoy the support of a battery at Sangley Point.[4]

Montojo could have considered two other options: He might have given battle in the open sea, but this course would have invited disaster. He might also have simply fled the Manila area, forcing Dewey to pursue him. Had he exercised foresight and stockpiled coal and provisions at various locations, he could have "drawn the American squadron after him in a search which might have been a long one. . . . Although there was almost the certainty of final destruction, this destruction would not have been in Manila Bay, and this fact might have saved the Philippines to Spain." However, this option met with strong opposition from Governor-General Basilio Augustín and the local populace, who placed their faith in the ability of Montojo's squadron to make an effective defense against an American naval attack.[5]

Admiral Montojo left Subig Bay at 10:30 A.M. on Friday, April 29 and steamed directly to Cavite, where he anchored in Cañacao Bay in a mere eight meters of water to await the arrival of Dewey. At 7:00 P.M.

the next day he learned that the American had reconnoitered Subig Bay
that afternoon and was headed towards Manila. At midnight the sound
of gunfire was heard in the vicinity of Corregidor—the entrance to
Manila Bay—and a report arriving at 2:00 A.M. on the morning of May 1
confirmed that an exchange of fire had occurred there. Despite the overwhelming indications that a naval engagement would ensue on May 1,
Montojo and many of his officers went to the city of Manila on the
night of April 30. Indeed, some did not reboard ship until after the
beginning of the battle. Montojo's uncertain and listless activities during the week prior to May 1 reflected his conviction that he had no
chance of resisting Dewey successfully. He lacked the necessary ships,
artillery, and mines to make a sound defense at Cavite. Only vast
miscalculation by his American counterpart would allow him to avert
devastating defeat.[6]

On the afternoon of April 30 Commodore Dewey had indeed reconnoitered Subig Bay, acting on the information from Consul Williams.
The position at Subig Bay was potentially strong. Lying about thirty-
five miles north of the entrance to Manila Bay, it flanked any force that
might threaten that area and posed a definite threat to Manila's
maritime communications with any other point ashore. When he arrived near Subig Bay, Dewey first sent in the cruisers *Boston* and *Concord* to investigate, adding the cruiser *Baltimore* when he received a
false report of gunfire. Montojo was not there. To one of his officers
Dewey exclaimed in glee, "Now we have them!" At 6:24 P.M. he set
off for Boca Grande, the main entrance to Manila Bay.[7]

Dewey prepared carefully for the movement through the entrance to
Manila Bay. Hoping to achieve surprise by not waiting until morning,
he intended to run in at night, with lights masked and gun crews
prepared to fire. The position he intended to pass was naturally strong;
if well defended, it could have proved difficult to handle. Two
points—Punta Gorda to the north and Punta Restinga to the
south—overlooked the entrance, and two islands lay in the mouth of
the Bay—Corregidor, the more northerly one, rising about six hundred
feet, and the smaller Caballo, rising about four hundred feet. Two
channels existed: one, to the north and running between Punta Gorda
and Corregidor Island, was called Boca Chica. The main passage, Boca
Grande, ran between Caballo Island and Punta Restinga. Its effective
width was only about three miles, however, because of a large rock
north of Punta Restinga known as El Fraile Island.

Dewey had to consider possible difficulties with mines in the Boca
Grande channel and artillery batteries on the adjacent land. Although
generally lacking sound intelligence concerning the Spanish defenses,

he had information that mines had been laid. However, Dewey decided that mines could not really pose difficulties in Boca Grande because of the channel's depth and the likelihood that both the contact and electrical varieties of mine would deteriorate rapidly in the tropical waters. He decided that the value of the objective far outweighed the risks of passage. Enemy batteries posed a more serious problem; by April 29 seventeen guns had been mounted in six different locations covering the entrances to the Bay. Of these, nine muzzle-loading weapons—three each at Punta Gorda, Corregidor, and Punta Restinga—did not constitute a truly serious threat because they could not be reloaded quickly enough to threaten speedy modern vessels. Two breech-loading guns at Punta Lassisi were too far away to create difficulties. The danger lay in the six breech-loading guns mounted on Caballo and El Fraile islands, at least when the ships would pass within a mile and a half of these locations. Dewey believed that these batteries, if well served by efficient crews, could give the American squadron "a very unpleasant quarter of an hour," but he did not hesitate in deciding to run past them, assuming that he would remain within range only for that brief period in the dark of the night.[8]

At about midnight on April 30 Dewey successfully entered Manila Bay. His squadron approched Boca Grande in single column, moving on a course about a half mile north of El Fraile and two miles south of Caballo, which would allow it to avoid the San Nicolas shoals inside the Bay but did expose it to the enemy's most concentrated fire for the longest period of time. As Dewey's flagship, the *Olympia*, slid by the batteries, lookouts observed no signs of life in the area. Only when the last vessels passed was there action. Three shots came from the battery of 4.7-inch guns mounted on El Fraile, but caused no damage to the squadron. With a few rounds of return fire from the *Boston, Concord, Raleigh,* and *McCulloch,* the brief engagement came to an end. Dewey had survived his potentially most difficult maneuver; he now concentrated on locating the enemy squadron. Nathan Sargent expressed surprise at the failure of the Spanish defenders to fire as much as possible on the passing ships or mass a considerable number of small craft—particularly some twenty-five gunboats available to them—for an attack on the American squadron as it passed through Boca Grande. Dewey also wondered why the batteries at Boca Grande did not fire much. He heard later that the men assigned to the batteries were absent from some of the locations that evening, since the Americans were not expected to enter under cover of darkness. It is more probable, however, that the lack of enterprise around Boca Grande reflected the defeatism of the Spanish commanders.[9]

As Dewey moved up the bay towards the city of Manila, proceeding slowly at about eight knots so as to avoid an engagement before dawn, he arranged his squadron for the impending battle. Leaving behind the revenue cutter *McCulloch*, the supply-ship *Zafiro*, and the collier *Nanshan*, he retained six fighting ships in column. He had no armored vessels, but four were good protected cruisers possessing relatively formidable guns—the *Olympia, Baltimore, Raleigh,* and *Boston.* The others were the unprotected cruiser *Concord* and the gunboat *Petrel.* Dewey's squadron displaced 19,098 tons and disposed of fifty-three heavy guns, including ten eight-inch breech-loading rifles. There were 1,611 crewmen aboard.

In Cañacao Bay, south of Manila, Montojo had anchored his squadron in an irregular crescent-shaped line stretching eastward from just inside Sangley Point to shoal water near Las Piñas. His line of battle from west to east consisted of two unprotected cruisers—the *Reina Cristina* and the *Castilla,* a wooden vessel—and five gunboats—the *Don Juan de Austria, Don Antonio de Ulloa, Isla de Cuba, Marqués del Duero,* and *Isla de Luzon.* Two other gunboats—the *General Lezo* and *Velasco*—were out of repair, anchored in nearby Bacoor Bay with the transport *Manila.* Montojo's squadron displaced but 11,328 tons and carried a mere thirty-seven heavy guns, of which the largest were seven 6.3-inch rifles.[10]

A comparison of the two squadrons reveals an overwhelming disparity of strength in favor of the Americans. The six American vessels outweighed the seven Spanish vessels by 7,770 tons, although crew strengths were roughly comparable. Four of the six American ships—all constructed of iron or steel—were "protected"—that is, they had armored decks. None of the Spanish ships were protected, and the largest one, the *Castilla,* was made of wood. Five of the American ships equalled or surpassed the speed of the two swiftest Spanish ships. The most notable difference, however, was in armament: Dewey's eight-inch guns outranged all of the Spanish weapons. Nine of the Spanish guns were muzzle-loading and therefore difficult to reload speedily. And the secondary batteries on the American vessels included 135 light guns, while the Spanish ships carried but 110. The American squadron had well-trained and disciplined crews with excellent commissioned officers in charge, whereas the Spanish squadron was in a much less satisfactory state. Some American commentators have attempted to minimize the difference in strength between the two squadrons on the grounds that the Spanish vessels were compensated since they usually were stationary during the naval engagement and therefore more able to direct accurate fire at the American squadron, but this argument ignores the patent facts that a moving target is more difficult to hit than a stationary target and that the American guns far outranged those of the Spaniards.[11]

These calculations do not take into consideration the Spanish batteries at Manila. Chadwick later counted 226 guns of all types in the area, of which 164 were muzzle-loaders. Only twelve were modern breech-loading weapons, the most powerful being four 9.4-inch (24 cm.) guns. Captain Mahan once postulated that one gun ashore was worth four afloat, and on this basis Spanish firepower at Manila clearly exceeded that of the Americans. But in this situation the normal calculation had no meaning. Only three of the Manila batteries actually were engaged on May 1, but they proved highly ineffective. The only artillery capable of firing continuously on the American squadron was the battery at Sangley Point, consisting of two 5.9-inch (15 cm.) breech-loading rifles, and the Cañacao (or Ulloa) battery, which had only one 4.7-inch (12 cm.) breech-loading rifle.[12]

Given the imbalance between Spanish and American firepower, the failure of Montojo to locate his squadron under the covering fire of the land batteries at Manila was most important in determining the outcome; it deprived Spain of any chance for victory. However, even if Montojo had fought adjacent to Manila, the Americans might have stayed outside the range of the heavy Spanish guns and used their eight-inch guns, which outranged anything on the Spanish ships, to batter the enemy from long distance. Dewey anticipated that Montojo would await attack in an anchorage off Manila under the guns of the city. But when he steered in that direction in the early hours of May 1, he observed only a few merchant ships. Turning to starboard towards Cavite and traveling about two or three miles off the mainland below Manila, he brought the Spanish squadron near Sangley Point under observation and prepared to attack. At 5:05 A.M. the Manila batteries opened fire, but their shells passed harmlessly overhead. The *Boston* and *Concord* then fired two rounds each at the shore positions, but thereafter paid no attention to them. Dewey wished to conserve his ammunition; no resupply was closer than seven thousand miles. In any event, he had identified the enemy squadron rather than land fortifications as his objective, in accordance with Captain Mahan's views on this subject.[13]

THE NAVAL COMBAT

The first phase of the naval battle now began. At just about the time when the Manila batteries opened up, two mines exploded harmlessly in front of the American ships. Dewey at first thought that they had been activated prematurely; later he heard that they had been fired to clear the way for a torpedo attack by two Spanish launches, a report that proved to be incorrect. At 5:15 A.M. the enemy squadron and its supporting artillery batteries opened fire on the American ships. Dewey now closed up his column of ships to form a lateral line at intervals of from two hundred to four hundred yards, laying a course at eight knots, to converge on the enemy rather than approach one by one—an effort to confuse the Spanish gunners. When the squadron reached the five-fathom mark, Dewey turned westward to run by the Spanish line, a maneuver that brought his port batteries to bear. At 5:40 A.M., when the *Olympia* closed to within five thousand yards of the enemy, at about two and a half miles away, Dewey calmly turned to its commander and said, "You may fire when you are ready, Gridley." An eight-inch shell fired from the flagship's forward turret signaled the rest of the squadron to commence firing. The American squadron continued moving westward to a location just north of Sangley Point, whereupon it "countermarched" on the reverse course—a means of bringing the starboard batteries into action. Because the range had been shortened to about two thousand yards, Dewey had surrendered a tactical advantage: Had he stayed at the maximum range of his eight-inch guns, the Spanish shells could not have reached the American ships. During the first phase of the battle, Dewey made five runs by the Spanish squadron, three to the west and two returns to the east. The later runs, particularly the last one to the west, were at somewhat shorter range because it was discovered that the water depth was somewhat greater than indicated on the charts.

At 7:00 A.M. Montojo ordered his flagship, the *Reina Cristina,* to leave its mooring and attack the *Olympia,* a desperate effort to change the course of the battle. This hopeless venture came to an unhappy end; not only was the *Reina Cristina* a slower vessel—it could make but thirteen knots at best, while the American vessel was capable of seventeen—but, more important, the Spanish flagship became vulnerable to the fire of the entire American squadron. Its gallant but quixotic attack having failed, the *Reina Cristina* returned to the Spanish line with mortal wounds. Montojo soon transferred his flag to the *Isla de Cuba.*

At 7:30 A.M. Dewey received a report from Captain Gridley that the *Olympia* had only fifteen rounds of ammunition left for each of its five-inch guns, and he immediately broke off the action, retiring to confer with his captains. He explained the situation thus in his *Autobiography:* "It was a most anxious moment for me. So far as I could see, the Spanish squadron was as intact as ours. I had reason to believe that their supply of ammunition was as ample as ours was limited. Therefore, I decided to withdraw temporarily from action for a redistribution of ammunition as necessary. For I knew that 15 rounds of 5-inch ammunition could be shot away in five minutes." Later on it was reported, quite erroneously, that Dewey had withdrawn at this time simply to permit his sailors to have breakfast. Although the ships did take advantage of the break to take their morning meal, Dewey's motive was certainly to evaluate his supply of ammunition.[14]

When Dewey finally received accurate information, he realized that his squadron was in excellent condition and that the enemy was *in extremis*. Gridley's report about the ammunition supply of the *Olympia* proved garbled; the truth was that each of the five-inch guns had fired only fifteen rounds. The Spanish marksmanship, as anticipated, had been poor indeed; the *Olympia, Baltimore, Boston,* and *Petrel* had all been hit but had sustained little serious damage. No Americans had been killed in this phase of the action; the only casualties had occurred on the *Baltimore,* with two officers and six enlisted men sustaining wounds. Even as the American ships were withdrawing, it became obvious that the Spanish squadron had sustained irremediable damage and many casualties. At 8:00 A.M. Montojo ordered all vessels capable of getting under way to move southward from Cañacao Bay to near the roadstead at Bacoor for a last stand. His ships were to be scuttled before being surrendered to the Americans. While Dewey lay off to the northwest, he sent a message to Augustín in Manila warning that he would shell the city if its batteries did not cease firing. No further projectiles came from that quarter.[15]

At 11:16 A.M. the American squadron resumed the action, and the battle came rapidly to its grisly conclusion. Now only the battery at Sangley Point and the guns of the *Don Antonio de Ulloa* returned Dewey's fire. The gunboat was soon silenced. Unfortunately for the defenders of Cavite, the guns at Sangley Point could not be lowered to fire at ranges less than two thousand yards; presumably those mounting them never anticipated that an enemy might approach to within that range. As a result, until the battery was silenced, it simply fired harmlessly over the American squadron. Dewey, remembering later the four 5.9-inch guns that had been taken from Sangley Point to Subig Bay, felt that if they had been available on May 1 the American squadron might have sustained much more damage. At about 12:15 P.M., a white flag unfurled at Cavite, reported by the *Petrel,* led to the end of the American attack. At 12:30 P.M. the attack ended, "the [Spanish] batteries being silenced and the ships sunk, burnt, and destroyed." At this point Dewey sent the *Concord* to deal with a merchant ship anchored near Bacoor, and the *Petrel* was ordered to finish off any Spanish war vessels still afloat in Cavite harbor. Lieutenant Edward M. Hughes and seven sailors of the *Petrel* launched a whaleboat and set fire to a number of ships scuttled in shallow water, at the same time taking possession of some small tugboats and launches.[16]

The final reckoning demonstrated the extent of Spanish tragedy and American triumph. Three of Montojo's ships—the *Reina Cristina, Castilla,* and *Don Antonio de Ulloa*—had been sunk during the battle. The *Petrel* fired the *Don Juan de Austria, Isla de Luzon, Isla de Cuba, Marqués del Duero, Velasco,* and *General Lezo.* Of the latter vessels the first three were later raised, repaired, and placed in the American service. Spanish casualties were severe, despite Montojo's efforts to minimize them by fighting the battle in shallow water. His command suffered 161 killed and 210 wounded, a total of 371 casualties. Much of this loss occurred on the *Reina Cristina,* which alone had 130 killed and 80 wounded. The American squadron suffered minor material damage and no fatalities. Only 9 men had been wounded—8 on the *Baltimore* and 1 on the *Boston.*[17]

Although the American squadron had gained a great victory, its gunnery at Manila Bay left much to be desired. During the battle Dewey's ships fired 5,859 shells but made only 142 hits, a ratio of only 2.42 percent. Most of the hits were recorded on vessels that sunk during the combat—39 on the *Reina Cristina,* and 37 each on the *Castilla* and *Don Antonio de Ulloa.* The *Olympia* fired 317 shells from its main batteries (eight- and five-inch guns) and had 630 rounds of ammunition left after the battle. The *Boston* fired 210 rounds from its eight- and six-inch batteries, retaining 386 unexpended rounds. The *Baltimore* was less active, its eight- and six-inch batteries firing 195 shells and retaining 665. Lieutenant Bradley A. Fiske, who viewed the battle from a mast on the *Petrel* as he determined ranges with his stadimeter, summarized the general disappointment: "Our practice was evidently much better than that of the Spaniards, but it did not seem to me that it was at all good." He attributed the difficulty to "uncertainty about the true range, and the fact that each gun captain felt it was incumbent upon him to fire as fast as he could." Lieutenant John M. Ellicott, who conducted a careful investigation of the Spanish ships after the battle, made some observations of the damage that were later to influence American naval construction: The iron and steel plates on the unprotected sides of the Spanish vessels did not slow the American projectiles enough to explode them. It was also apparent that eight-inch shells had much more effect for their size than those of lesser caliber. Gun shields struck from a distance of over 2,500 yards were dangerous to those supposedly protected by them. He concluded that ships had left the action because of conflagration and casualties to personnel rather than sinking, which occurred later on.[18]

AFTERMATH

Once victory was assured, Dewey made a number of post-battle dispositions. At 2:00 P.M. he took his squadron to an anchorage just off the Luneta, a bayside park of Manila, notifying Spanish authorities that he would destroy the city if its land batteries opened on his ships. He later moved back to Cavite, fearing a surprise attack. When the request to use the city's cable to Hong Kong was refused, he had the *Zafiro* cut the connection on May 2. It was not to return to service until August 22, ten days after the eventual end of the war. This deed greatly interfered with communication between Dewey and his superiors in Washington, a circumstance that correspondingly restricted central control of his activities and gave the American commander marked freedom of action. On May 2 the garrison at the Cavite arsenal raised the Spanish flag, explaining that the white flag of the previous day had indicated only a temporary truce. To this challenge Dewey reacted immediately; the arsenal was forced to surrender. When its garrison evacuated the place, Americans occupied it and continued to do so for the rest of the campaign. Dewey afterwards claimed that his victory on May 1 firmly established American authority in Manila Bay. "From the moment that the captain-general accepted my terms [not to fire on the American squadron] the city was virtually surrendered," he insisted, "and I was in control of the situation, subject to my government's orders for the future." A base had been seized seven thousand miles from home that could be held indefinitely.[19]

News of the victory at Manila came slowly to the anxious leaders in Washington. Dewey did not send the revenue cutter *McCulloch* to Hong Kong with dispatches until May 5. Meanwhile, incomplete information was dribbling out of Madrid by way of London. By May 3 it appeared that Dewey had gained a great victory, and McKinley told Charles G. Dawes that, when official notification came, he would make Dewey an admiral. McKinley was "much pleased at the outcome at Manila as he issued the orders a week ago for the fleet to proceed to Manila and destroy the Spanish ships." When Dewey's first dispatches reached Washington on May 7, confirming earlier reports from Europe, wild celebrations took place. Dewey was immediately given his promotion, and Congress voted $10,000 for a Tiffany sword to be presented the victor and bronze medals to be awarded his men. However, the decisive victory also posed some problems for the war leaders. The news "Induced a frenzied demand to mop up the Spanish forces in Cuba and the Philippines, and end the war at once," tasks not easily accomplished, because the United States Army was in no position to take the field. And a vast Dewey "craze" swept the nation, which enthusiasm contributed later to a brief "Dewey for President" campaign that came to nothing. For the moment, however, the craze sustained popular support for the war, advanced so auspiciously on May 1 many thousands of miles away from its principal theater.[20]

As was the Spanish custom, Admiral Montojo was subjected to a court-martial upon his return to Spain. His *post mortem* of the battle laid heavy stress on his squadron's relative weakness. He dwelt on the inadequacies of his vessels, guns, and crews, and on the importance of forestalling a bombardment of Manila. For this *apologia* there is some support. Most of the Spanish resources committed to the Philippines before May 1 had been designed to counteract the land operations of Filipino insurgents, who lacked any capability to fight at sea. Montojo's ships were not designed to fight modern ships of the classes included in Dewey's squadron. Montojo's counsel, Captain Víctor M. Concas, defended the decision to give battle at Cavite. Subig Bay was a more logical location, but it had not been fortified properly. Concas also stressed the failure of the home government to provide reinforcements. Recognizing that Montojo might instead have fled Manila to prolong the contest, he noted that this course would have encountered stern opposition from Governor-General Basilio Augustín and the citizenry of Manila. The court-martial convicted Montojo of dereliction of duty, but his sentence was merely to be separated from the service. There were extenuating circumstances; he had fought bravely and sustained a severe wound.[21]

Dewey later criticized Montojo severely. He believed that the Admiral should have remained with the Spanish squadron on the night of April 30 instead of attending a reception in Manila. It seemed to him "most incomprehensible" that the batteries at Boca Grande had not fired on the passing American squadron or that smaller ships had not tried to damage his ships in the narrow waters there. He was surprised that neither the *Isla de Cuba* nor the *Isla de Luzon* had attempted to make a torpedo attack during the action, since both were equipped with two torpedo tubes. Dewey did not mention the most obvious error, one that Spanish authorities have emphasized: Montojo should not have offered battle in Manila Bay. Whatever the ultimate outcome, he might well have delayed defeat and seriously hampered Dewey by withdrawing to other places in the archipelago. The adverse political consequences of this withdrawal would have been far less damaging than those that flowed from the sudden and dramatic outcome of May 1. And from a strictly naval point of view, Montojo should have fought under the guns of Manila rather than at Cavite, regardless of the damage that might have resulted to the city.[22]

Dewey's operations have received universal approbation. One admiring authority, Nathan Sargent, summarized the principal reasons for the smashing victory very well: "Admiral Dewey's success was due to his exhaustive preliminary studies of the situation, to his careful foresight and preparations at Hongkong, to his wise consultations with his captain[s], and their mutual consideration of every contingency which might arise, to his analytical diagnosis of all the ominous rumors of Spanish preparation, and finally to his celerity and virtual surprise of their position at an hour when he was least expected." He might also have mentioned the sad condition of the Spanish defenses. Given the relative strengths of the two squadrons and the tactical errors of Montojo, Dewey should have achieved a decisive victory. Since he made no serious mistakes in pursuit of his objective—the Spanish ships—he emerged victorious. William R. Braisted argues the tactical benefits that might have accrued to Spain, had Montojo fled Manila, but he recognizes the reasons why the enemy commander did not choose this course. "Distracted by internal unrest and by the irresolute government in Madrid, the Spanish authorities in Manila were perhaps too weak to order a retreat." Thus, a combination of Spanish pride and impotence smoothed Dewey's path to immortality.[23]

The American victory at Manila Bay constituted a prelude to later land operations in the Philippines, but for the moment attention shifted to the Caribbean Sea, destined to become the main theater of war. Even before Dewey had left Mirs Bay, Admiral Sampson's North Atlantic Squadron was steaming across the Straits of Florida to blockade Cuba. Naval operations in the Antilles, as in the Philippines, were preparing the way for the employment of the United States Army.

☆ SIX ☆

The Blockade of Cuba

On April 22, 1898 Admiral Sampson got underway at Key West with his squadron in double column, setting a course for Havana, less than 100 miles distant. Captain Robley D. Evans, commanding the *Iowa*, recalled the departure clearly: "In less than four hours from the receipt of the order the navy showed its state of readiness by actually starting for the enemy's coast. Fortunately for the country, we were in much better shape than the people thought we were." Readiness was necessary; to establish an effective blockade of Cuba was no easy task. Upon arriving that same day at Havana, Sampson prepared to close other ports as well. On the next day, April 23, he sent ships eastward to blockade Matanzas and Cárdenas, and westward to shut up Mariel and Cabañas. A patrol was sent out to watch the waters between Havana and Bahía Honda. Four days later Sampson managed to blockade Cienfuegos, a port on the southern coast of Cuba with good rail connections to Havana that was well situated to receive supplies from Mexico or points in the southern Caribbean. Sampson was, however, unable to maintain a continuous blockade of the more easterly ports on the north coast, particularly Nuevitas, Sagua la Grande, and Caibarién, due to a lack of ships that forced President McKinley to withhold issuance of a proclamation of blockade for the entire south coast of Cuba and Puerto Rico until June 28. Curiously enough, the United States never was to proclaim a blockade of Santiago de Cuba.[1]

108

ESTABLISHMENT OF THE BLOCKADE

On April 26 President McKinley issued a proclamation reflecting traditional American regard for the rights of neutrals on the high seas during time of war. The United States would honor the Declaration of Paris of 1856, which outlawed privateering. Neutral flags would cover enemy goods except for contraband, and noncontraband items belonging to neutrals carried in enemy ships would not be subject to confiscation. While blockades had to be effective to be binding, the navy would exercise great care in making searches at sea. Only the clearest grounds for suspicion would lead to interference with mail steamers. Spanish merchant ships in the United States were given until May 21 to depart and granted immunity from seizure, subject only to certain normal limitations: They could not transport members of the armed forces, could load only enough coal to travel to their home ports, and could not carry contraband or despatches. These privileges were extended to Spanish ships that had set sail for the United States prior to April 21.[2]

The war with Spain turned on efforts to prevent by means of the blockade the enemy from reinforcing and resupplying its army in Cuba and possibly to exhaust that force sufficiently to avoid the need for extensive deployment of troops against it. The blockade was also designed to end all forms of commercial exchange between Spain and Cuba. If Spain felt compelled to send out a naval relief expedition, its forces would have to be operating some three thousand miles from their only available bases. The blockade had one serious disadvantage in that it imposed hardships on Cubans, but its adverse effect on the Spanish troops was considered sufficient compensation for this. A Spanish soldier who served around Cienfuegos, Manuel Corral, later reported that his rations remained steady for about a month after the war began, but then he stopped getting his customary portion of coffee and wine; later on sugar ran out, and eventually he was left to fend for himself. It is impossible however to estimate accurately the full potential of Sampson's operation against Spanish maritime communications. Blockades by their nature are slow to take full effect, and the war was to last less than four months.[3]

During the first few weeks of the campaign Sampson and his subordinate commanders labored unceasingly to improve the blockade. Communication between various units of the blockading forces had to be perfected. Blockading techniques in general had to be observed and improved, and the task of coaling the vessels required constant attention. Ports that remained unclosed had to be scouted, and vessels moving on the high seas had to be intercepted and investigated for possible contraband, particularly ships out of Jamaica or Mexico seeking to enter harbors on the southern shore of Cuba. As prizes began to accumulate, it became necessary to make arrangements for adjudicating cases and allocating prize money; distribution of the spoils took place in the United States Navy until 1900. The blockaders had to supervise the visits of all neutral vessels to Cuban ports. Above all, efforts were made to augment the blockade squadron.

Although Sampson did not receive authority to bombard forts defended by heavy cannon, he could attack light land batteries firing in support of vessels he wished to capture. On April 28 two ranking commodores were placed under Sampson's command, one to administer the base at Key West and the other to serve as his deputy with the blockading squadron. This measure allowed the Admiral to concentrate on preparations for operations that might become necessary if Cervera's squadron ever appeared in the war zone.[4]

During the course of the blockade no less than fifteen engagements took place at ports other than Santiago de Cuba. For example, on April 27 Sampson took three vessels to Matanzas—the *New York*, *Puritan*, and *Amphitrite*—and shelled a battery there, a notable event because in the engagement American ships came under fire for the first time during the war. On May 11 small boats from the *Marblehead* and *Nashville* cut two cables off Cienfuegos under heavy enemy fire. They did not sever a third line—an omission that allowed the Spanish garrison to maintain telegraphic communication to Spain by way of Jamaica throughout the war. On the same day the navy suffered its first reverse when a torpedo boat, the *Winslow*, ventured into the harbor at Cárdenas. It immediately drew fire from a Spanish gunboat and some light guns on shore, and the revenue cutter *Hudson* had to tow the disabled American vessel out of the harbor. In this action a line officer and four enlisted men were killed, and three other enlisted men suffered wounds. (This was the only United States Navy line officer killed in action during the War with Spain.) Later in May Captain Caspar F. Goodrich, commanding the *St. Louis*, managed to cut several cables in the vicinity of Santiago de Cuba, Guantánamo, and Môle St. Nicolas. On June 13 the auxiliary cruiser *Yankee* fought a spirited engagement at Cienfuegos with a Spanish vessel and land batteries. Similar engagements occurred sporadically until the end of the war.[5]

Although the Spanish government at times alleged that the blockade of Cuba was ineffective and therefore illegal, postwar inquiries revealed that only a few vessels succeeded in running past the American squadron. According to Severo Gómez Núñez, the most authoritative Spanish commentator, only two ships got out of Havana—one on June

23 and the other on July 23. Eight ships entered Cuban ports between June 17 and July 31—four from Spain and the others from France, England, and Norway. Five of these vessels had sailed from Mexico, two from Spain, and one from Halifax, Nova Scotia. Had the war lasted longer, the blockade surely would have generated widespread deprivation inside Cuba.[6]

CHASE OF ADMIRAL CERVERA

On April 29 Admiral Cervera finally left St. Vincent in the Cape Verde Islands bound for San Juan, Puerto Rico—the location assumed at the Ministry of the Marine to be the most likely American objective at the outset of the war. His squadron included four armored cruisers—the flagship *Infanta María Teresa* (Captain Víctor M. Concas), the *Vizcaya* (Captain Antonio Eulate), the *Cristóbal Colón* (Captain Emilio Díaz Moreau), and the *Almirante Oquendo* (Captain Joaquín Lazaga). Captain Fernando Villaamil commanded a flotilla of three torpedo-boat destroyers—the *Plutón, Furor,* and *Terror.* Several other vessels under Cervera's command at St. Vincent—two transports and three torpedo boats—returned to the Canary Islands. For the most part the Spanish squadron was in poor condition. Cervera had an excellent ship in the *Cristóbal Colón,* but it was exceedingly vulnerable because it lacked its main battery of 10-inch guns. Three of the four armored cruisers carried defective breech mechanisms and unreliable ammunition for their 5.5-inch rapid-firing guns. Captain Concas later complained bitterly about poor machinery and inadequate stokers. The *Vizcaya,* long at sea, had a foul bottom, and its reduced speed slowed the pace of the other ships in the squadron. Cervera's base had to be the Canary Islands or Spain, because no adequate facilities for repairing damages and replenishing supplies existed in the Antilles. Captain Chadwick later drew an apt comparison between the Spanish Navy in 1805, just at the time of Trafalgar, and the navy in 1898: In each case Spain had a reasonable number of ships but was unprepared for a fleet action. "Spain was without the primal necessities of a fleet: without guns, without ammunition, without engineers, without coal, and even with the ships short of bread."[7]

When Cervera left European waters, he surrendered most of whatever advantage accrued to his squadron. The influential Mahan defined Cervera's force as a "fleet-in-being"—that is, one "the existence of which, though inferior, on or near the scene of operations, is a perpetual menace to the various more or less exposed interests of the enemy, who cannot tell when a blow may fall, and who is therefore

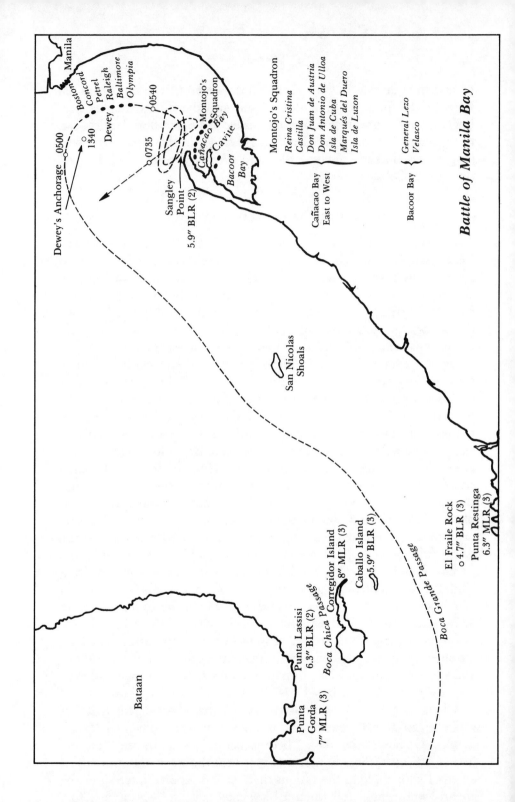

Manila

Boston
Concord
Petrel
Dewey Raleigh
Baltimore
Olympia

0540
0500
0735
1340

Dewey's Anchorage

Cañacao Bay
Montojo's Squadron
Cavite

Bacoor Bay

Sangley Point
5.9" BLR (2)

Montojo's Squadron

Reina Cristina
Castilla
Don Juan de Austria
Don Antonio de Ulloa
Isla de Cuba
Marqués del Duero
Isla de Luzon

Cañacao Bay
East to West

General Lezo
Velasco

Bacoor Bay

Battle of Manila Bay

San Nicolas
Shoals

Bataan

Punta Lassisi
6.3" BLR (2)

Punta
Gorda
7" MLR (3)

Corregidor Island
8" MLR (3)

Boca Chica Passage

Caballo Island
5.9" BLR (3)

Boca Grande Passage

El Fraile Rock
4.7" BLR (3)
Punta Restinga
6.3" MLR (3)

compelled to restrict his operations, otherwise possible, until that fleet can be destroyed or immobilized.'' Once Cervera was located, sufficient American forces would be concentrated to deal with him. His ability to threaten various objectives could then be cancelled, and the United States would attain freedom to maneuver vessels that otherwise would have been needed to protect locations deemed vulnerable to enemy raids. Captain Concas later justly complained that Cervera's departure for Puerto Rico ended the war because it divided the Spanish fleet. The squadron that went to the West Indies was so inferior to the opposing forces that it had no chance to avoid destruction. The remainder of the fleet, retained in Spanish waters, was incapable of effective offensive operations. If Cervera had been allowed to return to the Canaries or Spain, as he himself had argued, the total naval strength of Spain might well have interfered materially with American plans to move decisively against the Spanish Army in Cuba. Thus the blockade of Cuba played a truly important role in the campaign, because it forced the Ministry of the Marine to send out relief—a decision that all American planners had anticipated before the war. Cervera's outgunned ships would have to engage the combined naval forces of the United States far from a good base—the worst of all possible strategic circumstances.[8]

As long as Cervera's location could not be determined, the American fleet remained divided into two distinct forces. Commodore Schley's Flying Squadron stayed at Hampton Roads, Virginia, to guard against a possible Spanish descent on the east coast. It was but 2,350 miles from the Cape Verdes to San Juan, Puerto Rico, and from that port a mere 1,250 miles to Chesapeake Bay and 1,400 miles to New York. Once Cervera's position was ascertained, however, the Flying Squadron could be combined with the remaining ships of the North Atlantic Squadron blockading the north coast of Cuba. This convergence would concentrate overwhelmingly preponderant strength against Cervera's modest force.[9]

As soon as Cervera's departure became known at the Navy Department, preparations were made to intercept him. Because it was correctly assumed that the Spanish squadron was probably bound for either Puerto Rico or eastern Cuba, orders were issued on April 29 sending Captains Charles S. Cotton and Caspar F. Goodrich, commanding the *Harvard* and *St.Louis* (fast auxiliary cruisers leased from the American line), to the waters east of the Windward Islands. Two days later another fast cruiser, the *Yale*, was ordered to cruise off Puerto Rico. These three vessels were to report Cervera's arrival. If no sighting was made by May 10, the *Harvard* and the *St. Louis* were to proceed for telegraphic orders to Martinique and Guadeloupe respectively, and the

Yale was to visit St. Thomas on May 13. On May 3 the Department informed Sampson of its estimate that no large United States Army movement to Cuba should be expected for two weeks—presumably because none had been prepared—and no small force could leave an American port until the navy located Cervera. "If their objective is Porto Rico they should arrive about May 8, and immediate action against them and San Juan is authorized." In this event the Flying Squadron would move south to reinforce Sampson.[10]

Sampson decided to move eastward as soon as he learned of Cervera's departure, assuming that the Spanish squadron was bound for Puerto Rico. He believed that Cervera would run in to San Juan because coal and water could be obtained at that port, although he thought Martinique a possible objective because France might permit Cervera to coal there. (It was also conceivable that Cervera might attempt to intercept the battleship *Oregon*—then making its epic voyage around South America—which might call for a Spanish landfall at Martinique.) Sampson was convinced that Cervera did not intend to proceed directly to the American east coast; the Spanish squadron would surely encounter opposition there, without any access to a base at which to coal and make repairs. For his eastern deployment Sampson sought two battleships then with the Flying Squadron—the *Massachusetts* and *Texas*—but the Navy Department denied this request. On May 4 he left the blockade off Havana and moved towards San Juan with the two battleships *Iowa* and *Indiana*, the armored cruiser *New York*, the two ocean-going monitors *Amphitrite* and *Terror*, the two unprotected cruisers *Detroit* and *Montgomery*, the torpedo boat *Porter*, the collier *Niagara*, and the armored tug *Wompatuck*. The monitors and the torpedo boat had to be towed—a complication that was to lead to serious delays.[11]

The Navy Department showed some concern when it learned of Sampson's eastern movement, but did not veto it; such interference might discourage Sampson. Besides, it was learned that Captain Chadwick, Sampson's Chief of Staff, had sent letters home in which he intimated that the department had improperly interfered with the movements of the North Atlantic Squadron. The outcome was a cable sent May 5 that reached Sampson three days later: "Do not risk crippling your vessels against fortifications as to prevent from soon afterward successfully fighting the Spanish fleet." At the same time Long wrote a letter to Sampson reiterating his desire that the Admiral avoid operations that might weaken his squadron. After the war Mahan, who agreed with Chadwick that Puerto Rico was a truly important advance base, criticized Sampson's desire to proceed eastward as far as that island. If the Admiral was to move further east than the Windward Passage, he would abandon a central position with reference to three strategic locations—San Juan, Puerto Rico and Cienfuegos and Havana, Cuba. Should Cervera slip past the American squadron at San Juan, he might cause serious damage.[12]

When Sampson received Long's cautionary message on May 8 off Cap Haïtien, he convened a meeting of his captains, at length determining to continue on—a decision that proved unpopular in Washington. Sampson realized that Cervera might indeed bypass him and threaten the blockade off Havana or raid the eastern coast of the United States, but he thought it of paramount importance to prevent him from obtaining coal and other supplies at San Juan. To support his operations he asked the Navy Department to send three fast scouts to St. Thomas and, again, to add the battleships *Massachusetts* and *Texas* to his force. Long promptly responded with information on the Spanish fleet and partial acquiescence. He told Sampson that the *Pelayo* and *Carlos V* were not expected to leave Cádiz for at least two weeks; more important, he reported incorrectly that Cervera had been sighted off Martinique. He agreed to hold the *Harvard, St. Louis,* and *Yale* at St. Thomas when their cruises were completed, but made no mention of the requested battleships. Another cautionary statement might have been a veiled hint to Sampson not to go further eastward: "Blockade [of] Cuba and Key West will be in danger if skipped by you Spanish squadron. Therefore you should be quick in your operations at Puerto Rico." As if to guard against possible charges of interfering unduly with operations in the field, Long concluded, "In everything the department has utmost confidence in your discretion. The department does not wish to hamper you." If Long had hoped that Sampson would reconsider his decision, he must have been disappointed: The American squadron resumed its tortuous voyage eastward, experiencing serious delays because of having to tow the monitors.[13]

As Sampson headed for San Juan, Cervera's squadron approached Martinique, and on May 10 Captain Villaamil called at Fort de France with the destroyers *Furor* and *Terror* to obtain information about fuel supplies and Sampson's movements. The Naval War Board had ordered the *Harvard* to patrol east of Martinique until May 10, assuming that day to be the extreme outside date for the landfall of Cervera, but their estimate was too short; the Spanish passage from the Cape Verdes had been much slower than anticipated because of the need to avoid damaging the fragile destroyers. However, Villaamil had an unhappy time in Fort de France. The French authorities denied him coal and also attempted to detain him in port because of the presence of the *Har-*

vard. Villaamil managed to get away with the *Furor* but had to leave the unseaworthy *Terror* behind. On May 12 Villaamil reported a budget of bad news to Cervera. Cuba was blockaded; Sampson was at San Juan; no coal was available in Martinique.[14]

Cervera now faced a critical decision: Where should he go next? He chose not to proceed directly to San Juan, because he did not wish to encounter Sampson. There was no point remaining near Martinique, because the much-needed coal was unavailable there. He could go to Santiago de Cuba, which had not been blockaded, or try to reach Havana, where an American squadron barred the entrances. Both of these options were ruled out: Santiago de Cuba did not have the required supplies, and a voyage to Havana might precipitate an engagement with the North Atlantic Squadron. Cervera finally decided to steam further westward to the Dutch island of Curaçao. He had word that a collier had been sent there to refuel his ships, and he had no fear of encountering a strong enemy force in that area.[15]

When Cervera arrived at Curaçao on May 14 his hopes for coal were disappointed, and he made haste to move on. He did not find a collier there, and the Dutch governor allowed him just forty-eight hours in port, authorizing the purchase of only 600 tons of coal for the *Vizcaya* and the *Infanta María Teresa*. Captain Concas spent the evening with the two ships in Curaçao harbor while the remainder of the squadron lay outside it. "Nothing can give an idea of the anxiety of that night of May 14," he wrote later, "when we interpreted every word we heard as an attack on our comrades, and we could not even go to their assistance, for the harbor of Curaçao, which is closed by a bridge, is completely cut off from the outside at sunset." Once again Cervera was forced into another maneuver, for he had to leave Curaçao.[16]

For his next landfall Cervera considered four options, and finally chose Santiago de Cuba. He could have gone to San Juan, his initial objective, but Sampson could have easily taken that port. As for the other options, the blockading squadron guarded Havana—to which Sampson must return—and Cienfuegos could be easily closed and bombarded. By a process of elimination Cervera was brought to Santiago de Cuba. It was far from desirable, being distant from Havana and lacking necessary supplies, but was less dangerous than any of the others. Leaving Curaçao on May 15, Cervera proceeded slowly to Santiago de Cuba, arriving there at 9:00 A.M. on May 19. Lieutenant José Müller y Tejeiro, an artillery officer stationed at Santiago de Cuba, recalled the event: "The day when the fleet entered Santiago harbor was one of those beautiful mornings which are so frequent in tropical countries; not the slightest breeze rippled the surface of the water, not the least cloud was to be seen in the deep blue sky, and still, notwithstanding all that the local papers have said, very few were the people who came down to witness the arrival of the ships.'' This lackadaisical response reflected the general expectation of Spanish defeat that already suffused the outlook of the inhabitants, an attitude that existed everywhere else on the island.[17]

Cervera's situation—with no alternative but to visit Santiago de Cuba—had momentous consequences, because it allowed the American fleet to concentrate effectively as a unified force. Had Cervera, before the war began, gotten into Havana, he probably would have thus compelled Sampson to place one force in the Florida Straits to cover Havana, another on the American east coast to defend its ports, and a third eastward in the vicinity of Puerto Rico to interdict reinforcements coming from Spain. However, with Cervera in Santiago de Cuba, Sampson could take all his armored ships to that location, because there he could deal with both Cervera and possible reinforcements from Spain. (Lesser vessels could easily maintain the blockade of Havana.) It also meant that the United States, at least for the moment, could continue to postpone a land campaign at Havana, the center of Spanish strength.[18]

In a war riddled with ironies perhaps the most striking one was the ensuing, abortive decision of the Spanish government to authorize Cervera's return to Spanish waters. On May 12 Bermejo dispatched a message that permitted the squadron to leave the West Indies for the Iberian peninsula. Dewey's victory at Manila and Sampson's movement on Puerto Rico apparently had convinced the Ministry of the Marine that Cervera had been right all along. Unfortunately for the Spanish Admiral the day he received this message—May 19, the day he arrived at Santiago de Cuba—a new Minister of the Marine, Ramón Auñón y Villalón, sent word that he had withdrawn permission to return. Protests from the governor-generals of Cuba and Puerto Rico had forced this outcome. Both commanders argued that Cervera's departure from the West Indies would effectively destroy the will of their forces to continue resistance. But even if the order had not been cancelled, Cervera could not have undertaken a return voyage. Captain Concas summarized the reasons why: "We lacked the necessary colliers, without which it is madness in time of war to send a squadron out to sea, as it would be madness to send an army corps into a campaign without provisions and cartridges except such as the soldiers might carry in their knapsacks." He concluded mordantly, "The squadron was at Santiago.

By a miracle it had arrived there intact, and there was nothing to be done but to suffer the consequences of its departure from Cape Verde.''[19]

One of the remarkable failures of the war was the fact that the United States Navy did not finally ascertain the presence of Cervera at Santiago de Cuba until some ten days after his arrival there. The reasons for this tragicomic outcome contributed to an unseemly controversy after the war between Admiral Sampson and the commander of the Flying Squadron, Commodore Winfield Scott Schley.

At the same time that Cervera was seeking information in Martinique concerning the whereabouts of the American squadron, Admiral Sampson was completing his eastward movement from Havana to San Juan, Puerto Rico—a voyage of 1,130 miles that required eight days. On May 12 the American squadron bombarded San Juan. At 5:10 A.M. Sampson opened fire on the harbor and its fortifications without giving warning, although it was then customary to allow time to evacuate civilians from danger zones. After a brief action—during which the American ships inflicted relatively minor damage and return fire from the Spanish land batteries caused even less to Sampson's squadron—the attack was broken off at 7:45 A.M.[20]

Sampson had ascertained that Cervera was not at San Juan, and he knew that he must return without delay to a more central position. He later explained why he did not seize San Juan:

> The squadron would not have any great difficulty in forcing the surrender of the place, but the fact that we should be held several days in completing the arrangements for holding it; that part of our force would have to be left to await the arrival of troops to garrison it; that the movements of the Spanish squadron, our main objective, were still unknown; that the Flying Squadron was still north, and not in a position to render any aid; that Havana, Cervera's natural objective, was thus open to entry by such a force as his, while we were a thousand miles distant, made our immediate movement toward Havana imperative.

Why did he bother to undertake even a brief bombardment? He had in mind a form of reconnaissance, as he explained to Long on May 18: "I was determined to attack the batteries defending the port, in order to develop their positions and strength."[21]

The engagement at San Juan did include an act of individual heroism. One of the survivors of the *Maine*, Lieutenant Carl W. Jungen, had been

ordered to place a rowboat at the ten-fathom line off San Juan to ensure
that the attacking squadron would not run aground. This assignment
exposed his ship, the tug *Wompatuck,* to great danger, because
Spanish shore guns could cover the position quite easily. Nevertheless
Jungen performed this hazardous duty with great coolness. As it happened, not a single shot was fired at his vessel, which completed its
assignment successfully.[22]

What had Sampson accomplished? To be sure, he learned that
Cervera was not at San Juan. Also, as Captain Robley D. Evans noted,
the action gave the American squadron a baptism of fire: "Our men
received just what they most needed—practical demonstration of the
fact that it required a great many shots to seriously injure a modern
ship, and that every shell fired was not going to kill each individual
man who heard it screaming over his head." If nothing else, the action
at San Juan started the process that eventually brought Cervera to Santiago de Cuba. Secretary Long, however, did not think that the results
justified the risks. The American squadron had neither silenced the San
Juan's forts nor destroyed its coal supplies. While Sampson had "acted
with great prudence, as he could not afford to have his ships crippled,
in view of the possibility of an engagement with the Spanish fleet,"
Long opined privately, "still, the result strikes me as rather a failure,
and we await the results with deep concern." After the war Captain
Mahan criticized the voyage to San Juan as an eccentric movement for
which there was no real justification. "Our centre of operation had
been fixed, and rightly fixed, at Havana and Cienfuegos. It was subject,
properly, to change—instant change—when the enemy's fleet was
known to be within striking distance; but to leave the centre otherwise,
on a calculation of probabilities however plausible, was a proposition
that should have been squarely confronted with the principle [not to
undertake eccentric movements], which itself is only the concrete expression of many past experiences." This judgment still seems emi-
nently sound. By moving beyond the Windward Passage Sampson
deprived himself of centrality in respect to San Juan, Havana, and Cienfuegos. If Cervera had steamed directly for one of the latter two ports,
he could have made his landfall before Sampson could have intervened.[23]

After the bombardment of San Juan Sampson set his course westward
for Cap Haïtien on the northern coast of Haiti, where on May 16 he
learned that the Spanish squadron had been observed at Curaçao on
May 14 and that he had orders to return to Key West. He did not reach
his base there until 4:00 P.M. on May 18.[24]

Meanwhile the Navy Department was taking vigorous action to locate

Cervera and maneuver the Flying Squadron for a possible engagement. Sampson, at sea and out of reach for long periods, could not perform these duties. Accordingly, on May 13 Commodore Schley was ordered to take the Flying Squadron to a point off Charleston, South Carolina, whence he could either reinforce Sampson or support the Cuban blockade, depending on Cervera's decisions. Off Charleston he received orders to join Sampson at Key West. He arrived there on May 18, at 1:00 A.M.[25]

At the same time the department was searching vigorously for the Spanish squadron. After Cervera had been observed at Martinique, the protected cruiser *Minneapolis* and auxiliary cruiser *St. Paul* were ordered to scout in Haitian waters, particularly in the vicinity of the Windward Passage, thereby ensuring that the enemy would not slip unobserved around the eastern end of Cuba en route to Havana. When the word came that the Spanish squadron had touched at Curaçao, the *St. Paul* was diverted to Key West. It was then decided to send both these vessels—along with the *Harvard,* another fast auxiliary cruiser—to the gulf of Venezuela, there to cover a possible sortie into that region. However, these orders were cancelled when Sampson, learning of Cervera's movements, arranged for the auxiliary cruisers *Yale* and *St. Paul* to cover the Windward Passage between Cuba and Haiti while the *Harvard* would patrol the Mona Passage between Santo Domingo and Puerto Rico. The *St. Louis,* another fast auxiliary cruiser, was sent to St. Thomas. Even this rearrangement underwent modification: The *St. Paul* and the *Yale* proceeded to Cap Haïtien to await orders while the dynamite ship *Vesuvius* and protected cruiser *Cincinnati* steamed in the Yucatan Channel between western Cuba and Yucatan. These arrangements, entirely prudent though they were in guarding the approaches to Havana where the blockading squadron was concentrated, turned out to serve no purpose, because Cervera did not pass through any of the three passages under observation. Instead, he sailed directly to Santiago de Cuba from Curaçao.

On May 17, one day before Schley and Sampson were to arrive at Key West, the Navy Department decided its next dispositions in the West Indies. Since it appeared that Cervera's mission was to supply Havana, it became necessary to blockade the southern Cuban port Cienfuegos with its rail connections to the north. The Flying Squadron would perform this duty. From this station Schley also could cover the Yucatan Channel. Sampson received authority to stage operations at either Havana or Cienfuegos and also to modify details of the plan. Long summarized the reasons for these arrangements thus: "With Sampson before Havana and Schley at Cienfuegos, the armored vessels of the United States would be in a position from which they could strike either for the defense of our own blockade and coast, or engage in an offensive movement, combined or separate, against the enemy's squadron.'' At long last it had become possible to bring the Flying Squadron into close proximity with Sampson's ships and the probable location of Cervera. Captain Mahan, who as a member of the Naval War Board participated in this decision to place the armored ships off Havana and Cienfuegos, explained later that Cervera's movement to Santiago de Cuba was considered an improbability, because that place, unlike Cienfuegos, was inaccessible by land. "This forecast of the Board received justification," he argued, "by the subsequent statement of the Spanish Minister of Marine in the Cortes, that the squadron went there simply because there was no other port to which it could go,—an inability, real or presumed, which the Board could not know.'' The Board believed that San Juan was Cervera's objective; should he be reported there, it wanted to put four fast cruisers off that port to provide intelligence. The navy took a comparable step, when it heard that the Spanish squadron was at Santiago de Cuba, sending four fast ships to that city.[26]

After his arrival at Key West on May 18 Sampson received Schley on board the *New York* and arranged for the Flying Squadron's movement to Cienfuegos. This force was to include the best available ship, the *Iowa*, along with the *Massachusetts, Texas,* and *Brooklyn.* A number of small vessels were also attached to offset Cervera's torpedo-boat destroyers and ensure effective communication with headquarters. At the meeting, as Schley testified much later, Sampson instructed him not to risk his ships against fortifications until the navy dealt with the Spanish squadron. Cervera was presumed to be somewhere in the gulf of Venezuela, making for Cienfuegos. Curaçao was not mentioned.[27]

The meeting of May 18 initiated a series of events that led to serious misunderstanding between Sampson and Schley during the war and to acrimonious public controversy after its conclusion. In temperament Schley was expansive and prone to seek public notoriety, Sampson withdrawn and shy of popular acclaim. The commander of the Flying Squadron was one of the seventeen senior officers who had been passed over for the command of the North Atlantic Squadron when it was given to Sampson. Events would soon reveal whether Schley was prepared to accept this subordinate role.[28]

On May 19, when Schley left Key West for Cienfuegos, rumors began to circulate that Cervera had run in to Santiago de Cuba, and very soon confirmation was causing reaction in the Navy Department. The official in charge of the telegraph office in Key West, a Mr. Hellings, had close contact with a Cuban telegraph operator in Havana loyal to the insurgents, who from time to time secretly transmitted information concerning Spanish activities. On May 19 the Cuban telegrapher reported correctly that the Spanish squadron had anchored in the harbor of Santiago de Cuba. When this intelligence reached the Navy Department, orders to close on Santiago de Cuba went out to two of the three fast auxiliaries—the *St. Paul, Harvard,* and *St. Louis*—then assigned to patrolling in the Caribbean Sea. The protected cruiser *Minneapolis* was also assigned to this duty. All except the *St. Louis* received this instruction. Early on the morning of May 20, the Navy Department advised Sampson that it was taking the report about Santiago de Cuba very seriously, and suggested that he send Schley immediately to that port, leaving one vessel behind at Cienfuegos. Sampson, at first doubtful, sent a message to Schley at Cienfuegos informing him of the rumor but instructing him to stay there. The Flying Squadron, which had been moving at a snail's pace to Cienfuegos, received this word on May 22, shortly after it arrived. (Dispatch boats leaving for Cienfuegos a day after Schley's departure reached there on the same day as the Commodore.) Had Cervera decided to go in to Cienfuegos rather than Santiago de Cuba, he would have arrived there before the Americans.[29]

Sampson soon realized that the reports concerning Santiago de Cuba were probably correct, and he took energetic action. Orders went out to Schley replacing those he had received on May 22: "Spanish squadron probably at Santiago de Cuba—4 ships and 3 torpedo boat destroyers. If you are satisfied that they are not at Cienfuegos, proceed with all dispatch, but cautiously, to Santiago de Cuba, and if the enemy is there blockade him in port." Sampson sent the armed yacht *Hawk* with this message, assuming that the ship should reach Schley at about 2:00 A.M. on May 23. As it happened the vessel did not reach Cienfuegos until 7:30 A.M., thus frustrating Sampson's intention that Schley reach Santiago de Cuba on May 24. Information to Schley included word that the Admiral intended an eastward move of some two hundred miles to a point off Cay Frances in the Bahama Channel so that he might intercept the Spanish squadron if it attempted to approach Havana from that direction. Sampson left for this destination on May 23, taking with him the *New York* and *Indiana* as well as six lesser vessels. He wanted to go no further east than necessary, so that he could return speedily to Havana should Cervera attempt to run in there from the west. Schley presumably was on his way to Santiago de Cuba; the Spanish squadron might therefore steam northward on a course west of the Flying Squadron and pass unobserved through the Yucatan Channel.[30]

Schley, however, did not leave Cienfuegos when he received Sampson's dispatch, because he persisted in the belief that Cervera was actually in that harbor. As he approached within thirty or forty miles of the port, he had heard what he took to be guns firing a salute, supposedly part of the Spanish squadron's reception in port. (Well after the war he stated, "That of course was a mere guess. I did not go and look at the chart.") When he arrived off Cienfuegos, he allowed a British merchant ship, the *Adula,* to enter the port, hoping that upon its exit he could learn more about Cervera's location. When the *Adula* came out, it reported accurately that Cervera had gone into Santiago de Cuba on May 19 but incorrectly that he had left there on May 20. Putting this information together with the belief that he had heard guns, Schley reached the fallacious conclusion that Cervera was at Cienfuegos. On May 23 he reported himself unconvinced that Cervera was not at Cienfuegos. He had seen smoke in the harbor that might well have signaled the presence of the Spanish squadron. "Under such circumstances it would seem to be extremely unwise to chase up a probability at Santiago de Cuba reported via Havana, no doubt as a ruse." He would therefore remain where he was, coaling his ships and continuing his observations. He had no doubt that the Spanish squadron, if not in the harbor at Cienfuegos, was still headed either for it or Havana. To compound his error further, Schley did not investigate lights observed on the shore at night. Captain Evans, commanding the *Iowa,* also noted this signal. He knew that arrangements had been made to communicate with Cuban insurgents ashore in response to such signals, but took no action because he thought that Schley knew what to do. Commander Bowman McCalla, commanding the unprotected cruiser *Marblehead,* had earlier arranged the signalling system to occur at Sabanilla Point, thirteen miles west of Cienfuegos. When McCalla arrived at Cienfuegos on May 24, he learned that Schley thought Cervera was there. Obtaining permission to investigate the signal from shore, he made a landing and ascertained from Cuban insurgents that the Spanish squadron was not in the harbor of Cienfuegos. That evening, at 7:45 P.M., Schley finally sailed eastward towards Santiago de Cuba, departing almost two days later than expected—a dilatoriness that might have been disastrous indeed.[31]

Sampson did not learn of Schley's delay at Cienfuegos until 9:30 P.M. on May 26; meanwhile the Navy Department had become more and more convinced that Cervera was at Santiago de Cuba. On May 25 Sampson returned from his station near Cay Frances to a point somewhat closer to Havana, hoping to provide more effectively against the possibility that Cervera might come around the western end of Cuba. On the same day the Navy Department sent an order through

Môle St. Nicolas to Captain Charles S. Cotton—commander of the *Harvard*—that directed Schley to investigate Santiago de Cuba. Meanwhile Captain Charles D. Sigsbee, now in command of the *St. Paul* off Santiago de Cuba, captured a collier, the *Restormel*—the very ship sent from San Juan to Curaçao with coal for Cervera. This event seemed to confirm the report that the Spanish squadron was at Santiago de Cuba. It is surprising that none of the American cruisers ordered stationed off Santiago de Cuba established Cervera's presence there. The *Yale* reconnoitered the area on May 21 and the *St. Paul* arrived the same day. Two other fast ships, the *Harvard* and *Minneapolis*, took station off Santiago de Cuba on May 23. The *Harvard* left the next day for Môle St. Nicolas with despatches intended for Schley, but the other three ships remained—still unaware that their quarry was close by.[32]

On May 26 Schley finally arrived off Santiago de Cuba—only to depart almost immediately. When the *Yale, St. Paul,* and *Minneapolis* sighted the Flying Squadron, they joined it, leaving the entrance of the harbor uncovered from 6:00 P.M. on May 26 until 5:00 P.M. the next day, when the *St. Paul* returned to the area. Schley's tardy arrival resulted from his slow speed; he averaged only about seven knots per hour, for a voyage of forty-four hours. After just a few hours off Santiago de Cuba, and without making an effort to reconnoiter the harbor, he issued orders at 7:45 P.M.: "Destination Key West via south of Cuba and Yucatan Channel as soon as squadron is ready. Speed 9 knots." Schley explained that heavy seas on the south coast of Cuba had prevented necessary coaling, and that he therefore decided to fall back to Key West. This course greatly surprised the doughty Captain Evans of the *Iowa:* "I felt reasonably sure that Cervera was in Santiago," he wrote later, "but concluded that the commodore had better information than I on the point. My natural inference was that the Spanish ships had left Santiago and gone to the westward, and that we were going after them." A conversation at the time, presumably by megaphone, between Evans and Captain John Philip of the *Texas* reflected their feelings.

Referring to the order just received to return to Key West, Evans asked, "Say, Jack, what the devil does it mean?"

"Beats me. What do you think?"

"Damned if I know, but I know one thing—I'm the most disgusted man afloat."

Schley's explanation for his departure made no sense to Evans. Secretary Long agreed. He claimed later that the Commodore had enough fuel to remain off Santiago de Cuba, and had been unable to transfer coal from his collier to his ships only on May 25 and May 26, in part because he was en route to Santiago de Cuba from Cienfuegos on those two days.[33]

One can imagine the reaction in the Flying Squadron that must have followed Schley's next decision: After steaming westward for a day, he stopped his squadron at 7:30 P.M. on May 27 and drifted until 1:00 P.M. the next day! This extraordinary behavior extended by four days the period beyond the time Sampson had anticipated Schley's arrival at Santiago de Cuba—and the Commodore was still not where he was supposed to be. He had shown that he was either unwilling or unable to accept his subordinate role gracefully.[34]

Schley's inexcusable vacillation precipitated a spate of anxious efforts to ensure that the Flying Squadron proceed to a position off Santiago de Cuba and remain there. On May 27 Long cabled to Schley his belief that it was the "most absolutely urgent thing" to find out whether Cervera was at Santiago de Cuba. He announced that if the Spanish squadron was there an expedition of ten thousand troops would be sent to assist the navy. Having received word of Schley's coaling difficulties, Long sought to stiffen his backbone: "You must surmount difficulties regarding coaling by your own ingenuity and perseverance," he argued. "This is a crucial time, and the Department relies upon you to give quickly information as to Cervera's presence and to be ready for concerted action with the army." Sampson would then escort a convoy of troop transports to Santiago de Cuba, probably by way of the Windward Passage: "Cervera must not be allowed to escape." Captain Mahan later wrote that the Naval War Board concurred in the content of Long's message but did not compose its peremptory language. He was careful to record that, as far as he could recall, "there was no divergence of opinion between the Department and the [Naval War] Board, as a board, during that trying period of uncertainty as to the movements of Commodore Schley." Mahan also held that, while the Naval War Board was confident that Cervera was at Santiago de Cuba, it could not advise departure of the army expedition until the location of the enemy was confirmed beyond doubt.[35]

The desire of the Navy Department to blockade Cervera at Santiago de Cuba stemmed from the realization in Washington that this accomplishment would secure the fundamental goal of the campaign in the West Indies—command of the sea. If Spanish naval opposition could be eliminated, the United States could operate at will against both Cuba and Puerto Rico.

On the next day, May 28, Secretary Long sent another anxious cable to Schley, once again ordering him to remain at Santiago de Cuba. He inquired about the feasibility of seizing Guantánamo Bay, not far to the east, for use as a sheltered coaling station. If the Flying Squadron was forced to leave the vicinity of Santiago de Cuba, Schley was authorized to sink a collier in the entrance of the harbor. Either of two circumstances only could justify his departure: "if it is unsafe [for] your squadron, or unless Spanish division is not there." This message probably resulted from receipt that day of Schley's notice that he intended to return to Key West. When President McKinley received this news, Long remembered that the Commander-in-Chief allowed his face to fall. The Secretary of the Navy considered May 28 "the darkest day of the war." He later wrote that Schley's decision stemmed from insufficient reserves "of that unswerving steadiness of purpose and nerve which is the essence of supreme command, and of which Farragut is an example."[36]

On the next day, May 29, equally urgent orders went out to Schley reflecting growing alarm at his erratic behavior. "It is your duty to ascertain if the Spanish fleet is in Santiago and report," cabled Long. "Would be discreditable to the Navy if that fact were not ascertained immediately. All military and naval movements depend upon that point." Long confided to his diary the reasons for using such pointed language: Schley's despatches to the Navy Department reflected "indecision and indications of inefficiency on his part and the possibility of his starting back from Santiago de Cuba." He was particularly annoyed at the Commodore's failure to find out positively whether Cervera was actually at Santiago de Cuba.[37]

During this same period Admiral Sampson also made every effort to ensure that Schley would proceed to Santiago de Cuba and remain there. On May 27 he sent him word via the armed yacht *Wasp* of numerous indications that the Spanish squadron was at Santiago de Cuba. "You will please proceed with all possible dispatch to Santiago to blockade that port. If, on arrival there, you receive *positive* information of the Spanish ships having left you will follow them in pursuit." Like the Secretary of the Navy, Sampson was rapidly losing confidence in the commander of the Flying Squadron and employing increasingly curt language in orders to his subordinate. Perhaps he also had decided to take advantage of a message from the Navy Department that specifically placed the Flying Squadron under his orders, correcting any ambiguity that might have existed earlier. After consulting several of his senior officers, Sampson decided to instruct Schley to sink a collier in the mouth of the harbor at Santiago de Cuba. Through the captain of the protected cruiser *New Orleans* at Môle St. Nicolas, Sampson sent Schley a sharp order, telling the Captain, "You will . . . direct him to remain on the blockade of Santiago at all hazards, assuming that the

Spanish vessels are at that port." And Schley was ordered to block the entrance of the harbor with the collier *Merrimac,* the details of this operation being left to his discretion. After reiterating to the Captain of the *New Orleans* the utmost importance of preventing Cervera's escape, Sampson administered a dose of soothing syrup: "Say to the Commodore that I have the utmost confidence in his ability to carry this plan to a successful conclusion, and earnestly wish him good-luck." When Sampson returned westward to Key West on the next day, May 28, he cabled once again to Schley through Môle St. Nicolas, "The Spanish squadron must be blockaded at all hazards. . . . If Spanish squadron has left Santiago immediate pursuit must be made." Sampson's growing sense of urgency stemmed from receipt of information on May 28 that the United States government planned to send an expeditionary force composed of about ten thousand troops to Santiago de Cuba. As soon as Cervera's presence was definitely ascertained, Sampson was to escort transports by way of the Windward Passage to a landing about eight miles east of the objective. This operation could not be undertaken, however, if Schley allowed Cervera to escape.[38]

While all this activity was taking place, Commodore Schley finally went to Santiago de Cuba and ultimately blockaded Cervera in port. After receiving information from the *St. Paul* that led him to assume that Sampson was en route to Santiago de Cuba, he turned around and arrived at that port on May 28. The next morning, at long last, the *Massachusetts* sighted a Spanish man-of-war near the harbor entrance. Reporting on May 29 to the Navy Department, Schley mentioned the presence of the *Cristóbal Colón,* the *Infanta María Teresa,* and two destroyers. He believed that the other armored cruisers were also in port, although he had not yet observed them. Complaining once again about lack of fuel, he asked, barring an engagement in two or three days, to be relieved so that he could coal elsewhere, perhaps at Gonaives or Port-au-Prince.

The ten-day meander of the Flying Squadron perplexed no one more than Schley's subordinates. Captain Evans noted later, "As there had been no conference of commanding officers, we were all completely bewildered as to what this peculiar maneuvering might mean." He considered a deadly parallel: "Some of us, remembering the fate of Admiral Byng, felt that if Cervera was really in Santiago and got one of his ships away and on to the coast of the United States, while we were tinkering at the machinery of a collier, the world might be startled by another dreadful court-martial sentence." An investigation might well have resulted if Schley had not finally managed to blockade Cervera in port. Secretary Long later wrote, "Undoubtedly it is a fair criticism of the department that Schley was not relieved at once and an inquiry ordered." In all probability the Navy Department and the President did not proceed immediately against Schley because they wished to avoid the political difficulties that might stem from court-martialling a well-known and much-admired naval officer during a national emergency.[39]

After the war, when Schley and Sampson engaged in a public quarrel over this episode, a board of inquiry was appointed to investigate the actions of the Flying Squadron and its commander, and the majority report roundly criticized his operations of May 19–29: Commodore Schley had shown "vacillation, dilatoriness, and lack of enterprise." The board criticized most strongly Schley's actions connected with fuel problems: "His official reports regarding the coal supply and the coaling facilities of the Flying Squadron were inaccurate and misleading." The report might have noted other errors. Schley had not consulted his captains; he had violated not only the letter but the spirit of orders; he showed little or no enterprise in the search for the enemy; he ignored the most elementary principles of reconnaissance. Here was a jolly tar indeed, but one who manifested few of the qualities needed in an officer charged with important responsibilities in wartime.[40]

Not content with his earlier bumbling, Schley committed another cardinal error at the outset of the blockade of Santiago de Cuba when he missed a golden opportunity to attack the *Cristóbal Colón,* Cervera's proudest vessel. It was anchored near the entrance to the harbor, and an immediate movement by Schley could have brought it under fire. After waiting for two days, Schley finally decided to run in towards the entrance with the *Iowa, Massachusetts,* and *New Orleans.* Approaching to a range of about seven thousand yards at 2:00 P.M. on May 31, he fired for only ten minutes at the *Cristóbal Colón* and the batteries guarding the harbor entrance. The Spanish ship and shore batteries returned fire until 3:00 P.M., but neither side scored a hit. In his report of this action, the first in a series of bombardments that took place at intervals during the blockade of Santiago de Cuba, Schley wrote that he had "developed the fact that the Spanish vessels are in the harbor and that the fortifications are well-provided with long-range guns of large caliber." This statement glossed over his timidity. His brief effort posed no danger to the *Cristóbal Colón,* certainly a most lucrative target worthy of an attack in force by everything available on the blockade. It is true that Schley was under orders not to risk armored vessels against shore batteries without good reason, but he was definitely authorized to take action for reasonable cause. Had he acted quickly and decisively, seeking to surprise the Spanish ship—which, it should be remembered, lacked its main battery—he might have achieved a brilliant success. As it was, the only discernible result was that Cervera ordered the *Cristóbal Colón* to leave its exposed anchorage, posting instead the *Vizcaya* close enough to the entrance to thwart a surprise attack.[41]

The Spanish squadron had wasted many opportunities to leave Santiago de Cuba unobserved; Schley escaped severe criticism and perhaps even disgrace only because Cervera had chosen to remain in port rather than leave for another location before the American squadron could establish a blockade. It had become apparent immediately upon Cervera's arrival that Santiago de Cuba did not have the coal and supplies the Spanish squadron required for a long voyage. Captain Concas reserved some of his bitterest prose for a description of the city and its inhabitants: "Nothing can be compared with the disastrous situation of Santiago on the day of our arrival, and the stupendous ignorance of the Spanish residing there must be counted among the most disastrous features, for they had no conception whatever of the true condition of things." Since the city lacked communication by land to any areas except its zone of cultivation and the distant towns of Manzanillo, Holguín, and Guantánamo, and had no secure communications by sea because of the American naval presence, it had resigned itself to its fate. Concas disgustedly summarized the uncooperative attitude of the local business community: "The merchants, all of whom were Spanish, had ceased ordering goods, as they anticipated the country's defeat, and no one was willing to endanger interests, the fate of which was very uncertain, or to furnish goods on credit not knowing who would pay in the end." Governor-General Blanco, ensconced at Havana, realized that Cervera was in the most precarious circumstances. Reporting soon the Admiral's landfall to Minister of War Correa, he argued that the squadron could not remain long at Santiago de Cuba without being blockaded in port. Had the *Pelayo*, the *Carlos V*, and the torpedo-boat flotilla accompanied the other ships, the naval reinforcement might have been effective, but its modest actual size meant that it "must elude encounter and confine itself to maneuvers which will not compromise it and which can not have great results." He did not conceal his anger at the fact that Cervera had brought no provisions, weapons, and ammunition.[42]

When Cervera learned on May 23 that twelve American vessels lay off Cienfuegos and that Sampson had started eastward along the north coast of Cuba with his armored ships, he realized the need for a crucial decision. Since May 21, American ships had been observed off the entrance of the harbor, these being the *Minneapolis, St. Paul, Harvard,* and *Yale.* On May 24 Cervera proposed flight to San Juan, but a council of his captains decided against this course because of the slow speed of the fouled *Vizcaya*. The official record of the meeting recorded the intention to abandon movement to Puerto Rico in favor of remaining at Santiago de Cuba, where the squadron would "refit as far as possible from the stores to be had here, and take advantage of the first good opportunity for leaving the harbor, at present blockaded by superior forces." Explaining this decision to General Arsenio Linares, commander of the Spanish garrison at Santiago de Cuba, Cervera claimed that any move would "only be a matter of changing this harbor for another where we would also be blockaded." He had to come to Santiago de Cuba rather than other possible ports, he continued, because he thought it had much-needed provisions, coal, and stores. That he had in mind the functions of a "fleet-in-being" became apparent in another comment to Linares: "I flattered myself that I could keep the better part of the hostile fleet busy here, which is the only effective service that can be expected of this small and poorly equipped squadron." All this information he wished Linares to transmit to Blanco; it would explain his inaction. On the same day, May 25, he cabled a bitter and foreboding statement to Auñón, the new Minister of the Marine who had replaced Bermejo a week earlier: "I qualified our coming here as disastrous for interests of the country. Events begin to show I was right. With disparity of forces any effective operations absolutely impossible." Cervera's situation was indeed desperate; his thoughts at this time reflect a dispirited, hopeless mood, one that certainly must have worked against any display of special ingenuity or enterprise on his part.[43]

On May 26, for one brief moment, Cervera reconsidered his decision to stay at Santiago de Cuba, but he soon found reasons not to go out. Probably because he knew that he would have to either leave soon or never, he ordered departure for San Juan at 5:00 P.M. At 2:00 P.M., however, he heard that three hostile ships, absent since the previous day, had reappeared outside the harbor—the *Minneapolis*, *St. Paul*, and *Harvard*. Reconvening his captains for another council of war, he learned also of the possibility that the *Cristóbal Colón* might not be able to clear a rock at the bottom of the channel off Punta Murillo because of heavy swells. Once again a majority opposed a sortie and Admiral Cervera accepted their views, although Captains Concas and Joaquín Bustamante disagreed, arguing that the dangers of remaining in the harbor exceeded the risks of departure. In their dissenting statement the two captains envisioned that failure to leave would lead to either a hopeless battle or capitulation. Concas later claimed that he had favored a sortie primarily for political reasons. He believed that the home government "was determined that the squadron should be destroyed as early as possible in order to discover some means of attaining peace at any early date''; therefore the squadron should act immediately "not because it was logical but because we would receive definite and military order [*sic*] to do so under still worse conditions." In retrospect, however, Concas concurred with Cervera's decision to await a propitious opportunity for departure, but of course "such opportunity never presented itself, as it never does when the disproportion of forces is so great and when all the fundamental principles of naval strategy have been disregarded." Although available evidence does not validate Concas's thesis concerning the motives of the Liberal ministry, his strictly strategic arguments against remaining at Santiago de Cuba were certainly cogent.[44]

Cervera had one last opportunity to escape from Santiago de Cuba when the Flying Squadron made its inexplicable march and countermarch west of the Cuban port. He could have run around the east coast of Cuba through the Windward Passage and sneaked into Havana past Sampson, who was then in the vicinity of the St. Nicolas Channel. A more intelligent course would have been to proceed to San Juan for coal—he had only a small supply left—and then return to Spain. But both options became academic when, on May 29, Schley finally took station on the blockade of Santiago de Cuba, and, on June 1, Admiral Sampson arrived with his forces.[45]

To be sure, on June 8 Cervera again convened his captains to consider a plan for a nocturnal sortie prepared by his Chief of Staff, Captain Bustamante. The destroyers would leave port first, steering towards the American battleships blockading the harbor. Other Spanish ships would then exit and flee in various directions. Confusion would permit 50 percent of the squadron to make its escape. Concas thought the scheme feasible, provided the fast armored cruisers *New York* and *Brooklyn* were not on station; if they were present, he proposed that the entire Spanish squadron sortie as a unit at the time of the full moon. But once again the other commanders opposed an attempt to break out of Santiago de Cuba.[46]

Thereafter the naval forces at Santiago de Cuba took part in efforts to improve local defenses. General Cervera and Linares reached an understanding that some of the sailors from the squadron would be used on land as infantry should the Americans make an attempt on the city. They also talked of mounting some of the larger guns from the Spanish vessels at the entrance of the harbor to threaten the blockading forces, notably 6.3-inch Hontoria guns, but nothing came of this plan. Cervera's inertia in practically all dimensions was not the least of the reasons why the armed forces of the United States, despite errors of their own, were granted an opportunity to strike a decisive blow against Spain at Santiago de Cuba.[47]

When Sampson had reached Key West on May 28, he had learned of Schley's intention to leave Santiago de Cuba, news that caused him to move with his armored vessels to the probable location of the Spanish squadron. His squadron now included the *Oregon,* which he had found awaiting him at Key West—a most welcome surprise because it was the most powerful vessel in the fleet. Secretary Long had addressed several queries to him: After Schley returned to Key West how long would it take them to get to Santiago de Cuba? How long could his forces maintain a blockade of that port? Should the harbor at Guantánamo Bay be occupied and then used as a sheltered coaling station? Long reported that Schley still had not observed Cervera at Santiago de Cuba, although all other sources indicated his presence there. Sampson responded immediately that he could reach Santiago de Cuba in three days and blockade indefinitely. He thought it feasible to seize the harbor at Guantánamo Bay. If he departed with just the *New York* and the *Oregon,* allowing other ships to follow as fast as they could, he would be at his destination in two days. If Schley had really started westward, instead of waiting at Key West for him he wanted to intercept him and order the Flying Squadron back to Santiago de Cuba. After some delay—to an extent that led Sampson to prod the Navy Department—Long approved his plan to proceed with two ships, recommending immediate seizure of Guantánamo. Before Sampson left Key West, it was definitely established that Schley had returned to Santiago de Cuba and inaugurated a blockade. Long cabled him, "Hold on at all hazards," adding that the *New York, Oregon,* and *New Orleans* were en route to support him. Before Sampson left Key West at 11:00 P.M. on May 30 he sent instructions to Schley, beginning with congratulations but ending with a caution: "Maintain close blockade at all hazards especially at night, very little to fear from torpedo-boat destroyers. Coal in open sea whenever conditions permit." Hoping to alleviate fueling difficulties—the concern that Schley had emphasized above all others—Sampson asked his subordinate to determine the potential of Guantánamo Bay as a coaling station.[48]

Sampson's vessels moved eastward uneventfully to the Windward Passage and then around eastern Cuba to the south shore, arriving off Santiago de Cuba at 6:30 A.M. on June 1. His command included the battleship *Oregon,* the armored cruiser *New York,* the converted yacht *Mayflower,* and the torpedo boat *Porter.* Already present at the destination were the armored ships of the Flying Squadron—the battleships *Massachusetts, Iowa,* and *Texas* and the armored cruiser *Brooklyn*—

along with the protected cruiser *New Orleans*, the unprotected cruiser *Marblehead*, the auxiliary cruiser *Harvard*, and the colliers *Sterling* and *Merrimac*. Here was a formidable force, one incomparably superior to the beleaguered Spanish squadron inside the harbor of Santiago de Cuba.[49]

After the blockade was at last established at Santiago de Cuba, preparations for the expedition of the United States Army proceeded at feverish pace. Sampson received a despatch from Long on June 1 reporting Washington's intention for twenty-five thousand men encamped at Tampa to embark as soon as confirmation was received that Cervera was securely blockaded in port. Meanwhile Sampson was to select beachheads. The navy should assist the landing, with the proviso that Sampson should not endanger the crews of his vessels taking part in operations ashore. At the same time the Navy Department attempted to deceive the Spanish government concerning its strategy. It sent to the naval attaché in Paris, Lieutenant Sims, a false report that intelligence operatives were to allow to fall into hands of the Spanish government, instructing him,

> Give to secret agent this false information. The intended landing in Cuba has been delayed by dissensions arising between U.S. Army and Navy authorities, as to the proper place of landing, the former desiring Matanzas, the latter wishing Cienfuegos to be seized, to save necessity of blockading. It is expected that the latter will prevail, but meanwhile operations will be delayed.

Sampson was also asked to request that General Calixto García, the Cuban insurgent commander in the Santiago de Cuba region, assemble his forces behind the city. He was to receive ''5,000 stand of ammunition.'' All this activity indicated imminent land operations.[50]

BLOCKADE OF SANTIAGO DE CUBA

As soon as Sampson arrived at Santiago de Cuba he began efforts to sink the collier *Merrimac* across the harbor mouth and thus bottle up the Spanish squadron. He had developed this idea before leaving Key West for Santiago de Cuba, and in Washington the Naval War Board lent its support. If Cervera could not exit from the harbor, his vessels would be captured when the city fell to the army expedition. Sampson realized that if under these circumstances Cervera attempted to come out of the harbor, it would be to flee rather than offer battle. It was conceivable that, instead of closing the harbor, the navy might have stormed it in the manner of Farragut. What deterred Sampson—who would have liked to attempt such an enterprise—was his fear that mines might have been laid at the entrance. Electrical mines could be exploded from firing stations on shore; if these locations could be captured, then he could eliminate the threat. Also, seizure of the ground at the harbor's entrance would permit removal of the sunken collier at an appropriate time later in the campaign. The plan to sink the *Merrimac* in the channel was a temporary expedient to hold Cervera in port prior to the arrival of the expeditionary force, at which time landing operations could minimize the risks of entering the harbor. Sampson had specific instructions not to use armored vessels against fortifications unless the circumstances justified the risk. He exercised due caution, given the situation as it appeared to him at the beginning of June. If the port was closed down, he would not have to worry about the security of his squadron, then anticipating the task of dealing with Spanish reinforcements, particularly the armored ships *Pelayo* and *Carlos V.* Moreover, most of his forces could then be detached for other offensive operations, possibly a movement against the Canary Islands or the coast of Spain. Secretary of War Russell A. Alger later leveled severe criticism at Sampson for his caution at Santiago de Cuba, implying that the Admiral sought to shift the burden of difficult operations from his squadron to the United States Army. This argument has no validity. Sampson correctly desisted from an attack because of the mines and batteries that had to be passed in order to storm the entrance. If these obstacles could be eliminated by means of land operations, he was fully prepared to take action.[51]

The entrance to the harbor at Santiago de Cuba posed serious problems to an invader. Steep bluffs rose at the outer channel. To the east the elevation reached 207 feet, and on it were the Morro Castle and a battery. To the west the elevation was a bit lower at 174 feet; there rested the Socapa battery. The channel reaching northward followed a meandering path varying in width from 350 to 450 feet; twists in the channel prevented observation from outside for any distance through its course. Along the channel were additional batteries—the lower Socapa battery on the western side, and the Estrella and Punta Gorda batteries on the eastern side near its northern end. Smaller guns mounted in the lower Socapa battery and elsewhere along the channel were designed to cover that water. Twenty-four larger guns intended to fire out to sea were also mounted in the four batteries. Of these weapons fourteen were muzzle-loading. Only ten were breech-loading, the largest of which were two 6.3-inch guns at the upper Socapa battery. Two lines of electrical mines had been placed in the channel—a rank of seven, controlled from firing stations at Estrella and Socapa Points, and a rank of six that could be exploded from Socapa Point and Cay Smith, an island

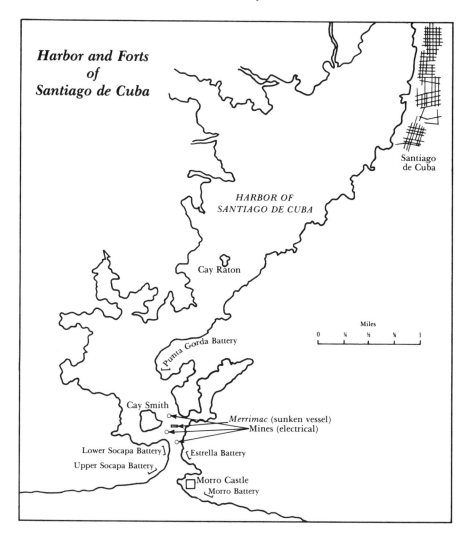

Harbor and Forts
of
Santiago de Cuba

Santiago
de Cuba

HARBOR OF
SANTIAGO DE CUBA

Cay Raton

Miles

0   ¼   ½   ¾   1

Punta Gorda Battery

Cay Smith

Merrimac (sunken vessel)
Mines (electrical)

Lower Socapa Battery
Upper Socapa Battery

Estrella Battery

Morro Castle
Morro Battery

in the channel. The mines posed the most serious problem for Sampson's armored vessels, more so than the land batteries, which a determined bombardment could have silenced.[52]

Admiral Sampson entrusted the blocking operation—sinking the *Merrimac*—to Naval Constructor Richmond Pearson Hobson, and preparations went forward at a furious pace. It was planned initially for the night of June 1–2, but delays forced postponement for a day. Hobson proposed initially to get the *Merrimac* into the channel by means of a ruse, running in with a Spanish flag at the mast, and sinking the vessel at the narrowest part of the passage. Sampson rejected this plan because the channel was exceedingly long and treacherous. Hobson then resorted to surreptitious entrance; he would allow the ship to drift past the Morro Castle and then anchor it at the proper location where electric mines would sink it. Ten explosive devices, each containing seventy-eight pounds of gun-powder, would be lashed to the port side of the *Merrimac* about ten feet below the waterline. Anchors would be stowed fore and aft, and axes used to cut them loose at the proper moment. Six sailors would make the attempt, with Hobson in command. Since the *Merrimac* was 333 feet long, proper positioning would surely preclude the passage of large vessels. [53]

At 3:00 A.M. on June 3, with the moon in its last hour, Hobson started his extraordinary voyage. The operation began well; the *Merrimac* managed to penetrate the channel to a good distance before it came under observation. Then Spanish shore batteries and guns on nearby picket ships opened fire. Hobson later reported that the Spanish defenders exploded six of the submerged electric mines in the first line (controlled from the firing station at Estrella Point) and two in the second line (Socapa Point) in an attempt to stop his ship. As luck would have it, a Spanish shot cut the steering gear, making it impossible for the crew to sink the ship at the planned location. To add insult to injury, the Americans were able to explode only two of the attached mines. Anchors were gotten out, but the stern anchor was shot away and the bow anchor line parted under the strain. The ship finally came to rest too far up the channel to pose a serious obstacle—a fact that was not ascertained for several days. Miraculously, Hobson and all seven of his men—one had stowed away for the attempt—were unscathed, though captured. The young officer's courageous exploit caused a great sensation and made him a national hero. Sampson recommended his promotion and immediately began efforts to recover him and his crew by means of a prisoner exchange. [54]

Hobson's brave failure forced the squadron off Santiago de Cuba to rely entirely upon a close-in blockade to prevent the escape of Admiral Cervera. The Navy Department made every possible effort to support the blockade, recognizing, in the words of Captain Mahan, that it had "no reason to apprehend for the moment an attack upon United States harbors; . . . the decisive center of war, at present, is off Santiago." Sampson could hope to sustain a close-in watch because of a combination of circumstances: The narrow channel precluded the exit of more than one ship at a time; the entrance lacked sufficient artillery; and Cervera did not have small, fast vessels such as torpedo boats to threaten large ships at a short distance from shore. [55]

On June 2 Sampson issued the first of a series of orders specifying the tasks of the blockading squadron. His ships were separated into two groups. Schley commanded one of the divisions, including the *Brooklyn, Massachusetts, Texas, Marblehead,* and the armed yacht *Vixen.* The Admiral himself commanded the other division, which contained the *New York, Iowa, Oregon,* the auxiliary cruiser *Mayflower,* and the *Porter.* These divisions would form an arc around Morro castle, Schley to the west and Sampson to the east, keeping at a distance of six miles during the day and closer in at night. Sampson specified the appropriate response, should Cervera attempt a sortie: "If the enemy tries to escape, the ships must close and engage as soon as possible, and endeavor to sink his vessels or force them to run ashore in the channel." He had no real fear of the enemy's artillery. "It is not considered that the shore batteries are of sufficient power to do any material injury to battle-ships." [56]

Sampson later modified his arrangements for operations at night, reflecting his concern that Cervera might be able to take advantage of darkness unless the blockaders took special precautions. On June 7 the Admiral issued general instructions that reorganized the defense, ordering three picket launches to locate themselves about a mile from the Morro. Further out, at a distance of two miles, three small vessels were to form a line—the *Vixen, Suwannee,* and *Dolphin.* The remaining ships would lie in an arc at a distance of four miles from the Morro. Why did he wish to maintain an unusually close blockade? "The end to be attained justifies the risk of torpedo attack, and that risk must be taken. The escape of the Spanish vessels at this juncture would be a serious blow to our prestige, and to a speedy end of the war." On June 8 Sampson made another modification, one that proved extremely important: He ordered the *Iowa, Oregon,* and *Massachusetts* to take turns of two hours each night at a station about two miles from the channel entrance, training their powerful searchlights up the channel. In addition, the *Brooklyn* and *Texas* to the west and the *New York* and *New Orleans* to the east were to take two-hour turns sweeping the coastline at either side of the entrance with their searchlights. After a few trials, the Americans perfected the performance of this hazardous duty. It greatly lessened the likelihood of a night sortie and worked against a successful torpedo attack. Why did not the shore batteries fire on the vedettes and the battleships that now lay well within range? Captain Concas later explained that the only modern guns at the entrance were two 6.3-inch breech-loading rifles in the Upper Socapa battery, for which the defenders had only a hundred rounds of ammunition. The Spanish commanders naturally did not wish to expend it except in case of an extreme emergency. However, even if the guns had been free to fire it might not have mattered, because, as General Linares informed Cervera on June 11, the beams of the searchlights reached all the way to the city, some four or five miles from the entrance. Thus presumably the battleships could have illuminated the channel from even further out.[57]

The close-in blockade of Santiago de Cuba was to play a most important role in the Cuban campaign of 1898, as Captain John Philip, commander of the *Texas,* noted succinctly: "It was the blockade that made the [sea] battle [of July 3, 1898] possible. The battle was a direct consequence of the blockade, and upon the method and effectiveness of the blockade was very largely dependent the issue of the battle. . . . Unremitting vigilance by night and day was an absolute necessity." Because the blockade duty was arduous, Admiral Sampson began to urge early land operations at Santiago de Cuba. His force expended tremendous effort on the blockade, and its dedication eventually was to be repaid.[58]

One of the curiosities of the Cuban campaign is the fact that not until June 13 did Sampson obtain conclusive evidence that all the ships supposedly with Cervera were in fact at Santiago de Cuba. On June 11 Lieutenant Victor Blue of the *Suwannee* was put ashore to make a visual reconnaissance of the bay and the ships in it. The need for this reconnaissance stemmed from a report that a Spanish armored vessel was on the loose somewhere in the Caribbean. If this was true, the ship might threaten the convoy of transports about to bring American troops to Santiago de Cuba. After going ashore at Aserraderos, Blue located the headquarters of the local Cuban insurgent commander, General Jesus Rabí. There he acquired a guide, Major Francisco H. Masaba y Reyes, and transportation in the form of a mule with whom to journey to a point northwest of the bay with a panoramic view of the harbor. After passing through the enemy lines, he was able to observe the Spanish squadron on the morning of June 12. His report of June 13 finally established beyond doubt that Cervera had four armored vessels and two destroyers.[59]

While the blockading squadron was awaiting the American expeditionary force it occasionally bombarded the batteries at the entrance to the bay. On June 6, for example, Sampson sent four of his armored vessels—the *Texas, Massachusetts, Iowa,* and *Oregon*—to interfere with Spanish efforts he thought might be underway to remove the *Merrimac* from the channel. From 7:30 A.M. to 10:30 A.M. the four ships fired on the batteries, opening at a distance of about six thousand yards from the Morro and closing to nineteen hundred yards. This operation convinced Sampson that the shore batteries did not pose serious difficulties. However, the capture of the forts he saw as a task for the army. Captain Evans summarized the navy's views on the bombardment:

"We all knew that it was impossible for any naval force to destroy them [the batteries] because of their location and commanding positions." He believed that a land force could capture them easily with naval support. On June 6 the Spanish defenders took casualties of nine killed and thirty-three wounded. One shell struck the old *Reina Mercedes*, causing a mortal wound to its second-in-command, Don Emilio Acosta. When he was hit, the brave Acosta smiled and said, *"Esto no es nada. Viva España!"* ("This is nothing. Long live Spain!") The day's operations prompted Sampson to send an optimistic but urgent telegram to the Navy Department: "If 20,000 men were here city and fleet would be ours within forty-eight hours. Every consideration demands immediate army movement; if delayed city will be defended more strongly by guns taken from fleet." This latter prediction, however, did not come true. Cervera did not remove guns from his ships for use ashore because he continued to contemplate departure. And he could have fired from the ships themselves against attacking land forces.[60]

A novel aspect of the bombardment began on June 14 with the arrival of the American dynamite gunship *Vesuvius*. This ship had three tubes that fired charges of guncotton weighing each over a hundred pounds, the impulsion coming from pneumatic pressure. A contemporary description reveals why the *Vesuvius* did not prove effective: "Its tubes are stationary and cannot be trained, so the aiming is done by the man at the wheel, who brings the *Vesuvius'* head in the direction where it is desired to send the shell." It was technically feasible to correct the aiming problem, but the difficulty inherent in extending the range of the dynamite tubes precluded further development of this type of weapon.[61]

Bombardments took place on several other occasions with results similar to those of June 6. To interfere with reported Spanish efforts to strengthen the fortifications at the harbor entrance, several vessels moved in on June 16 and inflicted casualties—three killed and eighteen wounded—at the Morro and Socapa batteries. A few days later, with the landing of the expeditionary forces on June 21–22, some shelling was employed. This kind of naval action, however, played a strictly limited role in the campaign at Santiago de Cuba—an outcome in keeping with the advice of contemporary strategists who never tired of reiterating that armored vessels should be employed against enemy ships rather than fortifications on land.[62]

One of the most important American military activities in Cuba prior to the arrival of the expeditionary force from Tampa was the successful landing of a Marine Corps detachment at Guantánamo Bay. The possibility of using Guantánamo Bay as a naval base, particularly for

coaling, had been discussed before Sampson arrived at Santiago de
Cuba. On May 31 Captain Sigsbee, commander of the *St. Paul,*
strongly recommended that the navy seize the bay and that American
troops occupy its shores, pointing out that a "great advantage in favor
of that Bay is that the land thereabouts is much lower than elsewhere,
and therefore does not offer the usual facilities of the region for a
plunging fire on vessels and troops from surrounding hills." On June 3
—possibly in response to an inquiry from Commodore George C.
Remey at Key West—the Naval War Board recommended that a battalion of marines encamped at Key West be used at Santiago de Cuba.
On June 7 the unit embarked on the *Panther* for active operations.
Meanwhile, on the same day, the navy moved into Guantánamo Bay.
The auxiliary cruisers *Marblehead* and *Yankee* left the blockading
squadron and entered the outer harbor of Guantánamo. A Spanish
gunboat there, the *Sandoval,* was forced to withdraw to Caimanera. A
few old smoothbore Spanish guns located on Cayo Toro, an island
separating the outer and inner harbors, offered no threat to the
American vessels. A small force of marines and sailors landed at Playa
del Este and destroyed the cable station located there. On June 9 Commander Bowman H. McCalla returned to Guantánamo with the
Marblehead to prepare for the arrival of the Marine battalion.[63]

Land operations beginning on June 10 at Guantánamo Bay were
completely successful. The First Marine Battalion—including 24 officers
and 623 enlisted men under the command of Lieutenant-Colonel
Robert W. Huntington in five rifle companies and an artillery battery—landed on June 10 at the east side of the outer harbor and occupied a hill there about 150 feet high. On June 11 the camp came
under attack, and combat ensued for three days. On June 12 about sixty
Cuban insurgents reinforced the Marines. By June 15 the eastern shore
had been cleared of Spanish troops, at the cost of only six American
lives. No more fighting took place in the area, and it proved a truly
useful anchorage for coaling and other operations during the rest of the
campaign. Some six thousand Spanish troops remained in the vicinity
of Guantánamo but did not interfere further with the Marines. The
Marines remained at Guantánamo until August 5. During this period
only 2 percent of the command became ill, and no one died of
disease—a remarkable record in comparison with that of the American
troops encamped around Santiago de Cuba. On June 14 Commander
McCalla reported that the Spanish defenders had mutilated three
Marines, but this charge was later withdrawn when it was realized that
Mauser bullets had caused the damage.[64]

Shortly after his arrival at Santiago de Cuba Sampson began to urge that an army expedition be sent to that city at no very distant date. Service on the blockade was onerous, and he could divine no impediment to the safe arrival of land forces. The expedition had still not appeared by June 17 when, admitting finally the failure of the *Merrimac* to block the channel, Sampson concluded, "I again urge earnestly army move with all possible celerity. Fine weather may end any day." By this time the expedition was at sea, having cleared Tampa on June 14. It arrived at Santiago de Cuba on June 20.[65] The blockade had served its purpose, ensuring American command of the sea in the Caribbean so that the land expedition could proceed in perfect safety to its destination. It held Cervera in port, making the city a desirable objective for the army. However undramatic, it provided the key to victory in Cuba.

ORIGINS OF ADMIRAL CÁMARA'S EXPEDITION

While the opposing squadrons were developing their activities in the Caribbean Sea the Spanish Ministry of the Marine sought desperately to bring the remainder of its fleet to combat readiness, an enterprise to which the Navy Department in Washington devoted anxious attention. The destruction of Admiral Montojo's squadron at Manila stimulated Madrid to consider sending out naval reinforcements capable of challenging Dewey's position. On May 8 Minister of the Marine Bermejo informed Admiral Manuel de la Cámara, who commanded the Spanish ships remaining at Cádiz after the departure of Cervera, of the necessity to prepare the battleship *Pelayo*, the armored cruiser *Carlos V*, and the auxiliary cruiser *Alfonso XII* for sea duty in ten days. He had in mind a mission he deemed "extremely important and far-reaching." These ships could be employed in operations elsewhere than the Philippines: They might attempt a raid on the eastern coast of the United States—a means of supporting Cervera's operations in the Caribbean. They might possibly be sent to reinforce the Spanish squadron directly. Or, finally, they might be retained in Spanish waters to deal with a potential visitation of the enemy. All these possibilities were considered in the United States Navy Department, which made strenuous efforts to keep itself informed about Madrid's plans for its employment. Secretary Long urged the naval attachés at London and Paris, Lieutenants Colwell and Sims, to redouble their efforts to obtain information.[66]

Reports from American consuls soon established that the larger Spanish vessels were fitting out at Cádiz and that other units were being prepared in various Mediterranean ports. Cámara probably did intend to go out to the Philippine Islands, although it was also thought possible that his destination would not be decided on until Cervera had completed his operations in the Caribbean. The Navy Department passed this information on to Dewey at Manila with the caution, "Means of receiving intelligence from Spain are very unreliable." As soon as the Navy Department learned of the probable presence of Cervera at Santiago de Cuba, Long cabled anxiously to Colwell and Sims, "Very urgent to know certainly the motions of *Pelayo* and other armored Spanish vessels. Have they sailed, or when will they sail and where?" Secretary of State William R. Day, obviously in fear that the vessels at Cádiz might depart for the Caribbean, ordered the American minister in Portugal to protest any attempt of Spanish men-of-war to coal in the Portuguese Azores. Lieutenant Sims reported that the *Pelayo* and *Carlos V* were still at Cádiz but could put to sea at an early date. He expected reports soon from a special agent whom he had sent to Cádiz. Two days later he gave notice that his spy had confirmed the presence of all ships at Cádiz. Their probable destination was the Philippines, but Sims thought this report suspicious because it was bruited about so frequently.[67]

While the Navy Department attempted to ascertain the mission of the Spanish ships fitting out at Cádiz and elsewhere, the Spanish Ministry of the Marine took action to organize its forces for future operations. The new Minister of the Marine, Auñón, issued a detailed order to Admiral Cámara on May 27, dividing the Spanish home fleet into three divisions, each with a given mission. Admiral Cámara was to take command of Group I—a force that included the armored cruiser *Carlos V,* three auxiliary cruisers, and a despatch boat—and attack a city on the American coast, preferably Charleston. This mission completed, he would go to San Juan, Santiago de Cuba, or Havana. The principal purpose of the raid would be to divert the attention of the United States Navy from the Caribbean and force a division of its forces, although it would serve also to retaliate for "unjustifiable acts of the enemy." If the raid succeeded, it would aid the movements of Cervera and of Group III, the latter a force of three auxiliary cruisers intended to take American prizes in the Antilles at the latitude of Cape St. Roque, and which might also link up with Cervera's squadron. Group II included the battleship *Pelayo,* the old battleship *Vitoria,* and three destroyers. It was assigned to defend Spanish waters, cruising between 30° and 36° N. in the Atlantic—a means of screening the Canary Islands and the Spanish Peninsula against a possible American attack.[68]

A few days later Sims reported garbled versions of this plan obtained through espionage. On June 1 the Navy Department heard that one of Sims's agents had learned that the vessels at Cádiz were to proceed to the West Indies. When arrangements were complete, the force would attack the American coast between Charleston and New York in order to create a diversion and to achieve a *coup d'éclat*. Another squadron would soon depart for the Philippine Islands. Spanish leaders were confident that the United States could not seize either Santiago de Cuba or Havana. The next day Sims reported again: Another agent had ascertained from the Spanish ambassador in Paris that the ships at Cádiz were indeed bound for the West Indies. To confirm this intelligence Sims would send an agent to Madrid who had connections with Spanish naval officialdom. However, he stated that Spanish failure to complete repairs on the ships at Cádiz was keeping them in port. This last report was more accurate than the earlier one.[69]

To deter any movement of the Spanish ships at Cádiz, whether to the Caribbean or the Philippines, the Naval War Board arranged to plant a report in Spain through intelligence agents. On June 1 Sims received secret instructions:

> Give out the following information; probably false, possibly true. As soon as Cervera's squadron is destroyed, an American fleet of armored vessels and cruisers will be detached against Spanish ports and the coast of Spain generally. The Americans seem to be especially incensed against Cádiz, and doubtless that place will come in for a taste of actual war.

On June 11 another such "plant" was ordered; the then Assistant Secretary of the Navy, Charles H. Allen, instructed Sims to "give as secret information intended to reach Spanish Ambassador that charts of Spanish coast have been issued to U.S. Battleships and a number of fast cruisers." Sims soon reported that this information was "apparently causing great anxiety" in Madrid.[70]

The Spanish government finally made its decision; it ordered Cámara to the Philippines, but decided to retain considerable naval strength in Spanish waters to defend against a possible American descent. On June 15 Minister of the Madrid Auñón directed his commander at Cádiz to proceed via the Suez Canal and the Indian Ocean to the Philippines, taking with him the armored ships *Pelayo* and *Carlos V*, the auxiliary cruisers *Patriota* and *Rápido*, and two transports with troops aboard—the *Buenos Aires* and *Panay*. Various other vessels would accompany the squadron as far as Suez and then return to the peninsula. Cámara was directed to ensure "the security of our sovereignty in the archipelago," but at the same time to exercise due caution, avoiding "notoriously unfavorable encounters" so as to preclude a "useless sacrifice of the squadron." This decision to move eastward rather than to the Caribbean took the principal remaining units of the Spanish

Navy away from the strength of the United States Navy, projecting them into a region where there might be greater probability of success. Minister of War Miguel Correa informed Auñón that Cámara must leave immediately "in order to calm anxiety of public opinion and raise spirit of fighting forces through knowledge that reinforcements are coming." Although Sims's agents reported confidence in Madrid that Cámara would enjoy success, the decision to send him to the Philippines rather than the Antilles suggests that the inner councils of government were quite pessimistic, at least about the ultimate outcome of the war.[71]

The voyage of Cámara, which began on June 16, was to have marked effects on American strategy during the next phase of the war. While the United States army was finally bringing troops to Santiago de Cuba, the Navy Department was maturing plans to dispatch a powerful squadron of American ships to Spanish waters and take measures to guarantee the safety of Admiral Dewey's squadron at Manila.[72]

The early operations of the United States Navy, which succeeded in establishing command of the sea in the waters surrounding the Antilles and the Philippines, exercised a profound influence on the future course of events. They made possible the dispatch of three army expeditions—one to Santiago de Cuba, another to Manila, and a third to Puerto Rico—that were able to reach their destinations without fear of enemy opposition. These naval activities ensured that Spain would find it most difficult to aid its distant colonial possessions in the Caribbean Sea and the Western Pacific Ocean. This general outcome had been envisioned almost from the beginning of planning in the United States. When the navy had seized command of the sea, the army would presumably destroy enemy opposition ashore. For this development to occur, however, the United States would have to mobilize a large volunteer force—one that did not exist at the outset of the war.

☆ SEVEN ☆

Mobilization of the United States Army

V ery little had been done to prepare the United States Army for war before the beginning of outright hostilities. Sufficient numbers of .30 caliber Krag-Jörgensen rifles were available to supply the regular army and enough .45 caliber Springfield rifles for the volunteer forces; during the weeks just preceding the declaration of war improvements had been made on the coastal defenses. Beyond these merest beginnings little had been done. Secretary of War Russell A. Alger summarized the situation starkly: "There was in the supply bureaus absolutely nothing for the troops included in the first call [for volunteers], and for the other troops provided for during the last days of April, nor for the additional forces created between the 10th and 25th of May, aggregating 249,000 men, exclusive of the regular army in its original status." Alger blamed this situation on restrictions in the Fifty-Million-Dollar Bill; had that measure not narrowly confined the War Department to defensive measures, much more might have been accomplished between March 9 and April 23. The Secretary did not explain why the Navy Department had been able to prepare much more actively than the Army.[1]

On the eve of war the United States Army numbered only about twenty-eight thousand men, scattered in small detachments across the country. The forces of the regular army included twenty-five infantry regiments, ten cavalry regiments, and five artillery regiments. Many officers had been assigned to colleges as instructors in military science or attached to militia units as advisers. No organization larger than a regiment existed, and most units were of smaller size. The state militias included many more troops, but were of doubtful utility. In 1897 the militia numbered about one hundred fourteen thousand officers and men, of whom one hundred thousand belonged to the infantry. Poorly trained, badly equipped, and lacking personnel trained to support combat arms, the militia's responsibilities were unclear because of its ill-defined legal status. Although the President possessed authority to mobilize state forces for federal service, no procedures had been established to accomplish this purpose.[2]

THE DEPARTMENT OF WAR IN 1898

To the War Department fell the burden of creating an army, but the Department was improperly organized for the task. At the top of the military hierarchy was the President in his constitutional role as Commander-in-Chief. His principal civilian subordinate was the Secretary of War. In 1898 Russell A. Alger of Michigan, a veteran of the Civil War who had become a successful businessman and politician, held this position. An affable, egotistical man who made a good appearance, sporting both mustache and goatee, he lacked qualities of leadership. Vain, selfish, and sometimes lazy, he often proved evasive in difficult situations. He lacked administrative experience in large organizations—a serious handicap when he was called upon to preside over a rapid expansion of the army. The principal military officer in the War Department was the commanding general of the army, almost always the senior Major-General on active duty. In 1898 Major General Nelson A. Miles of Massachusetts, another veteran of the Civil War who had gained fame as an Indian fighter, occupied this billet. Although Miles had many commendable qualities, he grew irascible with age and proved unable to work harmoniously with both colleagues and superiors. Highly ambitious and possessed of a monstrous ego, Miles easily confused his own interest with high principle. Graham A. Cosmas writes, "He was courageous but pompous and conceited, politically ambitious but gullible and naive." This "brave peacock," as Theodore Roosevelt called him, designed his own uniforms and regularly paraded a chestful of medals.[3]

Alger and Miles dealt with ten bureaus in the War Department, each bureau being assigned a particular administrative function with a Brigadier General in charge. Career officers provided leadership in each of the bureaus, advancing in strict seniority. Only three bureaus had enlisted men: about five hundred Engineers, sixty Signal Corpsmen, and seven hundred Medical Corpsmen. During the late nineteenth century almost all important decisions in the army emanated from the bureaus. This extremely centralized system of administration created mountains of paperwork and long delays. Line units chafed under this restrictive bureaucracy because it deprived local commanders of the power to act independently. According to Cosmas, it "kept senior officers from broad thinking and coordinated planning."[4]

Another administrative monstrosity besides the bureau system that plagued the War Department was the working relationship between the Secretary of War and the commanding general, which precluded both from functioning properly. The Army Regulations of 1895 specified the duties of each official in deceptively simple terms: the commanding general was authorized to give orders to the "military establishment . . . in that which pertains to its discipline and military control." The Secretary of War conducted the fiscal affairs of the army, working through the various bureaus. Orders from the President and the Secretary of War "relating to military operations or affecting the military control and discipline of the Army" were to be sent through the commanding general. Under this arrangement the commanding general did not exercise direct control of any bureaus except the Adjutant General's department and the Inspector General's department. He controlled the fighting units; only those staff officers detailed to service in the field came under his command. No one knew to what extent the commanding general was subject to the direction of the Secretary of War. In practice these two officials acted independently, considering themselves *de facto* equals beneath the Commander-in-Chief. Most of the time, however, the Secretary of War enjoyed a certain advantage, because the commanding general did not have sufficient personal staff and lacked influence over the bureaus. Usually the bureau chiefs lined up with the Secretary to preserve their prerogatives against the inroads of the commanding general. Although the Secretary could issue direct orders both to line and staff officers, he did not exercise fully effective control because no general staff existed through which to develop plans or provide general supervision of the army. Given their specialized functions, the bureaus were ill equipped to deal with overall military policy.[5]

The Adjutant General often prospered in this situation. His control of personnel matters made him the most powerful of the bureau chiefs. To retain influence, most incumbents in this office allied themselves with the civilian Secretary against the commanding general. The result was general rivalry throughout the army between the line and the staff officers, a circumstance that often caused operational deficiencies. The Adjutant General in 1898, Brigadier General Henry Clark Corbin, was an immensely talented officer with experience reaching back to the Civil War. Political influence had brought him to the attention of the executive branch during the tenure of Presidents Hayes and Garfield. Unusual administrative talents, personal charm, tact, and forcefulness placed Corbin in a powerful position within the War Department, disadvantaged because of the personal and administrative drawbacks of both Alger and Miles.[6]

For a number of years prior to the outbreak of war with Spain a group of reform-minded officers agitated for structural changes in the War Department to eliminate undue centralization and confusion in command authority. Among their proposals three stood out: decentralization of command authority to lower levels in the chain of command; regular interchange of officers between the line and the staff; and establishment of a general staff such as had been created in most European armies during the later nineteenth century to provide central planning. The reformers did not achieve a consensus on the question of relations between the civilian Secretary and the commanding general. If these changes had been made prior to the conflict of 1898, the army might have been better prepared to conduct operations efficiently in widely separated locations.[7]

The War Department was far less active than the Navy Department in anticipating possible hostilities with Spain, taking no really significant actions until the very last weeks before the declaration of war. It had no office specifically charged with planning. Moreover, the nation's civilian leadership was seeking peace, expecting to settle matters amicably with Spain.[8] Of great importance here also was the general assumption that in the event of war with Spain the army would play a part subordinate to the navy's.

PREWAR PLANS AND PREPARATIONS

The tendency of the army to minimize strategic planning stemmed naturally from national developments in the post–Civil War period. Reflecting the influence of Captain Mahan, Admiral Stephen B. Luce, and other naval intellectuals, the navy began emphasizing fleet action rather than coast defense and commerce raiding, but no comparable change occurred in the army, probably because little was happening to raise questions about its traditional defensive mission—protection of the homeland and its outposts from external attack. The army contemplated offensive action only if called upon to help the navy occupy enemy territory during a foreign war. This outlook led to the concept of a highly professional regular army during time of peace that could be expanded rapidly in time of war by having recourse to the militia. In contrast, prevailing doctrine in Europe emphasized large standing armies based on conscription. The efforts of reform-minded officers—most of them disciples of Brevet Major General Emory Upton—to gain acceptance of an "expansible army" made little progress prior to 1898.[9]

This idea—that the army would play a subordinate role in a war with a nation such as Spain—accounts for much of the temporizing that took place in the War Department until mid-April, 1898. The navy had recognized early in the emergency that, should war with Spain materialize, it would have to accept major responsibilities: For example, it took immediate advantage of the Fifty-Million-Dollar Bill, passed on March 9, 1898, to acquire additional ships and personnel and prepare the fleet for combat. No directives had come from the White House, to either the army or navy, but this fact did not inhibit the Navy Department. If war should come, whatever its scope, the navy's mission was quite apparent—to fight the Spanish fleet, destroy Spain's merchant shipping, and attack the enemy's colonies and even its home coast. By contrast, the army's mission would vary depending on the nature of the war: If the President stressed supply of the Cuban insurgents, the army would have to do little. If major overseas expeditions became necessary, the War Department would have to expend much greater energy. Since the executive branch had not settled these questions in advance, the War Department lacked clear guidance. It might have seized the initiative, but it did not have an organization and leadership capable of taking decisive steps. Secretary Alger interpreted the Fifty-Million-Dollar Bill narrowly, assuming that its stress on defensive measures precluded him from using his allocation of about $19 million for other purposes. The War Department therefore spent about $10 million on coastal defenses through its Ordnance Department, and another $5.5 million through the Engineer Department for the same purpose. Much smaller sums were assigned to the Medical, Quartermaster, and Signal Departments.[10]

When the army finally began to plan for operations, it worked on the assumption that it would be called upon to organize a relatively compact force of no more than seventy-five to one hundred thousand men—the number needed to support naval operations. The earliest estimates of probable numbers emanated from an interservice board appointed by Alger and Long that included two men each from the army and navy. A board proposal of April 4 called for a blockade of Cuba and a small expeditionary force to occupy one of the island's eastern ports, this location to be used to supply the insurgents. The board did not anticipate a large-scale invasion of Cuba, but if one should take place it would not occur until after the rainy season, at least six months in the future. For an attack on the Spanish stronghold there, Havana—certainly the most appropriate objective in the event of extensive operations—the board decided on a force of fifty thousand troops. It also proposed an attack on Puerto Rico to prevent Spain from using that strategic island as a base for operations elsewhere in the Caribbean. This plan confirmed earlier impressions in the War Department that the army would be asked to play only a modest role in a conflict with Spain. And the Cuban insurgents could be expected to approve a plan that emphasized their role in land warfare. General Miles became particularly interested in supply of the insurgents as the primary approach because of his fear that tropical conditions would pose great difficulties for American troops.[11]

To acquire sufficient personnel for the modest operations it expected to conduct, the War Department worked through friendly congressmen—particularly Representative John A. T. Hull (Republican from Iowa), Chairman of the House Committee on Military Affairs—to legislate its plan for an "expansible army" into existence. The army wished not only to deal with the current emergency but to bring about permanent change. Along with changes in the table of organization for infantry regiments, the War Department proposed the enlargement of the regular army from twenty-eight to one hundred and four thousand troops. Introduced in the House of Representatives on March 17, the Hull Bill soon encountered insurmountable opposition from legislative supporters of the state militia. They correctly assumed that, if passed, the bill would largely exclude the militia from service in a possible Cuban campaign and, over time, minimize the role of state volunteers in the framework of national defense. On April 7 an unlikely coalition of pro-militia legislators—southern Democrats still resentful of the army's activities during Reconstruction and Populists who opposed the current use of the armed forces against strikers—managed to refer the Hull Bill to committee, ending its chances of passage.[12]

Those who urged adequate preparation for war with Spain saw in this outcome confirmation of their view that the Administration lacked resolution. Theodore Roosevelt, for instance, complained bitterly about the absence of overall strategic planning. Perhaps inadvertently he put his finger on one of the principal reasons why the War Department had done little or nothing: "The President doesn't know what message he will send in [to Congress] or what he will do if we have war." He could not imagine how militia could be used effectively in Cuba, but guessed correctly that the army would have to find ways to manage this.

The defeat of the Hull Bill left no alternative to the use of militia.

On April 9 General Miles offered a plan that provided for an army of over one hundred sixty-two thousand men—one that would yield an expeditionary force of a hundred thousand troops. He wanted to enroll fifty thousand volunteers from the various states, who—along with a regular army enlarged to sixty-two thousand troops—would provide the manpower necessary for overseas operations. His proposal also called for an additional fifty thousand auxiliary troops drawn from the militia and other sources to man coastal defenses. These provisions constituted a basis for negotiations with Congress.[13]

Before Congress took any further action, the War Department decided to concentrate the regular army for possible operations in the Caribbean, in tardy recognition that hostilities might occur soon. On April 15 twenty-two infantry regiments were ordered to three ports in the Southeast—New Orleans, Mobile, and Tampa—and six cavalry regiments and most of the army's artillery units were dispatched to Camp Thomas, Tennessee (located in Chickamauga Park). These places were chosen because of their proximity to the probable theater of operations and their favorable climate. Very quickly units began to move from over eighty posts. Commanders were chosen for the four centers— Major General John R. Brooke for Camp Thomas, and Brigadier Generals William R. Shafter, John J. Coppinger, and James F. Wade for New Orleans, Mobile, and Tampa respectively. In the next few weeks, however, some infantry regiments were diverted to Camp Thomas and most of the troops designated for Mobile and New Orleans were sent to Tampa. While this brought almost all of the regular army together in two locations, it did not guarantee much training in combined operations because most of the infantry was separated from the calvary and the artillery.[14]

As this movement was taking place the War Department entered into negotiations with representatives of the state militias to clear the way for Congress to provide additional personnel. The plan that emerged from these discussions envisioned a volunteer army to serve beside the regular army. An initial call for volunteers between the ages of eighteen and forty-five would be confined to members of the National Guard, with quotas for each state according to population. Entire Guard units could enter the federal service under their own officers. With the militia accepting federal service, the War Department would exercise considerably enhanced control of its units, called up for three years or the duration, should the struggle end within a shorter period of time. Only one officer of the regular army could be assigned to a volunteer regiment, but efficiency boards would review the qualifications of volunteer officers. The President would appoint all staff officers and general officers of volunteers, but power to select lesser officers would remain with governors of the states. It was also decided to form certain national organizations of volunteers—a concept that later produced three cavalry regiments, one of which became the fabled Rough Riders. Recognizing that large formations would have to be deployed, the planners had the bill to be sent to Congress provide for the organization of army corps consisting each of three divisions. Each division would be made up of no more than three brigades, and a brigade would include no more than three regiments. This proposal was presented to Congress, and became law on April 22. Only two changes were made as it went through the legislative process, both of slight consequence: The term of service for the volunteers was fixed at two years, and the number of volunteers to be enrolled in special units was limited to three thousand men.[15]

Acting under the authority granted in this law, the act of April 22, President McKinley issued the first call for volunteers on the very next day. Instead of specifying sixty thousand men as the War Department had planned, he asked for one hundred twenty-five thousand—the approximate strength of all the existing militia units. Possibly McKinley took this step to avoid President Lincoln's error at the outset of the Civil War in not calling for a sufficient number. Perhaps also he hoped to impress Spain with the military potential of the United States; Madrid might thus even seek a settlement without actual combat. Whatever his reasons, the President's decision to proceed in this fashion added to the confusion that had already inhibited the army's preparations for war. Earlier, the Administration's hopes for a political settlement with Madrid had interfered with active planning; later, the necessity of making a political deal with the National Guard created further difficulties. The helter-skelter activity of the War Department in the coming weeks and months can be traced largely to these circumstances.[16]

On April 26 Congress completed action on another piece of legislation that would help shape the United States Army during the war with Spain, one expanding the size of the regular army. (This step would not be taken until the Act of April 22 had satisfied the powerful lobby of the National Guard.) The authorized strength of the regular army was increased to 64,719 men, although only 180 additional places for commissioned officers were created—a provision that took into account the disproportionate number of officers permitted in the peacetime cadre. Congress specified the form of the regular army's expansion: Each infantry regiment was to increase the number of battalions in wartime to three, each of these to include four companies. The law also specified the size of the basic units in the various combat branches: An infantry company would have 106 men, a cavalry troop 100 men, a heavy artillery battery 200 men, a light artillery battery 173 men, and an engineer company 150 men. Another provision of this law granted an increase of 20 percent in pay during the war.[17]

While Congress was creating legislative authority for the expansion of the army, the War Department finally began to consider plans of operation against Cuba. On April 18 General Miles had made a proposal characteristic of his strategic recommendations throughout the war. He was not sanguine about immediate prospects for a large-scale expedition to Cuba, raising two objections: The rainy season would create serious difficulties, given the size of the enemy force, which he estimated at about eighty thousand men—the remnant of an army that at one time had numbered two hundred fourteen thousand men. Moreover, he noted "the possibility of our own Navy not being able to keep the waters between our own territory and that island clear of hostile ships or fleets." Instead of major operations at the outset of hostilities, he proposed that the United States mobilize a small force of regulars for deployment to Cuba when the navy would secure command of the sea. If these troops were properly used, the War Department would not have to organize other units. Miles felt certain that "by using such force as might be necessary to harass the enemy, and doing them the greatest injury with the least possible loss to ourselves, if our Navy is superior to theirs, we can compel the surrender of the [Spanish] army on the island of Cuba with very little loss of life, and possibly avoid the spread of yellow fever over our own country." The next day two members of an army-navy board met with the Cabinet to discuss the readiness of the armed forces. Captain Albert S. Barker reported the navy as fully prepared, but Lieutenant Colonel Arthur L. Wagner of the army admitted that volunteer units would require at least six or seven weeks of training before they could be expected to fight well in offensive actions. Like General Miles, he expressed concern about tropical disease during the rainy season.[18]

On April 20 President McKinley held a council of war at the White House. Present were Secretaries Alger and Long, Admiral Sicard and Captain Crowninshield of the navy, and Generals John M. Schofield and Miles of the army. It was then that McKinley learned of the army's inability to take the field immediately in considerable force. Miles reported that troops could not be ready to campaign in Cuba for about two months, reiterating his qualms about sending an expedition until the navy had dealt with the Spanish fleet. Secretary Long, obviously annoyed, drew the inescapable conclusion that the navy would have to bear the initial burden of the war. The public, he thought, might not accept this course: "I am inclined to think that if war actually comes, the country will demand that our soldiers make a landing and do something."[19]

Such, then, was the situation on the eve of war with Spain. Theodore Roosevelt wrote to Captain Robley D. Evans, "If only the Army were one-tenth as ready as the Navy, we would fix that whole business in six weeks before the sickly season was well under way, but what will happen now I don't know." To former Secretary of the Navy Tracy he complained, "It goes without saying that our Army should long ago have been prepared, and that we should have had forty or fifty thousand men, regulars, backed by militia that had spent at least a month in camps in instruction, ready to move from Mobile next Saturday [April 23]." He obviously was thinking of the contrast of the navy's planning exercises, especially the emphasis on taking decisive action in the Caribbean before Spain could reinforce Cuba and Puerto Rico.[20]

Certainly the failure of the President to press for extensive prewar preparations and campaign planning inhibited the War Department during the last months before the war but important internal weaknesses in the department and the army itself also played a significant role. Its principal directorate, in the persons of Alger and Miles, manifested no real qualities of leadership at this critical moment. The army lacked both an officer corps experienced in the command of large units and enlisted personnel trained for conventional warfare. There was no general staff to direct the war effort, and the system of bureaus in the War Department was not organized to support major land campaigns such as one against Spain.

Fortunately the navy was in a markedly different state; as we have seen, it was prepared to act immediately against both Cuba and the Philippines. Admiral Sampson's North Atlantic Squadron was poised to blockade Havana and Commodore Dewey's Asiatic Squadron was ready to attack the Spanish squadron at Manila. These operations were intended partially to buy time in which to correct the deficiencies of the army; this was all the more feasible because the forces of Spain were in no condition to interfere with determined United States action on land or sea. Like McKinley, Sagasta had expected a peaceful settlement, a circumstance that inhibited effective Spanish preparations to withstand American operations; but an even more imposing reality stood in Spain's way—the demoralization of her forces because of the lengthy, fruitless, and sanguinary efforts to suppress the insurrection in Cuba.

RECRUITMENT OF THE ARMY

The legislation of April 26, providing for expansion of the regular army, more than doubled its size. On April 1 it had included 2,143 officers and 26,040 enlisted personnel—a total of 28,183 men. Its wartime maximum was set at 65,700 officers and men. However, enlistment during the war did not produce the full authorized strength. Strict medical standards may have played some part in this outcome, but more important was the preference of most eligible recruits for service in volunteer units. About twenty-five thousand men were added to the regular army during the war, selected from some one hundred two thousand applicants. Recruits were simply assigned to the existing units of the regular army for training. The strength of the regular army rose from 44,125 men in May to 58,688 men in August.[21]

To obtain its needed large mass of manpower the War Department relied upon volunteers, a procedure in keeping with tradition. The first call for volunteers, issued on April 23, brought the many militia organizations already in existence at the state level into federal service. These units included 115,627 men, of whom 9,376 were officers. A remarkably high percentage of the men in the militia agreed to accept federal service for two years unless discharged sooner. When Company A, Second Massachusetts met on April 19 to consider its course, even before the first call had been authorized, Sergeant W. A. Plummer led off with a "ringing speech" calling on members of the unit to volunteer for federal service. After others spoke "the Captain called for a rising vote upon the great question, and be it said to the everlasting credit of the members, every man rose in the affirmative." Additional enlistments filled the resulting vacancies in the militia units. The most important case of refusal to volunteer for federal service was that of the Seventh New York, a National Guard organization with a storied past. In this case, the principal objection was to the idea of serving under the command of regular army officers, especially those who had gone to West Point. One member of the regiment expressed himself clearly on this point: "To fight for my country as a volunteer in the regiment that I love would be a glorious pleasure, but to serve in the Regular Army and do chores for some West Pointer. . . . Well, I would rather be excused."[22]

On May 25, 1898 President McKinley issued a second call for volunteers on the same terms as the first, this time seeking seventy-five thousand men—an action that, along with certain special arrangements in a law passed by Congress on May 11, completed the provisions for manpower during the war with Spain. This legislation of May 11 permitted the enlistment of a volunteer brigade of engineers, to include no more than three regiments with a strength of thirty-five hundred men. More important, the President was empowered to raise up to ten thousand federal volunteers who possessed immunity from tropical diseases; this authority permitted organization of ten such "immune" regiments. All told, some 216,500 volunteers were authorized during the war; when combined with the regular army of 65,700, the total of authorized regulars and volunteers would reach 282,200 men. In actuality 8,970 officers and 173,717 men enlisted under the first and second calls from the various states, and another 763 officers and 16,992 men served as United States Volunteers. The volunteers of all types numbered 200,442; about 136,000 of them never left the country. The strength of the volunteer army rose during the war months as follows: May—124,804; June—160,524; July—212,094; and August—216,029. A grand total of 263,609 men served in the army during the war with Spain. The overall size of the armed services—including the United State Navy at a strength of 24,123 men and 1,751 officers (as of June 30, 1898)—reached about 290,000.[23]

No difficulties were encountered during the war in obtaining sufficient manpower. Popular enthusiasm at the outset of the conflict led to patriotic responses everywhere in the country. As one might expect, a certain number of rather bizarre offers were made to the War Department. The country did not accept the services of William F. ("Buffalo Bill") Cody, who published an article entitled "How I Could Drive Spaniards From Cuba With Thirty Thousand Indian Braves." Frank James, brother of the outlaw Jesse James, wanted to be placed in charge of a company of cowboys for service against Spain. The *New York Journal* proposed the formation of a regiment composed of great athletes, having in mind such luminaries as the boxers Bob Fitzsimmons and Jim Corbett, the football player "Red" Waters, and the baseball star "Cap" Anson: "Think of a regiment composed of magnificent men of this ilk! They would overawe any Spanish regiment by their mere appearance." Martha A. Shute of Colorado proposed to organize a cavalry troop consisting of women only. To enumerate this lighthearted list is to demonstrate the contrast in the mood of the nation during 1898 with that of 1917 or 1941.[24]

The legislation of April 22 and April 26 reflected a compromise between the War Department and the National Guard concerning the appointment of officers for volunteer units. The President was authorized to designate general officers and staff officers for divisions and commissioned officers for the units of the United States Volunteers. Governors of the several states appointed all other officers. As it turned out, the

White House made about a thousand selections, an onerous task indeed, because it was inundated with about twenty-five thousand applications. Although many political pressures were brought to bear, McKinley attempted to decide commissions on the basis of merit; for this reason professional soldiers fared well. Of 26 major generals appointed, 19 had had experience in the regular army. At the brigadier level, 66 of 102 appointees had been regular officers. Most of the generals chosen from civilian life could boast of service during the Civil War or in the militia. The most notable purely political appointments were those of Joseph Wheeler and Fitzhugh Lee, both former Confederate officers; McKinley had in mind here a gesture of sectional reconciliation. He bowed to partisan pressure in granting commissions to the sons of certain Republican wheelhorses, including the offspring of former President Benjamin Harrison, former Secretary of State James G. Blaine, and Secretary Alger himself.[25]

Some surveys of the composition of the volunteer units made in 1898 reveal certain general characteristics. The average age of volunteers for Company K, 1st Connecticut, was between twenty-three and twenty-four; the company's overall range was from nineteen to forty-five. In the 161st Indiana, the average was about twenty-six years of age. For 9,901 men in Illinois examined because they wished to enlist in that state's National Guard, the average age was twenty-four and two-third years. In Indiana the average height was five feet eight inches and the average weight 149 pounds. Members of the Connecticut company came from a wide variety of occupational backgrounds: There were 24 clerks or salesmen, 5 machinists or industrial workers, 4 students, 4 stenographers, and 3 electricians; only one or two men represented other occupations. With the Indiana regiment, the more rural setting produced different occupational backgrounds: The unit included 296 farmers, 118 clerks, 362 common laborers, 413 skilled laborers, 47 professional men, and 25 merchants. Only 8 men in the Connecticut unit had left wives and children at home. In the Indiana regiment only 128 of the 1,191 men had wives. That organization also had a preponderant number of native-born Americans—1,265 against 54 foreign-born. These statistics suggest that the average volunteer of 1898 was white, youthful, unmarried, native born, and of working-class background. They were not as representative of the overall population as would be the conscripts of the two World Wars or the Korean War, but they were enthusiastic, patriotic, and energetic. In the Connecticut company only 1 member later reported regretting his decision to join the unit, and only 14 said they would not enlist again. Just 2 admitted to having volunteered for love of the Cubans. The volunteer army enlisted with a will, and was to go off to fight after an extraordinarily short period of preparation.[26]

From eight to ten thousand blacks entered the volunteer army, supplementing the four black regiments of the regular army. Many of these black volunteers were enrolled in the four regiments of "immunes"— the Seventh, Eighth, Ninth, and Tenth United States Volunteer Infantry. Only three states—Alabama, Ohio, and Massachusetts—had black volunteer regiments available for duty under the first call. Company L of the Sixth Massachusetts was the only such outfit to experience combat during the war with Spain. When the second call for volunteers went out, five states accepted black units—Illinois, Kansas, Virginia, Indiana, and North Carolina. Just three of these units permitted black commissioned officers—the Eighth Illinois, the Twenty-Third Kansas, and the Third North Carolina. The regular regiments of blacks—the Ninth and Tenth cavalry and the Twenty-Fourth and Twenty-Fifth Infantry—were ordered to Tampa, and they became an important part of the Fifth Army Corps. All four were part of the expedition eventually sent to Santiago de Cuba.[27]

TRAINING CAMP

Very soon after volunteer units were collected in the various states, most were dispatched to training camps in the southeastern United States—the region closest to the most likely theater of operations—although some units from the western states were sent to California for shipment to the Philippine Islands. The regular army, as outlined above, had preceded them in this movement. General Miles had planned to retain the volunteers in their home states long enough to organize them properly, after which they would be concentrated for incorporation into larger units. However, when the situation in the Philippine Islands and the Antilles developed more rapidly than anticipated, it was decided to concentrate the volunteers in a few large camps so that they could be deployed at an early date. The largest encampments were at Camp Thomas, Tenn., and Camp Alger, Virginia (near Washington, D.C.). Troops destined for the Philippines gathered at the Presidio, near San Francisco. Troops intended to join the projected expedition to Cuba concentrated principally at Tampa. But other motives than availability for overseas deployment influenced this decision to collect both the volunteers and regulars in a few places: Not enough experienced regulars were available to supervise training at a large number of scattered locations. Also, as an investigating commission reported after the war, "removal of regiments from State camps

has the advantage of avoiding the disturbing influences of home locality." Concentration of the army permitted training in the management
and maneuver of larger units—an important consideration because
hardly any officers and men, except for the few remaining veterans of
the Civil War, had experienced training, much less operations, in units
larger than regiments. Finally, Secretary Alger noted that the brigading
of regiments from the great geographical divisions of the country
worked against "clannishness and provincialism, and the result was a
homogeneous army."[28]

On May 7, 1898, the War Department formed the volunteer and
regular regiments into several corps. In effect there were seven in
number. One of these, the Sixth Army Corps, never materialized, however. Another corps, the Eighth Army Corps, was created in June to include troops destined for the Philippine Islands. Only two of these
organizations went overseas as operational units—the Fifth Army Corps
to Santiago de Cuba and the Eighth Army Corps to Manila. The expedition to Puerto Rico was drawn from several of the remaining
corps.[29]

The War Department's attempt to mobilize a large army in a very
brief time without adequate prewar preparation was bound to result in
serious difficulties. For example, when the Sixth Illinois assembled at
Camp Turner, near Springfield, Illinois, it experienced what many
other volunteer units were encountering at the same time: "Disorder
prevailed, and it was impossible to learn anything regarding our future
movements. . . . Accommodations for lodging were poor, and we were
initiated in our soldier life by turning in on plank and cement floors
with newspapers for coverings." The most basic supplies were hard to
obtain: "Fully one half of the men had not the first mark of a soldier in
their dress, and excepting the officers, hardly a man was visible who
possessed a complete uniform." Confusion attended almost all aspects
of the mobilization during its earlier phases. More serious problems
arose later, particularly in respect to health. Much of this difficulty was
attributable to the system of requisition then in use to obtain supplies:
The bureaus of the War Department were supposed to fulfill requests
routed to them from commanders in the field. This approach might
have worked, had there been sufficient lead time and a clear understanding concerning the functions of the various field organizations.
Unfortunately neither of these preconditions materialized, and a
chaotic situation obtained for a good while. General Miles conceived of
the corps principally as an aggregate of administrative organizations
preparing troops for assignment to separate field commands. The officers leading these organizations, however, developed an entirely dif-

ferent view: They thought they were training troops for service under their command in the field. This confusion was never clarified; for this reason the corps commanders "maneuvered for front-line assignments, intrigued constantly for supplies and staff, and failed to equip their camps properly for long occupation." It would have been best for the army to establish divisional camps within its several geographical commands to provide training; corps should have been formed only when troops were sent overseas as part of expeditionary forces. Had there been a well-prepared administrative organization for the conduct of training, the army might have minimized the confusion that was to compound its difficulties during the early weeks of the war.[30]

The troops who went overseas to Cuba, the Philippine Islands, and Puerto Rico departed the United States for the most part before serious problems developed in the training camps, but most of the volunteers never left the country, and they eventually experienced serious epidemics of dangerous diseases at home. Since the corps commanders typically thought of themselves as preparing expeditions rather than operating training camps, they had made no provision for long-term placement, and filthy conditions eventually developed in most locations. Lieutenant Colonel Alfred A. Woodhull, a deputy surgeon general of the army, commenting on conditions at a particularly hard-hit place, Camp Thomas, summed up the most serious problem: "The refuse from the thousands of animals and other insoluble debris of the camp add to the aerial and indirectly to the aqueous pollution. A few of the regiments attempt to burn their kitchen garbage in extemporized furnaces, but there has been no systematic arrangement, as might easily have been made, for formal crematories." The result was an outbreak of typhoid fever along with frequent cases of diarrhea. The overcrowded conditions, lack of proper hygienic instruction and supervision, and absence of necessary supplies and equipment made pest-holes of the training camps. By September 30, 425 soldiers had died at Camp Thomas. The figures elsewhere were: Jacksonville—246, Camp Alger—107, and San Francisco—139. The death rates were actually quite a bit lower than those experienced in training camps during the early months of the Civil War, but the fact remains that disease proved far more deadly in 1898 than Spanish bullets. Out of 5,462 deaths in the armed services in 1898, only 379 resulted from combat.[31]

The resulting public outcry destroyed the reputation of the Surgeon General, Brigadier General George M. Sternberg, who had previously attained considerable notoriety as an epidemiologist and bacteriologist. He was guilty of an elementary error: He assumed that his duty had been completed when he issued orders. Because he failed to follow his instructions with inspections and other expedients, catastrophic situations developed in the training camps. In any event the Medical Corps was much too small to contend with the situation during the summer of 1898; even if Sternberg had shown considerable initiative, it is unlikely that he could have prevented much of the sickness.

The circumstances of the troops did not improve when they went overseas. Sternberg himself summarized the experience of the expedition that went to Santiago de Cuba: "The infection [typhoid fever] was carried by the Fifth Army Corps from Tampa to Santiago where, under the unfavorable conditions affecting the troops in the trenches, its rapid spread, together with the occurrence of yellow fever and the general prevalence of malignant malarial fevers, occasioned the utter breakdown of the health of that command." No one had yet discovered that mosquitoes carry malaria, yellow fever, and other deadly tropical diseases. Doctors knew that typhoid fever came from polluted water, but they were not aware of its highly contagious nature. Nevertheless, great improvement in sanitary conditions was finally brought about after the first few months of confusion, and this demonstrated that the army could control typhoid fever, diarrhea, and various other camp diseases. The mortality rate of the army had risen to 5.89 per thousand in September, 1898, but dropped to 1.51 per thousand in November and to .71 per thousand by April, 1899—in great part because of improved sanitation, although certainly the decline in troop strength after August and the onset of winter had some influence. This improvement did not foreclose a great public clamor that began before the end of the war and continued for many months thereafter, reinforced by the reports of returning veterans.[32]

Graham A. Cosmas skillfully summarizes the various circumstances that combined to prevent the War Department from making effective prewar preparations in many areas. The controversy over army legislation stemming from the activities of state militia organizations caused measurable delay. The army lacked an experienced cadre large enough to train a huge force of volunteers, and possessed few stockpiles of essential material. It suffered from unsound structure and cumbersome administration. It was impossible in the few weeks available to prepare three rather large expeditions for duty overseas. Had the army accomplished more prior to the outbreak of hostilities, the outcome would have been different, but its lassitude flowed largely from the general presumption that diplomacy would produce a peaceful settlement. Even if the war had been more strongly anticipated, it would have been assumed that land forces would play a distinctly secondary role. On top of all this, some time passed before President McKinley made certain critical strategic decisions necessary to permit efficient mobilization and deployment.[33]

The public was largely unaware or uncaring, as were all-too-many of their political representatives. Finley Peter Dunne's Mr. Dooley summarized the mood of ordinary folk thus: "Iv coorse, they's dissinsions in th' cabinet; but they don't amount to nawthin'. . . . We're all wan people, and we look to Gin'ral Miles to desthroy th' Spanish with wan blow. Whin it comes, trees will be lifted out be th' roots. Morro Castle'll cave in, an' the air'll be full iv Spanish whiskers." When delays ensued, some politicians, including Senator William E. Chandler (Republican from New Hampshire), a former Secretary of the Navy and a leading war-hawk, decided that the Administration really wanted to avoid combat. "I am inclined to think," he told a newspaper publisher on May 8, "there is a scheme to end the war without a fight with the Spanish fleet and without capturing Porto Rico. At any rate something paralyzes movement—not rash movements but reasonable movements." What Chandler either did not know or refused to admit was that no land force yet existed with which to engage the enemy. More important, however, was the lack of a definite strategic plan; more than a month was to pass before President McKinley would commit himself to a clear-cut course of action vis-à-vis Cuba.[34]

EVOLUTION OF STRATEGY: MAY, 1898

Even before the declaration of war, Secretary Alger confessed to the President that the army could not mount a major expedition to the Caribbean for some time to come, a revelation that led to planning for only modest preliminary efforts. On April 29 Major General William R. Shafter was ordered to Tampa, from where he was eventually to proceed to a landing on the southern side of Cuba with a force of six thousand regulars. After landing at Cape Tunas, about seventy miles east of Cienfuegos, he was to move inland far enough to contact the forces of the insurgent General Máximo Gómez and issue supplies to them. He would then return to the coast, re-embark, and steam to the northwestern coast of Cuba. After making contact with the blockading squadron, he was to supply the insurgents in that part of Cuba. However, if he learned that Admiral Cervera's squadron had arrived in the West Indies, he was to return immediately to the nearest safe port in the United States. "It is not expected," read his orders, "that you will penetrate further into the interior than to form a junction with General Gómez, to render him all assistance possible, and you are not expected to have your command on the island of Cuba but a few days. . . . This expedition is in the nature of a reconnaissance in force, to give aid and succor to the insurgents, to render the Spanish forces as much injury as possible, and avoiding serious injury to your own command." Such an operation would demonstrate enterprise, thereby placating public opinion, but would not over-commit the army.[35]

On the same day these orders were given, however, news of Cervera's departure from the Cape Verdes reached Washington, and the plans were changed almost immediately. On April 30 the War Department cancelled Shafter's orders to proceed to Cuba; however, he was asked to continue preparations for a modest expedition to be undertaken when the situation permitted movement. Henry Adams—an improbable commentator—summarized the situation very well in a letter written in far off Constantinople: "Logically, a squadron putting itself in such a position, ought to be destroyed to the last man; but things do not always or instantly result according to logic, and if the Spanish squadron succeeds in escaping destruction, and still more if it does us serious injury, and destroys our sea-power, there is a long story between us." No prudent President would authorize movement of troops into the Caribbean region until the navy had established command of the sea. Although Shafter was thus detained at Tampa, the War Department made other serious attempts to supply the Cuban insurgents. On May 10 Captain Joseph H. Dorst left Tampa with a few troops on board the side-wheeler steamer *Gussie,* bound for the northern coast of Cuba in an attempt to land supplies at several points west of Havana; but upon arrival two days later he encountered resistance and was forced to return to his base without completing the mission. On May 17 the stubborn Dorst went out again. Proceeding to Port Banes on the northern coast, he successfully delivered a large amount of supplies to a contingent of Cuban insurgents on May 26–27. This accomplishment was all that the army could point to by way of land operations in Cuba during the first two months of the war.[36]

A council of war convened at the White House on May 2 to decide on a new plan for operations in Cuba. On hand in addition to the President were Secretary Alger and General Miles for the army and Secretary Long and Admiral Sicard for the navy. The group decided that an expedition should be landed at Mariel, about twenty-six miles west of Havana. A good harbor existed there, and it seemed possible to establish a fortified position in the vicinity, from which a land attack could be launched against Havana. It would be easier to escort convoys to Mariel than to Cape Tunas on the southern coast. This plan closely followed the proposal of the joint army-navy board presented on April 4, except in the major respect of contemplating deployment of a rather

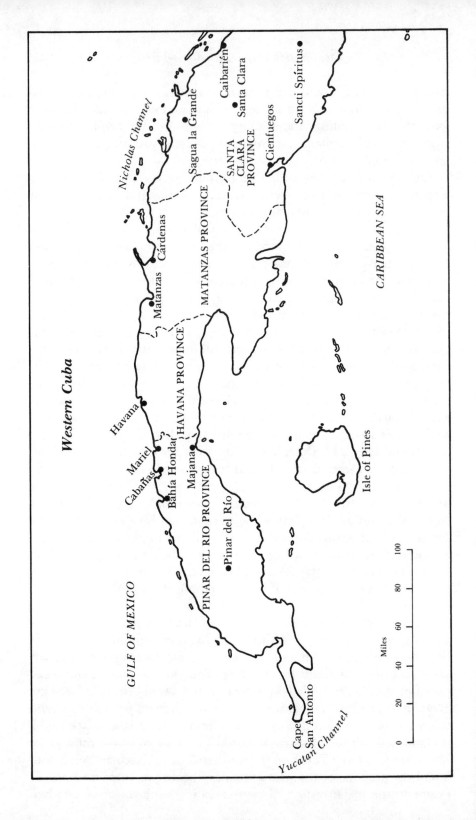

Western Cuba

GULF OF MEXICO

Nicholas Channel

CARIBBEAN SEA

Caibarién
Santa Clara
Sancti Spíritus
Sagua la Grande
Cienfuegos
SANTA CLARA PROVINCE

Cárdenas
MATANZAS PROVINCE
Matanzas
HAVANA PROVINCE
Havana
Mariel
Bahía Honda
Cabañas
Majana
PINAR DEL RIO PROVINCE
•Pinar del Río

Isle of Pines

Cape San Antonio
Yucatan Channel

Miles

0   20   40   60   80   100

large land force to Cuba at an early date. Preparations to put this scheme into effect began immediately: Shafter sent Brigadier General Henry W. Lawton to Key West for consultations with naval authorities; the results led the prospective commander to report optimistically on his ability to put the Mariel operation into effect.[37]

However, the plan of May 2 soon passed into limbo. On May 6 Admiral Sicard, acting for the Naval War Board, informed Secretary of the Navy Long that the army could not meet its commitments. He proposed that Long communicate to the War Department on the matter, presumably to hasten action. That very day, at a meeting of the Cabinet, Long presented a letter to Alger reiterating the agreement that had been reached earlier and urging an early date for the troop movement. At this juncture the Secretary of War took umbrage. "He intimates," wrote Long, "that the War Department will take care of itself without any interference from the Navy. I meet this with good nature, and simply suggest that my purpose is to show the readiness of the Navy, as I do not wish the impression to go abroad that there is any delay on our part." He then summarized the state of affairs: The "generous and sanguine" Alger had been the principal proponent of preparedness, but "for two months he has been saying that he would have his army ready in ten days—whereas, in fact, not a volunteer has left his state, and in my judgment there has been a striking lack of preparation and promptness." Long was certain that "if the Army would put fifty thousand men across upon Cuban soil, we could have Havana and the Island of Cuba at once." Alger reacted in a curious way to Long's needling: On May 8 he ordered General Miles to place himself at the head of seventy thousand men and proceed immediately to the capture of Havana! Why he did so cannot be ascertained with certainty. Surely he must have known that the troops for such an operation were not yet available. Possibly he sought to embarrass General Miles, with whom he was on increasingly bad terms.[38]

General Miles finally bestirred himself, and his initiative was to lead to a new set of orders for Shafter. Upon receipt of Alger's ridiculous instructions, the commanding general went to the White House and succeeded in getting President McKinley to call off the enterprise. His argument for cancellation reflected his assessment of the enemy strength at Havana and the general strategy required for the United States to prevail: He estimated that the Spanish garrison included about one hundred twenty-five thousand men, and that it had the support of 125 guns placed in strong positions. At the moment the United States lacked the ammunition required for a force of seventy thousand men. Moreover, it would be most unwise to move against Cuba until the navy

achieved command of the seas. Miles also adduced a tactical consideration: "The policy of storming heavily fortified positions had long since
become obsolete." He showed himself a devotee of surprise flanking
movements rather than frontal attacks. At this point early in May Miles
still entertained the general objections against an immediate operation
on land that he had raised on April 18. He wanted to make careful
preparations for a land campaign in Cuba, devoting special attention to
the problems of waging war in a tropical environment. On May 9 he
sent a new order to Shafter, directing him to seize Mariel or some other
point on the northern coast of Cuba, "where territory is ample to land
and deploy [the] army." Troops would be sent as soon as possible, from
Camp Thomas and other places. The principal purpose here was to establish a bridgehead from which forces could eventually move on the
prime objective, Havana, and its large garrison. This plan struck a compromise; it provided for early land operations, thereby satisfying
popular demands for action, but did not call for an early assault on the
center of enemy strength.[39]

The orders of May 9 immediately ran afoul of difficulties. When
Secretary Long heard of the orders he reacted vigorously. "I learn to my
utter amazement that it [an attack] is to be made tomorrow," he confided to his diary, "and not a word has been said to me about furnishing a convoy." After he complained to the President, a meeting
with Alger and Miles led to postponement of the expedition until the
navy could complete arrangements for a convoy. "Our ships are all
ready," noted Long, "but we must have at least some notice when and
where they are wanted." The expedition was thus delayed until May
16. In the meantime, Shafter was asked to send twelve thousand men to
Key West, where transports en route from New York were to take them
aboard. At the same time, five regiments of regulars were ordered from
Camp Thomas to Tampa. However, Washington soon learned that Cervera had been sighted off Martinique, and therefore the movement to
Mariel was cancelled until further notice, although Shafter's buildup
continued at Tampa amid general recognition that the army could
make no movement across water until the navy dealt with the Spanish
squadron.[40]

During the early days of May President McKinley and his advisers
concerned themselves not only with these plans for Cuba but with the
question what to do further in the Philippine Islands. In this regard the
mordant Henry Adams, after learning of Dewey's brilliant success at
Manila, for once abandoned his world-weariness, writing exuberantly to
his friend John Hay, American ambassador at the Court of St. James's,
about the decisions facing McKinley:

What does he want next? What should I want, in his place? To clear out the West Indies! That is as good as done! Hawaii! He can take it with a word! What of the East? What of Europe? By the horns of the moon, I know not where the ambition of the man may stop, for he holds the sceptre of the world—if Schley puts in his work.

The President did not think in such grandiose terms, but the victory at Manila Bay clearly would exercise a most important influence on basic military strategy for the future. On May 2, when it was first decided to send an expedition to Cuba, the President also directed the dispatch of land forces to the Philippines. On May 3 General Miles proposed an expedition of five thousand men to secure the city of Manila, and on May 6 some regular units and certain regiments of volunteers were ordered to concentrate at San Francisco for shipment across the Pacific. As the month of May passed the proposed expedition to the Philippines grew apace. By May 29 Major General Wesley Merritt had been appointed to the command of twenty thousand men—ultimately designated the Eighth Army Corps—with the mission of seizing Manila.[41] These preparations were intended to encourage a negotiated end to the war by intimating to the Liberal ministry that delay would result in increased American demands.

The uncertainty associated with the changing plans of operation complicated the task of the War Department, which was further complicated by the fact that the general policy of rapidly expanding the army conflicted with the special preparations of two relatively small but elite expeditions designed to conduct imminent operations in Cuba and the Philippines. McKinley's course, argues Cosmas, "left the Army's administrators in a dilemma, for to discharge effectively the latter task—invasion—they would have to neglect the former—arming, clothing, and equipping the large mass of reserves." The peacetime unpreparedness of the previous generation combined with the special exigencies of the current emergency to preclude smooth execution of ambitious military plans. Had the War Department been charged only with preparing either the small expeditions or the large volunteer force, efficiency might have materialized quickly, but to attempt both tasks at the same time was to ensure continuing difficulties. Another element worked against effectiveness in the War Department: The aforementioned prewar doctrine—enunciated by Emory Upton and institutionalized by Major General John M. Schofield—that assigned to the army a severely limited role in offensive wars overseas. The navy presumably would carry the main burden in such conflicts. For this reason the War Department's planning always centered on a small regular force rather than a mass levy. This circumstance, as Cosmas notes, "contributed to administrative chaos when it collided at the last moment with the desires of both President McKinley and the National Guard for greater numbers and a share of commands for non-regulars."[42]

McKinley's actions as Commander-in-Chief had significant effects on the war with Spain. At the outset he had tended to accept advice from the War and Navy Departments. This approach soon proved impracticable because of the unreliability of the leadership of the War Department and the need to consider the domestic political circumstances in making strategy and arranging its execution. Alger's bungling soon became apparent to the President. More important, however, was the question of policy: McKinley had done everything imaginable to avoid the war; after it began, he sought both to limit the conflict and end the fighting at the earliest moment, with the least expenditure of blood and treasure. His early decision to send expeditions to Cuba and the Philippines was intended not to escalate the conflict but to end it. McKinley hoped that vigorous American operations during the initial stages of the conflict would induce Spain to accept an early defeat. It is conceivable—nay, probable—that he wanted to prepare land expeditions quickly in the hope that they would not even have to complete their assignments, particularly the seizure of Manila. This overarching concept—the threat of immediate and vigorous attacks on the periphery of Spanish power to force an early victory—did not materialize suddenly. It emerged gradually during the month of May as the President grasped the opportunities opened to him by the naval operations in the Philippines and the Antilles—that is, the defeat of Montojo at Manila and the blockade of Cervera at Santiago de Cuba. Here was a most impressive demonstration of the ways in which command of the sea could create attractive strategic possibilities in the service of policy.

At the outset of the war McKinley had in mind domestic political considerations rather than imperialistic motives. He wanted the war over quickly so he could return to national projects that he wished to complete in fulfillment of campaign promises made during the critical campaign of 1896—particularly the preservation of sound money and reform of the tariff. McKinley, as we have seen, had been forced into the war because of irresistible popular demands. During the military struggle, writes Ernest R. May, "his aim was to check, subdue, or master the irrational element in domestic opinion. The real enemy to him was not the Spaniard but the Democrat, and the true measure of his strategy came, not at Manila Bay or off Santiago or on San Juan Hill, but in November, 1898, when the electorate gave his party majorities in both the House and the Senate and in November, 1900, when he was re-elected by nearly 900,000 votes.'' McKinley worked to preserve his command of the country, and the leadership he aspired to exert was that required to restore good times, not create an American empire.[43]

McKinley showed the strain of these responsibilities early in the war, but soon rallied and exerted his authority as Commander-in-Chief to ensure control of events. On May 15 a secretary, George M. Cortelyou, summarized his employer's situation thus:

> The President is again looking careworn, the color having faded from his cheeks and the rings being once more noticeable about his eyes. The strain upon him is terrible. Uncertainty as to the whereabouts of the Cape Verde fleet; the growing unrest and threatening character of the European situation,—these, coupled with the many difficulties constantly arising as a result of the short-sighted policy which for so long a time has been pursued by the Congress, leaving the country poorly prepared for hostilities, make the burden upon the executive shoulders a heavy one. Added to these things is the struggle for place among the ambitious gentlemen who desire to serve their country in high-salaried and high-titled positions. And then, too, the present conditions are attended by the usual differences and bickerings among the officers of the army and navy, which in certain high quarters are altogether too apparent.

Hoping to improve his control of daily events, the President established a war room next to his White House office with telegraphic connections to those military installations reachable by wire—including, eventually, the front at Santiago de Cuba. Secretary Long described the situation in the White House during the war months: ''Often of an evening members of the cabinet would gather at the White House discussing the campaign in the Philippines and West Indies, staying often beyond midnight.'' Information poured in and orders poured out. ''There was constant telegraphic communication in the executive departments with our army and navy officers, and in one room was a map so arranged with little moveable flags that a glance showed the position of our several ships and of our army forces.''[44]

McKinley could hardly avoid deep involvement in tactical and logistical details of the conflict as well as larger questions of policy and strategy. Secretary Alger rarely exhibited competence, and was continually in conflict with General Miles. Secretary Long sometimes vacillated when confronted with differences of professional military opinion. McKinley's biographer, Margaret Leech, summarized the consequence: ''Between the Army and Navy, the President was at all times the liaison and mediator. As Commander-in-Chief, he alone possessed the authority to compose the disputes that led to a stalemate in every program of united action.'' To achieve his purposes McKinley held frequent meetings with his military and naval advisers. Alger, Miles, and Adjutant General Corbin usually represented the War Department, while Long, Sicard, and occasionally Captain Mahan attended for the Navy Department. Because Alger and Miles were so unreliable, General Corbin became an ''unofficial Chief of Staff'' to McKinley and therefore exercised influence much beyond that of a conventional bureau head.[45]

If McKinley found himself in difficulties in Washington, the situation in Madrid was far more desperate, given the string of unrelieved American military successes during April and May. However, through the early stages of the war, the Liberal ministry showed no inclination to seek an immediate end to it. It continued efforts to acquire diplomatic support from great powers of Europe—a cause of concern to the McKinley Administration. Public opinion in Spain had predictably supported the decision to fight, fed in part by the notion that the Americans were poor soldiers. More astute observers, however, immediately realized that Spain had little or no chance of victory and the war might well bring on major domestic upheavals—even to the extent of a revolution—but some time had to pass before the government could safely invite negotiations. Still, as McKinley hoped, certain of those in power began early to urge peace upon Sagasta. Among them was Don Eugenio Montero Ríos, one of the most powerful political leaders in the Liberal Party, who proposed on May 8 that the government immediately begin direct discussions with Washington. Sagasta considered this proposition but rejected it, hoping to rally support in European capitols and thereby strengthen his hand. For the most part, political leaders publicly professed optimism, especially members of the Conservative Party—although the opinion of the Duke of Tetuán, the former Foreign Minister, sounded hollow indeed. He told a British diplomatist in Madrid that he expected ''disaster at sea from want of preparations as at Cavite but that the U.S. will not find it easy to take Cuba and Puerto Rico where there are seasoned troops and ample supplies.''[46]

Within the cabinet in Madrid the shock of the early defeats caused a crisis. Those politicians who prior to the war had urged concessions to the United States, especially the Liberal Moret and Foreign Minister Gullón, found themselves under attack, as did Minister of the Marine Bermejo, who was saddled with the responsibility for the disaster at Manila and the unpromising naval situation in the Antilles. To confirm his leadership for the next phase of the war, Sagasta appealed for national dedication and then reorganized his government. Ostensibly he sought to stiffen the nation's resolve, but he perhaps also hoped to strengthen his capability to negotiate a settlement with Washington later on. The Duque de Almodóvar replaced Gullón at the Foreign Ministry and Vicente Romero Girón superseded Moret as Minister for the Colonies. Captain Auñón, who earlier had been particularly anxious to send Cervera to the West Indies, took the helm at the Ministry of the Marine. From a political point of view among the most important appointments was that of Germán Gamazo, one of the moderate leaders in the Liberal Party, who agreed to accept a cabinet post (Minister of Development). By this device Sagasta dealt with an important element in his party that would have to be consulted about future decisions for war or peace. Moret told a British friend that Sagasta's reorganization of the Liberal ministry represented a triumph for conservative military elements in Spain, predicting, incorrectly, that Sagasta would soon depart and General Martínez de Campos, victor in the Ten Years' War, would assume leadership.[47]

Resolved to continue the struggle at least for the moment, the Spanish government issued a "Red Book" on May 19 in which it made public its diplomatic correspondence with the United States during the period April 10–21, 1898, hoping in this manner to publicize its prewar endeavors for peace and curry favor in European capitals.

Just as the reorganized Liberal ministry began its work, Cervera arrived at Santiago de Cuba with his forlorn squadron—an event that profoundly influenced the future policy of the Americans, because it posed the possibility of avoiding a large-scale campaign in Cuba. The President certainly hoped to minimize land warfare. His secretary, Cortelyou, reflected McKinley's attitude in commenting on a letter to the President from some parents of soldiers, asking him not to send troops to Cuba during the rainy season. "If some of the malcontents who are shouting 'On to Cuba' could see some of this correspondence, from all parts of the country," wrote Cortelyou, "they would not be so ready to proclaim their views as the only correct ones and to represent the President as lacking in strength of character or foresight." Even that doughty advocate of overseas expansion, Senator Henry Cabot Lodge—who was desirous of early operations in the Pacific—approved a deliberate pace in the Caribbean. "As to Cuba I am in no sort of hurry. Our troops are fresh and raw. They ought to be hardened up. They also stand sadly in need of equipment and all this takes time." He did not think the delay would interfere with overseas expansion. "Unless I am utterly and profoundly mistaken," he concluded, "the Administration is now fully committed to the large policy that we both desire." Roosevelt, however, did not like the sound of Lodge's comments on

Cuba. Writing from San Antonio, where he had joined the First Cavalry, U.S. Volunteers—soon to become known as the "Rough Riders"—he trumpeted to Lodge, "I earnestly hope that no truce will be granted and that peace will only be made on consideration of Cuba being made independent, Porto Rico ours and the Philippines taken away from Spain."[48]

Whatever Lodge might have thought, McKinley's course in the wake of Cervera's arrival at Santiago de Cuba suggests that his purpose was not to follow a "large policy" but to bring the war to an end as soon as possible, a goal that would work *against* overseas expansion. It is most probable that he sought to increase Madrid's interest in opening peace negotiations by posing multiple threats to Spain's colonial empire. Sagasta might then look for a negotiated settlement to avoid the loss of other parts of the empire besides Cuba, particularly the Philippines. If Cervera was eliminated at Santiago de Cuba and preparations made for early land operations at Manila, Spain might capitulate before the Americans had to mount a bloody and expensive campaign against the center of Spanish strength in Cuba—around Havana.

As soon as word of Cervera's arrival at Santiago de Cuba reached Washington, the War Department joined the effort against the Spanish squadron. On May 20 a brief message went to Admiral Sampson: "Army expect to have within a few days about thirty transport steamers at Tampa, Fla., please take such means as you think proper for guarding them." On May 25 he received further information: About thirty thousand troops on forty transports would have to be escorted from Tampa to Santiago de Cuba; some armored vessels should accompany the convoy in order to cover the landing. Meanwhile General Shafter, sensing the probability of imminent action, recommended that the Fifth Army Corps be made up primarily of the regular regiments then at Tampa, along with some volunteer units. This course seemed sound, he cabled, because he anticipated "an early advance" and thought "the first battle will be the decisive one and . . . the best troops should bear the brunt, supported as strongly as possible by the volunteers."[49]

On May 26 President McKinley convened a crucial council of war, including Miles, Alger, Long, and the members of the Naval War Board. This group made one of the most important decisions of the conflict: It abandoned the idea of an attack on Havana—planned earlier in May but suspended when Cervera appeared in the West Indies—so that the army could send expeditions to Santiago de Cuba and Puerto Rico. This course represented a partial victory for General Miles, who had long advocated an indirect approach rather than a frontal attack on the center of Spanish power at Havana. Orders from Washington immediately alerted army and navy commanders. Miles instructed Shafter to load twenty-five thousand men on his transports, along with necessary artillery and a squadron of cavalry. As soon as definite word was received concerning Cervera's location, he was to move to Santiago de Cuba. (Few in Washington doubted that the Spanish squadron was at Santiago de Cuba, but the incompetent Schley had not yet confirmed its presence there.) On May 27 both Sampson and Schley were sent details of the proposed movement. As soon as Cervera was positively located at Santiago de Cuba, troops would depart immediately from Tampa to land some eight miles east of the Cuban city; Sampson would be expected to escort fifteen or twenty transports along the northern coast of Cuba eastward to the Windward Passage and thence to Santiago de Cuba, taking with him for this purpose the armored vessels *New York, Indiana,* and *Oregon,* along with lesser vessels required to thwart possible attacks by torpedo boats. Monitors and other vessels could maintain the blockade of Havana. When the landing had been made at Santiago de Cuba, Sampson was to return all available ships to the northern blockade. Probably because Long wanted to make certain that the War Department adhered to its engagements, he summarized the agreement of May 26 in a letter to Alger: "On receipt of . . . information [that Cervera has been located], the movement to Santiago should be made without a moment's delay, day or night." He asked Alger to inform him whether "the troops will be ready to embark as soon as I give you the above information, for which we are waiting; and, in that case, to advise me at what point my convoy will report for the purpose of convoying the troops."[50]

Meanwhile General Miles, acting on instructions received on May 26, produced a plan of campaign for the Caribbean theater. Writing the next day to Secretary Alger, he outlined views that were to exert considerable influence at the time: Troops should proceed immediately to Santiago de Cuba. If during the interim the Spanish squadron had been captured or had escaped, Miles wanted to move the expedition quickly to Puerto Rico, bypassing operations in Cuba. Like Captains Chadwick and Mahan, he felt that Puerto Rico would provide a good base for future naval operations, especially those aimed at interdicting Spanish reinforcements: "We will be able to land a superior force [on Puerto Rico], and I believe that a combined effort will result in capturing the island, with the garrison, provided it is done before it can be reenforced from Spain." He noted that Key West was much closer to San Juan than was Cádiz, a spatial reality that favored American operations there. After victory had been attained at either Santiago de Cuba or Puerto Rico, the commanding general proposed a more elaborate operation in conjunction with the insurgents. From ten to fifteen thousand troops would land on the northern coast of Cuba and march westward toward Havana, on the line Nuevitas–Puerto Principé–Santa Clara. "These movements," he maintained, "can all be accomplished during the rainy season, through a country comparatively free from yellow fever, well stocked with cattle, and having grass sufficient for our animals." While this overland movement was taking place—requiring mostly cavalry and artillery from the regular army—elements of the volunteer army would land near Mariel or Matanzas and prepare for an assault on Havana. Miles also planned to use a deep-water port on the northern coast as a means of supplying the Cuban insurgents, who would in turn support his cavalry campaign in the interior.

Miles offered a clear rationale for operations on the periphery of Spanish power during the summer and fall, prior to massing for an assault on Havana: "The advantage of this movement will be that the army and navy will act in concert and close unison; that it does not divide our navy, and that it will utilize our most available military force [the regulars] in the best way during the time of the year when military operations are most difficult." Once again Miles favored operations that outflanked or enveloped the enemy at weak points, depending heavily on early deployment of the small but well-trained regular army in cooperation with the navy.[51]

General Miles manifested much more interest in the Cuban insurgents than did other American leaders, a consideration that influenced his plan of May 27 and later operations at Santiago de Cuba. On April 9, more than two weeks before the declaration of war, he had dispatched Lieutenant Andrew S. Rowan on a mission to insurgent headquarters in Cuba, seeking to establish contact for possible future cooperation. After going first to Jamaica, Rowan landed on the southern coast of Cuba; crossing the Sierra Maestre mountains, he located General Calixto García at Bayamo on May 1. The Cuban leader decided to send a three-man commission to the United States with Rowan— General Enrique Collazo, Colonel Carlos Hernández, and Lieutenant Colonel Gonzalo García Vieta. This delegation sailed from Nuevitas and, after passing through Nassau, proceeded to Washington for discussions with American officials—discussions that helped Miles mature his plan for a campaign in northern Cuba. These early contacts led to the later assistance from the insurgents around Santiago de Cuba when the navy blockaded Cervera. On May 29, Secretary Long informed Schley of this plan, instructing him to request General García to "assemble his forces in rear of Santiago and our army division will take with them to Santiago five thousand stand of arms and ammunition for Cubans." On June 2 Miles sent a letter to García by way of Colonel Hernández requesting cooperation. It reached García on June 6, and the Cuban general responded promptly through United States naval channels: He would move quickly to support the American landing at Santiago de Cuba; he would treat the "wishes and suggestions [of General Miles] as orders."[52]

President McKinley did not, however, accept all the recommendations of the commanding general; instead he extracted certain elements that would help force the quickest possible victory. He decided to attack Santiago de Cuba immediately with an expedition composed mostly of the regular army units encamped at Tampa. As soon as possible thereafter he planned to invade Puerto Rico, relying for this on the troops deployed at Santiago de Cuba and supplements from the United States. McKinley rejected a cavalry venture in northern Cuba. Movement on Havana would not take place until the fall; at that time Major General Fitzhugh Lee's Seventh Army Corps, training at Jacksonville, would be ready for action.

Secretary Alger later pinpointed the weaknesses of Miles's proposal to march through northern Cuba. The distance by sea from Key West to Nuevitas was some four hundred miles, a much longer stretch than the ninety miles between Key West and Havana. Moreover the distance between Nuevitas and Havana along the proposed line of march was about three hundred fifty miles. Extended communications would pose very difficult logistical problems. Why march this distance across land when the troops could just as easily land only a few miles from Havana under the protection of naval gunfire?[53]

As soon as Schley confirmed that Cervera was penned at Santiago de Cuba, orders went from Washington to Tampa directing the immediate departure of the army. On May 29 Shafter was told to get his men aboard transports and to "telegraph when you will be ready to sail with naval convoy." Commodore Remey, commanding at Key West, received notice to provide escort. On May 30 Shafter received a direct order from Miles: "Admiral Schley reports that two cruisers and two torpedo boats have been seen in the harbor of Santiago. Go with your force to capture garrison and assist in capturing harbor and fleet." Shafter's adjutant, Colonel Edward J. McClernand, later pointed to this message as the real start of the Santiago de Cuba campaign. On May 31 Shafter finally received a detailed order governing his later operations: He was directed to proceed in convoy to Santiago de Cuba and land either east or west of the city. Once ashore, his forces were to "move to the high ground and bluffs overlooking the harbor or into the interior, and cover the Navy as it sends its men in small boats to remove torpedoes, or, with the aid of the Navy, capture or destroy the Spanish fleet now reported to be in Santiago harbor." He was enjoined to "cooperate most earnestly with the naval forces in every way, agreeing beforehand upon a code of signals." When finished at Santiago de Cuba, he was to move to Puerto de Banes and await orders for "future important service," presumably the invasion of Puerto Rico. The message concluded: "When will you sail?"[54]

As Shafter's mission was being defined, the Navy Department decided to offer certain advice to the army. Long suggested to President McKinley that Shafter sail on the convoy commander's ship to ensure "concert of movement, so necessary and difficult in a combined operation." Hoping to interdict attempts by the Spanish defenders to reinforce the planned landing point, he also proposed that two to three thousand troops land ahead of the main body at Jaraguá—a place just east of the harbor entrance—and seize a bridge there. If this operation was completed at night, the rest of the expedition could land further east the next day without worrying about efforts to repulse them. Long opposed any use of seamen from the blockading squadron for such operations as the landing at Jaraguá. Clearly he hoped to modify those aspects of Shafter's orders of May 31 that seemed to contemplate naval landings, arguing, "The primary object of the expedition is the capture or destruction of the enemy's fleet in this port, which would be most decisive of the war. Therefore, the U.S. Squadron should not be weakened by the loss of skilled men in view of so important a possible naval action." After the substance of Long's letter was communicated to Alger, the Secretary of War replied rather acerbically, "I beg to reply that the major-general commanding the expedition will land his own troops. All that is required of the navy is to convoy and protect with the guns of the convoy while the military forces are landed."[55]

This episode is of interest in two respects. It constituted a link in the chain of events that was to interfere with interservice cooperation at Santiago de Cuba. Moreover, it revealed that the navy construed the land expedition as designed simply to help capture or destroy Cervera's squadron. This conception ran counter to the army's planning, which fixed the ultimate capture of the city as the expedition's central objective—an accomplishment that would necessarily also result in the surrender or destruction of Cervera's squadron. The difference was that the navy was concerning itself only with Cervera's ships, while the army was concentrating not only on the ships but on the city's garrison. Adverse consequences were to flow from this variance in objectives during the later stages of the campaign.

Politicians as well placed as Henry Cabot Lodge did not realize it, but the War Department was making all efforts to send Shafter quickly out to Santiago de Cuba with the units available at Tampa. Lodge had informed Theodore Roosevelt that the Administration was pursuing a deliberate policy, but Adjutant General Corbin had already telegraphed Shafter in terms that indicated the War Department's commitment to celerity: "The Secretary of War desires an early report on progress made, the number of men and organizations going with you, and when you will get away." Shafter replied optimistically; he intended to depart with eighteen to twenty thousand troops on Saturday, June 4. Anticipating an early embarkation, the Naval Board recommended that a number of "press boats"—vessels that news organizations chartered to follow developments—be detained in port to enhance security. This recommendation was accepted, and Shafter received orders to put it into effect. It was, however, difficult to control such craft because most of them were powerful seagoing tugs or swift steam yachts. Of fifteen to twenty such vessels, the Associated Press alone maintained four.[56]

The confusions of the moment stemmed from President McKinley's desire to exert immediate pressure at every available point on the periphery of Spanish power, hoping to force an early peace. This strategy accounted in great part for the War Department's intensive effort to place the Fifth Army Corps in Cuba rapidly. To some degree this course also reflected the navy's pressure for early assistance at Santiago de Cuba, given the difficulties of maintaining a close blockade indefinitely at that location. The hard-pressed Shafter bent every effort to move on Cuba without even the least unnecessary delay.

EIGHT

Tampa

At Tampa General Shafter worked feverishly to load necessary supplies and troops aboard transports, but he was not able to meet the timetable of the War Department. On June 4—the intended day of departure—he had to report that he could not depart before the evening of June 6, giving as reasons the tardy arrival of troops from Chattanooga and Mobile and difficulties encountered in loading. General Miles, who had come to Tampa to help expedite Shafter's departure, attempted to explain the delay to Secretary Alger: Over three hundred railroad cars had arrived in the Tampa area, but because invoices and bills of lading had not been received, no one knew what was in them. "The officers are obliged to break open seals and hunt from car to car to ascertain whether they contain clothing, grain, balloon material, horse equipments, ammunition, siege guns, commissary stores, etc.," he informed the Secretary of War. "Every effort is being made to bring order out of confusion. . . . Notwithstanding these difficulties this expedition will soon be ready to sail." Alger did not like this line of argument, wiring back curtly, "Twenty thousand men ought to unload any number of cars and assort contents. There is much criticism about delay of expedition." Certainly he reflected the Administration's wish to exploit the golden opportunity at Santiago de Cuba. "Better leave a fast ship to bring balance of material needed than delay longer," concluded Alger. Shafter responded in some irritation, drawing particular attention to the lack of proper facilities for handling materials in the Tampa region. "Could have put the troops on and rushed them off," he informed the Secretary of War, "but not properly equipped, as I know the President wishes them. I will not delay a minute longer than is absolutely necessary to get my command in condition, and start the earliest moment possible."[1]

On June 5 and 6 a curious episode took place that further exacerbated the already strained relations between General Miles and Secretary Alger. Probably in response to the Secretary of War's ill-concealed criticism the General telegraphed petulantly: "This expedition has been delayed through no fault of any one connected with it. . . . I request ample protection while at sea for this command from the navy." More interesting, however, is the remainder of this message:

> This enterprise is so important that I desire to go with this army corps, or to immediately organize another to go with it to join this, and capture position No. 2 [Puerto Rico]. Now that the military is about to be used, I believe it should be continued with every energy, making the most judicious disposition of it to accomplish the desired result.

Alger made no response to this proposition, explaining later that he and President McKinley had already given Miles the choice of leading the expedition to Santiago de Cuba or organizing another for Puerto Rico. The commanding general therefore was forced to decide for himself what role he wished to play. Alger later observed maliciously, "General Miles did not command the Santiago expedition, and that he did not was his own mistake or misfortune. He lost the opportunity to command in the greatest land battle of the war." Miles should have phrased his message of June 5 to force a response from the Secretary of War—but he did not do so, and failed to repeat his proposal prior to Shafter's departure. Perhaps to cover himself, Alger telegraphed Miles on June 6, "The President wants to know the earliest moment you can have an expeditionary force ready to go to Puerto Rico large enough to take and hold island without the force under General Shafter." This request further indicates the President's desire to pursue the war with great energy as a means of encouraging a peace overture from the Spanish government. After receiving Alger's message Miles devoted himself principally to the task of preparing the Puerto Rican expedition. He remained in Tampa until Shafter's departure for Cuba. Although his official orders to organize the Puerto Rican venture were not issued until June 26, he made many preparations well before that date.[2]

On June 5 and 6 Miles and Shafter reported that the Santiago de Cuba expedition would probably leave on June 7, and on that day feverish efforts were made to get the troops aboard the transports at Tampa. The Navy Department joined the chorus of those exerting pressure on Shafter, responding to Sampson's urgent recommendation that land forces appear without delay at Santiago de Cuba. During the evening of June 7 a perfect barrage of telegrams passed between Washington and Tampa, the War Department issuing peremptory orders to Shafter to depart and the harrassed commander giving reasons for his failure to comply. At 7:50 P.M. General Corbin informed Shafter that the President wanted him to go with no less than ten thousand men. At 8:50 P.M., however, Alger wired, "Since telegraphing you an hour since the President directs you to sail at once with what force you have already." Two more messages followed, Alger saying, "You will sail immediately, as you are needed at destination at once. Answer," and Corbin adding an explanatory word: "Information from Sampson says he has practically reduced fortifications [a reference to the bombardment of June 6], and only awaits your arrival to occupy Santiago. Time is the essence of the situation. Early departure of first importance." Shafter finally made response—in three different telegrams: At 9:00 P.M. he reported that he would sail in the morning with whatever he had on board, when he could get up steam. At 9:52 P.M. he indicated that he had been loading troops for a day and a half and that the situation had been satisfactory during the last day. Finally, at 10:15 P.M. he sent a message that must have been received with great relief in the White House: "I expect to have 834 officers, 16,154 men on transports by daylight, and will sail at that hour. Will wire particulars before starting."[3] Only by the morning of June 8, 1898, after a truly helter-skelter embarkation, was the expedition ready to leave Tampa.

General Shafter had gained command of the expedition to Cuba almost by accident. His qualifications for command in 1898 were hardly impressive. After compiling a good record in the Civil War, he entered the regular army and campaigned extensively in the Indian wars. In 1897, by dint of seniority, he attained the rank of Brigadier General. This circumstance led to his appointment as Major General and commander at Tampa at the outset of the emergency. He enjoyed the confidence of Alger, Miles, and Corbin, and manifested no political ambitions. But he had a serious physical problem—obesity. One writer described him aptly as a "sixty-three year old fat and gouty veteran who looked like three men rolled into one—or, as a quip said, a floating tent." In common with all other senior officers he had never had an opportunity to command large formations. When this inexperience combined with the confusion of the early weeks of the war, Shafter lost control of the situation—a reality that became apparent at Tampa. He survived only because he was blessed with a competent staff. Cosmas notes that at Tampa Shafter "did little to bring order to his base; he failed to draw clear lines of responsibility for staff officers and troop commanders; at times he overlooked important details." Fortunately his efficient subordinates compensated in part for the commander's failings, and Shafter gave them latitude. George Kennan recorded an experienced officer's estimate of the situation that developed in Tampa: "The fact of the matter is, they simply got all balled up, and although they worked hard, they worked without any definite, well-understood plan of operations." The responsibility for this situation rested with the War Department as well as Shafter, but a more competent officer might have minimized errors in this admittedly difficult situation.⁴

INTERLUDE IN TAMPA

While the regiments, particularly the volunteer outfits, made their way to the training camps, the nation responded enthusiastically, detecting in the new war an opportunity to demonstrate that it had healed the extraordinarily painful wounds of the Civil War. Whereas in 1861 onlookers had attacked the Sixth Massachusetts when it passed through Baltimore on its way to Washington, D.C., in 1898 the regiment was treated to a massive civic reception in that city. One observer considered it "the most dramatic event of the war upon American soil. For it was not a mere reception and patriotic demonstration. It was the new national spirit rising Phoenix-like from the ashes of '61. It was not Baltimore and Massachusetts alone joining hands, it was the meeting of the conservative representatives of a New South and a New North under circumstances of the deepest import in a national crisis."⁵

Colonel Leonard Wood, commander of the First Volunteer Cavalry—the Rough Riders, best known of the volunteer outfits—gained a similar impression when he passed through New Orleans on the way to Tampa. "New Orleans was very enthusiastic," he reported to his wife, "streets full of people and best of all an American flag in the hands of all. The cost of this war is amply repaid by seeing the old flag as one sees it today in the South. We are indeed once more a united country." Wood's assistant, Lieutenant Colonel Theodore Roosevelt, expatiated at greater length on the same theme: "Everywhere we saw the Stars and Stripes, and everywhere we were told, half-laughing, by grizzled ex-Confederates that they had never dreamed in bygone days of bitterness to greet the old flag as they now were greeting it, and to send their sons, as now they were sending them, to fight and die under it." Any number of other observers remarked on this phenomenon. A member of the First Ohio, travelling from Camp Thomas to Tampa, noted, "At every station crowds of people poured out to bid us Godspeed on our way to war. Ovation after ovation was given to the boys in b[lue] once so hated in this sunny Dixie land." Like other observers he noted the conspicuous presence of the national colors. "Our grand 'Old Glory' was prominently displayed at nearly every town, binding closer the link of affection of our North and South, now united in the common cause of national honor and national pride."[6]

The theme of national reconciliation appealed to a legion of popular poets, who were recording the war in their inimitable manner. One rhymester offered a poem entitled *Blue and Gray Are One:*

> Hurrah for the East and the West!
> The nation is one, undivided and free,
> And all of its sons are the best.

Truly the emotional impact of the national crusade must have deeply affected numberless Americans. The chaplain of the Twenty-Fifth Infantry, a black regiment, reflected the opinion of the moment, even imagining a constructive impact on race relations: "I believe that this war will very greatly help the American colored man of the South," he maintained, "and result in the further clearing of the national atmosphere."[7]

However inspirited by their trip, the troopers soon felt a decline of enthusiasm upon arrival at Tampa. The reigning confusion caught the attention of the correspondents following the army's fortunes. One of them, Poultney Bigelow, created a national sensation when he reported in the May 28 *Harper's Weekly* that troops had been concentrated at Tampa to provide an opportunity for training in large formations, but that the senior commanders had never seen their commands. "We have for this war laid out a complicated system of army organization, and intrusted the working of it in most instances to men who scarcely know the manual of arms." From reports of this nature the country realized that all was not well at Tampa. This insight was to encourage a strong proclivity ever after to dismiss as of no account the entire military experience of the war with Spain, a tradition that found its most effective spokesman in Walter Millis, whose influential book of 1931, *The Martial Spirit*, dwelt on the ridiculous and bizarre aspects of the war.[8]

Bigelow's report and others like it were fairly accurate—however ill they might have fallen upon patriotic ears—but behind the external confusion was not simply the inexperience of the troops and their commanders but the inherent difficulties in attempting to send out a major expedition from Tampa on unduly short notice. This Gulf city had been selected because it had shipping facilities and was the closest available port to Cuba. Its prime shortcoming, however, was inadequate rail connections to the North. Just two railroads reached Tampa proper, and only a single track connected it to Port Tampa several miles further south. Since Florida was far from the major industrial centers, almost all the supplies for the expedition had to come over this inadequate system. At one point during the period when Shafter was attempting to embark from Tampa, he explained his difficulties to Corbin primarily in terms of problems with the railroad: "The main cause for delay has been in the fact that great quantities of stores have been rushed in promiscuously, and with no facilities to handle or store them," he cabled the Adjutant General. "The last ten miles before reaching the wharf is a single track and very narrow space in which to work. The capacity of this place has been greatly exceeded." Repeating his complaints on June 7, he concluded, however, "Except for loss of time . . . it is not going to do any harm, as Mr. Cervera seems to be very safely bottled up, waiting to be called down." Secretary Alger later defended the choice of Tampa as a port of embarkation, holding that given the time stresses confusion would have occurred anywhere. After all, he maintained, Shafter eventually did depart from Tampa and arrive at Santiago de Cuba in basically good order. Had the convoy "been obliged to cross an open sea hundreds of miles farther, and [made] subject to dispersion by storms or attacks by ships of the enemy," the outcome might have been far less satisfactory. He did not attempt to explain why trains destined for Tampa were backed up as far north as Columbia, South Carolina. Charleston, South Carolina, would have made a better port of embarkation; it had much better facilities than Tampa and was not so distant from northern centers of production.[9]

Tampa was certainly an unprepossessing town in 1898. A reporter described it in most uncomplimentary terms: "A city composed of derelict wooden houses and drifting in an ocean of sand; a dreary city where the sand has swept the paint from the houses, and where sand swamps the sidewalks and creeps into the doors and windows." The sand was indeed everywhere. "It is a city where one walks ankle-deep in sand, and where the names of avenues are given to barren spaces of grubby undergrowth and palmettoes and pines hung with funeral moss." One of the rare amenities of the city was a new hotel of outlandish design— "a giant affair of ornamental brick and silver minarets"—erected by a local entrepreneur, Henry Plant. A number of officers and their families took rooms at Plant's hotel, along with newspapermen, foreign military attachés, and others involved in some way with the expedition. When Colonel Wood brought the Rough Riders to his campground, he "found everything confused and in a most frightful mix. Streets packed with soldiers and a foot deep in real beach sand." The situation stirred his emotions: "Confusion, confusion, confusion. War! Why it is an advertisement to foreigners of our absolutely unprepared condition. We are dumped into a grove of short stumpy ground in the dark and our animals on an adjoining place filled with 2100 loose animals which made the putting down of picket lines, etc., necessary."[10]

Inadequate facilities prevented much extensive training during the stay of the Fifth Army Corps at Tampa, but other types of activity made lasting impressions on the men there. One trooper remembered acquiring knowledge of a game associated with blacks: "It was the teamsters, and the Ninth and Tenth Cavalry, the only Negro cavalry regiments, that taught us northerners craps. Before the war with Spain, craps was not prevalent as a white man's game. But it did not take us long to catch on. Before we embarked from Tampa, even the soda water counters and ice-cream stands just beyond camp had a layout chalked on a poncho, with a soldier running the crap bank." The same observer, a member of the Seventy-First New York Volunteers, also recalled that liquor was not obtainable to blacks in Lakeland, a community near Tampa that some of the regiments used as a campsite. "Public sentiment rigorously enforced this law, for Lakeland was dry on principle—the principle of 'Plenty of bourbon for the white man, but no gin for the nigger.'" Scattered racial incidents might have led to more serious trouble had the Fifth Army Corps remained long at Tampa. One of the Rough Riders reported "a good deal of feeling between the white and colored soldiers." Rough-and-tumble fighting occurred, and some blacks were killed. Also, "a colored house of prostitution was burned down yesterday by a party of white soldiers who had been attacked by the inmates armed with pistols, soda bottles, etc." The spirit of national unity aroused at the beginning of the war obviously did not succeed in completely submerging racial tension within the army.[11]

For most of the units the stay at Tampa was mercifully short, but their difficulties did not end when they departed the sandy Gulf port. The Quartermaster General of the army, Brigadier General Marshall I. Ludington, experienced great difficulty in obtaining suitable troop transports. The navy had preceded the Quartermaster General into the market for such vessels, utilizing much of its share of the $50 million appropriated on March 9, 1898 to acquire auxiliary cruisers. The shallow waters around Cuba and Puerto Rico further limited Ludington, precluding the use of vessels with considerable draft. International law did not permit transfer of foreign ships to American registry after the beginning of hostilities, so Ludington had to depend solely on ships flying the American flag. Finally, he did not receive accurate information concerning the army's needs because of the general confusion that obtained throughout May. For all these reasons Ludington was forced to rely on vessels built primarily for the coastal trade—most of them dirty, run-down, and cramped. Thirty-eight ships were ultimately rounded up, a fleet presumably capable of transporting about twenty-five thousand troops to Cuba. It developed, however, that they could actually load only about sixteen thousand men, with supplies and livestock (2,295 horses and mules). Lieutenant John D. Miley, Shafter's competent aide-de-camp, sardonically described the consequences: "It was very evident that many organizations would have to be left, and the frantic efforts for places on the transports were only equalled by similar efforts to get back to the United States after the expedition had been in Cuba a short time." There was insufficient time to refit the troopships adequately for military purposes. The chief surgeon of the Fifth Army Corps, Lieutenant Colonel Benjamin F. Pope, later reported, "The ships had stands of rough lumber bunks, usually three tiers high, sometimes four, built into the holds and lower and main decks. The packing of these bunks was so close that there was hardly room to pass between them, while in too many instances, with the closure of the hatches, light and air would have been wholly excluded and suffocation quickly result." Sanitary problems materialized in these circumstances. The Inspector General, Colonel Charles R. Greenleaf, noted that the ships "were overcrowded to such an extent that the men could not properly attend to the ordinary wants of nature, or keep themselves reasonably clean. The cooking arrangements were defective and the fresh air and water supply were entirely inadequate." Such were the transports available on short notice for the shipment of the Fifth Army Corps to Santiago de Cuba![12]

The scramble to board the transports that took place on the night of June 6 left a deep impression on those who took part in it. Many were the exploits required of a unit to guarantee itself a place on a troop ship. The Ninth Infantry, a regiment of regulars, apparently stole a wagon train from the Sixth Infantry, also of the regulars, to get to the dock at Port Tampa. Men of the Seventy-First New York commandeered a train at bayonet point, thus depriving the Thirteenth Infantry of its transportation to the boarding platform. Nothing daunted, the Thirteenth proceeded to locate an empty train and a wood-burning locomotive, and managed to get to Port Tampa ahead of two other regular regiments.[13]

Theodore Roosevelt demonstrated special initiative ensuring that the Rough Riders made the voyage to Santiago de Cuba. He and Colonel

Wood managed to locate some coal cars; in these the Rough Riders, however ingloriously, rode to the dock. There the two leaders learned from Miles and Shafter that they should find their assigned craft immediately and board it; otherwise they would be left behind. (Probably the harassed commanders had been reading those insistent telegrams coming from the War Department ordering departure without delay.) In any case Roosevelt and Wood managed to locate the Quartermaster General, who assigned them a transport, the *Yucatan,* with the advice to "seize her instantly, if we hoped to keep her." This counsel proved sound, for it turned out that the vessel had also been allotted to the Second Infantry and the Seventy-First New York. Roosevelt proved equal to this disconcerting situation: "Accordingly I ran at full speed to our train; and leaving a strong guard with the baggage I double-quicked the rest of the regiment up to the boat, just in time to board her as she came into the quay, and then to hold her against the Second Regulars and the Seventy-First, who had arrived a little too late, being a shade less ready than we were in the matter of personal initiative." Such were the expedients required in the absence of sound planning.[14]

Adversity stimulated others to bizarre improvisations. The Second Massachusetts spent a night on the pier awaiting their ship. Their historian recorded for posterity the exploit of Private "Dido" Hunt, Company G, on that occasion: Hunt's "foraging instincts . . . became active, and as a result he and several members of that company passed the long hours of the night very comfortably." In a nearby freight yard Hunt located two barrels. Stealthily cutting a hole in one of them, he discovered a supply of bottled beer. "Satisfying himself in the only proper manner that there was no mistake, he acquainted the members of his squad and a few others with his find and soon an impromptu picnic was in progress. Under the very noses of the sentries, the contents of that barrel of beer disappeared before morning, and to those in on the secret the night passed very pleasantly." With this kind of activity some ever-resourceful soldiers succeeded in minimizing—though they could not eliminate—the frustrations of a thoroughly confused loading operation.[15]

GHOST SQUADRON AND DEPARTURE

On the morning of June 8 Shafter finally was able to report to the War Department that his transports were loaded and under way—only to receive later that day a most disheartening order from Washington. As his ships were en route to a rendezvous outside Tampa harbor in the Gulf of Mexico that afternoon, an urgent message arrived: "Wait until

you get further orders before you sail. Answer quick." At 4:06 P.M.
Shafter responded, "Message received. Vessels are in the stream, but
will be able to stop them before reaching the Gulf." The situation
leading to this unexpected development had been reported to Washington earlier that day from Key West. A despatch boat, the *Eagle,*
reported that while passing through the St. Nicholas Channel it had
sighted two Spanish men-of-war—an armored cruiser and a destroyer.
Another vessel, the *Resolute,* confirmed this report. Following the advice of the Naval War Board, the Navy Department immediately
ordered Admiral Sampson at Santiago de Cuba to send two fast armored cruisers through the St. Nicholas Channel and thence to Key
West; these powerful ships would reinforce the naval escort assigned
to protect the convoy of transports. "We mean to start this expedition
as soon as convoy is strong enough, the delay being only temporary,"
cabled the Assistant Secretary of the Navy, Charles H. Allen, to the
commander of the North Atlantic Squadron. At the same time the
naval commander at Key West, Commodore Remey, received orders to
scout for the Spanish vessels. All this activity reflected the concern that
Miles summarized in an anxious telegram to the War Department—
Miles was generally anxious about such events: "If that report is true,
Spanish vessels could be within six hours of the loaded transports now,
and there to-morrow. Have ample measures been taken by the Navy to
insure their safety?" Thus began the episode of the "ghost squadron."
It forced a six days' delay in Shafter's departure.[16]

Admiral Sampson soon solved the puzzle of the "ghost squadron."
On June 9 the *Dolphin* arrived at Santiago de Cuba with the news that
the *Eagle* had reported the presence of two Spanish warships off the
north coast of Cuba. On June 10 the *Yankee* came in from Môle St.
Nicolas and reported that it had seen a formation of eight vessels including a battleship. The next day, however, five American ships
appeared—the *Yosemite, Panther, Armeria, Scorpion,* and *Supply.*
Sampson immediately realized that the *Eagle* had mistaken for enemy
vessels the last three of this group, along with an English ship, the
Talbot, that had also been in the area of the sighting. From the beginning Sampson had been skeptical of the report, confident that no Spanish warship had escaped undetected from Santiago de Cuba. He thus
did not detach armored vessels for service with the convoy from
Tampa—nor did he take kindly to the whole episode, observing tartly,
"Delay [in sending the expedition] seems to me most unfortunate."[17]

However, in response to an urgent request from the Navy Department, Sampson took steps to determine positively that none of
Cervera's ships had escaped from the harbor at Santiago de Cuba.

Lieutenant Victor Blue conducted a reconnaissance and established beyond doubt that all six of the Spanish vessels remained at their anchorages in the bay. Captain Chadwick, writing to Secretary Long, expressed the irritation that the "ghost squadron" aroused among those on the blockade: "If I can be allowed to say anything, it is that we should go on and do our work without paying any attention whatever to rumors and loose talk—let us strike energetically, decisively, quickly and we need fear nothing in the way of possible raids or phantom squadrons." Despite the cogency of this remark, it is difficult to criticize the War Department for holding the convoy at Tampa until the falsity of the report had been determined beyond doubt.[18]

While the navy was tracking down the "ghost squadron," Shafter marked time. The War Department recommended that the units already embarked remain on their transports, and Shafter concurred in this suggestion because there was no available campground in the vicinity of Port Tampa. The transports pulled into the channel connecting the port to the gulf in order to find clean water in which the troops could swim. Meanwhile, the men took turns spending brief periods of time ashore. Theodore Roosevelt summarized the irritation of the Fifth Army Corps very well in a letter to his usual correspondent, Senator Lodge: His ship, the *Yucatan*, was anchored in a "sewer" and loaded with about a thousand men, although it could hold but half of that number comfortably. The commanders had given the deck to their enlisted personnel. "We officers have to sit in the cabin, and even several companies are down in the lower hold, which is unpleasantly suggestive of the Black Hole of Calcutta." After claiming that an unduly long delay would adversely affect the efficiency of his unit, he went out of his way to praise the way in which it had maintained morale. "We have a remarkably fine set; they never complain; but surely they should be put into action as soon as possible before letting some malignant disease break out in the crowds here on shipboard."[19]

While Roosevelt was stewing on the *Yucatan*, General Miles actively sought to interfere with the expedition to Santiago de Cuba. First he sent a message to the War Department in which he wondered whether the convoy should not have the protection of the entire navy on its way to either Santiago de Cuba, Puerto Rico, or Nuevitas. He obviously was contemplating the thought of cancelling the operation at Santiago de Cuba and turning to either the seizure of Puerto Rico or the Nuevitas-to-Havana campaign in northern Cuba. It might even be appropriate, if movement was judged "too hazardous," to "keep the troops in healthful camps . . . and assist the Navy to destroy the Spanish fleet" by releasing transports for service as auxiliary cruisers. After these remarkable proposals he concluded weakly, "It seems strange to be suggesting that the Army assist the Navy in this way, but I am sure we would receive most loyal support when the waters are safe for crossing with the Army." In another message Miles proposed a *ruse de guerre:* He wanted to let out false word of the convoy's departure; the escort would then proceed alone over the planned route, hoping to encounter the ghost squadron. He asked whether it was wise to send out transports until the navy had neutralized Spanish ships in Caribbean waters. Finally he inquired whether he ought not to prepare the expedition for Puerto Rico—another hint that he wished to cancel the movement on Santiago de Cuba. To these messages the Secretary of War replied in terms that could not have failed to annoy Miles: "The President directs me to say that no change of plan will be made; that expedition no. 2 [Puerto Rico] must be organized as rapidly as possible. We are looking for transports, and [I] am satisfied that the Navy will take care of that problem. Give nothing out." Washington was determined to send expeditions to both Cuba and Puerto Rico, and in that order. Thus came to grief the commanding general's latest effort to alter the plan of campaign.[20]

Patience with Miles had run out in Washington; George Cortelyou recorded on June 8 that McKinley was "solicitous to the last degree for the welfare of our troops and sailors, but he is determined not to delay the prosecution of the war a day longer than necessary." The President realized, apparently more clearly than many professional soldiers and a good number of the civilians around him, that an immediate attack on Santiago de Cuba might assist wonderfully in achieving his principal desire—a rapid end to the war. At least it would ensure general and lasting control of the Caribbean Sea; at most it would force Sagasta to sue for peace. He did not propose to let the meddlesome commanding general interfere with his purpose.[21]

As soon as it became clear that the "ghost squadron" did not exist, the convoy made final preparations for departure. General Miles, indefatigable, tried once more to influence the plan of campaign, proposing that the transports proceed around the western tip of Cuba and then eastward along the south coast to Santiago de Cuba rather than eastward to the Windward Passage and around the eastern tip of the island to Santiago. He gave as reasons the possibility that "the water may be smoother and the fleet in less danger from torpedo boats on the south side." To this proposal Alger gave a polite but curt response: "After careful consideration I am of opinion that the question of route should be left to judgment of General Shafter and Commodore Remey." This time the Secretary of War did not find it necessary to cite the President as authority for his position. On the evening of June 12 Shafter arranged to begin his movement at daylight the next day; he would meet the escort proceeding northward from Key West outside of Tampa Bay on June 14.[22]

The convoy sailed without incident. Reporting to President McKinley on the departure of June 14, Miles accented the bright side of the delay, claiming that it allowed Shafter to improve his situation and offered additional time for the Cuban insurgents to converge on Santiago de Cuba. In contrast, Theodore Roosevelt, preparing for departure, recorded bitter thoughts about his stay in Tampa: "The confusion and lack of system and organization here surpass belief," he wrote one of his sisters. Provided the expedition went to Santiago de Cuba, he believed that "the hard fighting of the individual regiments and regimental commanders will carry us through, but the interminable delays and the vacillation and utter absence of efficient organization are really discouraging." To another sister, however, he wrote with his normal ebullience, "The navy has had all the fun so far, and I only hope that peace will not be declared without giving the army a chance at both Cuba and Porto Rico as well as the Philippines."[23]

The convoy that organized outside Tampa Bay on June 14 was no mean formation. Its twenty-nine transports and six support vessels carried 819 officers and 16,058 enlisted men. Of the latter only 2,465 were volunteers; the regulars dominated the campaign at Santiago de Cuba, although after reinforcements arrived there the number of volunteers increased to 7,443. No fewer than 2,295 animals accompanied the expedition—959 horses and 1,336 pack and draft mules. Artillery was in short supply; aboard ship were sixteen 3.2-inch light field guns, eight 3.6-inch field mortars, one Hotchkiss rapid-fire revolving cannon, and four Gatling guns. The naval escort included the *Annapolis*, *Helena*, and *Castine*—which met the transports at Havana—and the *Indiana* (armored), *Detroit*, *Panther*, *Yosemite*, *Bancroft*, *Vesuvius*, *Scorpion*, *Wasp*, *Eagle*, and *Wompatuck*—all of which joined at the Dry Tortugas west of Key West. The escorts travelled about sixteen hundred yards in advance and at the sides of the columns of transports, these at three-hundred-yard intervals in three columns about eight hundred yards apart. Two barges to support landing operations were taken in tow. One of these was lost on the north coast of Cuba, a happenstance that created difficulties later on.[24]

The great majority of the men who flocked to the colors in 1898 never went overseas; while Shafter's expedition was sailing towards the little Cuban city where Admiral Sampson was waiting impatiently many hopeful heroes were languishing in training camps—and continued to do so throughout the long summer and well into autumn. A doctor who served with the Twelfth New York Volunteers at Camp Thomas later summarized the situation: "An army of over two hundred thousand men of as gallant fellows as ever shouldered a musket or drew a sword sweated for four months under the Southern sun under all the tension of expectation and the demoralization of disappointment, only to see the war, for them, come to an inglorious end." Humor helped relieve the boredom, inconvenience, and frustration of camp life. The historian of an Indiana regiment, the 161st Volunteers, remembered when a stranger approached a guard and asked, "Are you a sentinel, sir?" The soldier responded: "No, I am a Swede." At Pablo Beach, Florida, Colonel William Jennings Bryan, commanding a Nebraska regiment, waited in vain for orders to the front. (McKinley had allowed his Democratic opponent a commission but granted him no opportunity for derring-do.) One day someone told the boy orator of the Platte that a rattlesnake with seventeen rattles had been killed in his camp. " 'Oh, no,' replied Colonel Bryan, 'it couldn't have been in my camp. It must have been in the Second Virginia. If it had been in my camp it would have been sixteen to one.' "[25]

Sometimes, alas, demon rum seems to have provided solace. At Camp Alger a local moonshine became known as "two-step," because after drinking it no one could take more than two steps without falling over. In one volunteer regiment, the Fifteenth Minnesota—located at Camp Meade, Pennsylvania—the officers took the drastic step of forbidding the sale of alcohol in the regimental canteen. Unfortunately, reported the chaplain, "the favorable results were not so pronounced as they would have been had surrounding regiments been as considerate of their men, or as neighborly as courtesy demands; for either in spite of, or in ignorance of the timely warning of the war department, many regimental authorities set about preparing their commands for service in the tropics by inculcating them with alcohol, and the saloons established by these regiments were as freely open to men of other regiments as their own." As always in the history of warfare, virtue found itself on the defensive in training camps.[26]

Two other regiments of United States Volunteer Cavalry were raised besides the Rough Riders, but neither went to war, and some of their frustration found expression in doggerel laments. As it whiled away the war at Camp Thomas, the Third United States Cavalry, known as "Grigsby's Cowboys" after their commander, produced a rhyme to be sung to the tune of "Marching Through Georgia":

We are waiting, Uncle Samuel, an even thousand strong;
We are waiting for the "forward march" to hump itself along;

We are waiting for a chance to fight for country, right or wrong,
And not camp down here in Georgia. . . .
We are cavortin' as camp rangers and doin' park police,
A buildin' repytashuns as pious men o' peace,
And our sweetheart's farewell letter has tatters in the crease,
But still we are camped here in Georgia.

Not to be outdone, the other regiment of volunteer cavalry, known as
"Torrey's Rocky Mountain Riders," produced eight comparable lines:

With gusto, guns and horses galore,
Torrey led his terrors off to war;
He marched them up and marched them down,
But only around the camp and town.
Never a glimpse of Spanish foe,
But days, weeks and months of woe;
No battles to fight, no laurels to win,
So, he marched them home again.

One can only reflect, upon reading this verse, on the meaning of
Milton's famous line, "They also serve who only stand and wait."[27]

Despite the confusion that accompanied the preparation of the expedition to Santiago de Cuba, the War Department managed against
great odds to put together a relatively large force in a remarkably short
period of time—a force that could reasonably be expected to make a
useful contribution at Santiago de Cuba. It exceeded by some seven
thousand the number of troops Sampson had thought necessary for operations against the Spanish adversary. The expedition was sent out
long before its units approached true operational efficiency—a consequence of calculated political judgment on the part of President
McKinley. He proved willing to sacrifice optimum preparations in favor
of early operations, acting in the belief that vigorous campaigns in both
the Caribbean and Western Pacific against Spain's most important colonial possessions—Cuba, Puerto Rico, and the Philippine Islands—
would help force an early end to the war. Once the issue had been
joined, he settled upon a military strategy designed to break Spain's
control of Cuba so as to end the conflict in the shortest possible time, at
the least possible cost, and with minimal complications during and after
the struggle. Although he may never have heard of Karl von Clause-
witz, he consistently applied that military philosopher's most sacred
principles. During the war with Spain the United States government
subordinated strategy to policy in a relatively disciplined manner. Time
would tell whether McKinley's overall plan of operation would bring

about the desired political outcome. Historians who emphasize the confusion of May and June, 1898 neglect the fact that the army accomplished an extensive mobilization, however helter-skelter, and that sound political considerations dictated haste. In May and June, 1898 McKinley correctly traded efficiency for speed. Had the country been better prepared for war in April, he might not have been forced into such a trade. Under the circumstances, there is more to praise than to ridicule in the army's mobilization for the Caribbean campaign.[28]

NINE

Beginnings of the Campaign at Santiago de Cuba

On June 20 the American convoy from Tampa appeared off Santiago de Cuba. Captain Anibal Escalante Beatón, aide to the Cuban insurgent General Calixto García, almost half a century later still remembered his feelings on that day: "No other scene could be grander or more thrilling than that moving spectacle . . . after three long years of struggle in the jungle, between incessant marches through savannahs and forests, at a great distance from civilization and fighting constantly with an enemy a thousand times better equipped." The moment of deliverance had come.[1]

A different more buoyant mood existed in the United States. One poet writing in the *Cleveland Plain Dealer* summarized American attitudes in a composition entitled "Don't You Hear Your Uncle Samuel?"

> Land of garlic and tortillas,
> Land of xebecs and mantillas,
> Land of mules and smuggled bitters,
> Land of raisins and of fritters,
> Land of Pedro and of Sancho,
> Land of Weyler and of Blanco,
> Land of bull fights and pesetas,
> Land of dusky senoritas,
> Land of manners still and haughty,
> Land of Isabella naughty,

Land of Bobdil and Hamil,
Don't you hear your Uncle Sam'l?
   "Git!"

Soon, however, the braggadocio of the bumptious republic would undergo an acid test.[2]

On board the crowded, uncomfortable transports, brave spirits such as Theodore Roosevelt anxiously awaited the imminent campaign. "It is a great historical occasion," he wrote, "and I thrill to feel that I am part of it. . . . If we are allowed to succeed (for we certainly shall succeed, if allowed) we have scored the first great triumph in what will be a world movement." He had in mind that "large policy" he and Henry Cabot Lodge so eagerly espoused. Roosevelt's commanding officer, Colonel Leonard Wood, surveying the "great peaceful maritime picture" presented by the convoy as it moved around the eastern end of Cuba, also sensed the significance of what lay ahead: "Hard it is," he wrote his wife, "to realize . . . that this is the first expedition our country has ever sent overseas and marks the commencement of a new era in our relations with the world."[3]

Below decks less philosophical enlisted men drank, as they will do, despite high prices and doubtful merchandise. A. D. Webb, a member of Troop A of the Rough Riders, noted the price of whiskey on the *Yucatan*—it sold at $20 a gallon. Beer retailed at 25¢ the small pint. Somewhat ruefully, Webb stated that in earlier days he had "experimented with some pretty tough bug extract in Arizona, yet he can truthfully say that he has never tackled any red liquor that would come up to the standard of this rat poison sold right here on board this government ship."[4]

The passage from Tampa to Santiago de Cuba passed without untoward incident, although it tried the endurance of the troops. Captain Henry C. Taylor managed the convoy well—although Captain Alfred Thayer Mahan later complained that the navy should have been given full control of the operation. "The committing of transport service to the Army is radically vicious in theory," Mahan insisted, "and directly contrary to the practice of the most experienced nation, Great Britain." An army surgeon, Major Louis A. La Garde, recalling the difficulties of the passage, recounted how the men on his ship had to remain aboard for nineteen days between loading at Tampa and disembarkation at Siboney. He believed that the "overcrowded condition of the ship for a long voyage, the inadequate ventilation and heat between decks, the hot, blue woolen uniform, and the sameness of the diet of the travel ration had begun to tell on the strength of the men," and "the overcrowding of the transports on the way to Cuba had much to do with subsequently reducing the effectiveness of the command." Small annoyances irritated some members of the expedition: Matthew A. Batson, Ninth Cavalry, complained that a board of survey had been held to assign responsibility for a bushel of rotten potatoes. "The conduct of the war up to this time fully convinces me of what I have long believed—" he confided to his diary, "that Army officers as a rule get into a routine way of doing things to an extent that really unfits them for their own profession. Am I not an awful crank?" Lieutenant John J. Pershing of the Tenth Infantry summarized the attitude of most: "Better arrangements might have been made with more time and might have been necessary for a long voyage, but everybody was so eager to go and so fearful of being left behind at the last moment that almost any conditions would have been accepted without grumbling."[5]

The possibility of a surprise attack on the convoy had occurred to some. As Richard Harding Davis, a seasoned war correspondent, wrote: "We rolled along at our own pace, with the lights the navy had told us to extinguish blazing defiantly to the stars, with bands banging out ragtime music, and with the foremost vessels separated sometimes for half a day at a time from the laggards in the rear." To Davis the voyage reflected national character: "It was a most happy-go-lucky expedition, run with real American optimism and readiness to take big chances, and with the spirit of a people who recklessly trust that it will come out all right in the end, and that the barely possible may not happen. . . ." He might have been interested in a message that Matthew Batson sent to his wife when he finally arrived off Santiago de Cuba. Warning her that she should not accept the accounts she read in the New York *Journal* or *World,* he concluded, "Be assured that I will not be rash and foolhardy, but if it comes to a question of bravery, I shall not be found wanting and if I fall it will be while doing my duty."[6]

Back in Washington, George M. Cortelyou, forever solicitous, noted the anxious President's attempts to keep abreast of the situation. "In the evenings before retiring he goes to the war-room and studies the dispatches." He thought that McKinley had provided remarkable wartime leadership and had shown himself "the strong man of the Cabinet, the dominating force; but with it all are such gentleness and graciousness in dealing with men that some of his greatest victories have been won apparently without any struggle." The campaign just ahead would tax McKinley's powers to their limit.[7]

SPANISH PREPARATIONS AT SANTIAGO DE CUBA

Well before the beginning of the war, the Spanish garrison at Santiago de Cuba had begun preparations to defend itself. The Spanish historian Severo Gómez Núñez rather sarcastically observed that after

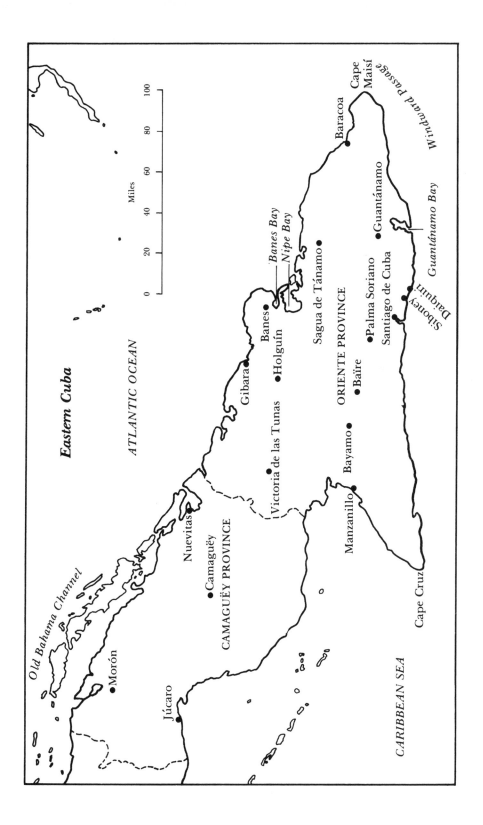

Eastern Cuba

Admiral Cervera took his squadron there the Americans made no secret of their intention to attack the place. "Besides being logical, a consequence of events, the newspapers of the United States had been proclaiming it publicly, *urbi et orbi.*" Early in April the Governor-General of Cuba, Don Ramón Blanco y Erenas, notified the commander in eastern Cuba, Lieutenant General Arsenio Linares Pomba, that Santiago de Cuba had been chosen as an American objective. How could it be defended against American naval operations coordinated with an insurgent attack on land? Linares gave some thought to concentrating all the troops under his command there, but eventually it was decided to leave in place the troops garrisoned at Sagua de Tánamo, Baracoa, Guantánamo, Holguín, and Manzanillo—a total of almost 24,500 men. By June 20 Linares had under his direct command around Santiago de Cuba a force that numbered only 319 officers and 9,111 enlisted men, many of whom were in debilitated condition. (American intelligence only slightly overestimated the number there.) The Spanish total grew by 1000 men when a contingent of sailors, about two-thirds of Cervera's crews, came ashore on June 22 under the command of Captain Joaquín Bustamante. About one-third of the Spanish force consisted of Cuban loyalists—militia and volunteers—who were not fully reliable. The garrison was organized into a division composed of two brigades under General of Division José Toral and General of Brigade Joaquín Vara del Rey, both destined to play memorable roles in the approaching campaign.[8]

Many authorities have criticized Linares's failure to concentrate all his forces at Santiago de Cuba, but Lieutenant José Müller y Tejeiro, a naval officer present at Santiago de Cuba, pointed out the wisdom of this course. No supplies were available at Santiago de Cuba to support a force that would have numbered about thirty-five thousand men, and no real defense could have been made against an American attack under the covering fire of Admiral Sampson's powerful squadron. And if Linares had brought in the garrisons elsewhere, the entire Cuban countryside and all urban regions except Santiago de Cuba would have fallen into the hands of the insurgents. Of course, another possibility existed: Should the Spanish garrison have abandoned Santiago de Cuba and moved across country to Cienfuegos or Havana? Müller correctly ruled out any such movement. None could be made on water because the Americans exercised command of the sea, and the Cuban insurgents could have harassed a Spanish column along the land route to either city. Even if the Cuban insurgents desisted from action, roads were most inadequate and supplies lacking. If a march had been attempted, Müller estimated that eight thousand men might have been killed or captured—and to what purpose?[9]

As Müller pointed out, few resources were available for the defense of Santiago de Cuba, and it was cut off from the main Spanish army in Cuba by the insurgents. They controlled its land communications, and the American squadron dominated its sea communications. The Spanish troops in Cuba had been divided into five corps—three based on the cities of Havana, Cienfuegos, and Puerto Príncipe, a fourth on the *trocha* from Júcaro to Morón, and a fifth in eastern Cuba. Frustration piled on frustration, because Linares could not strengthen himself with elements of his own corps in nearby locations and Blanco could not reinforce him with units from other parts of Cuba, units numbering in excess of 70,000 effective troops. The Spanish regulars in Cuba represented the remnant of the 214,000 men sent there during the insurrection. Perhaps 27,000 of those presumed effective were actually *hors de combat* in hospitals. In any event, less than 10,000 regulars were at Santiago de Cuba when General Shafter appeared off the city with his expedition.[10]

Santiago de Cuba lies at the western end of a valley about twenty miles long stretching in an east-west direction and lying between the Sierra Maestre mountains to the north and the coastline. This valley broadens out from a narrow strip at Daiquirí—well east—to a width of about seven miles in the vicinity of El Caney and San Miguel. Several streams run to the sea through hilly and brush-covered terrain. Of these the tiny San Juan River is the most important, flowing roughly south about two and one-half miles east of Santiago de Cuba. That city lies at the upper end of a fine harbor over four miles long. From the harbor to the sea a narrow channel runs for about a mile, and over it loom two heights at an elevation of about sixty-five meters—the Morro on the east side and the Socapa on the west. Both points offer excellent observation seaward. Just north of the Morro heights lies another elevated area, Punta Gorda, that commands the channel.[11]

Life in Santiago de Cuba became almost unbearable during the blockade. No flour entered the port after April 21. A German vessel was able to unload 1700 sacks of rice originally intended for Havana, but no additional provisions came in after April 25. The city normally relied for much of its food upon a cultivated region nearby, but the Cuban insurgents had long since rendered it almost useless. The roughly forty thousand people in the city—about ten thousand troops and thirty thousand civilians—rapidly depleted the available supplies of food. Tomas Alvarez Angulo, one of the Spanish defenders, described his pathetic diet during the last weeks of the campaign: "a little watered coffee, in the morning, that scarcely tasted of coffee, and two meals, consisting of white rice, mixed with water, without any fat and without salt. At times they gave us uncooked or well-cooked corn amongst the rice." Lieutenant Müller remembered that horses, dogs, and other animals died on the streets and that no one removed their carcasses. "I also saw," he continued, "this is significant, on account of the fatal consequences that might follow—I saw, I repeat, a dog throw himself upon a smaller one and kill and devour him." Captain Concas reported that an infantry officer invited to Admiral Cervera's table "was unable to eat, such being the condition to which the stress of circumstances had brought these honorable defenders of Spain; a condition which affected all the military forces from the general down, while the Spanish in general and the commissary department in particular lived in a very different manner." Local merchants added to the difficulties of the garrison by hoarding scarce goods and raising prices for troops who had gone without pay for many months. All this made both defenders and noncombatants more vulnerable to tropical diseases—typhus, malaria, dysentery, and yellow fever. An American journalist who entered the city soon after its fall noted that, true to its prior repute, it gave the impression mostly of "dirt, disorder, and neglect":

> The gutters were open drains, broken here and there by holes and pockets filled with decaying garbage and dirty, foul-smelling water. Piles of mango-skins, ashes, old bones, filthy rags, dung, and kitchen refuse of all sorts lay here and there on the broken and neglected pavements, poisoning the air with foul exhalations and affording sustenance to hundreds of buzzards and myriads of flies; little rills of foul, discolored water trickled into the open gutters at intervals from the kitchens and cesspools of the adjoining houses; every hole and crevice in the uneven pavement was filled with rotten organic matter washed down from the higher levels by the frequent rains, and when the sea-breeze died away at night the whole atmosphere of the city seemed to be pervaded by a sickly, indescribable odor of corruption and decay.

Such was the inhospitable city where Spain and the United States tested their strength in 1898.[12]

General José Toral headed a joint committee of five members that did what it could to strengthen the defenses of the channel leading to the harbor. Early in April this group had decided to place electrical torpedo mines there so hostile vessels could not force passage into the bay. One row of seven mines was in place by April 21. Another line of six mines, located north of the first row, was laid by April 27. These thirteen mines were controlled from Socapa Point and an island in the channel called Cay Smith.[13]

No amount of mining in the channel could keep out an enemy force, should the Spanish garrison lose the Morro and Socapa heights. "If the enemy had taken possession of them," wrote Müller, "it would have been easy to remove the torpedoes and force the bay, and then the city and its defenders would necessarily have had to surrender." For this reason Linares concentrated much of his artillery in batteries located at the entrance of the channel and along its course. These emplacements included the Morro battery of seven old howitzers east of the harbor entrance; the upper Socapa battery of three old howitzers and two modern breech-loading guns west of the entrance; the Estrella battery north of the Morro with two old howitzers, two old muzzle-loading guns, and two modern breech-loading guns; and the Punta Gorda battery, still further north—made up of four modern breech-loading guns and two old howitzers. Captain Concas contemptuously noted that some of the old bronze weapons bore the date 1724. They lacked sufficient range and accuracy to fire effectively on the blockading squadron.[14]

Although the guns guarding the entrance were largely obsolete and the electrical torpedoes in the channel could not be relied upon, these defenses still posed a serious problem for an attacking naval force because the narrow channel was so difficult to navigate. Only one ship—proceeding cautiously—could pass through it at a time. Even if the mines were removed, naval guns on Cervera's ships in the harbor might sink a ship entering through the channel and thus block the passage. By the same token, the peculiarities of the channel meant that it was just as easy to keep ships in the harbor as out, especially if the blockading forces could outgun the defending batteries.[15]

While efforts were being made to frustrate an attack by sea, General Linares prepared three lines of defense on land. The outer line—really only a screen—was located between Daiquirí and Siboney, where the Spanish defenders believed that the Americans would attempt to land. Thinly manned and poorly fortified, this position could probably not be held for any great length of time against a determined attack. To the west of this screen ran two lines—one a special line about eight or nine miles long that anchored on a series of forts and blockhouses mostly to the north and east of Santiago de Cuba, and the other a much shorter line quite close to the outskirts of the city. These fortifications made up the principal defenses of Santiago de Cuba. Linares decided not to concentrate his forces in one position close to the city, because he wished to protect a railroad running north to the Sierra Maestre mountains and an aqueduct that brought in the city's water supply. The main line of defense began at Ermitano and passed southward through El Caney, San Miguel de Lajas, Quintero hill, and the hills of Veguita and La Caridad to the bay. If these positions could be held, troops in the city would at least not suffer unduly from lack of food and water. However, the Spanish commander lacked sufficient forces to safeguard both his communications to the interior and the approaches to the city.[16]

Surely the Spanish garrison at Santiago de Cuba faced a desperate situation. It could not expect major reinforcement from either Spain or elsewhere in Cuba because the American squadron controlled the sea and the Cuban *insurrectos* largely dominated Oriente province. The garrison and ships at Santiago de Cuba might have been left with options besides awaiting an American attack, if the Spanish effort had been coordinated properly at an earlier date. As it was, all that Linares could do was wait for Shafter. On June 20 Governor-General Blanco in Havana informed the Minister of War in Madrid, Miguel Correa, that unless Spain launched a diversionary raid against the American east coast to draw the blockading squadron away or dispatched a relief squadron to Santiago de Cuba itself, the situation would soon be resolved—in favor of the Americans. He claimed to have done all he could for Linares, but called it "a difficult undertaking, on account of his being entirely cut off, enemy being in complete control of the sea." Cervera might still run out to Cienfuegos or Havana, but Blanco preferred naval reinforcements from the Spanish peninsula. The squadron could then return to Spain. For the moment the governor-general recommended that he be given control of all naval and military forces in Cuba, including Cervera's command. On June 24 Correa and Minister of the Marine Auñón sent the necessary orders, and Cervera lost his freedom of action.[17]

Meanwhile Spanish politicians had begun to criticize the Sagasta Ministry. On June 22 the leftist José Canalejas, who had visited Cuba just before the war (where he received the notorious Dupuy de Lôme letter), rose in the Cortes to berate both Sagasta and his predecessor, Cánovas, because of their failure to make adequate preparations for war. The next day the conservative Romero Robledo rose to ask viciously why the squadron at Santiago de Cuba had not gone out to attack Sampson's blockade. Auñón, Minister of the Marine for only a month, answered lamely: Warships were not built to be sacrificed without the best reasons. "Squadrons are deliberately lost when some good results to the nation that possesses them, but they are never lost for sterile pleasure," he insisted in good Mahanian accents, "not even for the puerile satisfaction that the survivor or the outsider can say that the others perished with glory." To forestall further criticism of his war measures, Sagasta suspended the Cortes on June 24. The parliamentary squabble made painfully obvious the sense of powerlessness that overspread all Spain and Cuba as the American army poised for an assault on Santiago de Cuba. It is possible that the attitudes of the Cortes influenced Blanco's decision made only about ten days later to order Cervera out of the harbor at Santiago de Cuba.[18]

ARRIVAL AT SANTIAGO DE CUBA

While the Cortes was snarling at Sagasta, General Shafter's command arrived off Santiago de Cuba. Captain French Ensor Chadwick, Admiral Sampson's chief of staff, visited the army commander on the headquarters ship, the *Segurança,* to convey the navy's wishes concerning the forthcoming attack. Sampson wanted Shafter to seize the batteries located on the Morro and Socapa heights, so that he could then clear the mines out of the channel without interference; then he could safely force the entrance and engage Cervera's ships. Chadwick returned to the blockading squadron under the impression that General Shafter had accepted this plan. The Spanish defenders were anticipating an attack on the entrance, and Captain Concas later criticized Shafter for taking a different course. Had he not done so "there would not have been so great a loss of life, nor would the outcome of his expedition have been so uncertain," he argued, "in spite of the terrible conditions in which they found our troops as well as the defenses of the city."[19]

Sampson and his defenders ever after insisted that the navy was not worried about the batteries as such but simply about the mines in the channel, which could not be removed unless the Spanish guns were prevented from firing on a working party sent in to perform this task. Until the mines could be removed, the risk of entrance outweighed the advantage to be gained from it. Captain Mahan was among the most vociferous of those who opposed taking risks with the armored ships in the American squadron. "If we lost ten thousand men, the country could replace them; if we lost a battleship it could not be replaced," he insisted. "The issue of the war, as a whole and in every locality to which it extended, depended upon naval force, and it was imperative to achieve, not success only, but success delayed no longer than necessary." Another contemporary authority, Herbert H. Sargent, argued a parallel view: "Battleships and armoured cruisers are not built for the purpose of attacking fortifications and land forces. Their purpose is to gain and hold control of the sea." He claimed that the loss of one or two large ships would have shifted the naval advantage away from the United States, and that after the fall of Santiago de Cuba, the American position depended on keeping its squadron intact. Those who criticize the navy's proposals of June 20 argue that forts would have been most dangerous to assault by land; mines would have been difficult to remove from the channel in any case; the batteries at Punta Gorda, Estrella Point, and Socapa Point would still have been able to command the channel; and Cervera's ships could have engaged each entering ship separately, given the narrowness of the channel.[20]

On June 20 Sampson, Shafter, and General Calixto García met at the camp of the local Cuban commander, General Jesus Rabí, a full-blooded Indian, to concert landing plans. This headquarters was near Aserraderos, some eighteen miles west of the Morro. The ponderous Shafter mounted a mule to make the short trip from the beach to the camp, causing the Cuban Captain Escalante Beatón to comment wryly, "One had to have compassion for the poor mule, upon contemplating it giving profound groans [*pugidos*] of anguish during its ascension, because of the cargo with which it had been punished that summer morning!" Accepting the recommendation of García, Shafter decided to land his forces at Daiquirí on June 22. To support this effort the Cuban commander promised to concentrate about one thousand troops under General Demetrio Castillo Duany to attack the Spanish troops near the landing area, a part of Linares's outer defensive ring. Another force of about five hundred Cubans would make a demonstration at Cabañas, three miles east of the Socapa, to mislead the enemy into the belief that the landing would take place there. Sampson was to add to the deception by bombarding Cabañas, the Morro, and forts located at Siboney and Aguadores, near other possible landing sites. He would also shell the actual landing site, Daiquirí, prior to the movement. After the American troops had disembarked, Sampson would transfer García's troops from Aserraderos by sea to Daiquirí and to Siboney.[21]

Well before the conference at Aserraderos Shafter had made his decision to attack Santiago de Cuba from the east along a route that moved relatively far inland and away from the most effective support of the naval squadron. "These movements committed me to approaching Santiago from the east over a narrow road, at first in some places not better than a trail, running from Daiquirí through Siboney and Sevilla, and making attack from that quarter." He insisted that he had adopted "the only feasible plan" and that "subsequent information and results confirmed my judgment," despite the fact that the navy had urged quite a different approach. To Shafter's mind the obvious strategy was to attack the city itself at the upper end of the bay rather than the harbor entrance at the lower end. "It would have been the height of folly and endangered the safety of the army to have attempted to carry out the plan desired by the Navy," he insisted, "and it never for one minute met with my approval." This version runs counter to that of

Sampson, who claimed that Shafter had accepted the Navy's proposition conveyed by Chadwick on June 20 and that nothing had occurred at Aserraderos informing him of the army's interest in a radically different plan.[22]

Why did Sampson and Chadwick continue for several days to believe that Shafter intended to assault the heights at the harbor entrance rather than move inland and attack the city? Apparently they assumed that the city could not be successfully assaulted as long as Cervera remained in the harbor to support its defenders with concentrated naval gunfire. Reviewing the discussions of June 20 some years later, Chadwick concluded that incorrect information from both the War Department and García concerning the location of Spanish troops around Santiago de Cuba had led Shafter to change his plan. These reports indicated that the harbor mouth was heavily guarded, but the city had been left largely without defenders. Chadwick did not alter his original view that a coordinated land assault could have overwhelmed the Morro and the Socapa. The Marines attached to the blockading squadron—numbering about one thousand men—could have joined with about four thousand Cuban insurgents to seize the Socapa, where only four hundred defenders could offer resistance. At the same time Shafter could have sent about two thousand men against the four hundred Spanish at the Morro, leaving fifteen thousand troops to assault the city proper. In other words, careful army-navy planning would have permitted the invaders to attack the entrance and the city both. Chadwick did not take into consideration the possibility that Linares might reinforce the heights, should the Americans begin preparations to attack them.[23]

In any event the consultations of June 20 created misperceptions that contributed mightily to later interservice squabbles at Santiago de Cuba. Shafter had not developed his plan of operation beyond a decision to land at Daiquirí and advance along an inland route toward Santiago de Cuba. The navy did not realize that the land forces had no intention of attacking at the entrance to the bay. Later on Shafter claimed that tactical considerations forced rejection of the navy's plan. Between his force and the Morro, he wrote, lay "a rugged piece of country, devoid of water, covered with a poisonous undergrowth, and so impenetrable that the railroad running obliquely from Aguadores toward Santiago, and a trail would have been the only means of reaching it." Given the availability of naval support from the guns of the squadron, Shafter might have considered these two routes more than sufficient for his purposes, but he did not comment on this possibility. Instead he argued that the army's inland movement on Santiago de Cuba eventually succeeded in forcing Cervera out of the bay and thus contributed to the capture of the place.[24]

Shafter's decision to land at Daiquirí and strike obliquely inland towards Santiago de Cuba derived primarily from his conviction that he had to accomplish his mission rapidly. As part of his preparation for the campaign Shafter had read accounts of an English attempt to attack Santiago de Cuba in 1741. Lord Vernon's expedition landed at Guantánamo Bay—quite a distance east of its objective—from where it advanced on Santiago de Cuba. Vernon encountered slight Spanish resistance during his approach march, but some two thousand of his soldiers perished along the way—victims of tropical disease; after coming within sixteen miles of his destination, he was forced to withdraw. Shafter told Alger after the campaign that "with this example before him he realized that the sole chance of success would lie in the very impetuosity of his attack." In other words, he must seek a quick decision before disease defeated him. During postwar commentary on the campaign before an investigating commission, Shafter said that he had decided prior to arriving off Santiago de Cuba "that whatever we did at that season had to be done very quickly." Otherwise yellow fever might destroy his command. "I intended to go as far to the front as I could, until we met decided opposition, and then to make an attack." General Joseph Wheeler, testifying before the same panel, made a similar statement: "We all knew the country as yellow-fever country. We knew this malaria fever often affected even the natives, and it seemed that promptness of action was more essential than anything else." Wheeler, however, considered the opposing forces, rather than the city, as the main objective of the Fifth Army Corps. "Well," he said, "the fleet and the army were the objective points. After taking the fleet the army would be at our mercy." Why, in this connection, had not the Spanish army simply retreated into the interior? One of the Spanish generals, José Toral, later told Wheeler that his men were footsore and therefore unable to march, but the old Confederate guessed that the Spanish garrison "was unwilling to risk a fight with our troops in the open field." At any rate, it seemed unwise to move on the batteries at the entrance of the bay because this enterprise would have required more time than Shafter's plan. Of considerable interest in this connection also is the recollection of Shafter's adjutant, Lieutenant Colonel McClernand. He reported long after the war a pronouncement of the commander to a group of officers while en route to Santiago de Cuba: "We were a long way from the Civil War; . . . the country was no longer accustomed to hear of heavy losses in battle and would judge us accordingly." Shafter therefore "intended to get his Army in position around the city of Santiago and demand a surrender." McClernand argued that this notion of minimizing casualties played "a controlling part in the battle before the city."[25]

Certainly, too, the tactical difficulties of an attack on the heights must also have given Shafter pause, as he indeed argued after the war, although they were distinctly secondary compared with the need for speed. He had no heavy artillery with which to support such an assault, although he might have called upon Sampson for naval gunfire, as he was to do on other occasions during the campaign. He must have believed that the tactical dangers of his plan were not very imposing compared with those inherent in the navy's proposal, even if moving inland through the valley to the outskirts of Santiago de Cuba deprived him of close support from the American squadron offshore and also increased his logistical problems.[26]

But was there more to this matter? Some authorities attribute to Shafter no sense of coordinated warfare or joint operations, no understanding of the ways in which land and sea forces could operate in conjuntion. Others charge that Shafter did not wish to share the honors at Santiago de Cuba with the navy—that he aspired to capture the city and Cervera by himself. Why attempt a dangerous operation at the harbor's mouth merely to prepare the way for another glorious naval victory? Such allegations are difficult to substantiate, but they do seem plausible—if only as tertiary considerations—in the light of Shafter's behavior at the outset of the campaign and thereafter.[27]

Shafter's orders gave him considerable latitude. He was instructed to move, after landing either east or west of Santiago de Cuba, to the high ground overlooking the harbor or penetrate into the interior, in order to "capture or destroy the garrison there, and cover the navy as it sends its men in small boats to remove torpedoes, or with the aid of the navy, capture or destroy the Spanish fleet now reported to be in Santiago harbor." Tactical decisions were left largely to him, except for the proviso that he proceed expeditiously. Shafter was given sufficient flexibility to emphasize land over sea forces, and he followed such a course. Perhaps he did not fully realize the consequences of his decision to proceed inland toward Santiago de Cuba rather than attack the heights. And—although his course invited many discomforts and discontents—it was not a surprising departure. He had had little time to consider tactical questions thoroughly before arriving at Santiago de Cuba, because the President's strategy placed speed ahead of efficiency in priority—just as at Tampa. Also, Shafter did not possess accurate intelligence about the region around Santiago de Cuba and the Spanish forces awaiting him there. The circumstances in which the general labored and his personal shortcomings—he lacked real training and experience in the conduct of joint operations—combined to mar his performance as a commander. When all was done, he would have his victory, but this outcome obscured a considerable measure of frustration and failure along the way.[28] And yet a sympathetic authority, Graham A. Cosmas, believes that Shafter correctly divined President McKinley's intentions.

It seemed logical to attack Santiago de Cuba, because the Cuban insurgents could support American operations most effectively in eastern Cuba. From the first, General Miles had exerted himself to obtain information about the Cuban forces in Oriente province. Lieutenant Rowan had visited Cuba to accomplish just this purpose. Calixto García's command in the eastern department included three corps: Two of these were located in the vicinity of Santiago de Cuba; they encompassed six divisions, each composed of thirty-one regiments, each of which in turn were organized into fourteen brigades of about fifteen thousand men. Sixty-five hundred insurgent troops were in the immediate environs of Santiago de Cuba, and a thousand others were stationed near Guantánamo to contain the large Spanish garrison there. The remainder were situated west of Santiago de Cuba or in small detachments near towns such as Cienfuegos, Mariel, Sagua la Grande, and Baracoa. By 1898 García had forced the Spanish army in eastern Cuba into strictly defensive operations; troop movements outside strong points were avoided except to reinforce threatened locations or acquire supplies. This circumstance contributed a great deal to the ultimate American success at Santiago de Cuba. The naval blockade of Cuba had proved effective because the Spanish army had become dependent on exports from Spain, the Cuban *insurrectos* having denied it sufficient local resources. Three years of warfare had resulted in the loss of over one hundred thousand Spanish troops. Those who remained were debilitated, a circumstance that naturally deprived them of the ability to take the offensive.[29]

CUBAN-AMERICAN RELATIONS

The Cuban *junta* in New York, tireless in its support of the insurrection, recognized the political importance of lending full Cuban support to the Americans at Santiago de Cuba. Tomas Estrada Palma enjoined García to provide assistance in all feasible ways, although he also took care to urge that the General involve himself in "the total organization of the branches of civil administration" as a means to prepare the way for a future Cuban government. General Máximo Gómez, who believed that his mission had been largely accomplished with the intervention of the United States, supported this policy of accommodation. Estrada Palma expressed some worry about the United States Administration's refusal to recognize the insurgent government, but he also noted that General Miles had adopted the *junta's* recommendation that the Cubans be supplied with arms. Although García cooperated with the Americans, he suspected that the United States did not intend to recognize the Cuban government after the expulsion of the Spanish army. He offered this view to Estrada Palma just a week after Shafter arrived at Santiago de Cuba, but ended on an optimistic note: "I do not doubt that before concluding the campaign all the people of the United States will be convinced to leave to us conditions for governing ourselves and for organizing all the necessary institutions for realizing the ends of an independent state." Despite the policies of McKinley, public opinion, García felt, would work in behalf of Cuban independence.[30]

The consultations between American leaders and García on June 19 and June 20 arranged for movements of insurgent forces that proved most helpful during the campaign at Santiago de Cuba. Three thousand *insurrectos* remained in the vicinity of Guantánamo to keep the Spanish garrison from joining Linares. Another concentration of three thousand Cubans near Holguín was intended to prevent a force of approximately twelve thousand Spaniards in that vicinity from relieving Santiago de Cuba. The most probable source of relief for the beleaguered city was some six thousand Spanish troops at Manzanillo; about one thousand Cubans were detailed to watch this garrison. García himself would guard the northern entrance to Santiago de Cuba; he would conduct a diversion at Cabañas, and on the day of the landing would attack Spanish forces defending Daiquirí. Cuban troops located west of Santiago de Cuba at Aserraderos were to be moved by sea on American ships to Siboney, an operation to be conducted secretly so that Linares would not transfer the units protecting the western approaches of Santiago de Cuba to the actual landing place. When completed, this disposition of the insurgents seriously threatened Linares. Captain Concas summarized the consequences: "All communications were cut off, forests, roads, and mountains. Everything was infested by the Cubans, and even the west coast of the harbor itself was unsafe, the American army being relieved of this painful service." Thus, operations at Santiago de Cuba required coordination not only of the American army and navy but also of American and Cuban forces.[31]

However, the relations between the Cubans and Americans that had begun well deteriorated rapidly. General García had made a most favorable impression during a visit to Sampson's flagship on June 19, and the conference at Aserraderos the next day cemented this estimate.

Lieutenant Colonel Arthur Wagner wrote later that the Cubans had at first impressed him: "They were better disciplined and better equipped than I expected them to be, and their ready obedience of their officers, and their manifest good care of their arms more than neutralized the unfavorable impression created by their ragged attire and general tatterdemalion appearance." Thereafter, however, he revised his estimate: "It was not until a later date that I discovered that, whatever their merits as bushwhackers might be, they were practically useless in battle." Yankee soldiers rapidly grew to dislike the *insurrectos* because the Cubans, forced for years to live off the land, frequently appropriated discarded American equipment. Colonel John R. Bennett of the Thirty-Fourth Michigan Volunteers wrote home bluntly that he had "failed to find any Cubans who are not what you would call human vultures." Other observers were to echo many times his further comment: "They are mostly like our poor, low negroes of the south, only they have less principle. They steal everything they can get their hands on." Second Lieutenant John H. Parker, in charge of the Gatling gun detachment, openly expressed his racial prejudice:

> [The Cuban] is a treacherous, lying, cowardly, thieving, worthless, half-breed mongrel; born of a mongrel spawn of Europe, crossed upon the fetiches of darkest Africa and aboriginal America. He is no more capable of self-government than the Hottentots that roam the wilds of Africa or the Bushmen of Australia. He can not be trusted like the Indian, will not work like a negro, and will not fight like a Spaniard; but he will lie like a Castilian with polished suavity, and he will stab you in the back with all the dexterity of a renegade graduate of Carlisle.

A member of the Ninth Cavalry, Major Matthew A. Batson, expressed another straightforward view of the situation along with a dash of philosophy: "The Cubans in my opinion are not worth fighting for, but of course everybody knows that. However, we have not forgotten the Maine, and besides War is the natural state of mankind."[32]

This American distaste for the Cubans soon alienated the insurgent troops, already suspecting—however unjustifiably—that the United States might renege on its pledge to obtain Cuban independence. General Shafter did nothing to counteract this tendency; he slighted the Cubans in planning his attack, suggesting that they be used as common laborers. After the war he once told a reporter, "Why, these people are no more fit for self-government than gun powder is for hell." The Fifth Army Corps, broadly representative of American society at the end of the nineteenth century, vented upon the Cubans, many of whom were blacks, all the racial prejudice that had accumulated at home. Few stopped to consider the fighting qualities of the Cubans as partisan guerrilla irregulars. Forgotten were the privations that the *insurrectos* had endured for three years or the fact that they lacked anything but the most primitive equipment. The country took no notice of Shafter's refusal to assign them important responsibilities. American reporters quickly adopted the attitude of the army and communicated its prejudices to their readers at home. All this was of course thoroughly discreditable, however typical of the time; it poisoned Cuban-American relations at the outset of the campaign in the Antilles, casting a long shadow over the future.[33]

Cuban-American trust was ebbing rapidly in the earliest days of cooperation, and an event early in July—García's failure to prevent an important reinforcement by Spanish troops of the garrison at Santiago de Cuba—particularly undermined confidence in the insurgents. On June 22 Colonel Federico Escario, in command of about thirty-seven hundred Spanish troops, left Manzanillo to relieve Santiago de Cuba, a move that García had previously ordered General Salvador Hernández Ríos to resist with a thousand men. The route from Manzanillo to Santiago de Cuba—about 160 miles long—passed through most difficult terrain particularly suitable for guerrila harassment. Escario's march evolved into an epic of bravery and suffering. Proceeding by way of Palmas Altas, Bayamo, Baíre, and Palma Soriano, the Spanish column managed to reach Santiago de Cuba on the night of July 2, a day after the garrison there had fought battles at El Caney and the San Juan Heights. Along the way Escario's command fought perhaps as many as forty skirmishes with the insurgents. Twenty-one Spaniards were killed and seventy-one wounded; many other soldiers fell out along the way from sickness or exhaustion. The severest fighting took place at Aguacate on July 1, where seven of Escario's men were killed and forty-three received wounds. About thirty-three hundred men completed the march, and they have been honored ever since in Spain for their steadfastness and sacrifice.[34]

Well before Escario approached Santiago de Cuba, García had agreed to guard the western approaches to the city. On June 27 the Cuban general proposed to reinforce the position with two thousand men. Shafter's rejection of this recommendation imposed limits on García's ability to interdict Escario's movement. Despite this circumstance, the American army generally attributed the Spanish column's entrance into Santiago de Cuba to Cuban laxity and cowardice. García may indeed have fallen prey to overconfidence. On July 1 he informed Shafter, ''I will advance toward Santiago placing my forces so as to prevent reinforcement to enter in Santiago and will simulate an attack on the northern side of the city with the object of calling their attention to that side.'' This message showed no concern about insufficient strength. On July 4 Shafter reported Escario's arrival to General Wheeler in highly critical terms. He had been told that the Cubans would cover the road on which Escario finally entered Santiago de Cuba, but "Garcia must have withdrawn and given them free entrance.'' Reporting the incident to the War Department, Shafter noted that "Garcia was especially charged with blockading that road.'' He made no mention of the Cuban's earlier proposal to reinforce the roadblock, a convenient omission that typified the tendency of the Americans to minimize their own failings while emphasizing those of the insurgents.[35]

LANDING AT DAIQUIRÍ

All this early activity prepared the way for the initial operation of the campaign at Santiago de Cuba—the landing of the Fifth Army Corps. The point of disembarkation, Daiquirí, had no real harbor. Lying at a slight indentation in the shoreline below some high hills, its only docking facilities were a large steel pier and a small wooden dock built to accommodate the ships of an American mining company located in the vicinity. Linares had deployed only about three hundred Spanish defenders to this area, some of whom had been there a month prior to the arrival of the Americans. He scattered his forces in order to cover several potential beachheads along about thirty miles of coastline, and little had been done to prepare for an attack on Daiquirí. A Spanish eyewitness, Tomas Alvarez Angulo, remembered some trenches and parapets and perhaps four cannons in place. Highly critical of Linares's failure to order destruction of the piers, he expressed himself pungently: "Once more the characteristic unpreparedness!'' Some other historians have criticized Linares for not concentrating all his forces at Santiago de Cuba and resisting the American assault with all his strength. This argument ignores the difficulties that Linares would have encountered in completing the concentration and maintaining his troops at Santiago de Cuba, but it is fair to criticize the Spanish general for not using available capabilities effectively to inflict damage and create confusion. On this occasion, as on others to come, he missed golden opportunities to delay or discommode if not defeat the invaders.[36]

If Linares's preparations to defend Daiquirí were redolent of hopelessness—of that "moral inertia" noted by many students of the campaign—the American operation of June 22 reflected the helter-skelter of the concentration at Tampa. Leonard Wood, waiting to go ashore, wrote disgustedly to his wife, "You can hardly imagine the awful confusion and lack of system which meets us on every hand in this business." Nevertheless, he felt confident: "Somehow everything seems to go in a happy-go-lucky way." Like certain of his superiors in Washington, Wood worried that some European nation might yet intervene in behalf of Spain: It was fortunate that the United States had attacked "a broken-down power, for we would surely have had a deuced hard time with any other." There had been a full measure of unpreparedness on the American as well as the Spanish side. Shafter had failed to organize the landing carefully, but fortunately the navy filled the gap. Admiral Sampson issued an order on June 21 that lessened some difficulties, assigning Captain Caspar Goodrich, a competent naval officer, to assist the army; his yeoman service helped curb the general confusion.[37]

On June 22 all the planned feints and bombardments along the coastline took place, and the transports moved off Daiquirí to unload. These preliminaries did not proceed altogether smoothly. Brigadier General Jacob F. Kent's infantry brigade, still aboard transports, was ordered to accompany the naval vessels off Cabañas, and he was not recalled to the beachhead for three days. (His presence may have been forgotten.) The naval bombardment of Daiquirí itself proved relatively ineffective, but that did not matter because the Spanish defenders withdrew as soon as it began. However, the lack of good harbor and docking facilities at Daiquirí and the presence of heavy surf there posed serious obstacles by themselves to the landing, and other difficulties further enhanced the confusion. The captains of the transports proved extremely wary of maneuvers close to shore, a situation that lengthened the time required to get the troops ashore. The army had had little or no training and experience in landing operations. Most important, probably, was the absence of sufficient lighters and other small craft needed to mount such an operation. Only the willingness of the navy to use its small craft compensated for this serious deficiency, one that continued to plague the expedition for many days.[38]

Somehow the Fifth Army Corps straggled onto the beach. Midshipman Halligan of the *Brooklyn* was the first man ashore, at 10:00 A.M. By 6:00 P.M. some six thousand men had disembarked; an equal number landed the next day. At this point Shafter decided to land also at Siboney, about eight miles closer to Santiago de Cuba than Daiquirí. By June 26 almost all the troops were off the transports. To get the mules and horses on land it was necessary to put them in the water and let them swim. Major Batson of the Ninth Cavalry reported on this process to his wife: "It is pitiful to see the poor brutes swim from one boat to another. Sometimes they get nearly to the shore, then turn around and swim to sea. Of course a great many of them are drowned, and the beach is covered with dead horses and mules." The landing was not without its fatalities. Two black troopers of the Tenth Cavalry drowned at Daiquirí—Corporal Edward Cobb of Richmond, Virginia, and Private John English of Chattanooga, Tennessee. Captain William O. ("Bucky") O'Neill, the ex-mayor of Prescott, Arizona and one of the most picturesque of the Rough Riders, dove into the water in a brave but futile attempt to rescue the victims.[39]

Sergeant Horace W. Bivins of the Tenth Cavalry summarized very well the feelings of many as the landing ran its course: "We are in good shape and are ready to do our duty. We are not afraid to fight for our country's honor and for this cause; for we believe that it is a just one. *Tyranny*, tyranny is what Spain has kept imposing upon the Cubans for the last century." However, Bivins, a black, could not help noting that his regiment had not been "treated with much courtesy while coming through the South. God grant the time will come when this country will have power to enforce the teaching of the heavenly doctrine that all men are created free and equal." He was prepared to sacrifice his life: "If I die on the shores of Cuba my earnest prayer to God is that when death comes to end all, I may meet it calmly and fearlessly."[40]

Admiral Cervera reacted to the landing immediately. Reporting to Auñón, he argued that he could not hope to get away but would "resist as long as possible and destroy ships as last extreme." On June 25 he acknowledged an order placing him under Blanco's command, and sent along a catalog of his problems to the Governor-General: For his 5.5-inch Hontoria guns he had only 650 reliable rounds out of a total of 3000. The majority of the fuses were unserviceable. Three of his 5.5-inch guns were defective—two on the *Vizcaya* and one on the *Almirante Oquendo*. Most disastrous of all, the *Cristóbal Colón* lacked its heavy armament, and the *Vizcaya* was so badly fouled that it could only make a fraction of its rated speed. No Bustamante contact mines were available to block the channel, and there were little coal and provisions for the month of July. Cervera did not fail to remind Blanco, "Blockading fleet is four times superior; hence our sortie would be positively certain destruction."[41]

As if to confirm Cervera's desperate messages, Sampson strove to tighten the blockade and Washington officialdom bestirred itself to send the army reinforcements. The Admiral ordered his blockading squadron to exercise "utmost vigilance" on station, keeping ready for action and observing the harbor entrance. "If the Spanish admiral ever intends to attempt to escape," he concluded, "that attempt will be made soon." At home Secretary Long sought to hasten the departure of transports loaded with volunteers—particularly the Atlantic steamers *Yale* and *Harvard*—giving as his reason the Navy Department's desire "above everything that the War Department shall not be able to say they were delayed by Navy." General Corbin was already trying to bolster Shafter, ordering the return of empty transports to Tampa without delay and reporting that reinforcements would soon sail from Newport News aboard the *Yale* and *Harvard*.[42]

If the attempt to reinforce Shafter commanded attention in Washington, the most immediate problem at Santiago de Cuba was that of supply. The troops carried with them their personal equipment and a small amount of food, but many of their belongings remained on the transports. The difficulties of camping and marching on to forward locations led many soldiers to discard all but the most essential items of equipment, a shortsighted decision that was to add to their discomfort during the early days of the campaign. Inadequate preparations interfered with the landing of their equipment, ammunition, provisions, medical support, and artillery at Daiquirí and Siboney. Meteorological conditions compounded their problems; it was hot during the day, often chilly in the evening, and tropical downpours occurred regularly each day and sometimes at night. Shafter lacked sufficient wagons and enough mules to haul them. And the roads indicated on maps of the area between Daiquirí and Santiago de Cuba turned out to be mostly trails or narrow pathways. All these difficulties tended to drain the army physically and particularly make it susceptible to tropical disease endemic in eastern Cuba, especially dysentery and malaria. There simply had been no time to create an efficient service of supply. Had the navy not lent extensive aid, the logistical tangle might have become completely impenetrable.[43]

The army did not remember this assistance for long—a situation that naturally aroused annoyance in the navy. In December, 1898, the acidulous Captain Mahan, who had a very short fuse, wrote angrily to Secretary Long, pointing out General Miles's view "that the navy had in some way failed to meet its engagements to provide facilities for the landing of the army at Santiago." He wanted to remind his superior "that the department at the suggestion of the war board wrote to the war department, to know if such aid were wanted; and that the reply was that they would do their own landing, asking us only safe convoy to the spot." Between June and December, 1898, the two services got into several acrid debates arising directly out of events at Santiago de Cuba, thus publicizing a rivalry that interfered with effective coordination.

Mahan, forever jealous of the anvy's prerogatives, did not intend to let the army steal a march on his beloved organization. In this respect, as in many others, lack of institutional arrangements to ensure interservice cooperation precluded maximum efficiency.[44]

When ashore the Fifth Army Corps counted about seventeen thousand men in all, most of whom belonged to five large organizations—three divisions, an independent brigade, and a volunteer brigade. Brigadier Generals Jacob F. Kent and Henry W. Lawton commanded the two infantry divisions—each with about five thousand troops—and Major General Joseph Wheeler led the dismounted cavalry division of some twenty-seven hundred men. About eleven hundred regulars were organized into the independent brigade, under the command of Brigadier General John C. Bates. The only separate organization of volunteers, a brigade composed of Michigan troops, numbered about twenty-five hundred men and was under the command of Brigadier General Henry M. Duffield. Contrary to a general impression, volunteers composed only a small proportion of the Fifth Army Corps until after the decisive engagements of July 1. Just five regiments of volunteers took part in the early phases of the campaign—the First United States Volunteer Cavalry (Rough Riders), the Second Massachusetts, the Seventy-First New York, the Thirty-Third Michigan, and one battalion of the Thirty-Fourth Michigan. Given the hasty organization of the expedition, the War Department perforce had had to rely primarily on those units actually available—the regulars concentrated at Tampa.[45]

The Fifth Army Corps had remarkably little artillery support at Santiago de Cuba. The light artillery battalion, which had sixteen 3.2-inch field guns, saw considerable action, as did the Gatling-gun detachment of four pieces. Eight field guns of large caliber were taken with the expedition, but were not used because they could not be moved into appropriate firing positions. Other artillery included eight field mortars, a Hotchkiss revolving cannon, and an experimental dynamite gun. Of these elements, only one, the Gatling-gun detachment, was to make a significant contribution at Santiago de Cuba.[46]

The Fifth Army Corps has been accurately characterized as ''a collection of efficient small units, not as a fully integrated fighting machine.'' The regulars were well trained and had talented officers to lead them, but few of the commanders had ever headed large formations, certainly not brigades and divisions, and experienced staff officers were in remarkably short supply. Although the Rough Riders demonstrated great *élan,* other volunteer units performed less efficiently and with lower morale because they were granted little or no time to train and lacked modern equipment, particularly the Krag-Jörgensen rifle. Another critical deficiency hampered Shafter's command: the absence of adequate auxiliary support—engineers, medical corpsmen, signal units, reconnaissance troops, and transportation outfits. If the opposing Spanish force had been in truly combat-ready condition, the situation might have become dangerous indeed.[47]

SKIRMISH AT LAS GUÁSIMAS

As soon as a sizeable contingent of troops had been put ashore at Daiquirí, General Shafter began his approach march on Santiago de Cuba. Informing Admiral Sampson that he planned to move against the city as rapidly as possible, he asked only that the navy "keep in touch during the advance, and be prepared to receive any message I may wish to transmit from along the bluffs, or any of the small towns, and to render any assistance necessary." Shafter's orders to General Lawton—or, in his absence, the senior officer at the front—were to advance toward Siboney. He suggested that General Castillo's insurgents lead because they knew the terrain. If Lawton's division encountered no opposition, it was to encamp, entrench, and remain in position just west of Siboney, where it would cover the landing operations there. Kent's division would follow Lawton's, and Wheeler's would bring up the rear. Bates's independent brigade was ordered to support Lawton. The advance toward Siboney began on June 22—the date of the first landings—and was completed without opposition the following day. About six hundred Spanish troops retired as the Americans came up, and by 9:20 A.M. on June 23 Shafter learned that Siboney was in American hands, information that allowed him to begin landings there.[48]

One of the Rough Riders, Joseph Ogden Wells, recorded his impressions of the march to Siboney, a characterization that aptly described many another movement during the campaign around Santiago de Cuba. "Our march was like a pipe organ, having many stops. We were in full marching order; that means each man carries a carbine, a hundred rounds of ammunition, canteen, poncho, half a shelter tent, the army blanket, rations and other necessary articles we were obliged to have." The men's packs became especially irksome as the army encountered difficult terrain. "At last we could stand it no longer and we began to throw away our blankets; after the blanket went cans of meat, then our coats and underclothes, until some only had their guns and ammunition left, for these were essentials." The tendency of the soldiers to discard much of their burden led later to considerable priva-

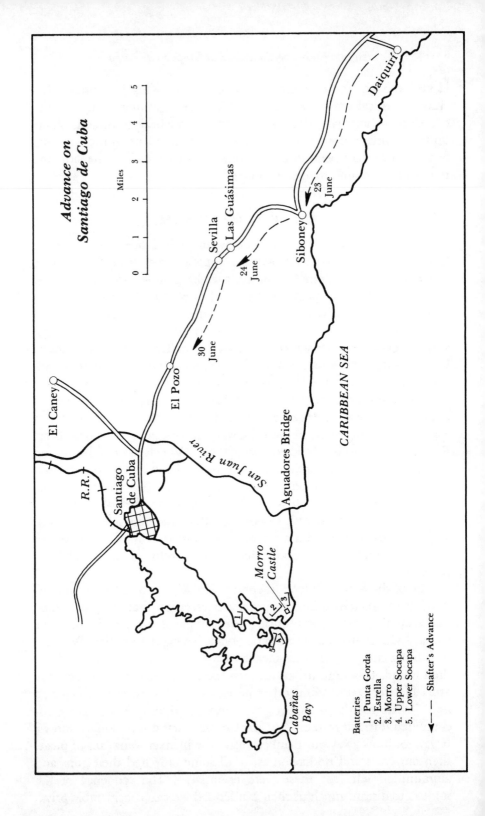

Advance on Santiago de Cuba

Miles

0 1 2 3 4 5

El Caney

R.R.

Santiago de Cuba

El Pozo

30 June

Sevilla

Las Guásimas

24 June

Siboney

23 June

Daiquirí

San Juan River

Aguadores Bridge

CARIBBEAN SEA

Morro Castle

2

3

1

4

5

Cabañas Bay

Batteries
1. Punta Gorda
2. Estrella
3. Morro
4. Upper Socapa
5. Lower Socapa

— — — Shafter's Advance

tion because it proved most difficult to advance supplies through the rough country to the front.[49]

At this stage General Wheeler, commanding the dismounted cavalry, launched a personal initiative that certainly exceeded Shafter's orders. The diminutive ex-Confederate, looking for all the world like a bewhiskered gnome, proved to be nothing if not energetic during his early moments in Cuba. When McKinley had asked Wheeler to accept a commission as Major General of volunteers, the old warrior mentioned his age, but the President waved this objection aside: "There must be a high officer from the south. There must be a symbol that the old days are gone. You are needed." This political consideration placed him in a critical position of responsibility at Santiago de Cuba, as the only Major General present besides Shafter. When Wheeler reached the vicinity of Siboney, a personal reconnaissance and information from the Cuban General Castillo revealed a contingent of Spanish troops located at Las Guásimas, about three miles northwest of Siboney. The enemy, numbering about two thousand, supposedly had a Krupp gun and were digging in, although the Cubans reported that the force intended to abandon the position. Brigadier General Samuel B. M. Young, who commanded one of Wheeler's brigades, proposed to conduct a reconnaissance in force the next morning (June 24) to develop the Spanish position. Wheeler gave permission, taking advantage of the fact that Shafter's orders had been directed to either Lawton or the "senior officer present." Shafter surely had intended the latter designation to apply only if Lawton was unable to act, but since Wheeler was the senior officer where he was, the wily veteran made a singular interpretation of the directive. He decided that it required him to entrench only if he met no opposition, a clear misreading of Shafter's intent. Accordingly Young was sent forward that evening with orders to reconnoiter Las Guásimas the next morning. Castillo promised to support this movement with eight hundred Cubans.[50]

Wheeler had decided to bypass Lawton's division so as to gain credit for the initial action on Cuban soil. Theodore Roosevelt airily obscured Wheeler's reckless and irresponsible initiative in his classic description of the Cuban campaign, *The Rough Riders:* "General Wheeler, a regular gamecock, was as anxious as Lawton to get first blood, and he was bent on putting the cavalry division to the front as quickly as possible." When Lawton learned of this scheme he attempted to alert Shafter, but the General was still offshore aboard the *Segurança* and could not be contacted in time to countermand Wheeler's orders. Shafter's actual wishes, as correctly divined by Lieutenant Colonel Arthur Wagner, were that the entire army should be disembarked and concentrated at Siboney, and that it should be supplied with requisite subsistence and ammunition before moving forward. Wheeler's initiative disrupted this rational deployment and led to serious logistical complications.[51]

Young's plan of attack required his two regiments of regular cavalrymen—the First and the Tenth—to advance northward to the right of his other regiment, the Rough Riders. The more easterly of the routes to Las Guásimas, pretentiously called the *Camino real* (Royal Highway), continued on to Santiago de Cuba. Young's regulars took this way. Colonel Wood and his Rough Riders used a mere path. About a mile separated the two columns, and no provisions were made to preserve contact between them. Richard Harding Davis, who accompanied the Rough Riders, pointed out some of the difficulties inherent in the plan: The troops had to make a strenuous night march to get into position, and were allowed only three hours of sleep before moving out early on the morning of June 24. Small-arms fire was likely to prove inaccurate because the rough terrain did not afford good views of the enemy, and as it happened none of the Rough Riders had ever fired their Krag-Jörgensen rifles.[52]

The Spanish commander at Las Guásimas, General Antero Rubín, had about fifteen hundred troops at his disposal. As the Cuban Castillo had reported, Rubín had orders to fall back on Santiago de Cuba in order to avoid being cut off. A Spanish advance party was placed astride the *Camino real,* with the main force deployed along a ridge of high hills. To the Spanish front rose a truly tangled woodland; General Young's report described it as a "mass of jungle growth, with wire fences, not to be seen until encountered, and precipitous heights as the ridge was approached."[53]

Young's difficult advance of about two hours began at 5:00 A.M. on June 24. Wood, commanding the left wing, remembered the beauty of the morning, the gentle breeze and cloudless sky. "It was difficult to imagine that we were rapidly approaching the enemy and about to engage in the first fight of the Santiago campaign." As the wings of the American formation approached the ridges where the Spanish troops awaited them, their inner flanks almost came together, so that a roughly solid line was formed for the assault. Wheeler and Young hurriedly examined the Spanish position and then ordered their troops to open fire. This action certainly proves that they had in mind something more than a reconnaissance in force.[54]

On the right the jungle, so difficult to move through, suddenly became a friend because it provided excellent cover. Young later claimed that the attack could not have succeeded except for the natural features of the battlefield and the coolness of his regulars: "Headway was so difficult that advance and support became merged and moved forward under a continuous volley firing, supplemented by that of two rapid-fire guns. Return firing by my force was only made as here and there a small clear spot gave a sight of the enemy." He was elated because he had observed no stragglers and because no one had fallen out to assist wounded men.[55]

On the left Colonel Wood and the Rough Riders moved forward with the regulars. Observing enemy fire falling on the units to his right, he ordered his men to return it. After posting a reserve troop to pin down the right flank of the Spanish position, he continued his advance. Soon after the action he wrote enthusiastically of "a most brilliant fight" to his wife: "It was exciting when the entire Spanish line would come up on the knee and pour in a volley at short range and if they would have shot as our people did we would have been wiped out, but one and all of our fellows went on obeying every command, ceasing firing and advancing in good order and pouring in a splendid fire when they were ordered." Lieutenant John J. Pershing, serving with the black troops of the Tenth Cavalry, recalled that his regiment lent valuable support to the Rough Riders at a critical juncture: After charging up the hill, "scarcely firing a shot, [the Tenth,] being nearest the Rough Riders, opened a disastrous enfilading fire upon the Spanish right, thus relieving the Rough Riders from the volleys that were being poured into them from that part of the Spanish line."[56]

After about two hours the Spanish troops began their prepared retirement, and Young's brigade rested on the ridges at Las Guásimas. American observers unanimously but incorrectly assumed that their attack had forced the enemy to retreat. Wood said that the Spaniards "broke and ran like sheep." Someone else reported that, when the Spaniards evacuated their positions Wheeler, the ex-Confederate, yelled, "We've got the damn Yankees on the run!" Whether he did or did not, it made marvelous newspaper copy back home, where sectional feeling dissolved, if only for a season, at the spectacle of American soldiers from the North and South, black and white, fighting shoulder to shoulder against an ancient enemy. No thought of pursuit crossed Wheeler's mind. As Wood wrote, "Our troops were too much exhausted and overcome with heat and hard work of the two preceding days to continue the pursuit. Had we had any mounted men or even fresh foot troops, I think we could have captured a large portion of their force, as they seemed completely disheartened and dispirited." Despite the post-battle exultation, the fight had had its anxious moments, and at one point Wheeler felt called upon to ask Lawton for reinforcements.

The Ninth Cavalry actually came up to the field, but it was not committed. A member of that unit, Major Batson, writing to his wife, roundly criticized the operation: "Some of these fellows will find out sometime or other that a handfull of Americans cannot clean out the whole Spanish Army." The Rough Riders, he said, had moved prematurely and had run into an ambush. "I tell you dear, it is a good thing we are not at war with England or Germany or France, for we would not last a week." Batson detested chaos: "No one knows anything. No one seems to be in command. Every fellow for himself. Can't find out anything." And yet no one could deny that an American force of about a thousand men had caused a Spanish rear guard of about fifteen hundred to abandon the ridges at Las Guásimas. Both armies suffered casualties in the skirmish: Sixteen Americans died and fifty-two were wounded, a rather large toll. The Spanish losses totaled ten killed and twenty-five wounded.[57]

Shortly after the skirmish newspaper accounts in the United States reported as fact the rumor recorded by Major Batson that General Young's force had been ambushed at Las Guásimas, but no evidence exists to support this allegation. Wood was correct in his denial: "All sorts of false reports have started to the effect that we were surprised etc., all of which are absolutely false." The Spanish versions of the fight do not mention an ambush. In all probability the confusion of the struggle in the dense undergrowth below the ridges at Las Guásimas led to the inaccurate reports. The American forces advanced in full knowledge that Spanish troops were ahead, and they actively sought to engage them.[58]

What resulted from the skirmish at Las Guásimas? Shafter held that it measurably improved the morale of his forces. "The engagement had an enspiriting effect on our men," he wrote later, "and doubtless correspondingly depressed the enemy, as it was now plainly demonstrated to them that they had a foe to meet who would advance upon them under a heavy fire delivered from intrenchments." After the war an investigating group appointed by President McKinley, the Dodge Commission, came to a comparable conclusion, even if it correctly decided that the little victory played an "unimportant role" in the campaign. In the flush of victory no one dwelt on the fact that General Wheeler had brought on an unnecessary engagement simply so that he could claim for himself and his command the distinction of having first engaged the enemy in Cuba. Alger asserted that the movement served a useful purpose, because it forced the enemy back upon its main line of defense just outside Santiago de Cuba and provided the American army with "a limited but most welcome area of open and well-watered country in which to rest and prepare for the final assault on the city." He neglected to observe, if he ever knew, that the Spanish force planned all along to withdraw upon any indication of an American attempt to get between it and the city. Castillo's report to Wheeler should have suggested the feasibility of simply turning on Rubín's flanks in order to cause a retreat. A flanking or enveloping movement would have been more appropriate than a frontal attack, which could have been disastrous if the Spanish had elected to stand and fight rather than pull back.[59]

In later years some students of the campaign argued that General Linares, who erred initially in failing to oppose the American landing, made an even more serious mistake in choosing not to defend at Las Guásimas. A check to the Americans might have gained time and seriously undermined their morale. Herbert H. Sargent pointed out the natural strength and strategic significance of the ridges at Las Guásimas, and also the lack of room for maneuver available to the Americans around Siboney. Chadwick, however, disagreed with this view: If Las Guásimas had been defended, it could have been brought under the fire of Sampson's squadron lying off the beach. "There was," he noted, "no point between Siboney and Santiago where such a stand could be taken without exposure to the fire of, at least, the heavier guns." However, since naval gunfire did not prove effective in other situations at Santiago de Cuba, his view is open to debate. In any case, the Spanish army abandoned the position at Las Guásimas, preferring to make a stand closer to its principal fortifications around Santiago de Cuba, and Shafter took advantage of the situation to push troops westward beyond Las Guásimas during the following week.[60]

The skirmish at Las Guásimas reinforced Shafter's commitment to approach Santiago de Cuba along an interior route, and therefore lessened the prospect of a land attack on the heights at the harbor entrance. Once advanced positions are taken, it is after all almost always difficult to abandon them even if they are unsatisfactory. The route to Santiago de Cuba by way of Las Guásimas had few merits; because of the difficult terrain and poor roads, Shafter could not supply his forces adequately along the tenuous line of communications running westward from Daiquirí and Siboney. This fact was to cost him dearly later in the campaign. Were the logistical problems of the interior route to Santiago de Cuba necessarily greater than the tactical difficulties associated with the navy's proposal to attack the Morro and the Socapa heights? It is difficult to judge. In any case, after Las Guásimas little likelihood remained that Shafter would alter his general plan of campaign to accommodate the wishes of Admiral Sampson.[61]

The events at Las Guásimas did not improve relations between the Americans and their Cuban associates. Castillo had promised to join the action, but his troops did not appear on the field. Roosevelt implicitly attributed this failure to cowardice, although Herminio Portell Vilá, a Cuban authority, states that the Cubans properly limited their contributions to providing intelligence and guiding the Americans through the woodland. Portell Vilá criticized Wheeler for violating his instructions, stressing the fact that Rubín had orders not to resist a serious American attack. Rather maliciously, the Cuban historian compared the skirmish of 1898 with a battle that had taken place at Las Guásimas during the Ten Years' War. Four hundred Spaniards were killed and another six hundred wounded in the earlier affray. Whatever the truth about the behavior of the insurgents, stories continued to circulate among the Americans that put them in bad odor. The Rough Rider A. D. Webb—last heard from as he drank "bug extract" on the *Yucatan*—related a story of Cuban cowardice in a letter to the *Arizona Bulletin* that had its counterpart in many another American newspaper:

> An insurgent major boarded our transport before we landed, and after looking us over said we were a fine looking lot of fellows but we needed machetas [*sic*] like his to cut our way through the Spaniards. During the fight [at Las Guásimas] he was seen "cutting his way" to the rear, and using his machete to beat his horse over the back. He has not been seen since.

However improbable this anecdote, it and others like it had considerable effect on millions of Americans who read them.[62]

Shafter did not reprimand Wheeler for having bypassed Lawton in order to attack at Las Guásimas, but he acted immediately to forestall further adventurism of this nature. His vaguely critical instructions to Wheeler after the skirmish deprived the old campaigner of new opportunities to indulge in tactical heroics and revealed his intentions: "Keep your front thoroughly picketed and also your right flank, and well in advance," Shafter cautioned, "but do not try any forward movement until further orders. From where you are now, or approximately there, I wish to advance in force, and will not move until all the troops are well in hand." The American commander planned an early attack, but did not want to risk defeat before he had deployed his forces and furnished them with necessary supplies.[63]

☆ TEN ☆

Battles of El Caney
and the San Juan Heights

The American victory at Las Guásimas prepared the way for a deployment against the Spanish main line of resistance just to the east of Santiago de Cuba. Shafter was anxious to engage the Spanish garrison, but he had to pause briefly in order to make essential preparations. He needed to maneuver troops into position, land supplies, build a line of communications, and decide on a plan of attack. When these tasks were completed, the Fifth Army Corps could then move against Spanish positions located on the San Juan Heights, a series of low-lying hills guarding the portals of Santiago de Cuba.

PREPARATIONS TO ATTACK SANTIAGO DE CUBA

Shafter informed Sampson that he would "advance on Santiago as soon as the command is all ashore, with sufficient rations and ammunition." On June 26 Sampson completed the transfer of García's three thousand troops by sea from Aserraderos to Siboney. Sampson had suggested earlier that García remain west of Santiago de Cuba to intercept reinforcements that might be sent to Linares from Holguín, but Shafter had another mission in mind for the Cuban insurgents. He thought seriously of moving García's troops along the coastal railroad and across a trestle at Aguadores into the vicinity of the Morro, a movement that would hold Spanish troops at the harbor entrance and implant the notion that the main American attack was to be directed at that point. A feint at Aguadores, he informed Sampson, would give "the impression we think the place is strong and intend to make our attack there, whereas we shall do it several miles to the North."

Meanwhile the first American reinforcements had arrived at Siboney. They were Michigan troops, who joined the brigade of volunteers under General Duffield's command. The War Department at this time dispatched the remaining elements of Duffield's brigade from Fortress Monroe and considered moving additional men from Tampa, although the necessary transports had not yet become available.[1]

Shafter decided to direct preparatory operations from the *Segurança* rather than ashore, because he believed that he could control the Fifth Army Corps most effectively from that location—a course that necessitated the designation of the senior officer ashore, General Wheeler, as immediate commander of the troops being concentrated around the village of Sevilla. To make certain that Wheeler held his position, Shafter sent him two direct orders on June 26. The first stated that some four thousand reinforcements were expected from the United States on the next day, a circumstance that would probably delay the advance. It concluded, "Get your men in hand, but make no forward movement." The second read, "Do not advance, but have the country, to the right and left of the road [to Santiago de Cuba], carefully reconnoitred." Despite Wheeler's impetuous action at Las Guásimas, he probably had no intention of acting on his own thereafter. An enlisted man from the Third Missouri Volunteers commented tellingly on the general's appearance at about this time: "Anyone that saw him there realized that he could not, and probably did not, take an active part in the battle." He was "diminutive in size and just a weak, old man. He probably was of some value in an advisory capacity, but nothing more." A lack of vigorous, experienced senior commanders adversely affected operations at Santiago de Cuba from first to last.[2]

By June 26 Shafter's plans had clarified to some degree. Informing Sampson that the Spanish were entrenching to prevent him from moving against the bay entrance south of Santiago de Cuba, he indicated his intention to attack in the area of El Caney northwest of the city, taking advantage of favorable terrain near the pipeline carrying water into the city. He hoped thus to get between the Spanish force and Santiago de Cuba, seeking to force the surrender of the city or drive the enemy toward the Morro. When this action took place, Sampson could locate it by listening to the army's guns. Shafter wanted the navy to prevent reinforcements from crossing the railroad trestle at Aguadores. However, he also wished to preserve the trestle, recognizing that he might need to use the railroad later on.[3]

The region around Sevilla proved trying to the army. It contained sufficient water to meet the needs of the troops, but yellow fever and malaria were endemic there, and the locality provided neither food for the soldiers nor fodder for their animals. Tropical downpours, hot days, and cool nights caused great discomfort, as did insects—mosquitoes, tarantulas, centipedes, and scorpions. Major Frederick E. Pierce of the Second Massachusetts commented particularly on another nocturnal marauder, the ubiquitous land crab: "They are harmless, and, we learned, good eating, but there is something so creepy, crawly and repulsive about them as they click, click over the ground, crawling backward as rapidly as forward, that I should indeed be hungry to try my appetite on one of them." The regulars were accustomed to difficult conditions in the field, but not the Volunteers. Theodore Roosevelt commented graphically on conditions in a letter to his sister: "I've had to sleep steadily on the ground; for four days I never took off my clothes, which were always drenched with rain, dew or perspiration, and we had no chance to boil the water we drank." He experienced difficulty obtaining food for his men. "We had hardtack, bacon and coffee without sugar; but last night we got some beans, and oh! what a feast we had, and how we enjoyed it." He also noted problems posed by the terrain. "So far the country is lovely; plenty of grass and great woods of palms . . . with mango trees and many others, but most of the land is covered with dense tropical jungle. This is what made it so hard for us in the fight [at Las Guásimas]." The suffering of the soldiers who had been wounded that day caused Roosevelt particular distress: "The wounded lay in the path, a ghastly group; there were no supplies for them; our doctors did all they could, but had little with which to do it; a couple died in the night, and the others we took on improvised litters to the landing place." Conditions of warfare in Cuba had begun to sober even the ebullient Roosevelt.[4]

To Alger Shafter expressed confidence that he could take Santiago de Cuba, although he might endure many casualties. "There is no necessity for haste," he argued, "as we are growing stronger and they weaker each day. The health of the command is reported to me by the surgeon as remarkable." Once again he felt called upon to restrain Wheeler: "Under no circumstances, unless you are attacked, must any fight be precipitated. . . . A waiting policy is one that we can afford, at least for a few days, to carry out strictly." Alger authorized Shafter to temporize as long as necessary to make adequate preparations for his attack.[5]

This pause did not sit well with the troops. One sergeant pungently expressed the feelings of those who wanted to move without delay:

Well, now, so this is what they call strategy, and you find it in the books. Well, damn Strategy! I've never read about it, but I am getting blooming tired of the demonstration of it. There's Santiago, and the dagoes, and here we are, and the shortest distance between two points is a straight line; which is something everybody knows, and don't have to study strategy to find out. I am in favor of going up there and beating the faces off them dagoes, and then let the war correspondents make up the strategy, as they seem to be the only ones who are worrying about it.

These sentiments spread by leaps and bounds as Shafter struggled during the last days of June to ready his command for a decisive action.[6]

General Shafter faced serious barriers to communication and difficulties in supplying the units destined to assault Santiago de Cuba. By ingenious methods cable connections had been established as early as June 21 between Guantánamo and Môle St. Nicolas. Direct communication already existed between Washington and the Môle. Later a cable was brought ashore at Siboney, providing connections to Playa del Este at Guantánamo Bay. Thereafter the Fifth Army Corps had a through connection to Washington, a most desirable arrangement. But nothing compensated for the lack of adequate landing facilities, transportation, and roads. Shafter summarized this disadvantage very well when testifying later on before the Dodge Commission about his logistical problems: "Well, Sir, that was the only difficult problem of that campaign. It was simply to get the bare necessaries of life to those men, and it taxed them to the utmost, the pack trains and all—the bare bread and sugar and coffee."[7]

The hastiness of the departure from Tampa soon began to make its effects felt. Because the army failed to provide itself with lighters, steam launches, and other vessels required to transfer goods from ship to shore, it was forced to contend with a bottleneck that could not be eliminated for several weeks. And two navy vessels were lost on the beach, creating additional stresses. Sampson complained that he had done all he could to make up for the army's deficiencies—"ruined many boats and worked many of our men beyond proper limit." He believed that the solution was to assign responsibility for landing operations to the navy, as in British practice.[8]

Secretary of the Navy Long put his finger on another difficulty—inefficient conduct by the War Department. "The Secretary of War bothers me now and then. He is like an unthrifty neighbor who wants to borrow the neighbor's shovel and hoe and horse." He was amused when Alger came to him to report that the army had gone ashore at Santiago de Cuba—thanks to the navy—but had no means of getting supplies and equipment on the beach. "He said he was going to send a tug and a lighter for this purpose, and wanted to know if I could furnish convoy for them." Long acquiesced, but then Alger said, "By the way, can't you lend me a lighter and a tug?'' Long agreed also to this request. Poor planning and lax administrative procedure explain why two weeks passed before Shafter could stockpile supplies only three days in advance of the need for them.[9]

Siboney and Daiquirí became the principal depots in the supply line of the Fifth Corps. Shafter used Siboney as his main base because of its proximity to Santiago de Cuba. He stored subsistence and landed reinforcements at this advanced location. Daiquirí served as storage point for ammunition, forage, land transport, and general supplies. Since horse-drawn wagons proved impractical, the army had to depend on seven mule-drawn pack trains to supply the entire front, as well as the Cuban insurgents, civilian employees, and prisoners of war. A railroad ran west from Siboney along the coast, but because of his decision to move into the interior Shafter had to rely almost entirely on the *Camino real,* a pitiful trail that never became more than a wagon road and most often resembled a rutted path. Several unbridged streams crossed it, forcing troops and wagons to ford at several points. The black loam in the region turned into sticky mud after rainfall—a circumstance that caused long delays when the rainy season began, about a week after the landing. Shafter tried to regularize movements between Siboney and the front, sending pack trains forward by night and returning them to his advanced base by day, but this procedure broke down when rains made streams unfordable and the roadway became choked with broken-down wagons. After tropical disease began to affect the packers and teamsters, a lack of manpower added to Shafter's difficulties. Theodore Roosevelt described the consequences for the units encamped around Sevilla. ''We were not given the proper amount of food,'' he complained, ''and what we did get, like most of the clothing issued us, was fitter for the Klondike than for Cuba. We got enough salt pork and hardtack for the men, but not the full ration of coffee and sugar, and nothing else.''[10]

One of the most serious consequences of the tangle at Siboney and Daiquirí was the decision not to deploy the heavy siege guns that had been brought with the expedition. Explaining to Alger that attempts to move them to the front would result only in blocking the road, Shafter reported his intention to rely solely on light artillery: ''I have four batteries at the front, and they are heavy enough to overcome anything the Spanish have.'' He promised that he would bring up the heavy artillery if he had to besiege the city, but he never managed to do so. To his credit Shafter foresaw certain needs that might be expected to materialize in the later stages of the campaign, and the War Department busied itself with plans to provide additional support.[11]

As Shafter struggled to get provisions and stores to his troops,

General Linares was working just as furiously to prepare for an American assault on Santiago de Cuba. He concentrated mainly on strengthening the city's outer line of defense—running from Escandel through El Caney, San Miguel de Lajas, Quintero Hill, Sueño, Veguita, the San Juan Heights, Chicharrones, certain lagoons, and the Aguadores River to a cove on the seashore. This activity, plainly visible to the American outposts, strengthened the case for an early attack. Captain Chadwick, ruminating on the errors of the campaign a few years later, stressed Shafter's failure to call for naval gunfire against the Spanish troops entrenching themselves on the line from El Caney to the San Juan Heights: "Day and night from the easy distance of 8,000 yards, half a hundred guns could have dropped a continuous shower of shell upon the position, making it absolutely untenable." The failure to consider this option revealed once again Shafter's refusal, whether from ignorance or design, to stress interservice cooperation at Santiago de Cuba.[12]

By June 30 Linares had completed his troop dispositions for the defense of Santiago de Cuba. In the probable area of the American attack he assigned 4,760 men to eleven strong points reaching from Dos Caminos, a mile north of the city, to Las Cruces, a point on the bay. He located 822 men at El Sueño, and exactly the same number along the line from San Juan Hill to Las Cruces. Several of the positions were behind the main line; for example, 140 men were situated at Fort Canosa, a half-mile east of San Juan Hill. Only 520 men were assigned to El Caney and 137 each to San Juan Hill and Kettle Hill, two rises on the San Juan Heights. The Spanish commander held 1,869 troops in reserve within Santiago de Cuba. A total of 3,389 troops were located west of the city at El Cobre, Mazzamorro-Monte Real, Socapa, around the bay, and in the mountain passes. At the Morro another 411 men awaited the American assault. The total Spanish garrison consisted of 10,429 men.[13]

Almost all students of the campaign at Santiago de Cuba have justly criticized these dispositions. Chadwick, for example, noted that Linares "attempted to cover every point of attack which imagination could suggest, instead of concentrating against the advance of an enemy who was to attack from the east, and whose advance could be over one or, at the most, two roads." Shafter had successfully concealed the removal of García from west of Santiago de Cuba, but, given the comparative weakness of the Cubans, the Spanish commander should still have transferred forces from the west to defend against the Americans, especially since he knew that Colonel Escario was approaching from Manzanillo. Because of Linares's extraordinarily unsound dispositions, only a minuscule number of his troops lay athwart the probable path of the assault.[14]

On June 28, when Shafter discovered that Colonel Escario was approaching Santiago de Cuba, he suddenly reversed his decision to build up at a certain leisure. The Spanish force was mistakenly reported to be under the command of General Pando and to number about eight thousand troops rather than the thirty-seven hundred men of actuality. It was assumed that this relief would reach the beleaguered city about July 2 or 3. Accordingly, the American commander decided to attack before that time. His first action was to post García and his men west and northwest of the city to prevent Escario's entrance. Shafter then ordered a reconnaissance of the Spanish positions just east of Santiago de Cuba to obtain needed information. This investigation concentrated on two locations, the town of El Caney and the San Juan Heights, both really outposts in advance of strongly manned positions. El Caney, a small hamlet, lies about six miles northeast of Santiago de Cuba. A strong defensive location, it boasted six wooden blockhouses to the northwest of the town, but the most important fortification was a stone fort called El Viso located about five hundred yards to the southeast. To approach it, American troops moving west from Sevilla could take a very poor road that branched northward off the route to Santiago de Cuba near a high hill called El Pozo. Another road to the southwest provided direct communication between El Caney and Santiago de Cuba. The San Juan Heights rise along the route to Santiago de Cuba, the *Camino real,* about two miles east of the city. Just north of that road lies a relatively low rise dubbed Kettle Hill. San Juan Hill rises about four hundred yards further southwest, a fairly imposing elevation about one hundred twenty-five feet high with a brick blockhouse at the summit. Just east of Kettle Hill and San Juan Hill flows a small stream, the San Juan River. About a thousand yards west of the San Juan Heights there was a strong line of fortifications. Many barbed wire entanglements, rifle pits, and trenches had been prepared on the Heights and to their rear.[15]

The reconnaissance of the Spanish positions made on June 30 proved spotty. Lieutenant Colonel Arthur Wagner later was scathing in criticism of it, arguing that the investigation of the region east of El Pozo resembled Moses's observation of the Promised Land from Mount Pisgah. He maintained that a "half-dozen small patrols, each under the command of an officer . . . directed to push forward until the enemy was touched upon or his position absolutely discovered, would have resulted in gaining information that would have saved an infinitude of trouble." Much more was learned about El Caney, where Brigadier

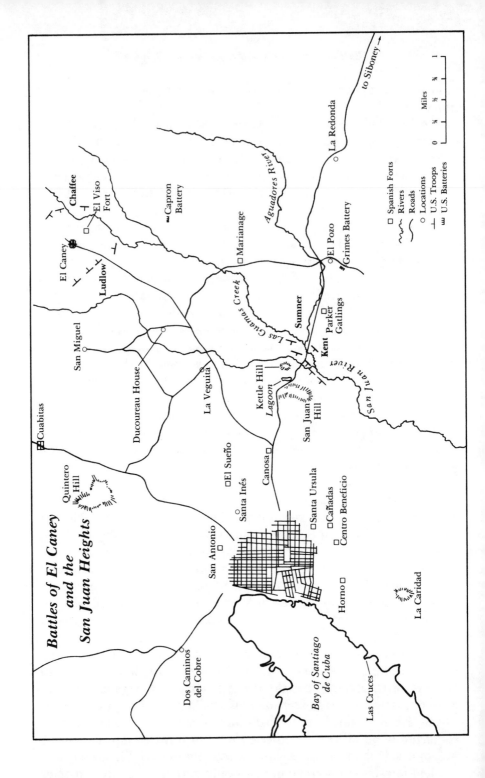

Battles of El Caney
and the
San Juan Heights

to Siboney

La Redonda

Chaffee

El Viso
Fort

Capron
Battery

Aguadores River

El Caney

Marianage

El Pozo
Grimes Battery

Ludlow

Las Guamas Creek

Sumner

San Miguel

Parker
Gatlings

Kent

Ducoureau House

La Veguita

Kettle Hill

Lagoon

San Juan
Hill

San Juan River

Cuabitas

El Sueño

Canosa

Quintero
Hill

Santa Inés

Santa Ursula

Cañadas
Centro Beneficio

San Antonio

Horno

La Caridad

Dos Caminos
del Cobre

Bay of Santiago
de Cuba

Las Cruces

□ Spanish Forts
〜 Rivers
⌒ Roads
○ Locations
┴ U.S. Troops
⊞ U.S. Batteries

Miles

0   ¼   ½   ¾   1

Generals Lawton and Adna R. Chaffee made extensive observations on June 28 and June 29. El Caney struck Shafter as an important location because it lay astride the road to Guantánamo. Also, Spanish forces could easily move from that vicinity to attack the flank of American units deployed in front of the San Juan Heights, or, alternatively, strike southward to cut American communications from Siboney to the front. On June 29 General Wheeler correctly reported that General Joaquín Vara del Rey held El Caney with a garrison of over five hundred troops, but he thought that the enemy would probably evacuate the position without a flight. If Vara del Rey remained, he could be driven out or captured without much difficulty.[16]

Shafter's information about El Caney and the San Juan Heights led him to plan two secondary attacks in support of a main assault on Kettle Hill and San Juan Hill. General Lawton's division, with General Bates's independent brigade in support, was ordered to attack El Caney at daybreak on July 1 At the same time General Duffield with his Michigan Volunteers was to demonstrate at Aguadores—the navy assisting—to trick the Spanish into believing that the attack would center on the heights at the harbor entrance. Duffield's feint was intended to discourage Linares from reinforcing the San Juan Heights with troops now located south of that position. The other infantry division, that of General Kent, and General Wheeler's dismounted cavalry division were to make the main attack on the San Juan Heights. General Lawton would come to reinforce Kent and Wheeler as soon as he had reduced El Caney, marching to join the battle along the road to Santiago de Cuba and taking a position on the right flank of the main assault force next to the dismounted cavalry. Shafter assumed that Lawton could participate in the main assault because he expected El Caney to fall in no more than two hours. The attack on the San Juan Heights would begin only after El Caney had been taken and Lawton had marched into position. On June 30, after the plan of operations had been issued, Lawton enjoined Shafter's adjutant, "McClernand, do not order the other divisions to attack until I get up. Give me time to reduce El Caney." This remark suggests that Lawton might possibly have anticipated delays in the operation at El Caney. One light artillery battery, under Captain Allyn K. Capron, would support Lawton at El Caney. Another battery, commanded by Captain George Grimes, would fire on the San Juan Heights from El Pozo. Two other light batteries, under Major J. W. Dillenback, were placed in reserve. After the surrender of El Caney to Lawton, García's insurgents were expected to interdict Colonel Escario's column approaching from Manzanillo, northwest of the city.[17]

Shafter intended to storm the San Juan Heights, rout the enemy, and capture Santiago de Cuba all in one fell swoop. Since this accomplishment would render the harbor untenable for Cervera, the principal objective of the expedition would have been attained—and by the United States Army. A successful attack on July 1 would not only preclude reinforcement of Santiago de Cuba from Manzanillo or Guantánamo but provide good docking facilities for American ships. Access to the harbor of Santiago de Cuba would lessen logistical problems and permit completion of the mission before disease could make serious inroads on Shafter's command.

Well before the engagement, however, Shafter's plan began to come apart. The three divisions did not begin the march to their pre-battle bivouacs until late in the afternoon of June 30. Because these movements were not completed until after midnight, many troops did not get proper food or rest. At the same time sickness took its toll of the principal commanders. Wheeler became sick, and General Samuel S. Sumner took over the dismounted cavalry division. Colonel Wood supplanted General Young, also taken ill, in command of the second brigade of dismounted cavalry; this arrangement left Lieutenant Colonel Roosevelt at the head of the Rough Riders. Shafter neither issued specific directions to his divisional commanders nor granted them discretion; he intended to direct the battle from a headquarters located more than a mile east of El Pozo, not realizing the difficulties of maintaining efficient communications with units scattered all the way from El Caney to Aguadores.

Shafter's inertia stemmed in part from illness. A chronic victim of gout, he reacted adversely to the heat and overexertion experienced on June 30, a circumstance that partially accounts for his failure to move closer to the action on July 1. He could observe both El Caney and the San Juan Heights from a high hill near his command post, but he did not obtain a full view of the terrain until he went to El Pozo after the assault. During the early morning of July 1, at 3:00 A.M., Shafter called in his adjutant, Lieutenant Colonel McClernand, and ordered him forward to El Pozo so that he could relay messages between the two attacking forces and general headquarters. Messengers and telephone lines would be used to transmit information and orders. Shafter's trusted aide-de-camp, Lieutenant John D. Miley, was sent forward to the San Juan Heights in order to coordinate operations in that area. This cumbersome system proved incapable of functioning properly on the day of the battle. For this reason staff officers had to make decisions without specific authority from Shafter, and small-unit commanders had to act without direction from superiors. At this juncture, then, the army's inexperience with larger formations—brigades and divisions—came home to roost. The battles of July 1 lacked real coordination; for the most part they "fought themselves."[18]

At daylight on July 1 General Duffield moved along the railroad toward Aguadores to conduct the planned diversion. Sampson had originally ordered his flagship, the armored cruiser *New York,* and the *Suwannee* and *Gloucester* to commence firing on Aguadores at 6:00 A.M., but this action was deferred until 9:20 A.M. because Duffield experienced considerable delay in getting into position. His troops detrained about a mile and one-half from the objective, an unnecessary precaution because the warships offshore could easily have provided cover at a more advanced point. The Michigan troops thus consumed considerable time marching toward Aguadores. When they arrived at the railroad trestle, a span of about seven hundred feet, they discovered that the Spanish had destroyed forty feet of its western end. None of Duffield's troops crossed the deep gorge, of course, and they never obtained good positions from which to direct fire on the Spanish defenders opposite. Only about two hundred seventy-five Spanish soldiers opposed the American force of twenty-five hundred. After desultory firing, Duffield withdrew at about 1:30 P.M. and returned to Siboney. Secretary Alger later claimed that this operation deterred Linares from reinforcing the San Juan Heights, but he cites no supporting evidence. The demonstration at Aguadores exercised little or no influence on the battles to the north.[19]

At El Caney General Lawton readied his division for an attack at 7:00 A.M. He expected to gain control of the Spanish position by 9:00 A.M., an accomplishment that would permit his troops to move southwest on the road to Santiago de Cuba to join the two other divisions of the Fifth Army Corps (Generals Sumner and Kent). The San Juan Heights would be assaulted at 10:00 A.M. Lawton placed his left—Brigadier General William Ludlow's brigade—astride the Santiago de Cuba road to cut off a possible retreat for the Spanish defenders. His right—Brigadier General Adna R. Chaffee's brigade—was located near the stone fort. He held his third brigade—under Colonel Evan Miles—in reserve. Capron's battery of light artillery—four 3.2-inch guns—was posted about twenty-three hundred yards south of El Caney. He would not have to deal with return fire because General Vara del Rey had no artillery. Capron opened at about 6:30 A.M., but his fire proved ineffective, the shots scattering. They were not concentrated on the principal ₛtrong point at El Caney, the stone fort El Viso. Only toward the end of the action, after Capron changed his position and gave full attention to El Viso, would the light artillery make a useful contribution. Clearly the guns should have been advanced further earlier, since they received no counter-battery fire. In any event more than these four light guns were required to provide sufficient support for a frontal assault on a naturally strong position such as El Caney. (The two artillery batteries held in reserve behind El Pozo played no real part in the battles of July 1.)[20]

At 7:00 A.M., as planned, Lawton's infantry opened with small arms on El Caney from ranges of six to eight hundred yards, attracting immediate return fire from well-sheltered defenders in entrenchments and blockhouses, and it soon became evident that El Caney would not fall easily. Lawton might have broken off the engagement then or continued it with a small force, proceeding with all or most of his men to the San Juan Heights, but he persisted in his full-scale attack. The morning wore on without indications that the garrison in El Caney was weakening, while casualties mounted on both sides. Given the stubborn resistance, Lawton decided to commit his reserve brigade and General Bates's independent brigade. Because the landing at Daiquirí had been unopposed and victory had come fairly easily at Las Guásimas, the Americans assumed that the Spanish soldiers would not fight well, even in a strong defensive position. They learned differently at El Caney.[21]

The Spanish garrison, armed only with Mauser rifles and lacking artillery support or rapid-fire weapons, sustained an untenable position for well over eight hours, despite the rain of fire that descended upon it throughout the action. Around noon the gallant Vara del Rey was killed, and two of his sons also fell that day. Only about five hundred twenty Spaniards held the position against Lawton's division of about fifty-four hundred men. All of the American troops, except for the Second Massachusetts Volunteers, were seasoned regulars. The volunteer outfit was handicapped during the battle because it had to use Springfield rifles, which required black powder. A few Cuban insurgents participated in the battle but limited their contribution to rifle fire at long range.[22]

Lawton's failure to overrun El Caney in good time had important effects on the deployment before the San Juan Heights. When McClernand first observed the delay from his post at El Pozo, he deferred the order to start the movements of the two divisions poised to attack Kettle Hill and San Juan Hill. When he then recognized that further hesitation would cause serious confusion, he finally authorized Sumner and

Kent to begin their movements. Sometime after noon Shafter ordered Lawton to break off the assault on El Caney and move to below the San Juan Heights, to his prearranged position to the right of the American line—the line that was supposed to sweep across those elevations and storm the city. Shafter later spoke frankly of his feelings at this stage of the battle: "I was fearful I had made a terrible mistake in engaging my whole army at 6 miles intervals, and I sent word to Lawton to come to Wheeler's right and help there." When the messenger, Captain J. C. Gilmore, Jr., delivered Shafter's order, Lawton resisted. Withdrawal at this late moment would constitute defeat; moreover, his brigades were so deeply committed that it might have been impossible to disengage. Shafter went along with Lawton's request to continue, and the attack on El Caney was pressed to a finish.[23]

At long last Capron's battery obtained the range of El Viso, and its fire opened the way for a climactic charge on that position that finally began bringing the engagement to a close. At about 3:00 P.M. the Twelfth Infantry from Chaffee's brigade finally overwhelmed the stone fort with the assistance of regiments from Miles's and Bates's brigades. Two hours more were required to end all resistance from the wooden blockhouses and entrenchments around El Caney. The Spanish force retreated only when it had been reduced to 80 men. Almost half the garrison had been killed or wounded—about 235 men—and about 120 were made prisoner. Of the original 521-man garrison only about 100 managed to get back to Santiago de Cuba, the other survivors having been dispersed during the retreat. American losses were numerically much heavier, although the total represented a small percentage of the troops engaged in the battle: 81 died and 360 suffered wounds. Over 14 percent of the Seventh Infantry endured casualties. Members of the Second Massachusetts had special praise for the Twenty-Fourth Infantry, a black regiment: "They knew no such word as fear, but swept up the hill like a legion of demons." When asked why his unit had taken no prisoners, one soldier replied, "What you talkin' 'bout, boss; we didn't come here to play basketball."[24]

Diverse evaluations were made of the struggle at El Caney. While Chadwick thought that both Americans and Spaniards ought to take pride in it "as an unsurpassed example of manly courage and military devotion," he maintained, as have many others, that Shafter should never have ordered a frontal attack on such a strongly fortified position. If El Caney had been ignored, or a relatively small force assigned the task of holding its garrison in place, Lawton's division would have been available for the main assault on the San Juan Heights, and Santiago de Cuba might have fallen that day. Secretary Alger, who felt that things had turned out well, made the truly curious argument that, had the attack on El Caney developed as expected, the assault on Santiago de Cuba would indeed have been pressed to a conclusion at the cost of many unnecessary casualties: "I shall always regard the unexpected delay in taking [El] Caney as one of the many incidents connected with the Santiago campaign in which the guiding hand of Providence seems to have interposed for America," he maintained stoutly. Lieutenant Colonel Wagner offered a more mundane defense of the operation, reiterating the need to protect the right flank at the San Juan Heights and cut off the road to Guantánamo, but he did not explain why these purposes could not have been accomplished without making a costly assault on an isolated and well-fortified but unreinforceable position. The Spanish authority Müller noted that the loss of El Caney deprived Santiago de Cuba of both its water supply and its zone of cultivation, but he maintained that these objects could have been attained without committing an entire division to a sanguinary peripheral battle, particularly if this maneuver divided the American army in the face of an undetermined number of defenders entrenched in a relatively unreconnoitered area.[25]

THE SAN JUAN HEIGHTS

The San Juan Heights commanded the eastern approach to Santiago de Cuba, and General Linares based his defense on this terrain. He developed a network of fortifications about four thousand yards in length anchored on San Juan Hill, part of a precinct (*recinto*) encompassing the area from Dos Caminos to Fort Punta Blanca. The Spanish had a good view of the places where the American forces would have to deploy prior to their attack. Linares established his headquarters at Fort Canosa, about a mile behind the heights. He believed that he could assign only about seventeen hundred men to hold the heights, assuming that the rest of his force would be needed to contain the insurgents and support the impending advent of Colonel Escario. Originally Linares posted very small contingents on San Juan Hill and Kettle Hill, but later he added reinforcements that brought the total number of soldiers there to 521. Three companies of the Talaveras regiment were moved from the districts of San Antonio and Santa Inés just north of Santiago de Cuba and placed in reserve. This group of 411 men, under the direct orders of the Spanish general-in-chief, had two pieces of artillery at its disposal—a 6.3-inch gun and a 4.7-inch gun. A contingent of sailors sent from the Spanish squadron to assist in the defense of the city supported Fort Canosa. Just behind this location a third line of mounted loyalist Cubans, 140 in number, screened the remaining Spanish forces assigned to the San Juan Heights—a reserve of about 4,350 troops composed of regulars, sailors, *voluntarios,* and firemen. Almost 1000 men of this reserve, however, were in hospitals.[26]

On June 30 Sumner's dismounted cavalry division bivouacked near El Pozo, and Kent's infantry division stationed itself astride the road to Santiago de Cuba somewhat further to the rear, the positions from which the two units would move into battle on July 1 against the Heights. At about 7:00 A.M. the first of Sumner's two brigades began its approach march along the main road to the city. Kent made preparations to follow with his three brigades. At about 8:00 A.M. Grimes's battery of four 3.2-inch light guns, posted near El Pozo, opened fire on the Heights at a range of about twenty-six hundred yards. Smoke from the black powder used by the Americans soon revealed the battery's position to the enemy, who, familiar as they were with the locale, had no difficulty obtaining the range of El Pozo. The Spanish guns firing from behind the Heights soon silenced the American artillery. As a result about eight thousand men had to struggle along a congested road directly before a strong position without appreciable artillery support.[27]

An inflatable hot-air balloon was raised and carried along the road, and Lieutenant Colonel G. McC. Derby, commander of the balloon unit, went aloft to make observations. When Derby located a small trail turning left (south) off the road to Santiago de Cuba, Kent was ordered to advance by that route to his assault position beneath San Juan Hill. This maneuver was designed to relieve congestion. Unfortunately, the observation balloon fully disclosed the American line of march and attracted a galling fire that caused numerous casualties. Colonel Wood, who described the advance as one made "in a dense mass wholly unprotected and without any definite plan of action," considered the balloon reconnaissance "one of the most ill-judged and idiotic acts" he had ever witnessed, and many others agreed with him. Richard Harding Davis described the plight of the troops exposed to enemy fire on the road:

> Men gasped on their backs, like fishes in the bottom of a boat, their heads burning inside and out, their limbs too heavy to move. They had been rushed here and there wet with sweat and wet with fording the streams, under a sun that would have made moving a fan an effort, and they lay prostrate, gasping at the hot air, with faces aflame, and their tongues sticking out, and their eyes rolling.

Troops in this condition were highly vulnerable to heavy fire from the enemy. At length Derby's balloon was disabled, but while in the air it contributed considerably to the list of casualties. If Shafter had earlier conducted a thorough reconnaissance of the region west of El Pozo, he would not have needed the balloon, and his troops could have deployed efficiently. A participant in the attack belonging to the Thirteenth Infantry, one of the organizations in Kent's First Brigade, reported afterwards that no one ''from the Division Commander on down had had an opportunity to examine the ground leading to the Spanish position or to reconnoitre that position to ascertain its physical geography and learn the number and direction of the Spanish works and how they were manned.''[28]

Certain geographic features influenced the planned deployment of the Fifth Army Corps prior to the assault on the San Juan Heights: Two streams cross the road to Santiago de Cuba east of the San Juan Heights. One is the Aguadores River, flowing north less than a mile from El Pozo, and the other the San Juan River itself, running south about six hundred yards in front of San Juan Hill. East of the San Juan River dense thickets impeded movement but offered cover. From the river to the base of San Juan Hill there stretched a valley overgrown with waist-high grass.

Sumner's cavalry division was expected to proceed over the road to Santiago de Cuba and then turn north into a position near the San Juan River from which it could move across Kettle Hill. The troops would then move past a lagoon and onward to the San Juan Heights proper. When Lawton's division would arrive after reducing El Caney, it would take up a position to Sumner's right and presumably attack the most northerly extension of the elevations to the front. Meanwhile, Kent's infantry division would turn south off the road in order to form for a movement across the meadow to San Juan Hill.[29]

This plan came unglued for two reasons: Lawton was detained at El Caney, and the two divisions assigned to overrun the San Juan Heights encountered unanticipated delays. The assault was supposed to begin at 10:00 A.M., but had to be postponed until well after noon. Even after Kent located the trail forking to the left off the main road and directed two of his brigades to take it to positions from which to march on San Juan Hill, progress proved agonizingly slow. To complicate the situation further, at this point there occurred one of the most unfortunate events of the day. Brigadier General Hamilton S. Hawkins, commanding one of Kent's brigades, ordered the Seventy-First New York Volunteers to take the lead into the assault position. When the First Battalion of this inexperienced regiment encountered severe fire, it recoiled on the units behind it. General Kent and some of his staff officers were able to prevent a wild flight, but the men of the Seventy-First failed to resume their advance; Kent had them leave the trail and lie down, so that the Sixth and Sixteenth Infantry, Hawkins's two other regiments, could move past the volunteers into positions just to the left of the road. Colonel Charles Wikoff, commanding a brigade that included the Ninth, Thirteenth, and Twenty-Fourth Infantry, managed to get his troops started into position at the left of Hawkins's brigade, although he was killed before he could complete his deployment. When the first two brigades of Kent's division got into line, Colonel Edward P. Pearson brought up the third brigade to support them. The Second and Tenth Infantry came up behind the slain Wikoff's brigade, he having been succeeded by Lieutenant Colonel Ezra P. Ewers in command, and the Twenty-First Infantry backed Hawkins. All this movement had to take place under plunging fire from the heights ahead. No American artillery or small-arms fire was directed on the enemy at this time, a circumstance that undoubtedly added to the casualties. Meanwhile the dismounted cavalry division struggled to its assault position below Kettle Hill. The first brigade, made up of the Third, Sixth, and Ninth Cavalry, anchored its left on the road. Slightly to the north, Colonel Wood brought his brigade into line—the First and Tenth Cavalry and the Rough Riders.[30]

At long last the two divisions were poised for the attack on the San Juan Heights. Shafter tersely summarized the situation: "After completing their formation, under a destructive fire, and advancing a short distance, both divisions found in their front a wide bottom in which had been placed a barbed-wire entanglement, and beyond which there was a high hill, along the crest of which the enemy was strongly posted." A British correspondent summed up what many must have felt at the time: "But this hill—the look of it was enough to stagger any man. Was this to be taken practically without the aid of artillery? Artillery should have battered, and battered, and battered the position, and then the infantry might have swept up at the run." Alas, there was no such preparation. "The infantry stood before the thing alone."[31]

At this point Lieutenant Miley, Shafter's aide on the scene, at the urging of General Sumner authorized a charge on his own responsibility, although Lawton had not arrived on the line and the San Juan Heights seemed to pose a truly formidable barrier. The Fifth Army Corps must attack or retreat; it could not sustain itself for long in the exposed positions below the Heights. Sumner's and Miley's decision, courageous and correct, started both divisions simultaneously across the bottomland to the front. The hour was about 1:00 P.M., some three hours after the planned time of the assault.[32]

On the left Hawkins's brigade moved toward San Juan Hill. As it stumbled through the high grass towards the slope leading up to the blockhouse atop the elevation, the most important action of the day took place. At 1:15 P.M. a Gatling-gun detachment—three weapons firing .30 caliber ammunition—opened on the Spanish positions atop the hill at ranges of six to eight hundred yards. Second Lieutenant John H. Parker, commander of this detachment, sustained his fire for only eight and one-half minutes, but it provided essential support while the Americans made their charge. The gunners poured fire on the hilltop at a rate of up to thirty-six hundred rounds per minute, and quickly forced the defenders to abandon their positions. As the Americans went up the Western slope, with the Sixth and Sixteenth Infantry in the lead, the enemy fled down the other side towards Santiago de Cuba. As Captain Leven Allen, commander of Company E of the Sixteenth, recalled the events, after he and the other junior officers got their units through various obstacles, he and his men started up the hill along with some troops from other units. About two-thirds of the way to the summit, he heard cries of "Come back!" and bugles sounding recall. This commotion apparently stemmed from fears that friendly fire directed at the summit would cause casualties. After much confusion Allen and other small-unit commanders resumed their advance and took possession of the summit.[33]

An inexplicable Spanish error benefitted the Americans. Enemy firing positions were located at the very top of the hill rather than at its "military crest"— that is, the point below the summit from which defenders could obtain an unobstructed view to the bottom of the slope. Private Charles Johnson Post of Company E, Seventy-First New York Volunteers, noted, "From the military crest to the actual crest was but twenty to thirty feet and no charge can be stopped within such a distance." Even if the Spanish defenders had remained in their positions, they could not have fired effectively on Americans moving up the hill. In any event, Lieutenant Parker's Gatling guns permitted General Hawkins to complete his charge successfully without engaging in a serious fire fight at the summit.[34]

As the infantry was storming San Juan Hill, Sumner's dismounted cavalrymen moved on Kettle Hill, a small elevation lying between them and the northern extension of the San Juan Heights. The Ninth Cavalry led, with the First Cavalry and the Rough Riders following closely. Lieutenant Colonel Roosevelt preceded his men on horseback. Forty yards from the top of Kettle Hill he had to dismount, but was among the first to finish the climb afoot. As in the case of San Juan Hill, the enemy had abandoned the summit by the time the first Americans reached it. No supporting fire was directed on Kettle Hill. From this elevation some of the troops paused to pour rifle fire on the southern crest of San Juan Hill. The remainder of Sumner's regiments, including three cavalry regiments—the Third, Sixth, and Tenth Cavalry—and a few men from other organizations moved forward near or on the south slope of Kettle Hill and kept advancing toward the more northerly part of San Juan Hill. During this action Sergeant George Berry of the Tenth Cavalry carried not only the colors of his own regiment but those of the Third Cavalry, shouting to his comrades, "Dress on the colors, boys, dress on the colors." Meanwhile the white officers of the Tenth, a black unit, suffered the heaviest casualties of any group of officers during the battle of San Juan Heights; eleven out of twenty-two were killed or wounded.[35]

Once on Kettle Hill Roosevelt obtained permission from General Sumner to join the advance on the northern extension of San Juan Hill. He and his troops flowed over a little valley to the front, moving past a small lagoon. "Long before we got near [the enemy entrenchements]," wrote Roosevelt, "the Spaniards ran, save a few here and there, who either surrendered or were shot down." When he reached the trenches on the summit of San Juan Hill, he claimed to have found them "filled with dead bodies in the light blue and white uniform of the Spanish regular army. . . . Most of the fallen had little holes in their heads from which their brains were oozing; for they were covered from the neck down by the trenches." In this respect T.R. may have exaggerated a bit; at least two participants reported that no trenches existed in this area. Colonel Alexander Bacon of the Seventy-First New York commented tartly, "These trenches being, then, imaginary, it is fair to argue that they were filled with imaginary, dead Spaniards." Roosevelt also claimed to have killed a retreating Spanish soldier at this point in the battle, shooting him at about ten yards' range with a pistol that had been aboard the battleship *Maine* when it went to the bottom. Roosevelt's brother-in-law, Commander William S. Cowles of the navy, had presented the weapon to him. Another participant in the attack also fired on a different Spanish soldier in the immediate vicinity of Roosevelt, but the leader of the Rough Riders did not learn of this act until later. Almost any veteran of combat would echo his comment on this circumstance: "It is astonishing what a limited area of vision and experience one has in the hurly-burly of a battle."[36]

After the battle American newspapers and magazines printed sketches that depicted a mounted cavalry charge on the San Juan Heights against a heavy concentration of Spanish troops. Margaret Leech corrected this thorough misrepresentation in summary terms: "There had been no massed attack; only thin lines of men in blue and a few in dusty brown, plunging across a meadow under the crackling rifle pits, trying to tear barbed wire with their hands or saw it with their bayonets." Death came to a good number. "Many of them quietly sank in the slippery, waist-high grass, or stumbled to pitch forward in its depths. The others waded on to climb the steep, sunny slopes." The action on Kettle Hill was the most important event in the life of Theodore Roosevelt. Leech wrote, "There was the stuff of which heroes are made in the bespectacled volunteer officer, charging the Spanish earthworks at a gallop, with a blue polka-dotted handkerchief floating like a guidon from his sombrero." The New York aristocrat later parlayed his performance in Cuba into a vice-presidential nomination that at length brought him into the presidency.[37]

Once in possession of the San Juan Heights the American attackers halted, instead of continuing on to Santiago de Cuba. The two divisions immediately began a confused attempt to strengthen the newly won position, fearing that the Spanish army might attempt a counterattack. No such effort materialized; the Spanish soldiers who evacuated the San Juan Heights fell back to strong defensive positions at the outskirts of the city, a line of fortifications much stronger than the positions on the heights. Since General Linares had suffered a serious wound, command devolved upon General José Toral. The events of July 1 dispelled the illusion that the Spanish defenders were incapable of determined resistance against a courageous army. The defenders at El Caney had been outnumbered by twelve to one, and the margin at the San Juan Heights was even greater—sixteen to one. But even had no obstacles presented themselves, the Americans could not have continued on to the city. The regiments were exhausted; artillery support was unavailable; and only a small part of the Fifth Army Corps had gotten into position for the assault. Only about three thousand out of over fifteen thousand effectives gained the Heights in the initial movement. Since the closest Spanish outposts were but a few hundred yards distant—well within rifle shot—the Americans began feverish efforts to entrench themselves.[38]

Shafter immediately reinforced the San Juan Heights, giving up all thought of capturing Santiago de Cuba in one bound. He found himself in a difficult position, because—as was to happen on numerous other occasions during the campaign—he had made no plans for strengthening the position his troops had seized, having expected to spend July 2 in Santiago de Cuba rather than a mile or so away on uninviting hillsides. His first report of the action to Washington conveyed the situation accurately: "We have carried their outer works and are now in possession of them. There is now about three-quarters of a mile of open country between my lines and city." He hoped to have his troops entrenched in considerable force by the next morning. "I regret to say that our casualties will be above 400. Of these not many are killed."[39]

Shafter soon discovered that he had grievously underestimated his losses. A total of 1,385 Americans fell; 205 men were killed and 1,180 wounded. Lawton's division suffered casualties of 81 killed and 360 wounded at El Caney. At the San Juan Heights Kent's division lost 89 killed and 489 wounded. The cavalry division under Sumner suffered the least, but still had 35 killed and 328 wounded. Officers were particularly hard hit; 22 were killed and 94 wounded. If the additional casualties inflicted on July 2 and 3—amounting to 9 killed and 125 wounded—are considered, casualties amounted to about 10 percent of the American forces engaged on July 1. Spanish losses—including the 235 casualties at El Caney— were 215 killed, 2 taken prisoner, and 376 wounded, for a total of 593. About 35 percent of the 1700 troops engaged against the Americans became casualties. Of the Spanish officers, 16 gave up their lives. Theodore Roosevelt explained why the American losses far exceeded those of the Spaniards: "It would have been very extraordinary if the reverse was the case, for we did the charging; and to carry earthworks on foot with dismounted cavalry, when these earthworks are held by unbroken infantry armed with the best modern rifles, is a serious task."[40]

Many students of Spanish strategy and tactics at Santiago de Cuba have been intensely critical of General Linares. Why did he not concentrate more troops at the San Juan Heights? Why did he not make use of naval guns, either by taking them ashore or having them fire from the bay? Only a minute percentage of the troops available to him were at El Caney and the San Juan Heights at the time of the American attack. If Linares had concentrated troops at appropriate places and used available artillery effectively, he might have stopped the Americans and forced them into defensive operations. There might then have ensued "a race between supply and the progress of the fevers in the area." This speculation assumes that the Americans would not have exploited tactical opportunities and the naval guns available to them. It also neglects the fact that General Linares would have had to prevent Cuban infiltration and protect civilians in Santiago de Cuba. Nevertheless, taking into consideration the various constraints on the Spanish commander, it seems he should have placed on San Juan Hill more than the 521 troops he had at the moment of the American attack. He should have used artillery fire to defend the position before the attack and harass it afterward. It is also difficult to understand why he did not order a counterattack. It is true that Linares was gravely wounded during the battle, but certainly this contingency should have been anticipated and arrangements made to ensure continuity of command.[41]

The failures of Linares somewhat obscured Shafter's mistakes on July 1. He did not have to attack El Caney in great strength. A holding attack would have been sufficient to immobilize the garrison there, and in any event victory at the San Juan Heights would force the Spanish troops at El Caney to withdraw or surrender. An unduly complicated plan and an entirely inadequate reconnaissance delayed the attack on the San Juan Heights and vitiated its power. If it had not been for Parker's Gatlings, Shafter might have come under severe criticism for failure to make proper use of his artillery and the guns of Sampson's squadron. Had Shafter avoided these mistakes, could Santiago de Cuba have been captured on one bound? It seems unlikely, because extensive fortifications and troop concentrations were placed just outside the city on the line of the planned attack. Overall, Shafter neglected to develop adequate command and control. The battles of July 1 fought themselves, particularly the struggle at the San Juan Heights. The outcome was by no means a complete American victory; the objective, after all, had been Santiago de Cuba itself.[42]

Once the battle reached a conclusion Shafter bent every effort to strengthen his position, an activity that continued through the night of July 1 and the next day. As for Lawton, after finally completing the reduction of El Caney he hastily set out for his assigned position on the right flank of the American line before the San Juan Heights. Just southeast of El Caney near a prominent landmark, the Ducoureau house, an advance guard drew fire from the enemy. Because of this unexplained opposition, Lieutenant Colonel McClernand ordered a change of route. Thus Lawton's arrival at the Heights was delayed until noon on July 2. Ironically, his eventual position on line was only about a mile from where the advance guard had attracted fire the day before. Bates's independent brigade, which had supported Lawton at El Caney, moved rapidly to the San Juan area and came into the line at its extreme left, linking up with Kent's division. General Duffield's volunteer brigade—including a unit that had just arrived, the Ninth Massachusetts Volunteers—went into the line with Bates. The Thirty-Fourth Michigan Volunteers were placed in reserve to the rear of Kent. García's Cuban insurgents took position just to the right of Lawton, but their lines did not extend sufficiently westward to block the Manzanillo road that passed through Dos Caminos.[43]

Shafter also relocated his artillery and the Gatling-gun detachment.

The light batteries were placed at appropriate sites behind the line of fortifications on the San Juan Heights, and Parker's Gatling guns were drawn right up to the front and employed there. Roosevelt accurately described their importance: "Indeed, the dash and efficiency with which the Gatlings were handled by Parker was one of the most striking features of the campaign; he showed that a first-rate officer could use machine guns, on wheels, in battle and skirmish, in attacking and defending trenches, alongside of the best troops, and to their great advantage." Some exchange of fire took place on July 2 and July 3, both sides suffering additional casualties, but the Americans made no further attempts to pierce the inner Spanish defenses—much stronger than those that had already been carried—and General Toral made no effort to counterattack.[44]

Black regiments, as at Las Guásimas and El Caney, made a signal contribution to the attack on the San Juan Heights. The Twenty-Fourth Infantry participated in Kent's charge on the blockhouse. The Ninth and Tenth Cavalry joined in the assault on Kettle Hill and the movement to the northern extension of the San Juan Heights. Lieutenant John J. Pershing—whose nickname "Black Jack" derived from his service with the Tenth Cavalry—summarized the views of most white officers in command of black troops on July 1: "We officers of the Tenth Cavalry could have taken our black heroes in our arms. They had again fought their way into our affections, as they here had fought their way into the hearts of the American people." Roosevelt reported later that he had threatened to shoot some blacks of the Ninth Infantry who had begun to drift away from the San Juan Heights, but firmness solved the difficulty. According to T.R., the "smoked Yankees"—a Spanish term for the American blacks—responded to the Rough Rider's commands thus: "[They] flashed their white teeth at one another, as they broke into broad grins, and I had no further trouble with them, they seeming to accept me as one of their own officers." He was prepared to acknowledge the work of black troops under the command of white officers. "Where all the regular officers did so well, it is hard to draw any distinction; but in the cavalry division a peculiar meed of praise should be given to the officers of the Ninth and Tenth for their work, and under their leadership the colored troops did as well as any soldiers could possibly do." George Kennan, a careful observer, was less patronizing and more unqualified in his judgment: "I cannot' refrain from calling particular attention to the splendid behavior of the colored troops," he wrote in *Campaigning in Cuba*. "It is the testimony of all who saw them under fire that they fought with the utmost courage, coolness, and determination." He reported Roosevelt as saying to a squad of blacks "that he never expected to have, and could not ask to have, better men beside him in a hard fight."[45]

The Fifth Army Corps paid a grievous price for its hasty preparations as it attempted to succor the men who fell wounded on July 1. Caspar Whitney, a *Harper's* correspondent reporting on the aftermath of the battle, drew a grim picture of the situation along the road to Siboney on July 2: "Dead men lying along the road, ghastly in their unstudied positions, men dying, men wounded, passing back to the division hospital, some being carried, some limping, some sitting by the road-side, all strangely silent, bandaged and bloody," The dross of combat lay all around. "Beyond the second crossing, the road was strewn with parts of clothes, blanket rolls, pieces of bacon, empty cans, cartridges; at the forks the marks of bullets everywhere—the trees shot through and through." Medical support was limited at best, and the choked roadway prevented many wounded soldiers from reaching assistance. Many men suffered greatly and many died before they could be brought to dressing stations or the hospital at Siboney. In a desperate effort to transport casualties to the rear the army resorted to improvised litters and wagons. Lieutenant Colonel Valery Havard, reporting on the use of mule-drawn wagons as ambulances, noted the grisly conse-quence: "If we consider the abominable condition of the roads, the unruly state of drivers and mules, and the great difficulty of procuring the means of preventing jars and jolts, it is not saying too much that the four or five miles of wheeled transportation from the battlefields to the field hospital cost the lives of not a few patients." Medical facilities brought to Siboney proved insufficient to meet the needs of the Fifth Army Corps. The service was overwhelmed at this point, when it had to deal with unexpectedly large numbers of casualties, and would be later when tropical disease began to take its toll.[46]

AFTER THE BATTLES

The battles of July 1 took much of the fight out of the American army, and particularly out of its commander. Müller could not refrain from musing about the striking inactivity of the Americans after El Caney and the San Juan Heights: "On the first of July the Americans fought . . . without protection and with truly admirable courage, but they did not fight again as they did that day." Instead, they entrenched themselves and assumed a defensive posture. "Did they think on that first day that all they had to do was to attack our soldiers en masse and put them to flight?" His speculation was perhaps all too close to the truth. As for Shafter, he was in poor health—suffering from both gout and malaria—and the failure to take Santiago de Cuba definitely depressed him. Margaret Leech wrote aptly, "One day's fighting had used up all his aggressiveness. He had broken his egg and spoiled his omelet; and, sick in mind and body, he shrank from exposing his army to further combat."[47]

Immersed in his own problems, Shafter failed to consider the truly desperate situation inside Santiago de Cuba. When the Americans halted to entrench themselves on the San Juan Heights, only about three hundred Spanish soldiers—of whom about a third were convalescents from the hospital—manned the positions immediately to the front. Toral attempted to remedy the situation; practically all the troops that had been garrisoned to the west (except those at the crucial Socapa heights) were transferred to the city. His hasty reorganization created a line of five or six miles between Dos Caminos and Punta Blanca. He managed to get fifty-five hundred men into positions along this line with another thousand in reserve. All his units, however, were in desperate straits: Less than two hundred rounds of ammunition remained for each soldier. The capture of Cuabitas had robbed the defenders of their water supply, and no more food could be brought in from the cultivated zone. What miserable rations remained in the city were distributed to them; civilians went without sustenance. Once the Americans gained control of the San Juan Heights, the city lay open to attack. From protected positions on the ridge small-arms fire and rapid-fire weapons could support an assault. If heavy siege guns were brought up, the Americans could shell Cervera's ships in the harbor. These circumstances certainly suggested to Toral abandonment of the city and retreat into the interior, but this option was not available: All routes to the north and west were cut off, and the Cuban insurgents controlled the countryside west of Santiago de Cuba.[48]

Shafter's activities during the two days following the battles at El Caney and the San Juan Heights reflected preoccupation with his own army's difficulties rather than adequate appreciation of the enemy's situation. He feared the Spanish forces might turn on his flanks or that enemy troops en route from Manzanillo might reinforce Toral. He recognized the terrible defect in his line of supply from Daiquirí and Siboney to the San Juan Heights, and feared that disease might soon create difficulties. Also, tropical storms—frequent visitors to the Caribbean during July—might seriously disrupt his maritime communications to the United States.

Seeking a way to improve his position, Shafter inquired of Wheeler about a plan to send "a division in rear of the left division [Kent] to clear out the forts along the entrance to the bay so as to let the Navy in and have the business over. Can it be done?'' Here was a striking reversal of attitude. If earlier Shafter hoped to claim for the army the limelight at Santiago de Cuba, the chastening effects of the battles led him to consider seriously a version of the scheme that Sampson had once unsuccessfully urged upon him. Wheeler, however, did not think that the Morro could be attacked easily. Because the Spanish positions provided excellent locations for artillery, he argued that an attack would result in great losses. Further serious bloodshed was one of the things that Shafter most wanted to avoid, so he immediately dropped all thought of attacking the entrance to the harbor.[49]

Shafter next gave serious consideration to retreat! At 7:00 P.M. on July 2 he called a conference of his generals and conveyed his impressions of the situation, saying to the assembled group, ''I have been told by a great many this afternoon that we cannot hold the position, and that it is absolutely necessary for us to retreat in order to save ourselves from being enfiladed by the Spanish lines and cut off from our supplies, as an attack by the Spanish with a few fresh troops would result in our utter defeat.'' He made much of the possibility that Spanish troops from Manzanillo were approaching Santiago de Cuba, and that others might come from San Luis, Holguín, and Guantánamo. Of this concern Chadwick wrote with ill-concealed disdain: ''The difficulties of transport experienced at the moment by the American army should have been assurance of the impossibility of concentrating 25,000 men [Spanish] by way of the mountain trails of Cuba.''[50]

Roosevelt later claimed that he opposed withdrawal and that Wheeler, sufficiently recovered from his illness to resume activity, supported him. ''No possible number of Spaniards coming at us from in front could have driven us from our position. . . . There was not a man on the crest who did not eagerly and devoutly hope that our opponents would make the attempt, for it would surely have been followed, not merely by a repulse, but by our immediately taking the city.'' Despite these brave words written many months after the event, Roosevelt did express considerable alarm in a letter written on July 3 to his friend, Senator Lodge: ''Tell the President for heaven's sake to send us every regiment and above all every battery possible. We have won so far at a heavy cost; but the Spaniards fight very hard and we are within measurable distance of a terrible military disaster; we *must* have help—thousands of men, batteries, and *food* and ammunition.'' He gave vent at this time to strong criticism of Shafter: ''Our General is poor; he is too unwieldy to get to the front.'' He was proud of his own performance at the San Juan Heights but sad about the casualties. ''For three days I have been at the extreme front of the firing line; how I have escaped I know not; I have not blanket or coat; I have not taken off my shoes even; I sleep in the drenching rain, and drink putrid water." Richard Harding Davis, a seasoned observer, also noted the fears of the troops before Santiago de Cuba at this time. "One smelt disaster in the air. The alarmists were out in strong force and were in the majority."[51]

With the exception of a brief message received in Washington July 2 indicating that he had underestimated his casualties, Shafter had failed to enlighten his superiors concerning the outcome of the battle and his prospects. The only information arriving in Washington came from newsmen. Alger remained with the President until 4:00 A.M. on the morning of July 3, waiting anxiously for news. Eight hours later the Secretary of War notified Shafter plaintively of this fruitless vigil with McKinley. Congratulating his general "most heartily" on his victory, he added, "I wish hereafter that you would interrupt all messages that are being sent to the Associated Press and others, and make report at the close of each day, or during the day if there is anything of special importance, at once." Clearly the home front was becoming decidedly anxious and impatient.[52]

About forty-five minutes after Alger sent this message, he finally received most discouraging word from Santiago de Cuba. Shafter reported the city so strongly defended that he could not make a frontal assault. For this reason he was "seriously considering withdrawing about five miles and taking up a new position on the high ground between the San Juan River and Siboney, with our left at Sardinero, so as to get our supplies, to a large extent, by means of the railroad, which we can use, having engines and cars at Siboney."[53]

This message caused the greatest consternation in Washington, because withdrawal in the face of the enemy would have been extraordinarily humiliating; it elicited immediate attempts to bolster the resolve of the commander in the field. McKinley and Alger left the decision to Shafter, but gave unequivocal indications of their desire that he remain on the San Juan Heights. "Of course you can judge the situation better than we can at this end of the line," they noted. "If, however, you could hold your present position, especially San Juan Heights, the effect upon the country would be much better than falling back." They promised reinforcements. Sensing Shafter's despondency, General Corbin sent a reassuring message: "You can have whatever reenforcement you want. Wire what additional troops you desire and they will be sent as rapidly as transports can be secured." To make good on this pledge the War Department feverishly spurred efforts to dispatch help. Brigadier General Guy V. Henry at Camp Alger, Virginia was ordered to send two regiments immediately to Cuba from Newport

News and transfer the rest of his command to Charleston, South Carolina for early shipment. All of these troops, amounting to about ten thousand men, had been intended for the projected invasion of Puerto Rico. Meanwhile Secretary Long searched for transports.[54]

Reports from Santiago de Cuba caused President McKinley to consider replacing Shafter on grounds of ill health. After meeting with Alger and Corbin he sent a message to Santiago de Cuba stating that if Shafter did not mend and General Wheeler also remained ill, the command should be transferred to the next ranking general. Later that day General Miles received orders to go to Cuba to be available in case of need. Full of plans for action at Santiago de Cuba—particularly a scheme to land at the west side of the harbor entrance, in accordance with Sampson's earlier proposal—the commanding general immediately dispatched a message to Shafter, announcing his impending advent with "strong reinforcements."[55]

Prior to the engagements of July 1, Shafter had been remarkably consistent in his reluctance to accord the navy any other than a subordinate role in operations against Santiago de Cuba. He had rejected out of hand Sampson's proposal that the army initially attack the forts at the harbor entrance, and he had not taken full advantage of the squadron's weaponry, limiting naval gunfire to bombardments on the day of the landing and in support of Duffield's feint at Aguadores on July 1. Chadwick later emphasized Shafter's failure to arrange a naval bombardment before the Fifth Army Corps moved on the San Juan Heights: "Had this been done it is probable that no action would have taken place outside of Santiago, and that the Spanish forces would have become so demoralized that the American troops could have entered the city at once with little difficulty." A general staff system in the War and Navy Departments, Chadwick decided, would have coordinated military and naval operations at Santiago de Cuba more effectively. Although naval gunfire against fortifications generally proved less efficacious than expected, the fact that Parker's Gatling guns contributed so importantly to the success at San Juan Hill lends credence to Chadwick's observation. Shafter's failure to try the squadron's guns against the Heights prior to his assault, if only to test their potential, stands out as a truly serious flaw in his conduct of the campaign.[56]

On July 2 Shafter suddenly reversed his course, asking Sampson to attack the forts at the harbor entrance. Reporting that he had experienced a "terrible fight" the previous day and that his lines were within a mile of the city, he continued, "I urge that you make effort immediately to force the entrance to avoid future losses among my men, which are already very heavy. You can now operate with less loss of life than I can.'' Sampson responded by telephone through his aide, Lieutenant Sidney A. Staunton. He minced no words in refusing to act alone. "Impossible to force entrance until we can clear channel of mines—a work of some time after forts are taken possession of by your troops. Nothing in this direction accomplished yesterday by the advance on Aguadores.'' Shafter's irritated rejoinder to Sampson's message reflected his unduly pessimistic estimate of the situation: "It is impossible for me to say when I can take the batteries at entrance to harbor. If they are as difficult to take as those we have been pitted against, it will be some time at a great loss of life.'' Probably Shafter's comment reflected Wheeler's advice. Neither seems to have realized that naval gunfire on the Morro and Socapa batteries, as well as others along the channel, might have vastly eased the task of assaulting the positions. Of course there was always the possibility that Cervera might then bring his naval guns into action against the American positions on the San Juan Heights. Shafter then cast a bitter aspersion: "I am at a loss to see why the Navy can not work under a destructive fire as well as the Army. My loss yesterday was over 500 men.'' (Apparently he still did not realize that his total casualties were well over a thousand.) Shafter requested that Sampson continue firing on Punta Gorda. His conclusion must have interested the Admiral: "I expect, however, in time and with sufficient men, to capture the forts along the bay.''[57]

Sampson then wrote a sensible letter to Shafter in which he clarified his reasons for not wanting to storm the entrance. He was not concerned about the Spanish artillery. The guns in the shore batteries posed no problems; they could fire only to seaward and were no match for the blockading squadron. What troubled him was the danger from mines known to have been laid in the narrow channel. For his ships to run into the harbor, it would be necessary to sweep this passage, a task that could not be accomplished unless the army first seized the heights. "It was my hope,'' he noted, "that an attack on your part on these shore batteries would leave us at liberty to drag the channel for torpedoes.'' Then, most deferentially, he stated, "If it is your earnest desire that we should force our entrance, I will at once prepare to undertake it. I think, however, that our position and yours would be made more difficult if, as is possible, we fail at our attempt.'' After briefly mentioning that he had already inaugurated counter-mining operations, he refuted Shafter's intimation that the navy was not prepared to make sacrifices like those of the army. "It is not so much the loss of men,'' he asserted, "as it is the loss of ships which has, until now, deterred me from making a direct attack on the ships within the port.''[58]

The Navy Department had to consider the overall strategic situation as well as the tactical problems Sampson faced at Santiago de Cuba. It had to bear in mind the resources required to mount operations against Puerto Rico and against Spanish naval units in European waters. It also had to take into account the contingency, however remote, that Spain might somehow obtain support from another naval power. The United States could not risk the loss of a single armored ship. Secretary Long expressed this concern clearly: "The attitude of Continental Europe forebade the reduction of our armored naval strength, because upon it we might have to rely for defense not only from the Spanish force in European waters but from an attack by the navy of another country." Shafter did not weigh his request in this light. Once again the lack of a general staff organized to concert strategy and further interservice cooperation impeded efficient conduct of the campaign at Santiago de Cuba.[59]

To straighten out the disagreement between the army and the navy Sampson sought a meeting with Shafter. He wanted to complete counter-mining operations in the channel and then send in the squadron. The Marines encamped at Guantánamo could be brought in to storm the Morro heights; better still, the army might attack the Morro while the Marines would operate against the Socapa batteries. Sampson decided to visit Shafter on the morning of July 3. When the General reported to Alger that the Admiral was coming to the front in order to consult on future operations, he also went out of his way to inform the Secretary of War that he had no intention of stepping aside: "I have been unable to be out during the heat of the day for four days, but am retaining the command." Just before 9:00 A.M. on Sunday, July 3 the flagship *New York* left the blockading squadron for the run eastward to Siboney, whence Sampson planned to travel to Shafter's headquarters. However, at about 9:35 A.M., the Admiral, standing on the quarterdeck of the *New York,* observed gunsmoke at the harbor entrance about seven miles distant. By a cruel strike of fate he had moved away from the blockade just before Admiral Cervera finally made his attempt to escape from the American grasp.[60]

On this very morning Shafter made an unexpected decision at the suggestion of his adjutant. Lieutenant Colonel McClernand recalled a conversation with Shafter on board ship while the Fifth Army Corps was proceeding to Santiago de Cuba in which the General had stated that, after getting the army into position around Santiago de Cuba, he would demand the enemy's surrender and then act according to developments. McClernand entered the tent where Shafter lay ill on his cot. "General," he said, "let us make a demand upon them to surrender." Shafter thought for a full minute—which unsettled the adjutant because it seemed to presage a rebuff—but Shafter finally said, "Well, try it." McClernand immediately prepared a demand for the surrender of the city, and it was dispatched to General Toral at 8:30 A.M. under a flag of truce. This message, formal and terse, wasted no words on amenities: "Sir: I shall be forced, unless you surrender, to shell Santiago de Cuba. Please inform the citizens of foreign countries and all men and women they should leave the city before 10 o'clock to-morrow morning." That afternoon, at about 6:30 P.M., Toral replied simply, "It is my duty to say to you that this city will not surrender and that I will inform the foreign consuls and inhabitants of the contents of your message."[61]

Between the time that Shafter sent his demand and the hour of Toral's rejection a dramatic transformation in the situation occurred at Santiago de Cuba: Admiral Cervera's squadron attempted to break through the blockade. After Shafter heard of Cervera's departure, he acceded to the urgent request of several foreign consuls that he permit noncombatants to leave Santiago de Cuba for El Caney. Toral was informed that the American bombardment would be delayed until July 5 so that civilians could evacuate the city—provided no attack was made on the Fifth Army Corps. At 7:31 P.M. on July 3 Shafter sent a cable to the War Department reporting that he had made a demand for surrender and that quiet had descended along the battle line. He gave as his opinion that "from news just received of escape of fleet am satisfied place will be surrendered." Apparently he did not yet know the extent of the damage that Cervera's squadron had sustained. After learning the truth, he told General Wheeler, "Now that the fleet is destroyed I believe the garrison will surrender, and all we have to do is hang on where we are and very soon starve them out."[62]

All thought of withdrawing from the San Juan Heights now vanished; Alger was relieved to receive a message in which Shafter stated flatly, "I shall hold my present position." Shafter elaborated his intentions on July 4: "I can hold my present line and starve them out, letting the noncombatants come out leisurely as they run out of food, and will probably be able to give such as are forced out by hunger food to keep them alive. I await your orders." The naval victory vastly encouraged the troops entrenched on the San Juan Heights. A regimental band, which had somehow managed to bring its instruments to the front line, played "The Star-Spangled Banner" and "There'll Be a Hot Time in the Old Town Tonight." Men cheered from one end of the front to the other, soaked to the skin from the persistent rain but happy indeed.[63]

A discordant note was sounded just after Cervera's departure, however, when Shafter learned that Colonel Escario with over three thousand troops had managed to enter Santiago de Cuba on the night of July 2. However, the flight of Cervera eased his mind as did news that reinforcements from the United States were on the way. Shafter had not completed his investment of the city to the north and west quickly enough to close the road from Manzanillo. He intimated at the time and later that García, assigned to guard the Manzanillo road, was at fault. For his part García informed General Gómez that he had not been able to restrain Escario, because this course of action required him to break contact with the right flank of the Fifth Army Corps; in other words, he lacked sufficient manpower to cover both Shafter's flank and the road from Manzanillo. Philip Foner claims that Shafter was really responsible for the entrance of Escario, because he had prevented despatch of a large force to harass the Spanish column along its line of march. In any event the Cuban insurgents did slow Escario sufficiently to preclude his arrival before the battles of July 1. Müller argued that, had the column entered the city earlier, the San Juan Heights could have been held against "almost the whole hostile army." Others, however, have observed that Escario's forces actually complicated the defense of the city, because they placed undue strain on limited supplies of food and ammunition.[64]

Soon after the war General Shafter summarized his views of the difficulties that developed on July 1. The only "hitch" had been Lawton's failure to reduce El Caney on schedule, but "as it turned out, it was better as it was, for had he been on the right on the Caney road at 10 o'clock, we should have taken the city of Santiago that day, and would have had none of the territory or outside soldiers that we got later." He neglected to add that, if the city had fallen on July 1, the Fifth Army Corps would not have been forced to endure considerable suffering thereafter. A member of the Sixteenth Infantry, John E. Woodward, in a diary entry on July 4 expressed relief at news that General Miles was on his way. "I hope he get[s] here on time," he began. "The heat is terrible on the men in the trenches & water is getting rather bad and if we advance much further I don't know what we will do for water." He was particularly exercised about the "*rotten* hospital service up here at the front." He did not know what would have happened "if it was not for Pvt Lemon Co F who was a physician."[65] Woodward might have taken comfort at the outcome of the naval battle that had just taken place the previous day. It vastly improved the prospects of the Fifth Army Corps entrenched on the San Juan Heights.

☆ ELEVEN ☆

The Sea Battle of Santiago de Cuba

The American victories at El Caney and the San Juan Heights, how-ever qualified, exposed Admiral Cervera's squadron to great danger. After the landing at Daiquirí the Spanish naval commander debated his future course with his superiors, torn between accepting battle with Sampson's squadron and the equally uninviting prospect of remaining at Santiago de Cuba. The martial events of July 1 forced a decision in favor of flight.

CERVERA'S PREPARATIONS FOR A SORTIE

On June 23, the day after the Fifth Army Corps began to land at Daiquirí, Admiral Cervera received an unwelcome message from the Ministry of the Marine that authorized him to sortie from the bay at Santiago de Cuba. Thereafter he devoted a great deal of time attempt-ing to avoid any such operation. On June 24 he argued in a meeting of his captains that the squadron could not hope to escape. A terse sum-mary of the proceedings supported the Admiral's opinion: "When each officer had stated his opinion on the present situation, it was unani-mously agreed that the sortie is now, and has been ever since the 8th in-stant, absolutely impossible." Of course, if the Spanish squadron could not fight at sea, it might support the forces on land. With this tactic in mind, the officer commanding the Spanish artillery at Santiago de Cuba inspected the guns aboard Cervera's ships on June 25 to determine how they might be used to protect the city. Captain Villaamil, commanding the destroyers, told one of his officers that the guns of the squadron should be emplaced around the city and all the seamen except skeleton crews landed to reinforce the army. When asked about the wisdom of a sortie, Villaamil responded, "I believe that such a determination will be a sad loss for the country, without honor or profit."[1]

Unfortunately for the squadron Governor General Blanco had committed himself to a sortie. He soon made known his opinion that Cervera "should go out from Santiago as early as possible whenever he may deem best, for the situation in that harbor is, in my judgment, the most dangerous of all." If the squadron surrendered without making a fight, "the moral effect would be terrible, both in Spain and abroad." Blanco's view was determinative, because Cervera had been placed under his command. The Admiral reacted immediately, giving vent to the desperate pessimism that he had manifested from the beginning: "I have considered the squadron lost ever since it left Cape Verde," he told Linares, "for to think anything else seems madness to me, in view of the enormous disparity which exists between our own forces and those of the enemy." He had a number of reasons for opposing a sortie: His ships would have to steam out of the harbor one by one, and he had no means of disguising their departure. "The absolutely certain result will be the ruin of each and all of the ships and the death of the greater part of their crews." Had there been any hope of escape, he would long since have made the attempt, although it would merely have changed the scene of action unless he could have managed to reach Havana, "where things might, perhaps, have been different." In a histrionic conclusion he expressed his personal views without the slightest equivocation: "I state most emphatically that I shall *never* be the one to decree the horrible and useless hecatomb which will be the only possible result of the sortie from here by main forces, for I should consider myself responsible before God and history for the lives sacrificed on the altar of vanity, and not in the true defense of the country." The admiral never thereafter varied from this attitude.[2]

Cervera's arguments once again failed to sway the Governor General. On June 26 Blanco informed him that he exaggerated the difficulties associated with a sortie, and proposed that the squadron go out at night in bad weather. To Cervera's conviction that Santiago de Cuba was certain to fall, he replied, "This is an additional reason for attempting the sortie, since it is preferable for the honor of arms to succumb in battle, where there may be many chances of safety." On the same day Minister of the Marine Ramón Auñón cabled his opinion that the squadron should attempt to run the blockade during the hours of darkness.

Cervera's counter was that an evening sortie would be more dangerous than one during the day because at night the American squadron moved close to the entrance of the channel. Apparently Blanco tired of these protests; on June 28 he gave the Admiral a direct order to leave Santiago de Cuba, either at a favorable opportunity or when the city seemed about to fall. To cover himself the Governor General took the precaution of clearing his decision with Madrid. Preparing to execute the order, Cervera attempted to have his shore party return to the ships. When Linares replied that he might be unable either to give due notice of disaster or release the crews, Cervera approached Blanco once again, reporting that he could not obey the Governor General's instructions without his seamen and asking for further instructions.[3]

At this point the battles of El Caney and the San Juan Heights took place, and Cervera was forced to consider his future course. When he convened his captains for another council of war, all agreed that conditions forcing departure had developed; but, since most of the crews were ashore, the proper course was to obstruct the entrance to the harbor so that Sampson could not force it, presumably by sinking a vessel in the channel. Once more Cervera sought to dissuade Blanco from ordering a sortie, reporting that General Toral required his sailors for the defense of the city. Besides, he added, "our sortie would look like flight, which is repugnant to all." These arguments failed to impress Blanco. His orders to General Toral left no more room for maneuver: "It is absolutely necessary to concentrate forces and prolong defense as much as possible, by every means preventing enemy from taking possession of harbor entrance before sortie of squadron, so as not to have to surrender or destroy ships." When Lieutenant Francisco Arderius, who had been ashore that day, described the land battle to Captain Villaamil, the commander of the destroyers expressed sadness that such sacrifices would not lead to a good end. When asked why, Villaamil replied that the squadron would have to depart and with its "certain loss" would end all chance of preserving control of "these lands that today are defended with so much . . . heroism." At 10:30 P.M. Blanco sent another order amplifying his previous instructions: Cervera was told to embark at the first opportunity, taking whatever route he deemed best. He mentioned that only three American ships blockaded Cienfuegos and that nine were then on station off Havana. Concerned about the possibility that the American army might soon seize the entrance to the channel, he asked Cervera to depart as soon as possible.[4]

Throughout the day of July 2 Toral attempted to shore up the city's defenses. Blanco ordered his commander at Santiago de Cuba to do all that was necessary to support Cervera's sortie, and also to hold out until reinforcements arrived from Manzanillo or Guantánamo. If he could not maintain himself, he should "gather all troops and loyal citizens, try to open a path, and fall back upon Holguín or Manzanillo, destroying what can not be taken and burning everything left behind, so that not the least trophy of victory will fall into the enemy's hands." Apparently he soon thought better of this order, instructing Toral to defend the city as long as possible and then link up with approaching relief columns. The most important consideration was the exit of the squadron, "for if Americans take possession of it Spain will be morally defeated and must ask for peace at mercy of enemy." A lost city could be reconquered, but "the loss of the squadron under these circumstances is final, and cannot be recovered." To Cervera he dispatched a final, crushing command: "In view of exhausted and serious condition of Santiago, as stated by General Toral, your excellency will reembark landing troops of squadron as fast as possible and go out immediately."[5]

At about 7:00 P.M. on July 2 Admiral Cervera gave his orders for the sortie. The squadron would leave around 9:00 A.M. the next morning, a Sunday, with the *Infanta María Teresa* in the lead. This vessel would engage the first available target. The three other armored vessels would follow—the *Vizcaya, Cristóbal Colón,* and *Almirante Oquendo*—and the destroyers *Furor* and *Plutón* would bring up the rear. Since the speedy *Brooklyn* was the most dangerous American vessel, the armored cruisers would give it preference as a target. The destroyers, utilizing their superior speed, would concentrate on escaping rather than fighting. Those ships running the blockade successfully were to steam for Cienfuegos or Havana. In his account of events at Santiago de Cuba Captain Víctor Concas emphasized the narrowness of the channel, a circumstance that forced the Spanish ships to go out one by one at a relatively slow speed. Therefore, each exiting vessel risked the concentrated fire of the American ships.[6]

A number of authorities have argued that Cervera should have sortied at night in accordance with the wishes of Blanco and Auñón. Commander Jacobsen, for example, thought the ships should have gone out under cover of darkness and steered in various directions, avoiding combat and reuniting at a prearranged rendezvous point. Cervera later explained his reasons for preferring daylight hours: The American squadron always closed up at night while one of the armored vessels, at a distance of less than a mile, illuminated the channel entrance with searchlights. Picket boats (vedettes), standing even closer in, provided additional observation. "Under these circumstances," claimed Cervera, "it was absolutely impossible to go out at night, because in this narrow channel, illuminated by a dazzling light, we could not have followed the channel and would have lost the ships, some by running aground, others by colliding with their companions." In any event, if some or all of the Spanish ships had gotten out of the channel, they would still have encountered the concentrated fire of the entire enemy squadron. Had modern artillery been available at the Morro and Socapa batteries, the American ships would have had to remain at a distance of five or six miles from the entrance, a circumstance that might have permitted a successful nocturnal sortie. However, Admiral Sampson, evaluating Cervera's decision later, decided that Cervera should have come out at night in bad weather. He might have counteracted the searchlights by shooting them out or employing his own. Sampson, it should be stated, did not mention the navigational problems that Cervera thought of such great significance. One thing is indisputable; the American decision to illuminate the entrance by night vastly complicated the task of the Spanish squadron. It was a simple but brilliant tactical improvisation.[7]

THE ACTION OF JULY 3

On Sunday, July 3, the weather proved clear and hot, with only a light northwest breeze to ruffle the smooth sea—a beautiful day for a desperate enterprise. Early that morning Captain Concas—who had become Cervera's chief of staff after Captain Bustamante was mortally wounded on July 1—made final observations at the channel. He noted that the *Brooklyn*, fastest of the American ships, lay further out than usual, leaving a gap in the western end of the blockade semicircle. This chance situation prompted Cervera to decide to run west for Cienfuegos. He now planned to ram the *Brooklyn* with the *Infanta María Teresa*, a deed that might assist the other vessels in making their escape. At 8:00 A.M. the flagship ran up a signal—*zafarrando de combate* ("Clearing for action")—and a little later *salir según orden prevenido* ("Leave following prepared order"). Then Cervera signalled *Viva España*. The hecatomb he had envisioned was at hand.[8]

The blockading squadron lying outside the channel entrance that morning was somewhat under its usual strength. The battleship *Massachusetts* and three other vessels—the cruisers *New Orleans* and *Newark* and the converted tender *Suwannee*—had steamed east to Guantánamo Bay for coal. Another armored ship, the cruiser *New York*, had left the blockade with Admiral Sampson aboard, accompanied by the armed yacht *Hist* and the torpedo boat *Ericsson*. As already mentioned, Sampson was bound eastward to Siboney, whence he would travel to General Shafter's headquarters. Seven vessels remained off the channel entrance, stretching in a rough semicircle. From east to west they were the converted yacht *Gloucester;* the battleships *Indiana, Oregon, Iowa,* and *Texas;* the armored cruiser *Brooklyn;* and the *Vixen,* another converted yacht. About eight miles separated the *Gloucester* and the *Vixen* at the ends of the semicircle. The Morro rose three or four miles distant from the ships. The blockading squadron had been going through its normal Sunday routine, including inspection, reading of the Articles of War, and divine service. Sampson's departure left Commodore Schley in command of the blockading squadron. Margaret Leech thought it remarkably ironic that "on that morning hour, of all the days and hours, [Sampson] should have been required to dance attendance on the bungling General; that Cervera should have chosen the westward course, carrying the battle ever farther from the American commander in chief, casting its honors to the insubordinate Commodore whose conduct he despised."[9]

The rival squadrons were vastly different in strength. That of Spain included only four armored cruisers and two destroyers, whereas the American squadron included four battleships, two armored cruisers, three converted yachts, and one torpedo boat. Cervera's ships displaced 28,280 tons, to 49,038 tons for Sampson's squadron. The Spanish ships had mounted only forty-two large guns to seventy-six aboard the American vessels—an imposing differential when it is recalled that a number of the Spanish guns were in disrepair and ammunition for certain of the weapons was unreliable. Only in crew complements was there virtual equality—2,261 Spanish sailors to 2,341 Americans. The difference in the strength of the two squadrons during the engagement was magnified because the Americans had an opportunity to destroy the enemy squadron in detail—that is, one at a time. Each Spanish ship had to exit the channel alone, exposing itself for some period to concentrated American firepower.[10]

Captain John Philip summarized the situation thus: As of 9:35 A.M., when the *Infanta María Teresa* came out, "Cervera's sally had been so long expected that when it actually came it was unexpected. I, for one, did not dream that, after declining the issue for a month, he would come out in broad daylight." The *Iowa* immediately raised Signal 250—"The enemy is attempting to escape"—and the American crews were rapidly called to quarters. Captain Henry C. Taylor told later of frantic reactions on the *Indiana:* Seamen assigned to the powder division were "throwing themselves down the steep ladder in their eagerness to reach their posts, until the ammunition deck was swarming with bruised and bleeding men, staggering to their feet and limping to their stations." On the *Oregon* a seaman remembered that when the *Infanta María Teresa* made its appearance "all of a sudden the Ordly made a dive for the Cabin head first, and told the old man [Captain Charles E. Clark] the Fleet was coming out of the Harbor. The old man jumpt up a standing." As the American ships cleared for action, the Spanish ships emerged from the channel at intervals of approximately ten minutes, about eight hundred yards apart, making eight to ten knots. The destroyers, last in line, appeared at around 10:10 A.M.[11]

For some ten minutes after the *Infanta María Teresa* came out of the channel it had to withstand the fire of the entire American squadron with only two of its own guns in operation, but it managed to force the *Brooklyn,* with the Commodore Schley aboard, into an extraordinary tactical error. Cervera steered straight for the *Brooklyn* because, as he reported later, "it was of the utmost importance for us to place this ship in a condition where she could not make use of her superior speed." The *Brooklyn* was on a west-northwest course, but it then executed a turn toward the northeast—*away* from the onrushing *Infanta María Teresa,* a maneuver that placed the *Texas* and the *Iowa* between it and Cervera's flagship. When the *Brooklyn* made this unexpected movement, the *Texas* had to back its engine to avoid a collision. The *Infanta María Teresa* then fled westward. Soon disabled by fire from the American squadron, Cervera's gallant flagship turned for shore and ran onto a small beach just west of Punta Cabrera at 10:35 A.M., only an hour after it had come out of the channel.[12]

The next two Spanish ships in line—the *Vizcaya* and the *Cristóbal Colón*—did not encounter as much initial opposition as the *Infanta María Teresa,* which drew most of the American fire at the outset of the battle. This circumstance allowed them to run further westward than the other ships. The fourth ship to appear, the *Almirante Oquendo,* was second to be destroyed. It turned towards the shore and struck the beach at 10:40 A.M. just west of the *Infanta María Teresa,* a result of American fire concentrated upon it after the flagship had been driven ashore. When the *Furor* and the *Plutón* finally came out of the entrance, they were engulfed in a hail of fire from the four American battleships present—the *Texas, Iowa, Oregon,* and *Indiana*—but the honor of dispatching both ships fell to the unprotected yacht *Gloucester,* whose skipper, Lieutenant Commander Richard Wainwright, had been on the *Maine* when it blew up in Havana harbor. The *Plutón* was beached at about 10:45 A.M. a little west of Cabañas; the *Furor* sank in deep water a few minutes later somewhat closer to Cabañas. A gunner on the *Oregon* remembered a counterpart on the *Furor,* "one of the bravest men I ever had the pleasure to look upon":

The Spanish gunner refused to leave his post. "That man must have known he was going to a shure Deth, he stood on Deck and cep firing at us all the time, and the last time I seen him he was Just going up in the air."[13]

Thus it fell out that by 11:00 A.M. only two Spanish ships remained in action—the *Vizcaya* and the *Cristóbal Colón*, both fleeing westward toward Cienfuegos. Since the *Vizcaya* had preceded the *Cristóbal Colón* out of the channel, it gained the lead at first, but the faster vessel soon passed it. For this reason the American squadron turned its attention next to the *Vizcaya*, and the doomed ship received fire from all the American armored vessels engaged—the four battleships and the cruiser *Brooklyn*. At about 11:15 A.M. the Spanish ship turned north for the shore, and ran aground on a reef just east of Aserraderos. Captain Clark, commanding the *Oregon*, later wrote of his emotions as the *Vizcaya* met its end: He experienced no exultation; perhaps he might have felt different, had his crew suffered casualties, but "as it was, the faces of the women and children in far-away Spain, the widows and orphans of this July third, rose before me so vividly that I had to draw comfort from the thought that a decisive victory is after all more merciful than a prolonged struggle, and that every life lost to-day in breaking down the bridge to Spain meant a hundred saved thereafter." Admiral Sampson, who by this time had joined the chase with the *New York*, now ordered the *Iowa* and the *Indiana* to resume stations off Santiago de Cuba. He feared that two Spanish ships remaining there, the unprotected cruiser *Reina Mercedes* and the gunboat *Alvarado*, might seize the opportunity to attack a group of American transports anchored at Siboney. This left the *New York, Brooklyn, Texas,* and *Oregon* to pursue the proud *Cristóbal Colón*.[14]

The last Spanish vessel afloat lacked its six ten-inch guns and therefore could not direct long-distance fire against its pursuers. Because it was unable to answer the American attack, a successful pursuit would seal its fate. The armored cruiser could make about 14.5 knots at its greatest speed, whereas its pursuers averaged somewhat less, but at about 1:00 P.M. the *Cristóbal Colón* began to lose speed. It had run out of its supply of good coal and had to use an inferior grade taken on at Santiago de Cuba. Very soon thereafter the *Oregon* obtained the range. Captain Paredes then decided to save the lives of his men rather than sacrifice them in a hopeless cause. About 1:15 P.M. he hauled down his flag and turned toward the shore, beaching his ship near the mouth of the Turquino River, about fifty miles west of Santiago de Cuba. Following a prearranged procedure, he had the valves of the ship opened, and it eventually filled with water—an act that directly contravened the laws of war.[15]

Surely the god of battle was with the Americans on July 3. Only one seaman was killed—Chief Yeoman George W. Ellis of the *Brooklyn*—victim to a shell fired from the *Vizcaya*. When he fell, some of the crew were about to throw his body overboard, but Commodore Schley stopped them, saying, "One who has fallen so gallantly deserves the honor of Christian burial." One other sailor, Fireman J. Burns of the *Brooklyn*, sustained a wound. Only three of the American ships—the *Brooklyn*, *Texas*, and *Iowa*—suffered damage, and none was punished severely. By contrast, according to Captain Concas, the Spanish squadron suffered 323 killed and 151 wounded out of 2,227 men—about 22 percent of the force. Cervera, however, had anticipated even greater casualties. A large number of Spanish sailors—1,720 officers and men—were taken prisoner. The remainder escaped detention; some 150 returned to Santiago de Cuba. Chadwick suspects, therefore, that the Spanish dead numbered 264. Captain Lazaga of the *Almirante Oquendo* died of a heart attack after his ship surrendered, and Captain Villaamil, commander of the destroyers, perished on the beach. Six years later his body was found and returned to Spain, where it was interred with military honors.[16]

The Spanish ships absorbed terrific punishment from the guns of Sampson's squadron; a count later established that 123 hits were made on the four armored vessels. The *Almirante Oquendo* was struck the most frequently by far—fifty-seven times. The *Infanta María Teresa* and the *Vizcaya* each received twenty-nine hits. The *Cristóbal Colón* was battered eight times as it left the harbor before passing beyond the range of the American ships. These statistics support Captain Concas's judgment that the critical disparity between the two squadrons on July 3 was primarily in gunnery. Sampson's gun crews had been given considerable target practice and had gained experience during the various bombardments prior to the naval engagement. In contrast, the Spanish ships had had almost no opportunity to practice with their 11-inch guns. They were also deficient in ammunition for the 5.5-inch guns, and what they had was often defective. One of the 5.5-inch weapons on the *Almirante Oquendo* blew out its breech-block, killing its entire gun crew. Admiral Sampson also drew attention to the numerous fires that broke out on the Spanish ships. Their wooden decks and superstructure burned easily, and the conflagrations there contributed greatly to confusion during the battle.[17]

However superior to the gunnery of the Spanish squadron, the American gun crews did not achieve an impressive percentage of hits, although it is doubtful that any navy could have done much better at the time. The *Brooklyn* fired 1,973 shells, the *Oregon* 1,903 shells, and the *Indiana* 1,876 shells, but only two of the largest size—twelve or thirteen inches—appear to have struck home. The percentage of strikes for various guns were: 2.3 percent for thirteen-inch and twelve-inch guns; 3.1 percent for eight-inch guns; 2.6 percent for six-inch and five-inch guns; and 1.1 percent for six-pound guns. These statistics, like those reported for the battle of Manila Bay, caused much concern, and stimulated efforts to improve gunnery after the war.[18]

During and after the battle many affecting scenes took place that engendered mutual respect between victors and vanquished. When Captain Evans received Captain Eulate of the *Vizcaya* on the *Iowa*, he chivalrously refused the Spaniard's sword. As Evans escorted his captive to a cabin, Eulate turned toward his burning ship and, raising his right hand, exclaimed: *"Adios, Vizcaya!"* Just as he spoke the forward magazine of the stricken ship blew up, and sent a column of smoke into the sky visible for many miles. After the crew of the *Infanta María Teresa* abandoned ship, a man suddenly appeared on deck and cried for help. Captain Concas remembered the reaction of the third boatswain, José Casado, who exclaimed, "I will not let that man die!" Entirely on his own initiative, Casado dove into the water and, reboarding the ship, "with utter disregard to the danger to his life, seized the man in distress, carried him down on his shoulders, and swimming with him to the shore, laid his precious burden on the beach." When Lieutenant Francisco Arderius, seriously wounded, was brought aboard the *Gloucester,* he received aid from one of the American sailors. Later he remembered having observed, "through the bandages that covered my eyes, tears in his, true tears, a most elevated representation of the compassion which that victorious enemy felt for our misfortune."[19]

In Washington an anxious President awaited word of the naval engagement. Finally, Sampson reported victory:

> The fleet under my command offers the nation as a Fourth of July present the whole of Cervera's fleet. It attempted to escape at 9:30 this morning. At 2 the last ship, the *Cristobal Colon,* had run ashore 75 miles west of Santiago and hauled down her colors. The *Infanta Maria Teresa, Oquendo,* and *Vizcaya* were forced ashore, burned, and blown up within 20 miles of Santiago. The *Furor* and *Pluton* destroyed within 4 miles of the port.

This boastful message was not well received in the United States. Intended as a parallel to General Sherman's famous Civil War message offering Savannah as a Christmas present, it struck a series of false notes. Emphasizing the role of Sampson, it did not mention other officers such as Commodore Schley, a fact that aroused annoyance when it became apparent that the Admiral had not played an important role in the combat. It surely dimmed the luster of Sampson's real achievement during the war. Only later was it learned that the admiral had not written the message; an aide had composed and transmitted it without prior clearance—but the damage had been done.[20]

Although Commodore Schley had indeed been the senior officer present when the Spanish squadron made its quixotic dash for freedom, certain important circumstances limited the significance of this fortuitous circumstance. Sampson's thorough and efficient conduct of the blockade had helped force the battle, and his sound tactical directions for coping with a Spanish attempt to escape ensured victory on July 3. As Secretary Long noted, the engagement "was the culmination of careful preparation on the part of Admiral Sampson," and the "exact action was taken that had been outlined by him previously." Indeed, Long did all he could to minimize Schley's contribution: "So well was the thing arranged that if Sampson had been a thousand miles away, and Schley had been in Europe, the movement would have been the same." In another place he extended this thesis, maintaining that Sampson at Santiago de Cuba "was as much in command as Grant at Chattanooga although Grant's generals were doing the actual fighting at Lookout Mountain and Missionary Ridge." Another reason for discounting Schley's claim for recognition as hero of the naval battle was his part in the maneuver that turned the *Brooklyn* away from the *Infanta María Teresa* at the beginning of the fight. Schley's "loop" allowed the *Cristóbal Colón* to gain important ground on the fastest of the American ships. The speedy Spanish ship might have escaped had it possessed a supply of good coal.[21]

After the war Schley defended his actions of July 3, claiming that the turn—prescribed initially by the commanding officer of the *Brooklyn*, Captain Cook—had been undertaken to place his ship in position to engage the enemy. It became evident, he told a postwar board of inquiry, that "we were steering on a diametrically opposite course. . . . The original plan had failed and . . . this Spanish fleet, in order and apparently at distance, had succeeded in passing the battleship line." He believed that his "loop," placing the *Brooklyn* on a course parallel to that of the Spanish ships, determined the nature of the battle thereafter. Concerning the *Texas*, he denied that he had run across her bow: "She was so distant that she never entered into my head at all as a menace or danger." A bit later, however, Schley offered a second explanation, maintaining that he made the turn to avoid getting caught in a crossfire from the *Vizcaya* and the *Cristóbal Colón*. When asked if this problem had been the sole reason for the loop, he replied, "The movement, of course, had two purposes—first, to avoid that [crossfire], and second, to continue the action. The *New York* being entirely absent, the *Brooklyn* that day had to take a very important lead, and if we had sacrificed her we might have lost the battle." Since Schley had erred so egregiously late in May in the attempt to blockade Cervera at Santiago de Cuba, he and his defenders were never able completely to dispel the suspicion that he had lost his composure at the outset of the battle, although the subsequent performance of the *Brooklyn* during the chase of the *Cristóbal Colón* at least partially redeemed earlier missteps. Whatever the merits of Schley's defense, it was fortunate that the Spanish ships had all chosen to flee towards Cienfuegos. If the destroyers had selected a southward course, they might have escaped, given their superior speed.[22]

Sampson proved loath to recommend decoration or advancement for Schley, although he was unstinting in praise of other officers. To Secretary Long he cabled on July 10, "I prefer leaving any question of reward for Commodore Schley to the Department." He suggested that his subordinate's performance during May ought to be considered in this connection. Prior to July 3 the Administration had been much annoyed with Schley, but the events of that day changed this somewhat. A friend of the President, H. H. Kohlsaat, wrote later, "McKinley told me he had Admiral Schley on the carpet to court-martial him for disobedience of orders in leaving Puerto Rico and going to Santiago, but his successful fight against Cervera so completely captured the imagination of the people they dropped the proceedings, as they would have been resented by the country." Whether or not this report is accurate, the reduction of Schley to fourth in the hierarchy of command in the Atlantic station prior to the battle of July 3 certainly supports the suspicion that his earlier performance had greatly lessened confidence in him.[23]

Fulsome praise of the navy came immediately from President McKinley and Secretary Long, views that accurately presaged the contemporary estimate. Sampson's summary of the action conveyed its character: "The method of escape attempted by the Spaniards—all steering in the same direction, removed all tactical doubts or difficulties, and made plain the duty of every United States vessel to come in, immediately engage and pursue. This was promptly and effectively done." He attributed the result to careful preparation: "I regard this complete and important victory over the Spanish forces as the successful finish of several weeks of arduous and close blockade, so stringent and effective during the night that the enemy was deterred from making the attempt to escape at night, and deliberately elected to make the attempt in day-light."[24]

The destruction of Cervera's squadron deprived Spain of its only naval force in Caribbean waters capable of contesting command of the sea. Cervera's fate allowed the United States to conduct operations thereafter throughout the region at times and places of its own choosing. And by eliminating the possibility of any challenge to American communications from the mainland to Cuba and Puerto Rico, the victory of July 3 portended major improvements in the blockade. Overseas it halted the movement of Admiral Manuel de la Cámara, who had left Cádiz and proceeded to the eastern Mediterranean Sea en route to the Philippine Islands.

TWELVE

Admiral Cámara
and the Eastern Squadron

On June 16 Admiral Manuel de la Cámara began his eastward voyage to relieve the Spanish garrison in the Philippines. His squadron included the battleship *Pelayo*, the armored cruiser *Carlos V*, and two merchant ships purchased from Germany armed with naval guns—the auxiliary cruisers *Patriota* and *Rápido*. Three destroyers also accompanied Cámara—the *Audaz*, *Proserpina*, and *Osado*—but these vessels had orders to return to Spain after escorting the expedition across the Mediterranean to Suez. Also with the squadron were two transports, the *Buenos Aires* and *Panay*, carrying four thousand troops, and four colliers laden with twenty thousand tons of coal. Cámara's orders directed him to proceed to the Philippine island of Mindanao. He could then decide whether to relieve the Visayas—those islands in the archipelago lying between Mindanao and Luzon—or attempt operations in the area of Subig Bay or Manila Bay. Auñón's directions cautioned Cámara "to avoid manifestly unfavorable encounters, considering as an essential point to avoid the useless sacrifice of the squadron and always to leave the honor of the troops without injury." Given the difficulties inherent in the mission and the manifest deficiencies of his squadron, Cámara received authority in certain circumstances to vary from his orders. To reach Mindanao from the Suez Canal steaming at an average speed of ten knots per hour, Cámara would have to voyage for thirty days. Since he would have to spend another ten days coaling and repairing vessels, the squadron could not hope to reach its destination until about August 17, assuming departure from the Suez area about July 8. However, its landfall at Mindanao would leave it some seven hundred miles distant from Manila, without, as Captain Chadwick correctly observed, "any real or actual purpose." Its only appropriate objectives could be Dewey's squadron at Manila and the American expedition sent to capture that city.[1]

Political calculations as well as strictly strategic considerations influenced the decision to dispatch Cámara. Shortly after the war ended, Auñón told the Spanish Cortes that, although he had decided the expedition could not really cope with Dewey, it was sent for "other reasons of an international order"—particularly the desire to retain the Philippines.[2]

Had the armored ships *Pelayo* and *Carlos V* reached the Philippines, they would have posed a serious danger to Dewey. Recognizing this possibility, the United States Navy Department ordered out two heavily armed monitors, the *Monterey* and the *Monadnock,* to strengthen the American squadron. For some time it was uncertain whether these slow seagoing monitors would arrive at Manila before Cámara.

ORIGINS OF THE EASTERN SQUADRON

When the Navy Department ascertained on June 17 that Cámara had passed through the Strait of Gibraltar bound for Suez, it began preparations to launch an expedition of its own. On June 18 Secretary Long ordered Admiral Sampson, then awaiting the arrival of General Shafter at Santiago de Cuba, to detail three of his armored vessels—the *Iowa, Oregon,* and *Brooklyn*—and four other ships for possible service in European waters: "They will be sent to coast of Spain in the event of Cadiz division passing Suez, Egypt." This maneuver would force the Spanish government either to accept uncontested attacks on its coastal cities or recall Cámara. At this point Secretary Long approved a recommendation from the Naval War Board that it make this plan known to the enemy through secret agents working for the naval attaché in Paris, Lieutenant William S. Sims. This planned "leak" was intended, wrote Long, "primarily to alarm Spain and to cause the recall of Camara, and secondarily to awaken Europe to the fact that the republic of the western hemisphere did not hesitate to carry war, if necessary, across the Atlantic." Once again, decision-makers in Washington manifested interest in the possibility, however remote, that some European state might come to the assistance of Spain. In preparing to send out the division of ships that eventually became known as the "Eastern Squadron," the Navy Department readied itself for any possible contingency, even if some officers suspected that Cámara lacked sufficient power to threaten Dewey.[3]

All this activity added to the responsibilities of Admiral Sampson, who was not only blockading Santiago de Cuba but supporting the Fifth Army Corps and sustaining the naval watch on other Cuban and Puerto Rican ports. He obtained additional authority when, on June 21, the Navy Department made important changes in command: The North Atlantic Squadron was redesignated the North Atlantic Fleet. Commodore John A. Howell, soon to be named second-in-command of this organization, was ordered to relieve Commodore John C. Watson and take charge of the blockade in the Caribbean on July 1 as commander of the First North Atlantic Squadron. On July 7 Watson received command of the Eastern Squadron. Commodore Schley—much in disfavor with both Sampson and Long—became commander of the Second North Atlantic Squadron on June 21, dropping to fourth in the chain of command. The Flying Squadron disappeared as a formal organization. Commodore George C. Remey retained command of the naval base at Key West. These sound arrangements clarified Sampson's authority and specified command responsibilities in harmony with the existing naval situation.[4]

As Admiral Sampson received the instructions to prepare the Eastern Squadron he also came under pressure to supplement the blockade against the northeastern and southern coasts of Cuba and Puerto Rico. Responding to word that the President wished to issue a proclamation of blockade for the entire south coast of Cuba from Batabanó to Cape Cruz, he notified the Navy Department on June 19 that he would prepare to cover the specified region and would send the *St. Paul* and *Yosemite* to San Juan, Puerto Rico. The next day he issued new instructions to ensure that commanders on the blockade adhere strictly to international law as interpreted by the United States. The importance of maintaining the naval watch became apparent on June 22 when the *Terror,* a destroyer that had accompanied Cervera from Spain as far as Martinique but had then gone to San Juan, tested the blockade. Captain Sigsbee, commanding the *St. Paul,* intercepted the ship and put a shell through its starboard side. The *Terror* managed to limp back into port; it remained out of action a month.[5]

Given his growing list of responsibilities, Sampson argued that he could not reasonably be expected to blockade additional ports. Because of the need to escort army convoys to Cuba his force was already too attenuated to maintain the blockade at a high state of efficiency, although he alleviated this somewhat by successfully recommending that certain ships patrolling the eastern seaboard of the United States be sent south to augment his command. Despite Sampson's views, the Navy Department persisted in its desire to expand the coverage of the blockade. Long noted various weaknesses and gave firm direction: "You must strengthen blockade, or claim [that it is] not effective enough will be made from abroad." Sampson then explained his situation in greater detail: He had wanted to improve the blockade of Cuba's south coast, but the demands on his forces had precluded its extension, and he had no doubt that Commodore Watson, commanding the blockade on the north coast, faced a similar situation. "The number of ships which must go to Key West for coal and for repairs must always be large," he noted, "and the army movements caused the temporary removal of twelve effective ships from their stations." Nevertheless he reported efforts to improve the blockade on both the south and north coasts so that it covered Nuevitas and Sagua la Grande. He also planned to attack some Spanish gunboats in the harbor at Manzanillo. On the next day, June 28, the State Department issued its second proclamation of blockade, extending coverage on the southern coast of Cuba from Cape Frances to Cape Cruz and also to San Juan, Puerto Rico. Neutral vessels were given thirty days to clear affected ports. This measure sought to end blockade running into Cuba from Mexico and other Central American locations. On July 1, true to his word, Sampson had the *Scorpion* and the *Osceola* attack Manzanillo. Overall, although the blockade never became completely effective, it served its purpose very well, even if its requirements gave constant concern to Admiral Sampson, whose need for ships constantly grew as new tasks were assigned to him.[6]

Meanwhile the Navy Department was tracking Admiral Cámara's voyage through the Mediterranean; the State Department lent valuable assistance in this respect, taking steps to erect diplomatic obstacles. On June 20 Secretary Long asked Secretary of State Day to have State Department representatives place "every possible impediment in the way of coal and other necessaries being supplied to [Cámara]." American consuls should "object strongly to the authorities in neutral ports, against either furnishing coal, or permitting the act of coaling within the waters under their jurisdiction." The basis for this action was to be a "plea that this is not a case of enabling a vessel to reach a home port, but of aiding and abetting a formidable expedition, destined to act in remote quarters of the globe against a squadron and land forces of the United States." Even if such complaints seemed unlikely to produce results, the agents were to protest in the hope of causing delays in Cámara's voyage. Day immediately issued instructions of this nature to consular personnel at stations along Cámara's probable route.[7]

On June 20 the Naval War Board recommended that the United States purchase the armored cruiser *O'Higgins* from Chile to keep it from falling into the hands of Spain, and at the same time expressed concern about the voyage of Cámara. Admiral Sicard noted that the United States must not only carry out extensive operations on both land and sea at very remote locations from the Caribbean to the Western Pacific, but must also defend its coast against possible raids. These requirements placed considerable strain on the fleet. "The success in both east and west depends upon control of the sea; that is, upon being constantly superior, in both quarters, to any probable combination of the enemy. . . . We have neither force enough to be constantly superior to him in all quarters, nor the power to anticipate his arrival in any one quarter, being ignorant of his destination." Since the monitors *Monterey* and *Monadnock,* en route to the Philippines, would more than compensate for the *Pelayo* and *Carlos V*—the only really strong units in Cámara's expedition—it seemed unlikely that the Spanish admiral would actually proceed to the Philippines, particularly because the coast of Spain would then lack a defense against American raids. It was imporant, however, to prevent Spain from obtaining the *O'Higgins,* because if it joined Cámara's squadron it might alter the strategic 'balance. For this reason the Naval War Board recommended its purchase, even at an exorbitant price of $6 million. The Board adduced a second reason for the purchase: "There may be questions pressing for settlement at the close of this war that would make the possession by us of one more formidable armored cruiser very desirable, even though we paid an excessive price for her." Once again the navy revealed its interest in larger questions of international politics and its appreciation of the influence that a powerful fleet might exert on the postwar settlement.[8]

When Secretary Long learned that Cámara had passed the island of Pantelleria, about halfway across the Mediterranean, he issued another order concerning the Eastern Squadron. Sampson was instructed to include the armored ships *Oregon* and *Iowa* in the squadron along with the auxiliary cruisers *Yosemite, Yankee,* and *Dixie.* Ships sent from the United States would replace these vessels on the blockade. When it was reported in Washington that the Chilean government had finally sold the *O'Higgins* to Spain, Long added the armored cruiser *Brooklyn* to the Eastern Squadron. Had this force ever left Santiago de Cuba, Sampson would have retained only four armored vessels—the battleships *Massachusetts, Indiana,* and *Texas* and the armored cruiser *New York.*[9]

All this activity finally elicited a protest from Sampson, a protest that led to altered orders from Washington. On June 26 the Admiral informed Long that he considered it "essential not to reduce this force too much for some few days, in view of the fact that the weather may compel me to coal at Guantanamo. Channel was not obstructed by the *Merrimac* and we must be prepared to meet the Spanish fleet if they attempt to escape." To hasten Cervera's defeat he was planning a torpedo attack on Spanish ships, but he did not really want to undertake this high-risk operation, and if authorized to retain his present forces, he would cancel it. He was acting on the assumption that Cervera's capture would end the war. This message had an immediate effect, and the Naval War Board recommended that Sampson be allowed to retain the *Oregon* and *Iowa* until the other vessels assigned to the Eastern Squadron were fully coaled, although preparations for eventual departure were to be expedited because "the Department is most desirous to get these vessels to the east via Spain." It became clear that the Department had no intention of disbanding the Eastern Squadron when Commodore Watson received orders to depart, with the *Iowa* as his flagship, as soon as Sampson gave a signal.[10]

Although Sampson managed to delay the expedition temporarily, the Navy Department paid careful attention to its preparation. On June 28 Long cabled Sampson to impress upon him "the urgent necessity to coal your armored ships rapidly, in order that Watson may sail as soon as possible eastward." As he recorded his efforts to dispatch Watson, Long expressed irritation at the slow development of affairs: "The war drags on and, I fear, is likely to drag on [further], although if we are successful at Santiago as we expect to be—and especially if we take Porto Rico,—we have things pretty much in our own hands." When Sampson seemed to hesitate, Long cabled once more, on July 1: "The prospective advance of Camara to the east makes it much to be desired Watson's squadron should commence to move. . . . The Department does not wish to weaken you, but diversion favorable for Dewey by operations positive is necessary." At this point, just as events at Santiago de Cuba were approaching a climax, the Navy Department found itself on the horns of a dilemma. It lacked sufficient armored ships to ensure security in both the Caribbean and the Western Pacific. Should it risk dividing its Caribbean forces to threaten the Spanish Peninsula?[11]

FATE OF CÁMARA'S SQUADRON

While the United States Navy prepared the Eastern Squadron, Admiral Cámara arrived at Port Said, Egypt, only to encounter considerable interference with his efforts to arrange passage through the Suez Canal. Reporting to Auñón, Cámara indicated his intention to coal before passing through the canal. At the same time news of his appearance at Port Said had been cabled to Washington. The American consul there soon reported that he had succeeded in stopping Cámara's coaling operations at Port Said and he did not anticipate their resumption. Lord Cromer, the British proconsul in Egypt, had received instructions from the Foreign Office to prevent delivery of coal to Cámara on the grounds that the Spanish squadron had a supply sufficient to permit its return to Spain. (The American consul was not aware of this.) Cámara was not allowed to fuel from Egyptian lighters within the three-mile limit, and was asked on June 29 to depart from territorial waters within twenty-four hours of his arrival. Passing this disturbing information on to Madrid, the Admiral announced his intention to tow the disabled *Pelayo* through the canal and coal in the Red Sea. After numerous exchanges between Cámara and Auñón on July 1, the Admiral was authorized to make his proposed movement, and he withdrew from Egyptian territorial waters to prepare for the operation. Meanwhile American authorities continued their efforts to prevent Cámara from obtaining coal at Red Sea ports such as Perim.[12]

The end of Cámara's eastward voyage was fast approaching. The outcome of the sea battle off Santiago de Cuba would result in his recall. On July 3 the Admiral received orders to proceed through the canal to the Red Sea, an operation completed July 5-6. Noting this movement, Lieutenant Sims in Paris also indicated that the three destroyers with Cámara would return to Spain. One of Sims's special agents in Madrid incorrectly reported to him that this latter development stemmed from the projected operations of the American Eastern Squadron, when in actuality it had been planned from the beginning. But he also noted accurately that Cervera had instructions to sortie at Santiago de Cuba. On July 6 Auñón ordered Cámara, by then in the Red Sea, to keep up steam; he could then, if necessary, return quickly to Spain. A somewhat later message announced the destruction of Cervera's squadron. On the next day the Minister of the Marine sent a definitive order commanding the expedition to return to Cartagena at all possible speed. A myth still lingers in Spain to the effect that Cámara had to retrace his steps because British and Egyptian machinations deprived the Spanish squadron of necessary fuel and supplies. Shortly after the war, however, Auñón specifically stated to the Cortes that Cámara had been recalled not only to save his vessels from possible destruction in the Philippines but to protect the shores of the homeland against a possible American attack. He might have mentioned that the expedition had considerable coal available in the colliers accompanying it. For his return Cámara received instructions to steam close to the Spanish coast "so as to be seen from the Spanish cities, exhibiting, when near them, the national flag, illuminated by search-lights, which are to be thrown upon the cities.'' This order was intended to calm fears that the coast had been left undefended against a possible American attack. Thus ended the abortive voyage of Admiral Cámara. Whatever other motives there might have been for his return to Spain, the American victory at Santiago de Cuba rendered his further movement eastward a strategic and political absurdity.[13]

Captain Mahan, looking back on this episode in 1906, showed considerable interest in it. Of Cámara's departure from Cádiz he wrote, ''The general military situation, constituted by Camara's movement eastward, is to my apprehension the most important and instructive of the whole war.'' Dewey had no armored vessels to counter the Spanish expedition except the monitor *Monterey*. At the same time, Sampson had only enough armored vessels to just discharge the multifarious duties assigned to him. For this reason the Navy Department faced a dilemma—''the dilemma of diminishing Sampson's squadron, with consequent risk of Cervera's escape, or of exposing Dewey to attack by superior force.'' This danger existed from the moment that Cámara got his squadron ready because, as Mahan observed, he ''occupied an interior position between the two American admirals.'' There was, however, another element to be considered: ''The Spanish cities being inadequately fortified, Spain was continually open to the check which we used, by the menacing organization of a division against them.'' Mahan was quick to note that ''the same unfortified position of our own coast imposed the improper station of the Flying Squadron in Hampton Roads, with its consequent too late arrival at Cienfuegos; and also the retention of Howell's vessels in the north [the coastal patrol], to the narrowing and the comparative ineffectiveness of the commercial blockade of Cuba.'' Given these considerations, the Naval War Board had advised the formation of the Eastern Squadron. Measurable publicity was given to this enterprise. ''Everything was done to impart apparent imminency to a movement which it was intended to postpone to the last moment, or until Cervera was destroyed.''

Mahan doubted that Madrid ever intended to have Cámara complete his voyage. ''The Philippines could not weigh against Cadiz, Malaga, or Barcelona. In fact, had Cámara got as far as Ceylon, Watson, appearing before any of those ports, and demanding his recall under penalty of bombardment, would have carried his point. There would have been no bombardment.'' Mahan believed that Cámara's movement to the Suez Canal and beyond was an elaborate bluff, suspecting that the Spanish Admiral may have sought to draw Watson away from Carib-

bean waters so as to ease the difficulty of Cervera's departure from Santiago de Cuba. In any event the retrograde movement of Cámara relieved the United States of its fears that Dewey might have to deal with
superior Spanish forces. And after the destruction of Cervera's
squadron, the United States Navy possessed enough armored vessels to
counteract the enemy fleet in Spanish waters.[14]

What, then, happened to the Eastern Squadron on its return? It was
not disbanded; on the contrary, it continued to prepare for active service in European waters. Although it never sailed, it played a not unimportant part in the events that brought the war with Spain to an early
conclusion.

FATE OF THE EASTERN SQUADRON

As soon as Cervera's defeat became known at the Navy Department,
efforts were resumed to prepare the Eastern Squadron for distant service. Asking for a report on Commodore Watson's supply of ammunition, Secretary Long informed Sampson, "Department attaches utmost
importance to the immediate preparation of Watson's vessels for departure." On July 6, before it was known that Cámara would return to the
Spanish Peninsula (he had just passed through the Suez Canal), the
Department noted that Sampson could add the *Iowa* to the Eastern
Squadron. The Admiral suggested the *Massachusetts* instead and proposed also to contribute the *New Orleans*. On July 7 orders came to
collect the *Iowa* and *Oregon*, along with the *Newark, Dixie*, and
Yosemite, at Môle St. Nicolas, there to await further orders. On July 8
both naval and diplomatic sources confirmed reports of Cámara's
return. Lieutenant Sims's agent in Madrid attributed the recall to fear
of the Eastern Squadron, and also reported that, although Sagasta appeared inclined towards a peace settlement, the Spanish premier hesitated because of possible opposition from naval officers. Presumably to
sustain pressure on Sagasta, the Navy Department redoubled its efforts
to send out Commodore Watson. On July 10 Sampson reported that
the Eastern Squadron could depart in two days, and the next day his
command was reorganized to reflect the changed strategic situation.
Commodores Schley and Howell would command two squadrons to remain in Caribbean waters. Watson's Eastern Squadron would include
the armored ships *Oregon* and *Massachusetts* along with the *Newark,
Dixie, Yosemite, Yankee*, a supply ship, and several colliers.[15]

At this juncture the Navy Department greatly upgraded the strength
of the Eastern Squadron, a step that elicited a protest from Admiral
Sampson: On July 12 Long informed Sampson that all armored vessels

except the monitors should accompany Watson's squadron as far as the Strait of Gibraltar. The monitors would support the planned invasion of Puerto Rico, awaiting the landing of troops at Port Nipe. Sampson soon made objections, claiming that the heavier armored ships should undergo extensive overhauling before attempting a long voyage. The *Iowa*, *Indiana*, and *New York* had been under steam for seven months and at sea in a state of readiness for six. "Of course," he continued, "I do not know the basis of the action of the Department. There may be overpowering reasons of which I am ignorant, but unless these exist, I recommend the Department to take this state of affairs into serious consideration." There followed a list of reasons for reviewing the order. Failure to make adequate preparations for an eastern movement might impair the navy's prestige, then at a high point. Ships were still needed to blockade Cienfuegos and undertake operations at Manzanillo, Batabanó, Gibara, and Nuevitas in order to cut off supplies moving to Havana and Holguín. Also, the monitors were unsuited to support the Puerto Rican expedition. All this comment led Sampson to an ominous conclusion: "If all the armored vessels and three converted cruisers were sent away, or expedition started for Puerto Rico conveyed by monitors, I foresee that the demands for naval assistance will cause us practically to abandon a large part of our blockade."[16]

Before Sampson's message arrived in Washington, orders had been prepared for the expanded eastern operation. The Navy Department now wished to send naval reinforcements to Dewey by way of the Mediterranean, the Suez Canal, and points east. To ensure against difficulties with Cámara, it was decided "to send . . . a covering squadron strong enough to guarantee against the possible efforts of all such armored ships of the Spanish Navy as may now be in condition for cruising in the straits of Gibraltar, and to hold any such force as Spain may collect blockaded in its own ports until our squadron for the East is well on its way." In short, two distinct squadrons were to be formed to proceed eastward under Sampson's command. After meeting colliers at the Azores, the combined force would coal either in Spanish or Moroccan waters. When Gibraltar had been passed, Watson would continue in command of the armored vessels *Massachusetts* and *Oregon* and the auxiliary cruisers *Dixie* and *Yosemite*. The covering squadron would include the armored vessels *New York, Brooklyn, Iowa, Indiana,* and *Texas* and the cruisers *Newark, New Orleans, Badger, Yankee,* and *Mayflower*. Its mission was to pin down the Spanish fleet until the Eastern Squadron had moved well beyond Gibraltar; then it would return to the western Atlantic. Despite the boldness of this conception, the Department reiterated the overriding importance of preserving the armored ships. "While any opportunity that may offer to destroy the enemy's armed ships must be used to the utmost, the vessels must not be exposed any more than may be imperatively necessary, to the fire of the coast fortifications." Sampson was to prepare energetically for the voyage and be ready to sail as soon as possible after receipt of orders.[17]

There then ensued a brief dialogue between the Department and Sampson, stemming from his concern about the condition of his ships. On July 16 the Admiral received a worried message: "Do you mean to say that the armored vessels you mention cannot in your judgment successfully make a voyage across the Atlantic and back in view of importance of re-enforcing Admiral Dewey?" Sampson replied that the *Oregon, Massachusetts, Newark,* and *Dixie* were ready to depart except for some additional loading of ammunition. Concerning the readiness of the armored vessels he stated that they could make the voyage but "they must be ready to meet all emergencies and this they are not in condition to do." Of them only the *Oregon* and *Massachusetts* were prepared for departure. All this left matters up in the air.[18]

The Naval War Board now considered the question in detail, concentrating on whether to dispatch one squadron or two. Suppose, began Admiral Sicard's memorandum on the question, another armored ship was added to Watson's squadron. In this circumstance he might have to accept a goodly amount of damage in an action with the Spanish fleet. Therefore a covering squadron would be ideal because it could cope with all possible contingencies. Nevertheless, should Watson proceed eastward with three armored vessels, it could be safely assumed that the American ships were inherently superior to their Spanish counterparts and possessed sufficient speed to pass rapidly through the region where they might expect an attack. Sicard was prepared to risk a voyage of three ships: "I feel personally so satisfied of the inferiority of our enemy, in the matter of ships and men, as demonstrated in the late operations against him, that I am willing to assume that the risk of passing Watson's squadron through the Straits and through the enemy's waters, is not one which need be seriously regarded by the Department in considering its plans; though I wish distinctly to admit that it is not the ideal campaign, as is the first one above mentioned."[19]

Sicard's views did not go unchallenged; no less a personage than Captain Mahan entered a powerful dissent. Now that the United States had control of the sea, he argued, it contemplated two operations: One was to mount the long-projected attack on Puerto Rico, seizing its capital San Juan. The other was to send at least two battleships to the Pacific Ocean as reinforcements for Admiral Dewey. To accomplish this task the United States would have to pass two armored vessels through

the very waters where Spain could most effectively concentrate its remaining naval strength. Because the three Spanish cities most exposed
to attack would be Cádiz, Málaga, and Barcelona, Spain's wisest course
would be "to concentrate the enemy fleet at Cadiz and with proper
scouting, throw it against US force in the straits or follow it closely
enough to bring about action before the US fleet causes any harm."
Spain could not avoid this course without sullying its honor, even if it
entailed the possibility of defeat. Adding the *Brooklyn* to the American
force would probably not preclude damage to at least one armored ship.
Given this analysis, Mahan concluded that control of the sea was "the
crucial feature of the whole situation. . . . While we unquestionably
possess it, as against Spain, we have no such margin as justifies a risk
without adequate gain." He drew a parallel conclusion concerning the
use of armored ships against San Juan. "The teaching of the war, so far,
is that such attacks are useless; and if we persist, we will get the further
teaching that they are dangerous to ships far beyond the point of any
possible gain from them." Ships should be employed against ships,
Mahan reiterated, because such operations promised a reasonable
return—something that could not be claimed for raids or bombardments directed against enemy ports.

Mahan concluded that either Watson should be sent with six armored ships to see him through the Strait of Gibraltar or the movement
should be postponed while the United States concentrated on the
Puerto Rican campaign. "However beneficial the effect upon our
diplomacy to reinforce Dewey, it is by no means equal to the injury to
our diplomacy caused by a couple of armored ships being disabled." Of
these possibilities he preferred prompt movement on Spain with six armored ships. The American squadron could not remain in the Caribbean Sea because of the hurricane season. "The whole war turns upon
the efficiency of the armored fleet; upon the same, turns the negotiations for peace, and the possible interference of foreign powers." The
Spanish would not challenge six ships, but "if they fail to attack two or
three, with their present force, in their own waters, they are utterly
disgraced." He was sure that Spain could not send ships to either raid
the American coast or disrupt trade in the West Indies. The enemy,
after all, had only two armored ships available, the *Pelayo* and *Carlos V.*
Why would Spain send its armored ships to American waters, when its
best chance would be to employ them in the Strait of Gibraltar?
Spanish successes in American waters during the absence of the American squadron would be quickly cancelled upon its return.

Mahan concluded that six armored ships should be sent to European
waters, with the *Brooklyn* remaining behind, but only two—the

Massachusetts and *Oregon*—should continue on to the Philippines. If the *Brooklyn* went to the Philippines with the *Massachusetts* and *Oregon* the outcome would be "less than desirable in case of complications with a third Power, which is the chief reason for now reinforcing Dewey." Here was an arresting analysis indeed. The third power in question was Germany; the presence of German warships in the Philippine Islands deeply concerned the Navy Department and the Department took this circumstance into consideration in deciding the movements of its principal ships. That Cámara was now on his way back to Spain meant that only the German squadron posed a threat to Dewey. In his general advice concerning both the diplomatic and strategic aspects of this question, Mahan adhered strictly to his earlier theories concerning the elemental importance of the battle fleet in relation to fundamental political objectives.[20]

Discussion of this question did not end with Mahan's analysis; the Naval War Board soon expressed its views on the specific nature of American naval operations in Spanish waters. What should the Eastern Squadron attempt to accomplish once the planned conquest of Puerto Rico had taken place? Should it contemplate occupation of the Canary Islands? Or should it occupy Ceuta, Spain's bastion in Morocco opposite the Rock of Gibraltar? Sicard's statement for the Naval War Board strongly opposed both proposals. Ceuta had been recently reinforced; besides, the United States had no need of it. The same considerations applied to the Canaries. As a general principle, the Board deprecated "further dispersal of our efforts, as we are already engaged at Cuba, Porto Rico, and the Philippines." In short, the Naval War Board believed that the only function of movement to European waters, aside from political and psychological effects, should be to escort Watson's two armored ships past the Spanish vessels at Cádiz.[21]

Sampson, who opposed the dispatch of a covering force with Watson, proposed to add either the *New York* or *Brooklyn* to the Eastern Squadron, along with the cruisers *Mayflower* and *New Orleans,* provided that ammunition for them arrived at Guantánamo. Watson supported this addition should the Department decide against sending a covering force. To assist in deciding the question, Long sought information concerning the *Pelayo* and *Carlos V,* then about to proceed westward from Cartagena to Cádiz.

For the moment the Navy Department delayed decisions concerning the Eastern Squadron, reacting to a series of new developments. Possibly in part to prepare for the conceivable arrival of Watson, on July 23 Auñón had ordered Cámara to return to Cádiz, showing himself to cities along the Spanish coast. One Spanish historian, Maura Gamazo, later maintained that this movement was intended to underline the Spanish peace initiative of July 22. On that day a proposal to end the war was sent from Madrid through the French government to the United States, but was not presented in Washington until July 26. Cámara arrived at Cádiz on July 27.[22]

Captain Mahan hatched a scheme to take advantage of the situation after receipt of the Spanish note, seeking a way to reinforce Dewey without endangering armored ships. Information had arrived from Lieutenant Sims that postponement of Watson's departure had strengthened Sagasta's peace initiative. Given this situation, Mahan suggested that the United States consider a bargain with Spain. Washington would delay the movement of all American armored vessels to Spanish waters provided Madrid allow two armored ships and supporting vessels to move unmolested through the Mediterranean Sea en route to the Philippines. "I should insist," he continued, "that those ships must go forward without delay, because we must increase our force in the Pacific; and that unless they accept this condition the fleet will sail as first proposed." The advantage of such a deal was that the United States could avoid a large squadron movement and encourage a peace settlement at the same time. Mahan's proposal came to the attention of President McKinley, who, when he sent it to Long, added an unusual and intriguing endorsement. "Dear Mr. Long: There are some good suggestions in the foregoing. Think of them. W. McK." However ingenious, this plan did not develop further.[23]

During the last few days of the war the Navy Department continued to prepare the Eastern Squadron, obviously seeking to counter Spanish delaying tactics during peace negotiations then taking place in Washington through the good offices of the French embassy. On August 2 Sampson received orders to sail three days later with both the Eastern Squadron and the covering force. In its final form the expedition was to include all the armored vessels and seven cruisers (the *Newark* and *Badger* if available, and the *New Orleans, Yankee, Yosemite, Dixie,* and *Mayflower*). Unreconciled to the maneuver, Sampson on August 4 proposed further delay. He wanted to send all or part of his force to San Juan until that city should fall to invading American troops. The city could fall into American hands in two weeks, terminating the war, provided that the army and navy cooperated in its reduction: "San Juan can be destroyed from the water and may yield without much resistance to a proper show of naval strength." This operation did not materialize, in part because of opposition from the army. Then, on the same day, Long cabled Sampson, "Negotiations are pending with Spain. Therefore do not sail with ocean fleet until further orders."[24]

The frustrating history of the Eastern Squadron now was coming to an end. When Sampson inquired whether he could assign its ships to the blockade, Long replied negatively on August 6: "Delay in fleet sailing is still uncertain. The ships must be held ready to depart at 12 hours notice and must not be distributed to the blockade." Once again Spanish delaying tactics during the peace negotiations had suggested the utility of maintaining the ability to launch the naval operation. Captain Mahan wanted to start the expedition without further ado, amazed as he was about the "procrastination and prevarication of the Spaniard." Drawing attention once again to the imminent arrival of hurricanes in the Caribbean Sea, he suggested that Spain might be stalling negotiations to prevent the Eastern Squadron from making its voyage.[25]

The American naval victory at Santiago de Cuba on July 3 decided the war with Spain because it guaranteed general and lasting command of the sea. Spain's remaining naval forces were insufficient to accomplish any of three possible missions—further operations in American waters, relief of Manila, and protection of the Spanish coast. As soon as possible thereafter, Sagasta recalled Cámara and moved for peace.

Even before Cervera's squadron had been destroyed, the Navy Department contemplated dispatch of the Eastern Squadron to strengthen the American position in the Pacific Ocean. Initially intended to reinforce Admiral Dewey against augmented Spanish forces, the squadron received a new mission after the naval victory at Santiago de Cuba and Cámara's retrograde movement from Suez to Cartagena and Cádiz: Henceforth it was deemed a means of strengthening Dewey against a third power, Germany, assumed to have designs on the Philippines Islands. As it happened, the Eastern Squadron never departed the Caribbean, because some of the vessels had to be used temporarily in support of local operations, particularly against Puerto Rico, and because negotiations to end the war were transpiring in Washington.

This episode of the Eastern Squadron is of considerable interest because the discussions of its possible movements cast important light on the nature of strategic thought during the war with Spain. The debate revealed the extent to which the peculiar characteristics of armored vessels posed limitations on their use. Their great value precluded employment in operations entailing considerable risk unless there was a chance to earn real dividends. Moreover, the lack of an important American base along the route from the West Indies through Suez to the Far East forced the United States to make extensive efforts to provide supply ships and colliers for the expedition.

The naval victory on July 3 did not remove the Spanish garrison from Santiago de Cuba. Shafter's army still faced the task of forcing surrender of the city, although Cervera's departure vastly simplified it. The situation of the Fifth Army Corps now had become somewhat anomalous, in that the expedition had been sent principally to deal with Cervera, not with the city of Santiago de Cuba and its garrison. Once on the ground, however, Shafter could hardly contemplate evacuation, a view upheld in Washington. Although on July 5 General Miles urged that the Fifth Army Corps be taken out of Cuba and used in the expedition against Puerto Rico, Shafter was instead left to decide how he would end Spanish resistance at Santiago de Cuba. The Cuban General Máximo Gómez also advanced a plan at variance with the desires of Shafter; he wanted to continue operations at Santiago de Cuba but at the same time send some ten or twelve thousand troops to Cienfuegos. The conquest of Cienfuegos would weaken Havana, which received supplies from that port, and also force the surrender of other places in the vicinity. There is no indication that Gómez's proposal, conveyed to an American naval officer on July 4, ever received consideration in Washington. The only troops available to execute it were those designated for Puerto Rico; their use at Cienfuegos or elsewhere in Cuba would have meant abandonment of a campaign that had been contemplated in Washington since before the declaration of war. As it turned out, no land operations in other locations materialized until Shafter completed his siege of Santiago de Cuba.[26]

THIRTEEN

The Siege of Santiago de Cuba

General Shafter's proclivity to besiege rather than storm Santiago de Cuba deepened after he learned of the victory at sea. When General Miles sent a message of congratulations and added the welcome news, "I expect to be with you within one week with strong reinforcements," Shafter replied, "I feel that I am master of the situation and can hold the enemy for any length of time." He was glad that the commanding general was coming to Santiago de Cuba; he could then see for himself "the obstacles which this army had to overcome."[1]

Meanwhile Shafter tried again to negotiate a surrender. As soon as news of the naval victory reached his headquarters he dispatched a message to General Toral reiterating his earlier demand. Noting Cervera's defeat and his ability to prevent Spanish reinforcements from entering the city, he suggested courteously, "To save needless effusion of blood and the distress of many people, you may reconsider your determination of yesterday. Your men have certainly shown the gallantry which was expected of them." To this letter Toral replied with equal courtesy, "The same reasons that I explained to you, yesterday, I have to give again to-day—that this place will not be surrendered." Toral's response meant that no immediate end to the campaign could be expected unless the Americans resumed the offensive, but Shafter showed no inclination to follow that course.[2]

At the urging of foreign consuls Shafter permitted civilians to evacuate Santiago de Cuba, a logical corollary of his threat to bombard the city. On July 4 refugees in large numbers began to move to El Caney. Eventually some twenty thousand of them gathered in that little town, the Americans doing what they could to supply them with food. Lieutenant John J. Pershing of the Tenth Cavalry recorded his impressions of the evacuation: "All day along the hot, dusty road leading from Santiago to El Caney, passed the long, white line; frail, hungry women carried a bundle of clothing, a parcel of food for an infant, while weak and helpless children trailed wearily at the skirts of their wretched mothers. . . . The suffering of the innocent is not the least of the horrors of war." Fewer than five thousand civilians remained in Santiago de Cuba. A Spanish officer commented that the city "presented the same aspect that Pompeii and Herculaneum must have offered. Not a single store was open, not even the drug stores. The desertion and solitude were complete." The British consul, Frederick W. Ramsden, drew another graphic picture of suffering in El Caney: "In some houses you will find fifty in a small room, and among them one dying of fever, another with diarrhoea, and perhaps a woman in the throes of child birth, and all that with not a chair to sit on or a utensil of any kind and all in want of food."[3]

After Cervera went out on July 3, the Spanish garrison in Santiago de Cuba only slowly grasped the magnitude of the disaster. Reports from the Morro on the day of the sortie seemed to indicate that Cervera had made good his escape. Blanco actually notified his commander in Cienfuegos that Cervera might be expected there. By nightfall, however, Toral had reported the bitter truth to Blanco and requested permission to close the entrance to the harbor. The enemy could force the entrance easily because the electrical torpedoes were almost all out of action. To prevent Sampson from coming in Toral proposed blocking the channel with a useless cruiser, the old *Reina Mercedes*. On the night of July 4, just before midnight, the attempt was made. Lookouts on the blockade watched the *Reina Mercedes* enter the channel; the American vessels as usual had closed up at darkness and illuminated the channel with searchlights. The *Texas* and the *Massachusetts* immediately opened fire, and both ships hit the old hulk. Despite the heavy fire the Spanish crew managed to sink the ship at the intended location, but the misfortune that had dogged the defenders at Santiago de Cuba once again manifested itself: When the ship came to rest, it lay east of the main channel near the Estrella cove so that it did not actually obstruct the entrance. As with the American attempt to obstruct the channel with the *Merrimac*, no amount of personal bravery sufficed to ensure success.[4]

One of the immediate tasks for the United States naval forces after the naval battle was to deal with the large number of Spanish sailors who fell into their hands. On the day of the battle the American squadron performed yeoman service in rescuing crews from the burning vessels. Those saved—except for the seriously wounded—were placed on the *Harvard* and *St. Louis* for transfer to the United States. Around midnight on July 4 trouble occurred on the *Harvard*. A line had been marked on the deck beyond which prisoners were not supposed to pass. One prisoner, possibly to escape the heat, either passed this line or appeared to make an attempt. When ordered to return, the Spaniard refused to obey; possibly the language barrier contributed to his behavior. A sentry then fired, an act that brought the remaining prisoners to their feet. Guards from the Fourth Massachusetts Volunteers responded to an alarm and poured a volley into the mass of about six hundred prisoners. Before order could be restored, six Spanish sailors lay dead and thirteen wounded. This truly unfortunate incident, much regretted by the Americans, marred an otherwise effective policy of good treatment. Admiral Cervera himself handsomely complimented his captors on their behavior, stating in a message to Blanco, "Our enemies have treated us and are treating us with the utmost chivalry and kindness. . . . They have even suppressed almost entirely the usual hurrahs out of respect for our bitter grief." He was glad to report that he and his men were "still receiving enthusiastic congratulations upon our action and all are vying in making our captivity as light as possible." Admiral Cervera and his officers were confined at the United States Naval Academy in Annapolis. The enlisted men were held near Portsmouth, New Hampshire, on Seavey's Island. Forty-eight disabled men were placed on the hospital ship *Solace* and later treated at Norfolk, Virginia.[5]

After the land battles of July 1 Shafter conceived the idea of returning certain wounded Spanish prisoners and also of exchanging some of his prisoners for Lieutenant Hobson and the men of the *Merrimac*. He persisted in these efforts until they were accomplished, apparently seeking to counteract assumptions that the Americans would mistreat and even kill prisoners. "I am satisfied," he reported, "that it [the return of wounded prisoners] will tend more to create dissatisfaction in the ranks of the enemy than anything I could have done, as the soldiers said we were fighting the church and were going to kill them." On July 5 he released four Spanish officers and twenty-four enlisted men without even requiring a *quid pro quo*. Then on July 6, negotiations for the return of Hobson were completed, and the hero and his men were exchanged for a like number of Spanish prisoners.[6]

EARLY SIEGE OPERATIONS

Despite the naval victory, General Shafter and the War Department continued to worry about the situation at Santiago de Cuba. The field commander thrust aside a suggestion from Washington that for reasons of health he might transfer his responsibilities to another officer. Secretary of War Alger then sent a considerate but pointed message through Corbin on July 4: "Being on the ground and knowing all the conditions, the Secretary of War directs you will use your own judgment as to how and when you will take the city of Santiago, but, for manifest reasons, it should be accomplished as speedily as possible." This statement was tantamount to proposing that Shafter attack the city rather than invest it, for siege operations would require a certain amount of time. It also reflected an important political consideration: President McKinley wished to maintain pressure on Spain at all possible points, seeking to hasten an end to the war. Corbin also wanted to know whether the Fifth Army Corps required reinforcements. Shafter was asked to respond quickly; if he did not need reinforcement, the Department intended to prepare the Puerto Rican expedition. Shafter already had anticipated this question in an anxious inquiry of July 4: "When am I to expect troops from Tampa?" Just before midnight the same day he telegraphed another, longer message in response to Corbin in which he referred to Escario's entry into Santiago de Cuba and reported nervously, "This puts a different aspect upon affairs, and while we can probably maintain ourselves, it would be at the cost of considerable fighting and loss." Nevertheless he showed no inclination to cut short his operations: "We have got to try and reduce the town, now that the fleet is destroyed, which was stated to be the chief object of the expedition." As to reinforcements he was quite explicit: "There must be no delay in getting large bodies of troops here." This correspondence precipitated the dispatch of General Miles to Santiago de Cuba with troops originally intended for the Puerto Rican expedition.[7]

Shafter did not rest content with his plea for reinforcements. He renewed efforts to have the navy storm the harbor entrance, an enterprise that appeared especially attractive after Cervera's departure and defeat. On July 4 he clearly expressed to the War Department his reason for proposing his operation: It was "necessary that the navy force an entrance into the harbor of Santiago not later than the 6th instant and assist in the capture of that place. If they do, I believe the place will surrender without further sacrifice of life." In another plaintive message he claimed, "If the Army is to take the place, I want 15,000 troops speedily, and it is not certain that they can be landed, as it is getting stormy. [The] sure and speedy way is through the bay. Am now in position to do my part." He prefaced his suggestion to Admiral Sampson with the claim that Escario's arrival had nearly doubled the size of the Spanish garrison, a serious misconception. He had to delay operations until July 6 or 7 in order to complete the evacuation of civilians and exchange of prisoners, but thereafter he wanted the navy to take action: "Now, if you will force your way into that harbor the town will surrender without any further sacrifice of life. My present position has cost me 1,000 men, and I do not want to lose any more."[8]

Shafter's actions after the naval victory reflected the various difficulties, real or imagined, that still weighed upon him. He overestimated the enemy's strength; he magnified petty concerns; he quailed at the prospect of further casualties to his forces; he feared that tropical disease might soon strike. It is hardly surprising that this uncertain performance eroded the confidence of the Fifth Army Corps in its commander. John E. Woodward of the Sixteenth Infantry minced no words in his private denunciation of the leader: "Gen Shafter is a fool and I believe should be shot. . . . We are now & have been handled by incompetent men and I sincerely hope that they may be made to suffer some day." He summed up the situation as he saw it in a pithy epigram: "Too much theory & too little horse sense." Theodore Roosevelt wrote at some length to Senator Lodge, excoriating the commander:

> Not since the campaign of Crassus against the Parthians has there been so criminally incompetent a General as Shafter; and not since the expedition against Walcheren has there been a grosser mismanagement than in this. The battle [of July 1] simply fought itself, three of the Brigade Commanders, most of the Colonels, and all of the regiments individually did well; and the heroism of some of the regiments could not be surpassed; but Shafter never came within three miles of the line, and never has come; the confusion is incredible. The siege guns have not yet been landed! The mortars have not even started from the landing place. Our artillery has been poorly handled. There is no head; the orders follow one another in rapid succession; and are confused and contradictory to a degree. I have held the extreme front of the fighting line; I shall do all that can be done, whatever comes; but it is bitter to see the misery and suffering, and think that nothing but incompetency in administering the nation's enormous resources caused it.

Roosevelt, a bit unstrung by the difficult campaign, might have exaggerated Shafter's errors. He had placed his finger on considerations that suggested a pause in land operations until the command was properly prepared for further action.[9]

After President McKinley consulted his principal military and naval advisers, he made certain important decisions. Efforts to reinforce the expedition at Santiago de Cuba went forward with utmost vigor, and Shafter received instructions to confer directly with Sampson about further operations. A message from Corbin contained a relatively explicit order to take the offensive: "Secretary of War instructs me to say that the President directs that you confer with Admiral Sampson at once for cooperation in taking Santiago. After the fullest exchange of views, you will agree upon the time and manner of attack." Clearly the Administration expected action; it wished to avoid a tedious siege operation. Before consulting Sampson, Shafter reiterated his earlier view that regardless of cost the navy should attack the harbor entrance. "If they do," he maintained, "I believe that they will take the city and all the troops that are there." Gone was his earlier determination to accomplish his mission with a bare minimum of naval support. Any other course, he now claimed, would involve "heavy losses." When the fighting would resume, Shafter intended to direct artillery fire on the enemy trenches before Santiago de Cuba, but he did not plan to extend the bombardment to the city itself, taking the presence of noncombatants into consideration. He then asked for further instructions, hoping that orders would issue from Washington strengthening his bargaining position with Sampson. Corbin's response was not encouraging. The Adjutant General sought to explain the reasoning in Washington that had prefaced the order to attack. Apparently, he began, Shafter did not believe that his forces were sufficient to assault Santiago de Cuba; therefore it was wise to await reinforcements, already on the way. Since only the commanders in the field could decide on the details of an attack, Shafter was ordered to agree with Sampson upon "a course of cooperation best calculated to secure desired results with least sacrifice." In retrospect this course seems fully justified; theater commanders must be accorded discretion in making tactical decisions. The difficulty in 1898 stemmed from inexperience and the lack of a coherent doctrine to guide command decisions required in joint operations.[10]

In messages to Admiral Sampson the head of the Fifth Army Corps emphasized the necessity of seizing Santiago de Cuba's harbor for use as a port; heavy surf was creating serious difficulties at Siboney. Secretary of War Alger encouraged Shafter, indicating that his field commander's actions had been "thoroughly approved" in the War Department. He had an idea: If the navy refused to force the entrance, the army might "take a transport, cover the pilot house in the most exposed points with baled hay, attach an anchor to a towline, and, if possible, grapple the torpedo cables, and call for volunteers from the Army—not a large number—to run into the harbor, thus making a way for the Navy." Alger asked for Shafter's views on this plan before making a decision. "One thing is certain," he concluded, "the Navy must get into the harbor, and must save the lives of our brave men that will be sacrificed if we assault the enemy in his intrenchments without aid." Meanwhile, Sampson received instructions to consult with Shafter, but the Navy Department showed little enthusiasm for the army's proposal. In directing Sampson to cooperate with the army, Secretary Long added an important qualifier: "Act according to your best judgment in the matter."[11]

Once again the Naval War Board provided important guidance in a draft order that it proposed to send to Sampson. "You are instructed not to risk the loss of any armored vessels by submarine mines, unless for the most urgent reasons, as the duration and result of this war will depend chiefly upon the superiority of our navy to that of the enemy." Shafter should attack the harbor's fortifications. "It has always been considered here that if you will batter the Morro and the army will assault and take it, they could hold the banks of the entrance and drive out the enemy's infantry from the vicinity of the mine field, thus enabling your boats, backed up also by the [squadron's] fire, ... to clear a channel through which your ships could enter and take the place." This proposal included a statement later dropped from orders sent to Sampson: "Department does not consider the capture of Santiago, or of the army defending it, to be a sufficient object for . . . a sacrifice [of armored ships]." To underscore the views of the Navy Department, Long sent a letter to Alger that expressed an identical viewpoint.[12]

Sampson remained unalterably opposed to an unassisted attack on the harbor. His comment on Shafter's request of July 5 left nothing to the imagination: "This dispatch shows a complete misapprehension of the circumstances which had to be met." Like his superiors in Washington, he rejected all proposed operations that entailed risk to armored ships without commensurate return, having in mind the requirements of the blockade and other commitments in the West Indies as well as the menace of Cámara's squadron, then in the eastern Mediterranean. Firmly of the opinion that Cervera's vessels constituted the only appropriate objective at Santiago de Cuba, he did not want to attack the city and garrison. Why squander resources to no good purpose? Captain Chadwick summarized the general principle that guided Sampson: "War is sacrifice—both of men and material. Of men there were plenty; of the all-important material—ships—there was but little." Sampson certainly did not lack the courage to assault the entrance; he had been most eager to attempt a much more dangerous attack on Havana. He simply did not believe that the risks at Santiago de Cuba should be accepted because he was convinced that the objective lacked significant importance. From the outset of the campaign he had urged Shafter to join in combined operations against the Morro and the Socapa to permit removal of mines from the channel. This plan had drawbacks as long as Cervera remained in the harbor; his ships might well have been able to sink an American vessel in the channel, blocking the harbor entrance, but this consideration no longer obtained after Cervera's departure. Under these circumstances the risk of the armored vessels might have been so reduced as to justify an attack.[13]

On July 6 Captain Chadwick invited General Shafter to arrange an attack on the harbor entrance, and the two agreed upon a plan. Chadwick presented a specific proposal, one developed earlier. The navy wished to use its Marines, numbering about a thousand men, to assault either the Morro or the Socapa. If this force moved on the Socapa, the army should move at the same time by way of Aguadores with two or three thousand men to seize the ground just north of the Morro. Sampson felt certain that this plan would achieve success. When the heights would have fallen into American hands, Sampson could use countermining equipment brought up from Guantánamo to remove explosives from the channel. After an unsatisfactory discussion in which Shafter contributed little but thinly disguised pique, the navy's proposal was adopted, but with an understanding that another attempt to force the surrender of the city would take place before any move would be made against the harbor. Beginning at noon on July 9, should Toral refuse another demand for surrender, the squadron was to fire large projectiles (eight- to thirteen-inch shells) at Santiago de Cuba every two minutes for an hour. Thereafter, for another twenty-three hours it would fire every five minutes. If this bombardment did not induce surrender, Sampson would land the Marines at Cabañas Bay; in company with available Cuban insurgents they would attack the Socapa. At the same time Shafter would assault the Morro—although for unexplained reasons this aspect of the plan was not made explicit in the minutes of the meeting. After the heights were occupied and the mines cleared from the channel, the squadron would enter the harbor. Shafter was to provide a map showing his positions so the squadron would not fire accidentally on his lines during the bombardment. He was also to complete telegraphic communications between Siboney and Aguadores so he could report on the accuracy of the squadron's fire on Santiago de

Cuba. Chadwick agreed to draft a letter to General Toral proposing once again that the Spanish garrison lay down its arms.[14]

Chadwick's letter attempted to relieve the Spanish general of the heavy burden resting on his shoulders. First he described the outcome of the naval engagement, offering Toral the privilege of sending emissaries to the Spanish prisoners aboard the *Harvard*—still at Santiago de Cuba—to confirm the accuracy of his statements. Then, noting that the navy would begin bombarding the city at noon on July 9 unless the garrison decided to capitulate, he insisted that he was making his proposal "in a purely humanitarian spirit" seeking to avoid further bloodshed, since the final outcome of further fighting was a foregone conclusion. Finally, he suggested that Toral refer the question to his government; to allow time for this consultation the Americans would delay the bombardment. Shafter accepted this draft, and it was duly dispatched to Toral. After the war Shafter denied that Chadwick had written this letter, claiming that a draft of his own prepared prior to the consultation of July 6 had been altered at Chadwick's suggestion to cater to Spanish feelings. "The whole matter was of so little importance that I never thought of it since," he informed General Corbin, "as it was not worth thinking about, although the Navy, in their desire to get personal credit for public service (which should be beneath any man, at least the making of it the main object of his existence) jumped at this episode as a drowning man would clutch at a straw." This statement reflects the extent to which relations between the army and navy had become strained at Santiago de Cuba.[15]

Shafter's report to the War Department of his conference with Chadwick catalogued the commitments of the navy and confirmed his desire to besiege rather than assault Santiago de Cuba. He had hopes that the threat of bombardment might induce Toral to surrender. Attack did not appeal to him because, although he thought he could achieve victory, it would come with "fearful loss." The capture of a few thousand men was not worth the casualties to be anticipated from an offensive, particularly when it appeared that a siege would eventually force the enemy to capitulate. In communicating to Sampson, he indicated his belief that Toral would indeed consult his government. However, Shafter also reported the spread of illness among the American troops. "If the result of the first day's bombardment is not decisive," he concluded, "it will be absolutely necessary for the Navy to break into the harbor at once." Meanwhile he did nothing to prepare an attack on the Morro. It is entirely possible that he did not believe himself committed to an active supportive role in the attack against the harbor heights, despite the arrangements made with Captain Chadwick.[16]

Shafter had taken advantage of the lull in the fighting not only to seek naval assistance and negotiate with Toral but to strengthen his lines. Nothing eased this activity more than the flight to Cervera. If the guns of the Spanish squadron had been employed against the San Juan Heights the American position might have become untenable, in which case Shafter would have been forced to either assault the city or withdraw out of range. Of course, had Linares or Toral decided to use naval guns against the San Juan Heights, the armament of the American ships could have been used in turn against Spanish positions and Santiago de Cuba itself. Shafter's acceptance on July 6 of the navy's proposal to bombard the city represented the general's tardy appreciation of the navy's firepower. The guns of the squadron could compensate for the army's inability to get heavy guns into position before the besieged city.[17]

After the battles of July 1 the Fifth Army Corps found itself required to care for a large number of casualties. On June 29 a field hospital had been set up about three miles east of Santiago de Cuba, but the principal medical facility was located at Siboney. Care provided at the field hospital itself constituted a notable improvement over the record of previous wars. A journalist who went to Cuba with Clara Barton as part of the Red Cross's efforts, George Kennan, attributed the increase in the percentage of wounded men recovering from wounds to the use of antiseptics—and also to the nature of the wounds resulting from the Spanish Mauser rifle. "In most cases," he noted, "this wound was a small clean perforation, with very little shattering or mangling, and required only antiseptic bandaging or care." It was still impossible, however, to operate successfully on soldiers who received abdominal wounds. The greatest difficulties of the medical service here were poor arrangements for the transfer of casualties from the battlefield to Siboney and insufficient medical personnel. Only three of the seven ambulances brought with the expedition were ashore by July 1. Mule-drawn army wagons were used as ambulances, but this expedient proved inadequate because of the impossible roads. As soon as the casualties could be moved from Siboney, they were put aboard the hospital ship *Olivette*. Two transports, the *Cherokee* and the *Breakwater*, were pressed into service as makeshift hospital ships.[18]

Colonel Charles R. Greenleaf, chief surgeon of the Fifth Army Corps, summarized the difficulties of the medical service: It lacked sufficient tentage for field hospitals and medical supplies, not to mention personnel. Greenleaf encountered great difficulty in unloading supplies, brought to Cuba on the hospital ship *Relief*. Given these difficulties, it was fortunate that casualties were minimized after July 1.[19]

After dealing with the initial influx of wounded soldiers, the medical service became increasingly concerned with tropical disease. From the first General Shafter's fear that his men would suffer grievously from yellow fever, dysentery, and malaria greatly influenced the plans of campaign. Although no great epidemic developed during the first few weeks at Santiago de Cuba, Shafter remained convinced that disease would eventually create serious difficulties. Medical experts in Washington shared this opinion. Before Colonel Greenleaf left for the front, he noted that health problems in the training camps were as nothing compared with those awaiting the army in Cuba. He was concerned about "long-continued and excessive daily heat of the climate, with rapid lowering of temperature at night; the necessary exposure to rain in the absence of tentage; the scarcity and poor cookery of food; the effect of prolonged physical exertion on the battlefield, inducing nervous exhaustion." Fortunately yellow fever, the most dreaded of tropical diseases, never became a serious concern. The principal threat came from malaria. Major Frank J. Ives, a volunteer surgeon at Santiago de Cuba, described the symptoms of what was often called "ephemeral fever": The victims would experience a sudden elevation of body temperature, rising to 104° or 105° F. The pulse rate would increase moderately; a severe headache, pains in the back and limbs, a flushed or swollen face, conjunctivitis, and "great prostration" would develop. The tongues would swell, and nausea and vomiting would accompany the fever. Patients would experience restlessness and difficulty sleeping. These symptoms would often subside after three to five days, and recovery take place, but the disease so debilitated its victims that they would be far less useful than before in the ranks.[20]

If Shafter never found a solution to these medical problems, the same can be said about his services of supply. The troubles stemmed from a lack of sufficient transports. Between June 6 and July 3 the War Department managed to charter only nine ships in addition to those used to ferry the expedition to Santiago de Cuba. Ship owners proved increasingly reluctant to offer their vessels, and they succeeded in blocking congressional attempts to facilitate transfers of registry. The navy came to the rescue, offering as transports three of the ocean liners it had leased— the *Harvard, Yale,* and *Columbia*—along with another vessel, the *Rita*. Most of the ships that sailed to Santiago de Cuba with Shafter's troops never made a second voyage, simply because they were not unloaded quickly enough. A majority of them returned to the United States only after the surrender of the city. Secretary Alger finally found a solution: He brought in a businessman from Detroit, Frank J. Hecker, who was asked to purchase a fleet of transports. Between June 20 and July 25 Hecker located fourteen vessels, almost all of them under foreign registry, and bought them for a sum of $16 million. These transports were put to some use toward the end of the campaign in the West Indies, and they helped meet increased overseas commitments after the armistice. Had Alger acted earlier to procure vessels, he might have avoided much of the delay and congestion at Santiago de Cuba.[21]

The services of supply came under criticism particularly when Shafter found it difficult to unload vessels upon arrival at Santiago de Cuba. He lacked tugs and lighters to transfer materials from ship to shore. Moreover, the captains were wary of approaching the beach, fearing damage to their ships. A message to Corbin reported, "Transports go off miles from shore and there is no way of reaching them or compelling them to come in. It is a constant struggle to keep them in hand." It was only due to the lighter *Laura*, lent by the navy, that the Fifth Army Corps could sustain itself. Shafter noted, "It is with the greatest difficulty that one day's food can be issued at a time." News of these difficulties, reported by correspondents, began to stir public outcries at home. On July 7 Corbin cabled that Richard Harding Davis in particular had criticized both operations and supply: "He says that some of the men in the trenches have been without food for forty-eight hours and without tobacco." The President, he continued, viewed such reports as unjust, but nevertheless "the country will of course be distressed by the account he [Davis] gives." Shafter replied that many soldiers had left their haversacks containing rations and their blanket rolls in stockpiles on the day of the battle, and it took some time to recover these items. Food had been brought up to the front line on the night of July 1. Nevertheless he confessed to certain difficulties: "[The troops] were without tobacco for several days, as it is only by the greatest exertion that coffee, sugar, meat, and bread could be gotten out. . . . They had full rations except for twenty-four hours, when there was no coffee." Although he rejected the reports of Davis, Shafter promised to make inquiries. Despite Herculean efforts, the inherent difficulties for the Fifth Army Corps of landing supplies and moving them over the difficult terrain between Siboney and Santiago de Cuba precluded efficient supply services throughout the brief campaign.[22]

On July 9 one of the Rough Riders, Lieutenant Sherrard Adams of Virginia, summarized his experiences in the trenches. He had not taken off his shoes or washed his face for a week. There was considerable sickness among his comrades, much of it the result of heat. "The boys are simply exhausted, having to work all night and lie in the sun all day in the trenches. We have to build our own fortifications, but we are getting along all right." His personal equipment had disappeared: "I have no coat, and have on a pair of ragged trousers. I have lost my cap, too.

Someone stole it and my saber." His commanding officer, Theodore Roosevelt, wrote much more bluntly to Henry Cabot Lodge, attributing the blame for the trials of his troopers to the high command: "It is criminal to keep Shafter in command. He is utterly inefficient; and now he is panic struck. Wheeler is an old dear; but he is very little more fit than Shafter to command." Unfortunately the situation did not improve as time passed and the siege dragged on.[23]

As always in war, comical incidents helped to relieve the sense of privation. "Dido" Hunt of the Second Massachusetts Volunteers, last heard from stealing beer on the dock at Tampa, once again entered into the history of the war. His commanding officer, General Ludlow, had purchased a cow from a local Cuban, and Hunt, as regimental butcher, was detailed to kill the animal. The executioner "fired again and again at the cow, the animal after each shot, looking about in a surprised manner as if wondering what the racket was all about. Finally one of the bullets hit the cow somewhere, and with a bellow of pain and fright, she ran off and disappeared in the darkness, leaving Private Hunt and the man who had been holding the rope gazing at each other." No one determined the fate of the cow, "although there were rumors that the animal had ended her career in the camp of one of the regular regiments, the men of which had a fresh meat supper that night." So much for the adventures of "Dido" Hunt.[24]

If Shafter made all too little progress in solving his logistical problems, he also experienced difficulty completing the investment of Santiago de Cuba. In the first days after the Battle of San Juan Heights his left flank did not reach the seashore, and his right flank did not extend far enough to block westward access to the city. Of particular importance was his failure to deploy all available artillery. To excuse these deficiencies Shafter pleaded lack of sufficient troops to cover the long front, which started at Aguadores on the beach and ran north around Santiago de Cuba to Dos Caminos west of the city. The War Department manifested considerable anxiety about Shafter's position, repeatedly suggesting the need to extend his lines, particularly the right flank. General Miles cabled on July 7 that an enemy movement around the uncovered right flank might cut his communications to Siboney and Daiquirí. Shafter could only respond with an inquiry as to when he might expect reinforcements. The next day, however, he expressed relative confidence. Having visited the front, he gave it as his opinion that his lines were "impregnable against any force the enemy can send." His new optimism found a reflection among the troops. A black soldier, Sergeant H. B. Bivins, Tenth Cavalry, wrote a friend on July 8, "The city is at our mercy; we can destroy it at any time." He recognized that the Fifth Army Corps had suffered numerous casualties and that it had to man a long line, but expressed confidence: "We have the Spaniards bottled up, the only chance they have to escape is to take wings and fly."[25]

Some improvements were made in the disposition of artillery. Four batteries of light guns were brought up to support the positions on the San Juan Heights—two behind General Lawton's division on the right (Capron and Parkhurst) and two others at El Pozo (Best and Dillenback). On July 9 the Chief of Artillery, Brigadier General W. F. Randolph, arrived at Siboney with the Fourth and Fifth Artillery, and he managed to get two more light batteries into the line (Taylor and Riley). The siege guns never came into play, but eight 3.5-inch mortars were readied for action (although not much ammunition was available). These half-measures hardly improved the confidence of front-line commanders, who remembered the consequences of ineffective artillery fire on July 1.[26]

Given the troubles of the Fifth Army Corps, Shafter's decision to besiege Santiago de Cuba and to parley with General Toral made sense from a strictly military point of view. On July 8 he summed up his present policy for the benefit of the War Department: "No assault will be made . . . from our present lines until the Navy comes into the city. I hope to be able to fire from intrenchments to drive the enemy inside the city." Shafter did not mention any commitment to assist Sampson's attempt on the Morro and Socapa heights or give any indication that he planned to follow the plan of July 6, preferring instead a naval bombardment of the city. If that effort did not cause the enemy to surrender, the squadron apparently would have to force the harbor without benefit of supporting action against the Morro.[27]

NEGOTIATIONS FOR CAPITULATION

On July 8 Toral presented a counter-proposition to Shafter. The Spanish commander offered to evacuate Santiago de Cuba, leaving the place to the Americans, in return for the right to march his forces unmolested to Holguín. On what basis did he suggest such a deal? He maintained that he held a reasonably good position. Even if his water were to be cut off, he had a supply stored in cisterns. Stocks of ammunition and food would suffice for some time to come. The threat of bombardment would affect only the Cuban population; his troops were encamped outside the city. Toral also noted that his troops were acclimatized, unlike the Americans.[28]

Shafter's reaction was to extend the truce for the moment and refer the Spanish proposition to Washington. To the War Department he cabled, "I have replied [to Toral] that while I have submitted the matter to my home Government I did not think his terms would be accepted. He makes this proposition to avoid danger to the city and useless shedding of blood." When the navy began its bombardment, Shafter was sure the Spanish garrison would agree to an unconditional surrender.[29]

General Corbin responded almost immediately with explicit directions: The President, he cabled, "instructs me to say that you will accept nothing but unconditional surrender and should take extra precautions to prevent the enemy's escape."[30] This order reflected McKinley's policy of unequivocally demonstrating to Spain the firmness of his commitment to the war and his intention to campaign unrelentingly at every opportunity. Certainly his posture accorded with the situation at Santiago de Cuba; Shafter had not suggested that he was incapable of backing up inflexible demands.

In the meantime Shafter held a consultation with his division commanders and shifted his ground, deciding to recommend acceptance of Toral's counter-proposition. To Alger he cabled four reasons for his change of view. An immediate surrender of Santiago de Cuba would release the harbor, permit civilians to reoccupy the city, avoid destruction of property, and free the Fifth Army Corps for service elsewhere. Two other considerations also entered into the decision: Noting that three cases of yellow fever had been discovered in the Michigan regiment at Siboney, he stated that if the disease began to spread "no one knows where it will stop." What about the Spanish garrison? Shafter dismissed this question: "We lose by this [Spanish movement to Holguín] simply some prisoners we do not want and the arms they carry. I believe many of them will desert and return to our lines." Obviously, Toral's arguments had made a considerable impression on Shafter and his division commanders. Once again the commander of the Fifth Army Corps appears to have lost his nerve. He might easily have interpreted Toral's message as a sign of weakness, but chose instead to emphasize his own difficulties rather than those of the enemy.[31]

A little less than two hours after Washington received Shafter's recommendation to accept Toral's counter-proposition, Corbin replied in terms that must have aroused great chagrin at Santiago de Cuba, cabling bluntly:

> I am directed to say that you have repeatedly been advised that you would not be expected to make an assault upon the enemy at Santiago until you were prepared to do the work thoroughly. When you

are ready this will be done. Your telegram of this morning said your position was impregnable and that you believed the enemy would yet surrender unconditionally. You have also assured us that you could force their surrender by cutting off the supplies. Under these circumstances your message recommending that Spanish troops be permitted to evacuate and proceed without molestation to Holguin is a great surprise, and is not approved.

Responsibility for damage to Santiago de Cuba, Corbin went on, rested not with the United States forces but with the Spanish commander. What was Shafter to do? "The Secretary of War orders that when you are strong enough to destroy the enemy and take Santiago that you do it." If he lacked sufficient force for this purpose, reinforcements were on the way. "In the meantime," concluded Corbin, "nothing is lost by holding the position you now have and which you regard as impregnable." Here was a ringing message indeed, and unmistakable in its thrust. Few American field commanders have ever received a directive more redolent of implicit criticism and explicit rebuff. McKinley wanted an early and definitive victory at Santiago de Cuba, and nothing had yet come to his attention to make him question the feasibility of such a triumph.[32]

This message forced Shafter's hand. He then took steps to execute his instructions. He immediately notified Toral that Washington had rejected the counter-proposition, and insisted upon an unconditional surrender no later than 3:00 P.M. the next day, July 10. If his demand was rejected, he would begin a bombardment at 4:00 P.M. To the War Department he then cabled, "My position is impregnable against any attack the enemy can bring against me, but I have not yet enough troops to entirely surround the town. The Cuban forces are not to be depended upon for severe fighting." To reassure McKinley and others that he would stand firm, he concluded, "Instructions of the War Department will be carried out to the letter."[33]

On July 10 Shafter finally managed to cover his right flank and make other dispositions to interdict all communication between Santiago de Cuba and the interior. The long-awaited reinforcements had begun to arrive, and were immediately deployed to the front. The First Illinois Volunteers and the First District of Columbia Volunteers were landed and placed to the right of the cavalry division, a step that allowed General Ludlow, commanding on the right flank under General Lawton, to control the Cobre Road. On the same day General García occupied Dos Caminos, as well as the cemetery of Santiago de Cuba (a little closer to the city on the Cobre Road). Other Cuban forces were placed in the rear to scout for any approaching Spanish reinforcements.

At this point Shafter informed Alger that he could not comprehend the War Department's solicitude about his right flank, because it had never been in danger of attack. He had extended the line only to ensure that Spanish troops in the interior could not emulate the march of Colonel Escario.[34]

Now that the American position had been reinforced with both troops and artillery, many in the Fifth Army Corps wished to force an immediate decision. Theodore Roosevelt belonged to this persuasion, writing bitterly to Henry Cabot Lodge of Shafter's "tacking and veering" in response to Toral's counter-proposition. He thought it would be a great misfortune to accept any other outcome than unconditional surrender, the situation having improved greatly since July 1. "We can probably get the whole Spanish army now," he concluded, "at the cost of probably not more than a couple of days' fighting, chiefly bombardment." Presumably he and others of militant mien believed that immediate resumption of military activity would settle affairs promptly, thereby obviating any danger of tropical disease.[35]

When General Toral rejected this latest demand for surrender, Shafter completed arrangements for a naval bombardment of Santiago de Cuba. He asked Sampson to begin firing at 4:00 P.M. on July 10, stating that he would report the fall of the first shells to assist the navy in obtaining the range. Fearful of error in the navy's aim, he noted, "It would be very disastrous for the morale of my men to have any of the shell fall near them and I think it would be better at first to put your shots in the western part of the city near the bay." For one hour on the afternoon of July 10 the *Brooklyn* and *Indiana* fired a few eight-inch shells at Santiago de Cuba—an effort that accomplished nothing. A much more extensive bombardment occurred on the morning of July 11, the *New York* joining the *Brooklyn* and *Indiana* in firing eight-inch shells into the city from 9:27 A.M. until 1:00 P.M. At that time Shafter ordered a cease-fire while he would make another attempt to obtain surrender of the garrison. He informed Sampson that the navy's shells had been accurate, but asked that heavier guns be utilized the next day should Toral again refuse to surrender. Once more he cautioned the admiral to avoid firing on his lines: "Be careful not to shoot beyond the town, as my troops are within 1½ miles of it, and you will be firing directly toward us."[36]

A board appointed later to investigate the results of the bombardment found that forty-six projectiles had damaged fifty-seven houses, but that a goodly number had fallen harmlessly into the water or beyond the target area. This outcome stemmed from Shafter's injunction to keep the bombardment well away from American positions.

'Had the ships been allowed to direct their fire more towards the center of the city,'' the board decided, ''the destruction would have been very great.'' However, Shafter and Alger later criticized the navy, calling the bombardment of July 10 and 11 ineffective—to which Captain Chadwick riposted vigorously: He noted that the bombardment had been stopped prematurely, before the squadron could use its larger guns. The outcome would have been devastating if all of the squadron's eight-inch guns had been employed, along with its eighteen twelve-inch and thirteen-inch guns. Sampson had ''an armament sufficiently powerful to have razed the city in a few hours and have made its site absolutely untenable to any body of men whatever.'' Chadwick's argument seems justifiable, but no further opportunity materialized to test his judgment. Although Sampson brought up the *Oregon* and *Massachusetts* from Guantánamo on July 13 to join in the bombardment, late on July 12 Shafter informed him that a truce still existed and that he should continue to refrain from firing on the city until further notice. As it turned out, no further combat took place at Santiago de Cuba between the end of the naval bombardment on July 11 and the formal capitulation on July 17.[37]

Shafter's churlish behavior toward the navy did not escape the attention of naval officers taking part in the campaign. Even the tactful Captain Caspar F. Goodrich, who had been most helpful to Shafter in landing troops and supplies, complained, ''Our sister branch . . . is a spoiled child and takes every exertion on our part as a matter of course. . . . Especially is it hard for us to put up with an irritating assumption of superiority.'' He was especially critical of the troop movement to Cuba: ''Some day a grave scandal will probably be unearthed. After getting the troops there the army was as helpless as a babe until the navy stepped in and landed them.'' The tension between the army and navy at Santiago de Cuba, stemming originally from disagreements about the proper means of reducing the city, reached new heights in the last moments of the siege.[38]

Negotiations resumed on July 11 that eventually would lead to the end of the Spanish resistance at Santiago de Cuba. On that morning Shafter received a message from the Secretary of War that played a considerable role in the eventual outcome: ''Should the Spaniards surrender unconditionally and wish to return to Spain,'' cabled Alger, ''they will be sent back direct at the expense of the United States Government.'' This truly unusual decision Alger later claimed to have urged as a means of expediting Toral's surrender. He insisted that it had many advantages: It would help obtain a decision before yellow fever became prevalent among United States troops; make a desirable impact on public opinion in Spain; impress the world as an act of generosity towards a defeated foe; demoralize other Spanish units in Cuba; and cost but little more than the price of maintaining a prison camp in the United States. (Such a camp had already been proposed, to be located at Galveston, Texas.) Shafter immediately passed this sweetener along to Toral, together with a renewed demand for unconditional surrender. The next morning he received word that his message had been referred to Governor-General Blanco.[39]

At this juncture General Miles arrived at Santiago de Cuba with a contingent of troops. As commanding general of the army, he might have superseded Shafter, but before leaving Washington he had voluntarily informed the President that he did not plan to assume command while the incumbent remained physically able to perform his duties. Accordingly, when Alger notified Shafter that Miles had departed for Cuba, he emphasized the limits of Miles's responsibilities. Corbin's message of July 8 stated, "Secretary of War directs me to inform you that General Miles left here at 10:40 last night for Santiago, but with instructions not to in any manner supersede you as commander of forces in the field near Santiago as long as you are able for duty." Alger obviously relished this restriction of Miles, a step consistent with his animosity towards the commanding general and his confidence in Shafter. Shafter's message reporting recovery of full health must have been intended to dispel any lingering feelings in Washington that he was incapable of retaining command.[40]

When General Miles arrived, he devoted his energies to planning an attack on the harbor entrance, the very enterprise Sampson had been advocating since the arrival of the Fifth Army Corps at Santiago de Cuba. The commanding general had given considerable thought to such an operation before leaving Washington. In his autobiography he stated flatly, "It was my purpose to land sufficient force on the west side of the harbor of Santiago and enfilade the enemy's line and take their position in reverse." After making arrangements with Sampson on the morning of July 11—the morning of the bombardment—to land his troops and receive supporting naval gunfire, he went ashore and made known his intentions to Shafter. Sampson assigned Lieutenant Richmond P. Hobson to the duty of coordinating the effort. As might have been expected, Hobson suggested that Miles land his troops on the eastern side of the harbor entrance and move against the Punta Gorda battery. The operation was to be prepared by noon July 14.[41]

Shafter, who had other ideas, continued to resist participation in the attack. On July 12 he reiterated to the War Department that the navy should assault the entrance by itself, emphasizing that he had growing supply problems and now had to deal with regular tropical rains. If the navy did not attack, and if the roads should become impassable, "we will simply have to take the town by assault, without regard to what it costs." These sentiments he communicated also to General Miles.[42]

Miles, however, joined Shafter in evincing a desire to avoid further action, as shown in two messages sent to Washington on July 12 (one from Shafter and the other from Miles). The two generals resuscitated the proposal to grant General Toral safe-conduct to Holguín in return for the surrender of Santiago de Cuba. Shafter stressed his concerns about casualties, supply, and tropical disease. He believed that he could seize the city, but if Toral fought—which he thought possible—"it will be at fearful cost of life." Miles reported Shafter's request, alleging that a siege might last for many weeks and that Shafter's troops were needed for operations elsewhere, presumably in Puerto Rico. He gave greatest emphasis, however, to the problem of tropical disease: "The very serious part of this situation is that there are one hundred cases of yellow fever in this command, and the belief of the Chief Surgeon [is] that it will spread rapidly."[43]

What motivated Shafter and Miles to abandon the policy of unconditional surrender? Apparently these latest proposals stemmed from the outcome of meeting with Toral. On July 12 Shafter informed the Spanish commander that he would extend the truce until midday July 13. He would not alter the location of any troops on his line, but would continue to advance troops who had recently arrived at Siboney to his fortifications. He suggested that Toral meet Miles and him under a flag of truce at 9:00 A.M. the next morning. Toral accepted this invitation, repeating his counter-proposition and informing Shafter of his need for "a solution . . . that leaves the honor of my troops intact; otherwise you will comprehend that I shall see myself obliged to now make defence as far as my strength will permit."[44]

No orders had been received from Washington when, on the morning of July 13, Miles and Shafter held their meeting with Toral. The commanding general of the army took the lead in the discussion, reiterating the terms that had been laid down previously: unconditional surrender and a promise to ship the garrison back to Spain. When Toral pleaded that Spanish law did not permit him to surrender as long as he possessed ammunition and food, Miles insisted that he must give up or accept the consequences. The parley produced an arrangement to extend the truce further until noon July 14, which would give Toral time to consult his government. Shafter's report of the discussion reflected guarded optimism: The Americans had made a "strong impression" on the Spanish commander. If he did not surrender, the navy would resume its bombardment with heavy guns. Nevertheless Shafter still remained anxious about disease, noting "a good deal of nervousness throughout the army on account of yellow fever, which is among us certainly."[45]

While the generals negotiated at Santiago de Cuba, Washington reconsidered their proposal to accept Toral's earlier conditions for the evacuation of Santiago de Cuba. Captain Mahan, taking part in these activities as a member of the Naval War Board, summarized their content in a series of communications to Secretary Long written after the war. Mahan himself was favorably disposed to the proposition, believing that possession of the city as against the enemy garrison satisfied the needs of the moments. But determined opposition came from President McKinley, who "took a very strong stand against acceptance; expressing himself not only vigorously, but with a certain vehemence very foreign to his usual manner." What considerations influenced the Commander-in-Chief? "He argued that the impression at home, and to an extreme degree abroad, would be most unfavorable to us, would tend to foreign complications and to prolong the war; for it would be assumed that such terms were extorted only from our sense of weakness." Nevertheless, the weight of professional military and naval opinion might have forced acceptance of the Miles-Shafter recommendation had not Mahan come to the rescue. As discussion continued, wrote Mahan, "the thought occurred to me, and was by me submitted, that our government should present as its terms the capitulation of the place and of the garrison, and the stipulation that the latter should be carried to Spain, with their arms, at our expense." Mahan erred in thinking that he was the first to propose this idea. Shafter had been authorized by Alger to advance it to Toral well before the meeting of July 13 at which Mahan claimed to have invented it. In any case McKinley deserves credit for both insisting upon unconditional surrender and agreeing to this proposal, lessening the enemy's humiliation through the return of the Spanish garrison to Spain at American expense.[46]

On that day the Secretary of War then sent Shafter reconfirmation of the previous decision to reject Toral's counter-proposition. "No modification of former order permitting the Spanish army evacuating Santiago under such conditions as proposed by Toral will be made," he stated positively. This instruction governed all further negotiations. At the same time Alger also informed Shafter, "The Secretary of the Navy will be consulted at once concerning the ordering of Sampson to assist you." Later that day, July 13, Shafter received permission through Miles to delay the assault on Santiago de Cuba until he learned the result of discussions with the Navy Department.[47]

In Washington Alger urged upon Long the army's view that the navy should make an unassisted attack on the harbor entrance. The Secretary of War offered four reasons to justify his request that Long "order the fleet off Santiago to at once force its way into the bay, if possible, to aid the Army in the capture of Santiago and the Spanish Army defending it": Heavy rains had made roads impassable, and Shafter might not be able to maintain his supply lines indefinitely. In addition, the rains made it most difficult to man the entrenchments on the San Juan Heights and elsewhere. Yellow fever had begun to spread rapidly. Finally, he cited Shafter's familiar plaint: "The character of the [Spanish] works is such that to take them by assault would be a terrible sacrifice of life." He reported Shafter as arguing that a cooperative effort would turn the capture of the city into "a comparatively easy matter." Long courteously acknowledged Alger's request but made no immediate response. Instead he cabled the proposal to Sampson and asked him to confer with Shafter. Two provisos gave Sampson considerable freedom of action: "Wishing to do all that is reasonably possible to ensure surrender of enemy," cabled Long, "I leave matter to your discretion." Also, he added, "battle ships must not be risked."[48]

Long's diary entry on this day summarized his mood: "We are all pained at the delays at Santiago. Our men are up to their knees in water one minute, and under the blaze of the sun the next." He summarized the course of negotiations neatly: "The commanding officers have been ordered over and over again to bring the matter to a head, but they delay—perhaps for good reason, although we are inclined to think the Spanish commander is tricking them along with truces and offers of terms of surrender."[49]

Long's message reached Santiago de Cuba at the same time as newspaper reports criticizing the navy for alleged inaction, a combination of events that finally shook Sampson's composure. Once again—this time in rather heated language—the Admiral opposed an attempt to force the harbor without first occupying the Morro and Socapa heights: "If the general chooses to ignore the sea approaches and to attack Santiago to the east and north that is his affair, but it should be clearly understood that his attack does not influence the situation at the harbor entrance, from which his left flank is distant not less than 4 miles." He had been ready for three weeks to take his proper part in an operation at the entrance, but would not move without appropriate support from the army. "To throw my ships to certain destruction upon mine fields would be suicidal folly, and I have not the force to form landing party strong enough to insure the capture of the forts." Noting reports published in the *New York Herald* concerning his disagreements with Shafter, he stated that the commander of the Fifth Army Corps had made no complaints to him.[50]

Sampson did not know that on July 13 Captain Mahan had argued the navy's case vehemently with representatives of the army. During a meeting that day concerning the possible dispatch of the Eastern Squadron to Spanish waters, Alger allowed himself to abuse the navy for its failure to storm the harbor at Santiago de Cuba. The Secretary's anger stemmed from his belief that undue priority had been given to operations in the Philippines. Margaret Leech noted, "He had worked himself into a wrathful conviction that the army in Cuba was being ignored and victimized by the Navy in general and Admiral Sampson in particular." There then ensued what Secretary Long called "a very pretty scrimmage. . .Mahan, at last, lost his patience and sailed into Alger; told him he didn't know anything about the use or purpose of the Navy, and that he didn't propose to sit by and hear the Navy attacked." Long reported, with a certain satisfaction, that the affair "rather pleased the President, who, I think, was glad of the rebuke." A bit later Alger visited the Secretary of the Navy and apologized for his outburst. This gesture touched Long, who noted that his colleague "seemed so dejected at the condition of the troops under the risk of yellow fever and at the burdens which are on them." The Secretary of War was "a sanguine, generous man, but the task—and it is a tremendous one—is too much for him." In any event Alger's and Mahan's outbursts, which came at a critical juncture during the campaign at Santiago de Cuba, again revealed the lack of any means for conducting joint operations.[51]

Still another bone of contention strained Sampson's relations with Shafter at this point. When the Admiral learned of the negotiations with Toral he insisted that the navy take part in them. To Shafter he gave notice of his desire to participate "in any conference held to arrange the terms of the surrender of Santiago, including the surrender of shipping and the harbor." He summed up his reasons simply: "Questions involved are of importance to both branches of the service." Shafter replied in a conciliatory manner; he would be glad to include a naval representative, but it would be difficult to inform the navy of meetings because of uncertainty about the timing of negotiations with the Spanish. To remedy this problem he recommended that Sampson send a naval officer to represent him at army headquarters. If this arrangement proved inconvenient, he would try to give notice sufficient to ensure that a naval officer could be present when Toral agreed to surrender. Sampson, of course, sought more than mere representation; he aspired to a substantive role in the discussions themselves.[52]

When Washington received reports of the meeting with Toral on July 13, specific instructions were sent to Miles concerning the surrender of Santiago de Cuba and its garrison. He could accept an arrangement that granted parole to the Spanish forces and allowed officers to retain side arms. Paroled soldiers would be returned to Spain at the expense of the United States. If this offer was refused, the Fifth Army Corps was to attack, unless the commanding general decided that a successful attack could not be made. He should consult with Sampson, and pursue joint operations on the basis of an agreement between the two services. Alger also cabled Shafter, "Your message announcing that unless your terms are accepted before noon to-morrow you will make an assault all along the line is received and approved. God bless you and your heroic army."[53]

Not only the Secretary of the Navy suspected that the Spanish commander had been playing for time rather than negotiating in good faith, but Shafter persisted in his belief that he could obtain a surrender without further combat. Lieutenant John D. Miley, the General's aide, reported that his superior received frequent advice to break off negotiations and assault Santiago de Cuba, but fortunately Shafter "allowed his better judgment to prevail." Miley laid heavy stress on the strength of the enemy's fortifications. He thought that if the Spanish defenders resisted another attack as strongly as on July 1 the result would have been "fearful to contemplate," an argument that Shafter advanced on several occasions during the negotiations themselves.[54]

As American forces developed the siege of Santiago de Cuba, the government in Madrid contemplated its course. After the defeats of July 1 and July 3 it became obvious that Toral faced a desperate situation. The garrison could be fed with boiled rice and rice bread, but this limited diet would weaken the troops. The mood in Santiago de Cuba itself was gloomy: "Everybody knew that calamity was not far off and was inevitable," wrote Lieutenant Müller, "for no provisions could be expected, either by land or sea." Escario's column swelled the number of defenders, although the Cuban home guards had largely disappeared after Cervera's departure. Even if the situation at Santiago de Cuba were to be retrieved, the Liberal ministry had to consider the consequences of other American operations—among them a sortie by the Eastern Squadron, an attack on Puerto Rico, and reinforcement of Dewey at Manila. If Spain continued to resist, it might fritter away all of the remainder of its imperial remnant. When Sagasta opened an exchange of messages with Blanco concerning the future, the Governor-General convened a meeting of his military commanders to arrive at his recommendation. This gathering decided that resistance should continue in Cuba regardless of the outcome at Santiago de Cuba. On July 9 Blanco cabled to the Minister of War that he could hold out for many months, and that the army wished as a matter of honor to fight on. To this unwelcome message Sagasta responded that in his opinion Spain had no alternative to capitulation, citing the danger to Puerto Rico, the Balearic Islands, the Canaries, and the Iberian peninsula itself and obviously bearing in mind possible operations of the Eastern Squadron. Moreover, future developments might lead to domestic tumult. Given the course of the war so far, to seek an immediate peace would be honorable; terms exacted after further calamities might prove unacceptable. Sagasta asked how the army would react to peace negotiations.[55]

Eventually the Liberal ministry overrode Blanco's objections. On July 12 the stricken General Linares, recovering from wounds received at the San Juan Heights, rehearsed the desperate situation of the garrison: It could neither flee the city nor receive reinforcements. ''The situation is fatal [and] surrender inevitable; we are only prolonging the agony; the sacrifice is useless; the enemy knows it, fully realizing our position.'' Shafter would merely sustain his siege, wearing out the Spanish troops and refusing to expose his own. Santiago de Cuba was not the legendary Gerona, a Spanish city that had defended itself nobly against French attack in the days of Napoleon. On the same day Minister of War Correa pleaded with Blanco to give assurances that the army in Cuba would abide by the decision of the government. Finally Blanco gave in, at least enough to permit action in Madrid. On July 14 he gave notice that the army would obey orders although it wished to continue the struggle. Should the government decide to seek peace, Blanco said, he would be compelled to resign his office. Sagasta then consulted a broad array of Spanish leaders. Only one, the intransigent Romero Robledo, opposed a peace initiative. To dampen sources of possible criticism, Sagasta closed the Cortes on July 14. He was now prepared to authorize both the capitulation of Santiago de Cuba and negotiations to end the war.[56]

On the morning of July 14, just before expiration of the truce, General Toral finally indicated his willingness to capitulate, a step that led to the last parleys. He sent a letter to Shafter mentioning his authority received from Blanco to negotiate ''capitulation on the basis of repatriation.'' He said he had word also that Blanco had applied to Madrid for final authority to surrender. Given the circumstances, the Spanish general proposed that he and Shafter appoint commissioners to arrange details. At noon on July 14 Toral not only personally reiterated the contents of this letter but expressed his desire to act for all the Spanish troops in the Division of Santiago de Cuba—those at Guantánamo and elsewhere. (This proposal greatly surprised the

Americans.) In reporting Toral's actions to Washington, Shafter noted that no formal surrender had yet taken place and asked how soon the Spanish garrison could be returned to Spain. Corbin indicated that this task could be accomplished very quickly. Shafter provided accurate information here, but Miles somewhat misrepresented the state of affairs in his messages to Alger. His report stated, "General Toral formally surrendered the troops of his army corps and division of Santiago on the terms and understanding that his troops would be returned to Spain." Shafter would appoint commissioners to work out details.[57]

Miles took a leading role during this period. Still preoccupied by the threat of tropical disease, he reported various measures to prevent the infection of his own command, which still remained offshore aboard ship. He indicated his intention to move on to Puerto Rico as soon as possible. To Shafter he wrote a letter that authorized the appointment of commissioners to treat with those of Toral and drew attention to the need for certain other arrangements: The refugees at El Caney should be allowed to return to the city, and it was necessary to provision them. The Red Cross relief ship, the *City of Texas,* now at Santiago de Cuba, should be allowed to enter the harbor and land supplies needed to sustain the civilians. All obstructions should be removed from the channel, by either the army or navy. (This latter proviso was an attempt to placate Admiral Sampson.) Although Shafter had acceded to Sampson's request for naval participation in the negotiation of the Spanish capitulation, the Admiral did not send a representative to army headquarters, probably because he was under the mistaken impression that the surrender had already taken place.[58]

CAPITULATION

The Spanish and American commissioners met for the first time on July 14 at 2:30 P.M. Generals Wheeler and Lawton and Lieutenant Miley represented Shafter. Two Cuban aides, Ramón Mendoza and Aurelius Maestre, interpreted for the Americans. Toral sent Escario, now promoted to General, Lieutenant Colonel Ventura Fontán, and Robert Mason, the British vice-consul—the latter serving as interpreter. The American commissioners presented a form of capitulation that included items agreed upon earlier, along with clauses restoring the city's water supply and permitting officers to retain their side arms. Toral's representatives wanted to insert provisions allowing the Spanish to take away their military records and authorizing Cubans who had served in the Spanish army to remain in Cuba. To the annoyance of the Americans, the Spanish commissioners, instead of completing the transaction then and there, returned to Santiago de Cuba. They came back later to request a day's delay, pleading their desire to consult General Linares. When the Americans demurred, suspecting the commissioners of delaying tactics, General Toral personally informed them that he could not surrender officially until Madrid sent formal permission. Only at this point, apparently, did it become clear to the Americans that they had misinterpreted Toral's earlier concession.[59]

There ensued a confusing delay. On the morning of July 15 Sampson asked Shafter to convey the terms of surrender and indicate when the Americans might occupy the harbor and city. To this inquiry Shafter replied, "Hitch in negotiations; we may have to fight for it yet. They wish to refer to Spain." Shafter also reported the delay to Miles and asked him not to depart, saying of his troops, "We may have to use them yet." The War Department then began to manifest anxiety. Corbin telegraphed, "The Secretary of War awaits with deep interest details of surrender. Delay not understood." To this message Shafter responded soothingly with accurate information: Toral had agreed to surrender; his hesitation was merely temporary. "The great point with the Spanish," he explained, "is that they be allowed to carry their arms with them to Spain, marching out of here and depositing them in my charge, but having them shipped with them to Spain." Miles, he continued, had been present when Toral announced his intentions and had noted that the Spanish action was "as absolute and as complete as possible." Shafter thought it impossible that the final arrangements would not materialize. Dissatisfied with this message, Alger observed that the Spanish commander might be stalling in expectation of early reinforcements. Shafter patiently explained that none were available to Toral; Cuban troops were covering all concentrations of Spanish troops in the vicinity. The American commissioners had no doubt of Toral's good faith. Reports had come in indicating that enemy officers were much pleased at the prospect of returning to Spain. However, the Generals were "afraid of the consequences with themselves unless terms of surrender are sanctioned by the Madrid Government."[60]

Shafter's intimation that he might permit the Spanish garrison to depart with their arms caused consternation in Washington. Any such arrangement struck leaders there as indicating that the American victory had been less than complete, an interpretation that might vitiate the impact of the surrender in Madrid and elsewhere. Alger immediately telegraphed in strong terms, "It is not possible you are entertaining the proposition of permitting the Spanish to carry away their arms. Such a suggestion should be rejected instantly." He reminded Shafter that he had been informed of the President's terms, and must adhere to them.

Shafter replied that he had made no concessions on this point. The Spanish arms would be surrendered, but the commissioners had asked Shafter to suggest to Washington that they be shipped to Spain eventually. "I regard this as a small matter that in no way binds the Government," he added, "but is one I would not let stand between clearing 20,000 Spanish soldiers out of Cuba or leaving them there to be captured later and probably with much loss to ourselves." Miles agreed with Shafter that the arms issue did not amount to anything; he informed Shafter that he cared little about it and that arrangements could be made for the United States to either send them separately or return them with the Spanish as part of their personal property. This reasonable attitude found no favor in Washington. Corbin immediately informed Shafter that McKinley and Alger were becoming impatient; they would disapprove any arrangement that allowed the garrison to depart with its arms. Then the Adjutant General, an old personal friend of Shafter's, offered some unofficial counsel: "The way to surrender is to surrender, and this should be fully impressed on General Toral. I send this as your friend and comrade, and not by authority, but you can be guided by it with entire safety."[61]

Washington need not have worried; the Spanish garrison was preparing to capitulate as soon as the official word they confidently anticipated would arrive from Madrid. On July 15, as anxious messages passed between Shafter and the War Department, Toral held a council of war to discuss the question of surrender. All sorts of reasons for giving up were adduced during this discussion: The city had little substantial fortification. Only eight thousand men were available to defend a perimeter of about nine miles. Units in given locations were in no position to support other units. Either antiquated artillery was wearing out or batteries had expended their ammunition. Cartridges for Mauser rifles were in short supply. The garrison had almost consumed its stocks of food. Sickness was growing on the lines outside the city, and water was hard to obtain because the enemy had cut off the source of supply. No new supplies could be expected because of the American blockade. No means of escape existed unless the garrison decided to accept battle in the most unfavorable circumstances. The enemy possessed not only forty thousand troops but considerable artillery and a powerful naval squadron. Further resistance would lead only to additional loss of life. The honor of Spanish arms had been satisfied, and an immediate surrender would ensure more favorable terms than might be available later. All these circumstances, presumably discussed for the record, led to a unanimous decision: "The necessity for capitulation has arrived."[62]

At 10:00 P.M. on July 15 Toral wrote a letter to Shafter reporting that he had received permission to sign a capitulation. As previously arranged, his commissioners would meet Shafter's representatives to edit the articles of capitulation. He specifically inquired whether the United States would allow his troops to return to Spain with their arms. At this point Shafter tersely cabled to the War Department, "Spanish surrendered; particulars later."[63]

President McKinley now dispatched to Shafter and his men the congratulations of the American people. "Your splendid command," he wrote, "has endured not only the hardships and sacrifices incident to campaign and battle, but in the stress of heat and weather has triumphed over obstacles which would have overcome men less brave and determined." McKinley then spoke of the fallen. "The hearts of the people turn with tender sympathy to the sick and the wounded. May the Father of Mercies protect and comfort them." That very day Charles G. Dawes had lunch at the White House with the President and First Lady, and he learned of the circumstances that had surrounded the negotiations in Santiago de Cuba as perceived in Washington. The President, Dawes reported, had forcefully opposed "too lenient terms of surrender." In response to a proposal that the Spanish be allowed to retreat to Holguín, McKinley had "wired as an ultimatum that the arms must be surrendered, but agreed that the troops should be transported to Spain. He withheld his telegram of congratulation to Shafter and his troops until he knew definitely that his terms were to be carried out to the letter." Then Dawes summarized the reason for McKinley's hard line: "The normal effect of the victory of Santiago might have been wholly lost if it had not been for the President's firmness."[64]

Throughout the campaign at Santiago de Cuba the President sought always to sustain the greatest possible pressure on the enemy. While seeking a clear victory there, he also was preparing for other operations—at Puerto Rico, Manila, and even in Spanish waters—as coordinated aspects of a cumulative effort to force an early decision. He had not wanted war; once it began he did everything possible to bring the struggle to an end at the earliest time with the least expenditure of blood and treasure. Throughout this period he carefully avoided actions that might encourage European intervention in behalf of Spain. The decision to send the expedition to Santiago de Cuba, however ill-prepared, now stood vindicated. The gamble had paid off.

Leonard Wood summarized very well the views of the men who had besieged Santiago de Cuba. Writing to his wife on July 15, he noted that an assault could have carried the city, but at the expense of perhaps three or four thousand casualties. He was pleased that the surrender covered not only the city and its garrison but all other enemy forces in eastern Cuba. Scornful of Shafter and patronizing about Wheeler ("Wheeler runs a news correspondence stand and while a dear old man is no more use here than a child"), he was glad that "we have whipped them and done it well but at many times the cost needed if we had our proper tools and a little brain matter at the top." To his wife he wrote graphically of the environmental problems that now confronted the Fifth Army Corps: "The heavy rains and the roads or rather trails are absolute canals of mud such as you never saw or imagined. Then our friend, the yellow fever, is behind us and the days of storms at sea in the region are near at hand." Supplies were low. "In short, my dear, having soundly thrashed the enemy, we are now in a struggle with nature and to a certain extent with disease." Like so many others at the moment of victory, Wood did not forget the human sacrifice. "Indeed this game of war is a sad one," he concluded, "and as one sees the graves of old friends in the army on almost every hill it forces home the cost of the victories."[65]

On July 16 there remained to General Shafter only the making of final arrangements with General Toral. Meeting for the last time at 4:00 P.M. on July 16, the commissioners two hours later signed the articles of capitulation. The word "surrender" was not used, because the Spanish word *capitulación* carries less pejorative content than *rendición*. This course of action continued the American practice here of manifesting utmost consideration for the feelings of the defeated enemy. General Wheeler explained later the reasons for this sensitivity: Toral proved more interested in simply recommending that the arms of his men be returned than in the actual deed. He sought "language complimenting him and his soldiers for their courage and chivalry." The proud general, if affronted, might have broken off negotiations. Wheeler learned from one of the Spanish commissioners of the future that lay before Toral: "As general commanding the forces, he would be held accountable for the surrender; . . . he would probably, even though he had received the consent of his Government to capitulate, have to answer for same before a court-martial at Madrid." For this reason he naturally wanted to avoid any statement in the articles of capitulation that might reflect on his personal courage or provide a basis for later charges.[66]

The articles of capitulation included ten clauses applying to all Spanish forces in the Division of Santiago, the area east of the line Aserraderos-Dos Palmas-Cauto Abajo-Escondida-Tánamo-Aguilera. Hostilities were to cease "absolutely and unequivocally." All Spanish troops and material were included in the capitulation. Toral agreed to remove all mines and other obstacles from the harbor. The Spanish command could render an inventory of all its arms and forces. Personnel would be returned to the Spanish Peninsula "with as little delay as possible." Officers could retain side arms, and troops their personal belongings. Military records could be transported out of Cuba. Cubans serving with the Spanish forces in various capacities could remain on the island after delivering up their arms and giving their paroles. Finally, "the Spanish forces will march out of Santiago de Cuba with the honors of war, depositing their arms thereafter at a point mutually agreed upon, to await their disposition by the United States government, it being understood that the United States commissioners will recommend that the Spanish soldier return to Spain with the arms he so bravely defended." This recommendation never received approval in Washington, but it served its purpose in expediting the final agreement.[67]

No naval officer signed the articles of capitulation, although Captain Chadwick was present at Shafter's headquarters, when the commissioners approved them. Sampson's chief of staff managed to prevent damage to a gunboat in the harbor, the *Alvarado,* which Spanish regulations required to be destroyed in the event of capitulation. Sampson had assumed that he and Shafter would jointly sign the articles of capitulation, bearing in mind the precedent established by the British at Louisbourg in 1758 when Admiral Boscawen and General Wolfe jointly received the French surrender. He reported later that when Chadwick arrived for the final meeting of the commissioners Shafter "peremptorily refused" his request to act for him. Shafter gave as his principal reason the fact that the terms had already been signed—apparently a reference to the preliminary agreement—but he also brought up another consideration that must have infuriated both Chadwick and Sampson. He noted that the Admiral had not mentioned the role of the army in reporting the naval victory of July 3. Sampson dismissed this argument scornfully: "There would have been as much reason for mentioning the Navy in the report of the land action of July 1." This episode, however petty in itself, contributed not a little to continued interservice squabbling at Santiago de Cuba after the Spanish capitulation.[68]

Toral's decision to surrender all the garrisons in the Division of Santiago de Cuba surprised the Americans. After the war Shafter testified that he had been "simply thunderstruck that of their own free will they should give me 12,000 men that were absolutely beyond my reach. I had no earthly chance of getting them." Toral, however, had considered the question from a perspective of deep despondency. During the negotiations with the American commission, he actually bared his feelings to Wheeler: "I would not desire to see my very worst enemy compelled to play the cards I have had to play during the last two weeks. . . . All my generals have been killed or wounded; I have not a single colonel left, and I am surrounded by a powerful army." He did not forget Sampson: "My men counted sixty-seven ships off the coast, all loaded with troops." When General Suárez Inclán defended Toral at his postwar court-martial, he gave considerable attention to this question. Since there was no hope for the other garrisons, he argued, why should Toral condemn them to additional privation? The military writer Gómez Núñez noted another motive: If they were surrendered along with the troops at Santiago de Cuba, the United States would have to bear the cost of repatriation.[69]

Toral's view that the war was all but over was far more realistic than that of Blanco, who bravely informed Madrid on July 17 that he could continue to resist—if he received munitions and provisions. "The fall of Santiago has no true military importance," he cabled, "and it can be said that the war still has not begun." If the enemy approached the Havana area, they would have to break through the *trocha,* an attack that would cost them dear. Blanco ignored the fact that, whatever its strictly military meaning, the surrender of Santiago de Cuba had imposing political significance. The complete collapse of all Spanish resistance in eastern Cuba definitely foreshadowed an early end to the war. Madrid had acquiesced to the capitulation with every intention of opening peace negotiations at the earliest possible moment.[70]

The formal capitulation took place on July 17. General Shafter and General Toral, each with an escort of a hundred men, met between the lines at 9:30 A.M. and confirmed the settlement. At noon the American flag was raised over Santiago de Cuba. All day the Spanish army marched out of the city, deposited its arms, and proceeded to a detention camp in the San Juan Heights. One unseemly event disfigured an otherwise well-conducted ceremony: Sylvester Scovel, an indefatigable and less than scrupulous reporter for the *New York World,* scaled the roof of the palace at Santiago de Cuba in order to appear in photographs of the flag-raising. When an American officer present divined Scovel's intention, he ordered the journalist to get off the roof. Scovel refused. When Shafter learned of his presence he gave an ominous order: "Throw him off!" Scovel then came down from his perch, and, infuriated, approached Schafter, yelling at him. He apparently struck at the General, although he probably did not make contact. For this misdeed he lost his correspondent's license.[71]

This event was only one of a series of skirmishes between General

Shafter and journalists covering the campaign at Santiago de Cuba. Unskilled in what now would be called press relations, Shafter became irritated when correspondents would report military movements he wished to conceal. The prying ways of reporters such as Richard Harding Davis and Sylvester Scovel greatly annoyed him, and he made no secret of his feelings. Naturally the newspapermen took reprisals, often in the form of animadversions upon Shafter's competence, some of which went well beyond the bounds of propriety. To the extent that these reports, justified or not, influenced the opinion of the public at the time and of historians later on, they undermined the reputations of the officers and men who campaigned at Santiago de Cuba. Shafter never managed to repair his relations with Richard Harding Davis; all he could do was refute the correspondent's accusations in communications to the War Department.[72]

The capitulation brought to the Fifth Army Corps a certain amount of booty, but it also saddled it with new responsibilities. The garrison surrendered about sixteen thousand rifles and three million rounds of ammunition. What food remained in Santiago de Cuba, mainly rice, fell into the hands of the victors. At the same time Shafter acquired responsibility for the care of some twenty-one hundred Spaniards hospitalized from wounds or disease. Moreover, he had to meet the needs of the Spanish prisoners held in the detention camp, along with those of the Cubans in the region—whether civilians or *insurrectos*. In this respect the American Red Cross—whose director, Clara Barton, came to Santiago de Cuba—performed yeoman service indeed. (The Red Cross ship *City of Texas* was the first vessel to enter the harbor.) Use of the facilities of the port of Santiago de Cuba greatly eased the task of meeting the needs not only of the American soldier but of conquered foe and Cuban ally.[73]

Although many difficulties still confronted them, the fighting men at Santiago de Cuba experienced a vast sense of relief when the Spanish garrison threw down its arms. Ogden Wells, a Rough Rider, did not fail to count the cost of victory: "As I glance down the line and see the many vacant places, I think of the comrades who are not present to exult in the reward of their bravery and my happiness gives way to sorrow." Colonel John R. Bennett of the Thirty-Fourth Michigan admitted that he had not yearned for more combat: "If we had been ordered to charge their works they would have piled us up 10 deep, and then we could never have reached them." He expressed great respect for the enemy's fortifications: "Their wire fences are a great defense, and had they not been pretty hungry, I rather think they would have been in possession of the city today.'' Few now questioned the wisdom of Shafter's decision to invest rather than assault Santiago de Cuba after the battles of July 1 and July 3. Despite numerous vicissitudes the campaign had been brought speedily to a successful conclusion with a minimum of casualties. The President's gamble had paid rich dividends. [74]

FOURTEEN

After the Capitulation at Santiago de Cuba

After General Toral's capitulation, General Shafter encountered some new and difficult problems. He became further embroiled in controversies with the navy. He had to round up all the Spanish garrisons in the Division of Santiago de Cuba and arrange their repatriation. To replace Spanish authority in the region, he was called upon to inaugurate a military government. Finally, and most urgently, he was forced to deal with tropical disease in epidemic proportions.

AFTERMATH OF THE CAPITULATION

Immediately after the surrender of Santiago de Cuba Shafter attempted to seize certain Spanish vessels in the harbor, even though the navy had indicated interest in them. This act precipitated another interservice quarrel. Despite a specific request from Sampson, nothing in the articles of capitulation provided for disposition of the Spanish ships. When Shafter inquired of Alger whether he should turn over the gunboat *Alvarado* and some merchant craft to the navy, the Secretary of War ordered him to take possession: "They belong to the army." Thus, when Sampson sent an officer to the *Alvarado*, he found that Shafter had already put his representative on board. This measure was too much for the Admiral. In high dudgeon he fired off a hot message to Shafter, noting that his ships lay within five hundred yards of the Morro, which he had frequently engaged but did not intend to take or claim. He expected comparable consideration from the army. "It should hardly be necessary to remind you," Sampson insisted, "that in all joint operations of the character of those which have resulted in the fall of Santiago, all floating material is turned over to the Navy, as all forts, etc., go to the Army." Shafter, however, refused to back down, informing the Admiral of his orders from the Secretary of War. Sampson then had recourse to the Navy Department, and Secretary Long promised to take up the question with President McKinley. Shafter then chose a conciliatory course, expressing a desire to avoid controversy over the ships. The next day Secretary Alger informed Shafter that prize law did not apply—meaning that neither service could profit from seizure of the vessels—and he ordered their transfer to the navy. Sampson thus won this minor tug of war, but at some further cost to interservice cooperation.[1]

Another matter continued to rankle the navy—the absence of a naval signature on the articles of capitulation. On July 19 Shafter adopted a soothing approach, informing Alger that it was not too late for Sampson to sign. He noted that he himself had not signed the document, the commissioners having represented him in their negotiations. (Since Toral had surrendered his forces directly to the army, Shafter had thought it appropriate to appoint a commission composed entirely of army officers.) On July 20 Sampson received authority from Secretary Long to sign the papers, but, when the Admiral attempted to take this step, Shafter reversed his previous position, arguing that he alone had received the Spanish surrender and that his commissioners represented him alone. To add insult to injury, he reiterated an argument bound to test the patience of Sampson: "I respectfully invite your attention to the fact that no claim for any credit for the capture of Cervera and his fleet had been made by the Army, although it is a fact the Spanish fleet did not leave the harbor until the investment of the City was practically completed and Cervera had sufficient losses on land on July 1st and 2nd, notably among them his Chief of Staff." Sampson finally gave up the fight, reporting Shafter's position to Long and even conceding that the General's point about Cervera might have some merit. He left the question to superiors in Washington.[2]

Musing over the disputes concerning custody of captured ships and the Spanish capitulation, Secretary Long tried to explain them. Ever hopeful of discouraging interservice rivalry, he nevertheless recognized "a good deal of indefinite feeling of inquiet on the part of the Army." He attributed this feeling to the fact that the navy at Manila and Santiago de Cuba had won two distinctive victories on its own, while the army's rather undramatic achievement at Santiago de Cuba owed quite a bit to naval support. Citing several salient instances in which the navy had lent assistance to the army—the loan of vessels, support for landing operations, and provision of escort for convoys—Long noted that he was doing what could be done to lessen tensions. "It is entirely natural that the Army officers should look for successes and be a little impatient that the Navy has secured so many," he concluded. "There are splendid fellows among them, and they will make a fine mark whenever they get the chance." Long did not, however, mention the most important reason why interservice rivalry had occurred so frequently at Santiago de Cuba: No effective institutional means existed within the American government to manage joint operations. The outcome in Cuba illustrated graphically the consequence of this failure to develop appropriate joint methods.[3]

Not only had General Shafter alienated the navy, he managed to prejudice relations with the Cuban insurgents around Santiago de Cuba. As the campaign developed, he usually bypassed General García. At the same time his men became increasingly critical of the *insurrectos,* who seemed to them more interested in picking up loose supplies than fighting the Spanish garrison. Behind the behavior of the Americans lay racial prejudice. As Margaret Leech put it, "This was a white man's army, with no use for foreign 'niggers.' " Shafter's relations with García reached a breaking point at the time of capitulation. He did not ask the Cuban commander to participate in the negotiations that ended the campaign, nor did he invite him to attend the formal ceremonies that took place on July 17. And after the surrender Cuban troops were not allowed to enter the city under arms—a measure taken to prevent violence, looting, and other infractions of public order. This course reflected the War Department's policy that, while the Cubans were to be treated justly, they "must recognize the military occupation and authority of the United States and the cessation of hostilities proclaimed by this Government."[4]

On the day of the capitulation García addressed a remarkable letter to Shafter in which he reviewed his grievances. Noting his exclusion from the ceremonies of capitulation, he also complained about Shafter's policy of retaining certain Spanish officials temporarily in office. He could accept American control of the area but not the continuing authority of the Queen Regent's officialdom. And nothing bothered him more than Shafter's refusal to allow Cuban troops to enter Santiago de Cuba under arms because of the possibility that they might abuse the Spaniards: "We are not savages ignoring the rules of civilized warfare," he insisted. "We are a poor, ragged army as ragged and poor as was the army of your forefathers in their noble war for independence, but like the heroes of Saratoga and Yorktown, we respect our cause too deeply to disgrace it with barbarism and cowardice." Following this rather heavy-handed comparison, he informed Shafter that he had submitted his resignation to General Gómez and was retiring with his forces to Jiguaní. To Gómez he explained that he could no longer follow the order to cooperate with the Americans; resignation was the only means available to protest Shafter's course.[5]

An effort by Shafter to placate the old Cuban leader probably had an opposite effect. He informed García that his policies stemmed from the fact that a war was in progress between the United States and Spain, and therefore it was "out of the question" for him "to take any action in regard to your forces with the surrender, which was made solely to the American army." He claimed to have given full credit to García and his men in reports of operations, and wished to acknowledge this assistance again.[6]

Somewhat later Shafter explained his course to the War Department, noting that the difficulties with the insurgents stemmed from García's desire to take control of the area around Santiago de Cuba. He had explained to the Cuban that he had no authority to address the general question of Cuban independence. Once again he brought up with Alger García's failure to prevent the entry of Escario into Santiago de Cuba; Shafter finally had to cover the roads west of the city himself, seeking to ensure the security of his forces, but García reacted negatively to this step. The Cuban scholar Emilio Roig de Leuchsenring, a particularly virulent anti-American historian, ascribes to Shafter a desire to strip the Cuban army of any credit for the victory in eastern Cuba. In many writings Roig has argued that in 1898 the United States actually sought to deprive Cuba of the independence that had been promised in the Teller amendment. While this interpretation is patently unsound, President McKinley's initial refusal to grant recognition to the Cuban government did ensure short-run difficulties with the insurgents until the United States clarified its future course. Had Shafter extended to García a modicum of the courtesy he lavished upon General Toral, he might have minimized the tensions that built up between the Americans and the Cubans. Later on, after Shafter left Cuba, Leonard Wood made efforts to placate the embittered García, and the old hero eventually accepted an invitation to visit the United States. After enjoying a public welcome in New York City and an interview with President McKinley, García died suddenly in Washington on December 11, 1898, at the age of seventy-one.[7]

Shafter was naturally anxious to repatriate the Spanish prisoners as soon as possible. On the day of the formal surrender he asked Corbin for ships to perform this duty, noting that their presence constituted a "source of embarrassment." He had in mind the difficulty of guarding and feeding a large number of prisoners as well as the possibility that sickness might break out among them. Although at one time he contemplated parole for the prisoners, he did not in the end insert this arrangement in the articles of capitulation because he decided it was unlikely that "we should fight them in Spain, and once there it does not seem possible that they can ever return." While awaiting word from Washington concerning arrangements to transport the prisoners, he assigned to the efficient Miley the task of gathering in all the Spanish garrisons in the Division of Santiago de Cuba—at Guantánamo and other locations. This process ultimately involved about twenty-four thousand men.[8]

To obtain ships for repatriation, the War Department adopted the unorthodox expedient of putting the job up for bids. A combine of British and German shipping companies, which included the Cunard the Hamburg-American Lines, proposed to charge $110 for each officer and $55 for each enlisted man or dependent. The total cost to the American government would have reached $1,312,915. However, a much lower bid came in from the Spanish *Transatlántica* company—$55 per officer and $20 per enlisted man or dependent—and *Transatlántica* received the contract. Between August 9 and September 17, 1898, it transferred 22,864 soldiers to Spain at a cost to the United States of $513,860. Arrangements were also made to return the naval prisoners confined in the United States. In this way a potentially difficult task was discharged quickly and effectively. This success vindicated the decision to offer repatriation at American expense as a means of encouraging the Spanish capitulation at Santiago de Cuba. The cost proved trifling in comparison with the military and humanitarian benefits that flowed from the arrangement.[9]

EPIDEMIC

While these events took place the American army, ironically enough, experienced its most trying days in Cuba, for tropical disease swept through the Fifth Army Corps and reduced it to a pathetic shadow of its former self. From the outset of the expedition its leaders had manifested constant concern about illness. The first case of yellow fever was identified on July 6, but the most serious epidemics materialized soon after in an onslaught of malaria and dysentery. The army generally realized the importance of proper sanitation and living conditions, but it was not yet known that mosquitoes transmitted yellow fever and malaria. As sickness developed rapidly during the latter days of the siege, the Chief Surgeon, Colonel Charles R. Greenleaf, and other medical officers made plans to prevent an epidemic. On July 12 Greenleaf proposed various expedients: Units ought to move their campsite every two days to a fresh location at least two miles distant from the previous bivouac. Cleanliness must be stressed, personal habits carefully controlled, and cooking subjected to close inspection. Strenuous efforts were decreed to avoid contact with both Cubans and Spaniards, considered carriers of the diseases. With reference to the anticipated expedition of the Fifth Army Corps to Puerto Rico, Greenleaf recommended limiting the amount of time spent on transports and avoiding overcrowded conditions. He also proposed to fumigate transports with burning sulphur before loading them. These recommendations reflected the special preoccupation of General Miles with the problem of tropical disease. Hoping to minimize sickness in his command, he even went as far as to keep almost all the troops that had accompanied him on transports anchored in Guantánamo Bay.[10]

Responding to reports from Shafter that yellow fever had begun to appear, the War Department took action. On July 13 Corbin forwarded its plan to ensure against epidemic conditions: Alger ordered Shafter to move his troops to high ground near the coast in locations with easy access to supplies. Each camp was to be kept well separated from the others. When a unit avoided any fresh cases of yellow fever for five days, it was to be returned to the United States or sent from Santiago de Cuba to some other location for additional field service. Cases of yellow fever were to be isolated, and none were to be placed aboard transports. To this instruction Shafter responded in obvious alarm, "Am I to understand from your telegram about yellow fever that Fifth Army Corps has to remain here through an epidemic of that disease?" Corbin responded soothingly that the message was intended simply to get the army out of the fever belt as soon as the Spanish garrison ended its resistance. "If later it is found advisable to bring your troops away," he closed, "it will be done." On the same day Alger directly conveyed his views, but in terms that appeared to contradict Corbin's clarification: "As soon as Santiago falls, the troops must all be put into camps as comfortable as they can be made, and remain, I suppose, until the fever has had its run." He then reported that two "immune" regiments had been ordered to Santiago de Cuba. "They, with the colored regulars, it seems to me, will answer to garrison the places as long as our forces have to remain there." The "immunes" were men who supposedly possessed immunity to yellow fever and other tropical disease. (It was commonly assumed, fallaciously, that black men from the south generally possessed such immunity.)[11]

Miles then began to take a hand. On July 14 he urged Shafter to isolate newly arrived troops in healthy camps to keep them free from infection and ready to deal with Spanish reinforcements that might be approaching from Holguín. Two days later he recommended that units change camps almost daily, preferably moving to ground near the railway between Siboney and Aguadores, where bathing facilities were available. Also, he suggested the burning of all structures that had been used to quarter Spanish troops. Anticipating the surrender, he wanted Shafter "to move the white troops on your line of communication on to the highest and healthiest ground, and let one or two regiments of colored troops do the provost duty and assist in the hospitals until the immune regiments can arrive." On July 16 the Twenty-Fourth Infantry, a black unit of the regular army, proceeded to Siboney and manned the hospital there. It performed yeoman service, caring faithfully for victims of the epidemic that soon overwhelmed the Fifth Army Corps. However, its experience destroyed the myth that blacks possessed special immunity to yellow fever. Of the 15 officers and 456 enlisted men of the Twenty-Fourth who arrived for medical duty at Siboney, only 3 officers were fit for duty and only 24 enlisted men free from disease when the tour was completed. At one point no less than 241 men of the regiment were sick. One of the last units to leave Santiago de Cuba, it marched out of its camp on August 26; only nine officers and 198 men were left.[12]

As soon as the Spanish garrison surrendered, the problem of disease assumed the highest priority. On July 17 Corbin telegraphed to Shafter that Alger expected him to concentrate on this matter. "How far will it be possible to place the command above fever belt and how soon?" Corbin expected an early answer. Shafter replied that he would take action as soon as he could, but that first he had to ensure against possible conflicts between the Spanish prisoners and Cuban insurgents. He wanted to begin transporting the Spanish as soon as individual ships became available, rather than wait until sufficient vessels had arrived to include all the prisoners in one large convoy. Miles retained his interest in the health problems, reiterating his view on July 18 that frequent changes of campsites would control disease.[13]

Intervention by the commanding general ultimately elicited a small outburst from Shafter. Ever since Miles's arrival on July 11, he had resented the advice and orders that came his way. Before Miles arrived Alger had informed Shafter that he was not to be removed from authority in any way. Miles's message of July 18 finally led to a complaint from Shafter: "Nothing will give me greater pleasure than serving under you, General, and I shall comply with all your requests and directions, but I was told by the Secretary that you were not to supersede me in command here." To this message Miles responded with courtesy but with vigor, insisting that he had no desire to displace the commander of the Fifth Army Corps. "Your command is part of the United States Army, which I have the honor to command, having been duly assigned thereto, and directed by the President to go wherever I thought my presence required, and give such general directions as I thought best concerning military matters, and especially instructed to go to Santiago for a specific purpose." For this little spat Secretary Alger must be held responsible. He had not fully clarified Miles's status in Cuba except as it had been conveyed to Shafter, a consequence of the embittered state of relations between the Secretary and Miles. Fortunately no further strain developed at Santiago de Cuba, because Miles soon departed with his command to Puerto Rico. However, the episode strengthened Miles's conviction that Alger was engaged in a conspiracy against him, one intended to preclude his effective participation in the conduct of the war.[14]

Shafter, remaining in command at Santiago de Cuba, did not find a solution to the problem of disease. Adding to his growing difficulties in this regard was the natural tendency of the soldiers, after the Spanish garrison had surrendered, to yearn for return to the United States. One camp song summarized these feelings perfectly:

> Snakes as long as Halstead Streat,
> Flies and skeeters that can't be beat.
> Oh, how we want to leave Cuba,
> Lord, how we want to go home!

The cumulative effect of improper clothing, poor food, limited shelter, and inadequate medical treatment began to debilitate the command. Theodore Roosevelt described the difficulties of diverting the troops: "We did everything possible to keep up the spirits of the men, but it was exceedingly difficult because there was nothing for them to do." Some tried to climb or hunt in the surrounding hills, but those who did so often found themselves ill the next day. Walter W. Ward of the Second Massachusetts Volunteers summed up the situation as it developed soon after the capitulation: Drills and daily inspections had to be ended because not enough men were present for duty. Men in the ranks would collapse and have to be removed to their tents. The fever found an ally in homesickness. Ward called it "nostalgia, . . . the bane of armies, . . . which in the Cuban campaign helped kill more men than the bullets of the Spaniards."[15]

Very soon commanders of volunteer units began to complain bitterly to political leaders in the United States. Colonel John R. Bennett of the Thirty-Fourth Michigan Volunteers, for example, wrote in extreme language to Governor Hazen Pingree of Illinois about the suffering that beset his men. "My command of 430 men all told has over 356 sick who are not able to even cook their own meals, and is perfectly disheartened, 14 having died in the past two weeks, and many more are to go if we do not get out of here very soon. God alone can realize the sufferings of these poor boys." He concluded with a comment that probably interested Governor Pingree: "Some one will have many lives to answer for because of mismanagement since the army started from the United States." Letters of this nature combined with newspaper reports to arouse public opinion in the United States, and calls for the return of the expedition began to materialize from many directions. Some officers even had the temerity to write directly to President McKinley in attempts to hasten the expedition's return to the United States. Lieutenant Colonel Charles Dick of the Eighth Ohio Volunteers reported an "appalling situation," and raised the specter of rampant yellow fever should the troops remain long in Cuba.[16]

For some days after the medical emergency began to mature at Santiago de Cuba, Shafter backed and filled; he did not make clear to the War Department the truly desperate threat to his command. On July 19, however, he requested a large number of additional medical personnel—five hundred hospital attendants, one hundred "immune" nurses, and a large number of "immune" doctors—along with the dispatch of two "immune" regiments. Sensing trouble, Corbin inquired anxiously, "Secretary War desires to know exact condition of your command as to yellow fever. How many regiments are affected?" Shafter reported three days later that his doctors could not agree on how many really had contracted yellow fever. He admitted only that every regiment had "more or less fever cases." As soon as he disposed of the Spanish prisoners, he planned to "put troops 20 miles inland on railroad and hope for improvement." Perhaps some of his subordinates had misled their commander. General Wheeler, for example, informed Shafter that his command, which had moved northward to higher ground, was improving in health and had not experienced yellow fever. He wanted more action: "I think the Cavalry Division would be of great service in Porto Rico." Although one of Wheeler's subordinates, Theodore Roosevelt, complained bitterly in private correspondence about the situation at Santiago de Cuba, he supported Wheeler's proposal to send the cavalry and other units to Puerto Rico, in a letter to no less a personage than the Secretary of War himself.[17]

At length Shafter became sufficiently alarmed to recommend drastic action. On July 23 he cabled to the War Department, "I think that at as early a day as possible the Fifth Army Corps should be rapidly moved to some point in the north. It could be done so quickly that but few would die in making the change, and once landed recovery would be speedy." So far, he added, the command had suffered "comparatively few deaths"; the immune regiments and a small naval force would suffice to maintain American control at Santiago de Cuba. As if to contradict himself, however, Shafter that very evening sent a message to Washington that minimized these problems. He did not think his situation alarming, although about fifteen hundred men were ill with fever. Of this number, he said, only about 10 percent had yellow fever. He could not, however, move troops to healthy locations outside the fever zone until the Spanish prisoners had been sent back to Spain and he had repaired the railroad going northward. Washington reported its willingness to undertake needed measures. Corbin informed Shafter, "The desire is to help you in every way possible. As soon as it can be done with safety, etc., it is the intention to bring the entire Fifth Corps home for rest and recuperation." Nevertheless Alger reported that he did not expect that the ships chartered to transport the Spanish prisoners would arrive at Santiago de Cuba for at least another week, and he also had to admit that a vessel assigned to carry two "immune" regiments from New Orleans to Santiago de Cuba had broken down.[18]

Shafter now began daily to report figures of sickness levels in his command, and they revealed a deadly pattern: On July 24 he noted 396 new illnesses, and on the next day about 500. Nevertheless he considered the situation somewhat improved, since about 450 men had returned to duty. On July 27 the total reported sick the previous day was given as 3,770, of which 2,924 were down with fever; new cases amounted to 639, but some 538 men had returned to duty. The next day, however, the numbers jumped strikingly. The total of all those sick was given as 4,122, of which 3,193 had fever; new cases had increased to 822, whereas only 542 men returned to duty. Although Shafter still was withholding frank information concerning the extent of the crisis in the Fifth Army Corps, the War Department reacted to these statistics. On July 28 Alger made a suggestion: "Would it not be well to encourage your command by telling them they will be moved north as soon as the fever cases subside? It would stimulate them, it seems to me, and that frequently is a tonic." He had chosen Montauk Point on Long Island in New York State as the location for a reception center. Meanwhile, the sick report for July 28 showed that almost one-quarter of the men at Santiago de Cuba were ill. Some 4,270 men were sick this day, of which 3,406 had fever; there were 696 new cases of fever, compared with a total of 590 returned to duty.[19]

As Shafter dallied, public concern mounted in the United States. Two transports, the *Seneca* and *Concho,* had been sent north to Montauk with fever victims aboard but without adequate medical supplies and personnel. Reports of the pathetic conditions on these vessels circulated broadly throughout the country and generated an immediate uproar. President McKinley immediately ordered an investigation, and Alger warned Shafter to avoid any further incidents of this nature. Shafter finally bestirred himself to request additional medical support, charging that the Surgeon General did not appreciate his difficulties; he announced to the troops the prospect of an early return to the United States, reporting its "very good effect on the men." Still he refrained from full disclosure of his difficulties.[20]

When Shafter finally decided to recommend drastic action, the War Department made an immediate response. On August 2 Shafter informed Corbin, "I am told that at any time an epidemic of yellow fever is liable to occur. I advise that the troops be moved as rapidly as possible while the sickness is of a mild type." He thought it possible to reduce the size of the garrison drastically, given the impending departure of the Spanish prisoners. The War Department had already begun to act, ordering Shafter earlier to send the dismounted cavalry division to high ground, but the message of August 2 took it by surprise. A conference was hurriedly held at the White House with the President, the Secretary of War, and Surgeon General George Sternburg, in attendance. When Sternburg insisted that yellow fever could not occur above a certain elevation, Alger reiterated the War Department's previous view to Shafter: He should move his command to high ground at the end of the railroad running north out of Santiago de Cuba, "where yellow fever is impossible." Asking for Shafter's advice, he noted that it would be "a long job at best to get so many troops away."[21]

When Shafter revealed the Secretary's views to his subordinate commanders, he evoked an angry reaction. All of them were convinced that the only proper course, given the extent of disease in their units, was to return immediately to the United States. They recognized the difference between the prevalent malaria and yellow fever, but they believed that troops who developed malaria would soon contract the more deadly disease. Theodore Roosevelt put this point dramatically in a letter to Henry Cabot Lodge, claiming that malaria would weaken his troops "until Yellow Jack does come in and we die like rotten sheep."

When the regular officers proved reluctant to make recommendations to Shafter, Roosevelt, a volunteer, decided to prepare a letter expressing the views of the group. He minced no words: "To keep us here," he wrote, "in the opinion of every officer commanding a division or a brigade, will simply involve the destruction of thousands. There is no possible reason for not shipping the entire command North at once." Not content with this statement, he concluded, "If we are kept here it will in all human possibility mean an appalling disaster, for the surgeons have estimated that over half the army, if kept here during the sickly season, will die."[22]

Meanwhile the other officers prepared a separate communication to Shafter, a statement that became known as the "round robin," in which they expressed, in less forceful language, views comparable to those of Roosevelt. Admitting that no epidemic of yellow fever yet existed, they deemed one likely to occur in the near future. No adequate facilities existed in the region north of Santiago de Cuba to house their troops as Alger had suggested, and in any event malaria was prevalent everywhere in the region through the rainy season. "This army must be moved at once or it will perish," concluded the missive. "As an army it can safely be moved now." Adding authority to this argument was a letter prepared by the surgeons of the Fifth Army Corps, in which they agreed with the comanding officers that the troops should be returned immediately to the United States, and that a move into the interior of Cuba would be both dangerous and impractical.[23]

Shafter quickly apprised the War Department of the "round robin," the opinion of the surgeons, and his own views. He agreed with his subordinates that it was impossible to move the Fifth Army Corps promptly and conveniently into the interior. The railroad was in disrepair and would not be usable for a week; in any event it could not move more than a thousand men per day, so that a transfer could not be completed before the end of August. He then stated flatly, "In my opinion there is but one course to take, and that is to immediately transport the Fifth Corps and the detached regiments that came with it to the United States. If it is not done, I believe the death rate will be appalling." Finally, at long last, Shafter had admitted the true state of affairs at Santiago de Cuba.[24]

Both the round robin letter and that of Roosevelt leaked to the press, an event that caused considerable anger in Washington. Shafter vehemently denied that he had given the texts to reporters at Santiago de Cuba, although a recent authority, Virgil C. Jones, claims that he did indeed allow them to come into the hands of the Associated Press. Whatever the truth, the documents were cabled immediately to the

United States and published throughout the country on August 4. This episode greatly embarrassed the War Department, already under criticism because of its earlier difficulties in preparing the nation for war. More important, it threatened to undermine delicate peace negotiations then underway, for on July 26 the Spanish government had delivered through intermediaries, a message to President McKinley, proposing an end to the war. Since that time McKinley had been negotiating through the French ambassador in Washington to conclude an armistice. The President was justly indignant at the disclosure of the round robin letter, because public knowledge of the army's plight might prejudice attempts to settle the war with Spain; fortunately nothing of the kind occurred. The officers at Santiago de Cuba, whether correct or not in their views, had a right to express them to superiors; their misstep was to let them be aired in public print.[25]

MONTAUK

Publication of the round robin letter did not force the decision to send the Fifth Army Corps to Montauk Point, that step having been taken already, but certainly the publicity of August 4 hastened the process. Orders came immediately from the War Department to evacuate the Fifth Army Corps from Santiago de Cuba; "immune" regiments would take over garrison duties. The news that their travail was almost over caused great joy in the ranks. The fever remained intense; between forty-two and forty-three hundred men were reported ill on August 1 and August 2. One of the Rough Riders, A. D. Webb, informed the *Arizona Bulletin* in a letter of August 4, "Nearly everyone in camp is fairly putrid with dysentery. Chills come around each day to shake the majority of us to see if we are still alive. When the chills get tired, along comes a most diabolical kind of fever which is warranted to turn a man up entirely in just three hours." Webb was ready to go home.[26]

On August 2 the War Department signed a contract with the Long Island Railroad providing access to several square miles of well-watered land and docking facilities at Montauk Point, Long Island—a critical first step in the development of a reception center there for the returning soldiers. Important problems immediately became apparent: Only one rail line reached Montauk from New York City, and no real facilities existed there for receiving supplies and handling large numbers of passengers. Moreover, the local roads were entirely inadequate for the needs of a large military installation. A sparsely populated region, eastern Long Island could not produce a supply of labor sufficient to build a camp overnight. Carpenters hired to put up buildings took advantage of the situation to demand high wages; work stoppages stemming from this circumstance slowed construction. If enough time had been available, a fine facility could eventually have been developed at Montauk, but the urgent decision to return the Fifth Army Corps precluded proper preparation. General Samuel B. M. Young arrived at Montauk on August 5 with orders to build both a detention camp to hold soldiers until declared free of illness and a hospital for disabled men. Before much progress could be made, however, about thirty-five hundred cavalry troops arrived from Florida, sent northward both to avoid typhoid and to help construct buildings at Montauk. Over five thousand mounts came with them. Their advent at Camp Wikoff—the name was in honor of an officer who had fallen at the San Juan Heights—actually interfered temporarily with construction, because of the facilities and manpower used to take care of them.[27]

When the first troops arrived on August 14—they left Cuba on August 7—Camp Wikoff was far from prepared for them. Neither the detention camp nor the hospital was able to provide adequate services, and days of terrible confusion ensued as additional transports came in. General Wheeler arrived from Santiago de Cuba on August 15 and assumed command. Soon critical press reports stimulated action. The War Department began doing everything possible to correct deficiencies. Private benefactors and charitable organizations launched an extensive campaign to supply food, clothing, and other necessary items. Eventually the situation at Montauk showed marked improvement, although the army never resolved all the problems of transport, housing, and medical treatment that surfaced. In an effort to raise morale, stimulate activity, and reassure the country, President McKinley visited the camp himself with Secretary Alger in tow; his constant interest helped to alleviate difficulties.[28]

The condition of the men who entered Camp Wikoff gave mute testimony to the ordeal they had experienced in Cuba. One observer criticized their unwillingness to adhere to normal standards of military behavior, not realizing that the troops could not conceivably do so. A more sympathetic view came from Major J. C. Powell, who pointed out that a rapid recovery of health and military efficiency could not be expected: ''What change has taken place has been gradual, for to the conditions of disease brought along with them was added . . . that of thorough exhaustion.'' As time passed by, men who were declared sufficiently recovered to travel were allowed to depart for their homes, a policy that lightened the burden at the camp, although it aroused public criticism when some men collapsed on their journeys. Newspapers, often unfairly, blamed the War Department. As one might expect, too much attention was given to the early difficulties at Camp Wikoff and not enough to later improvements.[29]

Camp Wikoff had but an ephemeral existence; by September 28 the last unit had been processed through. It received well over twenty thousand soldiers during its brief life. Of these only 257 died—mostly from effects of tropical disease—a rate of less than 2 percent, and a low number considering the privation experienced in Cuba and the state of medical knowledge at the time. In Cuba 514 men succumbed of disease in a much shorter period.[30]

The Fifth Army Corps passed into history on October 3, when it was formally disbanded at Camp Wikoff. General Shafter spoke with pardonable pride of its performance, noting particularly its superb discipline. He was pleased because no member had come before a court-martial. Taking into consideration its hasty formation and lack of training, it had indeed turned in a creditable performance. Its critics would do well to consider its accomplishments as well as its deficiencies, all in the light of the extraordinary demands placed upon it.[31]

When the volunteers returned to home they were well received, but often without the bubbling enthusiasm associated with homecomings after other American wars. Their countrymen took into consideration the debilitating effects of the campaign. A scene in Springfield, Massachusetts on September 27, 1898, when the Second Massachusetts Volunteers received a public welcome, was typical of the end of the affair for many troops: "There was no demonstrative welcome, for common sense told the people that it would have been the worst thing possible for the men whom the crowd wanted to honor. They were in no condition to endure such a welcome and what they wanted was to get to their homes or a resting place as quickly as possible." The effects of the epidemic were everywhere apparent. "On almost every face was the badge of the campaign against the pestilential fevers of Cuba and the sunken cheek-bones and emaciated forms bore eloquent witness to the hardships and sufferings that had been undergone. It had been no holiday excursion for the gallant Second." No holiday excursion indeed! Much of it had been hell. Yet, the soldiers could not resist a last bit of doggerel humor entitled *Hardships of War:*

> At Santiago he had lumbago,
> At Tampa the fever and chills;
> Before El Caney the weather was rainy,
> And there he had other ills.
> He reached Camp Alger and got neuralgia,
> And at Montauk the fever yellow,

But at home was the blow that laid him low,
His girl had another fellow.[32]

The campaign at Santiago de Cuba had been hastily decided upon, after Cervera had been penned up, as a means of applying immediate pressure on the enemy in a location as propitious for the Americans as it was unfavorable for the Spanish. Unable to mount an early campaign against Havana, the center of Spanish strength in Cuba, President McKinley wisely chose to conduct an operation in this peripheral location where a modest military accomplishment still might well yield important political results. Despite all the logistical and tactical bumbling associated with the expedition of the Fifth Army Corps, General Shafter accomplished his purpose. His combat losses—243 men killed in action and 1,445 wounded—were insignificant in comparison with the gains, a generalization that seems reasonable even if one adds the 771 men who died of fever in Cuba and at Montauk. When Sampson destroyed Cervera's squadron, he accomplished the principal military objective at Santiago de Cuba. The siege operation simply emphasized the McKinley Administration's determination to campaign actively in the field until Spain accepted American terms. The decision of the Liberal ministry in Madrid to authorize the capitulation at Santiago de Cuba was an aspect of a larger political decision—to seek an end to the war.

However, before Sagasta could open peace negotiations the Americans began still another campaign. The attack on Puerto Rico was undertaken as soon as possible after the victory at Santiago de Cuba. This enterprise constituted still another application of McKinley's overall strategy—to engage the enemy actively at locations far from his center of power where much could be achieved at small cost and in a short time. At some point, it was hoped, the cumulative effect of small, decisive victories at the enemy's periphery would force peace.

FIFTEEN

The Puerto Rican Campaign

Ever since Finley Peter Dunne's comic creation, Mr. Dooley, referred to the expedition to "Porther Ricky" as "Gin'ral Miles' gran' picnic an' moonlight excursion," historians have derided or at least neglected the conquest of Spain's other colony in the Caribbean Sea.[1] These reactions have obscured the role of this campaign in McKinley's strategic design for the war with Spain. And because the invasion of 1898 led to Puerto Rico's present status as a self-governing commonwealth of the United States, its history requires careful reconstruction.

Lying east of Hispaniola in the Greater Antilles, the rectangular island of Puerto Rico, about 3,435 square miles in extent, is about 108 miles across from east to west and about 40 miles from north to south. It is about 20 miles shorter than Long Island. In 1899 a census established its population at a little less than a million people—953,243, to be exact. Ponce (37,535 inhabitants), located on the south coast, was its largest city at the time, but the most important city was the seaport of San Juan (23,414 inhabitants) near the northeastern corner of the island, where the Governor-General maintained his residence. Other large concentrations of population were to be found in Utuado (31,000), Arecibo (30,000), Mayagüez (28,000); Yauco (25,000), Juana Díaz (21,000), and San Germán (20,000). About ten more cities boasted populations in excess of ten thousand people. A range of mountains crosses the island from east to west; near the sea, ridges and ravines running from the mountains open into broad, fertile valleys. The economy, predominantly agricultural, was based in this period on the cultivation of sugar cane, rice, and corn. Palm trees and orange trees grew in the lowlands. A system of narrow-gauge railroads, traversing a total of only 159 miles, linked certain coastal towns. There was only one important highway; it crossed the island for 70 miles from San Juan to Ponce, although the straight-line distance between the two cities is only 47 miles. A branch of this road ran south from Cayey to Guayama and thence east to Arroyo.[2]

Anti-Spanish agitation such as materialized in Cuba and the Philippine Islands did not occur in Puerto Rico, but certain local politicians did advocate various types of change in the relationship with the Spanish Peninsula. The most influential leader in this group, Luis Muñoz Rivera, favored autonomy for Puerto Rico within the Spanish empire. A black American-trained physician, José Celso Barbosa, also favored autonomy, but advocated different methods of achieving it. Only a few dissidents called for outright independence; they found a leader in José de Riego. And a not inconsiderable number of Puerto Ricans, known as *incondicionalistas,* favored maintenance of the existing relationship with Spain. Muñoz Rivera sought to obtain autonomy by negotiating with the Liberal Party of Sagasta, a somewhat less than glorious strategy to which Barbosa took exception. During the period from September, 1896 to February, 1897, Muñoz Rivera visited Spain and managed to strike a bargain with the Liberals. When this achievement became known in Puerto Rico, the *Muñocistas* in the faction favoring autonomy forced approval of the deal; the *Barbosistas* then bolted and formed a separate political organization.[3]

On November 9, 1897 Puerto Rico was granted home rule, as an aspect of Spain's decision to liberalize its Cuban policy, and an autonomic government soon materialized in the island. An irrevocable charter authorized an appointive Governor-General with relatively limited powers to preside as the representative of Spain over the government of Puerto Rico. An elected insular parliament would exercise real influence in affairs, and from its ranks a cabinet would be selected to provide executive direction. The Governor-General could not issue an order that lacked the signature of a local elected official. A certain measure of control over external as well as domestic policy fell to the insular government: It received authority to make treaties with foreign governments; and Puerto Rico was to be subject only to those Spanish treaties that its parliament chose to accept. Autonomy proved much more palatable in Puerto Rico than in Cuba because it represented a concession far beyond local hopes and expectations. On March 27 the

Puerto Ricans elected thirty-two members of parliament; the *Muñocistas* gained twenty-four seats and the *Barbosistas* (known as *puros*, to distinguish them from the compromising followers of Muñoz Rivera) elected but four representatives. Until the parliament met, the Governor-General retained authority. General Manuel Macías y Casado was appointed Governor-General on February 9, 1898, after the death of his predecessor. Macías declared martial law, and called grandiloquently for resistance against the American invaders: "Providence will not permit that in these countries which were discovered by the Spanish nation the echo of our language should ever cease to be heard, nor that our flag should disappear from before the eye. . . . Long live Puerto Rico, always Spanish. Long live Spain."[4]

The impending appearance of an American force off the shores of the island probably explains why the Governor-General finally called the parliament into session on July 17. Muñoz Rivera led the government, adopting a loyalist stance: "We are Spaniards," he said, "and wrapped in the Spanish flag we will die." The *Barbosistas*, however, refused to participate in the insular government. This reflected something of a political victory for Macías, who obviously hoped that the grant of autonomy would cement the loyalty of the Puerto Ricans.[5]

The Governor-General had pitiably few forces at his disposal with which to contest an American attack. Historians estimate the number of Spanish troops in Puerto Rico during the summer of 1898 at about eight thousand regulars. Of these men about five thousand were infantrymen, seven hundred artillerymen, and twenty-three hundred members of other branches—engineers, civil guards, and the like. Associated with this force were from seven to nine thousand "volunteers"—Puerto Rican militia, poorly trained and unreliable. The volunteers possessed only about nine thousand rifles. Puerto Rico was divided into seven military districts, each with a commander. The regular forces were scattered across the island in various cities. With the exception of a few guns at San Juan no artillery was available. Ponce and Mayagüez, the most important cities besides San Juan, had no defenses whatever. The naval forces defending Puerto Rico, numbering but 368 men, were even less imposing than the army. Macías controlled six vessels—two unprotected cruisers, two tiny gunboats, an auxiliary cruiser, and the destroyer *Terror*. Cervera had left the latter vessel at Martinique, and it later had tied up at San Juan. This forlorn flotilla could not hope to challenge the naval squadron that the United States could be expected to send into Puerto Rican waters, either to blockade coastal cities or support an invasion.[6]

The subject of Puerto Rico came up in only the briefest way in the

American diplomatic activity during the crisis leading to war. The island was mentioned in connection with Moret's efforts to negotiate a commercial agreement intended to regulate economic relations between Cuba and the United States. Woodford in Madrid was notified that the arrangement should cover Puerto Rico as well—hardly a vital instruction. Prior to the war almost all attention centered on Cuba; the United States did not develop a plan to annex Puerto Rico before the war or for some time thereafter.[7]

PLANS AND PREPARATIONS

Nevertheless, before the war both the War and Navy Departments gave some consideration to operations against Puerto Rico. On April 4, 1898, when the joint army-navy board presented its plan of campaign—a plan based on the assumption that the navy would carry the principal burden in the approaching conflict—it favored an attack on Puerto Rico to deprive the enemy of a useful base in the Caribbean Sea. Major General John M. Schofield—a retired commanding general of considerable reputation who had been called in for consultation during the prewar crisis—favored initial attacks on Puerto Rico and the Philippines rather than Cuba. Successes in those locations might eliminate the need to assault Spain's strongest colony. If operations against Cuba were to become necessary, General Schofield thought that they should occur only in the fall after the rainy season (from June to October), after the volunteer army had been sufficiently trained to undertake a major campaign. This view also figured in the strategic thought of Captain Mahan, who maintained in his postwar book on the war with Spain that Puerto Rico "would be invaluable to the mother country [Spain] as an intermediate naval station and as a base of supplies and reinforcements for both her fleet and army; . . . if left in her undisturbed possession, it would enable her practically, to enjoy the same advantage of nearness to the great scene of operations that the United States had in virtue of our geographical position." For this reason Mahan believed that Puerto Rico should have been the first *point d'appui*. Secretary Long partially supported this view: Had Spain been a more powerful adversary, it might have been sound strategy to move first against Puerto Rico. "Using it as a base," wrote Long, "we could have threatened his [the enemy's] communications and thus retarded, if not actually prevented, his relief of Cuba. Had he remained in occupation, he would have been in an excellent geographical position to defend Cuba and menace our ports." Why, then, not seize it at the outset? The Secretary of the Navy supplied a plausible explanation: "As the United States had no outlying colonies and no lines of communication to support, and our coast is distant only ninety miles from Havana, the Naval War Board rightly concluded that conquest of Porto Rico promised no results commensurate with the sacrifices such action would entail."[8]

The most important advocate of a Puerto Rican campaign was General Miles, who adopted a view almost like that of General Schofield. Believing that the war would develop as a largely naval conflict—"It was a question of whether our fleet would destroy the Spanish fleet or whether theirs would destroy ours"—he wished to delay operations in Cuba until the United States attained unquestioned command of the sea. He also placed special emphasis on minimizing the risk of tropical disease, most prevalent in Cuba during the rainy season. As a broad principle Miles thought it advisable to "operate against the Spanish forces by doing them the greatest amount of injury with the least to ourselves, harassing them during the sickly season, giving all the aid and comfort possible to the insurgents, and taking such places as we could during the rainy season or sickly season without endangering the lives of our own troops from disease." It was only a step from this view to another: "I was from the first in favor in taking Porto Rico, in order that the Spanish forces could not use it as a base against us."[9]

For these reasons, an assault on Puerto Rico exercised considerable appeal as an alternative to a campaign in Cuba during the early phases of the war. The comments of all who mentioned Puerto Rico prior to the war stressed its strategic significance. Talk of annexation, a political question, did not surface before the war. Shortly after hostilities started, however, the American consul at San Juan, Philip C. Hanna—who had withdrawn to nearby St. Thomas—recommended an early invasion on the grounds that "10,000 American soldiers landed in Puerto Rico can hold the island forever, because I am convinced, that a large number of Puerto Ricans will arise and shake off the Spanish yoke as soon as they are assured of help." A few days later he reported the number of Spanish troops in Puerto Rico with fair accuracy, once again stating that ten thousand troops could take the island; they could land at Fajardo or Ponce and march on San Juan, where the navy could join the assault. Hanna's proposal did not immediately strike a responsive chord in Washington, where all attention at the time was centered on the search for Cervera's squadron, then en route to the Antilles.[10]

It is possible, though, that Hanna's message had something to do with a secret mission sent to obtain information about Puerto Rico and its defenses. On May 5 the War Department ordered Lieutenant Henry F. Whitney to undertake a covert reconnaissance. Posing as an ordinary seaman on a British vessel, Whitney went to Ponce and investigated the area for some ten days. He left that port June 1, and by June 9 was back in Washington. Later General Miles paid handsome tribute to Whitney: "The information he gained concerning the position of the Spanish troops, the topography of the country, the character of the inhabitants, the resources and amount of supplies available, and especially his reports of the condition of the harbors, I afterward found to be most important."[11]

Puerto Rico first attracted public attention on May 12, when Admiral Sampson sailed to San Juan and subjected its defenses to a brief bombardment, but this attack constituted merely a passing episode in the larger enterprise of locating Admiral Cervera. Despite its strategic location, Puerto Rico did not enter importantly into American planning during the first month or so of the war because attention was riveted on Cuba and the Philippines. It is certain, however, that the small but influential group of public men who had absorbed the doctrines of Captain Mahan had not lost sight of the island. Henry Cabot Lodge, writing to Theodore Roosevelt on May 24, claimed that "Puerto Rico is not forgotten and we mean to have it." Roosevelt replied the next day, stating that no peace settlement should be made that did not include provisions for Cuban independence, detachment of the Philippine Islands from Spain, and annexation of Puerto Rico. There is no evidence, however, to indicate that serious discussion about taking the island had yet occurred within the McKinley Administration.[12]

Late in May, when it was determined that Cervera was indeed at Santiago de Cuba, interest in an attack on Puerto Rico grew rapidly. The island's strategic significance became most apparent if associated with a Cuban campaign centering on Santiago de Cuba rather than Havana. General Miles quickly reacted to the new situation in the Caribbean. On May 26 and 27 he advanced his plan (already discussed above in Chapter 7) calling for an attack on Puerto Rico along with a cavalry movement from Nuevitas on the north coast of Cuba towards Havana—both enterprises preliminary to a major assault on Havana at the end of the rainy season. This plan was consistent with Mile's inveterate preference for operations on the periphery of enemy power designed to obtain important victories at small cost. Strategists of a later generation, particularly Basil H. Liddell Hart, termed this general conception "the indirect approach." Apparently because of Miles's planning, General Roy Stone obtained information from Dr. Roberto Todd concerning the region around San Juan. However, as we have seen, instead of adopting Miles's plan the Administration decided to concentrate land forces immediately at Santiago de Cuba in order to destroy Cervera's squadron. This course would exert immediate pressure on

Spain, and promised an outcome that might lead to early peace negotiations. Nevertheless, President McKinley embraced the idea of mounting a second operation in the Antilles—an attack on Puerto Rico—following hard upon the conquest of Santiago de Cuba. Movement on Havana was postponed until autumn. Major General Fitzhugh Lee, preparing the Sixth Army Corps at Jacksonville, Florida, was designated to command the later operation against Havana. McKinley considered the effort at Santiago de Cuba as preliminary to the Puerto Rican invasion assuming peace had not yet been made. As early as May 31, General Shafter was informed that after completing his mission at Santiago de Cuba he should load his force on transports and "proceed to the harbor at Port de Banes [Cuba], reporting by the most favorable means for further orders and future important service." This service was to be a movement against Puerto Rico. On that day Lodge wrote again to Roosevelt, this time with accurate information: "The Administration are continuing very earnestly and I believe will soon undertake an expedition to Puerto Rico, which I believe is useful." He continued, in a vein that suggests he embraced the strategic thought of General Miles, "Let us get the outlying things first."[13]

Although General Miles did not succeed in peddling his cavalry campaign in Cuba to President McKinley, he busied himself with the Puerto Rican operation. On June 2, telegraphing from Tampa (where he had gone to help the Fifth Army Corps get off to Cuba), he informed Secretary Alger that an attack on Puerto Rico, which he deemed "highly important," should follow the campaign at Santiago de Cuba, provided the army and navy were in a position to continue. He wanted also to establish that the Cuban coastal cities Port de Banes or Nipe would make an appropriate rendezvous for troops moving to Puerto Rico. Miles then put in his bid for the command: "If it meets the approval of the government, as soon as this expedition sails another can be immediately organized to reinforce the first and make sure of the capture of number two [Puerto Rico], and I request that transportation be immediately secured for at least fifteen thousand men." Even before he received a response, Miles began to concentrate troops at Tampa for the expedition to "No. 2." On June 4 he received his answer. President McKinley himself wired, "The President wants to know the earliest possible moment you can have an expeditionary force ready to go to Porto Rico, large enough to take and hold the island, without the force under General Shafter." The President's purpose was unmistakable; he wished to sustain pressure on Spain hoping to avoid a dangerous campaign against Havana.[14]

President McKinley's decision had an immediate political effect. In the first enunciation of war aims since the outset of the conflict, on June 3 he secretly informed John Hay, the American ambassador at London, that the United States would require cession of Puerto Rico at the war's end rather than a monetary indemnity. This decision was made concurrent with the plan to follow the attack on Santiago de Cuba with an invasion of Puerto Rico. The demand for annexation stemmed from the specific situation in May, 1898, rather than prior design, although close observers had long sensed the strategic advantage that would flow from acquisition of the island.[15]

General Miles, nothing if not persistent, remained unreconciled to the President's considerable alteration of his grand design. On June 6 he once more attempted to sidetrack the expedition to Santiago de Cuba, proposing instead that he should assume command of the force at Tampa when it reached a total of thirty thousand men and take it to Puerto Rico. For the moment he would post a mere guard at Santiago de Cuba. When Puerto Rico had been taken, he would return to Santiago de Cuba and reduce it. After this the troops could move against any other objectives. (Miles probably had in mind his pet campaign westward across northern Cuba to Havana). To this suggestion the Secretary of War returned an instant rejection: "The President says no." Instead, McKinley urged "the utmost haste on departure of No. 1 [expedition to Santiago de Cuba], and also of No. 2, as indicated by you, but that No. 1 must be undertaken first." This capsule restatement of the general decision made on May 26 honored the sound premise that military action in the Caribbean should turn on the elimination of Admiral Cervera's squadron.[16]

Still the War Department pressed strongly for early organization of a separate Puerto Rican expedition. On June 7 Miles was ordered to ready thirty thousand men for departure in ten days; Corbin indicated that necessary transports would become available in that time. (Apparently the War Department had misconstrued Miles's message of June 6: The general did not contemplate a new force; he wanted to expand the army already at Tampa to thirty thousand to accomplish his abortive project.) On June 8 the War Department proposed a port other than Tampa as base for the Puerto Rican venture, taking into account the difficulties General Shafter had experienced in preparing the expedition to Santiago de Cuba. To this suggestion Miles returned a counterproposal: He wanted to move troops from Miami to Key West to supplement those embarked from Tampa.

At this point the sighting of the Spanish "ghost squadron" took place. It delayed Shafter's departure, which circumstance led Miles to revive his plan for operations in Puerto Rico and northern Cuba. To counter possible Spanish opposition on the high seas, he proposed that the entire navy accompany the expedition to Santiago de Cuba—or possibly to Puerto Rico or Nuevitas. Apparently what he really preferred was to let the navy deal with Santiago de Cuba by itself and to employ troops elsewhere. Once again Alger sent a chilling telegram: "The president directs me to say that no change of plan will be made." Instead, Miles was again ordered to organize No. 2 quickly.[17]

While Shafter completed his arrangements for departure, Miles lingered in Tampa a few days longer, continuing to debate strategy by telegraph with the Secretary of War. Alger persisted in his view that a new port of embarkation should be chosen for the Puerto Rican expedition, a more northerly location "where the weather is better and shipping facilities are ample." Miles retorted that the troops at Tampa were getting along well; he planned to draw additional men from Camp Thomas, Tennessee, to fill out his forces. When the War Department specified a date when transports would be available, Miles said, he would adopt it as his day of departure. He proposed, for reasons of health, to move troops based at Jacksonville to Fernandina. He also wanted to build up another contingent at Miami, where ten thousand troops could be accommodated in the near future. The men at Fernandina and Miami could be gradually transferred to Key West, where they could join the rest of the expedition as it steamed southward from Tampa for Puerto Rico. Once again he asked, "When will sufficient transports be available?" Alger asserted that, if possible, health considerations should take precedence in deciding troop locations; the President would allow men to be stationed in the best available places. Not to be outdone by his antagonist, Alger reiterated his favorite question: "When will our second expedition be ready?" Two days later the Secretary of War again proposed removing the troops remaining at Tampa to a more northerly location, and also noted certain hazards at Miami that he thought made the area unsuitable for stationing troops. Despite this pointed message, Miles reiterated his desire to prepare for Puerto Rico. Tiring of this sparring match, Alger finally obtained an order from President McKinley directing a troop concentration that varied somewhat from the one proposed by Miles: The commanding general was authorized to include all the troops then garrisoned at Tampa in his expedition. To them would be added a division based at Mobile under Brigadier General Theodore Schwan. Consolidated with scattered units from other locations, these troops would make a force of about twenty-nine thousand. Alger wanted to know if Miles desired additional men, and whether he planned to accompany the expedition to Puerto Rico.[18]

On June 15 Alger finally brought his telegraphic exchanges with Miles to an end, confirming his solution to the problem of troop concentration for the Puerto Rican expedition and arranging the return of Miles from Tampa to Washington. The Secretary of War informed the commanding general that no more troops would be ordered to Tampa and that those concentrated there would be brought north for shipment overseas. Thereafter facilities at the Florida port would be used only to send supplies and equipment to the Caribbean theater, not troops. In another telegram he ordered Miles to return without delay to Washington: "There are many matters that can be arranged better by personal contact than by correspondence. Answer." The extraordinarily stubborn Miles tried once more to delay: "I would request," he wired, "that all troops and war material now here remain until I see you, which will be in a few days." To this message Alger replied, "Important business requires your presence here. Report at once." Miles could only answer, "I leave by the first train 7:25 this evening."[19]

After returning to Washington Miles continued his obstructionism. On June 18 he met with the President, Alger, Long, and the Naval War Board to argue that troops and material designated as part of "No. 2" should concentrate at Tampa. McKinley continued to manifest great interest in an early invasion of Puerto Rico, a course consistent with his grand strategy, but the Secretary of the Navy wondered whether it might not be best to complete operations at Santiago de Cuba before starting another campaign. On June 24 Miles had the temerity once more to offer in a somewhat revised version his earlier plan to strike at Havana from eastern Cuba, proposing to seize Nuevitas for his base. From that city he would move inland. With the help of thirty thousand prisoners he expected to capture he would build a road at a pace of five miles per day to ensure good communications. This enterprise would continue until the end of September. Miles listed as advantages to be gained from this approach besides employment for prisoners of war the fact that cavalry could thus be used in the interior of Cuba and the likelihood that the army could avoid yellow fever in this region. As an alternative to this plan, he was prepared to concur in transfer of the troops then at Santiago de Cuba to a point west of Havana, presumably Mariel or some other port, to proceed from there to besiege the Cuban capital.[20]

Alger raised a number of cogent objections to both plans. Facilities at Nuevitas were not extensive enough to support a large expedition. Roadbuilding was not feasible in the interior of Cuba. The army would encounter serious difficulties in efforts to protect a long supply line deep in the interior. It was also unsound military practice to commit all the country's cavalry regiments in one location; some units might be required elsewhere. It made no sense to conduct a 350-mile march through undeveloped country to get into position for a campaign that would occur three months later, especially when it was remembered that "we could land under cover of our own battle-ships in a day, coming direct from the United States." Whether or not for these cogent reasons, Miles's harebrained scheme gained no support from the McKinley Administration.[21]

ORGANIZATION OF FORCES

On June 26 Secretary Alger issued detailed orders for the Puerto Rican expedition that governed two succeeding weeks of feverish activity. Three divisions were to be formed from the First and Third Army Corps. Along with two others created from the Fourth Army Corps, they would constitute a force of about twenty-seven thousand troops. Major General John R. Brooke would hold immediate command. When operations began, he would serve under Miles in company with two other senior officers, Major Generals John J. Coppinger and James H. Wilson. Troops that could be spared from Shafter's expedition at Santiago de Cuba would augment the concentration intended for Puerto Rico. Miles was ordered to prepare for departure from Tampa as soon as possible, after which preparation he was to request further instructions. At long last the commanding general showed an interest in getting his troops into combat, although he continued to advance eccentric views. On June 29 he informed Alger that he had placed some of his troops aboard transports and that others were ready to depart as soon as ships became available. He now advocated movement of his entire command to Santiago de Cuba. "If, on arrival at that place, they are not required," he wrote, "they should continue on to Puerto Rico without delay." On July 1, he advanced still another scheme, suggesting that available troops awaiting the movement to Puerto Rico make improved use of their time by seizing the Isle of Pines off the south coast of Cuba. Vulnerable to attack, the place could be used to support future campaigns in Cuba. Enjoying a good climate, it was a suitable location for hospitals, prison camps, supply depots, and possibly a base for cavalry operations on the larger island. "The one steamer now at Tampa can, with a battery of artillery and one regiment of infantry, take the island, land from two to six months' supplies, and return to Tampa inside of ten days, when the steamer should be ready to be used for any military purpose." Alger lost no time in disapproving this plan.[22]

Miles viewed the victories of July 1 and July 3 in Cuba as justification for an immediate attack on Puerto Rico. He believed that operations at Santiago de Cuba were primarily to accomplish "the forcing of the Spanish fleet out of the harbor and its destruction by the navy"—a view opposed to that of Shafter. On July 5, two days after the naval battle, he argued that the existing situation appeared "most favorable for proceeding immediately to Puerto Rico," an island "of the highest importance" because it was "the gateway to the Spanish possessions" in the West Indies. About four thousand of his men were aboard transports at Key West, and another seven thousand would soon become available at Charleston, South Carolina. In addition, he could draw on the twenty thousand troops then at Santiago de Cuba. If he lacked sufficient strength to conduct proposed operations in Puerto Rico, he could easily call for reinforcements. Miles now wanted to make haste; in this sense he had become reconciled to an important aspect of the President's strategic design.[23]

At this point the Administration's confidence in General Shafter reached a low point, and it was decided to send Miles and his troops to Santiago de Cuba. If necessary the commanding general could support the operations there, and he was expected to inaugurate the Puerto Rican campaign at the first opportunity. Two fast transports, the *Yale* and *Columbia*, awaited him with troops aboard at Charleston. On July 8 he boarded the *Yale* and left for Santiago de Cuba. Some of the units intended for his expedition were already en route to the Cuban city; on July 9–10 the First Illinois and the First District of Columbia Volunteers arrived at Siboney along with two regiments of regulars, the Fourth and Fifth Artillery. Miles came in on July 11.[24]

While at Santiago de Cuba General Miles devoted most of his energy to preparations for the campaign in Puerto Rico. He took extraordinary precautions to keep his troops free from tropical diseases. The medical state of Shafter's command made him decide not to take any troops who had served at Santiago de Cuba along to Puerto Rico. Keeping his own troops on board ship, he eventually moved his transports to the protected anchorage in Guantánamo Bay. Miles had his medical personnel develop strict procedures to minimize health problems. This sensible precaution helped maintain relatively good health in his command by comparison with Shafter's, although as it turned out Puerto Rico did not pose problems of this nature comparable to those in Cuba. On July 14 Secretary Alger informed the commanding general that the War Department was arranging the transport of twenty-five thousand additional men for his expedition and suggested that, when the capitulation took place at Santiago de Cuba, Miles should return to the United States and go to Puerto Rico with the main body of the expedition.

Miles may have interpreted this proposal as evidence of Alger's intention to deprive him of the Puerto Rican command. In any case his reaction was to press for an early departure to Puerto Rico with what troops
he could collect at Guantánamo Bay—only about thirty-five hundred.
At the same time he arranged to have other units intended for his expedition sail directly to Puerto Rico to join him there.[25]

On July 16 Miles matured his plan of operation. Visiting Admiral
Sampson to request naval support for the invasion of Puerto Rico, he
said that he would land at Fajardo, just below Cape San Juan at the
northeast corner of the island. From that beachhead he would operate
against San Juan. He then cabled to Alger that he had met with Sampson and intended to begin his campaign as soon as the navy could provide escort. Sampson agreed that Fajardo was an appropriate landing
place; Miles therefore requested that units embarking for Puerto Rico
from American ports steam to that location. Miles's plans for naval
escort contemplated protection not only of the transports leaving from
Cuba but of those moving from the United States. He also communicated to Alger his belief that none of Shafter's troops, beset by
tropical diseases, could be expected to join the attack on Puerto Rico.
However, unfortunately for Miles Sampson opposed the use of any armored vessels as escorts, bearing in mind the requirements of the
Eastern Squadron.[26]

The next day, July 17, a large number of telegrams passed between
Miles and Alger, the commanding general attempting to hasten his
departure for Puerto Rico and the Secretary of War leaning more and
more towards delay. Alger inaugurated the feverish exhange with a request for complete information about the proposed operation—"all
details, where rendezvous, and where you propose to land, and what
force required to make and maintain your initial landing." This information was needed to plan the routing of some nine thousand troops
and supporting units during the coming week. He concluded peremptorily, "Answer today; important." Miles responded that he had
available twenty-five hundred men on three transports at Guantánamo
along with the four batteries of light artillery and other units then proceeding to Santiago de Cuba. He wished to leave the next day for Point
Fajardo, about forty hours distant, and would do so when he and Sampson completed arrangements for this movement. Ultimately he wanted
to mass about thirty thousand troops. In another message he pointed
out that a strong naval force had been concentrated at Guantánamo
"preparing to go to Spain"—a reference to the Eastern Squadron. The
commanding general had been visited with another one of his bright
ideas: "Would it not be well to suggest a strong combined movement

on Porto Rico, to make sure of the capture of the island and the reduction of the forts there as speedily as possible, as its occupation will probably be all the assistance required of the Navy in the complete control of the islands in the West Indies?'' For sheer effrontery Miles may be unsurpassed in the annals of American military history; he breezily proposed nothing less than to divert powerful naval forces intended for an entirely separate enterprise to the service of his own campaign. After Miles's intentions were evaluated in the War Department, Alger indicated considerable disquietude. He wondered whether the commanding general had enough troops to conduct the campaign: "Your proposition to go to Porto Rico with 3,000 troops now afloat at Santiago does not seem best, in view of the fact that you could not be reinforced for a week or ten days." However, twelve thousand troops could be started now towards a rendezvous; he proposed that Nipe Bay serve this purpose. A final instruction must have confirmed Miles in his suspicion that Alger's real purpose was to deprive him of command: "Until this is settled you should remain where you are. Will cable progress every day."[27]

Alger's suggestion of Nipe Bay as a staging point for the Puerto Rican expedition stemmed from a recommendation of the Naval War Board a week earlier. On July 17 Long ordered Sampson to occupy Nipe Bay, who issued instructions to this effect the next day. On July 21 the *Topeka* and some small vessels accomplished this mission, but the enterprise went for naught, since Miles had settled on Guantánamo Bay as a rendezvous, and had clearly indicated his intention in communications to superiors in Washington. The failure of the War and Navy Departments to coordinate their activities in this respect constituted yet another example of inadequate cooperation between the services during the war.[28]

Finally, on July 18, the Administration decided to act; Corbin transmitted orders to Miles authorizing the expedition to Puerto Rico, with the understanding that reinforcements could not reach him for five to seven days. Sampson would receive instructions to assist in the action. Another specification here may be significant: "The Secretary of War futher directs that on your landing on the island Puerto Rico. . . you hoist the American flag." Was this requirement merely designed to dramatize the role of the army, or did it indicate an intention to annex Puerto Rico? It should be remembered that early in June, when a decision had been made to send out the expeditions to Santiago de Cuba and Puerto Rico, the Administration also covertly revealed its decision to annex Puerto Rico in lieu of an indemnity. Whatever the reason, the main import of the message was that Miles had gained sanction to pro-

ceed immediately to Puerto Rico with a small advance force. There he
would inaugurate operations, anticipating reinforcements that eventually would build his expedition to about thirty thousand troops. To
Alger he cabled briefly on July 19, "Order to go to Porto Rico received
last night. Will move as soon as navy is ready."[29]

As the War Department set about collecting transports for the Puerto
Rican expedition, General Miles pursued his efforts to obtain a powerful naval escort from Sampson. On July 18 the Admiral had received an
order from Secretary Long that guided his initial actions: "You will give
Miles such assistance as you and he may regard as necessary for landing
troops now on *Yale* and other transports at Porto Rico and maintaining
their landing." Miles was anxious to have a naval officer serve under his
command; for this duty he suggested Commodore Schley. This expedient, he felt, might minimize interservice squabbling of the sort that
had occurred during the campaign at Santiago de Cuba. On July 19
Long wired Sampson that the War Department had decided against the
rendezvous at Nipe Bay, and asked for a list of the ships going to Puerto
Rico with General Miles. Sampson, who was still discussing this question with the commanding general, did not answer this message—an
omission that led to complications later on. On that day Miles made a
specific request concerning the naval escort, asking Sampson for "a
strong force of naval vessels to accompany my transports, cover landing
[at Fajardo] from the same, protect the flanks of the military force during the occupation of that place, and render all assistance possible in
the movement from there to the investment and capture of the harbor
and city of San Juan." After requesting assistance in dealing with other
coastal towns, he made two other propositions—that the Marines encamped at Guantánamo be allowed to accompany him and that the
navy make a "strong demonstration" near San Juan as a diversion
before his force went ashore at Fajardo.[30]

When Sampson returned an unfavorable answer to Miles, there ensued a considerable row, conducted mostly by cable between Santiago
de Cuba and Washington. In his message to Miles on July 19 Sampson
stressed his orders to prepare the Eastern Squadron and the operation at
Nipe Bay, maintaining that these requirements precluded him from
providing all the vessels specified by Miles. On July 20 the Admiral
listed the force he had in mind: He would make available some of the
ships assigned to attack Nipe Bay (*Annapolis*, *Wasp*, *Leyden*) and also
the *Gloucester* and the three monitors *Amphitrite*, *Puritan*, and *Terror*.
Even without the monitors Sampson believed that the transports *Yale*
and *Columbia* with the protected cruisers *Cincinnati* and *New Orleans*
alone could cope with the defenders at Fajardo, unless the enemy

employed heavy guns. Miles exploded when he learned of Sampson's intentions. He immediately fired off a cablegram to the War Department in which he argued that should the *New Orleans*, which he wished to blockade San Juan, be absent from its station, his transports might come under attack from Spanish gunboats. The *Columbia* and *Yale* could not land unsupported without endangering the lives of the troops on board. Since the navy had concentrated numerous vessels at Guantánamo—intended for the Eastern Squadron—he asked that Sampson be ordered to provide a strong escort for the ten thousand troops he expected to have in hand within a week. This cable led to another from Long to Sampson, calling attention to Miles's complaint and adding, "Hasten adequate assistance as much as possible and report to the Department. Telegraph kind naval assistance Miles desires."[31]

The dispute was resolved only after President McKinley intervened directly. Writing to Secretary Long on July 20, he asked that the navy enlarge the escort for the Puerto Rican expedition:

> It is evident to me . . . that Admiral Sampson is not proposing to furnish such assistance as I have heretofore directed. He should send enough ships and strong enough as will enable General Miles to land his troops in safety, at Pt. Fajardo, Cape San Juan and to remain so long as their assistance is needed. General Wilson has already sailed from Charleston [on July 20] with orders to proceed to Pt. Fajardo. If your convoy is delayed he will reach Pt. Fajardo without any protection whatever, which must not be permitted. Wilson cannot be reached by wire. He has no guns on his ships. The Secretary of War says that General Wilson is due to arrive at Pt. Fajardo within three or four days. Prompt action should be taken to give Gen. Wilson protection on his arrival there. It seems to me a cruiser or a battleship, or both should be detailed for this duty. Please see that the necessary orders are issued at once.

Here was an unusually sharp and explicit order from McKinley. He had tired of interservice squabbling, and had to solve a real problem. Without early action General Wilson's contingent might steam into dangerous waters bereft of a naval escort. Ever hopeful of forcing an early end to the war, the President was anxious to avoid a serious military setback that might stiffen the resolve of Spain.[32]

The War Department lost no time informing Miles of the decision in Washington, and Long's order to Sampson on July 21 left nothing to the imagination: "The President directs you send ships of war enough and strong enough to enable Miles to land at Porto Rico and remain there as long as needed to render assistance or until further orders."

Miles was to receive the *Indiana* and *Newark* or comparable ships—immediately. And Secretary of the Navy wanted to know why his Admiral had not provided information about the escort. Sampson had no choice; he immediately added the battleship *Massachusetts* and the auxiliary cruiser *Dixie* to the list of vessels already specified for the escort. Acknowledging this assignment, Miles added, "I am ready to sail without delay, and hope to take advantage of the fair weather that usually prevails in Porto Rico during this month."[33]

Sampson was greatly angered at this outcome, judging that Miles required only a minimal escort for the voyage to Puerto Rico and landing operations. No available Spanish naval vessels could challenge the American ships he had specified earlier, and no batteries existed at Fajardo to oppose the landing. The detail of the *Massachusetts* would force still another delay in the departure of the Eastern Squadron. In his report to Long on July 22 the Admiral, obviously stung, pointed out that his orders concerning the Eastern Squadron and Nipe Bay left him with no ships for Miles's escort. He claimed to have answered all his telegrams. Long, always conciliatory, tried to make some amends: "Your dispatch of yesterday received and is of much value, showing that you have done all you could for General Miles, who has been deluging the War Department with requests for convoy." He cleared up the case of the missing message: "Our unanswered telegram was July 19th, in which we asked what vessels are you going to send to Porto Rico with Miles." In this fashion another interservice quarrel came to a conclusion. Sampson had behaved a bit childishly, perhaps reacting to earlier brushes with Shafter. Nevertheless, Miles should not have insisted on a naval escort far beyond his needs. McKinley acted properly in resolving the dispute, but came to an unsound solution.[34]

Miles finally departed from Guantánamo at 3:00 P.M. on July 21, planning to move north through the Windward Passage and then eastward along the north coasts of Hispaniola and Puerto Rico to Fajardo, where he intended to link up with the additional forces from the United States. Troops aboard the transports, dispirited because they had not been allowed to land in Cuba, took heart at the prospect of action in Puerto Rico. The naval escort included the *Massachusetts*, along with the *Dixie* and the armed yacht *Gloucester*. Troops were carried on the transports *Columbia*, *Yale*, and *Macon*, these vessels accommodating a total of 3,415 men. General Wilson's contingent, which had departed from Charleston on July 20, included about thirty-six hundred troops. On July 24 an additional twenty-nine hundred men under General Schwan left Tampa. Another four thousand at Newport News were preparing to depart for Puerto Rico, and a comparable group awaited other transports at Tampa. Alger, however, squashed Miles's request for the services of the Marines at Guantánamo: "I do not think well of your suggestion about marines," he cabled. "We have army enough for our work." When accumulated, the forces intended for Puerto Rico numbered about eighteen thousand men. This total fell twelve thousand short of the planned size, but compared favorably with the Spanish garrison on Puerto Rico, which Miles estimated at 8,233 regulars and 9,107 volunteers.[35]

OPERATIONS IN PUERTO RICO

Once out from Guantánamo Bay the erratic Miles made a truly surprising decision: He changed the objective from Fajarado to Guánica, a city on the southern coast of Puerto Rico. This action was highly questionable, because it posed unexpected and untoward problems of communication between Miles's headquarters, Washington, and the detachments of Wilson and Schwan proceeding to Fajardo. On July 22 Miles proposed to the senior naval officer present, Captain Francis J. Higginson, commanding the *Massachusetts*, that the expedition bypass Fajardo and move around the island along the eastern and southern coasts to its extreme opposite end to the port of Guánica—about twelve hours by sea. Miles gave as reasons for this change the fact that his movement to Fajardo had become known in Puerto Rico; that the deepwater harbor at Guánica provided excellent facilities; and that an unexpected landing on the south coast would achieve strategic surprise. "As it is always advisable not to do what your enemy expects you do to," he informed Higginson, "I think it advisable after going around the northeast corner of Puerto Rico to go immediately to Guánica and land this force and move on Ponce, which is the largest city in Puerto Rico." Either before or after completing this landing, he expected to receive reinforcements that would allow him "to move in any direction or occupy any portion of the island of Puerto Rico." Miles was acting on the basis of information supplied by Captain Henry H. Whitney. Whitney's espionage in Puerto Rico a few weeks earlier induced the commanding general to stress the favorable situation at Guánica and Ponce as against Fajardo.[36]

When this change of plan was discussed on the *Massachusetts*, Captain Higginson raised a number of cogent objections. After Miles reviewed his reasons for changing the landing place, citing an additional consideration not mentioned earlier—namely, that the population in the southern parts of Puerto Rico was much more disaffected from Spain than that of the north and, if given an opportunity, would

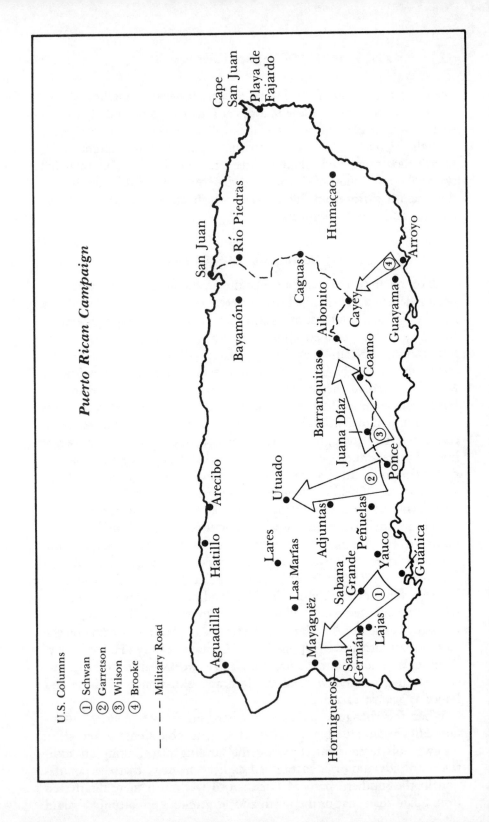

Puerto Rican Campaign

U.S. Columns
① Schwan
② Garretson
③ Wilson
④ Brooke
- - - Military Road

Aguadilla
Hatillo
Arecibo
Lares
Las Marías
Mayagüez
Hormigueros
San Germán
Sabana Grande
Adjuntas
Utuado
Lajas
Yauco
Peñuelas
Guánica
Ponce
Juana Díaz
Barranquitas
Coamo
Aibonito
Caguas
Bayamón
Río Piedras
San Juan
Cayey
Coamo
Guayama
Arroyo
Humacao
Cape
San Juan
Playa de
Fajardo

rally to the Americans—Higginson noted that he could not cover a landing at Guánica or protect a base there as effectively as at Fajardo. Moreover, he could not take the *Massachusetts,* the *Columbia,* and *Dixie* into Guánica because the harbor was too shallow. He was not sure that he could keep the sea in the event of heavy weather off the southern coast. Finally, he pointed to his lack of adequate charts, a circumstance that would restrict his ability to support operations on land. "On the east coast, from Cape San Juan to Point Algodon, [he could] approach close to the shore and cover with the guns of the fleet any position he wished to occupy, and, moreover, by placing a vessel on the north coast of Porto Rico just west of Cape San Juan, could obtain a cross fire over the land as far as Fajardo." This capability, of course, would seriously restrict the enemy's ability to sustain an effective defense and supply its forces from San Juan. Higginson also brought up another important consideration: "At Cape San Juan we were 30 miles from St. Thomas, where, in the absence of colliers, we could coal our ships and communicate with the Government." Miles left the *Massachusetts* that day without settling the issue. The next day he persisted in his proposal, and Higginson felt compelled to yield. Without making a demonstration at San Juan or Fajardo, a project to which some consideration had been given earlier, the expedition moved past its presumed landing place and continued on around the island to the southwest coast.[37]

Naval strategists later echoed Higginson's opposition to the change of plan. Captain Mahan, in a typically choleric letter to Secretary Long just after the war, condemned Miles's eccentric movement: "The Porto Rico landing I once told you, at Guanica, and the initiation of operations there, appears [sic] to me a military stupidity so great, that I can account for [these acts] only by a kind of obsession to vanity, to do a singular and unexpected thing." Chadwick mentioned some of the considerations underlying Mahan's criticism of the commanding general. He had "invested the Spanish with a much greater activity and initiative than their methods in Cuba justified. He would probably have found little opposition at Fajardo as did the ships which arrived there a few days later." There, a scant forty miles east of San Juan, Miles would have found good water and landing places. In addition, argued Chadwick, questions of terrain and distance should have been taken into consideration: "The change put between the American forces and the main Spanish position a much greater distance, and a mountain range which a determined enemy might have made impassible." A motive of Miles, unannounced at the time, might have been a desire to minimize the role of the navy during the Puerto Rican expedition. The commanding general informed Secretary Alger that "marching across the country, rather than under the guns of the fleet, will have in every way a desirable effect on the inhabitants of this country." It is true that at a later point in the campaign, Miles reacted powerfully against certain naval plans to conduct a bombardment of San Juan.[38]

Whatever the reasons for it, the decision to go to Guánica greatly complicated the operations required to conquer Puerto Rico. Whether Miles gained more by surprise than he lost by choosing a long and difficult route from his landing place to the center of Spanish resistance is a question that cannot be settled definitively, since the campaign came to a premature end before the American forces could reach San Juan. But the decision to bypass Fajardo was entirely consistent with the erratic behavior and suspiciousness that Miles manifested throughout the war. He was too unstable to hold a command of great importance; it is fortunate that the situation he encountered in Puerto Rico did not make undue demands on him.

In San Juan Governor-General Macías had received plenty of advance warning as he prepared to resist the American invasion. When Miles started for Puerto Rico, the Spanish defenders had been accurately informed about his strength and intentions. On July 25, before Miles made his landfall, the Colonial Minister Girón sent word from Madrid that the Americans intended to land either at Fajardo, Arecibo, or Ponce. Macías had orders from Minister of War Correa to offer resistance; a firm defense might strengthen Spain's bargaining position at the end of the war. However, when news spread throughout Puerto Rico that Miles was on the way, many inhabitants of coastal cities fled to the interior. At the same time units of Puerto Rican home guards (*voluntarios*) began to defect.[39]

Macías could choose between two obvious courses of action: He might concentrate all his forces around San Juan to defend the seat of government, or he might base his defense on strong points in the interior of the island. The first solution seemed more logical because the Governor-General had available only a small number of troops with limited supplies and could expect Puerto Ricans to mount local opposition to his forces in the interior. The second approach, however, would probably slow the pace of the American conquest—a political consideration of no small consequence. Faced with this dilemma Macías resolved it by rejecting both of the apparent options. He kept most of his forces in the north, where he expected the landing, but located battalions at two important coastal locations elsewhere—Ponce and Mayagüez—and placed another detachment at Caguas, astride the road between Ponce and San Juan. The latter force could maneuver quickly to any threatened locales. Other small detachments were scattered around the island to give the appearance that no turf would be abandoned to the Americans. Such were the Spanish dispositions with which the Americans would have to contend.[40]

On the morning of July 25 Miles made an uneventful landing at Guánica. After Captain Higginson ordered the *Gloucester* inside the harbor, a small force of sailors from that ship landed and dispersed a few Spanish defenders. No shots had to be fired as the Americans entered Guánica (nor did resistance materialize during subsequent landing operations at Ponce and Arroyo). The American flag was raised at 11:00 A.M. When Guánica had been secured, the transports steamed into the harbor and began disembarking troops and supplies. Miles later paid tribute to the efficiency of naval personnel at Guánica and elsewhere during the campaign.[41]

Realizing the importance of Ponce, some miles to the east, Miles immediately took steps to seize the city. Congratulating Captain Higginson on his successful operation at Guánica, he indicated that the navy should also take Ponce. To support this he ordered Brigadier General George A. Garretson, with six companies from the Sixth Massachusetts and one from the Sixth Illinois, to move on Yauco, a town six miles north of Guánica located on the railroad and highway to Ponce. After a brief skirmish at dawn on July 26—the first engagement in Puerto Rico—the Spanish defenders retired, and Yauco was occupied two days later, on July 28, enabling Brigadier General Guy V. Henry to march his troops across the highway to Ponce, arriving there that same day. Meanwhile, Miles had reported the victory at Yauco to Higginson and indicated that if Ponce were taken he would move transports there the following day. Accordingly, on July 27 Commander Charles H. Davis went ashore with a detachment of naval personnel at the Port of Ponce, two miles south of the main city. The next day in addition to Henry's contingent arriving by land, troops under the command of Major General James H. Wilson disembarked and occupied the city proper. (General Wilson had gone originally to Fajardo, but received word there that Miles had gone on to Guánica; with the *Annapolis* and *Wasp* as escorts, his transports arrived there on July 27, and Miles ordered him to Ponce the next day.) The Spanish garrison at Ponce retreated rapidly, moving northward toward San Juan along the military road. The commanding officer, Don Leopoldo San Martín y Gil, had been given orders to resist the landing, but had failed to execute them; obviously, any such effort would have served no rational purpose. Since no Spanish troops remained near the landing areas, General Henry concluded that the enemy was concentrating in the vicinity of San Juan.[42]

When Miles entered Ponce, he issued a proclamation insisting that the Americans came not as conquerors but as liberators and intended to respect personal and property rights—an action initiating a calculated campaign to attract Puerto Rican support. Miles gained considerable success in this endeavor; the overwhelming majority of Puerto Ricans collaborated with or at least failed to resist American activities, either because they welcomed the end of Spanish domination or because they decided to side with the strongest battalions. Of great importance during the campaign was the action of the Puerto Rican home guards: They deserted en masse, either to return home or join the Americans. This outcome naturally buoyed the spirits of Miles and his troops as they contemplated the next stage of the campaign. To Secretary Alger, the commanding general reported ebulliently, "This is a prosperous and beautiful country. The army will soon be in mountain region; weather delightful; troops in best of health and spirits; anticipate no insurmountable obstacles in future results." He was pleased to report that, so far, he had not lost a single man.[43]

General Wilson's arrival at Guánica raised Miles's strength to over seven thousand men, and within a week two more important reinforcements increased his command to above fifteen thousand: Brigadier General Theodore Schwan, departing from Tampa on July 24, came in on July 31 with some twenty-nine hundred men. Major General John R. Brooke, leaving Newport News on July 28, landed about five thousand troops at Arroyo, forty miles east of Ponce, on August 3–5. Some smaller contingents arrived later, but Miles finished the campaign with essentially the troops available as of August 5.[44]

Once established ashore at Guánica and Ponce, Miles developed an intricate plan of campaign to end Spanish resistance in Puerto Rico. Eventually he decided to send four distinct columns northward—three originating in the Ponce area and one in Arroyo—in order to approach the center of Spanish power around San Juan. One column under General Schwan would move forward on the left flank of the American advance, proceeding from Ponce to Mayagüez on the west coast and thence to Arecibo on the north coast. Another column would depart from Ponce under General Garretson and move due north to Adjuntas, Utuado, and Arecibo. This combined force would then come under the command of General Henry, ready to move eastward toward San Juan. Meanwhile General Wilson would lead a third column northeast from Ponce through Coamo against the strong point of Aibonito. On the right flank, General Brooke would move from Arroyo through Guayama to Cayey, seeking to get behind Aibonito on the road to San Juan, in order to make it untenable for the Spanish defenders.

Wilson and Brooke would then combine forces and drive together up the road, linking up near San Juan with the troops coming from Arecibo to seize the city. This complicated design stressed maneuver to isolate and outflank enemy positions. It avoided frontal assaults, a tendency in keeping with previous strategic proposals emanating from General Miles.[45]

On July 29 the Navy Department received a cable from Lieutenant Sims in Paris reporting suggestions made in the Spanish government that reflected a clear grasp of the American plan and its vulnerable aspects. A retired French officer had suggested to Madrid that "successful resistance could be made at Puerto Rico by attacking separate detachments before concentration." Had Macías heeded this and abandoned his attempt to maintain a military presence in all parts of the island and maneuvered his units so as to concentrate significant force at strong defensive positions in the central mountains, he might have been able to delay matters considerably. As it was, his resistance proved so weak that it undermined the home government's bargaining position during peace negotiations, which began in Washington as Miles arrived in Guánica. (When General Brooke arrived at Arroyo, he brought instructions to campaign vigorously despite current diplomatic exchanges that could lead to an armistice.) Because of his decision to land on the southern coast rather than in the region of San Juan, Miles risked considerable delay conquering Puerto Rico—which could have worked against an early settlement with Spain. After all, the President's purpose had been to strike as quickly and as vigorously as possible at the weakest defensive positions in both the Pacific and the Caribbean to force an early victory; nothing concerned McKinley more than avoiding a bloody attack on the center of Spanish power at Havana. Considering the approach he adopted, Miles was fortunate that Macías did not adopt a strategy designed to protract the conflict. Once Miles—a stubborn man with a one-track mind—adopted an opinion, it tended to remain immured in his consciousness. His strategic *idée fixe* was antipathy to frontal assault. If an energetic enemy commands a strong defensive position in depth—as became the rule during World War I—the avoidance of the "direct approach" has considerable merit, but it made no sense to Puerto Rico during 1898. The Spanish garrison proved incapable of attempting more than token resistance in all encounters of the campaign, a circumstance that flowed not only from the determination of individual American units but also from the universal decision of Puerto Ricans to support the invaders.[46]

Before Miles began the various movements of his campaign, he benefitted from bits of information gleaned in the field. Brigadier

General Roy Stone, an engineer officer, reported on July 29 that the enemy appeared to be concentrating two or three thousand troops at Aibonito, a strong position that could be defended effectively. General Wilson noted the same development and added that an advance guard was located at Coamo, a few miles southwest of Aibonito. On August 1 Stone provided additional information (obtained from a Puerto Rican, Don Clothilde Santiago, whose son was mayor of Aibonito): Some four thousand troops were "making great preparations in commanding positions" near Aibonito, and about a thousand troops were around Coamo. His informant had been close to the Spanish defenders; they believed they could hold Aibonito. He also noted, "They have mined the cliff in some places to blow it down upon the road." On August 5 Brooke advanced westward from Arroyo to Guayama. From there he could later move northward along a good road to Cayey, thereby getting behind Aibonito. At Guayama he had a sharp skirmish with the Spanish defenders, in which five men from the Fourth Ohio sustained wounds. This affray indicated that the enemy would make a stand in the region of Coamo, Aibonito, and Cayey. Miles, however, proceeded confidently, recognizing that he was in a position of great superiority. On August 8, responding to a request from the War Department for information concerning future needs, he stated, "I think enough troops have been ordered to Porto Rico. No more light batteries required." He also proved cooperative when the War Department asked him to return transports as soon as possible for use in transferring the Fifth Army Corps from Santiago de Cuba to Montauk Point.[47]

Miles had good reason for optimism; his forces were growing, whereas those of the enemy were in decline. Governor–General Macías realized that he was in desperate straits. To Minister of War Correa he explained his position in detail: Autonomy had no future in Puerto Rico. "The majority of this country [does not] wish to call itself Spanish, preferring American domination. This the enemy knows, and it is proved to him today by greetings and adhesions in towns that are going to be occupied." The strategic situation greatly favored the Americans. "Scarce forces remain only in some parts of the coast that at most can make an honorable retreat. Enemy master of the sea and with as many ships as he needs, can move his forces with ease and rapidity, displaying superiority everywhere." He drew the obvious conclusion: "The possession by him of all the coast, with exception of this place [San Juan], is easy and short operation." This news could not have encouraged the Liberal ministry to delay peace negotiations in hopes of a turn for the better in Puerto Rico.[48]

Miles, however, was not launching his offensive as soon as he had wished, because of the inadequate landing facilities at both Ponce and Arroyo—a circumstance that may have encouraged the navy to contemplate a project to end Spanish resistance in Puerto Rico before Miles could move on San Juan. On August 2 Commander Charles H. Davis of the *Dixie* reported his experience in Puerto Rico to Admiral Sampson. After sketching Miles's plan of campaign, he proposed an alternative means of seizing San Juan: "I am strongly of the opinion that San Juan de Puerto Rico could be taken by a fleet under your command and by a coup de main, without the assistance of the army and in advance of its approach from the South and the complete conquest of the Island of Puerto Rico accomplished by this means." He then specified the details of such an enterprise. Apparently Sampson thought well of this proposition. Did he not recall the inconclusive result of his bombardment at San Juan on May 12? Perhaps he remembered instead his jousts with Shafter and Miles at Santiago de Cuba. At any rate, two days later he broached the possibility of attacking San Juan to Secretary Long. If the movement of the Eastern Squadron to European waters could be delayed, its ships might be used against the city. Bearing in mind that the army might encounter "strong resistance from land side at the place," that San Juan's fall could end the war, and that two weeks would be required to complete a joint operation, he posed an alternative: "San Juan can be destroyed from the water and may yield without much resistance to a proper show of naval strength." The anti-army bias inherent in this proposal attracted the attention of Captain Mahan. Writing to Long on August 5, he argued that the armored ships had been entirely responsible for the favorable military situation. Noting that disease had completely demoralized the Fifth Army Corps, he ridiculed Miles's activities in Puerto Rico, concluding, "[His] line of operations . . . I have viewed from the first with great distrust, and the news is not calculated to justify his course in choosing the farthest point, almost, we could find from San Juan to land."[49]

The navy may have wished to execute Davis's plan, but all prospects for the operation collapsed when General Miles learned of it. After hearing that naval vessels at Ponce had been ordered to San Juan, he cabled immediately to the War Department, "In order that there may be no conflict of authority, I request that no aggressive action be taken against this place; that no landings be made or communication held with Spanish officials or forces on this island by the Navy." Clearly the suspicious commander feared that the navy might be planning to cut the army out of what minor glory remained to be accumulated in the war with Spain. The next day he sent an even more suspicious and importunate message to Alger. He was now "fully convinced" that Sampson had ordered naval vessels then off the south coast of Puerto Rico to move on San Juan and bombard the city. He objected to this enterprise on the grounds that it violated a presidential order against endangering the lives of innocent noncombatants. More important, however, the navy's plan represented to him "an interference with the work given the army by the President." When his forces arrived at San Juan he would welcome naval assistance against military targets there, but he opposed operations calculated to injure noncombatants. In a brisk conclusion he left no doubt of his desires: "The control of all military affairs on the land of his island can be safely left to the army." The Secretary of War for once lent support, cabling Miles, "Am assured there is no cause for your apprehension, but, for a certainty, positive orders have been issued preventing the move you suggest." In this fashion an effort of the navy that might have stolen the army's thunder in Puerto Rico was nipped in the bud.[50]

General Miles finally launched his offensive. One of General Wilson's staff officers, Augustus Peabody Gardner, seemed to welcome this development, writing to his wife on August 2, "The rumors of peace are thick, and everyone is more disgusted than ever. I am not bloodthirsty; but I should like to see a little real fighting after all the farce." On August 6 General Schwan received orders to thrust northward on the left flank of the projected sweep to San Juan. His Independent Regular Brigade included the Eleventh Infantry, two companies of the Nineteenth Infantry, Troop A of the Fifth Cavalry, and two batteries of light artillery—in all, 36 officers and 1,411 men. After passing through Sabana Grande and San Germán to Mayagüez, he was to go back into the interior and strike through Lares to Arecibo on the north shore. His instructions left no doubt about the mission: "You will drive out or capture all Spanish troops in the western portion of Porto Rico. You will take all the necessary precautions and exercise great care against being surprised or ambushed by the enemy, and make the movement as rapidly as possible, and at the same time exercising your best judgment in the care of your command to accomplish the object of your expedition." On August 8 General Brooke, commanding the right flank, received his orders: He was told to move rapidly but cautiously to Cayey. "Envelop or outflank the enemy rather than attack in front, and under no circumstances assault entrenched lines. Take every precaution against ambuscade and mined roads." Brooke was also enjoined to maintain a well-extended line, taking advantage of his superiority in troops. He was also to utilize his light artillery, dynamite guns, and an innovation in which Miles had great confidence—portable shields! The reason for taking Cayey was to isolate the Spanish position at Aibonito.

The reconnaissance of August 8 that led to the small engagement north of Guayama indicated that Spanish troops were entrenched some six or eight miles to the north on the road to Cayey. Brooke then spent several days preparing to attack this position.[51]

Meanwhile General Wilson's command experienced the first serious combat of the campaign, an engagement at Coamo on August 9 as the Americans moved along the road from Ponce toward Aibonito. Troops under the immediate command of Brigadier General Oswald H. Ernst executed a skillful flanking maneuver, following General Miles's prescription. The Sixteenth Pennsylvania, led by Lieutenant Colonel John Biddle, moved at night over a mountain trail and came out on the road to San Juan, north of the enemy position. Ernst then advanced, and a battle ensued in which the Spanish commander and his second-in-command were killed. The enemy suffered about 40 killed and wounded and 167 prisoners fell into the hands of the Americans. The road was now open to Aibonito.[52]

The next day, August 10, Schwan fought his first engagement. Leaving Yauco on August 9, he had moved through Sabana Grande and San Germán. At Hormigueros, seven miles south of Mayagüez, the garrison of that city—about fourteen hundred troops—accepted battle briefly, but to no avail. In the battle the Spanish defenders suffered about fifty casualties. The Americans had one killed and sixteen wounded. The hasty retreat of the Spanish forces allowed Schwan to occupy Mayagüez On August 11. Driving on toward Arecibo, he pursued the enemy in the direction of Lares and prepared to take it.[53]

As Schwan pushed rapidly towards Arecibo, the column under General Garretson moved along a mountain trail north of Adjuntas, a trail that General Stone's engineers discovered and managed to improve sufficiently to use. General Henry took command of this movement on August 13, but that very day he received an order to halt at Utuado.[54]

Meanwhile preparations were under way to attack the Spanish position at Aibonito. Miles informed Wilson on August 9 of an old road from Coamo parallel to the military highway along which infantry could move unobserved by night to a location north of Aibonito. All this was in keeping with Miles's persistent, almost obsessive, emphasis on flanking movements rather than direct assaults and on measures to avoid offering the enemy opportunities to surprise American forces. Wilson realized that the Spanish forces at Aibonito occupied a strong position. For this reason he wanted Miles to reinforce him at Coamo with Schwan's Independent Brigade. Meanwhile Colonel Biddle had discovered a footpath along a ridge south of Aibonito that would allow infantry to bypass the town and take it from the rear. Wilson wanted

Brooke to demonstrate against Cayey while this attack took place. Miles asked Brooke his opinion of the prospects for such an attack, "understanding, of course, that you proceed with strong force sufficient to avoid any surprise or flank movement of the enemy, and in such manner as to inflict the greatest injury on him, with the least to your own command."[55]

On August 12 Wilson notified Miles of his intention to advance; he planned to pass a force around Aibonito, at the same time sending a message to the town's defenders asking for its surrender. That afternoon Colonel Tasker H. Bliss advanced to Aibonito under a flag of truce to consult the Spanish second-in-command. That officer agreed to approach the Governor-General and report the result the next morning at 6:00 A.M. Bliss took advantage of his mission to reconnoiter the position ahead: "He describes the road as very crooked, a deep gorge on one side and a perpendicular wall on the other," Wilson informed Miles, "and. . . after it passes beyond our sight it is swept by rifle trenches as completely as it is on this side of the ridge." A brief exchange of fire between two forces, stemming from an American reconnaissance, further revealed the strength of the enemy's position. Wilson now decided to send General Ernst from Barranquitas on a march south over the Honduras River to strike the main road two miles east of Aibonito, a route that would still keep the Americans beyond the enemy's range. Meanwhile he intended to delay until he learned whether the negotiations with the garrison had borne fruit. The next morning Brooke had his answer; the Spanish commander informed Colonel Bliss that "if any further flags of truce are sent by us upon any condition whatever they will not be received and . . . if we wish to avoid further effusion of blood we should not move from the camps which we occupy." Wilson then decided to make his attack on the morning of August 13. The battle promised to be a serious struggle. Reinforcements from Caguas had been sent to the defenders at Aibonito, and two Plasencia guns were available. The force of thirteen hundred Spanish troops might well resist as stubbornly here as did their counterparts at El Caney and the San Juan Heights.[56]

However, before any further developments could occur, at 4:23 P.M. on August 12 General Corbin sent a telegram to General Miles informing him that representatives of the United States and Spain had signed a protocol in Washington and that all operations were to be suspended. This message halted the various columns then moving toward San Juan. Miles informed his subordinate commanders—and also Governor-General Macías—of the settlement reached in Washington, and no more combat took place in Puerto Rico. The victorious commander accurately summarized the state of affairs at the suspension of hostilities: "Please notice on map our troops occupy best part of Porto Rico. They are moving in such strong column in concert that nothing could check their progress." He was sure that only four more days would have been needed to overrun all of the island. "There were some unavoidable delays before the troops could be landed, but none after." Miles ignored the fact that the American columns had not yet engaged the troops at Aibonito and the large concentration around San Juan. Alger pointed out correctly that "at no place in Puerto Rico were the Spaniards encountered in large numbers, nor did they offer much resistance when met."[57] Miles's belief that he could have ended all opposition in four days was based on the assumption that the Spanish would prove as easily dealt with in the latter phases of the campaign as earlier. But in any event Macías had no means of making a lengthy defense. The outcome at Santiago de Cuba had deprived his army of the will to persist. Once ashore Miles wasted little time, and his constant progress gave the Spanish government no basis upon which to resist the United States demand that Madrid cede the island of Puerto Rico to it as part of the peace settlement. Miles might not have completed his operation as expeditiously as he thought, but it is improbable that he would have experienced undue delay.

Many of the difficulties that afflicted the expedition to Santiago de Cuba did not trouble the Puerto Rican expedition. Landing operations at Guánica, Arroyo, and Ponce went much more smoothly than at Daiquirí and Siboney. Medical problems posed no serious difficulties. The presence of an effective contingent of engineers assisted greatly in resolving problems associated with the landing and with such tactical situations as Garretson's march through the difficult country from Adjuntas to Utuado. Casualties were very light: In six engagements the Americans suffered losses of only seven killed and thirty-six wounded; Spanish casualties were about ten times as great. Miles properly ensured that his command did not alienate the Puerto Rican population. When General Roy Stone discovered that a soldier in General Wilson's column had defrauded a restaurant owner by passing Confederate money, he recommended harsh punishment: "It seems to me that nothing but a drum-head court-martial and a little cold lead will serve in a case of this kind if the guilty party can be found." As it happened, the offender, Private Louis J. de Haas of the Sixth Illinois Volunteers, was apprehended and given a general court-martial; he received a sentence of solitary confinement at hard labor for thirteen months in a federal penitentiary.

Another aspect of Miles's efforts to develop local support was his attempt to obtain the release of Puerto Rican political prisoners held in Spain and Africa.[58]

As in Cuba, however, American soldiers often developed a distinct aversion to the local populace, in great part because of their racial bias. One of the members of Schwan's Independent Brigade was especially vehement in his condemnation: He was not sure that "the average inhabitant of Puerto Rico is worth coddling. . . . A thick, stout cudgel or a bright sharp axe would be more effective than honeyed words in helping him cheerfully to assimilate new ideas." He judged that about a sixth of the people were well educated and about half of the rest might be shaped into "something approaching decency," but the rest would post great difficulties: "They are ignorant, filthy, untruthful, lazy, treacherous, murderous, brutal, and black." Attitudes of this nature inevitably affected the postwar occupation of Puerto Rico.[59]

Soon after the war ended, Miles had to evacuate the Spanish garrison in Puerto Rico. The protocol of August 12 authorized joint commissioners to arrange this and the matter progressed more or less efficiently to a conclusion. All Spanish troops were on their way home by October 21, 1898.[60]

During the last phases of the Puerto Rican campaign all manner of political pressure was exerted in Washington to send certain volunteer regiments into action. The War Department tried to contend with this interference by a policy of representing each state in at least one expedition. Corbin pointed out to Senator Henry Cabot Lodge, who wanted additional units from Massachusetts sent to Puerto Rico, that his state already had troops in the Caribbean whereas other states had none at all. "The pressure for this representation is of such character as to force the Secretary to equalize assignments among several states," he explained. Some protests were honored when the complainants adduced good reasons. Corbin decided to send an Indiana regiment from Camp Thomas to Puerto Rico when Senator Charles W. Fairbanks (Republican from Indiana) showed that troops from neighboring states such as Illinois, Michigan, Ohio, and Kentucky had gone overseas but none had from Indiana.[61]

However, when the fighting ended, political demands to bring the volunteer units home without delay were just as frequent. A message from Vermont offered "business as usual" as grounds for protesting the dispatch of a regiment from that state to Puerto Rico as part of the occupation: "Those of us who bid our sons godspeed when they enlisted in their country's service were prepared for any sacrifice they might make, even to life itself, and are now of the same mind; but when the war is over we feel their places will be at their homes and in their wonted places of business.'' These demands faithfully reflected the mood of troops in the field. A song of the Fourth Ohio Volunteers summed up the view in that unit:

> Lying in the guard house, awaiting my discharge—
> To hell with all the officers, the provost and the guard—
> When we get back to Circle Ville, as happy as a clam.
> To tell about the sow-belly we ate for Uncle Sam.
> Home, boys, home, its home you ought to be!
> Home, boys, home, in your own country!
> Where the ash and the oak and the bonnie willow tree—
> Where the grass grows green in God's country.

The views of the folks at home and the troops in the field were bound to force early decisions.[62]

Miles soon responded to the pressure from his troops. On August 23 he proposed to return a third of the force to the United States—not in whole units but in thirds of units—giving as reasons "severe rains; sickness increasing; many volunteers have strong reasons for going home; steamers returning empty." The War Department, however, had a different plan in mind: It proposed to release entire regiments at a time, mustering out one hundred thousand volunteers service-wide as soon as possible. However, Miles was authorized to send home only the volunteer cavalry of New York and Pennsylvania. But when the commanding general reiterated his proposal, the War Department bowed to his judgment. To help conduct the postwar occupation fresh units, both regulars and volunteers, were shipped to Puerto Rico. Once again supporters of the state militia had generated sufficient political pressure to sway the War Department.[63]

The campaign to conquer Puerto Rico, originally conceived to force Spain to the peace table before it became necessary to conduct extensive operations at Havana, ended most successfully, despite the curious behavior of General Miles. However, the outcome probably did not play a truly important role in forcing the negotiations that led to the protocol of August 12, simply because the course of the war before Miles landed at Guánica denied the Sagasta government any option of continuing resistance. The most important consequence of the short "moonlight excursion" was the annexation of Puerto Rico. Only a few would have imagined this outcome a few short months earlier. Puerto Rico came into the hands of the United States as an unintended by-product of the war. Whitney Perkins summarizes neatly the reason why the idea of annexation prospered after the declaration of war against Spain: "When the United States went to war with Spain in Cuba, it could not consistently permit Spanish rule to continue unchallenged in nearby Puerto Rico." Otherwise Puerto Rico might well have remained Spanish—as Martinique and Guadeloupe remained French and Trinidad and Jamaica remained British. American hegemony in the Caribbean Sea rendered these latter islands useless from a strategic point of view; there was no good reason to worry about the fact that they remained under European flags. The case of Puerto Rico was different, simply because of the situation in 1898. That island's historical experience as a colonial possession of the United States stemmed from historical accident rather than calculated design.[64]

☆ SIXTEEN ☆

Beginnings of the Manila Campaign

The campaign in the Philippines did not end with the early naval victory at Manila Bay; a siege lay in the offing, and Commodore Dewey made preparations for an extended stay. He summarized these measures succinctly: "The blockade of Manila must be established and enforced; immunity from surprise attack by the Spanish insured; Cavite arsenal must be occupied, its stores protected, and its precincts policed; and, generally, American supremacy and military discipline must take the place of chaos." On May 2 Dewey took his squadron to Cavite, a protected anchorage well beyond the range of the Spanish batteries at Manila, where he remained during the rest of the campaign. Next day a landing party occupied the Cavite arsenal, which provided some of the facilities required to maintain the American squadron in fighting trim. On the same date the *Baltimore* and *Raleigh* compelled the batteries at Corregidor to surrender, an operation that guaranteed safe passage in and out of the bay. Dewey also cut the cable connecting Manila and Hong Kong, thereby eliminating his telegraphic communications to Washington as well the defenders' to Madrid. To maintain contact with the outside world the revenue cutter *McCulloch* carried dispatches between Manila and Hong Kong. The supply ship *Zafiro* also plied the same route, circumventing neutrality regulations at Hong Kong and obtaining necessary goods to support the squadron.[1]

Dewey found himself in a peculiar situation: "I control bay completely and can take city at any time, but I have not sufficient men to hold," he observed soon after his victory. This situation required prompt consideration in Washington. On May 7 the Navy Department sent Dewey news of his elevation to Rear Admiral and informed him that the protected cruiser *Charleston* and auxiliary cruiser *City of Pekin* would soon come out to Manila with ammunition and supplies. Long added, "Will take troops unless you telegraph otherwise. How many will you require?" This request reflected a decision in Washington made as early as May 2 to provide troops for the seizure of Manila. Dewey received this message in time to respond from Cavite on May 13, "To retain possession and thus control Philippine Islands would require, in my best judgment, well-equipped force of 5,000 men, although United States troops sent by *Pekin* will be very useful to relieve the *Olympia* of guarding Cavite." He estimated the number of Spanish troops in Manila at about ten thousand, whereas the Filipino insurgents totaled about thirty thousand. Dewey later summarized the reason for his request: "We had the city under our guns, as Farragut had New Orleans under his. But naval power can reach no further ashore. For tenure of the land you must have the man with a rifle." Dewey now setled down to await the arrival of an army expedition.[2]

SPANISH DEFENSE AT MANILA

The Governor-General at Manila, Basilio Augustín, recognized that his garrison faced a desperate situation, but some optimism survived in the city based on the assumption that the home government would send assistance. Although Dewey had cut the cable to Hong Kong, the city maintained communication to Spain by other means, so that the needs of the garrison could be transmitted to the Peninsula without undue difficulty. As soon as the outcome of the May 1 naval battle became known, the walled city of Manila was evacuated, because the Spanish leaders anticipated a naval bombardment. Women and children were sent to the suburbs—most of them to Sampalong—and the deserted buildings within the walls were closed and placed under guard. Augustín then turned to other arrangements for defense of the city.[3]

Recognizing that his forces would face truly impossible odds if the Filipinos joined forces with the American invaders, the Governor-General took early action to maintain the loyalty of the indigenous population. On May 4 he created a Filipino militia and established a Consultative Assembly of Filipino notables to participate in the governance of the city. Pedro A. Paterno, who earlier had helped make the Peace of Biyak-na-Bató, was appointed head of the Assembly on May 9. Other members included Cayetano Arellano, Trinidad H. Pardo de

Tavera, and Pantaleon García. The Consultative Assembly convened its first session on May 28, and three days later Paterno issued a manifesto calling upon the Filipinos to collaborate with Spain. Presumably the Governor-General was prepared to grant autonomy in return for this loyalty. When Emilio Aguinaldo, leader of the Philippine independence movement, saw a copy of this document, he wrote on it, "You are pretty late"; on June 9 he issued a counter-manifesto that included a personal attack on Paterno. The Assembly met for the last time on June 13. It never accomplished anything of note, and was of doubtful loyalty. Several of the seventeen members later became prominent members of Aguinaldo's movement. The militia earlier had also failed to serve its purpose; insurgents had infiltrated it, and, when an armed uprising broke out late in May, it disintegrated almost immediately. These early wartime activities of the Spanish authorities at Manila suggest that they initially placed a certain amount of trust in the Filipinos. At the same time the home government recognized the importance of the native population. Segismundo Moret had sent word to Augustín on May 15: "Impressions Europe and American are that the natives distrust Americans. If you can manage to get them on our side victory is assured." This hope was disappointed; the Spanish garrison soon learned that it could expect little help from the local populace.[4]

Augustín had a fairly considerable force with which to fight both the Americans and the insurgents. About twenty-six thousand Spanish regulars and fourteen thousand militia were scattered throughout the archipelago. Some twenty-three thousand men were garrisoned at various locations in the main island of Luzon; of these nine thousand were at Manila. Small detachments provided local protection against bands of robbers in the countryside, some of which masqueraded as insurgent units. A leading Spanish historian, Severo Gómez Núñez, later argued that Augustín should have concentrated his troops at Manila for the defense of the city. Another writer, Ignacio Salinas, agreed with this view: If the provinces intended to remain loyal, troops were not needed in them; should they revolt, the insurgents would develop enough strength to prevail everywhere outside of Manila. Perhaps as many as four thousand troops did come to Manila from the countryside, but the rest remained at their stations. The Governor-General apparently assumed that, if he left the Spanish detachments in place, they could prevent a recurrence of the earlier insurrection. This belief proved ill founded; the government units were too small to hold out against the large concentrations of insurgents. Sixty-seven hundred Spanish troops eventually fell into the hands of the rebels.[5]

Most of the outlying garrisons surrendered to the insurgents during the summer of 1898, but a conspicuous exception occurred at Baler,

Luzon. A group of forty-seven Spaniards there under the command of Captain Enrique de las Morenas came under insurgent attack on July 1, 1898. When de las Morenas was killed, Lieutenant Saturnino Martín Cerezo assumed command. The defenders persevered even after Spain surrendered in August, 1898. In April, 1899, a group of American Marines under a naval officer, Lieutenant James C. Gillmore, went out to relieve Baler, but the unit was ambushed by the rebels and its members taken prisoner. Despite overwhelming odds and extraordinary privation, Martín Cerezo and his comrades, eventually reduced to a mere thirty, persevered against the insurgents for 337 days—until June 2, 1899. The resistance of the valiant Spanish band at Baler in defiance of hopeless odds is one of the proudest incidents in Spanish military history.[6]

When the Filipino insurgents began to organize themselves around Manila after the American naval victory of May 1, Augustín scattered his troops in numerous locations ouside the city to guard against attack, but this disposition proved untenable. Filipino action against these points forced the Spanish to fall back to a line of blockhouses just outside Manila. Fortifications called the Zapote line initially precluded a rebel invasion of Cavite province, but the defenders eventually had to evacuate these positions. The insurgents then conquered the province. Rail communications from Manila to all outlying provinces were soon interrupted; henceforth Spanish forces in Manila and in other parts of Luzon were unable to support each other. The insurgents constantly harassed Augustín's troops, but the Governor-General had his men successfully defend the city's water supply, protect the Manila batteries, preserve telegraphic connections with the Visayas, throw up defenses on the beaches north and south of the city, and improve communications between the city and the defensive perimeter. An entrenched camp was set up at San Juan del Monte and the artillery concentrated at Fort San Antonio Abad, a strong point close to the water's edge at the southwestern end of the line of blockhouses. These arrangements were intended to guard areas where attacks were most likely to occur. As Filipino and American pressure built up in July Augustín correctly anticipated an eventual assault on the city and did everything possible to strengthen his fortifications.[7]

The Governor-General realized, however, that he could not defend the city unless he received important reinforcements from Spain. On May 25 he stated this view unequivocally: "I need good cannons and ships of war to counteract those of the [American] squadron. . . . With an enemy within and outside I am in a very difficult and critical situation, since I lack force to counteract attacks by land and sea, and the assistance that the government offers me will arrive late." A Filipino attack developed against the outer defenses of Manila during the next two weeks, and Augustín argued more and more insistently that he could not continue to maintain himself without help. On June 8 Admiral Montojo supported his colleague's view in a message to Minister of the Marine Auñón: "We all await anxiously squadron and reinforcement; it is very urgent that they come before it is too late." Five days later Augustín cabled news of several insurgent victories. He could only conclude, "I insist on the doleful consequences at end of this situation because of scarce defense elements becoming exhausted and not receiving assistance."[8]

These messages had an important effect in Madrid; they eventually forced the dispatch of Admiral Manuel de la Cámara to the Philippines with supplies and reinforcements. Correa explained the Liberal ministry's reasons for taking action to Auñón: "I have received the gravest news from the Philippines. . . . The Government considers urgent [and] necessary departure squadron or part of it already gotten ready, to the end of calming anxiety [of] opinion, raising spirit [of] forces that fight, learning [of] departure reinforcements." When the garrison at Manila heard that Cámara had left Cádiz on June 16, its morale improved visibly. On June 21 a diarist wrote, "The effect that this semi-official news produces in the population can be calculated; every face is happy; every heart serene. No one now speaks of surrenders or of defeats; all speak of fighting and conquering."[9]

AMERICAN REACTIONS TO DEPARTURE
OF CÁMARA'S SQUADRON

As early as the middle of May rumors of a possible Spanish expedition to the Philippines began to reach both the Navy Department and Dewey's squadron at Manila. On May 12 Dewey reported a rumor that Spain's only battleship, the *Pelayo,* and another ship were en route to the Philippines. This rumor proved to have no foundation at the time, although on May 16 Long sent word to Dewey of "a possible Spanish expedition to operate about the Philippine Islands." This matter caused concern because Dewey lacked ships strong enough to individually contend with armored vessels such as the *Pelayo* and the *Carlos V.* On May 19 Secretary Long received a letter from Senator William E. Chandler (Republican from New Hampshire), commenting on Dewey's needs. The legislator proposed that the navy send out the *Monterey,* an oceangoing monitor with powerful weapons aboard—two twelve-inch and two ten-inch guns. "The *Monterey* in Manila's harbor mouth can stand off the Spanish fleet,'' he insisted. ''Twenty days have gone by [since the victory of May 1] and no ship has been sent to him [Dewey]; no supplies, no ammunition, no men, no nothing.'' For the moment Long did not act on this, contenting himself with sending a message to Dewey mentioning further reports that the *Pelayo, Carlos V,* and some transports were preparing to depart Spain for the Philippines. Noting, however, that other reports specified their destination as the eastern seaboard of the United States, he could only conclude, ''As our means of receiving intelligence from Spain are very untrustworthy, you are given this information for what it may be worth.''[10]

At this point the Naval War Board made a recommendation to Secretary Long that was greatly to influence later efforts to reinforce Dewey's squadron against the possible arrival of Cámara. In a memorandum on this question Admiral Sicard noted the necessity of arranging for ''the permanent defense'' of Manila, provided the government had ''the intention to hold the Philippine Islands or the port, and neighborhood of Manila.'' Since Dewey lacked armored vessels, the appearance of armored enemy ships in Philippine waters would force him to leave Manila Bay. Otherwise he might experience blockade and capture. And if during the interim American troops had landed at Manila, the navy would have to abandon them. As a long-term defensive measure the Board suggested that the army send heavy guns to Manila at once, along with materials required to emplace them. Of more immediate importance was its proposal of naval reinforcement: ''It is further recommended that the coast defense monitor *Monterey* be sent without delay to re-enforce Admiral Dewey, as the board understands that the harbor of San Francisco [the current base of the monitor] is unusually well fortified and armed, and we need therefore be under no apprehension of an enemy entering that port.'' Orders were issued the next day to put these recommendations into effect. Nothing was done however to mount guns at Manila, but preparations to dispatch the *Monterey* soon began. Dewey was given notice that the vessel would arrive around the end of July. At about the same time it was decided to send another monitor, the *Monadnock.*[11]

Meanwhile, Dewey began to manifest anxiety. On May 27 he requested information about the movements of Cámara and suggested that a battleship or armored cruiser be sent to counter the Spanish initiative. At the same time he inquired of the American consul at Gibraltar whether a Spanish squadron was being sent out and about its strength. On June 12 he reported various warships at Manila representing neutral powers and urged an early departure date for the *Monterey* and the *Monadnock.* Nathan Sargent has written that Dewey sent this message in response to the threatening behavior of a German squadron being concentrated at Manila, a powerful force that eventually surpassed that of Dewey. The Admiral must have been pleased to learn from the Navy Department that the Spanish ships had not yet left Cádiz and that great American efforts were being expended to prepare the two monitors for the long voyage across the Pacific. The *Monterey* was first out of port, clearing Mare Island, California for Manila via Honolulu on June 11.[12]

During the first three months of the war three considerations centered attention primarily on Cervera's squadron in the Caribbean Sea: Spain had no significant naval strength in the western Pacific; it appeared unlikely that Spain would expose its coastline to bombardment by sending Cámara to the Philippines; and the American navy wanted to avoid dividing its group of armored ships until it had ensured security in the West Indies. Concentration in the Caribbean was deemed the best means of protecting United States interests, not only there but in the Philippines as well. The situation altered after Cervera was blockaded in port at Santiago de Cuba and Cámara left Cádiz. The Navy Department now faced a dilemma: If it weakened Sampson's squadron to reinforce Dewey, it might allow Cervera to escape; if it retained all its armored ships in the Caribbean it might endanger Dewey. To escape this dilemma the Navy Department soon began to form a squadron to menace the coast of Spain.[13]

While the Eastern Squadron was being prepared, the Department depended primarily on the seagoing monitors to counter Cámara in the Philippines. Mahan later gave as his opinion that, "whether resulting from necessary preparations, or lack of early foresight on the part of the Department, or its advisers, or from concession to popular alarms, prevalent on the Pacific as on the Atlantic, the tardy despatch of these two vessels has remained on my mind as the only serious oversight chargeable to the [Naval War] Board." When Dewey learned that Cervera had been bottled up at Santiago de Cuba, he decided it would now be "folly" for Spain to send a squadron to the Philippines, but he did reveal a certain concern to Consul Rounsevelle Wildman at Hong King. Although he deemed the Spaniards "such fools one can never tell what they may do next," he was relieved to learn that the *Monterey* and *Monadnock* were on the way: "Without the two monitors they would be too strong for us." But he wanted even more help: "A strong squadron should at once threaten the coast of Spain." Writing again to Wildman, Dewey ventured the guess that Cámara would not materialize in Philippine waters, but he hoped that if the enemy did attempt the voyage the American monitors would arrive first. He knew that the *Pelayo* (9,000 tons) and *Carlos V* (9,200 tons) together more than matched his entire squadron. These Spanish ships mounted two 12.6-inch guns and four 11-inch guns. Dewey's largest weapons were 8-inch guns, and his entire force displaced only 19,008 tons. If the *Monterey* proceeded at its cruising speed of only six knots per hour, and if Cámara averaged about ten knots per hour, both would arrive in Philippine waters about August 1. As it turned out, the *Monterey* actually came into Manila Bay on August 4, a few days later than expected because of a delay at Honolulu. Had Cámara continued on to Manila, he would probably have beaten the *Monterey* and almost certainly beaten the *Monadnock,* which left on June 25 and came in on August 16. (The *Monadnock* required two days fewer than the *Monterey* because it encountered no difficulties along the way.)[14]

If Cámara should arrive in the Philippines before the monitors, how should Dewey protect his squadron? This question received increasing attention as Cámara voyaged across the Mediterranean to the Suez Canal. On June 27 Dewey had offered the Navy Department a solution he also mentioned to Wildman: "In my judgment, if the coast of Spain was threatened, the squadron of the enemy would have to return." The Naval War Board was just then completing plans for the sortie of the Eastern Squadron to Spanish waters. Long cabled this news to Dewey on June 29, listing the ships assigned to this force—to be led by Commodore Watson—and informing him that the Spanish government knew of its formation. On July 5 word went to Dewey that Cámara had passed through the Suez Canal and was expected in the Philippines.[15]

The Naval War Board had already begun to consider the proper course of action for Dewey, should Cámara actually arrive in Philippine waters. On June 19 it proposed that Dewey leave Manila Bay, and that the *Monadnock* follow a prescribed course so that it could easily be located east of the Philippines. It also suggested an alternative landing place for American troops then proceeding from the west coast to Manila, one that could be used if the Spanish regained command of the sea off the west coast of Luzon. For his part Dewey advised Brigadier General Thomas M. Anderson, who arrived at Cavite on June 30 with the first contingent of troops, to land only a few supplies; should Cámara arrive before the monitors, Anderson might have to make a hurried departure. The Admiral had no intention of accepting battle without reinforcements. Given reinforcement, Dewey had initially contemplated a defense in Manila Bay. But after July 14 he planned first to seize Manila, immediately upon the arrival of sufficient troops. With the city in his hands he could then deal with Cámara. Dewey later claimed to have developed still another scheme: After moving to the southern part of the Philippine archipelago, he would make a surprise attack on Cámara. "I should have steamed out to strike the enemy's ships, hopefully by surprise, when they were hampered by their transports," he stated in his autobiography of 1913, "throwing them into disorder at the outset of the engagement." He thought this strategy feasible because of his experienced crews. Whatever the truth of this assertion, his ultimate decision accorded with the ideas of the Naval War Board. On July 17 he notified the Navy Department that he did not expect the *Monterey* until August 5 and the *Monadnock* until August 15. "If necessary," he continued, "shall proceed with the squadron to meet the *Monadnock* to the east Cape Engano, Luzon." However, not long after Dewey settled upon his plan to leave Manila, he realized that the assistance from Spain would not reach Manila before the monitors.[16]

After the war Mahan summarized the consequences of the Board's and Dewey's decision. If Cámara left for the Pacific, the Spanish coast could be bombarded by the Eastern Squadron without fear of resistance. When Cámara arrived in the Philippines, he would have to engage two well-armed monitors. And even if he defeated Dewey's squadron, he would have to encounter the Eastern Squadron at some later date. General Anderson, upon learning of Dewey's intentions, decided simply to "take to the woods." He had six weeks' subsistence available and could easily take a defensible position beyond the reach of naval gunfire. However, all these arrangements went by the board when word came that Cámara had begun his retrograde movement to Spain.[17]

After Cámara turned back to the Peninsula, the Spanish garrison at Manila felt abandoned to its fate. Faced with large concentrations of insurgents and growing American forces, it lost all hope of avoiding defeat. One observer wrote, "The disillusion has been horrible, it has killed all our hopes, it has cut the electrical current that animates us, slackening our members. . . . Prostration invades us. . . . Today the city has capitulated morally." The future unveiled itself; Dewey's naval victory could not be undone.[18]

GERMANY AT MANILA BAY

Several other naval powers stationed ships in Manila Bay while Dewey was awaiting assistance. The day after the May 1 naval battle the first neutral man-of-war arrived, the British gunboat *Linnet,* and on May 5 the French *Brieux* anchored in the Bay. On May 6 the German cruiser *Irene* entered without acknowledging the presence of Dewey, and the transport *Darmstadt,* carrying replacements for the German squadron in the Far East, followed shortly after. The British cruiser *Immortalité* appeared on May 7. Two days later another German ship, the *Cormoran,* came in at 3:00 A.M., also without signalling its intentions, a procedure that caused considerable confusion. After its captain failed to heed an American steam launch sent to board the vessel, the *Raleigh* supposedly fired a shot across its bow (there's no official record of this). A Japanese vessel, the *Itsukushima,* dropped anchor on May 10. Two days thereafter Vice-Admiral Otto von Diederichs, commanding the German squadron in Asiatic waters, brought in his flagship, the *Kaiserin Augusta.* From then on the Germans kept at least two ships in Manila Bay; on June 18–20 two important additions arrived, the battleship *Kaiser* and the cruiser *Prinzess Wilhelm.* By June 27 the array of foreign ships included five from Germany, three from Great Britain, and one each from France and Japan. Germany's squadron, displacing 24,260 tons, was much superior in strength to that of Dewey.[19]

Years afterwards Dewey discussed the problems that arose from the presence of these neutral vessels, particularly those of Germany: "I knew that the intervention of any third power or group of powers while Sampson had yet to engage Cervera, or in the critical event of any setback to our arms, might have brought grave consequences for us, while the Philippines were a rich prize for any ambitious power; or, if they remained Spanish, they were still under the sovereignty of a nation which could hardly be expected to play an important part in the affairs of China." However, if this concerned him in 1898 he made no great issue of it in correspondence with the Navy Department. To be sure, on June 12 he reported the arrival of three German ships and several others under various flags, coupling this news with a request that the Department hasten the departure of the *Monterey* and the *Monadnock.* If Dewey had in mind the German build-up as well as the threat of the Cámara expedition, his cable did not express this view.[20]

What lay behind the presence of the large German squadron at Manila? On May 14, the German ambassador to Great Britain, Count Hatzfelt, had a conversation with his American counterpart, the courtly John Hay. The German began by denying that his country had any unfriendly feeling toward the United States. His government merely desired a few coaling stations; perhaps some arrangement along this line could be made as part of a Philippine settlement. He also mentioned Germany's interest in another Spanish possession, the Caroline Islands. Hay replied simply that he could provide no information about the eventual disposition of the Philippines. In his report to the State Department he noted his statement to Hatzfelt that "the inclination of the President was to a liberal and even generous treatment of Spain, when peace comes to be arranged; but that of course such treatment became more and more difficult with every additional day of war.'' After talking with Hatzfelt, Hay discussed German interests in the Far East with the British ambassador to Germany, who happened to be in London and who assured him that "whatever appearance may indicate, the German Government will take no practical steps which would bring them into any serious disagreement with us."[21]

On the same day in which Hay conversed with Hatzfelt, the German Foreign Minister, Prince Bernhard von Bülow, proposed to Emperor Wilhelm II that a German admiral proceed to Manila and obtain information that might be useful in determining Germany's future policy. This suggestion was soon put into effect. At the same time he counseled against hasty action; Germany should do nothing to precipitate a coalition of nations against it. Curiously, Bülow's comments stemmed from a report that the Filipinos might invite a German prince to become their king! On May 18 the Foreign Minister explained to Admiral Alfred von Tirpitz the purpose of the order to be sent out to Diederichs. Diederichs could "form for himself on the spot an opinion of the situation of the Spaniards, the attitude of the natives, and any outside influences which may make themselves felt with regard to the reorganization of conditions there." On June 2 Diederichs received orders to visit Manila and gather information about the mood of the Filipinos and the influence of neutral powers on political change in the archipelago. No further instructions, either political or naval in character, were sent to him, a fact that led the historian Thomas A. Bailey to conclude that he was not supposed to interfere with American operations but merely to be present if the United States decided not to annex the Philippine Islands. The order of June 2 accounts for the build-up of German strength as of June 20, when Diederichs welcomed the *Kaiser* and the *Prinzess Wilhelm* to Manila Bay. This unnecessary show of strength led to American misconceptions concerning the motives of the German squadron. However, Diederichs apparently attempted in personal relations at Manila to follow his instructions. On July 7, for example, Lieutenant Thomas M. Brumby, Dewey's aide, visited the German Admiral to present a list of American complaints about the behavior of his command. Diederichs replied soothingly that he had no desire to interfere with American operations. He felt that Dewey had conducted the blockade "in the mildest way possible and he did not want to embarrass him in the slightest." Brumby went away convinced of the German's sincerity and "personal probity."[22]

On the very day of Brumby's visit, however, an untoward incident inaugurated a period of severe strain between Dewey and Diederichs. The American Admiral sent two ships, the *Raleigh* and *Concord,* out to Isla Grande in Subig Bay to investigate a complaint from the insurgent leader, Emilio Aguinaldo, that the Germans were interfering with Filipino operations in that area. The ships came upon the German cruiser *Irene* in Subig Bay, but it departed when they came in view. Later it was alleged that, in its haste to leave, the *Irene* had slipped its cable, but the naval historian William R. Braisted notes that no conclusive evidence was presented to support this claim. Captain Joseph B. Coghlan of the *Raleigh* found no indication at Subig that the Germans had indeed trifled with the Filipinos. The Spanish garrison on Isla Grande surrendered to Coghlan in order to avoid falling into the hands of the insurgents; the American later turned the prisoners over to the Filipinos, apparently acting on orders from Dewey.[23]

On July 10 Diederichs sent his aide, Captain-Lieutenant Paul von Hintze, to the *Olympia* with explanations of the German actions that Brumby had brought to his attention on July 7, but he also registered a complaint, a step that caused a famous outburst. When the German officer stated that the Americans had no legitimate reason to stop the *Irene,* Dewey lost his temper. Ensign Henry V. Butler, who was present, recalled in 1930 what followed:

> Dewey: "Does Admiral von Diedrichs [sic] think he commands here or do I? Tell your Admiral if he wants war I am ready."
> German officer [Hintze] to Lt. Brumby: "Mein Gott! What is the matter with your Admiral?"
> Brumby: "Nothing, he means every word he says and you better tell your Admiral exactly what it was."

Diederichs might have taken offense at this blunt and certainly ill-advised challenge; but he chose not to do so, and after further discussion of neutral rights and obligations the situation improved markedly. According to Bailey the German Admiral realized that Dewey was under considerable strain; this circumstance explained and even excused his churlish behavior.[24]

The legal dispute centered on what measures could legitimately be taken to establish the identity of a neutral vessel. On July 11 Dewey wrote to Diederichs insisting upon plenary powers in this respect: "Her colors alone do not establish that identity, for it is a common ruse of war to hoist false colors." To this claim the German Admiral made objection: "The conclusion in your communication, in which you claim the right of boarding (*droite de visite*) men-of-war flying a neutral flag, is a demand which does not agree with the principles of maritime law as understood by me." Dewey then stated his views more clearly: "What I claim is the right to communicate with all vessels entering this port, now blockaded by the forces under my command." Diederichs accepted this interpretation, certainly less onerous than a claim to the right of visit, but extended his own position: Identification of a neutral vessel could be made by observing its contour as well as its flag. "This cannot be changed by the fact that ships engaged in war, on approaching an enemy's port, may have abusively hoisted neutral flags." With this communication the debate came to a close, Dewey having receded to a reasonable view in accordance with general practice.[25]

The German-American tempest in a teapot began as a misunderstanding and ended as an enduring myth. Unquestionably the eminent scholar Thomas A. Bailey is correct in his judgment that Diederichs had no intention of interfering with Dewey at Manila Bay: "His insistence upon what he conceived to be his rights during a blockade, together with the disproportionate strength of his fleet, gave a sinister aspect to German intentions." All this was later blown up into a legend that Germany had designs on the Philippines; that Diederichs did all he could to inhibit American movements; and that only Dewey's firm resolve avoided serious trouble right then and there with the minions of the Kaiser. Dewey and his associates had been much too quick in jumping to conclusions, a proclivity that Diederichs noted in his report to Berlin: "The Americans refuse to trust our loyalty, especially since my arrival at Manila, and their suspicion is being strengthened by the circulation of rumors to the effect that Manila is being supplied with provisions by His Majesty's ships and that there will be more energetic meddling in the war on our part in the near future." No such interference took place. One of John Hay's British friends, Cecil Spring Rice, described a conversation with a German friend, Prince Metternich, concerning Germany's intentions: When the Prince denied any German desire to challenge the United States, Hay said that "the disparity between the interests and the force sent to protect them was sure to excite remark, especially in view of the published desire of the Germans to get a coaling station." Nevertheless Hay felt sure "that Germany has no desire whatever to provoke a conflict—rather the contrary—that the Authorities are alarmed at the state of public feeling in America which is attributed wholly to British press intrigues—and that they are anxious to explain the presence of the German ships at Manila." This judgment of July, 1898, now enjoys the support of conclusive historical investigation, but the legend of malign German interference at Manila Bay refuses to die.[26]

PREPARATION OF THE ARMY'S EXPEDITION TO MANILA

While Admiral Dewey occupied Manila Bay, the War Department developed a plan of operation for the Philippine Islands and dispatched a sizeable expeditionary force to join the navy in reducing Manila. Without question news of Dewey's victory of May 1 greatly influenced decision-making. Prior to this time no thought had been given to army operations in the Philippines, but as early as May 3 General Miles recommended sending volunteer army units to occupy Manila. The next day President McKinley ordered various organizations to assemble at San Francisco for this purpose. At the same time Secretary Long began preparations to transport the expedition. The protected cruiser *Charleston* was assigned to accompany a transport, the *City of Pekin,* which was to carry the initial contingent of American troops to Manila. Bearing in mind the need to develop communications across the Pacific Ocean, Long ordered the commander of the *Charleston* to stop at Guam, southernmost island in the Spanish-held Marianas Islands, then known as the Ladrones. He was to capture the place, imprison military forces found there, and destroy fortifications and enemy vessels. "These operations should be very brief," admonished Long, "and should not occupy more than one or two days." Control of a central point on the long passage from the Hawaiian Islands to the Philippines would minimize the chance of Spanish interference between the United States and Manila.[27]

Some historians interpret these activities as an early indication of McKinley's intention to annex the Philippines, but no direct evidence supports this view. The real reason was the stimulus that Dewey's victory gave to McKinley's strategy to win the war. When word of the triumph at Manila came to Washington, the Administration realized that pressure on this outlying colonial possession of Spain, weakly held and difficult to support against an American attack, would help force an early termination of hostilities. Lieutenant William Warren Kimball had mentioned this motive when, in his war plan of 1896, he proposed a Philippine campaign as part of a war with Spain. Secretary Alger had this political consideration in mind when he wrote later that preparation for the Philippine expedition "was part of the general plan of campaign in further prosecution of the measures adopted by this government for the purpose of bringing about honorable and durable peace with Spain." It is what Secretary Long meant by his statement, "When the war broke out, our duty was to strike the hardest blow we could, and so we struck at Manila. There was not a moment after that when we could abandon Manila, because our military hold there was one of the most strenuous elements which brought Spain to terms." Operations in the Philippines remained secondary to those in Cuba and Puerto Rico, but they were part of the overall strategy of making cumulative attacks at the periphery of Spanish power to force an early end to war. Interest in annexation flowed from the outcome of operations in 1898; it played no role whatsoever in shaping the military and naval planning of the United States prior to the war or during its early moments.[28]

On May 12 Major General Wesley Merritt, the second-ranking officer in the United States Army, was selected to assume command of the Philippine expedition, and there then ensued a week of discussion concerning the makeup and mission of his forces. On May 13 Merritt wrote directly to President McKinley arguing for a larger force than previously contemplated and for inclusion of a large contingent of regulars. He insisted that volunteer units from the western states—contemplated for assignment to the Philippines—would be less well drilled than those from the East: "I fell that I would be doing the country, the forces in Manila harbor, and myself a great injustice to attempt to carry out your wishes with a smaller force or one differently constituted." He wanted not 5,000 troops but 14,000 men—6,050 regulars, 8,050 volunteers, and 300 engineers—about 12,000 effectives. He had in mind sending out his expedition in two roughly equal detachments. On May 15 Merritt raised the question of the purpose of his mission: "I do not know yet whether it is your desire to subdue and hold all the Spanish territory in the islands," he wrote McKinley, "or merely to seize and hold the capital." He also posed another problem: "It seems more than probable that we will have so-called insurgents to fight as well as the Spaniards, and upon the work to be accomplished will depend the ultimate strength and composition of the force."[29]

The War Department's immediate response was to accept Merritt's proposal for a larger force. As early as May 13, in ordering an officer to San Francisco to help prepare the expedition, General Corbin stated, "It is now thought that it will probably consist of about 12,000 men, or one army corps." At just this time Dewey's request for 5,000 troops arrived in Washington. Since the Admiral mentioned a Spanish force in excess of 10,000 men and many more Filipinos, General Miles recommended on May 16 a total expedition of over 15,000 men, one that would include 12,975 volunteers from the western states along with the regular units Merritt had requested (except for two infantry regiments). Meanwhile, however, Merritt muddied the waters; he complained publicly of his distaste for volunteer troops and asked that regular units then in Florida be diverted to his expedition. He also criticized Miles's letter of May 16 in angry terms; the force recommended was "unsuited to the ends to be accomplished, and insufficient in efficiency for the expedition to the Philippines,'' which was expected to conquer "territory 7,000 miles from our base, defended by a regularly trained and acclimated army of 10,000 to 25,000 men, and inhabited by 14,000,000 people, the majority of whom will regard us with the intense hatred born of race and religion.'' Miles stoutly defended his position, holding that Merritt exaggerated the size of the Spanish garrison and the population of the Philippines; the proposed force was after all over three times the size of the one requested by Dewey. Finally, he noted that the expedition was "not expected to carry on a war to conquer an extensive territory,'' its purpose being simply to provide "a strong garrison to command the harbor of Manila, and to relieve the United States fleet under Admiral Dewey with the least possible delay.''[30]

At length clear decisions concerning the size and mission of the Philippine expedition ended this unseemly but minor imbroglio. Merritt proved conciliatory, explaining to one of the President's secretaries that remarks attributed to him in the New York newspapers were "in every way incorrect and unauthorized. I had intended to take no notice of them but am told that they are taken seriously in Washington.'' To assuage the General a few additional regulars were added to his expedition along with a much-respected volunteer unit, the Tenth Pennsylvania. Counting additional volunteer units from the western states, the total force assigned to Merritt eventually numbered over twenty thousand troops. On May 19 President McKinley issued orders for the Philippine expedition. Dewey having established himself in Manila Bay, an army of occupation was being sent "for the two-fold purpose of completing the reduction of Spanish power in that quarter and giving order and security to the islands while in the possession of the United States.'' Merritt was enjoined to proclaim upon his arrival that he had come not to make war but to ensure the security of the inhabitants—a provision no doubt intended to placate the Filipino insurgents. Although Merritt's military powers were absolute and supreme, whenever feasible, local laws would remain in force.[31]

Nothing in these orders suggests that McKinley had as yet developed long-range plans for the Philippine Islands. As Graham A. Cosmas writes, he probably had not yet made up his mind. The President believed in "the self-controlling nature of war"—that it has a dynamic of its own to which one can only respond. His instructions merely directed an appropriate follow-up to Dewey's victory—in Cosmas's words, "exploitation of a successful attack with fresh forces. If that exploitation led to territorial conquests, the President would decide what to do with them after the shooting stopped.'' The complication was that a military campaign in the Philippines was more likely than not to entail long-term entanglements, and Merritt received no guidance about avoiding measures that might lead to such complications.[32]

The War Department bent every effort to send out the first contingent of the Philippine expedition, a step that accorded with both the military situation and the larger political purposes of the United States. On May 25 three transports left San Francisco, carrying five companies of the Fourteenth Infantry and two volunteer regiments, the First California and Second Oregon—a total of 2,491 officers and men. The *Charleston* had cleared port three days earlier. Brigadier General Thomas M. Anderson commanded this initial contingent of the expedition. He had orders to confer fully with Admiral Dewey at Manila and to keep his troops under the protection of the navy's guns until the arrival of the main force under Generals Merritt and Elwell S. Otis. In a word, he was to perform the normal functions of an advance party.[33]

The voyage of the *Charleston* and the three transports across the Pacific to Manila Bay was notable not only because it was the first such venture in American history but because it resulted in the initial territorial conquest of the war. After calling at Honolulu, the convoy covered the 3,337 miles to Guam, the most southerly island in the Marianas, in sixteen days. A small island, only 225 square miles in extent with a population of 9,630, Guam was strategically located at a point thirteen to eighteen hundred miles from the East Indies' northeastern periphery and five major east Asian ports—Yokohama, Shanghai, Canton, Hong Kong, and Manila. The prospect of taking Guam titillated the troops aboard the transports, although few had prior knowledge of the island. A warrant officer with the expedition remembered long afterward the question of the day: "What about Guam and where is it anyway, and what do we want of it?" Arriving off Guam at Agaña, the island's seat of government, at daybreak on June 20, Captain Henry Glass of the *Charleston* found no vessels of any kind in port. He then proceeded to San Luis d'Apra. After ascertaining that a ruined fort guarding the outer harbor was unmanned, he took the *Charleston* into the harbor, firing a few rounds at another unoccupied fort located at Santa Cruz to obtain its range. At this point two local officials and a naturalized American citizen who lived in San Luis d'Apra came out to greet and board the *Charleston*. They were under the misapprehension that the shots fired earlier were a salute, and they had come to apologize for their inability to return it. Captain Glass then informed them that Spain and the United States were at war. The next day he put a small force ashore and brought the Governor of Guam to the *Charleston* to arrange the surrender (the island had a garrison of only sixty troops). Glass took these men with him along with the civil leaders when he departed on June 22. In this simple fashion the United States acquired an island that became an important link in its chain of communications to the western Pacific.[34]

Anderson's contingent arrived at Manila on June 30. As it made its way there General Merritt and two capable assistants, Brigadier Generals Elwell S. Otis and Henry C. Merriam, worked feverishly to prepare the remainder of the expedition for embarkation. The methodical procedure followed in organizing the Eighth Army Corps—the designation given Merritt's command on June 21, 1898—contrasted markedly with the confusion that ruled earlier in Tampa as the Fifth Army Corps attempted to get off to Santiago de Cuba. This variance stemmed mainly from an important difference between the two situations: Shafter had to move rapidly to a location that had been decided upon hastily; Merritt could proceed more deliberately "to approach an objective clearly defined for weeks." Still, Merritt and his associates possessed more administrative talent than Shafter and his staff. The camp at San Francisco was properly organized, and the well-equipped units held there for shipment were given useful training prior to their departure. Although Merritt thought the command assigned to him was beneath the dignity of his rank, he worked assiduously to energize the War Department and whip his troops into excellent condition for the Philippine campaign.[35]

Because of careful work in San Francisco the additional contingents of troops were dispatched in good order to the Philippines. The second group—3,586 troops with Brigadier General Francis V. Greene in command—left in three transports on June 15. It included components of regulars from the Eighteenth and Twenty-Third Infantry and several volunteer units—the First Colorado, the First Nebraska, the Tenth Pennsylvania, and two batteries of the Utah Volunteer Artillery. It arrived at Manila Bay on July 17. A third contingent—4,847 troops loaded on seven transports with Brigadier General Arthur MacArthur in immediate command—left San Francisco during the period June 25–29. General Merritt accompanied this group. It included the remaining components of the Eighteenth and Twenty-Third Infantry, the Third Field Artillery, a company of regular engineers, and four volunteer outfits—the First Idaho, the Thirteenth Minnesota, the First North Dakota, and a battalion of the First Wyoming. Merritt arrived at Manila Bay on July 25, and MacArthur came in on July 31. The three contingents of the Eighth Corps reaching Manila prior to the end of the war comprised 407 officers and 10,437 men. Modest artillery support totaled sixteen light field guns, six small mountain guns, and an assortment of rapid-fire weapons, including Gatling guns. Two additional contingents did not arrive until after the end of the war. Brigadier General Elwell S. Otis left San Francisco on July 15–19 with 3,030 troops on three transports, and Brigadier General Harrison G. Otis sailed July 23–29 with 1,735 troops on two transports.[36]

The voyage to the Philippines required slightly over a month's time, broken only by a brief respite at Honolulu; for the most part the trip proved tedious but bearable. A member of the Second Oregon recalled shipboard routine: "Among the Oregon Volunteers were many young-sters who soon began to suffer from that old complaint, homesickness. The regiment of ten companies and band were poorly quartered on the vessel, there being no regular troop transports as yet, down in the storage holds. One company at a time was brought up to upper decks for fresh air and exercise, remained one or two hours and then back below. The masters or Captain of the transports frequently and forcibly expressed themselves at being obliged to loiter behind the slow-sailing "Charleston," which appeared several miles ahead like a great, grey turtle. The transports . . . were all up to date passenger liners, greyhounds of the Pacific."

Some problems materialized chiefly during the early voyages. Refer-ring particularly to the second contingent under General Greene, a naval officer pointed out some specific difficulties, including failure to place a naval officer in control, inability of army officers to grasp the dividing line between military control of troops and nautical command, and assumption of nautical control by land officers. One consequence was development of unsanitary conditions: "The troops were not clean in their persons, because no bathing regulations were adopted and the regular 'scrub and wash clothes' was unknown. Lice and other vermin were rampant. The men spit on the deck, threw waste food on deck, and defecated there without regard to the expostulations of the officers of the transport [*Valencia*]. The soldiers ran aloft as they pleased and exposed themselves to the risks of falling overboard. A guard was mounted, it is true, in certain parts of the ship, but as no reports were made to the officer of the deck, numerous accidents might have hap-pened without his knowledge in time to avert them. The men were lined up like convicts to receive their food, when mess arrangements might easily have been made."

Nevertheless, no truly serious problems materialized even during the earlier voyages, and the transports put into service later were managed much more carefully than the *Valencia*. As in so many other instances during the war with Spain, experience proved a sound teacher. Notwithstanding, early impressions of chaos remained fixed in many memories, perpetuating the illusion that the war had been badly conducted from first to last.[37]

ANNEXATION OF THE HAWAIIAN ISLANDS

As the Eighth Army Corps moved across the Pacific Ocean to Manila Bay, Congress took an important step; after over a half-century of involvement in the affairs of the Hawaiian Islands, in July, 1898 the United States annexed them. The most recent previous effort to acquire sovereignty of the island group had taken place the previous year. On April 5, 1897, the Minister representing the Hawaiian Republic in Washington proposed negotiations to arrange annexation. Difficulties with Japan over immigration and with American sugar-refining companies over tariff levels underlay this *démarche*. In due course President McKinley submitted a treaty of annexation to the Senate. The Japanese Minister in Washington, Toru Hoshi, made an immediate protest, giving three reasons for disapproval: Maintenance of the status quo in Hawaii was essential to good understanding among the Pacific powers; annexation might prejudice the rights of Japanese nationals in Hawaii; an American takeover might postpone settlement of Japanese claims stipulated in treaty obligations of the Hawaiian Republic. Toru Hoshi was at pains "to state most emphatically and unequivocally that Japan has not now and never had . . . designs of any kind whatever against Hawaii." Secretary of State John Sherman quickly rejected all three arguments, and, after the Department of State made its explanations, Japan withdrew its objections to the treaty of annexation. The Japanese protest was largely to satisfy domestic opinion, hoping to calm fears that Japanese immigrants in Hawaii might experience mistreatment. It is not known whether the government in Tokyo learned of secret instructions given at this time to the American naval commander in the Hawaiian area to hoist the flag and establish a provisional protectorate should Japan manifest warlike intentions.[38]

Although there was no sign that Tokyo either desired or expected a crisis in Hawaii, President McKinley may have thought differently. In discussing the treaty of annexation with Senator George F. Hoar (Republican of Massachusetts) he reportedly expressed real concern. "We cannot let these Islands go to Japan," he argued. "Japan has her eye on them. Her people are crowding in there. I am satisfied they do not go there voluntarily as ordinary immigrants, but that Japan is pressing them in there in order to get possession before anybody can interfere.'' Something had to be done to prevent Japan from gaining control. McKinley conceivably might have simply been making an argument he thought would appeal to the dubious senator from Massachusetts, later a leading anti-imperialist; but in any event many Americans at the time had begun to wonder whether Japan's expansionist ambitions might extend to the Hawaiian group.[39]

The treaty of annexation languished in the Senate until the war with Spain broke out, at which time the need for a Pacific port of call en route to the Philippines drew attention once again to the strategic importance of the Hawaiian Islands, screening the American west coast and the projected isthmian canal. On May 4 a joint resolution was introduced into the House of Representatives providing for their annexation. Sponsors believed it would be easier to obtain a simple majority in both houses of Congress than a two-thirds vote in the Senate alone. This procedure had a precedent; it has been used in 1845 to acquire Texas. President McKinley publicly supported the resolution after it became clear that it had broad support throughout the country and Congress. At the time he said to George Cortelyou, ''We need Hawaii just as much and a good deal more than we did California. It is manifest destiny.'' After Congress debated the question, the joint resolution passed through both houses by majorities of two-to-one or better. Opposition came from Representative Thomas (''Czar'') Reed (Republican from Maine), the Speaker of the House, and others, but the emotions of the war overwhelmed those who offered objections. On June 15 the House passed the measure by a vote of 209 to 91; the Senate did the same on July 6 by 42 to 21. When the President signed the joint resolution on July 7, the deed was done.[40]

On August 12, by coincidence the day on which the war with Spain came to an end, a ceremonial transfer of sovereignty took place in Hawaii as the United States assumed control. This outcome solidified American communications to the western Pacific, an important consideration in postwar discussions regarding disposition of the Philippine Islands. The sharpening of opinion during the war with Spain about the role of the Hawaiian Islands in America's national strategy is well summarized in Marilyn Young's statement, ''Prior to the Spanish-American War, most expansionists saw Hawaii as a defensive position, not as a stepping-stone. After the war, Hawaii became a stop on the way to Asia, not an end in itself.''[41]

By the end of July, 1898, the armed forces of the United States were poised to seize control of Manila and its environs, an outcome no one had foreseen prior to Dewey's victory on May 1. The campaign in the western Pacific developed as one aspect of President McKinley's attempt to force Spain out of the war quickly by exerting pressure on its most important colonial possessions. Military exigencies in 1898 finally completed a process that had stretched out across half the nineteenth century—the American absorption of the Hawaiian Islands. Close observers might already have begun to question the cost of these activities, especially if they had known the details of international diplomacy during the summer of 1898 and had grasped the significance of Emilio Aguinaldo's movement in the Philippines. For the moment, however—and especially after the victory at Santiago de Cuba—the military and naval energies of the United States concentrated on ending all Spanish resistance in the distant Philippine Islands.

SEVENTEEN

The Rise of
Emilio Aguinaldo

As the Americans prepared to seize the city of Manila, they found themselves more and more concerned with the Filipino insurgents, who were proving increasingly uncooperative. Upon his arrival at Manila on June 30, General Anderson with the assistance of Admiral Dewey selected a campsite on the beach a few miles south of the city. The First California occupied the site on July 15, and it was duly christened Camp Dewey. After the arrival of General Greene and the second contingent on July 17 about four thousand men were at this position. It was well located to serve as a base for operations against Manila because it lay along the road to that city from Parañaque. The southwestern end of Governor-General Augustín's line of fortifications lay between the American position and the city. When General Merritt arrived on July 25, he discovered that the Filipinos had surrounded Manila but had not attempted to storm the city. He also learned that relations between the Filipino and American forces had become tense, even if the two armies were ostensibly associated in the same cause.[1] What led to this situation?

PHILIPPINE INSURRECTION OF 1896–1897

If the insurrection in Cuba seriously strained the resources of Spain, so had another colonial disturbance—a less successful but still troublesome rebellion against Spanish authority in the Philippine

Islands. For many years the great religious orders of Roman Catholicism—particularly the Dominicans, Augustinians, and Franciscans—had exercised extraordinary influence in the government of the Philippine Islands. They held huge tracts of property in the countryside, particularly on the island of Luzon, and title to important commercial properties in Manila and other cities. This general situation created tension between the Spanish friars and the Filipino clergy. From this special irritation there developed by stages a movement that ultimately turned into a quest for independence.

In 1872 Governor-General Rafael de Izquierdo imposed a series of unpopular measures that, reversing a progressive colonial policy inaugurated under the Spanish Republic of 1868, led to a brief uprising. A group of Filipino plotters planned to mutiny on January 20, 1872, but a Spanish soldier learned of the scheme from a Filipino friend and gave warning. At the appointed time workers in the naval arsenal at Cavite rose against authority, but Spanish troops put down the uprising ruthlessly. The authorities blamed Filipino priests for the act, and some clergy were among the eighteen participants who later went to their executions. Other conspirators were banished to the Caroline Islands. According to John R. M. Taylor, a perceptive observer, this outbreak may have also reflected Filipino irritation at Spain's newly expanded presence in the islands, a result of the recent opening of the Suez canal, which allowed fast ships to reach Manila from Barcelona in thirty days. A new colonial bureaucracy materialized at this time, exerting pressure on the inhabitants of the Philippines at just the moment when they desired less imperialist control.[2]

In the wake of the uprising at Cavite a nationalist movement sprung up among patriotic Filipinos residing in Spain and in time spread back to the archipelago itself. A group of writers, among whom Dr. José Rizal became prominent, provided inspiration and leadership. Also of note were Pedro A. Paterno and Marcelo H. del Pilar. Rizal's influential novels (*Noli me Tangere,* 1886 and *El filibusterismo,* 1890) and the journalism of del Pilar, who managed an expatriate newspaper in Barcelona called *La solidaridad,* played an important role in what historians later called "the period of propaganda." Rizal and his associates—dubbed *ilustrados*—opposed armed insurrection, favoring instead advancement through education and suasion. They were interested especially in accelerating economic development. Instead of rejecting Spanish civilization, they advocated assimilation of Filipinos into an hispanicized culture. In 1892 Rizal, who had returned to the Philippines, organized the *Liga filipina* to further the nationalist movement. The league's announced aims revealed its stress on peaceful agitation for Filipino development. Rizal, however, was soon banished from Luzon to distant Dapitan, a port in Mindanao, a setback that precluded effective development of his league.[3]

On the day that Rizal was banished from Luzon, July 7, 1892, an organization was founded that later was to play a much more imposing role in the nationalist movement than the *Liga filipina*. It was called the *Katipunan*, a Malay word meaning "Society of the Sons of the People." Marcelo H. del Pilar helped organize it, but leadership eventually fell to one of the charter members, a young night watchman from the working class named Andrés Bonifacio. A clandestine organization, the *Katipunan* derived much of its inspiration from the Masonic movement. One of its historians, Teodoro Agoncillo, wrote that it "adopted the principles of Masonry in such a way as to be easily understood by members who belonged to the lowest stratum of society." Appealing mostly to the uneducated and the poverty-stricken, it advocated violent revolution against Spanish authority. Apolinario Mabini, who later rose to a position of great influence within the nationalist movement, claimed that the *Katipunan* would never have emerged if Spanish authorities, particularly the monastic orders, had permitted political organizations to function openly and allowed the educated middle class to act without undue restraint. The working class favored the moderate program of the *Liga filipina* and remained faithful to it for a long time, the more radical *Katipunan* gaining broad influence only when the *Liga* failed to provide leadership. John R. M. Taylor, an unfriendly commentator, summarized the goals of the Katipunan succinctly: "The poor were to have their brothers' wealth distributed among them; the native priests were to succeed their peninsular preceptors, and the native clerk his peninsular superior; the ambitious Spanish or Chinese mestizo would no longer have to give way to men of unmixed Spanish blood; out of race hatred and envy and blood lust there was to be born, by slaughter and pillage, a Malay republic."[4]

Bonifacio became president of the *Katipunan* on January 1, 1896 and lost no time in planning an armed uprising, to begin with a surprise massacre of Spanish authorities. Unfortunately for him a *katipunero* from the Visayas, Teodoro Patino, at his sister's urging revealed the plan to an Augustinian monk, Father Honorio Gil, on August 19. Bonifacio immediately fled to the hills of Balintawak in Caloocan, a town near Manila, and from there issued the *grito de Balintawak* ("cry of Balintawak"), calling the Filipinos to revolution. His organization immediately began military operations against the Spanish garrison of Luzon. In the province of Cavite, a main center of dissidence, leadership of the local insurgents eventually fell to a young man from Kawit named Emilio Aguinaldo y Famy. Of mixed Tagalog and Chinese blood, he came from a fairly well-to-do family of landowners. He had studied law briefly at the College of San Juan in Manila and had served as municipal captain of his community. Like many other leaders of the insurgents he was an official of the *Katipunan.*[5]

The then Governor-General, Ramón Blanco y Erenas, caught unawares, proved unable to snuff out the insurrection quickly. Having only four thousand Spanish troops and about two thousand Filipinos in hand, he at first asked Madrid for only one thousand reinforcements, but supplemented this request when he recognized the full extent of the uprising. On August 30 a sharp fight took place in San Juan del Monte, a suburb of Manila, in which a force of one hundred Spaniards killed approximately ninety insurgents. On that day Blanco declared that insurrection existed in a number of locations scattered widely through several provinces in Luzon—Manila, Bulacan, Pampanga, Nueva Ecija, Tarlac, La Laguna, Cavite, and Batangas. In the beginning the insurrection was largely confined to the Tagalog tribe, centered in these very provinces. Blanco drew in forces from other locations in the islands to Manila and, beginning in October, received reinforcements from the Spanish peninsula. He did not yet feel strong enough to take to the field; meanwhile the insurrection continued to spread throughout Luzon. On November 8–9 the insurgents repulsed a Spanish attack on Noveleta and Binkayan, inflicting many casualties. Aguinaldo commanded the Filipinos in this engagement; his victory led to his rapid elevation in the insurgent leadership.[6]

Despite the actions that had already occurred, Blanco hoped to use peaceful methods in bringing the insurrection to an end, but Cánovas soon replaced him with the more militant General Camilo de Polavieja, a man of different ideas. The new Governor-General made his position clear when he took office: "For those who are loyal," he announced, "I have nothing but sentiments of affection and protection; for the traitors, no punishment seems to me adequate and commensurate for the magnitude of the crime which they have committed against their King and Country." To underline his position he ordered the execution of the blameless José Rizal. Rizal's tragic death on the fashionable Paseo de la Luneta before a firing squad on December 30, 1896, gave the *insurrectos* their first martyr. Rizal, ultimately true to his middle-class background, was supposedly reconciled to the Church and married his mistress, an Irish schoolteacher, just before his execution, but some authorities dispute this claim. By the middle of January, 1897, Polavieja had assembled about twenty-five thousand reinforcements from Spain—enough to launch operations against the insurgents. The

Filipino citizenry in Cavite province were concentrated by the Spanish in five war zones, each with an army and a commander. General Lachambre, the Spanish field commander, fought fifty-seven battles against the insurgents in this period, including a major engagement at the Zapote bridge on February 17. Polavieja's well-conceived plan of operation and Lachambre's sound execution drove the insurgents from the field. When General Fernando Primo de Rivera succeeded Polavieja on April 25, 1897, the Filipinos were unable to wage conventional warfare in any form.[7]

At this critical juncture a struggle for power developed among the insurgents that was to have profound consequences for the later history of the nationalist movement. On April 20, 1897, Aguinaldo, who had by then risen to the command of the insurgent army, ordered the arrest of Bonifacio. A court-martial convicted the *Katipunan* leader and prescribed his execution. Aguinaldo then apparently sought to pardon his rival, but certain supporters, notably Generals Mariano Noriel and Pío del Pilar, objected to this course. The question was settled when, on May 10, a squad led by Lázaro Macapagal executed Andrés Bonifacio and his brother Procopio. Having thus eliminated the "Father of the Philippine Revolution," Aguinaldo retreated into the mountains of La Laguna de Tabayas and Bulacan, where his forces went over to guerrilla warfare. Primo de Rivera finally brought Aguinaldo at bay at a strong position called Biyak-na-Bató, about sixty miles north of Manila in mountainous Bulacan.[8]

During all this struggle, Aguinaldo had by 1897 put together a fairly comprehensive political program, well summarized in a proclamation of June printed in the Tagalog language. Recalling the long tradition of opposition to the monastic orders, the list of aims began with a call for expulsion of the friars and division of their property equally among Spanish and Filipino secular clergy. Second, Spain must concede to the populace a large measure of autonomy, both political and economic, along with freedom of the press and religious toleration. Third, civil servants must receive equal pay for equal work, regardless of whether they were peninsular or Filipino in origin. Fourth, all lands that the friars had appropriated must be returned to the original owners. Finally, legal reforms must guarantee equitable treatment of Filipinos. Aguinaldo had not yet adopted independence as an overt political objective; his program still reflected goals that had emerged during the period of *ilustrado* propaganda.[9]

In August, 1897, Pedro A. Paterno, one of the early Filipino nationalist leaders in Spain, arranged negotiations between Aguinaldo and Primo de Rivera. Aguinaldo made proposals closely resembling those he had publicized earlier, and in addition asked for a cash payment of three million Mexican pesos. In the interim, while negotiations were taking place, he would agree to a cease-fire if Primo de Rivera provided food for his troops. For his part the Spanish Governor-General dangled the prospect of certain modest reforms. Paterno carried Aguinaldo's proposals and Spanish counterproposals back and forth between Manila and Biyak-na-Bató for several months. One of the insurgent leaders, José Alejandrino, informed an Austrian sympathizer, Ferdinand Blumentritt, that Aguinaldo did not intend to scuttle the nationalist movement, no matter what came of his negotiations with Primo de Rivera: "In case peace is accepted," he claimed, "it will be only for the money involved which we propose to use for the purpose of promoting immediately another decisive revolution." He thought that Primo de Rivera understood the intentions of the insurgents, but "inasmuch as he acts purely for personal interest and does not care about the welfare of his country, it does not matter to him if, after obtaining a personal triumph in having temporarily pacified the Philippines, the Deluge comes." Whatever the motives of the parties, they reached agreement after Primo de Rivera obtained permission from Madrid to offer a bribe. On December 4, Segismundo Moret, the new Minister for the Colonies, had cabled, "Given financial state and possible complications, pacification is most important." The home government, now in the hands of Sagasta, did not wish to perpetuate difficulties in the Philippines, given its problems of great import elsewhere.

The Pact of Biyak-na-Bató, concluded on December 14, 1897, was actually contained in three separate documents. It provided for the banishment of Aguinaldo and twenty-seven companions to Hong Kong in return for a payment of 800,000 Mexican pesos in three installments—400,000 immediately, another 200,000 after seven hundred firearms had been surrendered, and a final 200,000 after the *Te Deum,* the traditional hymn of thanksgiving, had been sung in Manila to signify the end of the insurrection. Primo de Rivera was to declare a general amnesty and expend another 900,000 pesos to indemnify Filipinos who had suffered injuries. Aguinaldo apparently also expected the Governor-General to institute certain moderate reforms along the lines of those he had proposed at the outset of negotiations, but these measures were not specified in writing.[10]

What came of the Pact of Biyak-na-Bató? Upon his departure from Luzon, Aguinaldo received his 400,000 pesos. After his arrival at Hong Kong on December 31, 1897, he deposited his money in a bank, set up housekeeping with his exiled companions, and awaited an opportunity to resume the Philippine revolution. Primo de Rivera handed over another 200,000 pesos to leaders of the insurrection who remained in the Philippines, but he never delivered the final 200,000 pesos to anyone. On January 25, 1898, he declared a general amnesty. He failed, however, to institute most of the desired reforms. Alejandrino, who accompanied Aguinaldo to Manila in May, 1898, informed his correspondent, Blumentritt, that the insurgents did not really desire reforms; such improvements might interfere with their goal of independence. Although at this time the Spanish government was instituting sweeping changes in the Antilles, Alejandrino did not want any such treatment for the Philippines: "I hope that those who are directing the public affairs in Spain will not grant any reform to the Philippines, as this would be a very sensible act on the part of crazy persons." He wished that Liberals such as Moret would soon leave the scene, preferring Conservatives of Silvela's persuasion, who could be relied upon to resist change in all forms. As for the Pact of Biyak-na-Bató, he commented scornfully that when Primo de Rivera had gone "abuses will again be committed and then revolution will break out anew." Alejandrino looked forward with great anticipation to that day.[11]

Americans paid very little attention to the Philippine insurrection; their gaze was riveted on Cuba. But the events in far-off Luzon exerted an important influence on the policies of the Spanish government. The difficulty in the Philippines was among the circumstances that influenced Madrid to make a temporizing and in some ways even conciliatory response to continuing American insistence that something be done to resolve the internal problems of Cuba.

After the Pact of Biyak-na-Bató uneasy peace settled over the Philippines, but the insurgents soon resumed their activity. In March and April, 1898, several outbreaks of violence occurred, apparently stemming from local initiatives rather than central direction: A serious uprising in the province of Zambales during March and violence thereafter in northern Luzon and the island of Cebu signalled the rebirth of the insurgency. Earlier, in February, the American consul in Manila, Oscar F. Williams, reported that calm had not returned to the Philippines after Aguinaldo's banishment: The situation seemed somewhat like that in Cuba. "War exists, battles are of almost daily occurrence, ambulances bring in many wounded, and hospitals are full. Prisoners are brought here and shot without trial, and Manila is under martial law." He anticipated insurrection: "Insurgents are being armed and drilled, are rapidly increasing in numbers and efficiency, and all agree that a general uprising will come as soon as the governor-general [Primo de Rivera] embarks for Spain, which is fixed for March." Later in March

Williams indicated that the rebellion appeared to be gaining momentum: The insurgents were "getting arms, money, and friends, and they outnumber the Spaniards present and soldiery probably an hundred to one." Although exaggerated in tone, Williams's reports demonstrated that the spirit of insurrection remained very much alive on Luzon.[12]

AGUINALDO AND THE AMERICANS

The insurgents first contacted representatives of the United States late in 1897. Before the Pact of Biyak-na-Bató was concluded, a Filipino named Felipe Agoncillo called on the American consul general in Hong Kong, Rounsevelle Wildman, to propose an alliance between the insurgents and the United States. It was to be timed to the moment "when the United States declares war on Spain, which, in Mr. Agoncilla's [sic] judgment, will be very soon." For the moment Agoncillo suggested that the United States provide arms; they would be paid for when the insurgent government gained diplomatic recognition. As collateral security he offered "two provinces and the custom-house at Manila." This proposal aroused no interest in Washington. Thomas F. Cridler, the Third Assistant Secretary of State, threw some very cold water on it in his reply of December 15, some six weeks after Wildman's initial notice: "You may briefly advise Mr. Agoncilla, in case he should call upon you, that the Government of the United States does not negotiate such treaties and that it is not possible to forward the desired arms and ammunition. You should not encourage any advances on the part of Mr. Agoncilla, and should courteously decline to communicate with the Department further regarding his alleged mission." However restrained this message, it conveyed more than a little criticism of the consul general for having had any dealings at all with Agoncillo.[13]

Emilio Aguinaldo, living as an exile in Hong Kong, had his first contacts with Americans in March, 1898, after Commodore Dewey and his squadron arrived at that port. Later he claimed to have held a series of secret conferences with Commander Edward P. Wood of the *Petrel*, during which the American officer sought to induce him to return to the Philippines and lead a new attack on the Spanish government with the United States providing assistance. Wood supposedly went out of his way to disclaim any desire of the United States to acquire the Philippines. Before these negotiations could be completed, Aguinaldo maintained, and an understanding put in writing, Aguinaldo had to leave Hong Kong. There is, however, no evidence to confirm this story. Although Wood did have some conversations with the insurgents, it is highly probable that the rebel leader misrepresented their content as part of an effort to account for the decline in friendly relations between the Americans and insurgents that took place in succeeding months.[14]

On April 7, 1898, Aguinaldo left Hong Kong on the first leg of a journey to Europe, hoping to thus avoid legal problems resulting from a suit by one of his followers. (Isabelo Artacho had asked the courts to order payment to him for services rendered as Secretary of the Interior in the now defunct insurgent government of 1897, the funds to come from the money that Aguinaldo had received from Primo de Rivera). If Aguinaldo had given as much credence to his talks with Wood as he later claimed, why would he have planned to travel as far from the Philippines as Europe? He could not have failed to realize that relations between Spain and the United States had reached a serious crisis. If he had been about to make a deal with Wood, it seems wholly probable that he would have set out for a relatively nearby point—perhaps Japan. John R. M. Taylor wrote in this connection, "The importance of his presence near the Philippines in case of war did not occur to him, or if it did occur to him anything which he could obtain there from the aid of the United States probably seemed for the moment of little consequence compared with escaping from his wrangling companions with enough money to live on in Paris." It was truly unfortunate for the cause of Filipino independence that leadership should have fallen to a man who manifested remarkably little foresight and acuity not only at this time but throughout his ascendancy. Most successes of the Philippine revolution are attributable not to Aguinaldo but to certain talented advisers—among them Apolinario Mabini, who was not with him in Hong Kong.[15]

Next occurred one of those extraordinary strokes of fortune that alter the course of history. The ship Aguinaldo was on called at Singapore around April 21, just as Spain and the United States broke with each other, and through the initiative of an English adventurer, Howard W. Bray, the Filipino leader was brought into contact with the American consul general, E. Spencer Pratt. Bray, sympathetic to the insurgents, arranged a conference with Pratt that took place in the Filipino's lodgings on April 24. Aguinaldo's traveling companions, Gregorio H. del Pilar and José M. Leyba, also joined the discussions. Pratt apparently urged the Filipinos to cooperate with the American squadron at Hong Kong. Although careful to explain that he could not make commitments for the United States, he certainly manifested considerable sympathy for the insurgent cause and may even have discussed an alliance of some nature. At length Aguinaldo agreed to return to Hong Kong—provided he received an invitation from Dewey. Pratt then telegraphed to the Commodore, about to leave for Manila Bay,

"Aguinaldo, insurgent leader, here. Will come Hong Kong [to] arrange with Commodore for general cooperation insurgents Manila if desired." Dewey responded laconically, "Tell Aguinaldo come soon as possible." On April 26, the day before Aguinaldo left Singapore, he had another discussion with Pratt in which he expressed the hope that "the United States would assume protection of the Philippines for at least long enough to allow the inhabitants to establish a government of their own, in the organization of which he would desire American advice and assistance." This statement implied Filipino independence under some form of American protection. Pratt had no authority to accept any such proposition. Reporting the discussion to Washington, the consul general recorded his response: "These questions I told him I had no authority to discuss."[16]

However, Aguinaldo and his associates later claimed that Pratt had committed the United States to Filipino independence and an American protectorate. Bray confirmed this, maintaining in a telegram to Senator George F. Hoar of Massachusetts on January 12, 1899, "As the man who introduced General Aguinaldo to the American Government through the Consul at Singapore, I frankly state that the conditions under which Aguinaldo promised to cooperate with Dewey were *independence* under a protectorate. I am prepared to swear to this." Whatever the truth about the oral discussions, the American consul general did not enter into a formal arrangement. But—in the words of Teodoro Agoncillo, who correctly summarized this episode—"Pratt, acting on his own and without any official instructions from the American State Department, made it appear that he shared Aguinaldo's expression of Filipino aspiration, namely, independence."[17]

Admiral Dewey later explained his connection with these events in testimony before a Congressional committee in 1902: He had cabled Aguinaldo to return to Hong Kong simply to quiet the persistent Filipinos. "They were bothering me," he complained. "I was very busy getting my squadron ready for battle, and these little men were coming on board my ship in Hongkong and taking a good deal of my time, and I did not attach the slightest importance to anything that they could do, and they did nothing." None were willing to accompany him to Mirs Bay when he left Hong Kong: "There had been a good deal of talk, but when the time came they did not go. One of them didn't go because he didn't have any toothbrush." When asked whether Pratt had conveyed Aguinaldo's wishes to him, Dewey answered, "If by that you mean to bring out that I in any way knew that Aguinaldo was to cooperate with me for the independence of the Philippines I never received any letter of that kind. I don't remember when I first did hear from Pratt." He was at pains to minimize the importance of his exchanges with the consul general at Singapore: "I don't think I kept copies of Mr. Pratt's letters, as I did not consider them of much value. He seemed to be a sort of busybody there and interfering with other people's business and I don't think his letters impressed me." In his autobiography, written much later, Dewey reported only that he had received a cable from Pratt on April 24 concerning Aguinaldo's willingness to come to Hong Kong, if invited; Dewey had requested his return, "as it was possible that he might have valuable information to impart at a time when no source of information was to be neglected." One member of the Filipino group in Hong Kong did sail with Dewey to Manila: José Alejandrino. He, Andrés Garchitorena, and Teodoro Sandico accompanied Rounsevelle Wildman on a launch that visited the *Olympia* on April 27, the day Dewey was to leave Mirs Bay for Manila. The Commodore, anxious to depart, complained to Wildman for causing him delay, and then said to Alejandrino, "I cannot wait for your companions; if you three want to come, I will take you along." Alejandrino went; the others stayed in Hong Kong, awaiting the arrival of Aguinaldo.[18]

Dewey explained to the Congressional committee that he had dealt with the Filipinos only to accommodate Pratt, Williams, and Wildman. Did these officials, Dewey was asked, have the power to force Aguinaldo upon him?

> Yes, they had in a way. They had not the official power, but one will yield after a while to constant pressure. I did not expect anything of them; I did not think that they would do anything, I would not have taken them; I did not want them; I did not believe in them; because, when I left Hong Kong, I was led to suppose that the country was in a state of insurrection, and that at my first gun, as Mr. Williams put it, there would be a general uprising, and I thought these half dozen or dozen refugees at Hong Kong would play a very small part in it.

Dewey was convinced that, had he been able to seize Manila immediately after his victory of May 1, the Americans would have been accepted as liberators. When asked how long this feeling would have endured, he replied, "I don't know how long it would have continued, perhaps the insurrection was bound to break out, but there was no insurrection then, and I think they would have accepted us; I think so." Given Dewey's political naiveté, it is hardly surprising that he should have gotten into increasing difficulties with the insurgents during the summer of 1898.[19]

On May 4 Aguinaldo, who finally had returned to Hong Kong on May 1, met with his associates to decide his future course. Consul

Wildman argued that the Filipino leader should return to Luzon, but Aguinaldo demurred, arguing that he ought first to make a written agreement with the Americans; otherwise Dewey might force him into prejudicial decisions. The unanimous views of his colleagues, however, forced him to follow Wildman's advice. Aguinaldo then sought passage on the *McCulloch* on its return to Manila after delivering Dewey's first despatches to Hong Kong. Lieutenant Brumby, the Commodore's aide who brought the messages, refused permission, but Dewey subsequently authorized Aguinaldo's return to the Philippines when the *McCulloch* next sailed on May 16. Aguinaldo landed at Cavite on May 19.[20]

Dewey later gave two reasons for his decision to permit Aguinaldo's trip. In 1902 he told congressional investigators that he had been harassed into the deed. Why were the Filipinos so annoying? "God knows, I don't know," exclaimed the Admiral. "I let them come over as an act of courtesy, just as you sometimes give money to a man to get rid of him; not that I expected anything from them." He reminded the investigating group that he had been led to assume that upon his arrival thirty thousand Filipinos would rise against the Spanish oppressors. Eleven years later, however, he mentioned another motive: "Obviously, as our purpose was to weaken the Spanish in every legitimate way, thus hastening the conclusion of hostilities in a war which was made to free Cuba from Spanish oppression, operations by the insurgents against Spanish oppression in the Philippines under certain restrictions would be welcome." These two considerations are not mutually exclusive. It seems possible that both influenced the admiral's behavior.[21]

AMERICAN-FILIPINO COLLABORATION,
MAY–JULY, 1898

After Aguinaldo's advent at Cavite the American war with Spain became intertwined with the Philippine revolution, a consequence in part of Dewey's carelessness and the overzealousness of three American consuls. Whatever Pratt or Wildman might have said to Aguinaldo, neither was authorized to act for the United States. If the Filipino leader thought that the consuls had power to negotiate, he was certainly in error. And Aguinaldo certainly read far too much into the actions of the American commander. Dewey had made no promise, direct or indirect, to the Filipino leader, but he failed to weigh the political consequences of his actions—a weakness that eventually led to grievous misunderstandings. Only after Aguinaldo's arrival at Cavite did Washington become even vaguely aware of what had passed between the leader of the insurgents and American representatives in East Asia.

William R. Braisted correctly notes that the controversy about what actually occurred in these curious conversations has "partially hidden the fact that neither the responsible authorities in Washington nor the insurgents were aware of the real intentions of the other until each side was committed to policies between which there was no compromise."[22]

When Aguinaldo arrived at Cavite, he conferred with Dewey and ultimately adopted the Admiral's recommendation that he lead a rising against the Spanish garrison. Taylor reported the American as saying to Aguinaldo, "Well, now go ashore there; we have got our forces at the arsenal of Cavite, go ashore and start your army." Aguinaldo departed Dewey's presence, only to return and say, "I want to leave here; I want to go to Japan." After spending that night on the *Olympia*, Aguinaldo disembarked again, and finally began to organize his followers. He claimed later that Dewey had promised him independence, but available evidence does not support his assertion. On May 20, for the first time, Dewey mentioned Aguinaldo in a report to the Navy Department: "Aguinaldo, the rebel commander in chief, was brought down by the *McCulloch*. Organizing forces near Cavite and may render assistance that will be available."[23]

What actuated the Filipinos to collaborate with the Americans? If José Alejandrino is to be believed, they acted out of expediency. Writing on May 19 to his regular correspondent, the Austrian Ferdinand Blumentritt, Alejandrino explained why he had traveled to Manila with Dewey: He had been sent by the group in Hong Kong, which had accepted the American statement that the United States did not have designs on the Philippines. "I need not tell you that we do not have entire confidence in these promises, but we thought—I don't know if with or without reason—that the only way to counteract the intentions of the Yankees was to arm ourselves, taking advantage of the occasion which presented itself to be in agreement with them to help us carry out the arms-smuggling expeditions to the Philippines and get the arms that they will provide us with." Presumably to justify actions that he thought Blumentritt might criticize, Alejandrino concluded, "I want to inform you that even without our help the Yankees could take over the country and do whatever would best suit them, and the only manner to counteract their intentions is that we be sufficiently armed. It is with this idea that we help them. Naturally, I say this in confidence." The Filipinos, then, decided to cast their lot with the Americans because it seemed the most practical choice. If the insurgents should break with the United States later on, they would have strengthened themselves for whatever might transpire in the future.[24]

The Americans never offered much more than encouragement and a few arms to the insurgents. Dewey supplied perhaps a hundred rifles, some cannons, and ammunition, taking this course, he said later, because "we had a common enemy, and of course I wanted his [Aguinaldo's] help." When Dewey learned that the Eighth Army Corps was on its way to Manila, he asked Aguinaldo to evacuate the town of Cavite. After some hesitation the insurgents pulled back to Bacoor. When in 1902 Dewey was asked why he had armed the Filipinos, given his belief that Manila would surrender to the American forces without much resistance, he stated, "Well, I permitted it as a good military act, a proper military act. The Filipinos were our friends, assisting us; they were doing our work. I believed then that they would be so thankful and delighted to get rid of the Spaniards that they would accept us with open arms." The situation in Manila Bay influenced his action: "I was waiting for troops to arrive, and I felt sure that the closer they [the Filipinos] invested the city the easier it would be when our troops arrived to march in. It turned out as I expected, and we need not have lost a man." When pressed to explain further his dealings with Aguinaldo, Dewey drew a striking analogy between the situation in the Confederacy during the American Civil War and that in the Philippines: "I was in the South in the Civil War, and the only friends we had in the South were the negroes, and we made use of them; they assisted us on many occasions. I said these people [the Filipinos] were our friends, and 'we have come here and they will help us just exactly as the negroes helped us in the Civil War.'" He expressed his belief that Aguinaldo did not have independence in mind during the early stages of the American siege at Manila.[25]

On May 26 Dewey received his first political instructions from Secretary Long, a message that governed American relations with Aguinaldo thereafter. Although the Secretary of the Navy granted the Admiral considerable discretion, recognizing that he possessed information not known in Washington, he laid down a general standard of behavior: "It is desirable, as far as possible, and consistent with your success and safety, not to have political alliances with the insurgents or any faction in the islands that would incur liability to maintain their cause in the future." Some historians interpret this instruction as conscious preparation for eventual annexation of the Philippine Islands, but a much more plausible view is that McKinley simply wished to avoid unnecessary entanglements while waiting for the situation to develop further. His attitude toward Aguinaldo's movement was consistent with his refusal to recognize the Cuban insurgents. A policy of caution would hold open options for a time, preserving freedom of action at a later date.[26]

Replying to Long's instruction, Dewey reviewed his prior activities and once again described his anomalous situation. On June 3 he cabled a flat statement to Long: "Have acted according to the spirit of the Department's instructions therein [cable of May 26] from the beginning, and I have entered into no alliance with the insurgents or with any faction." There followed a succinct summary of the military situation: "This squadron can reduce the defenses of Manila at any moment [by bombardment], but it is considered useless until the arrival of sufficient United States forces to retain possession." Dewey did not later justify his failure to request guidance concerning relations with Aguinaldo, any more than Secretary Long ever explained Washington's tardiness in sending them.[27]

By May 24 Aguinaldo had consolidated his position in the insurgency sufficiently to proclaim himself dictator in what he called a "dictatorial government" to rule during the initial stages of renewed insurgency. At this juncture he promised to deliver power eventually to a president and cabinet appointed by a constituent assembly; that body would be called into existence when the insurgents gained control of the Philippines. Aguinaldo's proclamation also praised the activity of the United States: "The great North American nation, the cradle of genuine liberty, and therefore the friend of our people, oppressed and enslaved by the tyranny and despotism of its rulers, has come to us manifesting a protection as decisive as it is undoubtedly disinterested toward our inhabitants, considering us as sufficiently civilized and capable of governing ourselves and our unfortunate country." He emphasized the importance of adhering to the rules of civilized warfare and specified punishments for Filipinos who committed crimes.[28]

The insurgents' effort began with the acquisition of arms. On May 27 a shipment from Amoy arrived—2,282 Remington rifles and 176,550 cartridges. Consul General Wildman made this purchase with 50,000 Mexican pesos provided by Aguinaldo. He also arranged for a second shipment, expending 67,000 pesos. but it was never delivered to the insurgents; no one has ever explained the disposition of the payment. Some arms stored away after the Pact of Biyak-na-Bató were recovered, and others came with Filipinos who deserted the Spanish service. Late in May, Felipe Buencamino and other ex-insurgents who had joined the Spanish militia went back to Aguinaldo, an event that signaled a general uprising in the Tagalog provinces. Somewhere between twelve and fourteen thousand Filipino soldiers in the Spanish service eventually joined Aguinaldo; they formed the backbone of his army. The insurgents also sought arms in Japan. A purchase was made there through the exertions of Mariano Ponce, who enjoyed assistance from the

Chinese revolutionary Sun Yat-sen and certain prominent Japanese, left
Nagasaki on July 18 on the merchantman *Nunobiki Maru*. However,
the vessel encountered a violent typhoon off Formosa and went to the
bottom.[29]

Aguinaldo's army began operations around Manila at the end of
May, about the same time that fighting broke out elsewhere in Luzon
and in Mindoro, the Visayas, and Mindanao. The most important
military movements took place under the direct control of Aguinaldo
and a group of trusted associates in the immediate vicinity of Manila.
Their first objective was to seize the province of Cavite, a step towards
the conquest of Manila. With remarkable speed the insurgents broke
the Bacoor-Zapote line, occupied important towns in the vicinity—Mandaluyong, San Pedro Macatí, Caloocan, and Parañaque—and laid siege to Manila proper. Certain important suburbs of
the city came under insurgent control—Paco, Malate, a part of Quiapo,
and Santa Cruz. Aguinaldo divided the district around Manila into four
zones under the command of high-ranking subordinates: General
Mariano Noriel was headquartered in Pasay, General Pío del Pilar in
San Pedro Macatí, Colonel Antonio Montenegro in Mariquina, and
General Pantaleon García in a zone including Navotas, Tambobong,
Novaliches, and Caloocan. Aguinaldo certainly hoped to capture
Manila before the Americans, but Dewey correctly decided that the
Filipinos lacked sufficient strength. Although the American Admiral
did avoid further entanglements with Aguinaldo that might prove embarrassing later on, he appears to have held the Filipino leader in a certain regard, once telling a group of congressional leaders, "I knew he
could not take the city without the assistance of the navy, without my
assistance, and I knew that what he was doing—driving the Spaniards
in—was saving our troops, because our own men perhaps would have
had to do that same thing." As to personal relations, the Admiral was
quite positive: "He and I were always on the most friendly terms; we
never had any differences. He considered me as his liberator, as his
friend. I think he had the highest admiration for us because we had
whipped the Spaniards who had been riding them down for three hundred years." If the Americans were not truly active supporters of the insurgents, they posed no obstacles to their operations.[30]

The insurgents' success in the field stemmed from both their own exertions and the weaknesses of the Spanish garrison. Governor-General
Augustín lost much of his available force of defenders when his Filipino
troops went over to Aguinaldo. American assistance played a significant
role, in that Dewey's presence allowed the Filipinos to use the waters of
Manila Bay. The Spanish garrison was bottled up in the city, what with

Dewey's blockading it by sea and Aguinaldo laying siege by land. These difficulties at Manila mirrored the general decline of Spain's power during the spring and summer of 1898 as the United States, benefitting from insurgencies in both Cuba and the Philippines, extended its operations. Taylor noted that the Spanish outposts in the Philippines rarely offered serious resistance to the insurgents: "Their officers seem to have felt that surrender was inevitable; that as they were doomed to pass as prisoners to the insurgents it would be well to pass without unnecessary loss of blood and with better terms than they could obtain after prolonged resistance." Had Spanish garrisons in provinces such as Laguna, Bulacan, and Cavite chosen to fight their way back to Manila, they might well have succeeded, but the will to make the effort simply did not exist. After the Spanish garrisons had been captured, the insurgents dominated all locales outside Manila.[31]

Taylor insisted that no sign of Filipino desire for an independent republican government manifested itself: "A determined and well-organized minority had succeeded in imposing its will upon an unorganized, heterogeneous, and leaderless majority." Still, Aguinaldo's military success provided a solid foundation for the establishment of civil government. On June 12 he formally proclaimed the independence of the Philippines, and on June 18 and 20 went a step further, issuing a decree creating municipalities and provinces and providing for their administration. On June 23 he founded a government, putting himself at the head of a revolutionary committee. Taylor described this arrangement as "a strong and highly centralized military dictatorship, in which, under the form of election, provision was made for the filling of all offices, by men devoted to the group which had seized the functions of government." The decree of June 23 organized four departments of government—(1) Foreign Relations, Marine, and Commerce; (2) War and Public Works; (3) Police and Internal Order; and (4) Treasury, Agriculture, and Industry. To provide a judiciary the decree of June 18 designated a committee of the Congress to serve as the "Permanent Commission of Justice." Aguinaldo formed his first cabinet on July 15. Baldomero Aguinaldo became Secretary of War and Public Works, Leandro Ibarra assumed the portfolio of Secretary of the Interior, and Mariano Trías became Secretary of Finance.[32]

At about this time one of the most important figures in the Philippine movement first came to prominence; Apolinario Mabini offered his services to Aguinaldo. However, when he learned that Aguinaldo had no formal written agreement with the United States, he opposed—unsuccessfully—the leader's decision to proclaim the independence of the Philippines: It was "premature and imprudent" to declare the intentions of the insurgents "because the Americans were concealing their true designs while we were making ours manifest." The Americans, Mabini held, would do what they could to frustrate independence. Despite Aguinaldo's rejection of this view, the talented Mabini soon became one of his trusted advisers, assuming responsibility for much of the planning that preceded the further organization of the civil government. Taylor aptly argued that "the ability of this man, his hatred of the rule of white men, his honesty, and his power of expression, made him a most valuable ally."[33]

Aguinaldo's activities at Manila were stimulating growing interest in Washington, and Dewey soon found himself responding to inquiries about the insurgents. On June 14 Secretary Long transmitted a definite order to provide detailed information: "Report fully any conferences, relations, or cooperations, military or otherwise, that you have had with Aguinaldo, and keep informed the Department in that respect." This request reflected awareness that not only did the insurgents represent a significant component of the military equation in the Philippines but it was probable that their presence would influence the postwar settlement. The McKinley Administration sought most of all to preserve its freedom of action. This desire is apparent in an interesting message that Secretary of State Day sent Consul Pratt in Singapore on June 16: "If, in the course of your conferences with General Aguinaldo, you acted upon the assumption that this government would cooperate with him for the furtherance of any plan of his own, or that, in accepting his cooperation, it would consider itself pledged to recognize any political claims which he may put forward, your action was unauthorized and can not be approved." This message undermines allegations that the government in Washington plotted with Aguinaldo during the war with Spain. Nor does it indicate that the United States had already decided to annex the Philippines.[34]

Dewey's response to Long's request for information must have been comforting. The Admiral affirmed that he had not undertaken joint operations with the insurgents, but that he had treated them as friends, "being opposed to a common enemy." He praised Aguinaldo, reporting that the Filipino "acted independently of the squadron, but has kept me advised of his progress, which has been wonderful." He had counselled the Filipino to wage war "humanely," and Aguinaldo had heeded this advice. Then came the most welcome news of all: "My relations with him are cordial, but I am not in his confidence. The United States has not been bound, in any way to assist insurgents by any act or promises, and he is not, to my knowledge, committed to assist us." Although Aguinaldo hoped to capture Manila, Dewey did not think this object could be accomplished without artillery. He offered a comparison of the Filipinos and the Cubans: "In my opinion, these people are far superior in their intelligence and more capable of self-government than the natives of Cuba, and I am familiar with both races."[35]

On August 6 word came to the State Department of the early diplomatic contacts with Aguinaldo from Rounseville Wildman himself: He and Oscar F. Williams had entered into discussions with Aguinaldo because the Filipino constituted a "necessary evil." The leader of the insurgents could at least be held responsible for events: "The other alternative was to allow the entire islands to be overrun by small bands bent on revenge and looting." Wildman insisted that he had avoided entangling commitments to Aguinaldo: "We made no pledges and extracted from him but two, viz. to obey unquestionably the commander of the U.S. forces in the Philippine Islands, and to conduct his warfare on civilized lines."[36]

When General Anderson arrived with the first contingent of American troops on June 30, one of his immediate tasks was to deal with Aguinaldo. In an interview with the insurgent on July 1, he learned of the rebels' military progress against the Spanish garrison, gaining the impression that his arrival did not please Aguinaldo, who hoped to take Manila himself with the assistance only of the American naval squadron. Anderson then set to work establishing working relations with the insurgents. Aguinaldo proved cooperative but independent. On July 9 Anderson reported the Filipino to be organizing his government and "trying to take Manila without our assistance. This is not probable, but if he can effect his purpose he will, I apprehend, antagonize any effort on our part to establish a provisional government." As the days passed, Anderson became more and more suspicious of Aguinaldo's purposes, despite the façade of cooperation. On July 18 he noted that, despite the outward courtesies of the Filipinos, "in many ways they obstruct our purposes, and are using every effort to take Manila without us." He also had begun to suspect—incorrectly—that the insurgent leader was trying to negotiate a deal with the Spanish leaders in Manila. However, acting on the advice of Admiral Dewey, he did not interfere with Aguinaldo's efforts to form a government. He wanted to avoid actions that might limit the prerogatives of General Merritt, scheduled to arrive soon. Like Dewey, he was gaining in his regard for the "natives": "These people only respect strength and firmness. . . . They are not ignorant, savage tribes, but have a civilization of their own; and though insignificant in appearance are fierce fighters, and for a tropical people they are industrious." And so it continued, with both Anderson and Aguinaldo maneuvering to accomplish their separate designs without unduly annoying each other. Such was the situation when General Merritt arrived and took command at Manila on July 25.[37]

General Merritt reported on the state of Filipino-American relations as they appeared upon his landfall. Of great importance was the anomalous fact that the insurgents held a line against Manila *between* the Americans and the Spanish defenders. He also noted that the Filipinos had developed an organized government and controlled many points in the Philippine Islands outside the area around Manila. Since his instructions provided that "the powers of the military occupant are absolute and supreme and immediately operate upon the political condition of the inhabitants," he decided to avoid direct exchanges with Aguinaldo until gaining possession of Manila. "I would not until then be in a position to issue a proclamation and enforce my authority, in the event that his pretensions should clash with my designs." These considerations led him to develop plans for an attack on the city that excluded the insurgents. Cosmas notes the consequence: "The siege of Manila developed into a curious triangular contest in which the American fleet and the Eighth Corps fought the Spaniards while simultaneously maneuvering to deny the Filipinos a share in the spoils of victory. The Filipinos meanwhile used the strategic situation created by Dewey's success to forward their own cause."[38]

☆ EIGHTEEN ☆

The Conquest
of Manila

W hen Admiral Dewey reported the arrival of General Merritt, on July 26, he claimed that the situation within the city of Manila was "most critical" and that the Spanish garrison might "surrender at any moment." His estimate was accurate indeed; almost everyone inside the city knew that if reinforcements failed to appear, the garrison could not survive a determined assault, particularly one that involved both Americans and Filipinos. When Augustín informed Madrid of Merritt's arrival, he proposed, on the assumption that peace negotiations with the United States had begun, that he be allowed to negotiate a truce; otherwise he expected an early assault on the city. Morale among the Spanish populace was at an extraordinarily low level. Food scarcities had developed earlier in July, and the situation became chaotic when American reinforcements materialized just as news came in that Admiral Cámara had turned back to Spain. One of the inhabitants recorded the mood in Manila at the end of July: "A great part of the population, civil as well as military, believed that it [the city] ought to be capitulated at the first intimation that the Americans made, since they considered the defense impossible, that it would occasion thousands of victims needlessly; for another thing, they added, the downright conduct of the homeland relieves us of all obligation to her." As in the case of Santiago de Cuba, the garrison at Manila manifested little inclination to resist the Americans very far outside the gates of the city.[1]

411

If Dewey correctly estimated the situation inside Manila, he also proved a sound prophet concerning relations with the Filipinos. "Merritt's most difficult problem," he informed Secretary Long, "will be how to deal with insurgents under Aguinaldo, who has become aggressive and even threatening toward our army." The Admiral exposed much the same view to Consul Wildman and added a comment that he did not pass on to Washington: "You cannot imagine what a relief it is to me to have some one share the responsibilities of this difficult position with me." Considering that General Anderson "was making a mess of his dealings with Aguinaldo," he presumably thought that Merritt would do better.[2]

PREPARATIONS FOR THE ASSAULT

Merritt's first task was to open a route through the insurgent lines so that he could attack the city. Because he did not wish to deal officially with Aguinaldo, a procedure that he felt might confer undue status on the Filipino leader and imply recognition of his government, he asked General Greene to negotiate an arrangement. President McKinley later summarized the reasons why Merritt avoided official contacts with Aguinaldo: "It was fitting that whatever was to be done in the way of decisive operations in that quarter [Manila] should be accomplished by the strong arm of the United States alone. . . . Divided victory was not possible, for no partition of the rights and responsibilities attending the enforcement of a just and advantageous peace could be thought of." This independent approach paralleled the policy adopted in the case of Cuba. It was a logical course, given the President's desire to maintain firm control of future developments and hold open all possible options. Fortunately for General Merritt his subordinate, General Francis V. Greene, achieved sufficient influence with the local Filipino commander, General Mariano Noriel, to be able to make appropriate arrangements without difficulty, and the insurgents agreed simply to move out of their entrenchments.[3]

On the night of July 29 the Americans occupied positions directly opposite the Spanish defenders on a line that stretched from the beach on Manila Bay to the road connecting Cavite and Manila known as the *Calle real*. On the left front of the American lines, at Malate, rose Fort San Antonio Abad, the southwestern anchor of Augustín's line. The next strong point to the east was the Blockhouse No. 14, whence fortifications continued north and then west around the outskirts of Manila. Greene found the insurgents' trenches unsatisfactory, so he dug a new line 270 yards long from the beach to the road and supported it with some guns from the Utah Battery. On the night of July 31 the Spanish defenders to the north fired on this position. American casualties in this incident amounted to ten killed and thirty-three wounded—more than the total inflicted by the Spanish defenders during the entire Puerto Rican campaign. Later exchanges of gunfire in this location led to additional casualties—five killed and twenty wounded. This development led Greene to extend the line almost a thousand yards eastward, so that ultimately the right flank rested on the Pasay road and an impassable swamp.[4]

The American assault was then postponed because of difficulties in landing further reinforcements commanded by Brigadier General Arthur MacArthur that arrived July 31, and because of an effort by Dewey to end Spanish resistance by negotiation. Adverse weather and inadequate landing facilities prevented MacArthur from getting his force ashore until August 7. When his contingent finally completed its disembarkation, the American force totaled 8,500 men. Meanwhile Merritt tried to get the navy to support his position with gunfire, but Dewey proved uncooperative. The Admiral feared that this action might bring on a general engagement, an outcome he wished to delay until the arrival of the monitor *Monterey* with its heavy guns. He also wanted to pursue certain delicate negotiations with the Spanish Governor-General then being conducted through an intermediary. Merritt showed little interest in these secret talks, which had become possible because foreign consuls in Manila had extended their good offices. On July 29 Dewey cabled optimistically to Long about arranging a Spanish capitulation: "From information which I consider reliable, Spanish Governor-General would surrender to the United States forces at once, were it not for insurgent complication. In any event, they must capitulate very soon. Merritt and I are working together to this end." Actually Merritt, although agreeing that the insurgents represented a problem, doubted that the city could be taken without a fight. When he informed the War Department that he would join Dewey in demanding the surrender of Manila, at the same time giving assurances that the Americans would protect the garrison from the Filipino insurgents, he also stated, "It may be important to have my whole force before attacking if necessary to hold insurgents while we fight Spanish."[5]

On August 4 the *Monterey* finally arrived, but Dewey still resisted an immediate attack, hoping that his secret negotiations would bear fruit. Merritt knew that the monitor's two twelve-inch and two ten-inch guns far outranged the Spanish batteries, and that the navy could direct enfilading fire on the enemy's positions, at least from Fort San Antonio

Abad to Blockhouse No. 14—a bombardment that would surely force the defenders to abandon their line. He urged immediate action, but failed to sway Dewey. To increase pressure on the city it was agreed on to issue an ultimatum on August 6 demanding surrender. This message would go to the new Governor-General, Don Fermín Jáudenes y Alvarez, who had replaced the discouraged Augustín. Sagasta wanted the garrison to hold out until he completed peace negotiations in Washington. Augustín's pessimism was such that Madrid, fearing that he might give up prematurely, decided to replace him.[6]

On August 9 the American commanders wrote the Spanish garrison once again, noting its hopeless situation and once again demanding surrender. Before making his reply, Jáudenes convened a meeting of his commanders. Seven voted to begin negotiations for surrender, and seven voted to hold out, even though most believed that they could not defend the city. Jáudenes broke the tie, deciding to pursue delaying tactics. He then informed the Americans that he had no authority to surrender and asked for time to consult Madrid through Hong Kong. On August 10 Merritt and Dewey rejected this proposition.[7]

As these letters passed back and forth, Dewey pursued separate negotiations with Jáudenes through the Belgian consul in Manila, Edouard C. André. General Anderson described André's simple procedure: "His method was to go to the Governor-General and get a statement, which he wrote down in a memorandum book; then he would go to General Merritt and Admiral Dewey and get a statement from them, which he would carry back to the Governor-General." Dewey also attempted to capitalize on a conversation between a Roman Catholic chaplain accompanying the expedition, Father William D. McKinnon of the First California, and Archbishop Nozaleda of Manila, a member of a civilian group concerned with the defense of Manila that on August 8 recommended the surrender of the city. At this juncture Jáudenes intimated to André that he would capitulate if the Americans agreed to a sham battle that would preserve the garrison's honor and if the Filipinos were restrained from entering the city.[8]

Jáudenes's proposal finally broke the stalemate. When André conveyed it, Dewey held a meeting with Merritt and some other officers. In his testimony of 1902 before a congressional committee, the Admiral explained the outcome: The Spaniards would surrender if Dewey conducted a token bombardment of one of the forts. "I selected one at Malate [Fort San Antonio Abad], away from the city. Then I said that I must engage that and fire for a while, and then I was to make the signal by the international code, 'Do you surrender?' Then they were to hoist a white flag at a certain bastion." At another point in his testimony

Dewey said, "It was all arranged and we need not have lost a man there. . . . [Jáudenes] was fearful that the Filipinos would get in." The sham battle stemmed from Spanish punctilio; this same barrier to surrender, it will be recalled, had existed at Santiago de Cuba. "[Jáudenes] said his honor demanded that. So I had to fire, to kill a few people." The agreement was never committed to writing. Dewey wrote in 1913, "Although there were some further negotiations concerning the terms of surrender, nothing was definitely agreed upon; while it was impressed on General Jaudenes that the generosity of the terms granted would depend on the brevity of his resistance. Indeed these pourparlers continued until the day before the capture of the city." Not long after the end of the war Dewey paid tribute to André in a cable to Secretary Long: "This gentleman acted as intermediary . . . carrying several important communications, among them a message from me to the Governor-General to the effect that if the numerous batteries on the water front of the walled city kept silent the city would not be shelled." He noted that the replacement of Augustín by Jáudenes seemed at the time to indicate the popularity of determined Spanish resistance; in the circumstances "it is much to the credit of Mr. Andre that his counsel prevailed, and that in the attack the city batteries did not fire."[9]

The Jáudenes-Dewey arrangement applied primarily to the American naval squadron; it did not preclude combat between land forces. General Anderson, who only learned of the informal agreement—from André himself—after the war, reported its final form as follows:

> If the fleet did not throw shells into the walled city or the Spanish part of Manila the Spanish artillery would not open on the fleet. There was no agreement, as the memorandum was read to me, that our land forces would not be fired upon. On the contrary, there was a statement that the honor or Spain required that there should be resistance, and that, under the Spanish army code, their officers surrendering without resistance or giving a parole would subject themselves to a trial by court-martial.

Anderson's view of the agreement differed from that of Dewey, who thought that naval fire on Fort San Antonio Abad alone would salvage the honor of the defenders. There is no question that the deal was made, despite later efforts to minimize its import or obfuscate its specificity. Because one of its purposes was to keep the Filipinos out of the city, the unwritten deal constituted collusion between Dewey and Jáudenes against presumed friends of the United States.[10]

In making arrangements for operations against Manila, General Merritt considered the informal agreement that Dewey made with

Jáudenes, but also recognized that the Spanish might not keep their part of the bargain. On August 10 he gave orders governing relations with the insurgents: No rupture was to occur. Commanders could request permission from insurgents to occupy their trenches, but, if such requests were refused, they were not to compel acquiescence. Artillery was to be placed in positions that would not provoke difficulties with the insurgents. The Spanish garrison had located some artillery at Fort San Antonio Abad—three 3.6-inch bronze field guns, four 3.2-inch bronze mountain guns, and two 3.2-inch steel mountain guns—a circumstance that had to be considered in planning the attack. General Anderson fortunately had no difficulty in getting the insurgents to leave the trenches immediately in front of Blockhouse No. 14, which cleared the way for an American attack on the left flank of the enemy's line. The entrenchments from which the Americans would assault the right flank of the enemy's line of fortifications at Fort San Antonio Abad had been completed earlier. Two brigades were organized to make the attack: General MacArthur would command the right of the American line; his troops before Blockhouse No. 14 numbered 196 officers and 4,904 enlisted men. General Greene commanded on the left of the Eighth Army line, leading 139 officers and 3,691 enlisted men. Merritt's battle order, issued on August 12, directed that Greene assault Fort San Antonio Abad following the naval bombardment of that position. MacArthur would attack Blockhouse No. 14, supported by fire from field artillery and boat guns. If the enemy offered strong resistance, Merritt did not intend to press the assault "until after the navy had made practicable breaches in the works and shaken the troops holding them." He planned a land attack with naval support because it was more humane than naval bombardment of the crowded city.[11]

Other arrangements were included to provide the means of accepting the Spanish surrender and preventing the insurgents from entering the city. Merritt was to board the *Zafiro* on the day of the battle. If the enemy displayed a white flag, as agreed upon between Dewey and Jáudenes, representatives of the United States army and navy would enter Manila to arrange the Spanish surrender. Meanwhile, when the hostile fire had stopped, American troops would move on the enemy lines. Merritt's orders specified, "It is intended that these results shall be accomplished without loss of life; and while the firing continues from the enemy with their heavy guns, or if there is an important fire from their entrenched lines, the troops will not attempt an advance unless ordered from these headquarters." When the surrender would take place, the *Zafiro* would land six companies of the Second Oregon, and this force would occupy the walled city. A special memorandum outlined measures to ensure that the insurgents would not enter Manila. "Forcible encounters with the insurgents in carrying out these orders will be very carefully guarded against," it read, "but pillage, rapine, or violence by the native inhabitants or disorderly insurgents must be prevented at any cost."[12]

BATTLE OF MANILA

At 8:45 A.M. on August 13 Dewey's vessels were deployed to various stations to begin the engagement. The *Olympia*, *Raleigh*, *Petrel*, and two smaller vessels—the *Callao* and *McCulloch*—moved off Fort San Antonio Abad. None of the crews on these ships had been informed that the ships off Manila would only fire on that fort. Three cruisers—the *Charleston*, *Boston*, and *Baltimore*—took stations opposite the Luneta batteries. The powerful *Monterey* moved further inshore, and the *Concord* stood off the mouth of the Pasig River. At 9:35 A.M. the *Olympia*, *Petrel*, *Raleigh*, and *Callao* opened fire on Fort San Antonio Abad, bombarding it slowly for an hour. No return fire came from the fort or the batteries defending the city. Lieutenant Bradley A. Fiske, aboard the *Petrel*, remembered later that he had planned to observe the fire of the *Monterey* on the enemy's artillery ashore. He was disgusted when he discovered after the engagement that "the officers of the *Monterey* had known for three days that there would be no fight."[13]

As the naval bombardment came to an end, the two brigades made their prearranged attacks. At 10:25 A.M. General Greene advanced on Fort San Antonio Abad. It proved to be unoccupied, but Spanish soldiers entrenched to the north in the town of Malate opened fire and inflicted some casualties. All told, Anderson's brigade lost one killed and fifty-four wounded. The Spanish fire soon ceased, and the Americans were able to move through Malate and across the bridges to Binondo and San Miguel. On the right, General MacArthur moved his troops up the Pasay road as soon as he heard firing to the left. Here the Americans attracted severe fire from blockhouses, trenches, and the woods. After a sharp fight Blockhouse No. 14 was occupied at 11:20 A.M. Moving on to Singalong, the brigade encountered resistance from Blockhouse No. 20. The fight that ensued at this location lasted until about 1:30 P.M., the brigade taking casualties of five killed and thirty-eight wounded. Shortly thereafter, MacArthur was able to move through the Paco district into the walled city.[14]

Almost all of MacArthur's losses were in vain because they were inflicted after the Spanish garrison had already indicated its desire to sur-

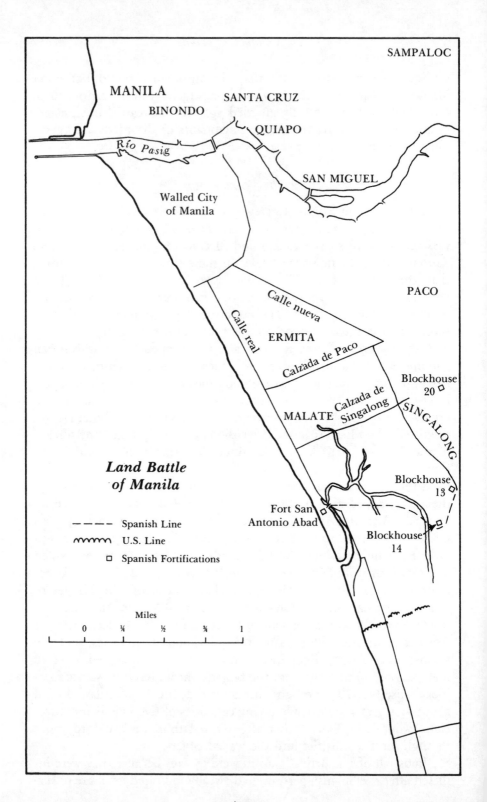

SAMPALOC

MANILA

BINONDO

SANTA CRUZ

QUIAPO

Río Pasig

SAN MIGUEL

Walled City
of Manila

PACO

Calle nueva

Calle real

ERMITA

Calzada de Paco

Blockhouse
20

MALATE *Calzada de Singalong*

SINGALONG

Land Battle of Manila

Blockhouse
13

Fort San
Antonio Abad

– – – – Spanish Line

〰〰〰 U.S. Line

▫ Spanish Fortifications

Blockhouse
14

Miles

0   ¼   ½   ¾   1

render. When Dewey completed his token bombardment of Fort San Antonio Abad, he steamed to a position off the walls of Manila. There, at 11:00 A.M., he hoisted the letters D.W.H.B., the international signal meaning, "Do you surrender?" Dewey recalled with some pride that he was the first to observe a response: "We had fifty people looking for that white flag; but I happened to be the first one who saw it. . . . We could not see the white flag—it was rather a thick day—but finally I discovered it on the south bastion; I don't know how long it had been flying there when I first saw it." Dewey was proved correct in his presumption that Jáudenes would honor the arrangements for surrender. At this point Lieutenant Colonel Charles A. Whittier of Merritt's staff and Lieutenant Brumby, Dewey's aide, went ashore to arrange terms with Jáudenes and Montojo. At 2:30 P.M. Brumby reported the surrender, but the Spanish standard was not taken down until the Admiral's aide raised the American flag at 5:43 P.M. The Second Oregon immediately took up duties as a provost guard, disarming the garrison and providing security in the walled city.[15]

During the battle two British vessels under the command of Captain Edward Chichester changed position to obtain a better view of the battle, an innocent maneuver that provided spurious support for the legend that the ships had been interposed between those of Dewey and the German squadron as a warning to Admiral von Diederichs. This supposed demonstration of Anglo-American solidarity was presumably designed to deter a possible German attack on the American ships. Despite the absence of evidence to bolster this misconception, it still lingers on. Thomas A. Bailey's explanation of this event, published in 1939, is unanswerable, but myths die hard.[16]

As expected, Aguinaldo and his troops proved less than cooperative. On the day before the battle General Anderson had notified the insurgent commander that his forces were not to enter Manila. When the fighting occurred on August 13, he confirmed this instruction, sending a brief message: "Do not let your troops enter Manila without permission from the American commander. On this side of the Pasig River you will be under fire." Nevertheless some four thousand insurgents moved into important positions in the suburbs of Manila, notably in Malate, Paco, and Ermita, an action that elicited another message from Anderson to Aguinaldo calling upon the Filipino leader to prevent "serious trouble" between his troops and the Americans: "Your forces should not force themselves into the city until we have received full surrender. Then we will negotiate with you." Aguinaldo, who remained at Bacoor because of fear that the Americans might imprison him, replied in disappointed terms: "My troops are forced by yours, by means of threats of violence, to retire from positions taken.'' He wanted Anderson to keep the American troops under control, but gave notice that he had issued orders designed to ensure cooperation. All this activity portended future difficulties.[17]

Had Jáudenes possessed full information about negotiations between Washington and Madrid during the period August 7–12 that finally resulted in cessation of hostilities, he might not have agreed to surrender so that the city would remain in Spanish control at the end of the war. But in the absence of such knowledge he had every reason to avoid a serious defense. The city lacked fortifications, artillery, and naval support capable of countering the Americans. The previous commander, Augustín, had failed to concentrate the troops available to him in the islands at the most threatened place—Manila—and thereby deprived himself of a formidable garrison. Meanwhile, he had also failed to maintain the loyalty of the Filipino populace, and the insurgent army grew rapidly. When the Zapote line was abandoned, the city's communications to the countryside were cut off, and the insurgents were soon able to invest the city. Defensive lines established in the immediate vicinity of the city were highly vulnerable to attack. Finally, because refugees were massed within the walled city, the Spanish commanders had to avoid an American bombardment. All these circumstances had come about before Jáudenes took power. He simply followed the inherent logic of the situation in arranging a relatively bloodless capitulation. Underlying the entire affair was the basic fact that Spain had been unable to succor Manila after the destruction of Montojo's squadron at Cavite on May 1. The will to resist the Americans had slowly ebbed away; Manila's garrison was in no mood to make a pointless sacrifice. It was fortunate that the operations of August 13 did not cause extensive casualties on both sides. It is of interest that the American commanders ashore and their troops did not know until afterwards that the Governor-General had agreed to give up after only a brief show of resistance.[18]

On August 14 a joint group of Spanish and American officers accepted a final agreement of capitulation that supplemented a preliminary document Merritt and Jáudenes had signed the previous day. Its provisions were relatively liberal, and no great difficulties stemmed from it. The Spanish troops were required to deposit their arms and remain in quarters under their own commanders until the signing of a peace treaty between the two nations. Officers were allowed to retain side arms, mounts, and private property. All public property was surrendered. In this connection lists of personnel, property, and stores were to be presented to the Americans in ten days. Questions of repatriation were to be referred to Washington; families of military personnel were to be allowed to depart at their own convenience. Officers would be supplied with rations and other necessary assistance, as though they were prisoners of war, until Spain and the United States agreed to a treaty of peace. All funds in the hands of Spanish officials were to be turned over to the victors. Finally, honoring their obligation to ensure the safety of Manila and its inhabitants against the insurgents, the Americans would make certain that "this city, its inhabitants, its churches and religious worship, its educational establishments, and its private property of all descriptions, are placed under the special safeguard of the faith and honor of the American army."[19]

The irony of this victory was that the battle occurred after a protocol had already been signed in Washington providing for cessation of hostilities. But word of peace did not reach the Philippines until August 16, because cable communications had not yet been resumed with Hong Kong. When Merritt sent news of the war's end to Jáudenes, the Governor-General then protested certain of the acts taking place under the terms of capitulation, basing his argument on the fact that the protocol had been signed prior to the battle at Manila. Merritt nevertheless insisted upon full execution of the terms, and the Spanish garrison completed its responsibilities under protest. The disparity in time between the signature of the protocol and the capitulation at Manila raised important questions of international law. If the victory came after the protocol had been signed, was it possible for the United States to claim that Philippine Islands by the ancient right of conquest? This issue came to the fore during the peace negotiations in Paris that began October 1, 1898, as arranged in the protocol of August 12.[20]

The summer campaign in the Philippine Islands bore no resemblance to the one concluded almost a month earlier at Santiago de Cuba. Sufficient time had been available to organize the expedition intelligently; for this reason the helter-skelter procedures that characterized the Cuban expedition never troubled the Philippine operation. By and large, interservice squabbles of the sort encountered at Santiago de Cuba did not measurably affect the course of events at Manila. Of great importance was the fact that serious difficulties with tropical disease did not materialize in the Philippines. Nothing was comparable to the epidemics of malaria, dysentery, and typhoid fever that overwhelmed the Fifth Army Corps at Manila. In the end the Spanish garrison chose not to make a serious defense such as that mounted at El Caney and the San Juan Heights. The only similarity between the two campaigns lay in the utter hopelessness of the Spanish situation. In both cases the

Spanish naval squadron present was destroyed, and the garrison left without hope of relief from Spain. Moreover, in both locales the Americans enjoyed important assistance from insurgents.

The capitulation at Manila concluded the war between Spain and the United States. With the receipt of the President's formal congratulations, the Eighth Army Corps settled into the duties of occupation, not realizing that its fighting days had hardly begun.[21] Few at the time imagined the extent to which the peace settlement to come would set the Filipinos and the conquering Americans against each other.

NINETEEN

Preliminaries of Peace

During the War with Spain in 1898 President McKinley consistently attempted to force peace in the shortest possible time and at the cheapest possible cost. To achieve this he adopted an "indirect approach," attacking the enemy's weakest positions at the periphery of its empire with the strongest available forces. If Spain were faced with determined opposition in several quarters, it might have to accept defeat without forcing the United States to attack its center of power in the Caribbean at Havana or ultimately the Peninsula itself. Whatever the tactical and logistical failings of the American forces, their strategic design was soundly conceived and well enough executed to obtain victory in a remarkably brief time. After the United States Navy seized command of the sea in the western Pacific and the Caribbean, three short campaigns—in Cuba, Puerto Rico, and Luzon—compelled the Liberal ministry in Madrid to sue for peace late in July, 1898.

PRELIMINARIES TO THE PROTOCOL

Before declaring war the United States carefully ascertained the attitudes of the great powers towards intervention in the Spanish–American controversy over Cuba. Spanish weakness, American strength, and unstable conditions in Africa and Asia as well as Europe militated against Madrid's efforts to enlist aid prior to the beginning of hostilities. Thereafter, American leaders continued to watch developments carefully, recognizing that decisions taken in London, Paris, Berlin, Vienna, Rome, and St. Petersburg might affect the course of the war. Ambassador John Hay's friend, Henry Adams, took it for granted that "diplomacy must now become pretty active." Surely, he thought, the United States could chase Spain out of the Antilles and acquire Hawaii at its pleasure. "But what of China? What of the East? What of Europe?" These were interesting questions indeed.[1]

Shortly after the first naval engagements, word filtered to Washington of British interest in an early peace. On May 8 John Hay reported an intriguing inquiry: "Member of British Government asked unofficially last night whether war would cease if Spain should offer through England to evacuate Cuba"—a development that stimulated the first real consideration of peace terms in Washington. After discussions at the White House, Secretary of State Day asked the ambassador whether Madrid had inspired the British inquiry and whether the United States should reply promptly. From London came word that the British official had been none other than the Colonial Minister, Joseph Chamberlain, but that his initiative did not stem from Spanish activity. Hay neatly summarized its meaning: "The significance of it consists in the indication it gives of the state of mind of the men at the head of affairs here, for they wish for a speedy termination of the war in the independence of Cuba, their certainty of our success, and their willingness to take a prominent part, if needed, in the work of pacification."[2]

Confirmation of Hay's estimate came in a memorable speech that Chamberlain gave in Birmingham on May 13. Among other things he said, "Our next duty . . . is to establish and maintain bonds of permanent amity with our kinsmen across the Atlantic." He concluded, "Terrible as war may be, war itself would be cheaply purchased if, in a great and noble cause, the Stars and Stripes and the Union Jack should wave together over an Anglo-Saxon alliance." A month later Chamberlain explained to the House of Commons that he did not contemplate a formal tie with the United States: "The Americans do not want our alliance at this moment," he noted. "They do not ask for our assistance, and we do not want theirs." Whatever Chamberlain's motives, the British Foreign Office showed no inclination to pursue policies that might conceivably alienate the United States.[3]

On June 3, almost a month after Hay first inquired of Day about peace terms, the Secretary of State suddenly spelled them out in a message to the embassy in London. The timing of this stemmed from the successful blockade of Cervera at Santiago de Cuba. Perhaps Spain might now accept defeat, having satisfied its honor and now being faced with further disasters. President McKinley's list of June 3, transmitted by Day, included four provisions intended to be communicated unofficially to Madrid through third parties. First, Madrid must evacuate Cuba and deliver title to the United States, so that Americans "could restore and establish order and hold until a stable government [is] established." Second, because the United States did not intend to exact a monetary indemnity, it required cession of Puerto Rico, an outcome that would satisfy "just and lawful claims" of its citizens stemming from the Cuban affair. Third, the Philippines would remain in Spanish hands except for "a port and necessary appurtenances, to be selected by the United States." Finally, Spain must cede a port in the Ladrones (Marianas) possessing a harbor and coaling station. Day concluded his message ominously; continued Spanish resistance might lead to material alterations in the American requirements. Obviously he hoped that when Sagasta learned of the terms he would open negotiations and thereby minimize losses. However, on June 14 Secretary Day altered the requirement concerning the Philippine Islands. Hay was informed that "the insurgents there have become an important factor in the situation and must have just consideration in any terms of settlement. It is most difficult without further knowledge to determine as to the disposition of Philippine Islands." This view reflected the resurgence of Aguinaldo then taking place around Manila with the benevolent encouragement of Admiral Dewey. Thus began the process that over the next few months would greatly revise Washington's policy towards the Philippines. Otherwise, the terms of June 3 remained remarkably stable.[4]

Nothing came of this indirect American pronouncement of war aims. When Hay reported on June 5 that Lord Salisbury was prepared to send the terms to Madrid by way of Vienna, Day immediately informed him that his list "was only intended to advise you of [the President's state of mind] and [was] in no sense to be a suggestion as coming from us." Action should stem from a British initiative; moreover, the United States did not wish to become obligated "by an arrangement made abroad or to admit European intervention in any form." Although the President would receive a message from Spain, the United States "must not be understood as suggesting or proposing overture of peace." In other words, Britain could proceed unofficially, but Spain must inaugurate discussions. When Hay told Salisbury of this requirement, the Prime Minister informed him that the British envoy in Vienna had already approached the Austrian Foreign Minister, Goluchowski, and had come away with the "impression that the minds of the Spanish Government were in such a state that they would offer or accept no terms which

would seem reasonable to us, except at the last extremity." Obviously
Madrid was not yet prepared to accept defeat.[5]

Salisbury did not convey to Hay certain additional items of information that came from Vienna somewhat later. The behavior of the
United States much exercised Goluchowski: "Henceforward Europe
must be prepared to deal with a power which would soon become as
formidable as it was unscrupulous and overbearing," warned the
Austrian. "We should all of us soon learn this to our cost, and more
especially as regards our economic relations with the New World."
Salisbury's informant concluded, "This, I may add, is a favorite theme
of Count Goluchowski." The Spanish-American struggle definitely
aroused continental misgivings about the future role of the United
States in world politics, but none of the great powers contemplated an
untoward intervention in the struggle during the summer of 1898.
Although Spain proved unprepared to negotiate in June, Salisbury's
willingness to convey the American terms confirmed the friendly disposition of Great Britain.[6]

Additional evidence of British benevolence materialized when Spain
around June 15 suggested an international occupation of Manila. The
Spanish ambassador in London intimated to Salisbury that the great
powers should assume control of the Philippine city and hold it without
prejudice to its ultimate disposition. Obviously Spain hoped that this
action would improve its prospects of retaining the Philippines.
Although Salisbury expressed sympathy, he indicated that Britain could
do nothing; such a measure would violate the duties of neutrality. On
June 15 he told Hay about the Spanish proposal, giving as reason for his
lack of responsiveness the claim that there was "no justification of such
breach of neutrality as this proceeding would involve." The Prime
Minister also volunteered the interesting information that only Austria
had exerted pressure in behalf of Madrid. Spain's initiative fared badly
in Paris also. Neither Gabriel Hanotaux nor his successor as Foreign
Minister, Théophile Delcassé, varied from a policy of strict noninterference, whatever their private views. In St. Petersburg, Count
Muraviev had shown some concern about the American attack in the
Philippines, going so far as to propose that France, Russia's ally, should
force Spain to end the war and should take the Pacific islands for itself;
but nothing came of this notion, because Paris refused to act. Germany
manifested some interest in the project to neutralize Manila, but Bülow
desisted when he learned that the other powers opposed it. Overall,
none of the great powers made serious efforts to interfere with
American purposes during the war with Spain. For this reason President
McKinley enjoyed considerable freedom of action in dealing with
Madrid.[7]

Writing to President McKinley after the naval battle of July 3 at Santiago de Cuba, Hay noted that the American victory should have ended the war, "but those Quixotes act more foolishly than ever. They want to force us, after killing them, to disfigure the corpse." He thought that the great powers showed a certain irritation with Spain for not fighting well and also for delaying peace overtures after it became clear that the United States had won. "We have never in all our history had the standing in the world we have now," he concluded, "and this, I am sure, is greatly due to the unfailing dignity, firmness, and wisdom you have shown in every emergency of the past year." Hay need not have worried that Spain would continue its resistance. Beginning on July 7 the naval attaché in London, Lieutenant Colwell—who had developed an intelligence service like that of his counterpart in Paris, Sims—detected indications of Spain's readiness to settle. These reports seemed confirmed when on July 14 Sagasta suspended constitutional guarantees in Spain, hoping thereby to muzzle domestic criticism of his initiative for peace. The persistent American siege of Santiago de Cuba had forced the Spanish Premier's decision to authorize the capitulation of that city and open negotiations for peace.[8]

On July 18 the Duque de Almodóvar del Río, who had replaced Pío Gullón as Foreign Minister in May, inaugurated the quest for peace. He asked his ambassador in Paris, Fernando León y Castillo, to propose that the French government authorize its ambassador in Washington, Jules Cambon, to present a communication to the United States government. Spain would settle on the basis of Cuban independence: "Our principal argument is the suffering imposed by the war upon the inhabitants of that Antille, now so totally blockaded that it is impossible for us to send food there." It was hoped that Cambon could proceed to procure from McKinley or Day "suspension of hostilities, as preliminary to definite negotiations, according to the instructions this Government transmits, in case the tenor of this message receives the approbation of the American Government." Besides the fundamental strategic reality—American command of the seas—there was realization also of the fact that Spain could not stimulate European intervention. Spanish business as well as other interests wished now to end the war before additional disasters, domestic and foreign, befell the nation. This decision to seek peace came just as General Merritt arrived in the Philippines and General Miles invaded Puerto Rico.[9]

There then ensued a tragicomedy of errors that delayed the Spanish initiative for no less than eight crucial days. On July 20 León y Castillo informed Almodóvar that the French government could not act immediately on the matter because the President was out of town, the Foreign Minister ill, and the diplomatic corps poised for a grand reception the next day. To this disconcerting message Almodóvar replied hastily: Not a moment was to be lost; "the capitulation of Manila, which may occur at any time; the occupation of other points in the Philippines; the attack upon Puerto Rico, and perhaps a landing on that island, are all contingencies which compel haste." (No message could have expressed more cogently the success of McKinley's cumulative strategy of widely separated attacks on the periphery of Spanish power at points where the United States possessed overwhelming advantages.) Thus bestirred, León y Castillo obtained French cooperation: On July 22 a letter from the Queen Regent intended for McKinley went to Cambon. María Cristina noted that war had come because her country had refused to grant independence to Cuba or withdraw troops from that island. Spain had fought for "but one object—the vindication of her prestige, her honor, her name." To avoid further horrors, Spain asked that President McKinley make known his terms for peace. Unfortunately this missive was further delayed: Sent in cipher, it could not be delivered until July 26 because the key to the cipher, unavailable in Washington, had to be obtained from the Spanish Consul General in Montreal.[10]

NEGOTIATION OF THE PROTOCOL

After receiving the Queen Regent's message, President McKinley convened the Cabinet to formulate terms for ending what John Hay at just this moment called "the splendid little war." As consultations began in Washington, intelligence from London and Paris—although inaccurate in some respects—correctly reported Spain's desire for an early settlement. Certain American terms were agreed upon without much debate, including three of the items identified in June—independence for Cuba, cession of Puerto Rico in lieu of indemnity, and cession of an island in the Ladrones, probably Guam. However, the question of the Philippines stimulated extensive discussion when various options found adherents within the Cabinet. Secretary of the Interior Cornelius Bliss, Attorney General John W. Griggs, and Secretary of Agriculture James Wilson favored annexation of the entire archipelago; Secretary of the Navy Long, Secretary of State Day, and Secretary of the Treasury Lyman J. Gage preferred merely to acquire a naval base there; neither Secretary of War Alger nor Postmaster General Charles Emory Smith took clear positions. Other possible options discussed were retaining the island of Luzon and leaving the others to Spain, or else restoring all the Philippines to the long-time owner.[11]

During this period, as communications poured into the White

House, President McKinley paid close attention to the views of the country, hoping to gauge public opinion accurately. He wished to avoid a split between himself and the great majority of Americans comparable to that of the immediate prewar months. The President's mail, however, did not reflect a clear consensus. One correspondent, Spencer Borden, argued forcefully for retention of all the Philippines, offering a rationale that closely approximated that the President developed much later on:

> It would be cowardly and pusillanimous for us to turn the islands back to Spain, giving them the power again to misrule the natives who have helped to make Admiral Dewey's position tenable. We would be equally despicable to ask Great Britain to take and care for them—which would make a greater row—and we must never permit these three bully nations that deprived Japan of the fruits of her victory over China [in 1895—Russia, Germany, and France] to play the game with us. There is only one logical course to pursue. Spain has shown herself unfit to rule her colonies, and these that have come into our possession as a result of war, must be held, if we are to fulfill our duties as a nation. If we do not want them as States, we must hold them in trust until they are capable of self-government, giving them the benefits of a Christian civilization which has reached its highest development under our republican institutions.

Others, however, offered equally vigorous criticism of overseas expansion, opposing even the acquisition of Puerto Rico. Moorfield Storey, the Bostonian who before the war had warned of the dangers of victory, and later played a leading role in anti-imperialist agitation, insisted now to Secretary Long that no lawyer could explain why Cuba should be given independence and Puerto Rico denied it. If, Storey said, when the Teller amendment was passed, "we meant to take Porto Rico then, and purposely limited our disclaimer to Cuba, we were not proposing 'an unselfish endeavor to fulfill a duty of humanity,' but a selfish war of conquest, and our declarations will not stand the sober verdict of history." As of the latter days in July, 1898, the voice of the people had not spoken with unanimity concerning disposition of the Spain's ex-colonies.[12]

While the Americans deliberated, Spanish leaders expressed concern—an understandable reaction because of indications that McKinley planned early conquests of Puerto Rico and Manila along with naval operations in Spanish waters. On July 27 Almodóvar complained to León y Castillo about General Miles's landing at Guánica, insisting that "the United States is unwarrantably attempting military aggression, without doubt the object of making more onerous the conditions of peace." Actually, Washington's purpose was principally to force the

early peace negotiations to a conclusion. Almodóvar then sent Cambon
a statement of Spain's position on annexations: He would accept the
loss of Cuba without reserve, although he preferred that the island be
ceded to the United States, but the Puerto Rican and Philippine questions should be dealt with differently. Spain accepted "the principle
of indemnification in reasonable proportion and measure," but,
Almodóvar noted, "the Spanish nation did not provoke the war, and
although fortune has been adverse to us this Government understands
that the conqueror should not be arbiter of territories foreign to Cuba
which have been attacked by the United States." The Liberal ministry
now realized that procrastination might entail unanticipated concessions to the United States.[13]

Cambon worked diligently in the Spanish interest, but entertained
no illusions about the difficulties that lay in his way. To Gabriel
Hanotaux on July 28 he reported realistically on the mood in Washington: "Unfortunately, Mr. McKinley's emotions are transitory, for he is
weak. There are wide divergences of opinion in his Cabinet, not as to
peace itself, but as to the conditions to be imposed on Spain." It was an
election year. "Politicians like Mr. Alger, the Secretary of War, would
sacrifice everything to the demands of the election committees; others
on the contrary, like Mr. Long, Secretary of the Navy, display generous
intentions." Cambon believed that Spain would gain nothing by
adopting the tactics of delay: "If the Madrid Cabinet procrastinates in
its reply and does not resign itself at once to certain necessary sacrifices,
such as Porto Rico, the conditions that will be imposed on it later will
be harder, and in proportion as the discussions are prolonged, circumstances will be less favorable to it." When the French envoy anticipated that McKinley might simply call him in to inquire about
Spain's conception of an appropriate settlement, he asked for power to
respond, informing León y Castillo that the United States intended to
press military operations vigorously until Spain accepted terms.[14]

On July 30 the President conveyed his terms of peace to Cambon:
Spain must relinquish Cuba and evacuate the island immediately. No
monetary indemnity would be exacted but, to satisfy claims made by
American citizens for loss and injury associated with the Cuban disturbance, he required the cession and evacuation of Puerto Rico and also
an island in the Ladrones to be selected later. Finally, for the same
reason—indemnification—the United States was "entitled to hold the
city, bay, and harbor of Manila pending the conclusion of a treaty of
peace."[15]

Cambon argued a bit. Giving notice that Spain would relinquish
Cuba, he asked for a plebiscite to determine whether the Cubans ap-

proved annexation to the United States. Of greater import was his state-ment that the demand for Puerto Rico conflicted with American profes-sions of disinterested concern. When Day reiterated that the United States asked no payment for damages, Cambon replied that the ces-sion of Cuba would constitute the richest of indemnities. McKinley did not yield in these matters, but agreed to change the wording of the Philippine clause as a means of soothing injured pride in Madrid. When Day withdrew to alter the official copies of the American demands, McKinley expressed regret that Spain had not come to terms immediatly after Dewey's victory at Manila Bay. "The conditions which we would then have demanded," he continued, "would have been less rigorous than those of the present, and so if my present demands are refused Spain would necessarily be exposed to greater sacrifices." He asked Cambon to stress this observation in communica-tions to the Liberal ministry. This was consistent with McKinley's earlier efforts to preclude traditional Spanish procrastination. The President also proposed that Washington serve as the site of the peace conference. When Cambon sought an immediate suspension of hostilities, McKinley stated that he would take this step only after Spain accepted the American terms. The Frenchman correctly described the President's posture: "While I deeply regret not obtaining greater concessions," he reported to León y Castillo, "[I] fear that the resolution of the White House will be irrevocable in the future."[16]

Those who talked with McKinley during this period agree that he largely controlled discussion of peace terms within his Administration. The Philippine question posed the only real uncertainty. Faced with conflicting advice, the President decided to postpone a decision. Charles Dawes summarized the situation aptly: "While the President is very conservative in his belief as to the policy of handling the Philip-pines situation, he wants the facts to be carefully considered, without the consideration involving the loss of any present advantage." Another associate, George Cortelyou, recorded an interesting anecdote: After the terms had been communicated to Spain, he remarked to McKinley that the note to Spain offered a good example of how a state paper altered as it underwent examination. The President then "took from his pocket . . . a memorandum in his own handwriting, made on the day of the receipt of the Spanish note, or at about that time, in which he stated what he would require as terms of peace. These . . . were ex-actly those which were finally transmitted." McKinley left no doubt that he had manipulated the Cabinet throughout the discussions to achieve a predetermined outcome.[17]

When Madrid learned of McKinley's desires, Cambon received instructions to seek changes. Almodóvar wanted to substitute something for the cession of Puerto Rico, contending that Spain had not started the war and that the responsibility for indemnification should fall to Cuba. He noted that in 1864, when Prussia and Austria took Schleswig and Holstein from Denmark, the duchies—not Denmark—had paid the indemnity. He also held that the provision concerning the Philippines lacked precision. Arguing that Spain would exercise sovereignty in the archipelago after the conclusion of hostilities, he insisted that "the temporary occupation of Manila, its port, the bay by the Federal Government is to continue only for the time necessary for an understanding between both countries regarding administration reforms." Such changes, he added, would be discussed by the Americans and Spanish only, a procedure that would exclude the Philippine insurgents.[18]

Cambon raised these questions at the White House on August 4, but made little progress. McKinley agreed to hold the peace conference in Paris rather than Washington and to exclude the Filipinos from negotiations concerning the Philippines. He held firm, however, on other matters. Seeking to engender some hope within the Liberal ministry concerning the Philippines, the President said, "The Madrid Government may be assured that up to this time there is nothing determined *a priori* in my mind against Spain; likewise, I consider there is nothing decided against the United States." There is no reason to question McKinley's sincerity in making this statement, although it was certainly intended mainly to encourage an early peace. When Cambon conveyed his personal assessment of the situation to Almodóvar, he observed gloomily, "I have foreseen that the President of the Republic would remain firm, and, since your excellency honors me by asking my personal opinion, I can not but persist in the idea that all vacillation will further aggravate the severity of the conditions." Obviously McKinley had convinced the French intermediary that he would brook no appreciable delay before asking even more of Spain.[19]

At this juncture an untoward incident occurred that might have given Spain some much-needed leverage. On August 4 the "round robin" of American commanders at Santiago de Cuba, which reported the desperate health situation of the American expedition, leaked the news to the press. President McKinley became infuriated when he read the stories, realizing that they constituted public notice of America's inability to hold the only territory so far surrendered by Spain. The public clamor for return of the troops from Cuba provided neither a dignified nor a firm context for conclusion of the negotiations with Spain. Cambon wrote later that, had he known of the situation earlier, he "might have been able to make use of it with Mr. McKinley to obtain better conditions for Spain." However, although the round robin did constitute a certain embarrassment, it is unlikely, given the imminent conquest of Puerto Rico and Manila, that Spain could have made much of the army's plight at Santiago de Cuba. If Sagasta had seized upon this development to delay matters, the American demands would certainly have become more onerous. The episode served primarily to reveal yet again the disadvantages flowing from indiscreet utterances of commanders in the field during delicate diplomatic negotiations.[20]

León y Castillo sensed the weakness inherent in the Spanish position. Having already agreed to give up Cuba, Almodóvar had surrendered his only bargaining chip. In addition, "with Manila in their possession, the future of the Philippines, which must be discussed in the projected conference, will remain absolutely at the mercy of the United States." Conceding that refusal to grant Cuban independence might mean further hostilities, he told Almodóvar that Spain must recognize the consequences of accepting the American terms at this time. The outcome of the pre-armistice negotiations would seriously restrict Spain's freedom of action later on.[21]

On August 7 Almodóvar initiated a final effort to modify the American demands. Cambon was asked to inform McKinley that constitutional constraints precluded Spain from evacuating territory before signing a peace treaty. And, the Cortes had to authorize any such settlement. More important, however, was a second ploy by Almodóvar. In a formal note to Day the Liberal ministry accepted the proposed terms concerning Cuba, Puerto Rico, and an island in the Ladrones, but made stipulations concerning the Philippine Islands. Although the Spanish Cabinet members agreed to discuss the question at a peace conference, "they did not *a priori* renounce the sovereignty of Spain over the archipelago, leaving it to the negotiators to agree as to such reforms which the conditions of these possessions and the level of culture of their natives may render desirable."[22]

Meanwhile all of Washington was reacting against Spain's delaying tactics. No one became more irritated than Captain Mahan. On August 7 he complained bitterly to Secretary Long about the failure to end the war promptly, prefacing his comments with note of a certain "incipient demoralization" within the American armed forces. This unsettling trend, stemming from "the absurd delay of Spain," might gather strength over time, eventually even crippling the navy. He wanted to force a settlement: "Why should not the President send for M. Cambon and civilly tell him the brute truth, viz: that we thoroughly understand that Spain is powerless before us owing to our relative naval supremacy; that she is unable to replace her navy; the delay is for many reasons inconvenient to us; that our terms are a minimum, and therefore an ultimatum; and for these reasons the offer of them, if not accepted, will be withdrawn at noon of next Wednesday [August 10].'' Mahan believed that this course would exact a decision from Madrid. If Spain did not accept the ultimatum, ''let it be known that the war is again on, and start Sampson's armored ships, whether toward Europe as proposed, or north (not for relaxation but for refit) and officers and men will all be contented—even happy.'' In calling for uncompromising diplomacy Mahan expressed not only his own sentiment but that of many others—including President McKinley, once again faced with a critical decision. It is of interest that behind Mahan's hard line lay not only a sense of America's incontrovertible military superiority but concern about morale in the fleet.[23]

When Cambon presented Almodóvar's latest views to Washington on August 9, he provoked a strong reaction. The French envoy reported later that both McKinley and Day became ''visibly annoyed'' as they read the Spanish communication. The President then proceeded somewhat along the lines that Mahan had suggested to Secretary Long, telling Cambon that he would not brook changes in the terms or accept limiting conditions. Cambon then attempted to prolong discussion by noting that the United States Senate lay under constitutional obligations similar to those of the Cortes, but McKinley proposed a procedure to bypass that problem: The two governments could simply sign a protocol explicating the terms and arranging a postwar conference. This executive agreement would not require legislative confirmation; it would merely halt hostilities on the basis of certain preliminary agreements. To hasten the immediate evacuation of Cuba and Puerto Rico the belligerents would appoint commissioners to oversee the process.[24]

Cambon gained nothing from last-minute efforts to soften McKinley's terms. On August 10 Day forwarded a draft protocol that McKinley later described as a ''virtual ultimatum.'' The Frenchman then recommended to Madrid that it accept the American proposal: ''I would express my conviction that if the Madrid Cabinet does not think it possible to accept this document Spain will have nothing more to expect from a conqueror resolved to procure all benefit possible from the advantages it has obtained.'' The terms of August 10 differed from those of July 30 only in the mention of commissions to supervise evacuation of the Antilles. In submitting the draft to Madrid, Cambon made as much as possible of certain alterations in wording, hoping by this device to enhance its palatability. He argued that the demand for evacuation of the Antilles was made only in principle, because of the arrangement to appoint commissioners. Since Article V provided for ratification according to constitutional forms, he considered the protocol merely a prior understanding regarding evacuation itself. To this specious reasoning Cambon added another more important point: Article VI included specific notice that hostilities were to end with the signature of the protocol. The Secretary of War had informed him that food would be shipped to Cuba as soon as the war came to an end, thus alleviating the suffering of the Spanish defenders.[25]

On August 11, at long last the Sagasta ministry accepted the inevitable, confirming the transaction proposed in Washington and consenting to end the war. After a cabinet meeting in Madrid Almodóvar authorized Cambon to sign the protocol for Spain. This act reflected his realization that the United States intended to force an even more drastic outcome if it did not now gain its ends. The garrisons at Havana, Manila, and San Juan, still unconquered, would eventually be forced to capitulate because they could not be resupplied or reinforced by sea. And further hostilities might well entail an attack on the peninsula itself.[26]

On Friday, August 12, at 4:30 P.M., President McKinley and Ambassador Cambon affixed their signatures to the protocol, and the three months' struggle came to an end. Don Eugenio Montero Ríos, soon to head the Spanish peace commission, later summarized the significance of the little ceremony in the White House: "This protocol, as one sees, made the catastrophe definitive and irreparable." It left only one great issue to be decided at Paris—the future of the Philippines. Of course, the outcome of the war ensured that the United States would hold the "whip hand" during the postwar parley; the Philippine question would actually be resolved in Washington rather than Paris.[27]

BACKGROUND OF THE PEACE NEGOTIATIONS

President McKinley quickly selected a peace commission. Secretary Day, who held moderate views about the disposition of the Philippines, was designated chairman of the group. To act for him at the State Department McKinley recalled the experienced diplomatist John Hay from London. Heretofore McKinley had been largely his own secretary of state; he was glad of the opportunity to transfer this responsibility to Hay, who was much more forceful than the self-effacing Day. To represent expansionist sentiment on the commission, McKinley chose a Republican party wheelhorse, Whitelaw Reid, publisher of the New York *Tribune* and former ambassador to France. Three members came from the Senate—which body is charged with giving advice and consent to treaties prior to executive ratification: Cushman K. Davis (Republican from Minnesota), the expansionist chairman of the Foreign Relations Committee, and William P. Frye (Republican from Maine) a "fiery jingo," represented the Republican majority; George Gray (Democrat from Delaware)—the ranking minority member of the Foreign Relations Committee, who professed strongly anti-expansionist views—completed the group. To serve as secretary to the commission McKinley designated one of the Assistant Secretaries of State, the international lawyer John Bassett Moore. At the outset, then, the majority—composed of Reid, Davis, and Frye—favored a "large policy."[28]

Sagasta faced a more difficult task than McKinley in designating plenipotentiaries. Four days after the end of the war, the Conservative Francisco Silvela, one of the Prime Minister's leading critics, inaugurated a painful Spanish self-examination of the disaster, maintaining in an influential statement that Spain was *"sin pulso"* ("without pulse") and that only a massive effort to reconstruct and dignify the action of the state could restore the country to vigor. On September 16 Silvela spoke again, placing blame for the defeat squarely on the shoulders of the Liberal ministry. The Conservative Party then refused to accept representation on the commission sent to negotiate in Paris, forcing Sagasta to rely on members of his own party and professional diplomatists. To head the delegation he chose one of the chiefs of the Liberal Party, the renowned Don Eugenio Montero Ríos, and two other party members, Don Buenaventura Abarzuza and Don José Garnica y Díaz. To provide diplomatic expertise, he named Don Wenceslao Ramírez de Villaurrutia y Villaurrutia, his Minister to Belgium. General of Division Don Rafael Cerero y Sáenz contributed military counsel. Emilio de Ojeda became secretary of the Spanish commission. Sagasta did not, however, select Almodóvar, in part because many Spaniards shared the sentiments of Manuel del Palacio, who composed a vicious quintain proclaiming that in a little more than seven months the Foreign Minister had "lost Cuba, Puerto Rico, the Philippines—and me!" Surely membership on the Spanish commission promised scant political reward. The diplomatist Augusto Conte wrote later that the discussion in Paris "was not properly a negotiation, because negotiation does not exist when one [party] exacts and the other concedes and signs."[29]

Early in September, Spain revealed a significant aspect of its bargaining position. Almodóvar claimed that the capitulation of Manila on August 13 was null, because it had taken place after the signature of the protocol in Washington, advising Cambon, "Those territories which the North Americans occupy in the Philippine Archipelago should be considered as ceded temporarily by Spain, without renunciation of her sovereignty, and not as conquered *manu militari* by a belligerent army.'' This difference, he maintained, was ''essential and the consequences are radically different.'' The American reply maintained, in defiance of most precedents, that suspension of hostilities began when notification reached commanders in the field; it mattered not whether the basis of American authority at Manila was the protocol or the capitulation because ''in either case the powers of the military occupant are the same.'' Almodóvar replied simply that the American note did not refute his contention.[30]

Public opinion in the United States was destined to exercise infinitely greater influence on the President's decisions concerning a peace settlement than arid legal formulas. The attitudes of the American people stemmed from the exhilaration of those events, beginning with Dewey's victory of May 1 and ending with Merritt's achievement of August 13, that thoroughly enmeshed the fortunes of the United States and the distant archipelago in the western Pacific. Although Dewey's enterprise and the subsequent decision to send a small expedition to Manila, constituted parts of a strategic design intended merely to force the early capitulation of Spain rather than to further American overseas expansion, these developments did raise the question of the ultimate political settlement. Various points of view, favoring or opposing acquisition, soon found expression across the nation. This wartime debate posed the possibility of annexing the Philippines, a consideration that had not played a part in the planning of operations at Manila.[31]

As early as May 9, 1898, a well-known writer named Horace N. Fisher had sent Secretary Long a prescient analysis arguing the case for annexation: Dewey's victory constituted ''an event of the first magnitude in the history of the Far East,'' one hardly less imposing than Clive's victory at Plassey that ensured British dominion of India. The great powers would not object to the advent of the United States in East Asia; they much preferred American control of the Philippines to Japanese. Then, reflecting an argument regularly offered at the time, Fisher justified expansion on the grounds that the United States required new markets for its burgeoning industrial production. ''Even now,'' he insisted, ''our domestic consumption can not take more than seventy-five per cent. of our manufactured products. . . . Hence the necessity of great foreign markets for such surplus, with the alternative of curtailment of production or of wages.'' Economic stringency posed serious dangers, including even class war in America. Declining wages already had produced unrest among workers, the result being a tendency to array labor against capital. He thought this outcome more dangerous to American institutions than overseas expansion. Finally, Fisher summarized the larger meaning of the war in the Philippines: "We have indeed come to the parting of the ways and must abandon our international isolation; that we have no foreign interests and responsibilities can no longer be seriously maintained." Here was indeed a powerful exercise in realism, one that could not fail to command the attention of those who heard it from various sources during the exciting summer of 1898.[32]

Some proponents of annexation offered powerful ethical justification for the policy. Another of Long's correspondents, the Rev. Jesse H. Jones, made such a case soon after Dewey's victory. Although he had opposed the war earlier, he was now prepared to make the most of it. The United States should retain the Philippines. "We have taken them by our might; we can not give them up except in utter weakness. . . . And besides we will be false to our duty to that people and to the whole human race to lead the way of freedom and progress, hope and prosperity." Contrasting American virtue and Spanish vice in the traditional manner, he concluded, "Spain must get off this hemisphere. She would not consent to be outgrown; she would have violence. Now she must go." Only in taking this path could that degenerate nation make adequate compensation for the destruction of the *Maine.* Here was an appealing line of argument indeed, associating overseas expansion with the civilizing mission that America has claimed for itself throughout its history, one that stressed duty and sacrifice rather than material benefit.[33]

If proponents of expansion appeared everywhere, a growing group of anti-expansionist advocates advanced opposing views. Another of Long's correspondents, William Endicott, Jr., developed two cogent arguments against annexation in general: The war had been waged to free Cuba, a humanitarian motive that precluded territorial grabs. Moreover, acquisition of overseas colonies would dictate a total change in the nature of American government, particularly because it would require a much-enlarged military establishment. "In my opinion," he continued, "the perils now confronting the republic are greater than at any time in its history, save only during the Civil War. It will be the part of a wise statesmanship to escape these dangers by returning to the traditions of the fathers." Sensitive to accusations of stodginess, he concluded, "It may be old fogeyism but I think George Washington is a safer counsellor to tie to than Senators Mason, Foraker and Lodge."[34]

However arresting the arguments of the anti-imperialists, they were difficult to sustain in the context of growing public sentiment for annexation of the Philippines. What lay behind this burst of emotionalism? Mr. Dooley had an opinion. Finley Peter Dunne recorded this exchange with Mr. Hennessey:

"We're a gr-reat people," said Mr. Hennessey earnestly.
"We ar-re," said Mr. Dooley, "We ar-re that, an' the best iv it is, we know we ar-re."

Burgeoning self-satisfaction, natural at a time of military success, surely affected popular attitudes as much as did arguments based on interest and duty. Senator Lodge, a central figure in the coterie of imperialists who favored expansion, observed during the months of war the mobilization of opinion in favor of taking the Philippines and other locations overseas. On May 24 he had informed Roosevelt, then in training with the Rough Riders, "Unless I am utterly and profoundly mistaken the Administration is now fully committed to the large policy that we both desire." This view stemmed from his knowledge of the energetic efforts within the War Department to send an expedition to Manila. Writing again on June 15, he reported in a similar vein, "The whole policy of annexation is growing rapidly under the irresistible pressure of events." Secretary Day had told him that everyone was agreed on the acquisition of Puerto Rico, the Philippine question being the only unresolved matter. A bit later, after dining with Mahan and Day, Lodge once again expressed his views: The President seemed "all right in his conception of policy," but he might not annex the Philippines if the war came to a premature end. "He is . . . very firm against European interference, but he is worrying over the Philippines—he wants to hold them evidently but is a little timid about it." A favorable straw in the wind was McKinley's order to occupy the island of Guam. If the President did not intend to take the Philippines, Lodge reasoned, why bother with the little island in the Ladrones? As far as he was concerned, the best argument for retention of the Philippines, and the one he thought most persuasive with the public, was "Whatever happens we cannot return to Spain the people whom we have set free. To hand Aguinaldo and his men back to Spain would be an act of infamy." As time passed, Lodge continued to modify earlier estimates of McKinley's instructions. By July 23 he had to admit to Roosevelt that the President, while firm on Cuban independence and annexation of Hawaii and Puerto Rico, had not really made a commitment concerning the distant archipelago: "He is not giving much consideration to the Philippines but the question in his mind is how much he will take there."[35]

The President was not yet decided on his course, a judgment confirmed by his willingness to postpone a final resolution of the issue until the peace conference convened in Paris. One visitor in July reported him as pursuing a policy of first gaining control of the Philippines, Ladrones, and Carolines; later on he would decide what to retain. At the moment he inclined toward keeping only the island of Luzon and fortifying Manila. Although lacking full information, McKinley as yet saw no advantage in taking all the Philippines. Ambassador Hay in London, adept as ever at reading McKinley's mood, reported British support for American annexation and reiterated his belief that the United States was at the pinnacle of its prestige in Europe. Perhaps to hedge his bet he also mentioned certain problems: One was the rapid rise in the islands of Aguinaldo and his adherents. "The more I hear of the state of the Tagalog population and their leaders the more I am convinced of the seriousness of the task which would evolve upon us if we made ourselves permanently responsible for them." He also raised the bogey of European intervention. "I have no doubt that Germany has been intriguing both with Aguinaldo and with Spain. They are most anxious to get a foothold there; but if they do it there will be danger of grave complications with other European powers."[36]

As the war came to an end Lodge noted further signs that McKinley was not yet committed to a "large policy." Writing to Henry White, a friend who was serving under Hay in London, he mentioned uncertainty in Washington, although he was sure that the American people would oppose return of the Philippines and Manila to Spain. "Public opinion is so pronounced that I do not see why there should be hesitation, and yet it looks as if it might be the intention to withdraw as much as possible, which would be to my way of thinking a great mistake, not only with a view to the interests of the country but on account of the immediate political effects." Obviously the partisan Lodge feared that the Republicans might suffer losses in the autumn elections if the Administration repudiated expansion. Others confirmed Lodge's reading of the popular view, such as the annexationist Senator Platt of Connecticut, who reported that nine-tenths of the people in his state wanted to retain all of the Philippines. "If I am to be guided by the views of the best people in the State and the large majority of the people," he concluded, "I shall be compelled to vote against any treaty which allows Spain to continue to exercise sovereignty over any of the inhabitants of those islands."[37]

The President had not yet found a solution to the Philippine puzzle. The signs and portents suggested that he might ultimately have to condone some expansion. Unsure of his final policy, McKinley sought to enlarge his knowledge of the situation in the Philippines. He asked that Dewey return to Washington and report in detail, but the Admiral did not wish to leave his post at a critical moment. As a substitute, General

Merritt was sent to Paris for consultations with the American peace commission. The inimitable Hay summarized the situation very well in his response to a letter from John Bigelow, a correspondent who urged the purchase of the Philippines: "I fear you are right about the Philippines, and I hope the Lord will be good to us poor devils who have to take care of them." He marvelled at Bigelow's desire to pay for the islands: "I should have expected no less of your probity, but how many except those educated by you in the school of morals and diplomacy would agree with you?"[38]

As the American peace commission prepared for departure to Paris, the President took another grudging step toward territorial expansion. Meeting the commissioners on September 16, he solicited their views. Senator Davis wanted to annex Luzon and Manila, hoping thereby to stimulate foreign trade; possibly Holland would take Mindanao, the Sulu group, and the Muslim regions. Senator Frye noted New England's objections to annexation, but favored taking the entire archipelago. Whitelaw Reid supported the two legislators. Only Secretary Day demurred, opposing territorial acquisitions elsewhere than the Caribbean. Senator Gray, who probably would have agreed with Day, did not attend the session. McKinley made certain interesting observations, as recorded in Reid's diary: "He believed the acquisition of territory was naturally attractive to the American mind . . . but thought it would probably be more attractive just now than later on, when the difficulties, expense and loss of life which it entailed, became manifest." What was he prepared to do? "He thought we could not possibly give up Manila, and doubted the wisdom of attempting to hold it without the entire island to which it belonged. Beyond this he did not seem inclined to go." If the President had already made up his mind to take all of the Philippines, he did all he could to conceal his view.[39]

McKinley's formal instructions to the American peace commission reflected the change in his position that had taken place since the early weeks of the war. "The plain teachings of history" justified independence for Cuba and the annexation of Puerto Rico. "It was not compatible with the assurance of permanent peace on or near our own territory that the Spanish flag should remain on this side of the sea." No such argument could sanctify annexations in the Pacific, but he maintained that the nation could not accept less than "the cession in full right and sovereignty of the island of Luzon." Transcendental influences were at work: "Without any original thought to complete or even partial acquisition, the presence and success of our arms at Manila imposes upon us obligations which we cannot disregard. The march of events rules and overrules human action." Although remaining entirely sensitive to the humanitarian motives that had led to the war with Spain, "we can not be unmindful that, without any desire or design on our part, the war has brought us new duties and responsibilities which we must meet and discharge as becomes a great nation on whose growth and career from the beginning the Ruler of Nations has plainly written the high command and pledge of civilization." With these lofty sentiments McKinley surely prefigured a formula for rationalizing a course of action—acquisition of an empire in the western Pacific—for which he had hitherto manifested no personal preference.[40]

McKinley's instructions dealt with various matters besides the Philippines. While confirming the evacuation of Cuba, Puerto Rico, and Guam, the commissioners were enjoined to reject a claim that Madrid might well advance—compensation for public property. "Cession of territory or the relinquishment of sovereignty over and title to it is universally understood to carry with it the public property of the Government by which the cession or relinquishment is made." The President brushed aside the Spanish claim that Jáudenes's capitulation of August 13 could not serve as the legal basis for acquisition of the Philippines. Insisting that Americans had in mind the common good rather than aggrandizement, he expressed willingness to establish equal trading privileges: "Asking only the open door for ourselves, we are ready to accord the open door to others." Additional directions required the commissioners to obtain the release of political prisoners relating to the insurgencies and to revive treaties with Spain suspended because of the war. Finally, McKinley stressed the need for speed in the negotiations, giving as his reason a wish to submit the treaty to the Senate at the beginning of the approaching legislative session. If the commissioners should desire additional guidance, they were authorized to communicate their needs—an arrangement that proved helpful later.[41]

Soon after the commission reached Paris, Reid received important intimations of European attitudes towards the United States. On September 28 the French Foreign Minister, Delcassé, went out of his way to note his careful adherence to the obligations of neutrals during the late conflict. American ambassador Horace Porter, present when Delcassé made this statement, interrupted to say that during the struggle "there had been no hint at any time of any concert with other powers against us." This general indication that France would pose no serious difficulties for the United States reflected the attitude of the other great powers. Despite lingering Spanish hopes, nothing happened to encourage the forlorn prospect of European intervention. Shortly after this talk with Delcassé, León y Castillo sought out Reid, his former diplomatic colleague, and virtually pleaded for mercy. Reid recorded him as saying, "They were poor and defeated, and it became a great and powerful nation like ours, in the moment of its first victory over a foreign power, to show itself as magnanimous as it had been successful." Not content with this effusion León y Castillo later added, "Do not forget we are poor; do not forget we are vanquished; do not forget that after all it was Spain that discovered America; do not forget that this is the first great war you have had with a nation on the continent of Europe, or with any foreign nation; that you have had an astonishing victory, and that you cannot complete it without showing magnanimity." These appeals revealed at the outset that Spain recognized its lack of substantive bargaining power. In the absence of diplomatic support from the great powers, it had to depend for mercy principally upon the good will of the conqueror.[42]

Just as the commission began its labors in Paris, the Filipino emissary Felipe Agoncillo appeared in Washington to argue the case for Philippine independence. On October 1 he had an interview with the President. McKinley merely listened; he suggested that Agoncillo present his views to the State Department in an unofficial memorandum. American representatives carefully avoided any actions that might fortify a Filipino claim that the United States recognized the regime of Aguinaldo. Foiled in Washington, Agoncillo then went to Paris in hopes of influencing events there, but failed to obtain even so much as a personal hearing with the American commissioners. Returning to the United States, he then sought unsuccessfully to see Secretary Hay. When the frustrated Filipino revealed his rebuff to the press, the State Department claimed that it had not received any official communications from him. Agoncillo's failure graphically demonstrated the inability of the insurgents to affect the outcome in Paris or Washington. The Filipino insurgency influenced the negotiations only in the sense that it was adduced as one of the reasons why the United States could not return the Philippines to Spain.[43]

Diplomatic activity during the war of 1898 reflected the fundamental political objectives of the two nations. McKinley worked to force peace upon Spain at the earliest possible moment, and Sagasta attempted to minimize the consequences of probable defeat. At the outset the United States had announced only one war aim—independence for Cuba. Accordingly, Spain's only objective was to retain sovereignty over the Pearl of the Antilles. Early in June, McKinley adopted additional war aims as part of a subtle attempt to bring Spain to the peace table. These requirements included annexation of Puerto Rico and an island in the Ladrones, presumably Guam, and acquisition of "a port and necessary appurtenances" in the Philippines. In the protocol of August 12 Spain accepted all of the American demands except the one dealing with the Philippines. McKinley's only deviation from his earlier policy was to defer disposition of the Philippines to a postwar peace conference. In the instructions provided the American delegation sent to Paris to conclude a definitive peace treaty with their Spanish counterparts, the President specified that the United States could not accept less than the cession of Luzon. This change of front reflected the outburst of popular expansionist sentiment that had materialized during the war and its aftermath. McKinley's directions concerning the Philippines were tentative. If the United States would not take less than Luzon, would it ultimately seek more? This question became the central preoccupation of the negotiators as they worked to conclude the Treaty of Paris during the latter three months of 1898.

TWENTY

The Treaty of Paris

Negotiating strategies at Paris became evident at the very beginning of the peace conference. Prior to sitting down with the Spaniards Whitelaw Reid convinced his colleagues that the American delegation ought to seek agreement on the issues settled in principle by the protocol of August 12, especially the independence of Cuba and the cession of Puerto Rico, before turning to the question of the Philippines. Day wanted to take up the latter immediately, but Reid's proposal prevailed in the American delegation. However, the Spanish commission decided to proceed differently. Seeking to retain control of the Philippines, it hoped to carry the legal argument that Spain still retained sovereignty over the archipelago. At the first session of the conference Eugenio Montero Ríos presented a remonstrance that noted Washington's refusal to permit Spanish attacks on the insurgents or allow the reinforcement of Spanish garrisons. He asserted that the United States had no right to take such actions because it was not sovereign in the Philippines. Montero Ríos advanced the claim that the capitulation at Manila, which took place after the signature of the protocol, could not serve as a legal basis for later negotiations concerning the disposition of the Philippines. At the second meeting of the peace conference on October 3 Day gave notice that the United States had already replied to Spain concerning the validity of the capitulation, insisting that the question lay outside the competence of the negotiators. He then presented proposals relating to Cuba, Puerto Rico, and Guam.

As Day spoke to the commissioners, Reid observed Montero Ríos, who "looked as if he was losing his last friend on earth. . . . The others obviously experienced considerable emotion also at being thus brought face to face with the results of the war [in] the Western Hemisphere."[1]

Like so many Spanish diplomatists before him, Montero Ríos took refuge in delay. Reid wrote McKinley that the Spanish leader was "so long-winded in Spanish that if he had equal command of one or two other languages he would be intolerable." The Spanish delegation hoped by lengthy disquisitions to both wear down American opposition and demonstrate to their countrymen that they had exhausted every possible means of restraining the greedy Yankees. Lacking an alternative course of action, Spain would place the United States in an indefensible position before international opinion by manipulating the plausible view that the Americans could not claim the Philippines by right of conquest. If the delegation could prolong negotiations, sympathy for Spain might develop among the great powers and conceivably pave the way to arbitration—a proceeding from which Spain might benefit. Sagasta may have sought to stall a decision at least until November, hoping that the American Congress elected in that month might force moderate terms upon McKinley. In any event the Spanish commissioners exploited every possible means of slowing a settlement.[2]

Sensing the intentions of the Spanish delegation, the Americans naturally attempted to force expeditious procedure. When Day learned that Spain wanted to take up certain minor questions raised by Spanish commissioners on the bodies then arranging the evacuation of Cuba and Puerto Rico, he immediately got Secretary Hay to agree that such matters should not come before the conference. After President McKinley asked Day to force an early departure of the Spanish garrison from Puerto Rico, the head of the American delegation clearly expressed his reasons for opposing this course: He realized that any discussion of such questions would cause delay. "It would open to them a door which . . . we hoped had been closed finally." Day was pleased when the two commissions agreed to procedures that limited the time devoted to any given issue. If either side made objections to a proposition advanced by the other, a brief could be filed presenting reasons for dissent. After the originator of the proposition had commented on the dissent, the negotiators would arrive at a decision—or else at an impasse.[3]

EARLY NEGOTIATIONS

Montero Ríos attempted to saddle the United States with the responsibility for the so-called Cuban debt, consisting of obligations of Cubans to Spanish citizens incurred during the Cuban conflict, a sum of about $400 million. He recognized that Spanish creditors were exceedingly unlikely to recover claims made on Cuba. Given the catastrophic financial crisis then afflicting Spain, this question took on great significance. The Spanish delegation preferred to transfer sovereignty over Cuba to the United States rather than simply to relinquish it, which transfer might impose liability for satisfaction of the debts upon the Americans rather than the Cubans. Montero Ríos realized that mere relinquishment of sovereignty over Cuba would give the United States "excellent ground for not accepting, or perhaps even discussing anything relative to the transmission of the Cuban debts and obligations which are now pressing upon Spain, so long as there is not a recognized entity which must accept them, and to whose account transfer must be made." Almodóvar supported Montero Ríos, instructing him to advocate transfer of sovereignty over Cuba to the United States so the treaty could specify "mutual rights and obligations"—meaning especially payment of the Cuban debt—with precision.[4]

On October 7 Montero Ríos brought the Cuban debt before the conference in tandem with the question of sovereignty, a tactic that provoked extended debate. Day quickly informed Washington of the American response: "Unless otherwise instructed we expect to take position at once that the Spanish proposals as to so-called Cuban charges and obligations . . . are excluded from discussion by the unconditional relinquishment of sovereignty and title pledged in the protocol of the 12th August. We also expect to stand upon language of protocol as to such relinquishment." This position gained approbation in Washington. The only opposition came from Senator Gray, who wanted to accept sovereignty over Cuba. He believed that tranfer of sovereignty would minimize complications when the United States set about "pacifying [the] island and restoring order in accordance with our own ideas." After a fruitless discussion on October 14, Day proposed to resolve the deadlock by simply drafting a clause providing for Cuban independence in language closely resembling that of the protocol, but this device proved unacceptable to the Spanish commission.[5]

Spanish officials in Paris now had recourse to an exercise in personal diplomacy. At an informal dinner Montero Ríos stated to Whitelaw Reid that Spain wished to realize sufficient money to finance economic development at home out of funds gained from the disposition of its colonies. León y Castillo then advanced the old argument that American acceptance of the Cuban debt would demonstrate magnanimity. Reid remained unmoved; he insisted that the United States could not be expected to pay for Spain's war against the Cubans. Mulling over the significance of his exchange with the Spaniards, he concluded that the overture indicated continuing unwillingness to accept American requirements concerning Cuba, Puerto Rico, and Guam. He suspected that the Spanish delegates hoped by persevering in their intransigence to force arbitration of the Cuban debt question, since they believed Spain would obtain more from an arbitrator than from the American commission.[6]

Recognizing that the Americans meant to hold firm, Montero Ríos proposed a rejoinder that would prevent a resumption of hostilities and cause minimal damage to Spanish sensibilities. To Almodóvar he suggested that Spain could merely announce that it bowed to the American demands under protest, given its inability to offer further armed resistance. He believed that McKinley would not resume the war, because in his scenario the Spanish commissioners would "accede to what is demanded, although we do not acknowledge the right of such demands and protest against their injustice." If his proposal was accepted, Spain would not resume diplomatic intercourse with the United States for an indefinite time; at the same time it offered "the advantage of saving our unfortunate country from new disasters." This abject solution reflected the impotence of the Spanish commissioners. Probably for this reason Almodóvar favored a different approach: Believing that the United States could not countenance a sudden end to the conference, he wanted to propose arbitration when negotiations reached an impasse. If the Americans refused, their actions would "serve to augment the justice of Spain in this contention." This procedure was hardly less abject than that advocated by Montero Ríos. Spain simply had to adopt highly undesirable policies because it lacked power to act otherwise.[7]

Putting Almodóvar's plan into execution, León y Castillo and an influential Spaniard, the Marqués de Comillas, explained the adverse consequences of a deadlock to Whitelaw Reid. Attempting to flatter the American, León y Castillo said, "You are the only diplomat there. It is the duty of a diplomat to find some middle way, to avoid the absolute failure of negotiations, to accomplish something." When Reid proved immovable, the two Spaniards suggested that the conference authorize a mixed commission to apportion the debts between Cuba and Spain. Much to the chagrin of his auditors, Reid adamantly opposed any such proceeding. Despite further Spanish efforts to press for transfer of sovereignty and American assumption of Spain's financial obligations, the American commission held firm. Becoming impatient, Day sought authority from Washington "to repeat that our position on the Cuban debt is final, and that if now again rejected nothing is left to us excepting to give notice of only one more meeting to close the protocol." Hay made no objection. When a meeting on October 24 produced nothing new, it appeared that the conference had reached an impasse.[8]

On October 25 Day suggested a concession of some significance, and thereby brought President McKinley directly into the discussion of the Cuban debt. A clause might be inserted into the treaty obligating the United States to use its good offices with Cuba in arranging compensation to Spain for the costs of having constructed internal improvements, all this "while not contracting any independent liability." A mixed commission could be created to determine obligations under this clause. If such an arrangement were made for Cuba, it would also have to be adopted in the cases of Puerto Rico, Guam, and the Philippine Islands. Day believed that there was merit in Spain's legal contention—namely, that local debts of certain classes could be passed on with transfer of sovereignty. He could not have been pleased when Washington returned a prompt and definitive veto of the project. Hay made no bones about the President's wishes: The United States would not assume any part of the debt or induce Cuba to satisfy any part of it. McKinley thought it "most desirable" that the commission "should adhere strictly to the terms of the protocol." If this course proved fruitless, the Americans could inquire into the Spanish position on local debts—particularly those related to internal improvements—and make recommendations. In the face of Spanish pressure the commission had wavered somewhat, but the President remained firm, as in several crises during the war. His steadiness forced Spain to act.[9]

After the unsuccessful discussion on October 24, Montero Ríos conceived the idea of trading a concession on the debt question for compensation of some sort in connection with the Philippines. To explore this possibility he once again made informal and private inquiries among the Americans. What he intended was simply to turn from the Cuban to the Philippine question, seeking compromise in this altered context. León y Castillo spoke to Ambassador Porter, and the latter agreed to transmit the Spanish suggestion to Day. The Spanish envoy then urged the necessity of compromise upon Reid, because "Montero Rios would be hooted in the streets of Madrid if he obtained no abatement of . . . terms." The American delegate uncharitably replied that he and his colleagues could not expect a welcome at home if they made such concessions, but eventually he hinted at the possibility of some such arrangement. He did not leave without warning León y Castillo that the American people now generally desired the entire Philippine archipelago, even if an influential minority opposed overseas expansion.[10]

Despite the not very promising outcome of the contacts with Porter and Reid, the Spanish commission proceeded with its plan to raise the Philippine question. Accordingly Montero Ríos accepted the American clauses for Cuba, Puerto Rico, and Guam, subject to the outcome of future discussion—which meant that his acceptance could be with-drawn later. Ojeda, the secretary of the Spanish commission, told Day after the formal session that Spain "accepted [the] articles in the hope of liberal treatment in the Philippine Islands," adding the obser-vation that "no government in Spain could sign [a] treaty giving up everything and live, and that such surrender without some relief would mean national bankruptcy." Day decided that Reid's hints to León y Castillo might have prompted the change in Spain's course. For his part Montero Ríos reported to Almodóvar that if no promise of compensa-tion materialized during the discussion of the Philippines, he would ask for suspension of the conference and propose submission of a document stating that, although Spain did not accept the American demands, it must bow to *force majeure*. This gesture constituted "the only road which prudence, combined with dignity, leaves Spain in facing a con-queror who would overthrow in this case the most elementary and sacred principles of justice." Noting the continued deterioration of Spain's position in those parts of the Philippines where the Americans had not penetrated, he concluded in long-suffering language: "The Commission nevertheless will continue struggling with all these misfor-tunes, unshaken in its design to save from shipwreck the interest and, to the last, the dignity of the country." Obviously he doubted that Spain could hope for much from the Americans, who obviously were not in a magnanimous mood.[11]

DECISION TO ANNEX THE PHILIPPINES

While it was debating Cuban questions with the Spanish commis-sioners, the American delegation was consulting various observers in preparation for the forthcoming discussion of the Philippines. General Merritt brought Dewey's noncommittal views to Paris; the Admiral did not take a definitive position concerning disposition of the archipelago, thereby irritating the expansionists on the commission. Merritt told Reid in private that Dewey's political ambitions perhaps were dictating prudence; the old sailor wished to avoid statements that could make him "unavailable as a candidate for the presidency." The General's own views were relatively circumspect, although he appeared to favor retention. Perhaps Merritt, too, harbored political ambitions. The com-mission also interviewed John Foreman, a British expert on the Philip-pines, who strongly advocated American annexation. Reid reported him as being so positive that the anti-expansionist Senator Gray "remarked to me laughingly that he couldn't get a bit of comfort out of the ex-amination even after he introduced such subjects as volcanoes and earthquakes." Another witness who made a distinct impression on the commission was Commander Royal B. Bradford, an American naval officer who expressed considerable concern about German naval ambitions in the Pacific. He wanted the United States to acquire not only the Philippines but also the Carolines and all of the Ladrones, not just Guam.[12]

The commission's investigations generally confirmed the previous outlooks of Davis, Frye, and Reid; they remained strongly in favor of annexing the entire archipelago. To buttress this opinion they offered a composite of views presented to the commission; these included the lack of a logical way to partition the islands; the fact that the whole island group could be defended as easily as a part; the probability that partition would cause turbulence among the indigenous population; the untoward consequences for commerce that might stem from partition; the belief that the United States had a moral obligation not to return the Philippines to a repressive power; and the claim that benefits would accrue to the Filipinos as a consequence of American sovereignty.

However, Senator Gray continued to oppose acquisition of the Philippines, advancing a number of reasons. The islands were not contiguous with the United States; possession would require an expanded navy; American labor might suffer from annexation; divisions might develop in the United States over what he called the "church question," a reference to the influence of the Roman Catholic Church; the United States had no obligation to the Filipinos even if it had conducted military operations in the Philippines against Spain; the American system of government did not include provisions for colonial administration of subject peoples; and annexation would sully the fine moral object of the war.

Day, in contrast, decided to favor somewhat more extensive acquisitions than before. He proposed the annexation of Luzon and certain adjacent islands to guarantee security in the China Sea. He also proposed to ensure free commercial intercourse throughout the archipelago so Spain could not alienate the remaining islands to another power. Many benefits would flow from this policy: "This gives us practical control of the situation, with a base for the navy and commerce in the East, and responsibility for the people to whom we owe obligation and those most likely to become fit for self-government." It limited, he maintained, the responsibilities of colonial administration without precluding territorial acquisitions in the future. "It does not leave us open to the imputation of following [an] agreement to negotiate with demand for whole [Philippines]." Day was closer in his views to the President than any other commissioner. It seems very probable that in resisting the extreme expansionists he thought himself to be supporting McKinley's more moderate outlook. In any event he was far removed from the majority on the commission.[13]

The views of the President, with whom the final decision lay, still remained fluid. At the end of September he talked with General Francis V. Greene, just returned from Manila, and these conversations helped shape his decision. According to Margaret Leech, McKinley "learned enough to convince him that it was to the interest of the United States to take the archipelago, and that no other disposition would give peace and prosperity to the inhabitants." Moreover, he gained in knowledge of the simmering conflict between American and Filipino troops at Manila, a subject of continuing concern in Washington.

In deciding his course the President gave little or no thought to the views of Spain; uppermost in his mind was the state of domestic opinion. To test the mood of the nation he decided to tour the Middle West. If the midwestern bulwark of the Republican Party favored annexation of the Philippines, he might safely ignore opposition evident in other parts of the country. McKinley's behavior strongly suggests that he well remembered his narrow escape from political disaster just prior to the war, when he had desperately sought an alternative to violence despite an overwhelming public clamor. Like so many chief executives, he found himself forced to a choice he did not wish to make. "We are in an anomalous position," he said. "The people want us to hold everything but the soldiers, forgetting that without them we could not hold anything."[14]

From October 11 to October 21 the President travelled extensively in the nation's heartland, seeking to ascertain the desires of the people. At Tama, Iowa on October 11 he probed cautiously, posing the issue of responsibility: "We want to preserve carefully all the old life of the nation,—the dear old life of the nation and our cherished institutions,—but we do not want to shirk a single responsibility that has been put upon us by the results of the war." On the same day in a speech at Boone, Iowa he raised another matter, the necessity for national unity: "We were all together in the fight; we must all be together in the conclusion. [Cheers.] This is not time for divided counsels. This is the solemn hour demanding the highest wisdom and the best statesmanship of every section of our country, and, thank God, there is no North, no South, no East, no West, but all Americans forever. [Great applause.]" Thus auspiciously the tour began, and the President warmed to his task.[15]

Encouraged by the reaction to these initial probes, the President spoke less and less guardedly as he traversed the Middle West. At Omaha, Nebraska, on October 12, during a visit to the Trans-Mississippi Exposition, he made the most publicized speech of the tour. Once again he insisted that the United States had not sought war: "To avoid it, if this could be done in honor and justice to the rights of our neighbors and ourselves, was our constant prayer." Although Americans had not asked for the challenges that arose in the aftermath of war, he sounded the note of responsibility. "Now, as then, we will do our duty." The next day, at Ottumwa, Iowa, he brought together the themes of national unity and responsibility: "We have been united up to this hour; we do not want to be divided now. And we want the best wisdom of the whole country, the best statesmanship of the country, and the best public sentiment of the country to help determine what the duty of the American nation is, and when that is once determined, we will do it without fear or hesitation. [Great applause.]" As the trip went on he allowed another element to creep into his public utterances—an appeal to the humanitarian instincts of the nation. At Springfield, Illinois he spoke explicitly on this subject. "We went to war, not because we wanted to, but because humanity demanded it. And having gone to war for humanity's sake, we must accept no settlement that will not take into account the interests of humanity. [Continued applause.]" And, finally, there was the theme of destiny, developed clearly in Chicago, Illinois on October 18: "My countrymen, the currents of destiny flow through the hearts of the people. Who will check them? Who will divert them? And the movements of men, planned and designed by the Master of men, will never be interrupted by the American people." Higher powers, therefore, were at work in connection with the Philippines. Who were Americans to stand in the way?[16]

As the tour came to a close McKinley blended the themes of humanity, duty, and destiny in a second speech at Chicago on October 19. The war with Spain had been waged to halt "oppression at our very doors," not to gain territory. "This noble sentiment must continue to animate us, and we must give to the world the full demonstration of the sincerity of our purpose." Duty, he insisted, decided destiny. "Destiny which results from the duty performed may bring anxiety and perils, but never failure and dishonor. Pursuing duty may not always lead by smooth paths, . . . but pursuing duty for duty's sake is always sure and safe and honorable." With these sentiments McKinley completed his consultation of the democracy. He returned to Washington prepared to make his decision concerning the Philippines.[17]

The President had learned what he set out to discover; the great mass of his supporters approved annexation of all the Philippines. Had McKinley followed his own predilections, it seems most unlikely that he would have kept all or even part of them. A few months later, when he

asked President Jacob Gould Schurman of Cornell University to make a
visit to the Philippines as head of a commission of inquiry, the academi-
cian demurred, saying that he opposed overseas expansion. The President responded quickly, "Oh, that need not trouble you. I didn't want
the Philippine Islands, either; and in the protocol to the treaty I left
myself free not to take them; but—in the end there was no
alternative." Among those options proposed were annexation of Manila
or Luzon only; Philippine independence; an American protectorate;
return of the archipelago to Spain; annexation by another power; and
partition among several powers. All of these were less acceptable to
McKinley than American sovereignty. In deciding the question the
President had not governed events; events had governed him. Remembering the hysteria early in 1898 after the sinking of the *Maine*, he
feared to contest the popular mood. Having almost lost control of the
nation before the war, he felt compelled to follow the people after its
end when the spoils were under discussion. To justify an uncomfortable
decision he developed the comforting themes of unity, humanity, duty,
and destiny.[18]

On one occasion several months later the usually circumspect President privately explained his reason for deciding to annex all of the
Philippine Islands. Henry S. Pritchett, a geographer, had become an acquaintance at the White House during the war, when he supplied maps
for the President's use. On May 2, 1899, in Pritchett's presence,
McKinley mused about the past. At the beginning of the war, he
began, he had opposed adding anything to the national domain, even
the Hawaiian Islands and Puerto Rico. Over time, however, he had to
face the consequences of declining to annex those strategic locations.
Their acquisition, he had decided, would constitute "the least dangerous experiment." At that point he was still "entirely opposed"
to taking the Philippines, but again eventually sensed the insufficiency
of various options. He first proposed to take only a coaling station. Next
he considered taking only Luzon. Finally, he decided that the course of
wisdom was to annex everything. McKinley apparently did not tell Pritchett why he changed his views, but the latter thought his motives quite
apparent: The President recognized that the American people desired
to annex the islands, and he believed that the country could perform
civilizing labors there—an enterprise that would have a purifying effect
at home. Did McKinley truly bare his soul to Pritchett? No one can be
certain, but this version of events comports more closely with available
evidence than the view that McKinley covertly pursued an expansionist
design from the beginning of the Cuban excitement. The pacific President, cautious to the core, genuinely opposed overseas expansion. He

accepted it eventually because over time, given the state of public opinion, he could divine no safe alternative.[19]

In the end many people of humane and conservative spirit who initially had resisted overseas expansion came to support it. Representative of this group was one of the most attractive public men of his times, Secretary of the Navy Long. On November 1, 1898, writing to a neighbor in Hingham, Massachusetts, he struggled to explain why he had decided to support the President, even though "all my instincts and prejudices are against anything like expansion in any respect." He preferred the United States "as it was in the first half of this century, provincial, dominated by the New England idea, and merely a natural outgrowth which for two hundred years had been going along in the lines of the Fathers." Unfortunately the rural paradise could no longer maintain itself. "I cannot shut my eyes to the march of events—a march which seems to be beyond human control." When the war began, Dewey had struck hard at Manila. Thereafter it could not be abandoned "because our military hold there was one of the most strenuous elements which brought Spain to terms." At the time of this statement of Long's, more than three months after the end of the fighting, no one thought that the archipelago would be either surrendered entirely to its inhabitants or returned to Spain. He agreed with McKinley that the United States had acquired a certain responsibility. The great difficulty was that "the Philippine group is practically an integrity, of which Manila is the heart." This fact militated against partial acquisition. Long would prefer to get rid of the Philippines and every other location except those on the North American continent, but at the same time he believed that opponents of overseas expansion exaggerated its dangers. "We have been expanding ever since the nation began. We have met and solved all the problems that have come with this expansion; we shall meet and solve any that may hereafter arise."

Someone had told him, continued Long, that the acquisition of Hawaii was the beginning of the end for the country, but he scoffed at this notion: "The beginning of the end occurred over an hundred years ago, when the Declaration of Independence was made." Someday the country would encounter insoluble problems, but until that time "the only [sound] statesmanship is to do the best that can be done under existing circumstances." What were those circumstances? "You and I don't want the Philippines," he continued, "but it's no use disguising the fact that an overwhelming majority of the people do, and among them is a vast number of most intelligent men and women, professors of colleges, heads of newspapers, clergymen. . . ." He took heart in the observation that if in America there was "political pulling and hauling and fraud and greed and meanness . . . there will also come the rapidly developing influence of Christian civilization and American enterprise and growth." Here then, was an arresting perspective. If McKinley habitually concealed his inner thoughts, Secretary Long and others of like persuasion did not. The Secretary's diary and correspondence of 1898 reveal fully his acceptance of expansion, even if he never became an enthusiast. If in so doing he erred, as many believe today, it was not because he was a fool, coward, criminal, or dupe. Many others travelled a similar road, including the President of the United States.[20]

Word of the President's decision reached Paris soon after his midwestern trip. On October 26 McKinley sent official notice that the American commission should negotiate annexation of the entire Philippine archipelago. Summarizing the other possible policies, he concluded that none were acceptable. Acquisition of Luzon alone, "leaving the rest of the islands subject to Spanish rule, or the subject of future contention, can not be justified on political, commercial, or humanitarian grounds." The United States must acquire the entire archipelago. "The President reaches this conclusion after the most thorough consideration of the whole subject, and is deeply sensitive of the grave responsibilities it will impose, believing that this course will entail less trouble than any other, and besides will best serve the interests of the people involved, for whose welfare we cannot escape responsibility." Two days later Secretary Hay added further information and guidance for the commissioners: The islands could probably be claimed by right of conquest, and the commissioners should not yield this point, although the question of annexation should be subject to negotiation as specified in the protocol. Presumably Hay realized that, having insisted on observing the letter of that document in dealing with other issues, it could not be ignored in treating the question of the Philippines. The Secretary did not fail to emphasize certain of the themes that McKinley had developed during his recent trip to the Midwest. "It is imperative upon us that as victors we should be governed only by motives which will exalt our nation. . . . Territorial expansion should be our least concern; that we shall not shirk the moral obligations of our victory is of the greatest. . . . The single consideration of duty and humanity" influenced the President.[21]

Senator Gray was downcast, confessing that "he felt as if he had made a mistake in coming." He soon concluded however that, although he would not conceal his personal views after returning to the United States, he felt bound while in Paris to support the President and the decisions of the commission.[22]

CONCLUSION OF NEGOTIATIONS

The delegates now possessed final instructions concerning the one question of policy in the September 16 directive that underwent notable change during the peace negotiations. On October 31 Day announced the American desire to annex all of the Philippines, noting that the United States would provide compensation to Spain for "necessary [public] works and improvements of a pacific character." This step confirmed the worst suspicions of the Spaniards. Montero Ríos expressed "amazement" at the scope of the demand, claiming that England, Germany, and Russia would not find this course "very much in harmony with the interest of each in the extreme Orient." León y Castillo decided that the United States wanted "to deny the Cuban debt and purchase the Philippines for the least sum possible." What was to be done? Almodóvar's orders were to delay: First, the commission should persist in retaining the islands. Then the line of defense would be to indicate Spain's willingness to rent "these colonies to development companies, under conditions which safeguard all interests." If the United States rejected this scheme, Spain could then demand suspension of negotiations so the commissioners could consult their superiors in Madrid. Almodóvar was thinking of the forthcoming vote in the United States: "Meanwhile, we shall see if the American elections by new conditions change the aspect of the negotiations." Outlining this scheme to León y Castillo, Almodóvar summarized his motives: "By means of these alternative propositions we shall be able to continue [negotiations] during the month until we see if the horizon improves." He had no illusions about the American purposes. "I consider . . . that the intention of the Americans is to annex everything of value in the colonial empire of Spain with the least sacrifice possible, and we should exert ourselves to prevent this."[23]

The uncertain situation in Paris led to some nervousness within the American commission. Senator Gray concluded that Spain might break off negotiations. Reid and Frye were more optimistic, basing their hopes for a successful outcome on the United States promise to compensate Spain for the cession, but neither was truly confident. Frye informed McKinley of his fear that negotiations might fail, proposing to offer $10 to $20 million in compensation: "If no treaty then war, a continued disturbance of business, and expenditure of a million dollars a day, and further loss of life." He also expressed concern because the United States had not seized the Caroline Islands—"infinitely more valuable than the Ladrones." If hostilities should resume, stated Frye, Dewey should take not only all of the Philippines but the Carolines.[24]

McKinley responded in soothing terms, noting his policy of generosity as long as this course did not compromise principle or duty. His commissioners were not "to disregard well-established precedents or make any conditions which will not be worthy of ourselves and merit the approval of the best judgments of mankind." Most important, he was fully prepared to offer "a reasonable sum of money in order to cover peace improvements which are fairly chargeable to us under established precedents." This statement must have eased the disquiet among the commissioners to a considerable degree, as it provided a means of propitiating the Spanish commission.[25]

However, at about this time the American commissioners decided that they could not establish the validity of the capitulation, and Day so informed Washington. "Captures made after agreement of armistice must be disregarded and status quo restored as far as practicable." The United States could annex the Philippines "only as indemnity for losses and expenses of the war." In this instance, however, the President proved adamant. Hay offered the curious view that "the destruction of the Spanish fleet on May 1 was the conquest of Manila, the capital of the Philippines." Apparently to stiffen the resolve of the commission, the Secretary of State reported McKinley's confidence that it would negotiate a settlement "on just and honorable grounds." Day could only answer that the commission had not yielded the claim for the Philippines based on the right of conquest, but that a majority of the commissioners did not believe its use in negotiations would result in a favorable outcome. He noted the obvious flaw in the claim that Manila had been conquered on May 1: "Subsequent military operations and capitulation no less than mutual acceptance of protocol preclude making demands upon that ground." Senator Davis insisted that indemnity, general military success, or the future security and welfare of the islands provided better grounds for cession than "perfected territorial conquest."[26]

During all these exchanges the President stood firm. Although he recognized the difficulties that his commissioners faced in Paris, he doggedly refused to relinquish the claim of victory as the basis for annexation. Its abandonment would cause a certain embarrassment, and nothing in the situation seemed to require the President to accept this and the attendant political disabilities. Also, firmness at this point would buttress his intention to reject unreasonable Spanish claims for compensation.[27]

Meanwhile the Spanish commission practiced the diplomacy at which it was most adept, the delaying policy prescribed by Almodóvar, although Montero Ríos proved less than happy with this course. On

November 4 the Americans received a Spanish document objecting to cession of the Philippines in which it was argued that Spain retained sovereignty in the Philippines and the United States could not raise a subject not mentioned in the protocol; nothing had occurred to justify expanded American demands. In communications to Almodóvar, Montero Ríos complained about the line he was supposed to take should the Americans reject the Spanish note. To propose making leases to development companies was to imply that Spain lacked capacity to administer the Philippines, and in any event the United States was most unlikely to accept any such arrangement because it offered no advantages. Almodóvar then told Montero Ríos that he should respond to an American ultimatum by simply asking for a suspension of negotiations. What could come of further delay? He hinted that help might materialize: "The interference of European interests is not impossible."[28]

On November 9, following its instructions from Washington, the American commission absolutely rebuffed the Spanish contentions and reiterated the arguments it had advanced earlier against them—an act that stimulated Spanish efforts to preclude a premature conclusion of negotiations. When Montero Ríos asked Almodóvar for instructions, acting on the impression that the Americans might well refuse to treat further, the Foreign Minister merely reiterated the basic views that Spain had advanced all along: Cession of Cuba relieved his country of responsibility for the Cuban debt, and the United States had never acquired sovereignty over the Philippine Islands. Should the Americans reject Spain's views on the Cuban debt, the Spanish commission should "declare that the right is reserved to treat with . . . [Cuba], solemnly declining all responsibility as to the claims of the creditors of such debt which may arise." As to the Philippines, "force, alone, which we can not resist, would oblige us to submit to the loss, but not until exhausting any other means to guard our rights." This statement indicates that, when pressed to the wall, the Spanish government intended to concede the issue. For his part Montero Ríos, concerned that the conference might soon break up, wanted to place the onus for this possible outcome on the Americans by proposing arbitration of the Philippine question (he knew that the United States would not accept this procedure). Almodóvar gave permission to make this suggestion. Should the Americans refuse, Montero Ríos was to suspend the negotiations. Clearly Madrid was at a loss to think of anything other than various expedients to gain time, hoping no doubt for a miracle.[29]

At this juncture the American commissioners, finding themselves in a quandary, requested instructions from Washington, at the same time sending along their views on the correct course of action. Day was still unreconciled to annexation of all the Philippines, arguing that control of Luzon and certain adjacent islands would provide sufficient support for naval and commercial operations. If the whole group was acquired, he recommended a payment of $25 million, taking into account the defeated adversary's bankruptcy and loss of colonial revenues. If necessary he was prepared to leave Mindanao and the Sulus to Spain. Frye remained firm for acquiring everything, proposing a payment of $10 million. If necessary, he would settle for Luzon, Mindoro, and Palawan along with one of the Carolines (Ponape). Spain, he felt, must release all political prisoners and ensure freedom of religion in all its Pacific possessions. It must also grant cable landing rights in the Pacific, the Canary Islands, Spain itself, and possessions elsewhere in Africa and the Mediterranean Sea. Senator Gray remained opposed to territorial acquisitions, but if the United States did expand, he favored "such reasonable concessions as would comport with the magnanimity of a great nation dealing with a weak and prostrate foe" rather than a policy of "forcible seizure." Whitelaw Reid wanted to take all of the Philippines, basing this policy on the principle of indemnity. If compromise became necessary, he proposed to leave Mindanao and the Sulus to Spain in return for the Ladrones and the Carolines. He too wanted Spain to guarantee religious freedom and free trade in the Philippines. If neither of these suggestions proved feasible, Reid urged still another option: The United States could take both the Philippines and the Carolines, offering $12 to $15 million for them. Most peremptory in his views was Senator Davis, who wanted the entire Philippines, Puerto Rico, Guam, and Cuban independence, all without compensation to Spain. Convinced that Spain was delaying settlement in hopes of eventual European intervention, he insisted, "We shall never get a treaty except as a result of such an unyielding ultimatum."[30]

After Hay considered this information he transmitted an instruction that was to guide the commissioners throughout the remaining negotiations. The United States, he began, was entitled to an indemnity, and Spain was able to pay. Also, the Filipinos could not be subjected to Spanish rule once again: "Willing or not, we have the responsibility of duty which we can not escape." The commissioners should thus insist on cession of the Philippines. As compensation they could offer $10 to $20 million, and even more if it was feasible to "get cession of a naval and telegraph station in the Carolines and the several cessions and guarantees, so far as applicable, enumerated in the views of Commissioners Frye and Reid." Partition of the Philippines could not be allowed; it would lead only to future embarrassments. The United States could conceivably yield on issues such as indemnity, trade, and commerce, "but the questions of duty and humanity appeal to the President so strongly that he can find no appropriate answer but the one he has here marked out." Hay counselled flexibility, but warned against Spanish procrastination.[31]

On November 21 the American commission presented an ultimatum. Somewhat earlier Montero Ríos had made his call for arbitration, but Day and his colleagues decided to state their requirements and give Spain a week to respond. No one knew whether Madrid would yield, but Reid professed to a certain optimism. Inside information in his possession indicated that the Queen Regent was ready to give in but Sagasta still hesitated; concession to the Americans might force his "permanent exile from power." Day reported activity on the other side intended to shake the resolve of the American commission, but President McKinley refused to bend, as firm in peace negotiations as in wartime councils. The ultimatum required that Spain accept $20 million for the Philippines. Both sides would relinquish claims of all classes, and Spanish traders could have free access to the islands for ten years. When these matters were arranged and final agreement reached on the clauses relating to Cuba, Puerto Rico, and Guam, the United States wished to take up several additional matters—a guarantee of religious liberty in the Caroline Islands, liberation of political prisoners in Cuba and the Philippines, annexation of the island of Kusaie in the Carolines along with cable landing rights elsewhere, and renewal of treaties in force prior to the war. Day specified that Montero Ríos and his colleagues must reply to this program by November 28, but was informed that a response would be forthcoming sooner. Day explained the situation tersely to President McKinley: "If the Spanish Commissioners refuse our proposition, . . . we shall give notice that our offer was final and nothing remains except to close the negotiation."[32]

The principal novelty in the ultimatum was the reference to the island of Kusaie, a result of naval considerations. Commander Royal B. Bradford had impressed the strategic significance of the Carolines and the Ladrones upon the commissioners. These island groups commanded the line of communications from Hawaii to the Philippines. In addition, the naval officer had predicted that Germany would take whatever did not fall to the United States. This argument led Reid, Davis, and Frye to urge the acquisition particularly of Kusaie—sometimes called Ualan—in the Carolines, although they considered other islands such as Ponape.[33]

Bradford was quite correct in his estimate of German intentions in the Pacific; Berlin was eyeing not only Mindanao and the Sulus within

the Philippine group but also the Carolines and the Samoas. Throughout the war indications of this appetite had come to the attention of the United States. Most important was the flurry associated with
Admiral Diederichs's presence at Manila Bay, but American officials
also noted other, less dramatic events: On May 14, for example, John
Hay had a conversation in London with Count Paul von Hatzfelt, the
German ambassador to the Court of St. James's, who while denying
that his nation was unfriendly toward the United States, also indicated
that it sought coaling stations in the Pacific. Something might be
worked out, said Hatzfelt, as an aspect of a Philippine settlement. He
mentioned the Carolines; probably he had in mind also Mindanao and
the Sulus: Concerning other locations, Germany would not oppose
American acquisition of the Hawaiian Islands but remained much interested in the Samoas. To all this information Hay remained noncommittal, stating only that he could give no word of eventual American
policy toward the Philippines. The President was disposed to
magnanimity—but less so with each passing day of warfare.[34]

In July the temporary chief of the German Foreign Office, Baron
Oswald von Richthofen, unofficially approached the American ambassador, Andrew Dickson White, with the suggestion that in return
for Germany's "good will" the United States should allow Berlin to acquire the Samoas, Carolines, and a naval station in the Philippines.
When the naval attaché, Commander Francis M. Barber, learned of this
conversation, he took umbrage and rashly cabled the Navy Department
that it should order "immediate doubling [of] Dewey's squadron via
Suez Canal as unofficial reply, to avoid future complication." This
political counsel from a naval source naturally aroused irritation in
Washington. Secretary Long immediately rebuked Barber: "You have
unintentionally exceeded your duties as Naval Attache in yesterday's
cable. The matter reported belonged only to the Ambassador to report
to the State Department." This exchange probably explains why Long
cabled Dewey on July 19: "Avoid military occupation of the Caroline
Islands or military interference with them."[35]

Ambassador White, however, did not leave well enough alone; at the
end of July he encouraged Richthofen to think that the United States
might discuss possible territorial dispositions in the Pacific with Germany. This initiative, completely unauthorized and undesired by
Washington, drew a message from Day that amounted to a reprimand.
The United States, White learned, had announced no Philippine
policy. "Under these circumstances, the suggestion contained in your
dispatch that we foreshadow . . . a policy in part or by indirection
through assurances given in advance to a neutral power cannot fail to be

untimely and embarrassing." Obviously the President objected to any activity at this time that might conceivably limit his freedom of action later on in deciding the ticklish Philippine question.[36]

Germany soon entered into secret negotiations with Spain for the purchase of various island groups in the Pacific, realizing that it probably could not strike a bargain with the United States. Around August 8 Richthofen heard from Madrid that Spain might dispose of all its overseas possessions. He then ordered inquiries about the Philippines as well as the Sulus, the Carolines, the Ladrones, and in the Atlantic the Canary Islands and Fernando Po. After learning of the August 12 protocol, Berlin concentrated on the Carolines and the Ladrones. On August 13 Richtofen ordered inquiries about Kusaie, Yap, and Ponape in the Carolines. This initiative led directly to a secret understanding between Germany and Spain, reached on September 10, that provided for cession of the three islands to Germany, conditional upon the outcome of Spanish negotiations with the United States concerning the Philippines. This arrangement was concealed from the American commission at Paris. It may not even have been known to Montero Ríos.[37]

German diplomats reacted immediately when the American commission began to consider acquisitions in the Carolines. The German envoy in Paris, Count Herbert Münster, went out of his way on several occasions to assure Whitelaw Reid that Germany had no present interest in the Philippines. On November 25 he went so far as to inquire whether Reid's name might be used in German negotiations concerning the Carolines with Madrid or Washington. Reid declined permission and immediately reported the incident to Day. Reid noted in his diary that the chairman of the commission appeared "impressed with the idea that this situation furnished one reason more for having as little delay as possible in completing our negotiations." Surely, provided the American commission performed competently in Paris, real difficulties would materialize only if European nations intervened in the settlement with Spain. Day and his colleagues would indeed have been exercised if they had known that Germany was actively contending for the Carolines at the end of November and had already made a preliminary secret arrangement to purchase them from Spain.[38]

After the American ultimatum of November 21 Spain carefully calculated its response. The commissioners in Paris divided, with Abarzuza and Villaurrutia arguing that the Americans would budge no further, and Montero Ríos, Garnica, and Cerero insisting on the possibility of further negotiations. Montero Ríos proposed either to offer both the Antilles and Philippines to Washington with the proviso that all debts be passed along with them or to make the cession with the understanding that the United States would underwrite the sum required to discharge the debts. If the Americans refused these propositions, he preferred to leave the islands to the United States, for lack of the ability to defend them, and end the negotiations without signing a formal treaty. The ultimatum placed Almodóvar in a quandary. In a cable to Montero Ríos he explained his difficulty: "If it were possible to investigate the real temper of mind of the American Government in case we retire without signing, we could decide with more certainty such a grave matter." What concerned him was the possibility, should the Spaniards walk out in Paris, that the United States might immediately resume hostilities, possibly against the Canary Islands or the Spanish coast itself. On November 24 Montero Ríos came up with three possible propositions to make to the United States, pursuing his general notion of making a cession in return for American assumption of debts. Receiving permission to submit his schemes to the American commission, Montero Ríos concluded that meeting with refusal would provide "one more proof of the abnegation of Spain to the limit consonant with her dignity and of the arbitrary and uncompromising attitude of the United States." No statement could be more indicative of the Spanish impotence.[39]

When the Americans received the Spanish propositions, they transmitted a summary of their views to Washington. Day, Davis, and Reid wanted to remain firmly behind the earlier ultimatum; Frye and Gray were prepared to leave Mindanao and Joló to Spain in return for Kusaie, although Gray preferred to take the entire archipelago and accept arbitration of the debt question. Once again President McKinley yielded not a whit. All he would do was remind the commission of his instruction sent November 13, in which he authorized them to offer additional compensation for an island in the Carolines. This action suggests that interest in the Carolines had quickened somewhat in Washington, presumably in response to the concern of the commission.[40]

However, as the Americans considered Montero Ríos's propositions, the Sagasta ministry finally brought itself to accept the ultimatum. On November 25 Almodóvar ordered his commissioners to sign the treaty and at the same time make appropriate protests. As one reason for this decision he cited the possibility that further delay might lead the United States to resume armed action against Spain. He referred also to possible domestic complications: "The Government . . . does not lose sight of the internal state of the country, whose restlessness is due to some extent, no doubt, to the international conflict pending; its duration provoking alarm in the prudent part of the nation, which desires that it be terminated, and serving as a constant stimulant to the agitators.'' From beginning to end the possibility of tumult at home had influenced Spanish behavior in dealing with the United States. Sagasta had accepted war to head off revolution; he sought peace for the same reason. The note of the Foreign Minister did not authorize negotiations concerning other topics—sale of the Carolines, cable landing rights, religious liberty, and renewal of treaties in existence before the war. When Montero Ríos received this instruction, he put up some resistance, asking whether Madrid would accept American agreement to one of his schemes—a plan to cede the Philippines without Mindanao and Joló for $50 million. Was this suggestion the result of his learning about minor differences within the American commission? Whatever the case, Almodóvar ordered his agent to sign the treaty without further discussion. If Spain left the negotiating table without further action, as Montero Ríos had proposed earlier, the deed ''might produce subsequent complications and even greater evils for our country, which is anxious to escape from this situation.'' He saw no choice except ''to succumb to force, accepting that [American] proposition, but as a whole, without analyzing or discussing any of its parts, which are all alike unjust.'' In this manner Almodóvar indirectly indicated willingness to accept the $20 million offered as compensation.[41]

Montero Ríos revealed the Spanish decision in a plenary session of the conference on November 28. After issuing his protest, he stated that Spain would sign a treaty embodying the final American terms. Reid described the somber session: ''The scene when they presented their answer to our ultimatum in the Salle des conferences was dignified and mournful. They looked and no doubt felt as if they were at the funeral of some dear one in the family.'' Nevertheless everyone behaved well; ''their courtesy was perfect; and I was proud of the considerate and perfect bearing of our people also.'' Montero Ríos, anxious to separate himself from the final discussions in Paris, asked permission of Almodóvar to return immediately to Madrid but apparently did not receive it, for he continued on until the end.[42]

For two more weeks the commissions discussed additions to the treaty, but few were made during this time. Spain sought commercial concessions in the Antilles in exchange for Kusaie, but nothing came of this. The United States offered to repatriate the Spanish troops in the Philippines, and Spain accepted this gesture. Arrangements were made to recover Spanish prisoners of war, including those held by the Filipinos, all in return for the release by Spain of political prisoners. Madrid successfully resisted a United States effort to specify that the Americans had the right to preserve public order in the Philippines between the conclusion of the treaty and its ratification. The Americans blocked Almodóvar's attempt to launch a new inquiry into the sinking of the *Maine*.[43]

On December 10, 1898, the two commissions formally affixed their signatures to the treaty of peace. Its seventeen articles reflected the one-sided outcome of the negotiations, although a much more Carthaginian settlement might have resulted had the United States taken full advantage of its bargaining position. On the two most contentious points of discussion—the Spanish effort to force American assumption of colonial debts and the American demand for the entire Philippine archipelago—the American commission forced a settlement, sweetening the outcome to some degree by granting compensation of $20 million for the Philippines. Charles G. Dawes well summarized the mood of those around President McKinley as the Paris conference came to an end: "Whatever the result to our Nation, the retention of the Philippines was inevitable from the first. No man, no party, could have prevented it." In contrast, Secretary Long, personally opposed to overseas expansion, wrote sadly to his wife, "If I could have had my way, I wouldn't have had the war, and I wouldn't have been burdened with Porto Rico or Cuba or the Philippines. They are an elephant, just as everything else is an elephant that disturbs the even tenor of our national way, but there they are, and my shoulder goes to the wheel." Many among the old gentry, whose world was slipping rapidly away, decided their course in the same mood. The world was bound to change after 1898.[44]

The most notable omission from the treaty was any mention of the Caroline Islands. Spain might conceivably have ceded all or part of the group had the Americans granted trading concessions in the Antilles, but Washington proved unwilling to take this step. Accordingly, Spain and Germany completed their negotiations on December 21, 1898, expanding the secret understanding of September 10. Germany acquired the Carolines, the Palaus, and the Ladrones (Marianas)—except for Guam—in return for twenty-five million pesetas. A formal treaty embodying the transaction was concluded on February 10, 1899 and ratified in June. Prince Bülow considered this purchase to be of great importance. Having acquired the Marshall Islands in 1895, Germany with the annexations of 1899 completed a chain of insular holdings in the Pacific that stretched north from the Bismarck archipelago to the Marianas. Bülow boasted that his country "now had a firm basis for our economic and general political development in Oceania." He could not anticipate the loss of these islands in the First World War and their later role in world politics.[45]

Harold and Margaret Sprout argue in their seminal study, *Toward a New Order of Sea Power*, that America erred mightily in not obtaining the Carolines in 1898, because these islands controlled communications to the western Pacific. Not content with the purchase from Spain, Germany added to its insular possessions when the tripartite dispute over Samoa was settled later in 1899. Britain agreed to withdraw its claim in return for compensation elsewhere—the Tonga group, certain islands in the Solomons, and territory in West Africa. Germany took the Samoan islands of Upolu and Savaii, and the United States obtained title to Tutuila and Manua. The German Admiral Alfred von Tirpitz coveted the Samoas because they lay on the route across the Pacific Ocean to the German concession in China at Kiaochow, were strategically located in relation to the projected canal across the isthmus of Panama, and could receive cable landings.[46]

If Germany's activities in 1898 and 1899 stimulated growing distrust of that country's intentions, the policies of Great Britain encouraged the notion that a tacit understanding or *entente* now governed American relations with its erstwhile mother country and antagonist. John Hay told President McKinley early in September, 1898 that as regards England "not the least of the results of your Administration [is] to have changed the condition of dull hostility which existed a year ago into a friendship firm enough to bear any test you might choose to put upon it." Hay exaggerated; his emphasis on close Anglo-American understanding was largely an advertisement of himself as his government's instrument in Britain during the war with Spain. And yet the climate had indeed altered in measurable ways. When Spain attempted to enlist British aid against the United States by dangling before Lord Salisbury certain land cessions near Gibraltar, the Prime Minister reaffirmed his settled policy of noninterference. And Britain had several good reasons for welcoming American control of the Philippines: R. G. Neale notes that in British eyes this outcome "would ensure the commercial policy desired in the area by Britain; it would prevent the disposition of the islands from becoming an occasion for European rivalry for concessions and counter-concessions; it would write *finis* to German ambitions in the area; and above all it would involve the United States territorially, and thus permanently, in the area close to that in which Britain in the past sought her diplomatic co-operation." Certainly, then, any study of the origins of America's involvement in the First World War must take into consideration the events of 1898.[47]

The United States Navy sought to compensate for the failure to acquire Kusaie when, on January 17, 1899, it laid claim to Wake Island. Commander Edward D. Taussig with the *Bennington* took possession of this lonely outpost despite Germany's claim that it was one of the Marshall Islands, basing his action on a visit paid there in 1841 by Captain Charles Wilkes. Lying between Midway Island and Guam, Wake Island provided a logical location for landing a trans-Pacific cable between Honolulu and Manila. Surely the acquisition of the Philippines imposed upon the United States in 1899 a whole new range of policy undreamed of a few short months before.[48]

THE SENATE AND THE TREATY

Good will generally reigned in the American commission at Paris, despite various disagreements over policy. Whitelaw Reid wrote to McKinley in praise of his colleagues; together they constituted "a singularly harmonious and agreeable Commission." Davis, Frye, and he had maintained almost identical positions; Day had become more and more comfortable with expansion; and Gray, "who generally starts out with every question by stating the Spanish side of it, generally lands on ours,—though often with many a protest and reservation." Reid was even willing to excuse the Delaware Senator's partisan views, because he was "really doing wonderfully well and personally he is most delightful, while nobody can help admiring his honest effort to be fair-minded and judicial." However, this bipartisan cooperation proved evanescent. Considerable controversy erupted when the treaty came before the United States Senate.[49]

At the onset of the debate it appeared that the public strongly endorsed approval of the treaty. When the New York *Herald* polled 498 other newspapers, it discovered that 305—61.3 percent—favored expansion. New England and the Middle States definitely leaned towards overseas acquisitions, and the West did overwhelmingly. Only in the South was there a bare majority against ratification. Of importance was the fact that two-thirds of those voting in the Senate must give consent to permit ratification. Some of the senators who would be called upon to consider the treaty were "lame ducks"; resigning or defeated in the Congressional election of November, 1898, they would still sit until March, 1899, when the new Congress, more Republican than its predecessor, would take over. However, legislative disputation over the treaty transcended party lines—a source of concern in the White House. For example, the stalwart Republican from Massachusetts, Senator George Frisbie Hoar, became one of the treaty's most energetic opponents. Some years after the controversy he recalled an interview with the President during December, 1898: After McKinley greeted him with "the delightful and affectionate cordiality" Hoar always found in him, he was asked, "How are you feeling this winter, Mr. Senator?" Hoar quickly replied, "Pretty pugnacious, I confess, Mr. President." This remark produced a reaction from the chief executive not unlike that noted by several others at one time or another during the McKinley Administration: "The tears came to his eyes, and he said, grasping my hand again: 'I shall always love you, whatever you do.'"[50]

Soon after the treaty was introduced into the Senate on December 10, various objections began to materialize. Senator George G. Vest (Democrat from Missouri) introduced a resolution adducing constitutional impediments. Nowhere in the Constitution, he argued, was there a grant of power authorizing the President to acquire territory to be held permanently as a colony; all land held by the United States must be prepared for eventual statehood. Another popular constitutional viewpoint found expression in a resolution offered by Senator William E. Mason (Democrat from Illinois) on January 7, 1899. He maintained that the principle of self-determination ruled out annexation. "The Government of the United States of America will not attempt to govern the people of any other country in the world without the consent of the people themselves, or subject them by force to our domination against their will." Then, on January 11, Senator Augustus O. Bacon (Democrat from Georgia) offered still another threatening resolution: He proposed that the United States announce that it planned to grant the Philippines independence "when a stable and independent government should have been duly erected." This approach, reflected earlier in the Teller amendment, worried McKinley's supporters, who recognized that the humanitarian motive in the declaration of war against Spain would surface among the arguments against the treaty. To head off Bacon's resolution the President decided to conciliate the insurgents, and organized a commission to do this. More difficulties arose when Senator Arthur O. Gorman (Democrat from Maryland)— who planned to seek his Party's presidential nomination in 1900 on an anti-imperialist platform—lined up all but a half-dozen Democratic senators against the treaty.[51]

These developments helped clarify the lines of battle. The Republicans were split into two factions, with a majority favoring consent and a relatively small minority opposing approval largely on anti-annexationist grounds. A curious division occurred among the Democrats: Quite a few wished to vote in the negative, but William Jennings Bryan, the defeated presidential aspirant of 1896, wanted to approve the treaty but thereafter extend independence to the Philippines. By this approach he tried to settle the issue of expansion once and for all so the election of 1900 would turn on domestic questions, at which time he wanted to campaign for free silver and against monopolies. Bryan's influence may have led some Democrats to support the treaty. McKinley circumspectly avoided taking a position on the ultimate disposition of the Philippines after annexation. This tactic helped supporters of the Administration hold certain wavering colleagues in line, but as the moment of decision approached in early February the outcome appeared in doubt.[52]

Just before the vote in the Senate, word came from the Philippines that fighting had broken out between Filipino insurgents and American troops. President McKinley immediately grasped the consequences: "It is always the unexpected that happens, at least in my case," he exclaimed. "How foolish these people [the insurgents] are. This means ratification of the treaty; the people will insist on its ratification." When the test came in the Senate on February 6, fifty-seven voted yea and twenty-seven nay. Had two more senators voted nay, the treaty would not have gained the necessary two-thirds margin. Bryan's maneuvers in favor of consent probably influenced the outcome, as did the beginning of the Philippine insurrection. Senator Lodge also played a role; he worked skillfully to bring four doubtful senators behind the treaty. McKinley deserves credit for intelligent preparation, particularly in deciding to appoint three senators to the peace commission and developing the more lofty of the pro-annexationist arguments—humanity, duty, and destiny. Even if the treaty had failed at this time, it seems probable that the new Senate would have voted for it. Seven who voted against the treaty on February 6 did not return in March. Later efforts to pass the Bacon amendment and another, less specific version sponsored by Senator Samuel D. McEnery (Democrat from Louisiana) came to nothing. The United States government thus committed itself to long-term occupation of the Philippine Islands, riding the wave of popular expansionist sentiment that swept all before it after the war with Spain. Once again popular emotions induced McKinley to enact policy he did not desire. This time he proved unwilling to risk the public wrath that had almost ruined him earlier when he resisted the nation's decision to make war on Spain.[53]

In Spain the treaty, considered a national humiliation, was attacked, as might be expected, much more severely than in the United States. When it came before the Cortes, it received 120 votes for ratification to 118 against, a margin too narrow to achieve legislative approval. The

Queen Regent then took matters into her own hands: She used her constitutional powers to override the Cortes, and the treaty was ratified on March 19, 1899. Ratifications were then exchanged and the treaty proclaimed in Washington, D. C., on April 11, 1899. Shortly after the Queen Regent acted, Sagasta fell from power and the Conservative Francisco Silvela took his place. The Liberal ministry had achieved its most important wartime objective, the preservation of constitutional monarchy and parliamentary government, but paid a price in the form of temporary banishment from power. Interestingly enough, several of the Liberals who played important roles in the events of 1898—including Segismundo Moret and José Canalejas—later became prime ministers, proof that their activities during the war with the United States did not ruin them.[54]

The defeat led many Spaniards to an orgy of self-criticism, a development that engendered an important national movement known as "Regeneration." The Spanish writer Pío Rioja set its tone with a famous remark: "Don't you think we're a sorry lot, we of '98?" Lord Salisbury agreed with him; he lost no time in classifying Spain among the "moribund nations." The loss of Cuba was no ordinary event in the history of Spain. It dealt a final blow to the glorious tradition of *reconquista.* Henceforth Spain would have to look elsewhere for national inspiration. Various literary figures, among them influential members of the distinguished group known as the "Generation of '98," developed a number of regenerative themes in widely read works. These included criticism of parliamentary government, the desirability of administrative and technical leadership by experts as against politicians, and demands for authoritarian government. The "Disaster of '98" was not the least of the several shocks that eventually were to undermine Spanish democracy and constitutionalism. Some Spaniards sought solace after 1898 in isolationism or Hispanicization. Others believed that the future lay in regional development—for example, preservation of the Basque, Catalonian, and Andalusian cultures. Another group favored Europeanization along cosmopolitan lines. Various reform movements received a fillip because of the war—feminism and educational change among them.[55]

Across the Atlantic acceptance of the treaty committed the American people to an imperial interlude. As early as February 16, 1899, President McKinley expressed the philosophy that was to govern his Philippine policy thereafter, as well as that of his immediate successors—Theodore Roosevelt and William Howard Taft. Speaking to the Home Market Club in Boston, he depicted himself not as conqueror but as liberator, not as master but as emancipator. The United States would establish order in the Philippines so that a "reign of reason" would begin to function. While less than specific about the long term, he denied selfish motives: "No imperial designs lurk in the American mind," he trumpeted. "They are alien to American sentiment, thought, and purpose. Our priceless principles undergo no change under a tropical sun. They go with the flag." McKinley determined to put down the Philippine insurrection and administer the islands for an extended period. Annexation of the Philippines, he reiterated, created national responsibility. Speaking again in Massachusetts—this time to the state legislature—he expressed his view boldly: "We may regard the situation before us as a burden or as an opportunity; but whether one or the other, it is here, and conscience and civilization require us to meet it bravely. Desertion of duty is not an American habit." McKinley himself probably considered colonial administration an undesirable burden, but in postwar America he proved unable to resist the unmistakable public desire for overseas expansion.[56]

Whitelaw Reid, fresh from his triumphs in Paris, joined the President in sounding the call to colonial responsibility. Speaking to the Lotos Club of New York City on February 11, 1899, he refused to speculate on the commercial opportunities that might materialize in East Asia, especially because of Aguinaldo's insurrection—"that irritation of a Malay half-breed's folly"—but he was prepared to argue that "nobody ever doubted that they would give us trouble. That is the price nations must pay for going to war, even in a just cause."[57] Trouble would indeed materialize in unwonted plenty. Not the least of it would be the task of suppressing an insurrection in the Philippines, a tragic outcome of the decision to annex that far-off archipelago thousands of miles across the broad Pacific Ocean.

Conclusion

It remains to summarize the course of the war with Spain.

The failure of Spain to quell the Cuban insurrection that began in 1895 led to growing difficulties with the United States. Two successive Presidents, Grover Cleveland and William McKinley, opposed to adventurism in the Caribbean Sea, sought through the extension of good offices to conclude the insurrection peacefully, but neither could ignore a gradual increase of American public interest in the Cuban struggle, a phenomenon that rekindled the congenital American aversion to the lingering Spanish presence in the New World. Prime Minister Antonio Cánovas del Castillo, leader of the Spanish Conservative Party, attempted to crush the Cuban insurrection by main strength, but his generals never concocted an effective antidote to the guerrilla strategy of the Cuban commander, General Máximo Gómez, and his cohorts in the countryside. When McKinley succeeded Cleveland in 1897, he moved beyond his predecessor's offer to mediate the conflict, and advocated a grant of home rule to the Cubans. When Cánovas was assassinated by an anarchist in August, 1897, his successor, Práxedes Mateo Sagasta, adopted such a policy. In doing so he was responding more to domestic pressures than to American demands: The Cuban insurrection, especially as it became protracted, exposed the consitutional regime established in 1875, the Restoration Monarchy, to attacks from reactionaries on the right, supporters of the Carlist pretender to the throne, and radicals on the left (adherents of the Republican Party). The principal bogey of the centrists, who dominated the Spanish Restoration, was an extremist coalition of Carlists and Republicans. This concern greatly influenced Spanish management of the Cuban insurrection. Sagasta's home-rule initiative was welcomed in Washington, but the Cuban insurrectionists rejected it flatly, recognizing in the concession a sign of weakness. Their continued intransigence might eventually bring a full measure of independence.

The destruction of the American battleship *Maine* at Havana in February, 1898 elevated the festering diplomatic controversy over Cuba into a serious threat of war. Prior to this the Cuban question had been but one of a number of public issues of interest to the American people; but after the *Maine* went down the fate of Cuba dominated the public consciousness. An ungovernable burst of popular emotion led to a universal demand for the independence of Cuba. Desperate to avoid hostilities but ultimately responsive to the voice of the people, President McKinley increased the price of peace, finally asking Madrid to grant Cuba full independence. He knew that Spain would be extremely loath to move beyond home rule for Cuba, the last jewel in what once had been the most imposing of New World empires. Sagasta's reaction was to temporize, at the same time seeking diplomatic support in the chancelleries of the other great powers. This diplomatic initiative went for naught: Spain had no claims on the great powers, having pursued a foreign policy of isolation in Europe, and none of the leading nations, then preoccupied with colonial conflicts in Africa and Asia, was prepared to risk the wrath of the United States. When Spain refused an ultimatum from Washington, McKinley reluctantly asked Congress to intervene militarily on behalf of Cuban independence—although he successfully opposed recognition of the insurrectionist government.

It must be stressed that nothing could have been more distasteful to the pacific McKinley than war. Aside from a pronounced personal aversion to violence, the chief executive's principal reason for opposing war was a desire to further his domestic political goals—improvement of the tariff laws and maintenance of a sound currency. He was dedicated not only to bringing about full recovery from the deep depression that had begun in 1893 but to preserving the future of private enterprise in America through salutary reforms. Although he believed that international adventurism might well subvert his program of domestic legislation, he feared to ignore the judgment of the people, for failure to respond to the massive public demand that the United States help liberate Cuba might strip him of effective power. Congress might conceivably supersede the President as it had President Andrew Johnson during Reconstruction. The Democratic Party might gain control of Congress in the autumn elections of 1898 and, even worse, elevate William Jennings Bryan to the presidency in 1900. Whatever his abilities, and they were considerable, McKinley lacked sufficient political courage to pursue a pacific policy beyond a certain point—and he reached that point in April, 1898. Compelling domestic influences were more important than international considerations in dictating McKinley's decision for war.

On several occasions during the nineteenth century the United States had been tempted to seize Cuba, but imperialistic motivations do not account for the decision to go to war in 1898. On the contrary, anti-imperialistic attitudes predominated throughout the crisis that eventually led to the conflict. Congress, to demonstrate this commitment beyond cavil, inserted the Teller amendment, a self-denying ordinance that repudiated all interest in acquiring Cuba, into the war resolution. What accounts then for that extraordinary burst of public sentiment, a true fire-storm of political emotion, for Cuban independence after the sinking of the *Maine?* Surely some Americans dreamed of finally evicting the "cruel Spaniard" from the New World. Others aspired to expand trade and investment in the Antilles, by this device disposing of excess production and capital at home—the so-called "glut"—and postponing the class warfare that seemed to threaten the country in 1896. Certain strategic thinkers hoped to strengthen the nation's grip on the maritime approaches to the Central American isthmus, where it was planned to construct an interoceanic canal. Still others were prone to romantic views about the virtues of acquiring an overseas empire, believing that only in this way could the United States fulfill its destiny as a great power and meet its responsibilities as the exemplar of political democracy and Christian faith to races deemed less fortunate and competent.

And yet none of these elements, alone or in combination, accounts for the American decision to go to war in April, 1898. McKinley chose to fight because he could divine no means of weathering the public enthusiasm for support for Cuban independence. The thought of a selfless war for Cuban freedom released pent-up emotions that had been building up among the American people for a generation or more, as the nation ineluctably acquired the capabilities of a great power. This process, involving fundamental social and economic changes, bred fear as well as hope, particularly during the economic downturn that began in 1893. An unfathomable, immeasurable, and paradoxical combination of confidence and insecurity suffused Americans in 1898. Irrational impulses rather than calculated strategic, economic, ideological, or religious considerations moved them to a great crusade in defense of *Cuba libre*. Very few Americans justified the decision to help Cuba as a self-interested grab for markets, empire, or an isthmian canal. When McKinley became convinced that he could no longer resist overwhelming public opinion, however irrational, he decided on force to secure self-determination for Cuba. This change of front he deemed necessary to maintain his leadership and that of the Republican Party, even if it threatened his program of domestic legislation.

The great irony of 1898 was that neither McKinley nor Sagasta wanted war. Both sought desperately to achieve a pacific solution. Madrid eventually decided to fight, although it could discern little prospect of victory, because an honorable defeat after spirited resistance might preclude revolution at home and preserve the Restoration Monarchy. Washington's decision for war was far less desperate, given the disparity between the military capabilities of the two nations, especially after it became evident that a debilitated Spain could not hope to obtain any form of support from the great powers of Europe. If President McKinley could not avoid war, he could at least seek a rapid victory and thereby avoid any more than the minimum of human, material, and political costs.

The war between Spain and the United States deeply affected three other peoples—the Cubans, the Puerto Ricans, and the Filipinos. The American intervention in 1898, culmination of a long, thirty-year campaign for Cuban independence, signalled the success of insurgent strategy, which was aimed at avoiding military defeat rather than achieving victory in the field, trusting that in time Spain would prove unequal to the task of sustaining control of Cuba. In contrast, the Puerto Ricans, not yet interested in independence, welcomed the Spanish grant of autonomy extended late in 1897; they became essentially passive bystanders in 1898, playthings of the conflict between the United States and Spain. In the distant Philippines an unsuccessful insurgency languished, slow to grasp the possibilities that war might open to it, however much it might yearn for independence.

Because the decision for war came as a surprise to statesmen in both Spain and the United States, each country had failed to make fully comprehensive plans and preparations for war. The principal reason for restraint was that almost everyone had anticipated a political settlement, but another consideration exercised important influence: Neither side had adequate forces in hand. All that Madrid could do, when it finally recognized that war was a distinct possibility, was to ready its decrepit fleet for service in the Caribbean and the western Pacific and ask its proconsuls in Cuba, Puerto Rico, and the Philippines to make whatever local dispositions were feasible without reinforcement or resupply from the homeland. Although the United States did possess an efficient navy that had been placed on a war footing and deployed for a possible war, its army was all but nonexistent. No extensive operations on land could be contemplated until the nation mobilized a large force of volunteers. Although it is true that all thought about war with Spain assumed the probability of a naval conflict that would require little activity on the part of the army, the overall unpreparedness of 1898 belies the thesis that President McKinley and others engaged in a conscious conspiracy to seize an overseas empire from Spain.

When Spain, however tardily, began preparations for war with the United States, it had little choice in deciding its strategy. Assuming that at the beginning of the struggle the Americans would probably menace its colonial possessions in the Caribbean and the Pacific, particularly Cuba, Puerto Rico, and the Philippine Islands, Spanish leaders realized that their armed forces must attempt to maintain maritime access to those places. If Spain failed to sustain its outlying garrisons, it must accept defeat. But to commit all its naval forces to those overseas locations would invite hostile engagements in adjacent waters and even against its coast. Lacking resources and time, the only serious movement that Spain could prepare before the war was a voyage of a small squadron to the Antilles.

Although the United States had not greatly strengthened its forces before February, 1898, the navy had engaged in sporadic strategic planning for several years. The planners stressed what was later called the "indirect approach"; the armed forces would attack on the periphery of the enemy's power, conducting operations that entailed the most cost to Spain and the least to the United States. War with Spain would turn on command of the sea. Since the United States had a respectable fleet, its first effort would be to engage the enemy's forces in Caribbean and Philippine waters. When the navy had attained victory at sea, the army could then attack the insular possessions of Spain. Ideally these campaigns would force an early capitulation, but, if they did not end the war, then—and only then—the scene of the battle would shift to the Iberian peninsula.

If this strategic design was to be pursued to its logical conclusion, hostilities would occur in three theaters. The primary theater—which the United States hoped would be the theater of decision—was the Caribbean Sea, particularly the islands of Cuba and Puerto Rico. After the navy established a blockade of the Antilles, it would undertake fleet operations to establish lasting general command of the sea. Then the army would land near Havana and engage the enemy's most important military concentration. It would also attack Puerto Rico, which, lying to the east of Cuba astride the line of communication from Spain, possessed obvious strategic significance. While these activities took place, the navy would assume the offensive in a secondary theater, the western Pacific Ocean, principally by engaging a Spanish squadron based at Manila. This attack was originally intended to seize a base and prevent any interference with American commerce. It would also exert pressure on Madrid to end hostilities. Prior to the war American strategic planners gave almost no thought to land operations or territorial acquisitions in the Philippines. If the combination of defeat in the Caribbean and the western Pacific Ocean did not force Spain to the peace table, then the navy might undertake operations in a third theater, the waters surrounding the Iberian peninsula. It might attack certain island groups, such as the Canaries and the Balearics, or possibly even Ceuta, across the Strait of Gibraltar from Algeciras. It could even bombard coastal cities of Spain, such as Cádiz, Málaga, and Barcelona.

At the beginning of the war neither Spain nor the United States was fully prepared to execute its strategic design. Large Spanish garrisons were located in Cuba and the Philippines, but the local insurrections had drained both forces. Troops in Puerto Rico, few in number, could not be expected to resist a determined American assault. The Spanish fleet, concentrated at Cádiz, was in serious disrepair and lacked well-trained crews. At the beginning of hostilities it could aspire only to maneuver a small squadron of armored vessels, one that could not hope to survive a direct engagement with the United States Navy, a modest but combat-ready force prepared to operate in both the Caribbean and the western Pacific. As for the United States Army, the minuscule regular army could be concentrated in Florida to prepare for modest operations in the Caribbean theater, but some time must pass before the War Department could hope to conduct large-scale enterprises against important concentrations of the enemy.

Although it appeared that the United States might conceivably encounter difficulties during the early stages of the war, no appraisal of forces could have led impartial observers to any other conclusion than that Spain was in a most desperate position. This reality encouraged President McKinley, once committed to war, to seek a quick and relatively painless victory, one that would result chiefly from operations by American naval forces far from the center of Spanish power. He knew that Spain did not want war and that Madrid could anticipate victory only in the most improbable circumstances. Desirous of minimizing postwar complications, McKinley identified only one war aim at the beginning of the struggle: the independence of Cuba. When this outcome had been assured, he would receive overtures of peace.

During the first six weeks of the war the outcomes of important naval operations led the United States to mature its strategic design. Commodore George Dewey's successful attack on Admiral Patricio Montojo's pathetic squadron in Manila on May 1 immediately stimulated planning for operations to seize Manila, an enterprise that had not been contemplated earlier. This project would increase pressure on Spain to accept an early defeat. McKinley authorized the seizure of Guam, southernmost island of the Ladrones (Marianas) group, to strengthen the long line of communication across the Pacific. The same purpose motivated the President's successful effort to annex the Hawaiian Islands in July, an unexpected conclusion to a complicated process reaching back to the 1840's. Meanwhile Rear Admiral William T. Sampson established an effective naval blockade of Havana and other Cuban ports.

The Spanish Admiral Pascual Cervera, who steamed westward from the Cape Verde Islands soon after the declaration of war with a small squadron of four armored cruisers and three destroyers, managed to avoid interception and enter the unblockaded Cuban harbor of Santiago de Cuba. Commodore Winfield S. Schley's Flying Squadron, after many vicissitudes, managed to bottle up the enemy force there. While the American navy attempted to establish command of the Caribbean Sea, a small army composed mostly of regular troops was concentrated at Tampa. Its initial mission was to make occasional raids on the coast of Cuba during the summer of 1898. There were no plans to engage the large Spanish garrison around Havana until a strong army of volunteers had been brought into existence.

As soon as McKinley learned that Cervera had been blockaded in port at Santiago de Cuba, he decided to launch certain relatively modest operations in the Caribbean without delay. The expeditionary force at Tampa would land at Santiago de Cuba where, with the help of the Cuban insurgents, it would assist the navy in capturing or destroying Cervera's squadron. The Governor-General of Cuba, Ramón Blanco, could not hope to succor the weak Spanish garrison at Santiago de Cuba, far removed as it was from Havana. Victory in southeastern Cuba would ensure general and lasting command of the Caribbean Sea and foreclose Spanish support of the Antilles. When the operation at Santiago de Cuba was completed, the American expeditionary force, augmented with reinforcements, would move on to Puerto Rico. There, too, resistance would be minimal.

This plan had obvious strategic advantages. It put Spanish forces under attack in two places in the Caribbean where the United States could mass preponderant strength, particularly if the local populations could be neutralized or won over—a foregone conclusion in Cuba and a definite possibility in Puerto Rico. The cumulative effect of these operations at Santiago de Cuba and Puerto Rico, when added to the impact of those completed or projected in the Philippines, might force Madrid to seek peace before it would become necessary to attack the strong Spanish position at Havana—envisioned as the ultimate objective in the Caribbean theater—or mount naval operations against the Spanish coast itself. Early in June, then, the United States had developed a quite explicit and detailed strategy. This mature design adhered generally to the scenario envisioned prior to the war, but had been adjusted to take into account the naval victory at Manila and the blockade of Cervera at Santiago de Cuba. It was fully consistent with the President's desires. Having failed to avoid war, he wanted a victory at the earliest possible time and at the least cost in blood and treasure, a success that would free Cuba and permit an early return to the domestic political agenda so dear to McKinley's heart.

Spain sought to frustrate the American design by sending out a second naval squadron, under Admiral Manuel de la Cámara, to relieve the Philippines or draw important American naval forces away from the Caribbean Sea. This forlorn project had little chance of success. It depended on the prolongation of Spanish resistance at Santiago de Cuba, Manila, and elsewhere, and on the unsound assumption that the United States lacked sufficient reserves of naval power to counteract it. After it became apparent that Cámara intended to sail eastward through the Mediterranean Sea and the Suez Canal to the Philippines, the Navy Department sent strong naval reinforcements to Dewey from the American west coast. It also organized the Eastern Squadron in Cuban waters to pursue Cámara or attack the Spanish coast.

The war was decided early in July. After helter-skelter but successful efforts to land the Fifth Army Corps near Santiago de Cuba, General William R. Shafter moved on the city. The assault of July 1 on El Caney and the San Juan Heights failed to carry the city itself, but it forced the Spanish garrison to abandon outlying positions. Shafter then dug in and laid siege to Santiago de Cuba, preferring to starve out the defenders rather than accept the losses that might result from additional assaults. These partial American victories of July 1 led Governor-General Blanco to order the Spanish naval squadron out of the city's harbor. When the gallant Spaniards sortied on the morning of July 3, the blockading American squadron destroyed every enemy vessel. The end of Cervera's squadron, along with unmistakable indications that the United States would soon attack Puerto Rico and Manila, caused Sagasta to recall Cámara, who had begun his eastward voyage, and prepare for peace negotiations. The garrison at Santiago de Cuba capitulated two weeks later on July 17. Although defeated, Spain had preserved its honor and the constitutional monarchy. Delays in reaching an armistice, which did not take effect until August 12, permitted American forces to execute a successful invasion of Puerto Rico and put troops into position for an assault on the city of Manila.

On July 25, a mere eight days after the capitulation at Santiago de Cuba, General Nelson A. Miles landed his expeditionary force at Guánica, Puerto Rico, and by August 12 these troops had all but completed the conquest of the second of the Spanish Antilles. The Spanish Governor-General Macías had few reliable troops and no naval units to dispose against the Americans. Miles launched several coordinated attacks from the southern coast with the intention of converging on San Juan, the principal center of Spanish strength in the island, located in its northeastern section. These operations were well advanced when the war came to an end. As President McKinley had intended, the Puerto Rican campaign played a significant role in deciding the Spanish government to seek an early peace. Its ultimate success made up for Miles's often erratic and irresponsible behavior as the senior officer of the army.

Early in June, 1898, in conjunction with the decisions to strike Santiago de Cuba and Puerto Rico, the President had developed a comprehensive set of war aims, adding several items to a list that at first had contained only the demand for Cuban independence. Hoping to encourage an early peace initiative from Madrid, he secretly made known demands for Puerto Rico and an island in the Ladrones, presumably Guam; in return for these concessions the United States would forgo a monetary indemnity. Also at this juncture McKinley indicated interest in a port in the Philippines, but made no mention of annexing the entire archipelago or any significant part of it such as the island of Luzon. However, this latter provision altered after McKinley obtained information about the insurgency of Emilio Aguinaldo and the public became interested in the Philippines. To lend cogency to his demand for an early peace the President warned that the list of war aims would expand further if Spain prolonged its resistance. McKinley's interest in Puerto Rico and Guam aroused little opposition at home, but the possibility that the United States might acquire all or part of the Philippines posed more serious questions and engendered extensive debate. Since the will of the people did not immediately become fully manifest, the President, although personally inclined to eschew annexation of the entire archipelago, postponed a final decision. Remembering his brush with political disaster during the spring of 1898, when he had initially resisted popular desires, he wished to avoid another such situation. In all probability, also, McKinley's refusal to decide his Philippine policy prior to the end of the war was intended to encourage an early Spanish capitulation.

The Liberal ministry's decision finally to sue for peace ultimately brought about a settlement. Sagasta entrusted negotiations to an intermediary, the French ambassador in Washington, Jules Cambon. To speed a conclusion McKinley intimated that delay might strengthen his disposition to annex all of the distant archipelago in the western Pacific. After some hesitation Spain accepted McKinley's terms as stated in June, but with one important exception: Sagasta agreed to grant Cuba its independence and cede Puerto Rico and Guam to the United States, but he was not required to accept a Philippine settlement. This question was reserved for consideration during a postwar peace conference scheduled to meet in Paris in October. A protocol signed on August 12 incorporated these decisions and provided for an immediate cessation of hostilities.

The last engagement of this brief war took place after the signature of the protocol. On August 13, Pacific time, just a few hours after the official end of the of the conflict but before word could reach the Philippines, an expeditionary force under General Wesley Merritt took possession of Manila after a confused battle that caused little damage to the participating forces. The Spanish commander, Governor-General Fermín Jáudenes, had previously agreed to capitulate after only a brief show of resistance, in return for protection from the Filipino insurgents. In May Dewey had introduced rebel leader Emilio Aguinaldo into the situation at Manila simply as a war measure, thoughtlessly failing to calculate possible future political costs. Aguinaldo rapidly reestablished his ascendancy in the movement for Filipino independence. When events revealed that the United States might replace Spain as sovereign in the Philippines, tensions developed between the insurgents and the American forces encamped around Manila, particularly after Aguinaldo greatly extended his authority over Luzon and elsewhere during June and July, 1898. Merritt's successful seizure of Manila further exacerbated tensions, and the strained relations spilled over into the immediate postwar months as the United States negotiated a definitive peace treaty in Paris.

When President McKinley issued instructions to the American peace commissioners appointed to negotiate the treaty with Spain, he temporized concerning annexation of the whole of the Philippines, specifying only that the United States would accept nothing less than cession of Luzon. While his representatives in Paris struggled to force Spanish concurrence in settlements of other matters, already provided for in the protocol of August 12—Cuban independence and cession of Puerto Rico and an island in the Ladrones—McKinley carefully probed public opinion at home. After a speaking tour of the Midwest in October, during which he developed various arguments to justify acquisition of overseas territories and engendered an enthusiastic response, he returned to Washington convinced that the American people strongly favored annexation of the entire Philippine archipelago. Despite personal reservations, he acceded to the views of the majority and ordered his peace commissioners to arrange the matter, citing as justification humanitarian concern for the well-being of the Philippine people, national duty to serve the general interests of civilization, and the destiny of the United States in world affairs.

Spain bargained desperately to obtain monetary compensation for the loss of the Philippines. Madrid had no other recourse except to resume the war, an option that was foreclosed when the other great powers continued to skirt involvement in the controversy. Eventually the United States offered $20 million in compensation for certain Spanish facilities in the Philippines, and the Liberal ministry reluctantly accepted this amount. This provision gave rise to the later misconception that the United States had purchased the Philippines outright for $20 million. The treaty of peace signed in Paris on December 10, 1898, fulfilled the war aims for which the United States had fought and added as spoils the whole of the Philippine Islands, Puerto Rico, and Guam.

A humanitarian crusade had attained its prime object, Cuban independence, but it had also stimulated expansionist appetites. Accordingly, the peace conference turned into an American territorial grab of significant proportions, something neither planned nor even anticipated before the brief conflict with Spain. Having begun to attain the capabilities of a great power a generation prior to 1898, the United States chose to emulate the international behavior of Europe for some years thereafter, albeit on a relatively modest scale. The obligations of empire soon forced the United States into activities overseas for which there were few precedents in the national experience.

Whatever the failings of William McKinley, he was neither a fool nor a knave. It is true that he lacked sufficient will to avoid a war he desperately opposed and postwar overseas expansion he personally deemed most problematic. But it is equally true that he demonstrated sound strategic insight during the conflict and full awareness of the need to relate the use of force to basic political objectives.[1]

The armed forces met the test of 1898. Although the army, unprepared for war, experienced difficulties during the early days of the conflict with Spain, especially at Tampa and Santiago de Cuba, its later performance helped rescue its reputation.[2] For the United States Navy the struggle was one of remarkable achievement, excepting Schley's meandering search for Cervera in May.

The most imposing short-run consequence of the relatively inexpensive struggle was a long, sanguinary, and expensive colonial conflict —the Philippine insurrection. Although an organized anti-imperialist movement had materialized in the United States late in 1898 to oppose the annexationist policies of the McKinley Administration, it gained only limited popular support and failed in its most ambitious enterprise —the attempt to persuade the Senate of the United States to withhold consent from the Treaty of Paris in January, 1899. Just as the upper house concluded debate on the treaty, fighting broke out near Manila between Aguinaldo's insurgents and the American garrison, under the command of General Elwell S. Otis. This development stemmed from Aguinaldo's decision to resist American sovereignty. It is most unlikely that any arrangement short of a nominal American protectorate or outright independence would have satisfied the Filipinos; undoubtedly, however, the United States might have dealt much more intelligently with the insurgents between August, 1898—the signing of the protocol—and January, 1899—the debate on the treaty.

The war with Spain exposed weaknesses in the organization of the United States armed forces and brought to public attention a whole range of international responsibilities that required improvements in national defense. These circumstances helped fuel a series of postwar investigations—most of them aimed at the army—that ultimately led to significant changes.

On September 26, 1898, President McKinley had formed a commission, headed by the railroad magnate Grenville M. Dodge, to inquire into various allegations of mismanagement leveled against the War Department. McKinley apparently hoped to calm the public prior to the autumn elections. After holding extensive hearings the Dodge Commission reported its findings on February 9, 1899. It found no corruption or intentional neglect of duty, but decided that "there was lacking in the general administration of the War Department . . . that complete grasp of the situation which was essential to the highest efficiency and discipline of the Army." Here was a tactful but direct reflection on the competency of the bumbling Secretary of War, Russell A.

Alger. The commission proposed that the War Department reduce paper work, stockpile necessary supplies, and develop schools of instruction to train personnel properly for wartime duty and ensure a supply of competent officers.[3]

In a separate action a court of inquiry looked into charges that the War Department had supplied troops canned beef injected with toxic chemicals. General Miles actively lent support to claims that boric or salicylic acid had been used to preserve meat. The Dodge Commission rejected this accusation. When Miles pressed for further action, a special court absolved the Commissary General of Assistance, Brigadier General Charles P. Eagan, of wrongdoing, but censured him for purchasing unduly large quantities of refrigerated beef. It dismissed as unwarranted Miles's charges about "embalmed beef."[4]

These investigations helped stimulate reform of the War Department designed to improve plans and preparations for war. Eventually Secretary of War Elihu Root established a general staff, the most important legislation in this move being a law of February 14, 1903. A few weeks earlier, on January 21, 1903, Congress passed the Militia Act, thereby improving procedures for training the militias of the several states. These changes ameliorated structural deficiencies in the War Department, particularly the unsound division of authority between the commanding general and the Secretary of War, and broke down the barriers that had inhibited appropriate war preparations prior to April, 1898. Secretary Root also improved relations between staff and line officers, and upgraded service schools. His reforms capped an important effort by the War Department to meet the new responsibilities thrust upon it as a consequence of the war with Spain.[5]

The Navy Department and its head, Secretary of the Navy John D. Long, escaped a general investigation because of successes during the war with Spain, but postwar controversy over the relative merits of Admirals Schley and Sampson led Schley to demand a court of inquiry. That court's report properly criticized Schley for "vacillation, dilatoriness, and lack of enterprise" during the days prior to June 1, 1898 when he was seeking Admiral Cervera. He was also criticized for his actions during the sea battle of Santiago de Cuba, especially the famous "loop turn." Although the dispute between Sampson and Schley did not lead to a general overhaul of the Navy Department, it helped publicize the need for new and improved vessels, adequate communications by means of bases and naval stations, and improved operational performance, especially in gunnery. Recognition that there had been inadequate provisions for planning led to the creation of the General Board of the Navy in 1900. However, the navy did not develop an organization comparable to the army's general staff until the creation of the Office of the Chief of Naval Operations in 1915. To coordinate interservice action the Joint Board of the Army and Navy was established in 1903.[6]

What of the new empire? The acquisitions of 1898 at first struck many Americans as justifiable, but to later generations they appear ill advised in most respects. Many were the disadvantages and dangers of enhanced entanglement in the affairs of the Pacific–East Asian and Caribbean–Latin American regions. The offsetting benefits of expanded trade and enhanced security did not materialize. Expansion proved costly in legal and moral as well as practical terms, leading to concern that territorial acquisitions overseas violated fundamental democratic principles of self-determination and peaceful resolution of disputes. Certainly possession of the territories conquered in 1898—Puerto Rico, Guam, and the Philippine Islands—was not essential to the security of the Western Hemisphere, and the United States did not require an overseas empire to exercise a salutary influence on world politics. These realities became evident during the early years of the new century, and the country soon turned away from the adventurism of 1898.

The most important consequence of the war with Spain was that it hastened the nation's acceptance of international responsibilities commensurate with its power. During the twentieth century the United States was to become deeply engaged in global affairs. It was to exert its strength frequently, including its military power, in many parts of the world—largely for defensive reasons. The episode of 1898 was almost the last in the history of American expansion. Careful study of the war with Spain helps buttress this judgment.[7]

Note on Sources and Authorities

Approximately one thousand published sources and authorities were consulted in connection with this study of the War with Spain in 1898. Many of these items are cited in the notes herein. This brief commentary identifies the most indispensable materials of a general character.

United States Foreign Relations. The principal published collections of documents are the microfilm reproductions of diplomatic correspondence issued by the National Archives and Records Service. (These publications are listed here on pp. 490ff. under "Abbreviations" in the notes.) The volume in the *Foreign Relations* series for 1898 is selective and incomplete: U.S. Department of State, *Papers Relating to the Foreign Relations of the United States, With the Annual Message of the President: Transmitted to Congress December 5, 1898* (Washington, D.C. 1901). For the peace conference at Paris, see U.S. Department of State, *Papers Relating to the Treaty With Spain*, Sen. Doc. No. 208 (five parts), 55th Cong., 2nd Sess. (Washington, D.C., 1899); and Howard Wayne Morgan, ed., *Making Peace With Spain: The Diary of Whitelaw Reid September–December 1898* (Austin, 1965).

The single most valuable secondary work on the international political aspects of the war with Spain is Ernest R. May, *Imperial Democracy: The Emergence of America as a Great Power* (New York, 1961). A useful collection of essays summarizing modern scholarship is Paolo E. Coletta, ed., *Threshold to American Internationalism: Essays on the Foreign Policies of William McKinley* (New York, 1970). Two important works on President McKinley are Margaret Leech, *In the Days of McKinley* (New York, 1959); and Howard Wayne Morgan, *William McKinley and His America* (Syracuse, N.Y., 1963).

United States Army. Three comprehensive collections of documents were published immediately after the war, all of them of great utility: U.S. War Department, *Annual Reports of the War Department for the Fiscal Year Ended June 30, 1898. Report of the Secretary of War. Miscellaneous Reports* (Washington, D.C., 1898); U.S. War Department, Adjutant General's Office, *Correspondence Relating to the War With Spain and Conditions Growing Out of the Same, Including the Insurrection in the Philippine Islands and the China Relief Expedition, Between the Adjutant-General of the Army and Military Commanders in the United States, Cuba, Porto Rico, China, and the Philippine Islands, From April 15, 1898, to July 30, 1902*, 2 volumes (Washington, D.C., 1902); U.S. Senate, *Report of the Commission Appointed by the President to Investigate the Conduct of the War Department in the War With Spain*, 8 volumes, Sen. Doc. No. 221, 56th Cong., 1st Sess. (Washington, D.C., 1900).

The most important secondary works treating the United States Army are French Ensor Chadwick, *The Relations of the United States and Spain: The Spanish-American War*, 2 volumes (New York, 1911; reprinted in New York, 1968); Graham A. Cosmas, *An Army for Empire: The United States Army in the Spanish-American War* (Columbia, Mo., 1971); and Walter Millis, *The Martial Spirit: A Study of Our War With Spain* (Boston, 1931).

United States Navy. The principal collection of documents is the second volume of U.S. Navy Department, *Annual Reports of the Navy Department for the Year 1898*, 2 volumes, Volume 1: *Report of the Secretary of the Navy. Miscellaneous Reports*, Volume II: *Appendix to the Report of the Chief of the Bureau of Navigation* (Washington, D.C., 1898).

Chadwick's classic work remains the best secondary treatment of the navy, but two other studies treating events in the Pacific Ocean possess special merit: Ronald Spector, *Admiral of the New Empire: The Life and Career of George Dewey* (Baton Rouge, 1974); and Nathan Sargent, *Admiral Dewey and the Manila Campaign* (Washington, D.C., 1947).

Spain. The Spanish government published three "Red Books" treating the diplomacy of the 1898 war: *Negociones generales con los Estados Unidos desde 10 de Abril de 1896 hasta la declaración de guerra* (Madrid, 1898); *Negociones diplomáticas desde el principio de la guerra con los Estados Unidos hasta la firma del protocolo de Washington* (Madrid, 1898); and *Conferencia de París y tratado de paz de 10 Diciembre de 1898* (Madrid, 1899). All were translated and published by the United States as *Spanish Diplomatic Correspondence and Documents, 1896-1900, Presented to the Cortes by the Minister of State* (Washington, D.C., 1905). Documents concerning naval activity are in Spain, Ministry of the Marine, *Correspondencia oficial referente á las operaciones navales durante la guerra con los Estados Unidos en 1898* (Madrid, 1899); and Pascual Cervera y Topete, *Guerra hispano-americana. Colección de documentos referentes á la escuadra de operaciones de las Antillas* (El Ferrol, 1899), translated and published by the U.S. Navy Department as *The Spanish-American War: A Collection of Documents Relative to the Squadron Operations in the West Indies. Arranged by Rear-Admiral Pascual Cervera y Topete* (Washington, D.C., 1899).

Spanish historians have not given sufficient attention to the 1898 war. The most helpful works were produced close to the event: Severo Gómez Núñez, *La guerra hispano-americana*, 5 volumes (Madrid, 1899-1902); and Víctor M. Concas y Palau, *La escuadra del Almirante Cervera* (Madrid, n.d.) translated and published by the U.S. Navy Department as *The Squadron of Admiral Cervera* (Washington, D.C., 1900).

Cuba. The National Archives of Cuba published two important collections of political documents: *La revolución del 95 según la correspondencia de la delegación cubana en Nueva York*, 5 volumes (Havana, 1932-1937); and *Correspondencia diplomática de la delegación cubana en Nueva York durante la guerra de independencia de 1895 á 1898*, 5 volumes (Havana, 1943-1946).

Perhaps the most useful secondary works dealing with Cuba are Philip S. Foner, *The Spanish-Cuban-American War and the Birth of American Imperialism 1895-1902*, 2 volumes (New York and London, 1972); Herminio Portell Vilá, *Historia de Cuba en sus relaciones con los Estados Unidos*, Volume 3: *1878-1899* (Havana, 1939); Marshall M. True, "Revolutions in Exile: The Cuban Revolutionary Party 1891-1898" (Dissertation, University of Virginia, 1965); Miguel Varona Guerrero, *La guerra de independencia de Cuba 1895-1898*, 3 volumes (Havana, 1946).

Puerto Rico. The most useful study of events in Puerto Rico is Carmelo Rosario Natal,

Puerto Rico y la crisis de la guerra hispanoamericana (1895-1898) (Hato Rey, 1975). For other information, see Lidio Cruz Monclova, *Historia de Puerto Rico (Siglo XIX)*, Volume 3, Part 3: *1885-1898* (San Juan, 1964).

Philippines. Among the most useful secondary studies are Teodoro Agoncillo, *The Revolt of the Masses: The Story of Bonifacio and the Katipunan* (Quezon City, 1956); Teodoro Agoncillo, *Malolos: The Crisis of the Republic* (Quezon City, 1960); Teodor M. Kalaw, *The Philippine Revolution* (Quezon City, reprinted 1969; first published 1925); and Gregorio F. Zaide, *The Philippine Revolution* (Manila, 1964; revised edition, 1968).

Abbreviations

AF. U.S. Navy Department. *Area File of the Naval Records Collection 1775–1910.* Microcopy No. 625, National Archives and Records Service. Washington, D.C., 1965.

ARWD 98. U.S. War Department. *Annual Reports of the War Department for the Fiscal Year Ended June 30, 1898: Report of the Secretary of War. Miscellaneous Reports.* Washington, D.C., 1898.

ARWD 03. vol. 3 U.S. War Department. *Annual Reports of the War Department for the Fiscal Year Ended June 30, 1903.* Volume 3: *Reports of Department and Division Commanders.* Washington, D.C., 1903.

BN 98. U.S. Navy Department. *Annual Reports of the Navy Department for the Year 1898.* Volume 2: *Appendix to the Report of the Chief of the Bureau of Navigation.* Washington, D.C., 1898.

Consular Despatches, Havana. U.S. State Department. *Despatches from United States Consuls in Havana, 1799–1906.* Microcopy T-20 (roll 132, volume 132), National Archives and Records Service. Washington, 1958.

CWS. U.S. War Department, Adjutant-General's Office. *Correspondence Relating to the War With Spain and Conditions Growing Out of the Same, Including the Insurrection in the Philippine Islands and the China Relief Expedition, Between the Adjutant-General of the Army and Military Commanders in the United States, Cuba, Porto Rico, China, and the Philippine Islands, from April 15, 1898, to July 30, 1902.* Volumes 1–2. Washington, D.C., 1902.

Diplomatic Despatches, Spain. Despatches From United States Ministers to Spain, 1792–1906. Microcopy No. 31 (rolls 122–125), National Archives and Records Service. Washington, D.C., 1957.

Diplomatic Instructions, Spain. Diplomatic Instructions of the Department of State, 1801–1906. Microcopy M-77 (roll 150 includes Volume 22 for June 17, 1895–March 9, 1900), National Archives and Records Service. Washington, D.C., 1946.

FO 185. Great Britain, Foreign Office. "Correspondence Between Foreign Office and Spanish Embassy in Madrid." Foreign Office 185, Public Record Office, London, England.

Foreign Relations, 1898. U.S. State Department. *Papers Relating to the Foreign Relations of the United States, With the Annual Message of the President: Transmitted to Congress December 5, 1898* (Washington, D.C., 1901).

IC. U.S. Senate. *Report of the Commission Appointed by the President to Investigate the Conduct of the War Department in the War With Spain.* Volumes 1–8. 56th Cong., 1st Sess., Sen. Doc. No. 221. Washington, D.C., 1900.

Notes From Spanish Legation. Notes *From the Spanish Legation in the United States to the Department of State: Spain, 1790-1906.* Microcopy No. 59, National Archives and Records Service. Washington, 1970.

Notes to Foreign Legations, Spain. Notes *to Foreign Legations in the United States From the Department of State, 1834-1906: Spain.* Microcopy No. 99, National Archives and Records Service. Washington, D.C., 1950.

NWC. U.S. Naval War College. Record Group 7: "Intelligence and Technological Archives, 1894 to 1945." Archives of the Naval War College, Newport, R.I.

PPC. U.S. State Department. *Records of the Department of State Relating to the Paris Peace Commission, 1898.* Microcopy T-954 (three rolls), National Archives and Records Service. Washington, D.C., 1965.

RG 38, Entry 100. U.S. Navy Department. Record Group 38, Entry 100: "Correspondence with U.S. Naval Attaches during the Spanish-American War." Volumes 1–2. National Archives. Washington, D.C.

RG 45, Entry 19. U.S. Navy Department. Record Group 45, Entry 19: "Translation of Messages Sent." National Archives. Washington, D.C.

RG 45, Entry 20. U.S. Navy Department. Record Group 45, Entry 20: "Confidential Letters 1893–1908 (Volume for July, 1894–March, 1900)." National Archives, Washington, D.C.

RG 45, Entry 40. U.S. Navy Department. Record Group 45, Entry 40: "Cipher Messages Received." National Archives. Washington, D.C.

RG 45, NRC 371. U.S. Navy Department. Record Group 45, NRC 371: Telegrams of the Naval War Board. Volumes 1–2. National Archives. Washington, D.C.

RG 45, NRC 372. U.S. Navy Department. Record Group 45, NRC 372: Correspondence of the Naval War Board. National Archives. Washington, D.C.

RG 80, E194. U.S. Navy Department. Record Group 80, Entry E194: Messages Received and Sent by the Naval War Board. National Archives. Washington, D.C.

RG 108, Entry 118. U.S. War Department. Record Group 108, Entry 118: "Letters Sent from Florida, Cuba, and Puerto Rico; May–Sept. 1898." Volumes 1–2 (Nos. 36 and 37). National Archives. Washington, D.C.

RG 108, Entry 119. U.S. War Department. Record Group 108, Entry 119: "Letters and Telegrams Sent from Florida and Puerto Rico; May 31–Sept. 7, 1898." Volumes 1–4. National Archives. Washington, D.C.

RG 165, Entry 310. U.S. War Department. Records of War Dept. Gen. and Special Staffs. Record Group 165, Entry 310. National Archives. Washington, D.C.

Spanish Diplomatic Documents. Ministry of State (Spain). *Spanish Diplomatic Correspondence and Documents, 1896-1900, Presented to the Cortes by the Minister of State* (Washington, D.C., 1905).

Ultramar Records. Spain, Sección de Ultramar (10), National Historical Archives, Madrid, Spain. (Includes material relating to the Colonial Ministry in its relations with Cuba, Puerto Rico, and the Philippine Islands.)

USAMHI. "The U.S. Army and the Spanish American War Era, 1895-1910." U.S. Army Military History Institute. Carlisle Barracks, Pa.

Notes

INTRODUCTION

1. Hyman G. Rickover, *How the Battleship "Maine" Was Destroyed* (Washington, 1976), 1–5.
2. For detailed accounts of the sinking of the *Maine*, see the story by its commander: Captain Charles D. Sigsbee, *The "Maine": An Account of Her Destruction in Havana Harbor* (New York, 1899); see also John Edward Weems, *The Fate of the "Maine"* (New York, 1899). Weems interviewed survivors of the disaster many years after the event. For reports of persons present at Havana, see Fitzhugh Lee to William R. Day, 15–16 February 1898, in U.S. State Department, *Despatches from United States Consuls in Havana, 1799–1906,* Microcopy T-20, National Archives and Records Service (Washington, D.C., 1958), roll 132 (hereafter cited as *Consular Despatches, Havana)*; Ishbel Ross, *Angel of the Battlefield: The Life of Clara Barton* (New York, 1956), 206. Other information is in Lee to Day, 16 February 1898, in U.S. State Department, *Papers Relating to the Foreign Relations of the United States, With the Annual Message of the President: Transmitted to Congress December 5, 1898* (Washington, 1901), 1,019 (hereafter cited as *Foreign Relations, 1898);* Blanco to Lee, 16 February 1898, *Consular Despatches, Havana,* roll 132; Sigsbee Report, 17 February 1898, in Record Group 45, Entry 40: "Cipher Messages Received," no. 2, 44, in the Naval Records Collection of the Office of Naval Records and Library, National Archives, Washington, D.C. (hereafter cited as RG 45, Entry 40); Stewart Woodford to John Sherman, 16 February 1898, in U.S. State Department, *Despatches from United States Ministers to Spain, 1792–1906,* Microcopy No. 31, National Archives and Records Service (Washington, D.C., 1957), roll 124 (hereafter cited as *Diplomatic Despatches, Spain);* Du Bosc to Sherman, 16 February 1898, in U.S. State Department, *Notes from the Spanish Legation in the United States to the Department of State: Spain, 1790–1906,* Microcopy No. 59, National Archives and Records Service (Washington, D.C., 1970), roll 29 (hereafter cited as *Notes from Foreign Legations, Spain).*
3. For Captain Vanaman's letter to his family, see *Area File of the Naval Records Col-*

lection 1775-1910, Microcopy No. 625, National Archives and Records Service (Washington, D.C., 1965), file 8, roll 226 (hereafter cited as *AF*). For Secretary Long's reaction, see Long Diary, 16 February 1898, quoted in Lawrence Shaw Mayo, ed., *America of Yesterday: As Reflected in the Journal of John Davis Long* (Boston, 1923), 163-164. Long believed that the ease with which a great battleship could be sunk ought to constitute a deterrent to war. On February 28, 1898, he noted in his diary Fitzhugh Lee's view that a mine had sunk the *Maine.* He himself, however, did not attribute responsibility to the Spanish Government. (Long Diary, 28 February 1898, *ibid.,* 172.) Captain Alfred Thayer Mahan counseled against jumping to conclusions about the cause of the sinking. See Robert Seager II and Doris D. Maguire, eds., *Letters and Papers of Alfred Thayer Mahan* (Annapolis, 1975), vol. 2, p. 592.

4. Olney to Cleveland, 19 February 1898, quoted in William James, *Richard Olney and His Public Service: With Documents Including Unpublished Diplomatic Correspondence* (Boston and New York, 1923), 307-308; Ernest R. May, *Imperial Democracy: The Emergence of America as a Great Power* (New York, 1961), 147.

5. For McKinley's remarks to Fairbanks, see Margaret Leech, *In the Days of McKinley* (New York, 1959), 168. For Dawes's report, see Dawes Diary, 21 February 1898, quoted in Bascom Timmons, ed., *A Journal of the McKinley Years by Charles G. Dawes* (Chicago, 1950), 145.

6. For correspondence related to the Spanish proposal of a joint investigation, see Lee to Day, 18 February 1898, *Consular Despatches, Havana,* roll 132; and Day to Lee, 19 February 1898, *ibid.* American authorities, however, did facilitate to some degree the activities of the Spanish investigators (see Day to Lee, 26 February 1898, *ibid.*; and Lee to Day, 28 February 1898, *ibid.*) For the American reasons for not accepting the Spanish proposal of a joint investigation, see Roosevelt to Long, 19 February 1898, quoted in Gardner Weld Allen, ed., *Papers of John Davis Long, 1897-1904* (Boston, 1939), 57. Roosevelt recognized that the public opposition to cooperation was an "absurdity," but he thought that in the heated atmosphere this attitude would have considerable influence. For a typical statement of the conventional view accepted in Spain, see Jerónimo Bécker, *Historia de las relaciones exteriores de España durante el siglo XIX (Apuntes para una historia diplomática),* Volume 3: *1868-1900* (Madrid, 1926), pp. 860-861.

CHAPTER I

1. For background about the origins of the insurrection of 1895, see Philip S. Foner, *The Spanish-Cuban-American War and the Birth of American Imperialism, 1895-1902,* Volume 1: *1895-1898* (New York and London, 1972), xxiii-xxiv.

2. For information concerning the Cuban revolutionary movement in the United States, see Ernest R. May, *Imperial Democracy: The Emergence of America as a Great Power* (New York, 1961), 69-70; Charles F. Chapman, *A History of the Cuban Republic; A Study in Hispanic American Politics* (New York, 1927), 75; Marshall MacDonald True, "Revolutionaries in Exile: The Cuban Revolutionary Party, 1891-1898" (University of Virginia dissertation, 1965), 35-68; and Foner, *Spanish-Cuban-American War,* vol. 1, p. xxi-xxii.

3. Martí's appointments to commands in Cuba included Generals Guillermo Moncada (Santiago de Cuba), Bartolomé Masó (Manzanillo), Julio Sanguily (Havana), Pedro E. Betancourt (Matanzas), García Ponce (Havana), and Francisco Carillo (Las Villas). (Foner, *Spanish-Cuban-American War,* vol. 1, p. xxii-xxiv.) For information on Martí's plans, see Charles H. Brown, *The Correspondent's War: Journalists in the Spanish-American War* (New York, 1967), 8; and Foner, *Spanish-Cuban-American War,* vol. 1, pp. 2-4, 14.

4. For information on the Manifesto of Montecristi see Foner, *Spanish-Cuban-American War*, vol. 1, pp. 4–6. See also Melchor Fernández Almagro, *Historia política de la España contemporánea*, Volume 2: *Regencia de doña María Cristina de Austria durante la menor edad de su hijo don Alfonso XIII* (Madrid, 1959), pp. 782–789. The Cuban patriot historian Emilio Roig de Leuchsenring deals with this episode in several of his works, particularly *El manifiesto de Montecristi, sus raíces, finalidades y proyecciones* (Havana, 1957).

5. For the landings see Foner, *Spanish-Cuban-American War*, vol. 1, pp. 7–9. For Martí's death, see *ibid.*, 11; Brown, *Correspondents' War*, 9; Enrique Piñeyro, *Comó acabó la dominación de España en America* (Paris, 1908), 98. For Martí's diary of the period 9 April–17 May 1895, see Máximo Gómez y Baez, *Diario de la campaña del mayor general Máximo Gómez* (Havana, 1941), 289–325. For Gómez's proclamation of July 1, 1895—in which he prohibited transport of goods to Spanish-held areas and ordered an end to production of sugar—see French Ensor Chadwick, *The Relations of the United States and Spain: Diplomacy* (New York, 1909), 408. Gómez announced that he would treat all who violated this policy as traitorous enemies, subject to trial upon capture. For additional information concerning Gómez's economically oriented strategy and his differences with Maceo on this question, see Chapman, *Cuban Republic*, 79–81; Foner, *Spanish-Cuban-American War*, vol. 1, pp. 21, 24–26, 106.

6. For an excellent account of the western movement, see Juan J. E. Casasús, *La invasión: sus antecedentes, sus factores, su finalidad: estudio crítico-militar* (Havana, 1950). The western campaign allowed Gómez to reiterate and extend the policy he had announced on July 1 (see his order of November 6, 1895, in Chadwick, *United States and Spain: Diplomacy*, 409). For Gómez's view on the importance of the western movement, see Casasús, *La invasión*, 131. For the international impact of the western movement, see Gerald F. Linderman, *The Mirror of War: American Society and the Spanish-American War* (Ann Arbor, Mich., 1974), 133. The western regions of Cuba were much more developed than the eastern ones, and therefore any campaigns there would have a real impact on production (David F. Healy, *The United States in Cuba, 1898–1902: Generals, Politicians, and the Search for Policy* [Madison, 1963], 405). For an effort to correct journalistic excesses, see George Bronson Rea, *Facts and Fakes about Cuba: A Review of Various Stories Circulated in the United States Concerning the Present Insurrection* (New York, 1897).

7. For general comments on the Cuban campaigns of 1895–1898, see Brown, *Correspondents' War*, 25; May, *Imperial Democracy*, 126–127; and Jack Cameron Dierks, *A Leap to Arms: The Cuban Campaign of 1898* (Philadelphia and New York, 1970), 11. The term *mambí*—plural, *mambises*—derives from a black officer at Santo Domingo, Juan Mamby, who fought for Dominican independence in 1846. Used first to describe the insurrectionists of 1868–1878, it was revived during the war of 1895–1898. (See Foner, *Spanish-Cuban-American War*, vol. 1, p. 31.) For information on expeditions to Cuba, see Chadwick, *Spanish-American War: Diplomacy*, 418; Foner, *Spanish-Cuban-American War*, vol. 1, pp. 17–18. An extended account of various expeditions is found in Ramiro Guerra y Sánchez et al., *Historia de la nación cubana*, Volume 6, Book 5: "Emigración y expediciones cubanas en la guerra de independencia (1895–1898)," (Havana, 1952), pp. 259–333.

8. For information on the Constituent Assembly of Jimaguayú, see Foner, *Spanish-Cuban-American War*, vol. 1, pp. 40–43; True, "Revolutionaries in Exile," 103–112; Miguel Angel Varona Guerrero, *La guerra de independencia de Cuba, 1895–1898*, (Havana, 1946), vol. 1, pp. 637–649; Fernández Almagro, *Historia política*, vol. 2, pp. 789–791; and Chapman, *Cuban Republic*, 82–83. Varona

Guerrero provides extensive information on the activities of the Cuban government in the above-cited work (pp. 661–672). True remains the authority on the more important activities of the *junta* in New York. For its propaganda activities, see "Revolutionaries in Exile," 133–164; for its military policy, see *ibid.*, 200–236; and for efforts to obtain support in South America (largely unsuccessful), see *ibid.*, 237–272. The indefatigable agent, Arístides Agüero, worked hard in that region but accomplished little. Failure to achieve victory and to negotiate a solution with Spain led the *junta* to concentrate increasingly on intervention by a third party—the United States.

9. Foner, *Spanish-Cuban-American War*, vol. 1, pp. 17, 26–31; Graham A. Cosmas, *An Army for Empire: The United States Army in the Spanish-American War* (Columbia, Mo., 1971), 77–78; and Chapman, *Cuban Republic*, 77.

10. F. Bonmatí de Codecido, *Alfonso XIII y su época*, Volume 1, Book 1: *1886–1906* (1943), pp. 106–108. For Cánovas's statement of March 8, 1895, see Marqués de Lema, *Cánovas, o el hombre de estado* (Madrid, 1931), 236; and Leonor Meléndez y Meléndez, *Cánovas y la política exterior española* (Madrid, 1944), 173. For a recent brief biography of Cánovas, see José Luis Comellas, *Cánovas* (Barcelona, 1965).

11. For the statement attributed to Martínez de Campos, see Bonmatí, *Alfonso XIII*, vol. 1, bk. 1, p. 109. For his strategy, see Foner, *Spanish-Cuban-American War*, vol. 1, pp. 33–34; Chadwick, *United States and Cuba: Diplomacy*, 407; Bonmatí, *Alfonso XIII*, vol. 1, bk. 1, p. 105. The figures for 1895 are in Foner, *Spanish-Cuban-American War*, vol. 1, p. 16. For 1898 figures, see Cosmas, *Army for Empire*, 76. Two classes of Cubans served with the Spanish army, *guerrilleros* (Cubans enlisted in the Spanish army) and *voluntarios* (members of the home guard) (Brown, *Correspondents' War*, 49). Martínez de Campos assumed command in Cuba on April 16, 1895.

12. For the Spanish song see Foner, *Spanish-Cuban-American War*, vol. 1, p. 35. The Spanish diplomatist was Augusto Conte (see his *Recuerdos de un diplomático*, (n.p., 1903), vol. 2, pp. 580–581. The British observer is quoted in Cosmas, *Army for Empire*, 76. For a first-hand account of training given Spanish recruits and the experience of their passage to Cuba, see Tomas Alvarez Angulo, *Memorias de un hombre sin importancia (1878–1961)* (Madrid, 1962), 178–193. Alvarez Angulo served in the garrison at Santiago de Cuba during 1898.

13. For information on Weyler's early activity, see Chadwick, *United States and Spain: Diplomacy*, 431; and Valeriano Weyler y Nicolau, *Mi mando en Cuba: historia militar y política de la última guerra separatista*, (Madrid, 1906), vol. 1, p. 25. The latter is a five-volume set; dedicated to Cánovas, it constitutes Weyler's *apologia pro vita sua*. For the reconcentration order of February 16, 1896, see Chadwick, *United States and Spain: Diplomacy*, 432; and Albert G. Robinson, *Cuba and the Intervention* (New York, 1905), 44–45. For the hoped-for effects of reconcentration, see Foner, *Spanish-Cuban-American War*, vol. 1, pp. 78, 81, 110; Weyler, *Mi mando en Cuba*, vol. 1, p. 11. For Ewing's order, see Chadwick, *United States and Spain: Diplomacy*, 493. Many Spanish defenders of reconcentration at the time and since have argued that no other means existed to cope with guerrilla warfare. (For example, see Manuel Corral, *El desastre! Memorias de un voluntario en la campaña de Cuba* (Barcelona, 1899), 40, 73. Corral claims that reconcentration would ultimately have forced a decision in favor of Spain had it not been for the intervention of the United States. Weyler's reconcentration order of October 21, 1896, for Pinar del Río, reflects his version of this policy in its fully developed form: All people outside of a designated line were to remove themselves to be within it by eight days. Anyone who failed to comply would be treated as a rebel. It was illegal to move provisions between towns without permission of the military. Those who violated this rule were to be tried as abettors of the insurrection. Owners of beef cat-

tle were to take their animals to towns where they would receive protection. Insurgents who came in voluntarily after eight days would receive care. (A copy of this decree was enclosed in Polo to Day, 5 April 1898, *Foreign Relations, 1898,* 739.)

14. For Weyler's strategy, see Gabriel Maura Gamazo, *Historia crítica del reinado de Don Alfonso XIII de Austria durante su menoridad bajo la regencia de su madre Doña María Cristina de Austria,* (Barcelona, 1919) vol. 1, p. 277; Valeriano Weyler y Lopez y Puga, Duque de Rabí, *En el archivo de mi abuelo: biografía del Capitán General Weyler* (Madrid, 1946), 99–100; Fernando Gómez, *La insurrección por dentro: apuntes para la historia,* 2d ed., (Madrid, 1900), 23–24, 39; and Foner, *Spanish-Cuban-American War,* vol. 1, pp. 78, 81.

15. For parallel views, see Cosmas, *Army for Empire,* 78–79; see also Chapman, *Cuban Republic,* 78.

16. For comments on reconcentration, see May, *Imperial Democracy,* 127; Foner, *Spanish-Cuban-American War,* vol. 1, p. 77. Chadwick argues that reconcentration was legal under the laws of war, but that destruction of property as practiced by the insurgents was not (Chadwick, *United States and Spain: Diplomacy,* 493–494). In any event, the terrible death rate in the zones of reconcentration resulted from crowding and lack of food (Chapman, *Cuban Republic,* 81).

17. For Spain's foreign policy, see José María García Escudero, *De Cánovas á la república* (Madrid, 1951), 112; Duque de Tetuán, *Apuntes del ex-ministro de estado Duque de Tetuán para la defensa de la política internacional y gestión diplomática del gobierno liberal-conservador desde el 28 de Marzo de 1895 á 29 de Septiembre de 1897,* (n.p., 1902), vol. 1, pp. 121–123; May, *Imperial Democracy,* 107; and Jesus Pabón y Suárez de Urbina, *El 98, acontecimiento internacional,* (Madrid, 1952), 33–35. For Cánovas's realistic views, see Charles Benoist, *Cánovas del Castillo: la restauration rénovatrice* (Paris, 1930), 34; and his isolationism, see Meléndez y Meléndez, *Cánovas,* 166. See also Julio Salom Costa, *España en la Europa de Bismarck: la política exterior de Cánovas (1871–1881)* (Madrid, 1967), 414–422; and Vicente R. Pilapil, ''Spain in the European State System 1898–1913'' (Dissertation, Catholic University of America, 1964), 13.

18. Before developing his message Cánovas supported efforts to revive Spain's alliance with Italy—an arrangement that had lapsed in 1895—hoping by this device to gain support not only from Italy but from Austria-Hungary and Great Britain. This effort attracted no interest. (May, *Imperial Democracy,* 108.) On July 9, 1896, Fernando de León y Castillo, a leading Spanish diplomat, suggested in the Cortes that Spain seek diplomatic help in Europe, a preliminary to Tetuán's efforts (see his speech of this date quoted in Fernando de León y Castillo, Duque de Muní, *Mis tiempos,* [Madrid, 1921], vol. 2, p. 94). For details of Tetuán's activity, see May, *Imperial Democracy,* 108–109. See also the pioneering account of Orestes Ferrara, *The Last Spanish War: Revelations in ''Diplomacy''* (New York, 1937), 19, 31.

19. For initial reactions of the United States, see H. Wayne Morgan, *America's Road to Empire: The War with Spain and Overseas Expansion* (New York, London, and Sydney, 1965), 10; Chadwick, *United States and Spain: Diplomacy,* 411–412; Wilfred Hardy Callcott, *The Caribbean Policy of the United States, 1890–1920* (Baltimore, 1942), 83. For discussion of the distinctions between insurgency and belligerency, see Horace Edgar Flack, *Spanish-American Diplomatic Relations Preceding the War of 1898* (Baltimore, 1906), 9–31. John A. S. Grenville and George Berkeley Young think that Cleveland and Olney were correct in seeking to avoid war, but believe that mediation, as opposed to recognition of Cuban belligerency, was an unrealistic approach (see their *Politics, Strategy, and American Diplomacy: Studies in Foreign Policy, 1873–1917* [New Haven and London, 1966], 200). For congressional activity early in 1896, see May, *Imperial Democracy,* 76–78; John Layser Offner, ''President McKinley and the Origins of the Spanish-American War'' (Dissertation, Pennsylvania State University, 1957), 40, 43, 47; Grenville

and Young, *Politics, Strategy, and American Diplomacy*, 194; Foner, *Spanish-Cuban-American War*, vol. 1, p. 191; Walter LaFeber, *The New Empire: An Interpretation of American Expansion, 1860-1898* (Ithaca and London, 1963), 290-292.

20. Entry in William L. Wilson Diary, 3 March 1896, is quoted in Festus P. Summers, ed., *The Cabinet Diary of William L. Wilson, 1896-1897* (Chapel Hill, N.C., 1957), 38.

21. For information on Olney's note of April 4, 1896, see May, *Imperial Democracy*, 92; Morgan, *Road to Empire*, 11; Foner, *Spanish-Cuban-American War*, vol. 1, pp. 193-197; and Grenville and Young, *Politics, Strategy, and American Diplomacy*, 189-193. For the Spanish reply, see Tetuán to Olney, 4 June 1896, in Henry James, *Richard Olney and His Public Service: With Documents including Unpublished Diplomatic Correspondence* (Boston and New York, 1923), 290-303. A Liberal commentator on Tetuán, the Conde de Romanones, later criticized the Foreign Minister for not taking advantage of the American offer (see his *Sagasta, o el político* [Madrid y Barcelona, 1930], 185-186). For Cleveland's reaction, see the unsigned memorandum quoted in Allan Nevins, ed., *Letters of Grover Cleveland: 1850-1908* (Boston, 1933), 717. Perhaps to reinforce his own viewpoint, Cleveland issued a fresh neutrality proclamation on July 27, 1896 (George Roscoe Dulebohn, *Principles of Foreign Policy Under the Cleveland Administrations* [Philadelphia, 1941], 56-58).

22. For information on the campaign of 1896 and the "Cuban planks" of the two major parties, see Paolo E. Coletta, ed., *Threshold to American Internationalism: Essays on the Foreign Policies of William McKinley* (New York, 1970), 22; and May, *Imperial Democracy*, 78.

23. For the full text of Cleveland's statement, see Chadwick, *United States and Spain: Diplomacy*, 475-483. See also Morgan, *America's Road to Empire*, 11-12; and Healy, *The United States in Cuba, 1898-1902*, 11-12. Recent estimates show that the United States had $10 to $30 million invested in sugar and about $10 million in manufacturing (see Foner, *Spanish-Cuban-American War*, vol. 1, p. 189). Estimates made during the 1890s were probably high. Of course, the Wilson-Gorman Tariff of 1894—which raised the tariff on sugar imported into the United States—greatly reduced profits from the sugar trade in the American market and strengthened the hands of the Cuban insurgents (see Leland Hamilton Jenks, *Our Cuban Colony: A Study in Sugar* [New York, 1970], 40). For well-documented arguments that American sugar interests did not play an important role in precipitating the war with Spain, see Richard D. Weigle, "The Sugar Interests and American Diplomacy in Hawaii and Cuba, 1897-1903" (Dissertation, Yale University,), 242-243. For an analysis of Cleveland's message, see Dulebohn, *Principles of Foreign Policy Under the Cleveland Administrations*, 56-58. For correspondence relating to Taylor's discussions with Tetuán and other Spanish leaders in early January, 1897, see Taylor to Olney, January 2, 5, 7, and 8, 1897, *Diplomatic Despatches, Spain*, roll 122. See also Olney to Taylor, 4 January 1897, in U.S. State Department, *Instructions of the Department of State, 1809-1906, Spain*, Microcopy No. 77, National Archives and Records Service (Washington, D.C., 1946), roll 150, vol. 22, p. 269 (hereafter cited as *Diplomatic Instructions, Spain*). (Both of these microfilm records are taken from Record Group 59, General Records of the Department of State.) For information concerning Cleveland's opposition to a resolution offered by Senator Donald Cameron (Republican from Pennsylvania), see True, "Revolutionaries in Exile," 307-308. See also Grenville and Young, *Politics, Strategy, and American Diplomacy*, 198. For the abortive confidential negotiations of E. F. Atkinson and Oscar B. Stillman, see *Ibid.*, 195-199. Donald K. Carson, "Richard Olney, Secretary of State, 1895-1897" (Dissertation, University of Kentucky, 1969), 159-160.

24. For the Lodge-Roosevelt exchange, see Lodge to Roosevelt, 2 December 1896, in

Henry Cabot Lodge and Charles F. Redmond, eds., *Selections from the Correspondence of Theodore Roosevelt and Henry Cabot Lodge, 1884-1918*, (New York, 1971 reprint edition), vol. 1, 240; Roosevelt to Lodge, 4 December 1896, in *ibid.*, 243.

25. McKinley's statement to Cleveland is quoted in Dierks, *Leap to Arms*, 14; see also Henry F. Pringle, *Theodore Roosevelt: A Biography* (New York, 1931), 165. Offner quotes Cleveland as saying after his talk with McKinley that no other interview had impressed him "as being so full of settled sadness and sincerity, and no other man ever gave me a stronger idea of his unyielding determination to do his duty when confronted by a great crisis" (Offner, "President McKinley and the Origins of the Spanish-American War," 97.) McKinley's pronouncement against war is quoted in Coletta, ed., *Threshold to American Internationalism*, 12–13. For the view that Europe might conceivably intervene in an American-Spanish confrontation, see May, *Imperial Democracy*, 118–120.

26. For Spanish internal politics in this period, see May, *Imperial Democracy*, 96–107. For a modern summary of the restoration, see José Luis Comellas, *La restauración como experiencia histórica* (Seville, 1977).

27. For Maceo's death, see Alvarez Angulo, *Memorias*, 169; Fernández Almagro, *Historia política*, vol. 2, pp. 314–315.

28. For Cánovas's statement of 1865, see Meléndez y Meléndez, *Cánovas*, 340. Benoist's statement is quoted in May, *Imperial Democracy*, 132. See also Melchor Fernández Almagro, *Cánovas: su vida y su política* (Madrid, 1951), 588–589.

29. For information about the *Unión constitucional*, see May, *Imperial Democracy*, 94. The *unión* was particularly committed to controlling tax and tariff policies in the interests of Spanish officialdom in Cuba and the manufacturing and commercial interests in Spain that benefited from trade and investment associated with the Pearl of the Antilles. For information concerning the activities of the small Socialist party in Spain, see Jack A. Clarke, "Spanish Socialists and the Spanish-American War: A Note," *Mid-America* 40 (October 1958): 229–231.

30. Cánovas is quoted in Walter Herrick, Jr., *The American Naval Revolution* (Baton Rouge, La., 1966), 201. Tetuán's activity is described in Fernández Almagro, *Historia política*, vol. 2, pp. 403–404. For Cánovas and the possible sale of Cuba, see León y Castillo, *Mis tiempos*, vol. 2, pp. 98–100; Lema, *Cánovas*, 210–212; and Gabriel Maura Gamazo, *Historia crítica del reinado de Don Alfonso XIII durante su menoridad bajo la regencia de su madre Doña María Cristina de Austria*, (Barcelona, 1919), vol. 1, p. 361.

31. For the Liberal position, see the manifesto published in *El Correo* (Madrid) on June 24, 1897, and reprinted in *Foreign Relations, 1898*, 592–595. Moret is quoted in May, *Imperial Democracy*, 160; Tetuán reproduced two texts of Moret's statement, one for release to the newspapers and the other an official version for publication approved by Sagasta (see Tetuán, *Apuntes de Tetuán*, vol. 2, pp. 80–114; see also Romanones, *Sagasta*, 186).

32. For Woodford's appointment, see May, *Imperial Democracy*, 123–124.

33. For the diplomatic exchange with Madrid prior to Woodford's arrival there, see H. Wayne Morgan, *William McKinley and His America* (Syracuse, 1963), 342–343; and Sherman to Taylor, 1 September 1897, *Diplomatic Instructions, Spain*, roll 22, 420. For congressional activity in this period, especially the effort of Senator John T. Morgan (Democrat from Alabama) to obtain support for a joint resolution providing for recognition of Cuban belligerency, see Chadwick, *United States and Spain: Diplomacy*, 491; and Everett Walters, *Joseph Benson Foraker: An Uncompromising Republican* (Columbus, Ohio, 1948), 144–145. See also Morgan, *America's Road to Empire*, 26. For Woodford's instructions and their importance, see Sherman to Woodford, 16 July 1897, *Foreign Relations, 1898*, 558–559; and Grenville and Young, *Politics, Strategy, and American Diplomacy*, 248–249.

34. For Woodford's discussions with fellow American envoys in Europe, see Andrew Dickson White, *Autobiography of Andrew Dickson White* (New York, 1906), vol. 2, p. 162; Woodford to Sherman, 30 August 1897, *Diplomatic Despatches, Spain,* roll 123; Woodford to McKinley, 10 August 1897, *ibid.,* roll 123; and May, *Imperial Democracy,* 126.

35. For the assassination of Cánovas del Castillo, see May, *Imperial Democracy,* 111; Alvarez Angulo, *Memorias,* 174–177; and Fernández Almagro, *Cánovas,* 623–625. Cánovas was only one of a long list of leaders assassinated by anarchists in this period: President Sadi Carnot of France was killed in 1895; Empress Isabel of Austria-Hungary fell in 1898; later killings included King Humberto of Italy and President McKinley in 1901. Woodford's course can be traced in his correspondence with President McKinley and his messages to the State Department, as in for example, Woodford to McKinley, 19 August 1897, *Diplomatic Despatches, Spain,* roll 123—which records his desire to delay his arrival in Spain; and Woodford to McKinley, 3 September 1897, *ibid.,* roll 123.

36. For Woodford's dealings with the Duke of Tetuán, see Lester B. Shippee and Royal B. Way, "William Rufus Day," in Samuel Flagg Bemis, ed., *The American Secretaries of State and Their Diplomacy,* (New York, 1929), vol. 9, p. 50; Sherman to Taylor, 17 September 1897, *Diplomatic Instructions, Spain,* roll 22, 427; and Woodford to Sherman, 20 September 1897, *Foreign Relations, 1898,* 565–568. See also Coletta, ed., *Threshold to American Internationalism,* 42.

37. For the circumstances that led to Sagasta's return, see F. Soldevilá, *Historia de España,* 2d ed., (Barcelona, 1964), vol. 8, p. 393; Jerónimo Bécker, *Historia de las relaciones exteriores de España durante el siglo XIX (Apuntes para una historia diplomática),* Volume 3: *1868–1900* (Madrid, 1926), pp. 853–854; May, *Imperial Democracy,* 160; and Romanones, *Sagasta,* 187. Woodford's concerns are expressed in Woodford to Sherman, 6 October 1897, *Diplomatic Despatches, Spain,* roll 123; and Woodford to Sherman, 16 October 1897, *Foreign Relations, 1898,* 581. For the replacement of Weyler, see Weyler, *Mi mando en Cuba,* vol. 1, p. 7; and Becker, *Historia de las relaciones exteriores de España,* vol. 3, p. 854. Besides Moret as minister for the colonies, the new Cabinet included Miguel Correa y García as Minister of War, Segismundo Bermejo y Merelo as Minister of the Marine, and Pío Gullón as Foreign Minister.

38. For the Spanish note, see Gullón to Woodford, 23 October 1897, *Foreign Relations, 1898,* 582–589 (the quotation is on p. 584). See also Woodford to Sherman, 26 October 1897, *Diplomatic Despatches, Spain,* roll 123.

39. For interpretation of Sagasta's motives, see Romanones, *Sagasta,* 189.

40. For *junta* viewpoints, see Estrada Palma to José Frías, 3 November 1897, *Correspondencia diplomática de la delegación cubana en Nueva York durante la guerra de independencia de 1895 a 1898* (Havana, 1943), vol. 1, pp. 147–149; Estrada Palma to R. E. Betances, 3 November 1897, *ibid.,* 150; Estrada Palma to Francisco de Arredondo, 10 October 1897, *ibid.,* 151–152. For the views of Gómez, see Juan Nido y Segalerva, *Historia política y parlamentaria de Excmo. D. Práxedes Mateo Sagasta* (Madrid, 1915), 898; and Gómez, *Diario,* 395. For his execution of Lt. Col. Joaquín Ruíz, see Leopoldo Horrego Estuch, *Máximo Gómez: libertador y ciudadano* (Havana, 1948), 203. Gómez never wavered in his views. See his comments made on February 12, 1898, in which he argued that autonomy was really a device intended to divide the Cubans and that foreign intervention would eventually decide the war's outcome. Emilio Roig de Leuchsenring, *Ideario cubano,* Volume 2: *Máximo Gómez* (Havana, 1936), 98. For Conte's views see his *Recuerdos,* vol. 3, p. 583. Conte held that Sagasta and Moret lacked the "valor" necessary in the situation. What was called for was not autonomy but an outright grant of independence. For Lee's views, see Lee to William R. Day, 23 November 1897, *Consular Despatches, Havana,* roll 131; this despatch is also published in U.S. House of

Representatives, *Consular Correspondence Respecting the Conditions of the Reconcentrados in Cuba, the State of War in That Island, and the Prospects of the Projected Autonomy,* 55th Cong., 1st Sess., House Doc. No. 406 (Washington, D.C., 1898), 8–9. Lee, of course, had taken this view much earlier (see his comment of March 17, 1897, to Assistant Secretary of State Day quoted in Morgan, *William McKinley and His America,* 341).

41. Woodford's notice of America's adherence to law in its dealings with filibusters is in Woodford to Gullón, 30 October 1897, *Diplomatic Despatches, Spain,* roll 123. For a typical report on suffering in Cuba, see that of A. C. Brice, consul at Matanzas, on October 15, 1897, in *Foreign Relations, 1898,* 596–597. For American comments on reconcentration, see Sherman to Woodford, 6 November 1897, *Diplomatic Instructions, Spain,* roll 22, 542–543; and Sherman to Dupuy de Lôme, 6 November 1897, in *Notes to Foreign Legations in the United States from the Department of State, 1834–1906: Spain,* Microcopy No. 99, National Archives and Records Service (Washington, D.C., 1950), roll 90, 349–351 (hereafter cited as *Notes to Foreign Legations, Spain*). For the Spanish reply, see Dupuy de Lôme to Sherman, 18 November 1897, *Notes from Spanish Legation,* roll 129. Woodford's reactions after Gullón's note are found, for example, in Woodford to McKinley, 7 November 1897, *Diplomatic Despatches, Spain,* roll 103 (in which the quotation can be found), Woodford to McKinley, 20 November 1897, *ibid.,* and Woodford to Sherman, 20 November 1897, *ibid.* Washington's statement that it would give Madrid reasonable time to implement its policies is in Sherman to Woodford, 20 November 1897, *Foreign Relations, 1898,* 611.

42. Woodford to Sherman, 24 November 1897, *Diplomatic Despatches, Spain,* roll 123; and Woodford to McKinley, 4 December 1897, *ibid.* For indications of modifications in Weyler's methods, see Dupuy de Lôme to Sherman, 6 December 1897, *Notes to Foreign Legations, Spain,* roll 29. For Blanco's strategy, see Maura Gamazo, *Historia crítica,* vol. 1, p. 362. The texts of the autonomy decrees and comments on them are in *Foreign Relations, 1898,* 617–644. See also Woodford to Sherman, 26 November 1897, *Diplomatic Despatches, Spain,* roll 123. For a defense of the decrees, arguing that they represented an important break with past Spanish tradition, see Rafael María de Labra, *Aspecto internacional de la cuestión de Cuba* (Madrid, 1900), 45–55. For a more negative view, emphasizing the ways in which Spain retained final authority, see Foner, *Spanish-Cuban-American War,* vol. 1, pp. 133–134. Foner does not answer Labra's contention that the decrees included all that the Cuban *autonomistas* had been asking for since 1879.

43. For comments on the President's message, see May, *Imperial Democracy,* 125–126, 161 (followed here); Healy, *The United States in Cuba,* 13; Sherman to Woodford, 6 December 1897, *Diplomatic Instructions, Spain,* roll 22, 543–544; and Woodford to Sherman, 7 December 1897, *Diplomatic Despatches, Spain,* roll 123. For Woodford's comment, see Woodford to McKinley, 11 December 1897, *ibid.*

44. For Lee's communications, see Lee to Day, December 13, 14, and 15, 1897, *Consular Despatches, Havana,* roll 131. For a later, even grimmer assessment of the situation, see Lee to Day, 8 January 1898, *ibid.*

45. For the relief project, see Day to Dupuy de Lôme, 18 December 1897, *Notes to Foreign Legations, Spain,* roll 90, 363–367; Day to Lee, 24 December 1897, *Consular Despatches, Havana,* roll 131; and Chadwick, *United States and Spain: Diplomacy,* 529. For Herbert Croly's assessment, see his *Marcus Alonzo Hanna: His Life and Work* (New York, 1912), 277.

46. May, *Imperial Democracy,* 162. For relevant correspondence, see Woodford to McKinley, 8 January 1898, *Diplomatic Despatches, Spain,* roll 123; Woodford to Sherman, 24 January 1898, *ibid.,* roll 124; Day to Woodford, 24 January 1898, *Diplomatic Instructions, Spain,* roll 124; Woodford to Gullón, 25 January 1898, *ibid.;* Woodford to McKinley, 28 January 1898, *ibid.,* roll 123; Woodford to

McKinley, 31 January 1898, *ibid.*; and Woodford to Sherman, 3 February 1898, *ibid.*, roll 124.

47. For discussion of information reaching Madrid, see May, *Imperial Democracy*, 164. May notes receipt in Madrid of discouraging word from both General Blanco and an important Spanish editor and politician, the radical José Canalejas. For Canalejas's visit in the United States, during which time he had an interview with McKinley and heard the President's protestations of peaceful intent, see Maura Gamazo, *Historia crítica*, vol. 1, p. 342. The Cuban *junta* planned demonstrations against Canalejas during his visit (Estrada Palma to Dr. R. E. Betances, 26 October 1897, *Correspondencia diplomática de la delegación cubana*, vol. 1, pp. 143–144). For Woodford's projected visit, see Offner, "President McKinley and the Origins of the Spanish-American War," 181–182. Woodford's report of his talks with the Queen Regent and Moret is Woodford to McKinley, 17 January 1898, *Diplomatic Despatches, Spain*, roll 123.

48. The autonomous governments began functioning in Cuba on January 1, 1898 and in Puerto Rico on January 15, 1898. For views on the failure of the autonomous regimes, see León y Castillo, *Mis tiempos*, vol. 2, p. 98; Olcott, *McKinley*, vol. 2, pp. 6–7. For Weyler's interpretation, see *Mi mando in Cuba*, vol. 1, p. 13.

49. For the movements of the *Maine*, see John D. Long, *The New American Navy* (New York, 1903), vol. 1, p. 135; Hyman G. Rickover, *How the Battleship "Maine" Was Destroyed* (Washington, 1970), 22–23. For Lee's views, see Lee to Day, 3 December 1897, *Consular Despatches, Havana*, roll 131. The consul general remained skeptical of Blanco's chances for success (Lee to Day, 7 December 1898, *ibid.*).

50. For information about the riot, see May, *Imperial Democracy*, 135–137; Lee to Day, 12 January 1898, *Foreign Relations, 1898*, 1,024; and Lee to Day, 13 February 1898, *ibid.*, 1,025. Lee's immediate reactions are reported in Lee to Day, January 13, 14, and 18, 1898, *Consular Despatches, Havana*, roll 131. For information about the Cabinet meeting of January 14, 1898, see John D. Long Diary, 14 January 1898, quoted in Margaret Long, ed., *The Journal of John D. Long* (Rindge, N.H.; 1956), 213. For messages relating to the dispatch of the *Maine*, see Day to Lee, 22 January 1898, in *Consular Despatches, Havana*, roll 131.; Day to Lee, 24 January 1898, in *Foreign Relations, 1898*, 1,025–1,026 (two messages); Lee to Day, 24 January 1898, in *ibid.*, 1,025; Lee to Day, 25 January 1898, *Consular Despatches, Havana*, roll 131; and Rickover, *How the "Maine" Was Destroyed*, 34. For correspondence arranging the visit with Madrid see three messages, from Woodford to Sherman on January 25, 27, and 28, 1898, in *Diplomatic Despatches, Spain*, roll 124.

51. Long Diary, 24 January 1898, quoted in Lawrence Shaw Mayo, ed., *America of Yesterday: As Reflected in the Journal of John Davis Long* (Boston, 1923), 153–155; also in Margaret Long, ed., *Journal of John D. Long*, 213–214. The belief still persists that McKinley sent the *Maine* to either heat up the situation in Havana or intimidate Spain. However, no evidence is available to support either claim. Long's account of the reasons for the mission, however simple, seems generally sound, although in all probability the McKinley Administration hoped that in some way the *Maine*'s presence at Havana would have a calming effect. It is also possible that McKinley also considered the annoyance that might be produced in the United States if violence in Havana were to adversely affect American citizens or interests there without his having taken prior steps to provide protection. Rickover argues that McKinley acted suddenly in dispatching the *Maine* in order to preclude Spanish objections. The action, he writes, was taken to guard American interests and "take advantage of whatever opportunities time might bring." (Rickover, *How the "Maine" was Destroyed*, 32).

52. For Sigsbee's initial reports, see Sigsbee to Long, 29 and 31 January 1898, *RG 45*, Entry 40. The quotation from Sigsbee's report is in Sigsbee to Long, 1 February

1898, *AF*, file 8, roll 26. For other reports indicating quiet in Havana, see Sigsbee to Long, 3 and 9 February 1898, *ibid.* Lee's desire to retain a battleship at Havana is stated in Lee to Day, 4 February 1898, *Foreign Relations, 1898,* 1,027–1,028. This message was sent in response to Day to Lee, 4 February 1898, *ibid.,* 1,027. For Lee's letter to Day of February 5, 1898, see *Consular Despatches, Havana,* roll 132.

53. For the reports from the *Montgomery,* see Converse to Long, February 3, 8, and 10, 1898, *RG 45,* Entry 40, nos. 2, 38, 35, 37; Converse to Long, 6 February 1898, *Foreign Relations, 1898,* 669–670. Lee and Sigsbee's views are in Lee to Day, 4 February 1898, *Consular Despatches, Havana,* roll 132; Sigsbee to Long, 8 February 1898, *Foreign Relations, 1898,* 673; and Lee to Day, 10 February 1898, *Consular Despatches, Havana,* roll 132. Sigsbee accurately argued that the practice of reconcentration was a logical response to guerrilla tactics: ''It is guerrilla war on both sides, and in a country where physical characteristics are ideal for the purpose. It is a war of blockhouses and marauding or scouting bands. The Cuban policy is to tire out all the Spaniards and to prevent such agricultural operations as will provide revenue to the Spanish government'' (Sigsbee to Long, 8 February 1898, *Foreign Relations, 1898,* 672).

54. Woodford to McKinley, 4 February 1898, *Diplomatic Despatches, Spain,* roll 123; and Woodford to McKinley, 7 February 1898, *ibid.* For Spain's reversion to a policy of mere delay—for which there were many precedents in Spanish history—see May, *Imperial Democracy,* 168. For a summary account of the failure of Spanish reforms in Cuba, see Offner, ''President McKinley and the Origins of the Spanish-American War,'' 160–183. For Woodford's later concern about war with Spain—which arose in the wake of the Dupuy de Lôme affair and the sinking of the *Maine*—see Woodford to Sherman, 12 February 1898, *Foreign Relations, 1898,* 1,011; and Woodford to McKinley, 19 February 1898, *Diplomatic Despatches, Spain,* roll 123.

55. For accounts of the Dupuy de Lôme letter, see Horatio Rubens, *Liberty: The Story of Cuba* (New York, 1932), 287–292. See also Foner, *Spanish-Cuban-American War,* vol. 1, pp. 233–234, which relies on Ruben's account. Relevant correspondence is Dupuy de Lôme to Gullón, 8 and 9 February 1898, in Spanish Ministry of State, *Spanish Diplomatic Correspondence and Documents, 1896–1900, Presented to the Cortes by the Minister of State* (Washington, D.C., 1905), 80–82 (hereafter cited as *Spanish Diplomatic Documents*); Day to Woodford, 9 February 1898, *Foreign Relations, 1898,* 1,008 (a cable giving notice of the letter and demanding the recall of Dupuy de Lôme); Woodford to Sherman, 11 February 1898, *ibid.,* 1,008–1,009; and Day to Woodford, 12 February 1898, *Diplomatic Instructions, Spain,* roll 22, 499.

56. For the text of the letter, see Dupuy de Lôme to Canalejas, December 1897, *Foreign Affairs, 1898,* 1,007–1,008.

57. For Long's views, see Long Diary, 10 February 1898, quoted in Mayo, ed., *America of Yesterday,* 162. McKinley's note is quoted in Morgan, *America's Road to Empire,* 43. For involved correspondence concerning the Spanish government's apology for Dupuy de Lôme's indiscretion, see Woodford to Sherman, 11 February 1898, *Foreign Relations, 1898,* 1,008–1,009; Woodford to Sherman, 12 February 1898, *ibid.,* 1,011; Woodford to Sherman, 14 February 1898, *Diplomatic Despatches, Spain,* roll 124; Woodford to Sherman, 15 February 1898, *ibid.,* roll 123; Woodford to Sherman, 17 February 1898, *Foreign Relations, 1898,* 1,014; Day to Woodford, 18 February 1898, *Diplomatic Instructions, Spain,* roll 22, 501–502; Woodford to Sherman, 19 February 1898, *Diplomatic Despatches, Spain,* roll 124; Sherman to Woodford, 27 February 1898, *Foreign Relations, 1898,* 1,018–1,020; and Woodford to Sherman, 8 March 1898, *Diplomatic Despatches, Spain,* roll 124.

58. For general comments on the reactions in Washington and Madrid after the sinking of the *Maine,* see Leech, *In the Days of McKinley,* 170–171; and May, *Imperial Democracy,* 164–165.

CHAPTER 2

1. For Dodge's view, see Dodge to McKinley, 21 February 1898, quoted in Stanley P. Hirshson, *Grenville M. Dodge: Soldier, Politician, and Railroad Builder* (Bloomington and London, 1967), 230. Godkin is quoted in William E. Armstrong, *E. L. Godkin and American Foreign Policy 1865-1900* (New York, 1957), 196. For the Secretary of the Navy's views, see Long Diary, 24 February 1898, quoted in Lawrence Shaw Mayo, ed., *America of Yesterday: As Reflected in the Journal of John Davis Long* (Boston, 1923), 168.

2. For Dawes's observations see Dawes Diary, 26 February 1898, quoted in Bascom Timmons, ed., *A Journal of McKinley Years by Charles G. Dawes* (Chicago, 1950), 145. For Roosevelt's assessment, see Roosevelt to Douglas Robinson, 6 March 1898, in Elting E. Morison et al., eds., *The Letters of Theodore Roosevelt* (Cambridge, 1951), vol. 1, p. 789.

3. Morse to Long, 6 March 1898, quoted in Gardner Weld Allen, ed., *Papers of John Davis Long, 1897-1904* (Boston, 1939), 68; and Bouvé to Long, 2 March 1898, in *ibid.*, 64.

4. Woodford to McKinley, 23 February 1898, *Diplomatic Despatches, Spain*, roll 123; and Woodford to McKinley, 26 February 1898, *Foreign Relations, 1898*, 665.

5. For Sagasta's electoral maneuvers, see Juan Ortega Rubio, *Historia de la regencia de María Cristina Hapsbourg-Lorena* (Madrid, 1906), vol. 3, p. 243. The date for the meeting of the Cortes was originally announced as April 25, but on April 14 it was moved up to April 20, a consequence of the great crisis that had materialized in recent days. For Woodford's analysis, see Woodford to Sherman, 28 February 1898, *Foreign Relations, 1898*, 666.

6. Sherman to Woodford, 1 March 1898, *Foreign Relations, 1898*, 666-669. Woodford did not receive this instruction until March 15, when he acknowledged it. See Woodford to Sherman, 15 March 1898, *Diplomatic Despatches, Spain*, roll 124.

7. For information on Moret's complaints and the American reaction, see Woodford to McKinley, 2 March 1898, *Foreign Relations, 1898*, 673-676; Day to Woodford, 2 March 1898, *ibid.*, 676; Woodford to Sherman, 3 March 1898, *ibid.*, 677; Woodford to Day, 4 March 1898, *Diplomatic Instructions, Spain*, roll 123; Woodford to Day, 6 March 1898, *Foreign Relations, 1898*, 678-679; and Day to Lee, 8 March 1898, *Consular Despatches, Havana*, roll 132. For Day's letter, see Day to Woodford, 3 March 1898, *ibid.*, 681.

8. For the origins and passage of the Fifty-Million-Dollar Bill and interpretations of its significance, see Ernest R. May, *Imperial Democracy: The Emergence of America as a Great Power* (New York, 1961), 149; Graham A. Cosmas, *An Army for Empire: The United States Army in the Spanish-American War* (Columbia, Mo., 1971), 73 (Cosmas's views are followed in the present account); Walter Millis, *The Martial Spirit: A Study of Our War With Spain* (Boston and New York, 1931), 115-117. For the views of the Secretary of the Navy, see Long Diary, 8 March 1898, quoted in Mayo, ed., *America of Yesterday*, 172-173.

9. Dawes's observations are recorded in Dawes Journal, 9 March 1898, in Timmons, ed., *Journal of the McKinley Years*, 145-146. Bryan is quoted in Paolo E. Coletta, *William Jennings Bryan*, Volume 1: *Political Evangelist, 1860-1908* (Lincoln, Neb., 1964), 221. (This is the first volume of an authoritative three-volume biography that finally meets the need for a fully detailed and reliable study of Bryan.)

10. Woodford to McKinley, 9 March 1898, *Foreign Relations, 1898*, 681-685.

11. For Du Bosc's views, see Du Bosc to Gullón, 25 February 1898, *Spanish Diplomatic Documents*, 88. He had been moved to comment by preliminary reports coming from Havana that a submarine mine had caused the explosion. This news, he noted, had "stirred up the greatest agitation until even the most important and conservative men have lost their heads." For the American report, see U.S. Senate, *Message From the President of the United States, Transmitting the Report of the*

Naval Court of Inquiry Upon the Destruction of the United States Battleship "Maine" in Havana Harbor, February 15, 1898, Together With the Testimony Taken Before the Court, 55th Cong., 2nd Sess., Senate Document No. 207 (Washington, D.C., 1898). For comments on the report, see Jack Cameron Dierks, *A Leap to Arms: The Cuban Campaign of 1898* (Philadelphia and New York, 1970), 20–21; and French Ensor Chadwick, *The Relations of the United States and Spain: Diplomacy* (New York, 1909), 561.

12. For the Spanish Report, see the translation in U.S. Senate, *Report of the Committee on Foreign Relations, United States Senate, Relative to Affairs in Cuba (April 13, 1898),* 55th Cong., 2d Sess., Senate Document No. 885 (Washington, D.C., 1898). For a summary, see Gullón to Polo de Bernabé, 27 March 1898, *Spanish Diplomatic Documents,* 102. See also Dierks, *Leap to Arms,* 21. What was the truth of the matter? No final determination can be made. The *Maine* was raised in 1912, towed out to sea, and scuttled. The most likely probability is that the ship's forward magazines were indeed triggered by an internal explosion, as the Spanish board contended. If an external weapon had triggered the explosion, who would have done it? Certainly Spanish authorities were the least likely to do anything of the sort; they desperately sought to avoid war. More likely perpetrators would have been either the Cuban insurgents, hoping by this method to precipitate American intervention in their behalf, or angry *incondicionalistas,* intransigent opponents in Cuba of any concessions to the insurgents. Recently Admiral Hyman G. Rickover arranged for a modern engineering analysis by Ib S. Hansen and David W. Taylor. The two argue convincingly that a primary explosion in the six-inch reserve magazine caused a partial detonation of other forward magazines. It is probable that a fire in Bunker A-16 caused by spontaneous combustion led to the explosion. (See, for the Hansen-Price report, Appendix A in Hyman G. Rickover, *How the Battleship Maine Was Destroyed* [Washington, 1976], 107–130.)

13. Dawes Journal, 22 March 1898, quoted in Timmons, ed., *Journal of the McKinley Years,* 147.

14. For a thorough and convincing analysis of Proctor's speech, see Gerald F. Linderman, *The Mirror of War: American Society and the Spanish-American War* (Ann Arbor, 1974), 42–43, 57–58. Some observers at the time thought that Proctor had gone to Cuba at the instance of President McKinley, but Linderman shows that this impression was incorrect (*Ibid.,* 54–55). Well before he made his speech, Proctor informed a correspondent of his real feelings: "I very much regret that we have not done more to aid the Cuban cause, but . . . it seemed to rest mainly with the administration, and the pressure of business interests has prevented possible action so far. The city interests have made strenuous protests against action that many have claimed would bring on commercial disaster, etc., just as there seemed to be a chance of returning to prosperity. I do not take any stock in this view of the case, but I have been helpless to do very much" (Proctor to Paul Brooks, 14 February 1898, quoted in *ibid.,* 50). Reed is quoted in Arthur Wallace Dunn, *From Harrison to Harding: A Personal Narrative, Covering a Third of a Century, 1888–1921,* (New York and London, 1922), vol. 1, p. 234. Dunn, however, is at points unreliable. In the absence of corroborating evidence, the historian must use his work with caution. Whether this particular incident really occurred or not, the statement is certainly consistent with the general picture of Reed that remains.

15. Dawes diary, 19 March 1898, quoted in Timmons, ed., *Journal of the McKinley Years,* 147.

16. For the brief discussion of purchase, see Woodford to McKinley, 17 March 1898, *Foreign Relations, 1898,* 685–688; Woodford to McKinley, 18 March 1898, *ibid.,* 688–692; and Woodford to McKinley, 19 March 1898, *ibid.,* 693. For information on the activities of María Cristina and McKinley regarding purchase, see May, *Imperial Democracy,* 149–150. May reports that McKinley also considered briefly the

possibility of Spain's retaining nominal sovereignty over Cuba with the United States developing a relation to Cuba-like that obtaining at the time between Great Britain and Egypt. (Turkey retained nominal sovereignty over Egypt, but Egypt governed itself under the supervision of Great Britain.) This arrangement proved unacceptable to both the fire-eaters of 1898 and the Cuban insurgents (*Ibid.*, 150). On Woodford's dealings in March, 1898, see *ibid.*, 166–167.

17. For these developments, see Woodford to McKinley, 19 March 1898, *Foreign Relations, 1898,* 692; Day to Woodford, 20 March 1898, *ibid.,* 692–693; Woodford to McKinley, 21 March 1898, *ibid.,* 695; Woodford to McKinley, 22 March 1898, *ibid.,* 696; and Woodford to McKinley, 23 March 1898, *ibid.,* 696–697. For the official text of the instruction, see Woodford to Gullón, 23 March 1898, *Spanish Diplomatic Documents,* 95. Woodford declared himself prepared to transmit any Spanish proposal to his government. See also, for a detailed account of this episode, Woodford to Sherman, 25 March 1898, *Foreign Relations, 1898,* 698–701.

18. For correspondence related to this development, see Woodford to McKinley (cable), 24 March 1898, *ibid.,* 697; Woodford to McKinley (letter), 24 March 1898, *Diplomatic Despatches, Spain,* roll 123; and Woodford to McKinley, 25 March 1898, *ibid.*

19. Woodford to Sherman, 25 March 1898, *Foreign Relations, 1898,* 698–701; Gullón to Woodford, 25 March 1898, *Spanish Diplomatic Documents,* 96–97; and Woodford to McKinley, 26 March 1898, *Diplomatic Despatches, Spain,* roll 123.

20. Margaret Leech, *In the Days of McKinley* (New York, 1959), 174–175. Day asked Lee to report on relief needs in Cuba (Day to Lee, 26 March 1898, *Consular Despatches, Havana,* roll 132.) McKinley's message to Woodford regarding the *Maine* is in Sherman to Woodford, 26 March 1898, *Foreign Relations, 1898,* 1,036–1,037.

21. For this information, see Dawes Diary, 26 March 1898, in Timmons, ed., *Journal of the McKinley Years,* 149. For an early recommendation that the navy be ordered to intercept the Spanish flotilla, see George C. Remey to Crowninshield, 18 March 1898, *AF,* file 8, roll 227.

22. Woodford to Day, 27 March 1898, incorporating text of Day to Woodford (telegram), 25 March 1898, *Foreign Relations, 1898,* 712–713.

23. For the procedural message, see Day to Woodford, 27 March 1898, *ibid.,* 711–712.

24. This interpretation is drawn from May, *Imperial Democracy,* 152–154. For information about the senatorial group opposed to war, see Dunn, *From Harrison to Harding,* vol. 1, p. 231.

25. Dunn, *From Harrison to Harding,* vol. 1, p. 147; Platt to H. Wales Lines, 25 March 1898, quoted in Louis A. Coolidge, *An Old Fashioned Senator: Orville H. Platt of Connecticut* (New York and London, 1910), 271–272; Dawes Diary, 27 March 1898, quoted in Timmons, ed., *Journal of the McKinley Years,* 149. Notable support for Cuba emanated from the south. One authority argues that Representative Joseph W. Bailey (Democrat from Texas), minority leader of the Democrats in the House of Representatives, reflected regional sympathy for Cuba's opposition to a despotic central government, presumably a legacy of the Civil War (Sam Acheson, "Joseph W. Bailey and the Spanish War," *Southwest Review,* 17 [1932]; 142–143). For another Southern expansionist's views, see August C. Radke, Jr., "John Tyler Morgan, An Expansionist Senator, 1897–1907," (Dissertation, University of Washington, 1953).

26. For the memorandum to the Spanish government, see Woodford to Sagasta, 29 March 1898, *Spanish Diplomatic Documents,* 106–107. For Woodford's views on the probable outcome—American acquisition of Cuba—see Woodford to McKinley, 29 March 1898, *Foreign Relations, 1898,* 718–721. See also Woodford to McKinley (cable), 29 March 1898, *ibid.,* 718; and Woodford to Day (letter), 30 March 1898, *ibid.,* 721–724.

27. For Day's views expressed to Woodford reporting tension in Washington, see Day

to Woodford, 30 March 1898, *ibid.*, 718. For Dawes's views, see Dawes Diary, 29 March 1898, quoted in Timmons, ed., *Journal of the McKinley Years*, 150.

28. Leech, *In the Days of McKinley*, 184–185. For the original account of Day's encounter with the unidentified senator, see Jennie Hobart, *Memories* (n.p., 1930), 61 (recollections of the wife of McKinley's Vice-President, Garrett A. Hobart). For the quoted poem, see Frank Arthur Putnam, *A Battle Call for Cuba* (Chicago, 1898).

29. Day to Woodford, 30 March 1898, *Foreign Relations, 1898*, 721.

30. For Polo's estimate of the situation in Washington, see Polo to Gullón, 27 March 1898, *Spanish Diplomatic Documents*, 101. For a similar appraisal, see Polo to Gullón, 3 April 1898, *ibid.*, 110. For Blanco's activities, see Polo to Day, 26 March 1898, *Foreign Affairs, 1898*, 705–710; Polo to Gullón, 28 March 1898, *ibid.*, 714–717 (two messages); and Polo to Day, 31 March 1898, *ibid.*, 725–726 (two messages). The State Department received Blanco's proclamation of the end of reconcentration on April 1. For the activities of the autonomic government, see Polo to Day, 1 April 1898, *ibid.*, 728–729.

31. For the report of the Spanish response, see Woodford to Day, 31 March 1898, *ibid.*, 726–727. For Woodford's later comments, see Woodford to McKinley, 31 March 1898, *Diplomatic Despatches, Spain*, roll 123; Woodford to McKinley, 1 April 1898, *Foreign Relations, 1898*, 727–728; and Woodford to Day, 2 April 1898, *ibid.*, 731.

32. Woodford to McKinley, 3 April 1898, *ibid.*, 732.

33. The Kaiser is quoted in May, *Imperial Democracy*, 196. For Bülow's action, see Bülow to Wilhelm II, 29 September 1897, quoted in E. T. S. Dugdale, *German Diplomatic Documents, 1871–1914*, Volume 2: *From Bismarck's Fall to 1898* (London, 1929), 496; Prince Bernhard von Bülow, *Memoirs of Prince Bülow*, Volume I: *From Secretary of State to Imperial Chancellor, 1897–1903* (Boston, 1931), 70–71, 255.

34. This interview was reported to Paris on January 5, 1898 (May, *Imperial Democracy*, 211).

35. For the reactions of France, see May, *Imperial Democracy*, 204–209. See also Fernando de León y Castillo, Marqués del Muni, *Mis Tiempos* (Madrid, 1921), vol. 2, pp. 105–106. For Austria-Hungary and Italy, see May, *Imperial Democracy*, 204, 212.

36. Taylor is quoted in a pioneering study of European diplomatic activity in relation to the War With Spain: Orestes Ferrara, *The Last Spanish War: Revelations in "Diplomacy"* (New York, 1937), 97. For Roosevelt's views, see Roosevelt to Francis Cruger Moore, 5 February 1898, in Elting E. Morison, ed., *The Letters of Theodore Roosevelt* (Cambridge, Mass., 1951), vol. 1, 768–769. For Bülow's view, see Bülow to Eulenberg, 15 March 1898, quoted in Dugdale, *German Diplomatic Documents*, vol. 2, p. 500.

37. Queen Regent of Spain to Queen Victoria, 17 March 1898, in George Earle Buckle, ed., *The Letters of Queen Victoria, Third Series, a Selection from Her Majesty's Correspondence and Journal Between the Years 1886 and 1901*, Volume 3: *1896–1901* (London, 1932), 236–237; Marquess of Salisbury to Queen Victoria, 1 April 1898, in *ibid.*, 239. Information coming to President McKinley constantly confirmed the view that Britain would take no action inimical to American interests. See, for example, William Osborne to McKinley, 22 March 1898, Papers of William McKinley, microfilm copy, Library of Congress, Washington, D.C., series I, roll 3. Osborne reported, "I have been delighted at the generous expressions of approval given over here towards your course, and I am satisfied that the Government of the English people would like some overture on the part of the United States towards closer relations with each other."

38. For the Spanish initiative, see Gullón to Representatives Abroad, 25 March 1898,

Spanish Diplomatic Documents, 99. For various diplomatic reports, exchanges, and instructions stemming from the Spanish initiative, see Salisbury to Barclay (United States), 29 March 1898, in *Records of the British Foreign Office,* Correspondence Between the Foreign Office and the British Embassy in Madrid, Foreign Office 185, box 863, Public Records Office, London, England (cited hereafter as *FO 185*). See also Rascón (London) to Gullón, 26 March 1898, *Spanish Diplomatic Documents,* 100; Hoyos (Vienna) to Gullón, *ibid.*; Villagonzalo (St. Petersburg) to Gullón, 27 March 1898, *ibid.,* 101; Mazo (Rome) to Gullón, 27 March 1898, *ibid.*; Méndez Vigo (Berlin) to Gullón, 28 March 1898, *ibid.*; Rumbold (Vienna) to Salisbury, 29 March 1898, *FO 185,* box 864; and Villagonzalo to Gullón, 30 March 1898, *Spanish Diplomatic Documents,* 107. For the exchange between Salisbury and Pauncefote, see Salisbury to Barclay, 29 March 1898, *FO 185,* box 863; and Pauncefote to Salisbury, 29 March 1898, *FO 185,* box 863. For some account of the period, see Lewis Einstein, "British Diplomacy in the Spanish-American War," *Proceedings of the Massachusetts Historical Society,* 76, (January-December, 1964): 35-36. For Spain's misconception of the result and the actual outcome, see Gullón to Representatives Abroad, 31 March 1898, *Spanish Diplomatic Documents,* 109; and May, *Imperial Democracy,* 171-172.

39. For notice to Madrid that the Vatican supported the proposed initiative by the great powers, see Merry del Val (Spanish ambassador to Vatican) to Gullón, 25 March 1898, *Spanish Diplomatic Documents,* 99-100. For Germany's role, see Dugdale, ed., *German Diplomatic Documents,* 503; Ferrara, *Last Spanish War,* 113-114; and May, *Imperial Democracy,* 215. For Rampolla's and Ireland's activity, see James H. Moynihan, *The Life of Archbishop John Ireland* (New York, 1953), 162.

40. Merry del Val to Gullón, 2 April 1898, *Spanish Diplomatic Documents,* 109; May, *Imperial Democracy,* 172-174; and Gullón to Merry del Val, 3 April 1898, *Spanish Diplomatic Documents,* 110. The Spanish government informed Britain of this proposal (Spanish Ambassador to British Government, 4 April 1898, *FO 185,* box 864). For the attitude of Minister of War Miguel Correa and Minister of the Marine Segismundo Bermejo—who with the Conde de Xiquena believed that the Americans sought war and therefore negotiations would be useless—see Gabriel Maura Gamazo, *Historia crítica del reinado de don Alfonso XIII durante su menoridad bajo la regencia de su madre doña Cristina de Austria* (Barcelona, 1925) vol. 2, p. 6; and May, *Imperial Democracy,* 168-169.

41. Day to Woodford, *Foreign Relations, 1898,* 732-733. For sound interpretation of Washington's response to the possibility of papal mediation, see May, *Imperial Democracy,* 153-154. See also Jerónimo Bécker, *Historia de las relaciones exteriores de España durante el siglo XIX (Apuntes para una historia diplomática),* Volume 3: *1868-1900* (Madrid, 1926), pp. 872-873.

42. Woodford to Day, 4 April 1898, *Diplomatic Despatches, Spain,* roll 124. For Polo's statement, see May, *Imperial Democracy,* 157. For reports of Ireland's later conversations with McKinley, see Polo to Gullón, 4 and 6 April 1898, *Spanish Diplomatic Documents,* 111-113. For additional information on the abortive project of papal intervention, see Jerónimo Bécker, *Relaciones diplomáticas entre España y la Santa Sede durante el siglo XIX* (Madrid, 1908), 388-389. See also Ferrara, *Last Spanish War,* 114-118.

43. For Dawes's views, see Dawes Journal, 4 April 1898, quoted in Timmons, ed., *Journal of the McKinley Years,* 152. Long's observations are in Long Diary, 4 April 1898, quoted in Mayo, ed., *America of Yesterday,* 176. Platt included his observations in Platt to John H. Platt, 2 April 1898, quoted in Coolidge, *An Old Fashioned Senator,* 226-227. Roosevelt's statements are in Roosevelt to Robert Bacon, 5 April 1898, quoted in Morison, ed., *Letters of Theodore Roosevelt,* vol. 2, p. 811; Roosevelt to Root, 5 April 1898, *ibid.,* 812-813; Roosevelt to William Tudor, 5 April 1898, *ibid.,* 812.

44. Orders went to both Woodford and Lee to prepare for early evacuation from their posts. (Sherman to Woodford, 4 April 1898, *Foreign Relations, 1898*, 733; and Day to Lee, 4 and 5 April 1898, *Consular Despatches, Havana*, roll 132.) For information about the decision to delay transmission of a message to Congress until April 11, see Lee to Day, 3 and 5 April 1898, *ibid.*; Day to Lee, 6 April 1898, *ibid.*; Long Diary, 6 April 1898, in Mayo, ed., *America of Yesterday*, 177; and Dawes Diary, 5 April 1898, in Timmons, ed., *Journal of the McKinley Years*, 152. For the message to McKinley, see Woodford to McKinley, 5 April 1898, *Foreign Relations, 1898*, 734–735.

45. Day to Woodford, 5 April 1898, *Foreign Relations, 1898*, 735. For Woodford's later activities, following news that the message would not go to Congress until April 11, see Woodford to Gullón, 6 April 1898, *Spanish Diplomatic Documents*, 111–112; Woodford to Day, 6 April 1898, *Foreign Relations, 1898*, 741–743 (three messages); Woodford to Gullon, 7 April 1898, *Spanish Diplomatic Documents*, 113; and Woodford to Day, 7 April 1898, *Foreign Relations, 1898*, 744.

46. Joint Note of the Powers, 6 April 1898, *Foreign Relations, 1898*, 740. For McKinley's response, see *ibid.*, 741. Polo's report of this interview is in Polo to Gullón, 7 April 1898, *Spanish Diplomatic Documents*, 113.

47. For evidence of the Austrian initiative in this matter, see Salisbury to Pauncefote, 2 April 1898, *FO 185*, box 863. See also R. G. Neale, *Great Britain and United States Expansion: 1898–1900* (East Lansing, Mich., 1966), 29. Ferrara presents evidence concerning the attitude of Great Britain in his *Last Spanish War*, 131–132. For the procedure of clearing the message with the White House before presenting it, see Pauncefote to Salisbury, 6 April 1898, *FO 185*, box 863; Pauncefote to Salisbury, 8 April 1898, *FO 185*, box 864. For a good account of the episode, see Charles S. Campbell, Jr., *Anglo-American Understanding, 1898–1903* (Baltimore, 1957), 30–32.

48. May, *Imperial Democracy*, 175–176. Notice of the Spanish decision to proclaim an armistice came to Washington in Woodford to Day, 9 April 1898, *Foreign Relations, 1898*, 746. For the end of reconcentration, see Alfred L. P. Dennis, *Adventures in American Diplomacy, 1898–1906* (New York, 1969), 71; Day to Woodford, 4 April 1898, *Foreign Relations, 1898*, 733; Polo to Day, 5 April 1898, *ibid.*, 737–739. For the armistice arrangements, see Gullón to Rampolla, 9 April 1898, *Spanish Diplomatic Documents*, 115; and Gullón to Debetsky (Austrian ambassador), 9 April 1898, *ibid.*, 114. For Blanco's decree, see Emilio Roig de Leuchsenring, *La guerra hispano-cubanoamericana fué ganada por el lugarteniente general del ejército libertador Calixto García Iñiguez* (Havana, 1955), 20–21; and Polo to Day, 11 April 1898, *Foreign Relations, 1898*, 750. For Spanish views, see Bécker, *Historia de las relaciones exteriores de España*, vol. 3, p. 874; and Juan Nido y Segalerva, *Historia política y parlamentaria del Excmo. D. Práxedes Mateo Sagasta* (Madrid, 1915), 917.

49. For the last flurry from Woodland, see Woodford to McKinley, 10 April 1898, *Foreign Relations, 1898*, 747; Woodford to McKinley, 11 April 1898, *Diplomatic Despatches, Spain*, roll 123. For the decision to send in the message, see May, *Imperial Democracy*, 157; and Day to Woodford, 10 April 1898, *Foreign Relations, 1898*, 749. Consul General Lee got away from Havana on April 9, eliminating that reason for delay (Lee to Day, 9 April 1898, *Consular Despatches, Havana*, roll 132). For the message itself, see Message to Congress, 11 April 1898, *Foreign Relations, 1898*, 750–760; the official congressional publication of the message is U.S. House of Representatives, *Message of the President of the United States, Communicated to the Two Houses of Congress, on the Relations of the United States to Spain by Reason of Warfare in the Island of Cuba*, 55th Cong., 2d Sess., House Document No. 405 (Washington, D.C., 1898). For analysis of the message, see David F. Healy, *The United States in Cuba, 1898–1902; Generals, Politicians, and the*

Search for Policy (Madison, Wis., 1963), 21–22; H. Wayne Morgan, *America's Road to Empire: The War With Spain and Overseas Expansion* (New York, London, and Sydney, 1965), 62. Some historians persist in the view that economic motives—such as declining trade with Cuba—influenced McKinley, but they are hard pressed for evidence to support this view. For an example, see Tom E. Terrill, "An Economic Aspect of the Spanish-American War," *Ohio History* 76 (Winter-Spring, 1967): 73–75. For cautionary warnings against over-exploitation of discrete documents, see Lewis L. Gould's excellent criticism of the use of the "Reick telegram" by historians in their attempt to undermine the view that businessmen were opposed to war during the *Maine* crisis ("The Reick Telegram and the Spanish-American War: A Reappraisal," *Diplomatic History* 3 [Spring, 1979]: 193–199).

50. For the Hobart-McKinley conversation, see Jennie Hobart, *Memories*, 60. Long's report of his talk with the congressman is in Long Diary, 6 April 1898, quoted in Mayo, ed., *America of Yesterday*, 177. For Cleveland's views, see Cleveland to E. C. Benedict, quoted in Allan Nevins, ed., *Letters of Grover Cleveland: 1850–1908* (Boston, 1933), 744. Storey's speech is quoted in Mark A. DeWolfe Howe, *Portrait of an Independent: Moorfield Storey, 1845–1929* (Boston and New York, 1932), 195.

51. Senator Platt's views are in Platt to John H. Platt, 7 April 1898, quoted in Coolidge, *An Old Fashioned Senator*, 278. For the delay because of the nature of the message, see May, *Imperial Democracy*, 157–158. For a parallel view of the inadequacy of the Spanish response to American pressure from the President's viewpoint, see John A. S. Grenville and George Berkeley Young, *Politics, Strategy, and American Diplomacy: Studies in Foreign Policy, 1873–1917* (New Haven and London, 1966), 262.

52. For Dawes's observations, see Dawes Diary, 12 April 1898, quoted in Timmons, ed., *Journal of the McKinley Years*, 153. For the abortive identic note, see Campbell, *Anglo-American Understanding*, 32–39; Bradford Perkins, *The Great Rapprochement: England and the United States, 1895–1914* (New York, 1968), 37–41; Neale, *Great Britain and United States Expansion*, 26–27; Ferrara, *Last Spanish War*, 144–150; and Einstein, "British Diplomacy in the Spanish-American War," 45–48. For Goluchowski's views, see Ralph Milbank to Salisbury, 20 April 1898, *FO 185*, box 864. For Muraviev's views, see May, *Imperial Democracy*, 132. Those of Hanotaux are recorded in Representative at Paris to Salisbury, rec. 20 April 1898, *FO 185*, box 864.

53. For Roosevelt's comments, see Roosevelt to Lodge, 14 April 1898, in Morison, ed., *Letters of Theodore Roosevelt*, vol. 2, p. 815. For Lodge's comment to Higginson of April 15, 1898, see John A. Garraty, *Henry Cabot Lodge: A Biography* (New York, 1953), 189. For the vote on the Foraker-Turpie amendment, see the model study by Paul S. Holbo, "Presidential Leadership in Foreign Affairs: William McKinley and the Foraker-Turpie Amendment," *American Historical Review*, 76 (July 1967): 1,327–1,328, 1,332. In the Senate the split along political lines was eighteen Republicans and thirteen Democrats and Populists for the amendment, thirty-two Republicans and five Democrats opposed (Healy, *United States in Cuba*, 23–24). For the requirement that Spain withdraw immediately from Cuba, see Charles S. Olcott, *The Life of William McKinley* (Boston and New York, 1916) vol. 2, p. 33–34. For Chandler's observation, see Chandler to Paul Dana, 19 April 1898, quoted in Leonard Burr Richardson, *William E. Chandler: Republican* (New York, 1940), 582.

54. For comment on the Teller amendment, see Healy, *United States in Cuba*, 25. For Reid's view, see Royal Cortissoz, *The Life of Whitelaw Reid*, Volume 2: *Politics-Diplomacy* (New York, 1921), 223.

55. For the text of the joint resolution, see *Foreign Affairs, 1898*, p. liv. See also French

Ensor Chadwick, *The Relations of the United States and Spain: The Spanish-American War* (New York, 1911), vol. 1, p. 55.

56. For Cortelyou's views, see his diary entry of April 16, 1898, quoted in Olcott, *McKinley*, vol. 2, 53–54. For Long's views, see Linderman, *Mirror of War*, 189.

57. For the report of the unidentified American observer in Madrid, see Crowninshield to Sampson, 30 April 1898 (enclosing intelligence report of 16 April 1898), in U.S. Navy Department, *Annual Reports of the Navy Department for the Year 1898, Volume 2: Appendix to the Report of the Chief of the Bureau of Navigation* (Washington, D.C., 1898) (hereafter cited as *BN 98*). Italics are added. The ultimatum to Spain was included in Sherman to Woodford, 20 April 1898, *Foreign Relations, 1898*, 763. The Queen Regent's comments to the Cortes are in Melchor Fernández Almagro, *Historia política del España contemporánea*, Volume 2: *Regencia de doña María Cristina de Austria durante la menor edad de su hijo don Alfonso XIII* (Madrid, 1959), 498–499. For the Queen Regent's decree declaring war on the United States, see U.S. State Department, *Proclamations and Decrees During the War with Spain* (Washington, D.C., 1899), 93–94. Carlos Ría-Baja's statement is in his *El desastre filipino: Memorias de un prisionero* (Barcelona, 1899), 59.

58. For Sherman's departure, see Leech, *In the Days of McKinley*, 153, 191; Dawes Diary, 24 April 1898, in Timmons, ed., *Journal of the McKinley Years*, 156. For Roosevelt's exit and Long's comment, see Long Diary, 25 April 1898, quoted in Mayo, ed., *America of Yesterday*, 186.

59. The first statement is quoted in Hermann Hagedorn, *Leonard Wood: A Biography* (New York, 1931), vol. 1, p. 141. The second is quoted in Linderman, *Mirror for War*, 185.

60. For Washington Gladden's views, see his *Our Nation and Her Neighbors* (Columbus, Ohio, 1898), 39.

61. For Richard Hofstadter's views, see his "Manifest Destiny in the Philippines," in Daniel Aaron, ed., *America in Crisis: Fourteen Crucial Episodes in American History* (New York, 1952), 198. For the influence of America's acquisition of great-power capabilities, see David F. Trask, *Victory Without Peace: American Foreign Relations in the Twentieth Century* (New York, London, and Sydney, 1968), 18–25.

CHAPTER 3

1. For Concas's views, see Víctor M. Concas y Palau, *The Squadron of Admiral Cervera* (Washington, 1900), 15.

2. For Cervera's assumption of command at Cádiz see Alberto Risco, *La escuadra del Almirante Cervera (narración documentada del combate naval de Santiago de Cuba)* (Madrid, 1920), 21. For the Gullón–Dupuy de Lôme exchange, see Gullón to Dupuy de Lôme, 16 December 1897, *Spanish Diplomatic Documents*, 51; Dupuy de Lôme to Gullón, 16 December 1897, *ibid.*, 52. For Gutiérrez Sobral's warning, see Juan Nido y Segalerva, *Historia política y parlamentaria del Excmo. D. Práxedes Mateo Sagasta* (Madrid, 1915), 931. This message is also reproduced and discussed in Severo Gómez Núñez, *La guerra hispano-americana: Puerto Rico y Filipinas* (Madrid, 1902), 114–116. See also Víctor Concas y Palau, *Causa instruída por la destrucción de la escuadra de Filipinas y entrega del arsenal de Cavite* (Madrid, 1899), 26–27. It is not clear to what meeting Gutiérrez Sobral referred, but the United States plan to move immediately on the Philippines in the event of war had been under discussion for many months. Since the Spanish government did not yet anticipate war, it probably did not give the message the attention it deserved. Of course, when Dewey appeared in early March at Hong Kong, it was well understood that if war came he would move on Manila.

3. For the exchange between Madrid and Washington, see Gullón to Dupuy de Lôme, 5 February 1898, *Spanish Diplomatic Documents*, 79; Dupuy de Lôme to Gullón, 7 February 1898, *ibid.*; Gullón to Dupuy de Lôme, 8 February 1898, *ibid.*, 80. For the movements of the *Vizcaya*, see Tomás Benítez Frances, *El 3 de Julio desde el "Vizcaya": El manuscrito de un combate* (El Ferrol, 1898), 41–45. After a visit to Havana the *Vizcaya* went with a sister ship, the *Almirante Oquendo*, to the Cape Verde Islands for a rendezvous with other armored vessels of the Spanish navy (*Ibid.*, 46–68). See also Walter R. Herrick, Jr., *The American Naval Revolution* (Baton Rouge, La., 1966), 217.

4. Cervera to Juan Spotturno, 30 January 1898, in Pascual Cervera y Topete, *The Spanish-American War: A Collection of Documents Relative to the Squadron Operations in the West Indies* (Washington, D.C., 1899), 12; and Cervera to Bermejo, 12 February 1898, *ibid.*, 22.

5. Bermejo to Cervera, 15 February 1898, *ibid.*, 24.

6. For this exchange, see Bermejo to Cervera, 15 February 1898, *ibid.*, 24; and Cervera to Bermejo, 16 February 1898, *ibid.*, 25.

7. Bermejo to Cervera, 23 February 1898, *ibid.*, 27; Cervera to Bermejo, 25 February 1898, *ibid.*, 27–28; and Cervera to Bermejo, 26 February 1898, *ibid.*, 30.

8. For the continuing exchange between the fleet commander and the Minister of the Marine, see Bermejo to Cervera, 4 March 1898, *ibid.*, 32; Cervera to Bermejo, 7 March 1898, *ibid.*, 35. For Villaamil's deployment, see Nido, *Historia de Sagasta*, 911. The flotilla consisted of the torpedo boats *Ariete*, *Razo*, and *Azor*; the destroyers *Plutón*, *Terror* and *Furor*; and the transport *Ciudad de Cádiz*. For American correspondence relating to the preparation and movements of the Spanish fleet, see Dyer to Roosevelt, 5 and 11 March 1898 (two messages), in U.S. Navy Department, Record Group 45, Entry 19: "Translation of Messages Sent," National Archives, Washington, D.C. (hereafter cited as *RG 45*, Entry 19). See also Day to Woodford, 12 March 1898, *Diplomatic Instructions, Spain*, roll 22, 521; Woodford to Sherman, 13 March 1898, *Diplomatic Despatches, Spain*, roll 124 (two messages); Woodford to Sherman, 14 March 1898, *ibid.*; Dyer to Roosevelt, 14 March 1898, *RG 38*, Entry 100; and Crowninshield to Commander in Chief, North Atlantic Station, 14 March 1898, *AF*, file 4, roll 33.

9. Cervera to Bermejo, 16 March 1898, in Cervera, *Spanish-American War*, 38.

10. The *Vizcaya* had come to Havana after a visit to New York. For the movements of the *Vizcaya* and the *Almirante Oquendo*, see French Ensor Chadwick, *The Relations of the United States and Spain: The Spanish-American War* (New York, 1911), vol. 1, pp. 25–26. Roosevelt urged unsuccessfully that steps be taken to prevent the two ships from leaving Havana. Roosevelt to Benjamin Tracy, 6 April 1898, in Elting E. Morison, ed., *The Letters of Theodore Roosevelt* (Cambridge, Mass., 1951), vol. 2, pp. 810–811. Correa's statement is discussed in Nido, *Historia de Sagasta*, 918. For Cervera's warning, see Cervera to Bermejo, 6 April 1898, in Cervera, *Spanish-American War*, 42–43. For an earlier message warning of the American threat to the Canaries, see Cervera to Bermejo (telegram), 4 April 1898, *ibid.*, 42. For Blanco's appeal, see Blanco to V. R. Girón, 7 April 1898, *ibid.*, 43.

11. For the exchange between Cádiz and Madrid, see Bermejo to Cervera, 7 April 1898, in Cervera, *Spanish-American War*, 43; and Cervera to Bermejo, 8 April 1898, *ibid.*, 44. Beránger's statement of April 6, 1898, is quoted in Chadwick, *Spanish-American War*, vol. 1, p. 40. For Víctor Concas's observation, see his *La escuadra del almirante Cervera* (Madrid, n.d.), 26. Bermejo's orders are in Bermejo to Cervera, 8 April 1898, in Cervera, *Spanish-American War*, 45–46. For concern about Puerto Rico, see Gabriel Maura Gamazo, *Historia crítica del reinado de Don Alfonso XIII durante su menoridad bajo la regencia de su madre Doña María Cristina de Austria* (Barcelona, 1925), vol. 2, pp. 17, 19.

12. For this information, see Francisco Arderius, *La escuadra española en Santiago de*

Cuba: Diario de un testigo (Barcelona, 1903), 30, 35; Risco, *La escuadra del Almirante Cervera*, 45; and Chadwick, *Spanish-American War*, vol. 1, p. 34. With the assistance of consular officials and Lieutenant Dyer—the naval attaché in Madrid—the Navy Department kept itself fairly well informed on the movements that eventually brought Cervera's ships together at St. Vincent in the Cape Verde Islands. See, for example, information in Dyer to Roosevelt, 8 April 1898, *AF*, file 4, roll 33, reporting correctly both Cervera's movement to the Cape Verdes and the departure of the two armored cruisers from San Juan for the same destination; J. B. Guinraes (Guimaraes?) to ———, 11 April 1898, *AF*, file 8, roll 228, reporting the names of the destroyers and torpedo boats at St. Vincent; Dyer to Chief Intelligence Officer, 16 April 1898, in Record Group 45, NRC 372; "Correspondence of the Naval War Board," 23–33, in the Naval Records Collection of the Office of Naval Records and Library, National Archives, Washington, D.C. (cited hereafter as *RG 45*, NRC 372); Philip C. Hanna (consul at San Juan, Puerto Rico) to Day, 16 April 1898 (from St. Thomas, Danish West Indies), *AF*, file 8, roll 228, reporting the departure of the *Vizcaya* and the *Almirante Oquendo* from San Juan: and Dyer to Roosevelt, 20 April 1898, *AF*, file 4, roll 33. One consul, the author Albion W. Tourgée, located at Bordeaux, sent a message to Day in response to orders concerning a Spanish gunboat at the mouth of the Garonne, supposedly sent there to prey on American shipping: "I am in mortal terror lest I should again be found guilty of undue levity in reference to official matter," he began, "but should you see fit to report this to the Hon. Secretary of the Navy, it would seem to me very appropriate to accompany it with the information that, as no American ship of any sort has entered the roadstead of the Garonne in three years, there would hardly be any place on the planet where a Spanish gunboat could do our commerce less harm" (Tourgée to Day, 8 April 1898, *AF*, file 4, roll 33). Of a total of about 15,000 officers and men in the Spanish Navy, some 2,200 were in Cuba and 1,500 in the Philippines; the remainder were in the Spanish peninsula. Some of Cervera's ships were apparently undermanned. (Chadwick, *Spanish-American War*, vol. 1, p. 44.)

13. For Cervera's objection to the Puerto Rican expedition, see Cervera to Bermejo, 19 April 1898, in Cervera, *Spanish-American War*, 49. For the decision of April 20, 1898, see *ibid.*, 52–54. See also Concas, *The Squadron of Admiral Cervera*, 27–28; and Arderius, *La escuadra española*, 37.

14. For Cervera's last efforts, see his *Spanish-American War*, 54–55. One consideration that probably influenced Sagasta's government was continuing pressure from Blanco to send aid. On April 22 Blanco reported to Correa, the Minister of War: "I must not conceal from your excellency that if people should become convinced that squadron is not coming, disappointment will be great, and an unpleasant reaction is possible. Beg that your excellency will advise me whether I can give them any hope of more or less immediate arrival of squadron" (Blanco to Correa, 22 April 1898, *ibid.*, 55). For a last-minute appeal, see Cervera to Bermejo, 22 April 1898, *ibid.*, 57. In a formal letter Cervera, probably for the record, spelled out in detail his objections to the Caribbean voyage (Cervera to Bermejo, 22 April 1898, *ibid.*, 56.)

15. For the conference at the Ministry of the Marine, on April 23, 1898, see Alberto Risco, *Apuntes biográficos del Excmo. Sr. almirante D. Pascual Cervera y Topete* (Toledo, 1920), 57. Captain Ramón Auñón apparently took the strongest position of those favoring the order to Cervera to leave for Puerto Rico. Only a month later he was to succeed Bermejo as Minister of the Marine. For the views of the various participants, see Cervera, *Spanish-American War*, 58–65. For the final order to depart from the Cape Verdes, see Bermejo to Cervera, 24 April 1898, *ibid.*, 64–65. Cervera had to leave Portuguese St. Vincent quickly because of the requirement under international law that belligerent ships of war must vacate neutral ports in time of war. For the efforts of Captain Lazaga, see Concas, *The Squadron of Ad-*

miral Cervera, 35. For those of Villaamil see *ibid.*, 33; and U.S. Navy Department, *Views of Admiral Cervera Regarding the Spanish Navy in the Late War* (Washington, 1898), 24.

16. Mahan, *Lessons of the War with Spain*, 95–96, 98–99.
17. For Germany's involvement, see John A. S. Grenville and George Berkeley Young, *Politics, Strategy, and American Diplomacy: Studies in Foreign Policy, 1873–1917* (New Haven and London, 1961), 283–284. For correspondence between Manila and Madrid, see Primo de Rivera to Moret, 3 March 1898, Records of the Minister for the Colonies (*Ministro de Ultramar*), *Ultramar* Section 10, Government of the Philippines 1839–1899, National Historical Archives, Madrid, Spain, bundles 5,302–5,303 (hereafter cited as *Ultramar Records*); and Moret to Primo de Rivera, rec. 4 March 1898, *Ultramar Records*, bundles 5,302–5,303 (dated 5 March by Concas in *La Escuadra de almirante Cervera*, 32). See also Fernando Primo de Rivera, *Discurso de Excmo. Sr. D. Fernando Primo de Rivera, Marqués de Estella, pronunciado en el senado el día de 11 de Junio de 1898 con motivo de ataques que le han sido dirigidos en el Congreso de los Diputados censurando su gestión como Gobernador general y General que fué de las Islas Filipinas* (Madrid, 1898), 15. See also Duque de Tetuán, *Apuntes del ex-ministro de estado Duque de Tetuán para la defensa de la política internacional y gestión diplomática del gobierno liberal-conservador desde el 28 de Marzo de 1895 á 29 de Septiembre de 1897* (n.p., 1902), vol. 2, p. 32.
18. Ignacio Salinas y Angulo, *Defensa de general Jáudenes* (Madrid, 1899), 25; and Severo Gómez Núñez, *La guerra hispano-americana: Puerto-Rico y Filipinas* (Madrid, 1902), 174.
19. Patricio Montojo, "El desastre de Cavite" (1898): Sus causas y sus efectos," MS 1326, pp. 6–8, in Library of the Spanish Naval Museum, Madrid; and Montojo to Bermejo, 24 March 1898, in Ministry of the Marine, *Correspondencia oficial referente á las operaciones navales durante la guerra con los Estados Unidos en 1898* (Madrid, 1899), 5–8. Montojo initially had at Manila the cruisers *Reina Cristina*, *Castilla*, *Don Juan de Austria*, *Isla de Luzon*, the gunboats *Bulusan* and *Panay*, and the transport *Cebu*. He recalled the *Isla de Cuba* from Iloilo, the *Elcano* from Joló, and the *Marqués del Duero* from Cavite.
20. For relevant correspondence, see Montojo to Bermejo, 26 March 1898, *Correspondencia oficial*, 8; Bermejo to Montojo, 27 March 1898, *ibid.*; Montojo to Bermejo, 29 March 1898, *ibid.*, 9–10; Montojo to Bermejo, 11 April 1898, *ibid.*, 12; Montojo to Bermejo, 12 April 1898, *ibid.*, 13; Bermejo to Montojo, 12 April 1898, *ibid.*, 15; Montojo to Bermejo, 15 April 1898, *ibid.*; Bermejo to Montojo, 17 April 1898, *ibid.*, 16; Bermejo to Montojo, 19 April 1898, *ibid.*; Montojo to Bermejo, 21 April 1898, *ibid.*; Montojo to Bermejo, 23 April 1898, *ibid.*, 16–17; and Bermejo to Montojo, 24 April 1898, *ibid.*, 17.
21. Montojo, "El desastre de Cavite," 11.
22. For Moret's message, see Moret to Primo de Rivera, 18 March 1898, in Tetuán, *Apuntes de Tetuán*, vol. 2, pp. 117–118; and Montojo, "El desastre de Cavite," 10. Moret waxed enthusiastic in early April when the possibility arose that the Pope might mediate the conflict over Cuba (Moret to Primo de Rivera, 4 and 8 April 1898, *Ultramar Records*, legajos 5,302–5,303). Correa's message of March 26, 1898, is mentioned in John R. M. Taylor, *The Philippine Insurrection Against the United States;* 5 vols. of galley proof never published), galley 5 AJ; and Montojo to Bermejo, 12 April 1898, *Correspondencia oficial*, 9. For the Moret and Montojo messages concerning Dewey's intentions, see Moret to Primo de Rivera, 9 April 1898, *Ultramar Records*, bundles 5,302–5,303; and Montojo, "El desastre de Cavite," 15. For the change of command, see Manuel Sastrón, *La insurrección en Filipinas y guerra hispano-americana en el archipiélago* (Madrid, 1901), 363; José Roca de Togores y Saravia, *Bloqueo y sitio de Manila en 1898* (Huesca, Spain, 1908),

185–186. These writers, both present in the Philippines at the time, thought that Primo de Rivera should have retained command. See also Taylor, *Philippine Insurrection*, galley 5AJ. One authority claims that efforts were made to keep Primo de Rivera in the Philippines in some capacity other than Governor-General—perhaps as field commander under Augustín—but arrangements to this end were not completed (Teodoro A. Agoncillo, *Malolos: The Crisis of the Republic* [Quezon City, P.I., 1960], 87–88). See also Correa to Augustín, 12 April 1898, in Tetuán, *Apuntes de Tetuán*, vol. 2, p. 119, for a cable authorizing the return of Primo de Rivera, giving as the reason the belief that there appeared to be no likelihood of an imminent rupture with the United States!

23. For information concerning Augustín's last-minute activities, see Taylor, *Philippine Insurrection*, galley 7AJ; Roca, *Bloqueo y sitio de Manila*, 22–23; and Salinas, *Defensa de Jáudenes*, 42. For Moret's final prewar message, see Moret to Augustín, 24 April 1898, *Ultramar Records*, bundles, 5,302–5,303.

CHAPTER 4

1. French Ensor Chadwick, *The Relations of the United States and Spain: The Spanish-American War* (New York, 1911), vol. 1, pp. 3–6; W. A. M. Goode, *With Sampson Through the War: Being an Account of the Naval Operations of the North Atlantic Squadron During the Spanish American War of 1898* (New York, 1899), 1; John Layser Offner, "President McKinley and the Origins of the Spanish-American War" (Dissertation, Pennsylvania State University, 1957), 182; Graham A. Cosmas, *An Army for Empire: The United States Army in the Spanish-American War* (Columbia, Mo., 1971), 75–76. Cosmas notes that intelligence about the insurrection in Cuba obtained in this period was both plentiful and accurate.

2. For Roosevelt's letter to Mahan, see Roosevelt to Mahan, 9 June 1897, in Elting E. Morison, ed., *The Letters of Theodore Roosevelt* (Cambridge, Mass., 1951) vol. 1, pp. 622–623. For his views on naval expansion, see Roosevelt to Bowman Henry McCalla, 3 August 1897, in *ibid.*, 636; and Roosevelt to Long, 30 September 1897, in *ibid.*, 695. His contacts with McKinley are noted in Henry Cabot Lodge and Charles F. Redmond, eds., *Selections from the Correspondence of Theodore Roosevelt and Henry Cabot Lodge, 1884–1918* (New York, 1971 edition), vol. 1, p. 277. For his letter to the Secretary of the Navy, see Roosevelt to Long, 20 September 1897, in Morison, ed., *Letters of Theodore Roosevelt*, vol. 1, pp. 684–685. For his comments to Lodge, see Roosevelt to Lodge, 21 September 1897, in Lodge and Redmond, ed., *Selections From the Correspondence of Roosevelt and Lodge*, vol. 1, pp. 278–279.

3. For the exercise assuming an Anglo-Spanish combination against a Franco-American alliance, see the report by Lieutenant Commander John B. van Bleeker and Lieutenant W. E. Reynolds in Archives of the Naval War College, Record Group 7, Intelligence and Technological Archives (1894–1945), Naval War College, Newport, R.I., UNOpB, box 21 (hereafter cited as *NWC*). For Train's exercise, see *NWC*, UNOpB, box 21.

4. "Situation in the Case of War With Spain" (1895), in *NWC*, UNOpB, box 21.

5. Lt. William Warren Kimball, (Staff Intelligence Officer, Naval War College) "War With Spain—1896," in NWC, UNOpB, box 21. For information on Kimball's plan, see John A. S. Grenville and George Berkeley Young, *Politics, Strategy, and American Diplomacy: Studies in Foreign Policy, 1873–1917* (New Haven, 1966), 272–276. See also articles by Grenville: "Diplomacy and War Plans in the United States, 1890–1917," *Transactions of the Royal Historical Society*, fifth series, 2 (London, 1961): 1–21; and "American Naval Preparations for War With Spain, 1896–1898," *Journal of American Studies*, 2 (April, 1968): 33–47. For a critique of

Grenville's argument that the planning of this period had a close connection with actual operations in 1898, see Ronald Spector, "Who Planned the Attack on Manila Bay?" *Mid-America*, 53 (April, 1971): 94–102. See also William R. Braisted, *The United States Navy in the Pacific, 1897–1909* (Austin, 1958), 22. Spector is critical of Kimball's plan, arguing that "It exhibited a simplemindedness about world politics and about the efficacy of naval power not untypical of many naval officers of the time." He emphasizes the point that the campaign at Manila was designed to force an indemnity and deter a Spanish campaign against American commerce. (Ronald Spector, *Admiral of the New Empire: The Life and Career of George Dewey* [Baton Rouge, La., 1974], 32–33.)

6. For information about the plan dealing with Anglo-Spanish opposition, see Spector, *Admiral of the New Empire*, 34. For the plan of November, 1896, see "Situation in Case of War With Spain," *NWC*, UNOpb, box 21. A clear copy of the November piece was prepared in December, 1896, and is located in the same place. For Taylor's comments, see "Synopsis of the War College Plan for Cuban Campaign in a War With Spain," *NWC*, UNOpB, box 21.

7. The signers of this plan included Rear Admiral Francis M. Ramsey, Chief of the Bureau of Navigation; Rear Admiral J. Bunce, Commander-in-Chief of the North Atlantic Station; Captain William T. Sampson, Chief of the Bureau of Ordnance; and Lieutenant Commander Richard Wainwright, Chief Intelligence Officer. For its text, and the dissent by Captain Henry C. Taylor (President of the Naval War College), see Grenville, "American Naval Preparations," 38–41. For additional comments, see Spector, "Who Planned the Attack on Manila Bay?" 96–97.

8. For this plan, see Grenville, "American Naval Preparations," 41–47. Spector notes the developments of January, 1897, in "Who Planned the Attack on Manila Bay?" 97–98. The new board included besides Lieutenant Commander Wainwright, the only other member of the earlier group, Rear Admiral Montgomery Sicard, Commander-in-Chief of the North Atlantic Station; Captain Arent S. Crowninshield, Chief of the Bureau of Navigation; Commander Charles O'Neil, Chief of the Bureau of Ordnance; and Commander Casper F. Goodrich, President of the Naval War College. Grenville argues that the changes in January, 1897, resulted from the absence of Admiral Ramsey and the influence of new members who sympathized with the views of the Naval War College (Grenville, "American Naval Preparations," 37).

9. This analysis reflects Ronald Spector's views. See his "Who Planned the Attack on Manila Bay?" 100–102. Spector shows that the Naval War College spent much of its time preparing plans to defend the coast against the British navy. He believes that the navy was as "confused and divided" as other groups of Americans in regard to the country's future in world politics. Attempting to counter the views of Grenville, he claims, "To assign to them [that is, the American naval officers] full responsibility for the American acquisition of the Philippines is as short-sighted as to attribute it to the intrigues of Theodore Roosevelt and Henry Cabot Lodge." For a recent summary of war planning prior to the war, see another work by Spector, *Professors of War: The Naval War College and the Development of the Naval Profession* (Newport, R.I., 1977), 88–100.

10. Roosevelt to Kimball, 19 November 1897, in Morison, ed., *Letters of Theodore Roosevelt*, vol. 1, p. 717; and Roosevelt to Kimball, 17 December 1897, *ibid.*, 743.

11. Roosevelt to Long, 14 January 1898, *ibid.*, 758–763. For Long's views, see Long Diary, 13 January 1898, in Margaret Long, ed., *The Journal of John D. Long* (Rindge, N.H., 1956), 212–213.

12. Roosevelt's views on foreign policy are in Roosevelt to William Astor Chandler, 23 December 1897, in Morison, ed., *Letters to Theodore Roosevelt*, vol. 2, p. 746.

13. For accounts of Dewey's appointment, see George Dewey, *Autobiography of George Dewey: Admiral of the Navy* (New York, 1913), 167–170; Margaret Leech,

In the Days of McKinley (New York, 1959), 159–161; and Spector, *Admiral of the New Empire*, 37–38. For Dewey's orders, see Commander Nathan Sargent, *Admiral Dewey and the Manila Campaign* (Washington, 1947), 3. For Long's later version of the appointment procedure, see his diary, 9 October 1898, quoted in Long, ed., *Journal of John D. Long*, 228. Authorities now agree that Roosevelt's role in this episode does not reveal him as pursuing a well-conceived scheme to bring about annexation of the Philippine Islands, a myth that still is repeated in some textbooks.

14. Roosevelt to Long, 16 February 1898, in Gardner Weld Allen, ed., *Papers of John Davis Long, 1897-1904* (Boston, 1939), 55; Roosevelt to Long, 21 February 1898, *AF,* area 11, roll 409.

15. Long Diary, 26 February 1898, *ibid.,* 169–170.

16. For the order, see Roosevelt to Dewey, 25 February 1898, *BN 98,* 23. The ancient *Monocacy* was a steamer deemed unfit for combat operations. The *Olympia,* a protected cruiser that served as Dewey's flagship, had been scheduled to return to the United States. Secretary Long liked and admired Roosevelt but became exasperated with him at times. On the day that "the very devil possessed him," Roosevelt had visited Long, moving the Secretary to record in his diary, "He is so enthusiastic and loyal that he is in certain respects invaluable; yet I lack confidence in his good judgment and discretion." For this reason he planned to return to work the next day. (Long Diary, 25 February 1898, in Lawrence Shaw Mayo, ed., *America of Yesterday: As Reflected in the Journal of John Davis Long* [Boston, 1923], 169.) For Roosevelt's self-appraisal, see William Henry Harbaugh, *Power and Responsiblity: The Life and Times of Theodore Roosevelt* (New York, 1961), 95.

17. For orders to the *Oregon* on March 7 and 12, 1898; April 6 and 30, 1898, see *BN 98,* 47–48, 52. Clark assumed command of the *Oregon* on March 17, 1898. See also U.S. Navy Department, *Annual Reports of the Navy Department for the Year 1898,* Volume I: *Report of the Secretary of the Navy; Miscellaneous Reports* (Washington, 1898), 5. For an account of the voyage by an enlisted man, see R. Cross, *The Voyage of the "Oregon" From San Francisco to Santiago in 1898 as Told by One of the Crew* (Boston, 1908). His remark about the voyage from San Francisco to Callao is in *ibid.,* 5. See also a recollection by Captain Clark in his *My Fifty Years in the Navy* (Boston, 1917).

18. News of Spanish efforts to purchase ships of war came in Henry White to Sherman, 26 February 1898, *AF,* file 4, roll 33. It came to White, an official at the American embassy in London, from Hiram S. Maxim. The Spanish inquiries had come to Armstrong's, a company that, according to Maxim, preferred to sell to the United States. For notice to the attachés, see Roosevelt to Lt. William S. Sims (Paris), 3 March 1898; Roosevelt to Lt. John C. Colwell (London), 3 March 1898; and Roosevelt to Lt. Albert P. Niblack (Rome), 7 March 1898, all in Record Group 38, Entry 100: "Correspondence With U.S. Naval Attachés during the Spanish-American War," 2 vols., in Records of the Office of the Chief of Naval Operations, National Archives, Washington, D.C. (hereafter cited as *RG 38,* Entry 100). For Brownson's mission see Long to Colwell, 6 March 1898, *AF,* file 4, roll 33. For ship purchases, see Goode, *With Sampson Through the War,* 7–9; Donald William Mitchell, *History of the Modern American Navy: From 1883 Through Pearl Harbor* (New York, 1947), 58; Charles Oscar Paullin, "A Half-Century of Naval Administration in America, 1861–1911," Part II: "The Navy in the Spanish-American War," *United States Naval Institute Proceedings* 40 (March-April, 1914): 419–420; John D. Long, *The New American Navy* (New York, 1903), vol. 1, p. 151; and Allan Nevins, *Henry White: Thirty Years of American Diplomacy* (New York and London, 1930), 313. The four liners were leased from the American Line, maintaining passenger service between New York and Southampton. The ships were named the *Paris, New York, St. Louis,* and *St. Paul.* The *New York* was renamed the *Har-*

vard and the *Paris* the *Yale*. (William H. Flayhart III, "Four Fighting Ladies," in Clayton R. Barrow, Jr., comp. and ed., *America Spreads Her Sails: U.S. Seapower in the 19th Century* (Annapolis, 1973), 195–214. This article discusses the wartime services of these vessels.)

19. Long, *New Navy*, vol. 1, p. 151; Chadwick, *Spanish-American War*, vol. 1, p. 41.
20. Roosevelt to Long, 15 March 1898, *AF*, area 11, roll 409. In a letter to Captain Alfred Thayer Mahan, Roosevelt commented on certain aspects of this plan the day before he met with the committee. He reported the President's desire to avoid war if at all possible. Roosevelt planned to emphasize a statement by Mahan that minor irritants should be ignored—he had in mind raids on the east coast—in favor of concentration in Cuba. Angry because he thought Spain had gained in naval strength relative to the United States in recent months, he wished that war had come a year and a half previously. He assumed that the *Pelayo* would come to the Caribbean, and it was for this reason that the battleship *Oregon* had been ordered there from the Pacific. He wanted in any case to fight before the Spanish destroyers reached Cuba. "But we won't," he lamented. "We'll let them get over here and run the risk of serious damage from them, and very possibly we won't fight until the beginning of the rainy season, when to send an expeditionary force to Cuba means to see the men die like sheep." (Roosevelt to Mahan, 14 March 1898, Papers to Alfred Thayer Mahan, Library of Congress, Manuscript Division, Washington, D.C., box 3; the letter is published in Morison, ed., *Letters to Theodore Roosevelt*, vol. 1, pp. 793–794.
21. For the order to establish the Flying Squadron, see Long to Commander-in-Chief, North Atlantic Squadron, 17 March 1898, *AF*, file 8, roll 227. Evans is quoted in Edwin Albert Falk, *Fighting Bob Evans* (Freeport, N.Y., 1939), 253.
22. Long for Commander-in-Chief, North Atlantic Squadron, 23 March 1898, *AF*, file 8, roll 227. See also Chadwick, *Spanish-American War*, vol. 1, pp. 22–23; and Herrick, *American Naval Revolution,* 230. Long was referring to Lieutenant William Cushing, who in 1864 sank a Confederate ironclad, the *Albemarle*, in a daring action on the Roanoke River.
23. For Long's office routine, see his diary, 15 March 1898, in Mayo, ed., *America of Yesterday,* 174. For a brief portrait of Long, see Charles Oscar Paullin, "A Half-Century of Naval Administration in America, 1861–1911, X: The Navy Department, 1897–1911," *United States Naval Institute Proceedings* 40 (January-February, 1914): 112. Paullin says of him, not unkindly, "His rusty silk hat and cheap suit of ready-made clothes contrasted oddly with the dress of his polished and well-groomed colleague in the State Department, the late John Hay." His administrative arrangements are described in Long Diary, 2 February and 20 May 1898, in Mayo, ed., *America of Yesterday,* 157, 195.
24. For Long's comparison of the Navy and War Departments, see his diary, 13 May 1898, quoted in Long, ed., *Journal of John D. Long,* 225. His views on Allen are in his diary, 11 May 1898, *ibid.*; Long, *New Navy*, vol. 2, p. 176.
25. Paullin, "The Navy in the Spanish-American War, 1898," 419–420. For lists of ships in commission and ships purchased, see Chadwick, *Spanish-American War*, vol. 1, pp. 397–403.
26. Information about the ships of the navy is found in several works. See Richard H. Titherington, *A History of the Spanish-American War of 1898* (New York, 1971 edition), 101–103; G.S. Clark, "Naval Aspects of the Spanish-American War," in T. H. Brassey, ed., *The Naval Annual, 1899* (Portsmouth, 1899), 127; Jack Cameron Dierks, *A Leap to Arms: The Cuban Campaign of 1898* (Philadelphia and New York, 1970), 35–36; Hyman G. Rickover, *How the Battleship "Maine" Was Destroyed* (Washington, 1976), 18.
27. For this information, see Long, *New Navy*, vol. 1, pp. 163, 207–208; Goode, *With Sampson Through the War,* 11; and U.S. Navy, *Annual Report for 1898,* vol. 1,

p. 5. For the public alarm that required provisions for coast defense, see Leech, *In the Days of McKinley*, 196; and *Foreign Relations, 1898,* lvi. Captain Sampson offered typical naval arguments against measures for coast defense, believing that Spain would not attempt to raid the east coast (Sampson to Long, 30 March 1898, *AF,* file 8, roll 227).

28. For naval intelligence arrangements, see Long, *New Navy,* vol. 2, p. 82; Chadwick, *Spanish-American War,* vol. 2, pp. 359–362; *BN 98,* 33. For the origins of the two special missions, see Long to Ensign William H. Buck, 28 April 1898, and Long to Ensign Henry H. Ward, 28 April 1898, in Record Group 45, Entry 20: "Confidential Letters, 1898–1908," in Naval Records Collection of the Office of Naval Records and Library, National Archives, Washington, D.C. (hereafter cited as *RG 45,* Entry 20).

29. Commander Richardson Clover, head of the Office of Naval Intelligence, also participated in early meetings. For information concerning the Naval War Board, see Richard Sedgwick West, Jr., *Admirals of American Empire: The Combined Story of George Dewey, Alfred Thayer Mahan, Winfield Scott Schley, and William Thomas Sampson* (Westport, Conn., 1971 edition), 216; Paullin, "The Navy Department, 1897–1911," 116–117; Sicard to Long, 24 August 1898, *BN 98,* 33. For Mahan's arrival in Washington, see Long Diary, 10 May 1898, in Mayo, ed., *America of Yesterday,* 190.

30. For Mahan's views, see Mahan to Long, 10 May 1898, in Allen, ed., *Journal of John D. Long,* 119–120. For Long's comment on Mahan, see Long Diary, 19 May 1898, in Mayo, ed., *America of Yesterday,* 194. For the Naval War Board, see Mahan to Dewey, 1 March 1900, quoted in Herrick, *American Naval Revolution,* 228. See also David Healy, "McKinley as Commander-in-Chief," in Paolo Coletta, ed., *Threshold to American Internationalism: Essays on the Foreign Policies of William McKinley* (New York, 1970), 86. Mahan's contribution to the Naval War Board is praised, and properly so, in Captain W. D. Puleston, *Mahan: Life and Work of Captain Alfred Thayer Mahan, U.S.N.* (New Haven, 1939), 202. In response to a request of the Navy Department in 1906 Mahan prepared a summary of the Naval War Board's activities. He concluded, "It should be remembered always that the Board of 1898 was an entirely new creation, extemporized on the moment for an urgent felt necessity. As a body, it had had no previous connection with the preparations of the Government, nor influence upon them; and the association with them of the individual members had been slight. The Board therefore approached the questions submitted to it without a formulated policy,—other than such knowledge as its members possessed of the leading principles of war,—and without previous mature consideration of the effect of this or that disposition on the whole theater of war,—of the relations of the parts to the whole. Among conflicting opinions of capable men,—and there were conflicts,—and diverse considerations of policy, the Board had only the general leading principles just spoken of to guide it; it began with no digested opinion of those special conditions, in the two countries, which might modify the application of principles." As an example of this latter point Mahan cited the retention because of domestic pressures of the Flying Squadron at Hampton Roads rather than its deployment to the Cuban blockade. (Alfred Thayer Mahan, "Narrative Account of the Work of the Naval War Board of 1898," 29 October 1906, in *NWC,* UNOpB. This document is published in Robert Seager II and Doris D. Maguire, eds., *Letters and Papers of Alfred Thayer Mahan,* (Annapolis, 1975), vol. 3, pp. 627–643.) For a summary of Mahan's views of the Board, see Robert Seager II, *Alfred Thayer Mahan: The Man and His Letters* (Annapolis, 1977), 370–371.

31. For general naval strategy, see Leech, *In the Days of McKinley,* 195; Healy, "McKinley as Commander-in-Chief," 89; and Long, *New Navy,* vol. 1, p. 166. The navy assumed initially that the army would be ready for active operations much

sooner than turned out to be the case (Edward Ranson, "Nelson A. Miles as Commanding General, 1895–1903," *Military Affairs* 29 [Winter, 1965–1966]: 183). For Chadwick's views, see his *Spanish-American War*, vol. 1, p. 91. It is true, however, that arrangements were made to patrol the waters of the American west coast (see Roosevelt to Long, 18 April 1898, *AF*, file 9, roll 319; and Lt. Commander Jefferson F. Moser to Roosevelt, 21 April 1898, *BN 98*, 135–136).

32. For this information, see Alfred Thayer Mahan, *Lessons of the War With Spain and Other Articles* (Freeport, N.Y., 1970 edition), 27, 29, 32, 107; Puleston, *Mahan*, 187, 202; and Seager, *Mahan*, 362–363.

33. For Sampson's plan to bombard Havana and capture it as Farragut had captured New Orleans in 1862, see Chadwick, *Spanish-American War*, vol. 1, pp. 64–65, 70–73; Robley Dunglison Evans, *A Sailor's Log: Recollections of Forty Years of Naval Life* (New York, 1908), 408; and Sampson to Long, 30 March 1898, *AF*, file 3, roll 227. For the rejection of this plan, see Chadwick, *Spanish-American War*, vol. 1, pp. 74–76; Falk, *Fighting Bob Evans*, 253–254; Long, *New Navy*, vol. 1, pp. 232–233; and Long to Sampson, 6 April 1898, *BN 98*, 171. Mahan cogently summarized reasons for not using armored vessels against land fortifications and batteries. "If it would have entailed even a remote risk of serious injury to an armored ship, it stood condemned irretrievably (unless it conduced to getting at the enemy's navy), because it would hazard the maintenance of the blockade, our chosen object, upon which our efforts should be concentrated" (Mahan, *Lessons of Our War with Spain*, 110). The restless Sampson believed, along with Admiral Sicard and Captain Chadwick, that if the flotilla of Spanish torpedo boats and destroyers in the Canary Islands set sail for the West Indies, the United States should consider the enterprise an act of war and send the navy immediately against Spanish vessels in Caribbean waters (Rear Admiral Albert Smith Barker, *Everyday Life in the Navy: Autobiography of Rear Admiral Albert S. Barker* [Boston, 1928], 275; and Sampson to Long, 29 March 1898, *AF*, file 8, roll 227). For Roosevelt to Evans, 20 April 1898, see Morison, ed., *Letters to Theodore Roosevelt*, vol. 2, p. 819.

34. For the Navy Department's initial scheme, see Long to Sampson, 6 April 1898, *BN 98*, 171. Sampson's counterproposal is in Sampson to Long, 14 April 1898, *AF*, file 8, roll 228. The commanding officer specified the vessels to be sent to the four northern ports in Sampson to Long, 18 April 1898, *AF*, file 8, roll 228. For correspondence relating to the inauguration of the actual blockade, see Long to Sampson, 21 April 1898, *BN 98*, 174, 175 (two messages). At the same time Long alerted all naval stations that the blockade had been ordered. It came, of course, before a formal declaration of war (*ibid.*, 175). For the formal proclamation of blockade, issued on April 22, 1898, see U.S. State Department, *Proclamations and Decrees During the War With Spain* (Washington, 1899), 75–76. For Sampson's promotion, see *BN 98*, 167.

35. The quotation is from Dewey, *Autobiography*, 178.

36. For activities at Hong Kong, see *ibid.*, 171–172, 180; Sargent, *Dewey and the Manila Campaign*, 5, 7, 9, 10; William Reynolds Braisted, *The United States Navy in the Pacific, 1897–1909* (Austin, 1958), 24–25; and Long, *New Navy*, vol. 1, p. 147. For relevant correspondence, see Long to Dewey, 21 March 1898, *BN 98*, 65; Long to Dewey, 5 April 1898, *AF*, file 10, roll 363; Dewey to Long, 6 and 9 April 1898 (two messages), *BN 98*, 66; Long to Dewey, 16 April 1898, *ibid.*; and Dewey to Long, 18 April 1898, *AF*, file 10, roll 363.

37. For Dewey's planning, see Laurin Hall Healy and Louis Kutner, *The Admiral* (Chicago, 1944), 157; Braisted, *United States Navy in the Pacific, 1897–1909*, 25; and Spector, *Admiral of the New Empire*, 43.

38. For the events surrounding the movement to Mirs Bay, see Wilsone Black to Dewey, 23 April 1898, *AF*, file 10, roll 363; Dewey to Long, 23 April 1898, *AF*, file 10, roll

363. For the movements of Consul Oscar F. Williams, see Sargent, *Dewey and the Manila Campaign*, 14; Patricio Montojo, "El desastre de Cavite (1898): Sus causas y sus efectos," MS 1326, Library of the Spanish Naval Museum, Madrid. For the scene in Washington, see Long, *New Navy*, vol. 1, pp. 181–182. The Secretary of the Navy had proposed that the President send the order earlier, on April 21, but McKinley refused because, although diplomatic relations had been broken, no state of war existed as yet (Healy, "McKinley as Commander-in-Chief," 89–90). For the sequence of events in Washington, see Lt. Humes H. Whittlesey to Long, 22 August 1901, *AF*, file 10, roll 363; and Spector, *Admiral of the New Empire*, 2.

39. For Roosevelt's letters, see Roosevelt to Henry White, 30 March 1898, in Morison, ed., *Letters of Theodore Roosevelt*, vol. 2, p. 805; Roosevelt to William Austin Wadsworth, 7 April 1898, *ibid.*, 814; and Roosevelt to Benjamin F. Tracy, 18 April 1898, *ibid.*, 818.

40. For the views of Dawes, see his diary, 22 April 1898, in Bascom Timmons, ed., *A Journal of the McKinley Years by Charles G. Dawes* (Chicago, 1950), 156.

CHAPTER 5

1. For Dewey's movement to Mirs Bay, see George Dewey, *Autobiography of George Dewey: Admiral of the Navy* (New York, 1913), 193–195; Ronald Spector, *Admiral of the New Empire: The Life and Career of George Dewey* (Baton Rouge, La., 1974), 48. See also Dewey to Long, 25 April 1898, *BN 98*, 67 (two messages). Dewey could remain in Mirs Bay, even though in violation of international law, because the Chinese, unlike the British at Hong Kong, had no means of enforcing its neutrality. For the orders, see Long to Dewey, 24 April 1898, *ibid.* See also Brayton Harris, *Age of the Battleship, 1890–1922* (New York, 1965), 58. Harris says that the message arrived at 7:00 P.M. (In dealing with the movement of messages between Washington and Hong Kong, it is important to know that the time differential is thirteen hours. Thus noon in Manila on April 25 is 11:00 P.M. on April 24 in Washington. Times given in this work are local times unless otherwise specified.) On April 15 Assistant Secretary of the Navy Roosevelt summarized for Secretary of the Navy Long the planned scenario in the western Pacific in the event of war: "Commodore Dewey will be directed to operate against Manila. Probably it will not be advisable for him to blockade, but he should certainly pick up the Spanish vessels, and probably he should take the forts defending Manila. The objection[s] to trying ships against forts until the Spanish vessels are destroyed which obtain on the North Atlantic coast do not obtain on the Asiatic Coast" (Roosevelt to Long, 15 April 1898, in Gardner Weld Allen, ed., *Papers of John Davis Long, 1897–1904* [Boston, 1939], 95.) Dewey, of course, had received word that Admiral Sampson was blockading the coast of Cuba, an operation described in Chapter 6. He was instructed in this message, "Await orders" (Long to Dewey, 21 April 1898, *BN 98*, 66). For information relating to Consul Williams, see Williams to Day, 4 May 1898, *AF*, file 10, roll 363. Williams left Manila on Saturday, April 23, arriving in Hong Kong on April 27. With the assistance of the consul general at Hong Kong, Rounsevelle Wildman, he hired a tugboat that took him to Mirs Bay. See also Walter Millis, *The Martial Spirit: A Study of Our War With Spain* (Boston and New York, 1931), 183; and Harris, *Age of the Battleship*, 59. For the stay at Mirs Bay, see John M. Ellicott, "The Naval Battle of Manila Bay," *United States Naval Institute Proceedings*, 26 XXI (September, 1900): 491.

2. For the voyage to Manila, see Dewey, *Autobiography*, 196; French Ensor Chadwick, *The Relations of the United States and Spain: The Spanish-American War* (New York, 1911), vol. 1, pp. 171–173; Bradley Allen Fiske, *From Midshipman to Rear-Admiral* (New York, 1919), 241; Dewey to Long, 27 April 1898, *BN 98*, 68; and

Henry F. Graff, ed., *American Imperialism and the Philippine Insurrection: Testimony Taken From Hearings on Affairs in the Philippine Islands before the Senate Committee on the Philippines—1902* (Boston, 1969), 8. The quotation describing Dewey is in Margaret Leech, *In the Days of McKinley* (New York, 1959), 159.

3. For the movement to Subig Bay, see Montojo to Bermejo, 25 April 1898, in Ministry of the Marine (Spain), *Correspondencia oficial referente á las operaciones navales durante la guerra con los Estados Unidos en 1898* (Madrid, 1899), 17–19; Montojo to Bermejo (telegram), 25 April 1898, *ibid.*, 21; Chadwick, *Spanish-American War*, vol. 1, p. 167. For Montojo's activity at Subig Bay, see Ignacio Salinas y Angulo, *Defensa del General Jáudenes* (Madrid, 1899), 24; Víctor M. Concas y Palau, *Causa instruída por la destrucción de la escuadra de Filipinas y entrega del arsenal de Cavite* (Madrid, 1899), 34; Donald Barr Chidsey, *The Spanish-American War: A Behind-the-Scenes Account of the War in Cuba* (New York, 1971), 74; Montojo report, *BN 98*, 89; Montojo to Bermejo, 29 April 1898, *Correspondencia oficial*, 25; Patricio Montojo, "El desastre de Cavite (1898): Sus causas y sus efectos," MS 1326, Library of the Spanish Naval Museum, Madrid. Dewey reported later that eighty mines had been laid and fifteen had been found on shore. These, he thought, had been pulled out by Filipino insurgents and the powder removed from them. (Dewey, *Autobiography*, 202.) There is, however, no Spanish confirmation that there were eighty mines there. Probably the ones he located were the Mathieson mines.

4. Montojo, "El desastre de Cavite," 12; José Roca de Togores y Saravia, *Bloqueo y sitio de Manila en 1898* (Huesca, Spain, 1908), 71–74; Montojo to Bermejo, 30 April 1898, *Correspondencia oficial*, 25–29; Teodoro A. Agoncillo, *Malolos: The Crisis of the Republic* (Quezon City, 1960), 103; and Chidsey, *Spanish-American War*, 76.

5. The quotation concerning the possible option of departing Manila Bay is from Chadwick, *Spanish-American War*, vol. 1, p. 76. See also Salinas, *Defensa del General Jáudenes*, 27.

6. Montojo report, *BN 98*, 90; Montojo to Bermejo, 30 April 1898, *Correspondencia oficial*, 29; Augustín to Correa, 30 April 1898, quoted in Fernando Soldevilla, *Año político, 1898* (Madrid, 1899), 186; and Roca, *Bloqueo y sitio de Manila*, 75. On the same day Augustín complained to the Minister of War, Miguel Correa, that Montojo had taken action without his consent (Concas, *Causa instruída*, 32–33). Perhaps it was this message that provoked one from Bermejo to Montojo, in which he stated, "Your return to Cavite has caused profound impression after your departure for Subig. In all your operations work always in accordance with Governor General for the defense of that colony." (Bermejo to Montojo, 30 April 1898, *Correspondencia oficial*, 25). See also Nathan Sargent, *Admiral Dewey and the Manila Campaign* (Washington, 1947), 47; and Ellicott, "Naval Battle of Manila Bay," 501. Ellicott thinks that Montojo did not expect that Dewey would arrive as soon as he did.

7. Dewey, *Autobiography*, 205; Sargent, *Dewey and the Manila Campaign*, 25–26; Chadwick, *Spanish-American War*, vol. 1, pp. 161, 171–173.

8. For the problem of the mines, see Dewey, *Autobiography*, 197–199; Russell A. Alger, *The Spanish-American War* (New York and London, 1901), 320; Sargent, *Dewey and the Manila Campaign*, 24; Agoncillo, *Malolos*, 99–100; and Charles H. Brown, *The Correspondents' War; Journalists in the Spanish-American War* (New York, 1967), 191. Chadwick stresses not only the depth of water but the strong tidal currents moving through Boca Chica and Boca Grande as creating difficulties for mining operations. Some warheads from Whitehead torpedos were laid near Caballo Island, but they had no effect on the action. (Chadwick, *Spanish-American War*, vol. 1, pp. 163–164.) For information about the batteries, see Dewey,

Autobiography, 198; Sargent, *Dewey and the Manila Campaign*, 23; and Chadwick, *Spanish-American War*, vol. 1, p. 163. Roca argues that, had a real effort been made to fortify the entrance, the Spanish defenders could have kept Dewey from entering (*Bloqueo y sitio de Manila*, 40).

9. Dewey, *Autobiography*, 209–210; Agoncillo, *Malolos*, 106–107; Sargent, *Dewey and the Manila Campaign*, 33–34, 47; John M. Ellicott, "The Defenses of Manila Bay," *United States Naval Institute Proceedings*, 26 XXVI (June, 1900): 282.

10. For the opposed squadrons, see data in Robert Wilden Neeser, *Statistical and Chronological History of the United States Navy, 1775–1907* (New York, 1909), vol. 2, pp. 250–251; and Donald William Mitchell, *History of the Modern American Navy: From 1883 Through Pearl Harbor* (New York, 1947), 67. Dates of construction are given in John D. Long, *The New American Navy* (New York, 1903) vol. 1, pp. 167–169. Other authorities give slightly variant data—e.g., Chadwick, *Spanish-American War*, vol. 1, p. 169. Chadwick lists the *Isla de Cuba* and *Isla de Luzon* as protected cruisers. Mitchell also lists them as protected cruisers and gives the same designation to the *Don Juan de Austria* and the *Don Juan de Ulloa*. By American standards, however, they are properly considered gunboats.

11. Long, *New Navy*, vol. 1, pp. 175–192; and Montojo report, *BN 98*, 90. For slightly variant figures, see Sargent, *Dewey and the Manila Campaign*, 28–29. He says that the American ships carried fifty-six guns under the four-inch type, whereas the Spanish carried forty-four.

12. Chadwick, *Spanish-American War*, vol. 1, pp. 28–29, 164. The guns at Manila included four 9.4-inch (24 cm.) guns; four 5.5-inch (14 cm.) guns; two 5.9-inch (15 cm.) guns; nine 8.3-inch (21 cm.) mortars; and eighteen 6.3-inch (16 cm.) guns (Sargent, *Dewey and the Manila Campaign*, 25). The three batteries at Manila that fired on Dewey were: one at the mouth of the Pasig River (two 6.3-inch MLR), one near Malate (two 9.4-inch BLR), and another at the south bastion of Manila (one 9.4-inch BLR). Only one of the two 5.9-inch guns at Sangley Point was mounted so as to bear on Dewey's squadron during the attack (Montojo, "El desastre de Cavite," 21–22).

13. Chadwick, *Spanish-American War*, vol. 1, pp. 170–171; and Sargent, *Dewey and the Manila Campaign*, 34.

14. For information concerning the first phase of the battle—from its initiation to Dewey's temporary withdrawal—see Dewey, *Autobiography*, 212–216; Sargent, *Dewey and the Manila Campaign*, 34–36; Montojo, "El desastre de Cavite," 34; Dewey to Long, 4 May 1898, *BN 98*, 69–70; and Chadwick, *Spanish-American War*, vol. 1, pp. 178–179. The quotation concerning withdrawal is in Dewey, *Autobiography*, 219.

15. Dewey, *Autobiography*, 217–220; Montojo report, *BN 98*, 92; and Dewey to Long, 4 May 1898, *ibid.*, 70.

16. Dewey to Long, 4 May 1898, *BN 98*, 92; Dewey, *Autobiography*, 221–223; and Sargent, *Dewey and the Manila Campaign*, 40. For an eyewitness account of the battle by an unidentified naval officer, see Thomas J. Vivian, ed., *With Dewey at Manila* (New York, 1898).

17. For the material losses, see Chadwick, *Spanish-American War*, vol. 1, pp. 202–203. For reports of the commanders of American vessels, see *BN 98*, 73–86. For reports of Spanish commanders, see *Correspondencia oficial*, 36–60. For casualties, see Neeser, *Statistical and Chronological History of the United States Navy*, vol. 2, pp. 250–251. Lieutenant John M. Ellicott of the *Baltimore* reported slightly variant figures for the Spanish ships—167 killed and 214 wounded—a total of 381 casualties; he includes casualties of the shore batteries. Montojo's report was seriously in error; he listed 75 killed and 281 wounded—a total of 356. (John M. Ellicott, *Effect of Gun Fire of the United States Vessels in the Battle of Manila Bay*

(May 1, 1898) [Washington, D.C., 1899], 13; and Chadwick, *Spanish-American War*, vol. 1, pp. 204–205.) A Spanish authority, Gabriel Maura Gamazo, reports that 25 Americans were killed and 50 wounded! See his *Historia crítica del reinado de Don Alfonso XIII durante su menoridad bajo la regencia de su madre Doña María Cristina de Austria* (Barcelona, 1925) vol. 2, p. 19.

18. For the calculations concerning shells fired, hits achieved, and expenditure of ammunition, see Chadwick, *Spanish-American War*, vol. 1. pp. 203–204. For Fiske's view, see his *From Midshipman to Rear-Admiral* (New York, 1919), 249. For a biographer's account of Fiske's experiences at Manila, see Paolo E. Coletta, *Admiral Bradley A. Fiske and the American Navy* (Lawrence, Kan., 1979), 55–56. For Ellicott's observations, see his *Effect of the Gun Fire in the Battle of Manila Bay*, 13.

19. Sargent, *Dewey and the Manila Campaign*, 42–44; Dewey, *Autobiography*, 226–227; and Leech, *In the Days of McKinley*, 207. Leech comments on the cable-cutting as follows: it "reflected an egoism no less arrogant because it was ingenuous. He [Dewey] desired to operate with a minimum of interference from Washington." One historian claims that Dewey cut the cable to avoid compromising his security; he thinks that Dewey acted because of a warning from Consul Williams, received on March 10, that the Filipinos had tapped the cable (Philip Yale Nicholson, "George Dewey and the Transformation of American Foreign Policy," [Dissertation, University of New Mexico, 1971], 93). The Spanish troops that evacuated Cavite retired to San Francisco de Malabón. (John R. M. Taylor, *The Philippine Insurrection Against the United States* [Washington, D.C., 1906], galley 8AJ). For Dewey's views on the effect of his action, see his *Autobiography*, 224. See also Dewey Testimony, 1902, in Graff, ed., *American Imperialism and the Philippine Insurrection*, 2.

20. Dawes recorded events in Washington after the victory at Manila in his diary for April 29 and May 3, 1898, in Bascom Timmons, ed., *A Journal of the McKinley Years by Charles G. Dawes* (Chicago, 1950), 157, 158. See also Leech, *In the Days of McKinley*, 204–205. Leech reports the post-battle pressures in Washington in *ibid.*, 209.

21. See Montojo's report of the battle, *BN 98*, 92. Concas discussed Montojo's activity in two works: One is *Causa instruída por la destrucción de la escuadra de Filipinas y entrega del arsenal de Cavite* (Madrid, 1899); he is also certainly the author of a book issued under the pseudonym "C. P."—which initials stand for his last name, Concas y Palau—entitled *Ante la opinión y ante la historia: El Almirante Montojo* (Madrid, 1900). The commander who surrendered the Cavite arsenal, Don Enrique Sostoa y Ordóñez, was also tried, but the verdict in his case was "free absolution" (Conde de Torre-Velez, *Defensa del Excmo. Señor Don Enrique Sostoa y Ordóñez, Ex-Commandante General del arsenal de Cavite . . .* (Madrid, 1899), 130.

22. For Dewey's views, see his *Autobiography*, 232–233. In the wake of the battle, however, Dewey was gracious in victory. When Montojo was court-martialed, he wrote to Dewey for answers to certain questions, obviously with an eye to his defense: Did Dewey agree that there had been no defenses at Subig Bay? Dewey agreed. Did he believe that the depth of Subig would have caused greater casualties than at Cavite? Dewey agreed. Was the Spanish defeat due not to unreadiness but to poor ships? Dewey hedged. He responded that the Spanish defense was "gallant in the extreme. The fighting of your flagship [the *María Cristina*], which was singled out for attack was in the traditions of valor of your nation." The exchange of correspondence between Dewey and Montojo is reprinted in Healy and Kutner, *The Admiral*, 190–191. Criticisms of Montojo are found in Roca, *Bloqueo y sitio de Manila*, 86; Maura Gamazo, *Historia crítica*, vol. 2, p. 11. Some accounts say that a Spanish vessel attempted a torpedo attack on Dewey's second run, but this claim is untrue (Spector, *Admiral of the New Empire*, 61).

23. For Sargent's views, see his *Dewey and the Manila Campaign*, 48. For Braisted's views, see his *The United States Navy in the Pacific, 1897-1909* (Austin, Tex., 1958), 26.

CHAPTER 6

1. Evans's observation is in his *A Sailor's Log: Recollections of Forty Years of Naval Life* (New York, 1808), 411. For information about the blockade, see Sampson to Navy Department, 27 April 1898, *BN 98*, 177; French Ensor Chadwick, *The Relations of the United States and Spain: The Spanish-American War* (New York, 1911), vol. 2, pp. 322-324; and W. A. M. Goode, *With Sampson Through the War: Being an Account of the Naval Operations of the North Atlantic Squadron During the Spanish American War of 1898* (New York, 1899), 35.
2. U.S. State Department, *Proclamations and Decrees During the War with Spain* (Washington, 1899), 77-78.
3. For the purpose of the blockade, see John D. Long, *The New American Navy* (New York, 1903), vol. 1, p. 229. For the effect of the blockade on the Cuban population, see Herminio Portell Vilá, *Historia de Cuba en sus relaciones con los Estados Unidos y España*, (Havana, 1939), vol. 3, p. 462. For the effect of the blockade on the Spanish forces, see Manuel Corral, *¡El desastre! Memorias de un voluntario en la campaña de Cuba* (Barcelona, 1899), 177. For a comparable report, see Tomas Alvarez Angulo, *Memorias de un hombre sin importancia (1878-1961)* (Madrid, 1962), 218. For Americans serving on the blockade, the duty often seemed boring. Dudley Knox, later to become a naval historian, reported to his sister from the U.S.S. *Maple*, "The blockading . . . is usually monotonous business. All prizes have disappeared from the sea." Knox to his sister, 11 June 1898, *AF*, file 8, roll 231.
4. The records in *AF*, file 8, include detailed correspondence relating to these matters. For Sampson's orders regarding land batteries, see Long to Sampson, 26 April 1898, *BN 98*, 177. For the orders concerning the two commodores, see Long to Sampson, 28 April 1898, *ibid*. Assigned under Sampson were Commodore George C. Remey to Key West and Commodore John C. Watson to the blockade.
5. For the engagement of April 27, see U.S. Navy Department, *Annual Reports of the Navy Department for the Year 1898*, Volume I: *Report of the Secretary of the Navy. Miscellaneous Reports* (Washington, 1898), 16. For the Cienfuegos engagement on May 11, see Walter Millis, *The Martial Spirit: A Study of Our War With Spain* (Boston and New York, 1931), 201; Goode, *With Sampson Through the War*, 83-86; and Chadwick, *Spanish-American War*, vol. 2, pp. 326-333. The reports of the officers who took part are in *BN 98*, 190-198. For the engagement at Cárdenas on May 11, see Goode, *With Sampson Through the War*, 83, 96-103; Chadwick, *Spanish-American War*, vol. 2, pp. 333-337; and Millis, *Martial Spirit*, 200. The reports of Commander Chapman C. Todd of the *Machias*, 11 May 1898; First Lieutenant Frank H. Newcomb of the *Hudson*, 11 May 1898; and Lieutenant John B. Bernadou, of the *Winslow*, 16 May 1898 are in *AF*, file 8, roll 229. For the cable-cutting of the *St. Louis*, see two reports by Captain Caspar F. Goodrich of 18 May 1898 and 27 May 1898, in *BN 98*, 209-210, 211; and Caspar F. Goodrich, "The *St. Louis'* Cable-Cutting," *United States Naval Institute Proceedings*, 26 (March, 1900): 158-166. Communications were never completely severed between Cuba and Spain, despite the interest of the Naval War Board in that outcome. See Rear Admiral Montgomery Sicard to Long, 23 May 1898, *AF*, file 8, roll 230. For the engagement of June 13 at Cienfuegos, see Chadwick, *Spanish-American War*, vol. 2, p. 338. For later engagements, see U.S. Navy Department, *Annual Reports, 1898*, vol. 1, pp. 16-17.

6. Severo Gómez Nuñez, *La guerra hispano-americana. La Habana: Influencia de las plazas de guerra* (Madrid, 1900), 133–134, 140–141. For a Spanish complaint about the illegality of the blockade, see Gullón to Representatives Abroad, 11 May 1898, *Spanish Diplomatic Documents,* 164. For a list of prizes taken by American ships during the war, see Robert Wilden Neeser, *Statistical and Chronological History of the United States Navy, 1775-1907* (New York, 1909), vol. 2, pp. 458–468.

7. For Chadwick's comment, see his *Spanish-American War,* vol. 1, p. 46. For information concerning Cervera's squadron, see Jack Cameron Dierks, *A Leap to Arms: The Cuban Campaign of 1898* (Philadelphia and New York, 1970), 46; Gabriel Maura Gamazo, *Historia crítica del reinado de don Alfonso XIII durante su menoridad bajo la regencia de su madre Doña María Cristina de Austria* (Barcelona, 1925), vol. 2, pp. 17–19; Víctor M. Concas, *La escuadra de almirante Cervera* (Madrid, n.d.), 168; Francisco Arderius, *La escuadra española en Santiago de Cuba: Un diario de un testigo* (Barcelona, 1903), 40. For the report of Cervera's departure, see J. B. Moore to Long (including unsigned telegraphic report from St. Vincent), 29 April 1898, *AF,* file 8, roll 228.

8. Alfred Thayer Mahan's definition of a "fleet-in-being" is in his *Lessons of the War With Spain and Other Articles* (Freeport, N.Y., 1970 reprint edition), 76. For Concas's view, see his *Causa instruída por la destrucción de la escuadra de Filipinas y entrega del arsenal de Cavite* (Madrid, 1899), 9. For comments on the strategic consequences of Cervera's movement to the Antilles, see Chadwick, *Spanish-American War,* vol. 1, p. 61; and Dierks, *Leap to Arms,* 45–46.

9. Chadwick, *Spanish-American War,* vol. 1, pp. 62–64. See also Dierks, *Leap to Arms,* 46–47.

10. For the orders to the scouting ships, see Long to Sampson, 29 April 1898, *BN 98,* 363; orders to Captains Cotton and Goodrich, 29 April 1898, *ibid.,* 360–363; orders to the *Yale,* 1 May 1898, *ibid.,* 365–366. For the Navy Department's estimate, see Long to Sampson, 3 May 1898, *ibid.,* 366. For a variant text of this message and additional information, see Chadwick, *Spanish-American War,* vol. 1, p. 216.

11. William T. Sampson, "The Atlantic Fleet in the Spanish War," *Century,* 57 (April, 1899): 887–888. Sampson probably shared the views of Captain Chadwick expressed in the letter from the Captain to Secretary Long on April 30, 1898: He wanted to attack San Juan. "In my humble opinion we should by this time be in possession of Puerto Rico, and Spain's base be thus three thousand miles further off. With the coal and machine shops at San Juan (Puerto Rico) destroyed and the place rendered untenable there would be no fear of any Spanish on this side; Cuba would then be an easy question" (quoted in Gardner Weld Allen, ed., *Papers of John Davis Long, 1897-1904* [Boston, 1939], 109). For another expression of this view, see Chadwick to Long, 10 June 1898, *ibid.,* 137. See also Goode, *With Sampson Through the War,* 61–62, for a discussion of the author, a war correspondent on the *New York,* had with Sampson as the eastern movement began. The Naval War Board considered the possibility that Cervera might be after the *Oregon,* but then decided not to send help because the likelihood of Cervera's seeking out the American battleship seemed less and because the board did not want to interfere either with Sampson's operations at Puerto Rico or with the covering operation on the east coast (Memorandum of the Naval War Board, 12 May 1898, *BN 98,* 52).

12. For the Navy Department's reaction to Sampson's planned movement to San Juan, see Albert S. Barker, *Everyday Life in the Navy: Autobiography of Rear-Admiral Albert S. Barker* (Boston, 1928), 284. Some of this concern stemmed from fears in the Department—later proved groundless—that the armored ships *Pelayo* and *Carlos V* might come to Cervera's assistance. For the instructions to Sampson, see Long to Sampson, 5 May 1898, *BN 98,* 366. See also Long to Sampson, 6 May 1898, *BN 98,* 367–368. For Mahan's views, see his "Narrative Account of the Work of the

Naval War Board of 1898,'' 29 October 1906, in the Archives of the Naval War College, Record Group 7, Intelligence and Technological Archives, 1894 to 1945, UNOpB, 8, 11.

13. These events are discussed in Chadwick, *Spanish-American War,* vol. 1, pp. 220–222.

14. For this information, see Arderius, *La escuadra española en Santiago de Cuba: Diario de un testigo* (Barcelona, 1903), 51–52; Víctor M. Concas y Palau, *The Squadron of Admiral Cervera* (Washington, 1900), 44. The experiences of an enlisted man are reported in Tomas Benítez Frances, *El 3 de Julio desde el ''Vizcaya'': El manuscrito de un combate* (El Ferrol, 1898), 69–99.

15. Arderius, *La escuadra española,* 57–58; Concas, *The Squadron of Admiral Cervera,* 45; and Chadwick, *Spanish-American War,* vol. 1, pp. 250–258.

16. Concas made his comment in *The Squadron of Admiral Cervera,* 49. For additional information, see Pascual Cervera y Topete, *The Spanish-American War* (Washington, 1899), 75–77. What happened to the missing collier? When the Ministry of the Marine heard that Cervera had touched at Martinique, it ordered the vessel, then at San Juan, to go there, but of course Cervera had moved on to Curaçao and the connection was never made.

17. For information on Cervera's decision to run into Santiago de Cuba, see Concas, *La escuadra de almirante Cervera,* 88–90; and Mahan, *Lessons of the War With Spain,* 165. Concas takes up this question in another of his works—*Sobre las enseñanzas de la guerra hispano-americana* (Bilboa, 1900), 11—in which he defends the performance of the Spanish Navy against the strictures of foreign writers, especially H. W. Wilson of Great Britain and D. Bonamico of Italy. For the observations of Lieutenant José Müller y Tejeiro, see his *Battles and Capitulation of Santiago de Cuba* (Washington, 1899), 27.

18. For the effect of Cervera's entering Havana, see Severo Gómez Núñez, *La guerra hispano-americana: La Habana,* 117, 120. See also Chadwick, *Spanish-American War,* vol. 1, pp. 64–65. For the view that the decision to enter Santiago de Cuba allowed the United States to postpone a difficult campaign at Havana, see Severo Gómez Núñez, *La guerra hispano-americana: Santiago de Cuba* (Madrid, 1901), 42–44.

19. For the Minister of the Marine's order, see Bermejo to Cervera, 12 May 1898, *Corresponcia oficial,* 126. For the order cancelling return, see Auñón to Commander, *Terror,* at Martinique and Marina de Santiago de Cuba, 19 May 1898, in Gómez Núñez, *La guerra hispano-americana: La Habana,* 137. See also Concas, *La escuadra de almirante Cervera,* 97–98. For the protests from Cuba and Puerto Rico, see Blanco to Moret, 17 May 1898, and Macías (Governor-General of Puerto Rico) to Moret, 18 May 1898, in Arderius, *La escuadra española,* 65. Auñón had been very strongly in favor of sending out Cervera in the first place; defending his wartime leadership in response to questioning in the Cortes by José Canalejas on September 10, 1898, Auñón attributed the decision to withdraw permission to return to the protests from Cuba and Puerto Rico (Ramon Auñón y Villalón, *Discursos pronunciados en el parlamento por el ministro de marina D. Ramon Auñón y Villalón durante la guerra con los Estados Unidos* (Madrid, 1912), 81–83. He may conceivably have sought to shift responsibility for the later defeat. The quotation by Concas is in his *The Squadron of Admiral Cervera,* 51.

20. For a full account of the bombardment of San Juan, see Chadwick, *Spanish-American War,* vol. 1, pp. 225–235. He reports these casualties: United States— seven wounded, one killed; Spain—thirteen killed, one hundred wounded. Some of the American projectiles carried beyond the military targets to the town, causing some civilian casualties. Sampson's postwar account is in his ''The Atlantic Fleet in the Spanish War,'' 890–891. For information on what took place within San Juan, see Angel Rivero Méndez, *Crónica de la guerra hispano-americana en Puerto Rico*

(Madrid, n.d.), 65–108; Macías tu Correa (Minister of War), 27 May 1898, in *ibid.*, 608–613. See also U.S Navy Department, *Sketches From the Spanish-American War by Commander J——* (Washington, 1899), 13–14. The author, a German officer named Jacobsen, criticized Sampson for attacking without due warning. Under international law Sampson was not obliged to give warning in an attack on strictly military targets, but would have to do so if attacking a city with a noncombatant population. Reports of commanders in the action are in *BN 98*, 370–382.

21. For the quotation about the reasons for departing San Juan, see Sampson to Long, 3 August 1898, *ibid.*, 460. The explanation for the bombardment made by Sampson is in Sampson to Long, 18 May 1898, *AF*, file 8, roll 229.

22. Edwin Albert Falk, *Fighting Bob Evans* (Freeport, N.Y., 1939 reprint edition), 270.

23. For the views of Evans see his *Sailor's Log*, 422. For the views of the Secretary of the Navy, see Long Diary, 13 May 1898, in Lawrence Shaw Mayo, ed., *America of Yesterday: As Reflected in the Journal of John Davis Long* (Boston, 1923), 193. Mahan's views are in his *Lessons of the War With Spain*, 168, and his "Narrative Account of the Naval War Board," 8. See also Goode, *With Sampson Through the War*, 86–87. Mahan's most recent biographer, Robert Seager, believes that Mahan erred; he thinks that "concentration in this instance was both unnecessary and a luxury" (*Alfred Thayer Mahan: The Man and His Letters* [Annapolis, 1977], 368).

24. Sampson to Long (from St. Thomas), 12 May 1898, *BN 98*, 384; Long to Sampson, 14 May 1898, *ibid.*, 387; and Sampson to Long, 18 May 1898, *ibid.*, 368–370. See also orders to U.S.S. *Yale* to report the sighting at Curaçao to Sampson in Long to *Yale* (at St. Thomas), 14 May 1898, *ibid.*, 387. See also Chadwick, *Spanish-American War*, vol. 1, p. 247.

25. These arrangements are discussed in John D. Long, *The New American Navy* (New York, 1903), vol. 1, pp. 246–248. For relevant correspondence, see Long to U.S.S. *Minneapolis* and Long to U.S.S. *St. Paul*, 13 May 1898, *BN 98*, 386; Long to Sampson, 14 May 1898, *ibid.*, 388; Long to Sampson, 16 May 1898, *ibid.*, 390–392; and Sampson to Long, 16 May 1898, *ibid.*, 392. The Naval War Board played a role in these events, advising the concentration of both Sampson and Schley at Key West and also the disposition of the lookouts (Mahan, "Narrative account of the Naval War Board," 9–10). It should be noted that on May 12 the Naval War Board recommended that no reinforcements be sent to cover the movements of the *Oregon* despite the possibility that Cervera might seek to intercept the American battleship on its northward voyage to join Sampson. The Board gave as its reasons that "The danger of her meeting the Spanish Squadron was now thought to be less than formerly, and it was undesirable to disturb Admiral Sampson's operations around Porto Rico or to leave the northern coast without its chief defense" (Memorandum of the Naval War Board, 12 May 1898, *RG 45*, NRC 372, 46).

26. For the order concerning the Sampson and Schley dispositions, see Navy Department to Remey, 17 May 1898, in Record Group 45, NRC 371: Telegrams Sent Out, the Naval War Board, vol. 1, 105, in the Naval Records Collection of the Office of Naval Records and Library, National Archives, Washington, D.C.), (hereafter cited as *RG 45*, NRC 371. Sampson received the message en route from Cap Haitien to Key West. It was delivered on May 17 by the U.S.S. *Dupont*. (Sampson to Long, 3 August 1898, *BN 98*, 462). For Long's views, see Long, *New Navy*, vol. 1, p. 251. Mahan's observations are in "Narrative account of the Naval War Board," 13–15.

27. For the meeting of May 18, 1898, see Chadwick, *Spanish-American War*, vol. 1, pp. 248–249. For arrangements made orally with Schley, see Sampson to Long, 18 May 1898, *BN 98*, 393. For the orders of 19 May 1898, see Sampson to Long, 3 August 1898, *ibid.*, 464. For Schley's account of the meeting, see U.S. Navy Department, *Record of Proceedings of a Court of Inquiry in the Case of Rear-Admiral Winfield S. Schley, U.S. Navy: Convened at the Navy-Yard, Washington, D.C., September 12, 1901* (Washington, 1902), vol. 2, pp. 1,343–1,344.

28. For characterization of Sampson and Schley, see Margaret Leech, *In the Days of McKinley* (New York, 1959), 197, 220–221.

29. For information about the receipt of the report about Cervera, see J. C. Willever to M. Marean, 19 May 1898, *AF*, file 8, roll 230. In the same place there is certification from Marean, dated October 10, 1901, that the telegram came into his hands about 4:00 P.M. on May 19, 1898. For the orders to the ships to go to Santiago de Cuba, see Long, *New Navy*, vol. 1, p. 257. See also Long to U.S.S. *Minneapolis* (at St. Thomas), 19 May 1898, *BN 98*, 393. This order read, "Proceed at once off Santiago de Cuba; the Spanish fleet reported there; Schley ordered there; find *Harvard* if practicable; she is somewhere off north coast of Porto Rico; proceed with off Santiago; her orders same as yours. Keep touch with Spanish fleet, communicate occasionally." For information about the Navy Department's desires after learning about the rumor and Sampson's response, see Long to Sampson, 19 May 1898, *ibid.*; Chadwick, *Spanish-American War*, vol. 1, pp. 266–269. For Schley's movements, see Long, *New Navy*, vol. 1, pp. 255–256.

30. For Sampson's reasons for finally accepting the likelihood that Cervera was at Santiago de Cuba, see Chadwick, *Spanish-American War*, vol. 1, p. 271. It seems probable that the Navy Department did not report the details of how it learned about Cervera's movement so as to protect its source. Sampson learned about this source independently in Key West. For the orders to Schley to move to Santiago de Cuba, see Sampson to Schley, 21 May 1898, *BN 98*, 466. See also Sampson to Long, 21 May 1898, *RG 45*, Entry 40, no. 2, 173. The mission of the U.S.S. *Hawk* is recounted in Sampson, *Spanish-American War*, vol. 1, pp. 274–275. For Sampson's eastern movement, see Sampson to Long, 3 August 1898, *BN 98*, 470. See also Long, *New Navy*, vol. 1, p. 254.

31. Schley's remembrance of the supposed salute is in U.S. Navy Department, *Court of Inquiry*, vol. 2, p. 1,347. For Schley's decision to remain at Cienfuegos and subsequent events, see Winfield Scott Schley, *Forty-Five Years Under the Flag* (New York, 1904), 268; Schley to Sampson, 23 May 1898, in Chadwick, *Spanish-American War*, vol. 1, pp. 281–282; *ibid.*, 297; Schley to Long, 30 May 1898, *BN 98*, 402–403; Long, *New Navy*, vol. 1, p. 262; and Evans, *Sailor's Log*, 428.

32. Sampson's movements are reported in Chadwick, *Spanish-American War*, vol. 1, p. 285. The orders to the U.S.S. *St. Paul* are in Long to Cotton (at Môle St. Nicholas), 25 May 1898, *BN 98*, 395. For the capture of the British merchant vessel *Restormel*, see Sigsbee to Long, 25 May 1898, *ibid.*, 410–412; Goode, *With Sampson Through the War*, 133; and Alberto Risco, *Apuntes biográficos del Excmo. Sr. Almirante D. Pascual Cervera y Topete* (Toledo, 1920), 100. For information about the vessels off Santiago de Cuba in the period May 21–26, 1898, see Cotton to Long (from Môle St. Nicolas), 25 May 1898, *BN 98*, 395; Long, *New Navy*, vol. 1, pp. 274, 278; and Chadwick, *Spanish-American War*, vol. 1, pp. 298–302.

33. For Schley's decision to return to Key West, see Long, *New Navy*, vol. 1, 274; Schley to Long, 30 May 1898, *BN 98*, 403–404. For Schley's difficulties with coaling, see Schley to Long (from Môle St. Nicolas), 25 May 1898, *ibid.*, 394; Chadwick, *Spanish-American War*, vol. 1, pp. 286, 293; Schley to Long (through Kingston), 28 May 1898, *BN 98*, 397. Evans reported his reaction to the order in his *Sailor's Log*, 429. The conversation between Evans and Philip is reported in Charles H. Brown, *The Correspondents' War: Journalists in the Spanish-American War* (New York, 1967), 262. For Long's views on Schley's capacity to coal, see his *New Navy*, vol. 1, pp. 276–277. See also Falk, *Fighting Bob Evans*, 295.

34. Long, *New Navy*, vol. 1, p. 280.

35. For the message, see Long to cable office, Môle St. Nicolas, for delivery to Schley, 27 May 1898, *BN 98*, 397. For Mahan's comments, see "Narrative Account of the Naval War Board," 16. The development of the plan to exploit command of the sea in the Caribbean, resulting from a successful blockade of Cervera, is discussed in Chapter 5.

36. For the message, see Long to U.S.S. *Harvard* (at Kingston) for Schley, 28 May 1898, *BN 98*, 397–398. For the secretary's appraisal, see Long, *New Navy*, I, 276.
37. For Long's message, see Long to Schley, 29 May 1898, *BN 98*, 399. For the Long Diary, 29 May 1898, see Margaret D. Long, ed., *The Journal of John D. Long* (Rindge, N.H., 1956), 226–227.
38. For the various messages to the Flying Squadron, see Sampson to Schley (via the U.S.S. *Wasp*), 27 May 1898, *BN 98*, 475; Sampson to Schley (via the U.S.S. *New Orleans*), 27 May 1898, *ibid.*, 476; Sampson to Schley, 28 May 1898, quoted in Chadwick, *Spanish-American War*, vol. 1, pp. 295–296. Sampson notified the Navy Department of his actions in Sampson to Long, 28 May 1898, *BN 98*, 398. For the order placing Schley under Sampson, see Long to Sampson, 24 May 1898, *ibid.*, 394. This information was conveyed to the Flying Squadron in Long to Schley, 24 May 1898, *ibid.* See also Chadwick, *Spanish-American War*, vol. 1, p. 285. Word of the plan to send troops to Santiago de Cuba came in Long to Sampson, 27 May 1898 (rec. 28 May 1898), *CWS*, vol. 1, p. 17.
39. Schley's decision to return to Santiago de Cuba, made on May 28, 1898, is discussed in Chadwick, *Spanish-American War*, vol. 1, 327–328; Millis, *Martial Spirit*, 235–236; and Long, *New Navy*, vol. 1, p. 280. Schley's initial report of the blockade is Schley to Long, 29 May 1898, *BN 98*, 400. Evans's observations are in his *Sailor's Log*, 429. For the views of his superiors, see Long, *New Navy*, vol. 1, p. 276; and Leech, *In the Days of McKinley*, 222.
40. The decision of the court of inquiry is reproduced conveniently in Long, *New Navy*, vol. 1, pp. 284–285. Admiral Dewey, who served as one of the panel members, presented a separate memorandum that defended Schley's activities, but he did not offer a convincing defense for these views (*Ibid.*, 286).
41. For the report of this action, see Schley to Long, 1 June 1898, *BN 98*, 427. For accounts of the bombardment and its outcome, see Arderius, *Escuadra española*, 89; Millis, *Martial Spirit*, 239; Dierks, *Leap to Arms*, 63; Chadwick, *Spanish-American War*, vol. 1, pp. 331–333; and Evans, *Sailor's Log*, 432.
42. For the early activity of Cervera in Santiago de Cuba, see Arderius, *Escuadra española*, 79–80; and Cervera to Auñón, 20 May 1898, in Cervera, *Spanish-American War*, 81. In the latter message Cervera noted, "Intend to refit ships in shortest possible time, because, in my opinion, Santiago will soon be in difficult situation if it does not receive aid." Concas's observations are in his *Squadron of Admiral Cervera*, 52. For Blanco's message, see Blanco to Correa, 20 May 1898, in Cervera, *Spanish-American War*, 81. He expressed similar sentiments in Blanco to Linares for Correa, 26 May 1898, *ibid.*, 94–95.
43. For the situation at Santiago de Cuba and the meeting of May 24, 1898, see *ibid.*, 88–89; Long, *New Navy*, vol. 1, p. 270–271; and Chadwick, *Spanish-American War*, vol. 1, pp. 311–313. For a list of the American vessels observed by the Spanish squadron off Santiago de Cuba in the period of May 21–31, see José Müller y Tejeiro, *Combates y capitulación de Santiago de Cuba* (Madrid, 1898), 75–81. For Cervera's communications, see Cervera to Linares, 25 May 1898, in Cervera, *Spanish-American War*, 91–92; and Cervera to Auñón, 25 May 1898, quoted in Chadwick, *Spanish-American War*, vol. 1, p. 313.
44. For the council of May 26, 1898, see *ibid.*, 95–98; and Long, *New Navy*, vol. 1, pp. 271–272. For the views of Concas, see his *Squadron of Admiral Cervera*, 57. It cannot be ascertained whether Concas actually had his political analysis in mind on May 26. He might have developed this view later on because of the policy of the Liberal ministry in early July. Müller stresses lack of coal and high ocean swells as reasons why the Spanish squadron did not go out in the period May 20–27, 1898 (Müller, *Battles and Capitulation of Santiago de Cuba*, 109).
45. The two options open to Cervera are discussed in Dierks, *Leap to Arms*, 185–189. See also Chadwick, *Spanish-American War*, vol. 1, 317–318; Müller, *Combates y capitulación*, 92. On June 1, Cervera proposed to Auñón that some effort be made

to divert the armored cruisers *Brooklyn* and *New York* to another location, a step that might make it possible to run the blockade. This suggestion implicitly testified to the strength of the American position. (Cervera to Auñón, 1 June 1898, in Cervera, *Spanish-American War*, 99.) Auñón lived in a dream world all his own. On June 3, in response to repeated appeals from Blanco for relief, he informed Cervera that it was necessary to send ships and troops to the Philippines. Cervera would be detached only temporarily for duty in the Pacific and would return soon to the Antilles with reinforcements! This fantastic scheme never materialized. (See *ibid.*, 100.) The Minister of War, Correa, asked Blanco his opinion of this scheme at the same time (Correa to Blanco, 3 June 1898, in Risco, *Apuntes biográficos*, 119–120).

46. For Bustamante's scheme, see Cervera, *Spanish-American War*, 102–103.

47. For naval support of land operations, see *ibid.*, 104–105; Arderius, *Escuadra española*, 110.

48. Sampson returned to Key West to improve his communications (Sampson to Long, 3 August 1898, *BN 98*, 477). The Long-Sampson exchange is in Long to Sampson, 28 May 1898, *ibid.*, 398; Sampson to Long, 29 May 1898, *ibid.*, 399; and Long to Sampson, 29 May 1898, *ibid.* Word of Schley's position is mentioned in Chadwick, *Spanish-American War*, vol. 1, p. 324. For the messages to Schley, see Long to Schley (via U.S.S. *Harvard* at Jamaica), 29 May 1898, quoted in *BN 98*, 401; and Sampson to Schley, 29 May 1898, quoted in Sampson to Long, 3 August 1898, *ibid.*, 478. The Navy Department sent two additional messages to Schley via Jamaica. One asked him about the location of the two armored cruisers not yet identified—the *Almirante Oquendo* and the *Infanta María Teresa*. Another informed him that he could obtain a good view of the harbor by landing someone at Sagua, twenty-five miles east of the city, with instructions to proceed to the heights at the north end of Santiago Bay (Long to Cotton for Schley, 30 May 1898, *ibid.*, [two messages]). On 31 May Schley reported the presence of another vessel of the *Vizcaya* class (Schley to Long, 30 May 1898, *ibid.*). For Sampson's departure from Key West, see Remey to Long, 30 May 1898, *ibid.*

49. Chadwick, *Spanish-American War*, vol. 1, pp. 325–385. Sampson had estimated his probable time of arrival as 4:00 A.M. on June 1 (Sampson to Long, 1 June 1898, *BN 98*, 402). The Navy Department remained greatly interested in ascertaining definitely the presence of all the Spanish ships supposedly at Santiago de Cuba. This desire related to the plans then afoot to send an army expedition. The Department did not want to send out the force in preparation at Tampa without ensuring that it would have smooth sailing to its destination. (Long to Sampson, 31 May 1898, *ibid.*, 401.) This message reads, "It is essential to know if all four armored vessels [are] in Santiago, as our military expedition must wait for this information. Report as soon as possible." Sampson responded three days later, "Some observations made to-day by a reliable Cuban, in accordance with my instructions made four armored vessels and two destroyers at Santiago. At that time repairs and more coal needed by them." (Sampson to Long [via Môle St. Nicolas], 2 June 1898, *BN 98*, 402.) This report was accurate. On June 3 Lt. William S. Sims, that energetic impresario of espionage in Paris, gave assurance that the Spanish squadron would remain at Santiago de Cuba because of the badly damaged condition of three vessels, particularly the *Cristóbal Colón*. He also noted that the ships remaining at Cádiz were in even worse shape. (Sims to Bureau of Navigation, rec. 3 June 1898, *RG 38*, entry 100.)

50. For word to Sampson of the projected expedition, see Long to Sampson, 31 May 1898, quoted in Sampson to Long, 3 August 1898, *BN 98*, 480. For the text of the false message to be planted in Spain, see Long to Sims, 31 May 1898, *RG 38*, Entry 100. Sims had prepared the way for this enterprise. Earlier he had cabled, "If you

desire at a suitable time to circulate misleading information relating to naval movements, I can accomplish it through special agent at Paris having amicable relations with the Spanish Ambassador at Paris.'' Sims to Bureau of Navigation, rec. 24 May 1898, *RG 38*, Entry 100. The agent referred to in Long's telegram was, of course, this man who knew the Spanish Ambassador, León y Castillo. Sims reported later, "Special agent at Paris stated that the Spanish Ambassador telegraphed Madrid yesterday false information concerning Matanzas and Cienfuegos'' (Sims to Bureau of Navigation, rec. 4 June 1898, *RG 38*, Entry 100). For the order to contact García, see Long to Sampson, 30 May 1898, quoted in Sampson to Long, 3 August 1898, *BN 98*, 480. Sampson received this message through Môle St. Nicolas on June 1.

51. At 9:00 A.M., only two and one-half hours after his arrival at Santiago de Cuba, Sampson sent the *New York* in towards the harbor mouth to make observations needed to plan the sinking of the *Merrimac* there. For comments on Sampson's motives, see Goode, *With Sampson Through the War*, 144, 146; and Chadwick, *Spanish-American War*, vol. 1, pp. 345–346. Chadwick notes that in 1904 the Japanese tried to close Port Arthur in a similar manner, a development he thought supportive of the tactical and strategic considerations in Sampson's mind at Santiago de Cuba. For the action of the Naval War Board, see Long, *New Navy*, vol. 1, pp. 268–269. Chadwick expressed his views at the time in a letter to the Secretary of the Navy: "Were the entrance to Santiago of a different character, *i. e.*, with low-lying land, we could easily force our way in, but it is extraordinarily narrow commanded by bluffs two hundred feet in height, and these bluffs occupied by an active enemy would render our action in this narrow inlet, but three hundred and fifty feet broad, planted with mines, very difficult and disaster there would be irretrievable. If we were sure to be left alone, we should of course try it at whatever risk; with the hope of the arrival of the army we of course wait'' (Chadwick to Long, 10 June 1898, quoted in Allen, ed., *Letters of John D. Long*, 134). For Alger's criticisms, see his *Spanish-American War*, 225.

52. Information about the harbor entrance is found in Dierks, *Leap to Arms*, 62; Gómez Núñez, *La guerra hispano-americana. Santiago de Cuba*, 63; and George Kennan, *Campaigning in Cuba* (New York, 1899), 56. Information concerning the batteries is taken from Müller, *Battles and Capitulation*, 19–20, 25; Major General Joseph Wheeler, *The Santiago Campaign 1898* (New York, 1898), 88; Chadwick, *Spanish-American War*, vol. 1, pp. 319–320. The 6.3-inch breech-loading Hontoria rifles at the Socapa and Morro batteries had been taken from the *Reina Mercedes*, an old cruiser moored at Santiago de Cuba. For the mines see Müller, *Battles and Capitulation*, 17–18.

53. Chadwick, *Spanish-American War*, vol. 1, pp. 337–340; Dierks, *Leap to Arms*, 64–65; and Sampson to Long, 3 June 1898, *BN 98*, 437.

54. Chadwick, *Spanish-American War*, vol. 1, pp. 341–346, 354, 358; Richmond Pearson Hobson, *The Sinking of the "Merrimac": A Personal Narrative of the Adventure in the Harbor of Santiago de Cuba and of the Subsequent Imprisonment of the Survivors* (New York, 1899), 95–97; Dierks, *Leap to Arms*, 67–68; and Sampson to Long, 3 August 1898, *BN 98*, 481. Concas claimed that he and Bustamante, an inventor of mines used by the Spanish Navy, opened some of the unexploded mines lashed to the side of the *Merrimac* and found the powder wet (Concas, *Squadron of Admiral Cervera*, 59). Arderius claimed that the Spanish government notified Cervera on May 28, 1898, that the Americans were planning to block the channel. This information led to precautions. Captain Villaamil sensed the possibility of an attack on June 2 and alerted Venancio Nardíz, commanding at the Socapa, to watch carefully that evening. (Arderius, *Escuadra española*, 92–93.) Sampson admitted the failure to block the channel in Sampson to Long, 17 June

1898, quoted in Sampson to Long, 3 August 1898, *BN 98*, 495. For an article treating Hobson's popularity and later career, see Barton Carr Shaw, "The Hobson Craze," *United States Naval Institute Proceedings*, 102 (February, 1976): 54–60.

55. For Mahan's statement, see Mahan for the Naval War Board to Long, 3 June 1898, *AF*, file 8, roll 231. For the reasons why it was possible to maintain a close blockade at Santiago de Cuba, see Fernando Soldevilá, *Historia de España*, 2d edition (Barcelona, 1964), vol. 7, p. 417.

56. For the order of June 2, see Chadwick, *Spanish-American War*, vol. 1, p. 348.

57. For the order of June 7, see *ibid.*, 357. For an order pulling together all blockade instructions, see Squadron General Order No. 10, 11 June 1898, *AF*, file 8, roll 231. For the order of June 3, see Chadwick, *Spanish-American War*, vol. 1, pp. 362–364; and *ibid.*, vol. 2, p. 185. For Captain Robley D. Evans's description of the difficulties associated with the searchlight tactic, see his *Sailor's Log*, 440–441. For the reason why the Spanish batteries did not fire on the close-in blockaders, see Concas, *Squadron of Admiral Cervera*, 59–60. See also Arderius, *La escuadra española*, 109–110. Chadwick pointed out the probability that the search lights would also have been effective from further out (Chadwick, *Spanish-American War*, vol. 1, p. 366).

58. For the views of Captain Philip, see Edgar Stanton Maclay, *Life and Adventures of "Jack" Philip, Rear-Admiral United States Navy* (New York, 1903), 264–265. A Spanish observer noted the strain on the Spanish crews that derived from the constant watch for a possible American attack on the channel (Arderius, *La escuadra española*, 104–105). Captain Chadwick, writing to Long on June 10, expressed his satisfaction with the efficiency of the blockade but also his desire for assistance: "We are now anxiously and not patient-mindedly awaiting the army. . . . Our blockade thus far has undoubtedly been effective; nothing has gone in or out since our arrival" (Chadwick to Long, 10 June 1898, in Allen, ed., *Papers of John D. Long*, 134).

59. Victor Blue to Lieutenant Commander D. Delahanty, U.S.S. *Suwanee*, 13 June 1898, *BN 98*, 444–445; and Sampson to Long, 13 June 1898, quoted in Sampson to Long, 3 August 1898, *ibid.*, 492. See also Chadwick, *Spanish-American War*, vol. 1, pp. 378–379.

60. For information about the bombardment of June 6, 1898, see *ibid.*, 351. For the reports of the captains participating in the action, see *AF*, file 8, roll 231. For Evans's views, see his *Sailor's Log*, 438. The anecdote about Acosta is in Arderius, *La escuadra española*, 100. Additional information about the bombardment is in *ibid.*, 97–101. For Sampson's message, see Sampson to Long, 6 June 1898, *BN 98*, 485.

61. The observation about the *Vesuvius* is in Goode, *With Sampson Through the War*, 171. Seven Spanish defenders were wounded in this attack (Herbert H. Sargent, *The Campaign of Santiago de Cuba* [Chicago, 1907], vol. 3, p. 198).

62. For the bombardment of June 16, see Sampson Order, 15 June 1898, quoted in Sampson to Long, 3 August 1898, *BN 98*, 493. For reports of the captains commanding participating vessels, see *AF*, file 8, roll 232. For information concerning bombardments and casualties inflicted, see Gómez Núñez, *La guerra hispano-americana. Santiago de Cuba*, 92; Müller, *Battles and Capitulation of Santiago de Cuba*, 153; and Sargent, *Campaign of Santiago de Cuba*, vol. 3, p. 198.

63. For Sigsbee's comments, see Sigsbee to Long, 31 May 1898, *BN 98*, 414. For information concerning the orders for the Marine battalion, see Remey to Long, 2 June 1898, *RG 45*, Entry 40, no. 2, 207; Sicard for Naval War Board to Long, 3 June 1898, *AF*, file 8, roll 231; and Charles Allen to Naval Base, Key West, 7 June 1898, *AF*, file 8, roll 231. For the operations of June 7 in Guantánamo Bay, see Brown, *Correspondents' War*, 279–280; John R. Spears, *Our Navy in the War With Spain* (New York, 1898), 260; and Bernard C. Nalty, *The United States Marines in the*

War With Spain (Washington, 1959), 9. See also Sampson to Long, 8 June 1898, quoted in Sampson to Long, 3 August 1898, *BN 98*, 488. For the return of the *Marblehead* to Guantánamo, see Chadwick, *Spanish-American War*, vol. 1, p. 356.

64. For the operations at Guantánamo, see Long, *New Navy*, vol. 2, pp. 5–6; Nalty, *Marines in the War With Spain*, 9–10; and Chadwick, *Spanish-American War*, vol. 1, p. 375. For correspondence, see R. W. Huntington to Colonel Commandant Charles Heywood, 17 June 1898, in U.S. Navy, *Annual Reports, 1898*, 838–839; McCalla to Sampson, 12 June 1898, *AF*, file 8, roll 231; and McCalla to Sampson, 19 June 1898, *AF*, file 8, roll 231.

65. For messages urging an army expedition, see Sampson to Long, 7 June 1898, *BN 98*, 488; and Sampson to Long, 17 June 1898, quoted in Sampson to Long, 3 August 1898, *ibid.*, 495.

66. For Bermejo's message, see Bermejo to Cámara, 8 May 1898, in *Correspondencia oficial*, 273. For the messages to Colwell and Sims, see Long to Attachés, London and Paris, 10 May 1898, *RG 38*, Entry 100.

67. For reports providing this information, see Carroll to State Department, 11 May 1898, *AF*, file 4, roll 33; Horatio L. Sprague (Consul at Gibraltar) to Assistant Secretary of State, 15 May 1898, *AF*, file 4, roll 33; and Sprague to Day, 15 May 1898, *AF*, file 4, roll 33. For the message to Dewey, see Long to Dewey, 19 May 1898, *RG 45*, NRC 371, vol. 1, 132. Long's message to Sims and Colwell is Long to Attachés, London and Paris, 20 May 1898, *RG 38*, Entry 100. For the information about the Azores, see Day to Long, reporting Day to Townsend (Minister at Lisbon), 20 May 1898, *AF*, file 4, roll 33. Sims's information came in Sims to Bureau of Navigation, rec. 21 May 1898, *RG 38*, Entry 100; and Sims to Bureau of Navigation, rec. 23 May 1898, *RG 38*, Entry 200.

68. Auñón to Cámara, 27 May 1898, *Correspondencia oficial*, 276–280. See also Chadwick, *Spanish-American War*, vol. 2, pp. 384–387; Risco, *Apuntes biográficos*, 116; and Cervera, *Spanish-American War*, 147–150.

69. For these messages, see Sims to Bureau of Navigation, rec. 1 June 1898, *RG 38*, Entry 100; and Sims to Bureau of Navigation, rec. 2 June 1898, *RG 38*, Entry 100.

70. For the first such message, see Allen to Sims, 1 June 1898, *RG 38*, Entry 100. The recommendation of the Naval War Board is in Sicard for the Naval War Board to Long, 1 June 1898, *RG 45*, NRC 371, vol. 2, 3.

71. Reports from consuls, ministers, and attachés during the first two weeks of June provided useful information to Washington, although some of their messages were contradictory. For examples see John H. Carroll (Gibraltar), 5 June 1898, *AF*, file 4, roll 34; he reported, "Positive Cadiz fleet stationary some days Spain fears destruction Peninsular commerce and Cádiz fleet; third fleet unavailable months"; Sims to Bureau of Navigation, 7 June 1898, *RG 38*, Entry 100; Townsend (Lisbon) to Day, 8 June 1898, *AF*, file 4, roll 34; Sprague to Day, 10 June 1898, *AF*, file 4, roll 34; Sprague to Moore, 12 June 1898, *AF*, file 4, roll 34; and Hay to Day, transmitted in Day to Long, 13 June 1898, *AF*, file 4, roll 34. Conflicting reports came in on June 14: The consul in Tangiers, Partridge, reported the Spanish fleet still at Cádiz, cabling, "Am satisfied not ready to sail. At present do not believe it is intended for America or Philippines." (Partridge to Day, 14 June 1898, *AF*, file 4, roll 34.) Sprague, however, reported accurately from Gibraltar, "Madrid telegram to local newspapers states Minister Marine leaves Cadiz today; departure fleet will soon follow" (Sprague to Day, 14 June 1898, *AF*, file 4, roll 34). The order to Cámara is Auñón to Cámara, 15 June 1898, *Correspondencia oficial*, 287–289. Cervera includes this message in his *Spanish-American War*, 151–154. See also Risco, *Apuntes biográficos*, 117; and Melchor Fernández Almagro, *Política naval de la España moderna y contemporánea* (Madrid, 1946), 205–206. Sims's report on the mood in Madrid stated, "Officers attached to vessels and intelligent Spanish citizens thoroughly believe we cannot land in Cuba or other Spanish possessions; also that

fleet at Cádiz will destroy a part of U.S. fleet for the reason that we cannot keep concentrated; we must defend certain points. All special agents have reported this confidence universal and complete.'' (Sims to Bureau of Navigation, rec. 13 June 1898, *RG 38*, Entry 100.)

72. The voyage of Admiral Cámara is discussed further in Chapters 12 and 16.

CHAPTER 7

1. Russell A. Alger, *The Spanish-American War* (New York and London, 1901), 13–14.

2. For this information, see French Ensor Chadwick, *The Relations of the United States and Spain: The Spanish-American War* (New York, 1911), vol. 1, p. 46; Graham A. Cosmas, *An Army for Empire: The United States Army in the Spanish-American War* (Columbia, Mo., 1971) pp. 5–6, 10–14. In 1897 only eighteen recruiting centers existed in the entire country, located at the larger centers of population and at military posts. This number had grown to only twenty-two by April 1898. The recruiting program had obviously not been geared to the needs of the nation during a serious emergency. Marvin A. Kreidberg and Merton G. Henry, *History of Military Mobilization in the United States Army, 1775–1945* (Washington, D.C., 1955), 150.

3. For information about Russell A. Alger, see Kreidberg and Henry, *History of Military Mobilization*, 58; and Margaret Leech, *In the Days of McKinley* (New York, 1959), 200. For Nelson A. Miles, see *ibid.*, 200–201; and Cosmas, *Army for Empire*, 61–62.

4. For the bureau system, see Cosmas, *Army for Empire*, 14–19, 26.

5. *Ibid.*, 22–24. For a brief description of the old army's organization, see James E. Hewes, Jr., *From Root to McNamara: Army Organization and Administration, 1900–1963* (Washington, D.C., 1975), 3–6.

6. Cosmas emphasizes the unusual importance of Corbin during the war with Spain. See his characterization in *Army for Empire*, 62–64. See also Leech, *In the Days of McKinley*, 236–237.

7. Cosmas, *Army for Empire*, 27–28.

8. Kreidberg and Henry, *History of Military Mobilization*, 150–151; and Russell F. Weigley, *History of the United States Army* (New York, 1967), 299.

9. This account closely follows Cosmas, *Army for Empire*, 36–45.

10. For the consequences of the lack of clarity in the mission to be assigned the army, see *ibid.*, 74–75. For the army's expenditure of about $16 million of about $19 million allocated to it in the Fifty-Million-Dollar Bill, see Alger, *Spanish-American War*, 8. See also Edward Ranson, ''Nelson A. Miles as Commanding General, 1875–1903,'' *Military Affairs*, 29 (Winter 1965–1966): 183; Chadwick, *Spanish-American War*, vol. 1, p. 49. Chadwick notes that the Medical, Quartermaster, and Signal Departments made no expenditures of their allocations up to April 23, 1898. Many critics have commented on the army's emphasis on coastal defense. Cosmas defends this activity as prudent, given the likelihood that Spain might have attempted to counter a blockade by raiding the coast. He notes that Spain actually contemplated such operations, but lacked the ability to undertake them. (Cosmas, *Army for Empire*, 86–87.) Of course, a more sophisticated planning agency might have recognized that Spain had little capability for such operations.

11. Cosmas, *Army for Empire*, 73–74, 81, 87–89. See also Graham A. Cosmas, ''From Order to Chaos: The War Department, the National Guard, and Military Policy, 1898,'' *Military Affairs* 29 (Fall, 1965–1966): 107.

12. *Ibid.*, 109–110, 115.

13. For Roosevelt's views, see Roosevelt to William Austin Wadsworth, 7 April 1898 in

Elting E. Morison et al., *The Letters of Theodore Roosevelt*, Volume 2: *The Years of Preparation* (Cambridge, Mass., 1951), 814. For Miles's plan, see U.S. War Department, *Annual Reports of the War Department for the Fiscal Year Ended June 30, 1898: Report of the Secretary of War—Miscellaneous Reports* (Washington, 1898), 19 (hereafter cited as *ARWD 98*); Kreidberg and Henry, *History of Military Mobilization*, 152; and Cosmas, *Army for Empire*, 97–99.

14. For information concerning this concentration, see Kreidberg and Henry, *History of Military Mobilization*, 152–153, 165–166; Corbin Orders, 15 April 1898, in U.S. War Department, *Correspondence Relating to the War With Spain and Conditions Growing Out of the Same, Including the Insurrection in the Philippine Islands and the China Relief Expedition, Between the Adjutant General of the Army and Military Commanders in the United States, Cuba, Puerto Rico, China, and the Philippine Islands, from April 15, 1898, to July 30, 1902* (Washington, D.C., 1902), vol. 1, pp. 7–8 (hereafter cited as *CWS*).

15. Kreidberg and Henry, *History of Military Mobilization*, 154–155, 164–165; Cosmas, *Army for Empire*, 100–102; and Chadwick, *Spanish-American War*, vol. 1, pp. 46–47. General Miles later complained that the Act of April 22, 1898 had an adverse effect on recruiting for the regular army because recruits perferred to serve with local militia units from their home areas. (Nelson A. Miles, "The War with Spain—I," *North American Review* 168 [May, 1899]: 517. The provision for the organization of three special volunteer regiments evolved from a proposal by the governor of Arizona to form a regiment of mounted riflemen. Senator Francis E. Warren (Republican from Wyoming), Chairman of the Senate Committee on Military Affairs, learned of this suggestion and proceeded to arrange for three special outfits. (Herman Hagedorn, *Leonard Wood: A Biography* [New York and London, 1931], vol. 1, p. 125.)

16. Kreidberg and Henry, *History of Military Mobilization*, 156; and Cosmas, "From Order to Chaos," 119. For the text of the call for volunteers made on April 23, 1898, see U.S. State Department, *Proclamations and Decrees During the War with Spain* (Washington, D.C., 1899), 76–77.

17. Cosmas, "From Order to Chaos," 119; Chadwick, *Spanish-American War*, vol. 1, pp. 46–47.

18. For the views of the commanding general, see Miles to Alger, 18 April 1898, *CWS*, vol. 1, pp. 8–9; and *ARWD 98*, 19. For the activity of Barker and Wagner, see Albert Smith Barker, *Everyday Life in the Navy: Autobiography of Rear Admiral Albert S. Barker* (Boston, 1928), 280.

19. Long Diary, 20 April 1898, in Lawrence Shaw Mayo, ed., *America of Yesterday: As Reflected in the Journal of John Davis Long* (Boston, 1923), 183. See also Leech, *In the Days of McKinley*, 201; and Cosmas, *Army for Empire*, 106–107.

20. For Roosevelt's comments, see Roosevelt to Evans, 20 April 1898 in Morison, ed., *Letters of Theodore Roosevelt*, vol. 2, p. 818; and Roosevelt to Tracy, 21 April 1898, *ibid.*, 819.

21. The law of April 26 at long last provided the organizational structure that General Upton and the progressive reformers had advocated for a generation. These units included twenty-five infantry regiments, ten cavalry regiments, five artillery regiments, and smaller contingents of specialized troops, most of whom were in the Medical Corps or Engineers. Each regiment included three battalions of four companies each. Authorized strength for an infantry company was 106 men. With its officers, the total strength of an infantry regiment was 1,274 men. The size of units varied somewhat in other branches: A cavalry troop included 100 men, a battery of heavy artillery had 200, a battery of light artillery had 173, and a company of engineers had 150. (For this information see Kreidberg and Henry, *History of Military Mobilization*, 149, 159–162; Cosmas, *Army for Empire*, 113; and *ARWD 98*, 144–151.)

22. For the proclamation calling for 125,000 volunteers issued on April 23, 1898, see U.S. State Department, *Proclamations and Decrees*, 76–77. For statistical information, see Kreidberg and Henry, *History of Military Mobilization*, 150; and Jack Cameron Dierks, *A Leap to Arms: The Cuban Campaign of 1898* (Philadelphia and New York, 1970), 41–42. For the activity of Company A, Second Massachusetts, see Alfred Seelye Roe, *Worcester in the Spanish War: Being the Story of Companies A, C, and H, 2nd Regiment and Company G, 9th Regiment M.V.M. During the War for the Liberation of Cuba, May–November, 1898* (Worcester, Mass., 1905), 10. For the incident about the Seventh New York, see Gregory Mason, *Remember the Maine* (New York, 1939), 76. In the Third Brigade of the New York National Guard, out of a total of twelve companies 46 of 47 officers volunteered, and 926 out of 988 enlisted men. In terms of percentages, about 98 percent of the officers accepted federal service, as did about 94 percent of the enlisted men. (James W. Lester, *History of the Second Regiment, New York Infantry, U.S.V.* [Saratoga Springs, N.Y., 1899], 5–6.)

23. For the proclamation of May 25, 1898, see U.S. State Department, *Proclamations and Decrees, 1898*, 78–79. For the authorized strengths and actual strengths achieved, see *ARWD 98*, 144–151; and Chadwick, *The Spanish-American War*, vol. 1, pp. 47–48. For the total strength of the volunteer army by months and additional information, see Kreidberg and Henry, *History of Military Mobilization*, 155–156, 160, 163–164. The latter authors include some men not counted by Chadwick, which accounts for the slight discrepancy in total figures between the two authorities. For the navy figures, see Chadwick, *Spanish-American War*, vol. 1, pp. 40–41.

24. The list is compiled by Charles H. Brown in his *The Correspondents' War: Journalists in the Spanish-American War* (New York, 1967), 159.

25. Cosmas, *Army for Empire*, 148–151. Margaret Leech reports that during the war with Spain the President made 1,032 appointments of volunteer officers. He also appointed 71 second lieutenants in the regular army, for which there were two thousand applications. (Leech, *In the Days of McKinley*.) A total of 387 regular officers served with the volunteer army. Kriedberg and Henry believe that the small number of available regular officers interfered greatly with the efficiency of the army during the war. (Kreidberg and Henry, *History of Military Mobilization*, 162).

26. These statistics are drawn from W. E. Biederwolf, *History of the One Hundred and Sixty-First Regiment, Indiana Volunteer Infantry* (Logansport, Indiana, 1899), 19; George B. Thayer, compiler, *History of the Company K First Connecticut Volunteer Infantry, During the Spanish-American War* (Chicago, 1900), 62–67, 339; and Nicholas Senn, *Medico-Surgical Aspects of the Spanish-American War* (Chicago, 1900), 339. Senn, incidentally, reported that the most common causes of rejection for physical reasons among applicants for enlistment in the Illinois National Guard were: hernia, varicose veins of lower extremities, poor physique, heart disease, imperfect chest expansion, loss of teeth, and flat feet (*Ibid.*, 26).

27. Willard B. Gatewood, Jr., *"Smoked Yankees" and the Struggle for Empire: Letters from Negro Soldiers, 1898–1902* (Urbana, Ill., Chicago, and London, 1971), 6–11; Cosmas, *Army for Empire*, 136–137; and Theophilus G. Steward, *The Colored Regulars in the United States Army* (New York, 1969 reprint edition), 87. Two black regiments were enlisted later on for service in the Philippine Insurrection—the Forty-Eighth and Forty-Ninth U.S. Volunteer Infantry. In all probability, had more opportunities been provided a much larger black contingent would have entered the service.

28. Alger, *Spanish-American War*, 26–27; U.S. Senate, *Report of the Commission Appointed by the President to Investigate the Conduct of the War Department in the War With Spain*, 56th Cong., 1st Sess., Doc. No. 221 (Washington, 1900), vol. 1, p. 119 (hereafter cited as *IC*). See also Cosmas, *Army for Empire*, 113–117, 131–132.

29. Chadwick, *Spanish-American War*, vol. 1, p. 49; and Kreidberg and Henry, *History of Military Mobilization*, 164–165. For the strength of the various corps at certain times during the period May–August, 1898, see *ibid.*, 165. The Eighth Army Corps was formed officially on June 21, 1898. The commander who had been designated for the Sixth Army Corps, Major-General James. H. Wilson, believed that he was the victim of a plot to deprive him of a command; the War Department never explained why it did not assign troops to this command. (Cosmas, *Army for Empire*, 132–134.)

30. Cosmas, *Army for Empire*, 141–143. For the experiences of the Sixth Illinois, see R. S. Bunzey, *History of Companies I and E, Sixth Regt., Illinois Volunteer Infantry from Whiteside County* (Morison, Ill., 1901), 109, 112. James A. Huston argues that the most serious error of 1898 was to give "undue priority of manpower mobilization over matériel mobilization." (See his *The Sinews of War: Army Logistics, 1775–1953* [Washington, D.C., 1966], 277.)

31. For information on health problems, see Walter Millis, *The Martial Spirit: A Study of Our War With Spain* (Boston and New York, 1931), 367; Cosmas, *Army for Empire*, 245–150, 264–274; and Leech, *In the Days of McKinley*, 300–304. Woodhull's observation is in his report, 7 August 1898, in *ARWD 98*, 764.

32. For the comment of the Surgeon General, see George M. Sternberg, "The Work of the Medical Department During the Spanish War," *ibid.*, 703. See also his *Sanitary Lessons of the War and Other Papers* (Washington, D.C., 1912).

33. Cosmas, *Army for Empire*, 110.

34. For the quotation from Finley Peter Dunne, creator of Mr. Dooley, see Russell F. Weigley, *History of the United States Army* (New York, 1967), 295. Chandler's remark is in Chandler to Paul Dana, 8 May 1898, quoted in Leon Burr Richardson, *William E. Chandler: Republican* (New York, 1940), 583. For comments on McKinley's delay in reaching a decision concerning Cuba, see David Healy, "McKinley as Commander-in-Chief," in Paolo E. Coletta, ed., *Threshold to American Internationalism: Essays on the Foreign Policy of William McKinley* (New York, 1970), 88–89.

35. For the order, see Corbin to Shafter, 29 April 1898, quoted in Alger, *Spanish-American War*, 44–45. See also Chadwick, *Spanish-American War*, vol. 2, p. 7; and Cosmas, *Army for Empire*, 111.

36. For the views of Henry Adams, see Adams to Elizabeth Cameron, 29 April 1898, in Worthington Chauncey Ford, ed., *Letters Of Henry Adams (1892–1918)* (Boston and New York, 1938), vol. 2, p. 173. For cancellation of Shafter's orders, see Cosmas, *Army for Empire*, 112; and Leech, *In the Days of McKinley*, 201–202. For the Dorst expeditions, see Alger, *Spanish-American War*, 43–44. See also Fred M. Mugger to Commodore J. C. Watson, 13 May 1898, *AF*, file 8, roll 229; Chadwick, *Spanish-American War*, vol. 2, pp. 10–12; and Cosmas, *Army for Empire*, 112. In his second expedition Dorst landed 7,500 Springfield rifles, 1,300,000 rounds of ammunition, and 20,000 rations at Port Banes, as well as some equipment, clothing, and livestock.

37. For the plan of May 2, 1898, see Cosmas, *Army for Empire*, 123; Alger, *Spanish-American War*, 46–47; and Leech, *In the Days of McKinley*, 214–215. Alger reported that Congress provided $350,000 to finance this operation. For Shafter's response, see John D. Miley, *In Cuba With Shafter* (New York, 1899), 5–6.

38. For the recommendation of the Naval War Board, see Sicard to Long, 6 May 1898, *RG 45*, NRC 371, vol. 1, p. 23. For the letter of the Secretary of the Navy, see Long to Alger, 6 May 1898, *BN 98*, 662. This letter stated that the size of the force to be sent to Cuba had been fixed at forty to fifty thousand men. For Long's assessment of Alger, see Long Diary, 6 May 1898, in Mayo, ed., *America of Yesterday*, 189. Long's assistant, about to leave the Navy Department to take up his commission as an army officer, was equally critical of the War Department. On May 7 Theodore Roosevelt expressed himself firmly: "The delays and stupidity of the Ordnance

Department surpass belief. The Quartermaster Department is better, but bad. The Commissary Department is good. There is no management whatever in the War Department. Against a good nation we would be helpless." (Quoted in Virgil Carrington Jones, *Roosevelt's Rough Riders* [New York, 1971], 29; see also Leech, *In the Days of McKinley*, 214–215.) For Alger's curious order to Miles, see *ibid.*, 216.

39. For the activities of Commanding General Miles, see Nelson A. Miles, *Serving the Republic: Memories of the Civil and Military Life of Nelson A. Miles, Lieutenant-General United States Army* (New York and London, 1911), 272–273. See also Nelson A. Miles, "The War with Spain—I," *North American Review*, 168 (May, 1899): 523–524; and Leech, *In the Days of McKinley*, 214–216. For the order to Shafter, see Corbin to Wade, 9 May 1898, *CWS*, vol. 1, p. 11. The order went through General James F. Wade because at that time he was the senior officer at Tampa.

40. For Long's actions, see Long Diary, 10 May 1898, in Mayo, ed., *America of Yesterday*, 192. For the orders to Shafter, see Corbin to Wade, 10 May 1898, *CWS*, vol. 1, p. 11. Shafter immediately objected to the orders to send men to Key West. He pointed out that water sufficient to support a large force there would have to made available before troops could go (Shafter to Corbin for Miles, 11 May 1898, *IC*, vol. 2, p. 876. For cancellation of the Mariel operation, see Alger, *Spanish-American War*, 47–48; Long to Alger, 13 May 1898, *BN 98*, 663; and Unidentified to Remey (at Key West), 14 May 1898, *RG 45*, NRC 371, vol. 1, p. 84 (this message stated baldly, "The Army movement on Cuba is suspended until objective of Spanish fleet becomes known").

41. For the views of Henry Adams, see Adams to Hay, 5 May 1898 in Ford, ed., *Letters of Henry Adams*, vol. 2, p. 175. For the plans to send troops to Manila, see Leech, *In the Days of McKinley*, 209–210; and Cosmas, *Army for Empire*, 119–121. Detailed analysis of decisions in May relating to the preparations for an army expedition to the Philippines is in Chapter 9 of the present book.

42. For the quotations, see Cosmas, *Army for Empire*, 136–311.

43. This account follows the analysis of Ernest R. May in his "McKinley (1898)," essay in Ernest R. May, ed., *The Ultimate Decision: The President as Commander-in-Chief* (New York, 1960), 96, 106–107.

44. Cortelyou Diary, 15 May 1898, quoted in Olcott, *McKinley*, vol. 2, pp. 54–55. For the description of the White House in 1898, see Long, *New Navy*, vol. 2, p. 149. See also May, "McKinley (1898)," 94; and Olcott, *McKinley*, vol. 2, p. 51.

45. Leech's observation is in her *In the Days of McKinley*, 233. For the meetings in the White House, see Healy, "McKinley as Commander-in-Chief," 87–88. Charles G. Dawes noted the growing difficulties with Alger, writing on May 5, "I am afraid Alger is endangering his position in the Cabinet by his actions and unwise talk. He maintains that his prerogatives are being encroached upon. Fortunately, for our cause at war, he tells the truth" (Dawes diary, 5 May 1898, quoted in Bascom Timmons, ed., *A Journal of the McKinley Years by Charles G. Dawes* [Chicago, 1950], 158).

46. For the early popular mood, see Tomas Alvarez Angulo, *Memorias de un hombre sin importancia (1878-1961)* (Madrid, 1962), 212–213. Diplomatic reports out of Madrid and elsewhere reported the private apprehensions of Spanish leaders, whatever their public pose. A report from Brussels reflected the views of the Belgian leadership as they observed the course of events in Spain from the perspective of a lesser European neutral: It was thought that a republic might come into being, forced by a possible outbreak of workers in Catalonia. Defeat of Spain might also cause disturbances in Portugal and even the creation of a unified Iberian republic. This development would not be well received in Great Britain. The Belgians too thought this outcome might have adverse effects on the European balance of power. (F. Plunkett to Salisbury, 30 April 1898, *FO 185*, Box 864.) For the private

proposal of Eugenio Montero Ríos, see his *El tratado de Paris: Conferencias pronunciadas en el círculo de la Unión Mercantil en los días 23, 24, y 27 Febrero de 1904* (Madrid, 1904), 7. For views of Tetuán, see Barclay to Salisbury, 16 May 1898, *FO 185*, Box 870.

47. For general accounts of political developments at this time in Spain, see Melchor Fernández Almagro, *Historia política de la España contemporánea*, Volume 2: *Regencia de doña María Cristina de Austria durante de la menor edad de su hijo don Alfonso XIII* (Madrid, 1959), 518–519; and Fernando Soldevilla, *Año político (1898)* (Madrid, 1899), 220–223. See also José María García Escudero, *De Cánovas a la república* (Madrid, 1951), 115; and Diego Sevilla Antrés, *Canalejas* (Barcelona, 1956), 223–224. The views of Moret are reported in Barclay to Salisbury, 17 May 1898, *FO 185*, Box 870. Sagasta may have wanted to appoint his envoy in Paris, Fernando León y Castillo, to the post of Foreign Minister, but the ambassador reported in his memoirs that he refused on the grounds that he would be most helpful in France—the French might be willing to mediate at a proper moment. Fernando León y Castillo, Marqués del Muni, *Mis tiempos* (Madrid, 1921), vol. 2, pp. 109–111.

48. For Cortelyou's views, see Cortelyou Diary, 22 May 1898, quoted in Olcott, *McKinley*, vol. 2, p. 55. For the exchange between Roosevelt and Lodge, see Lodge to Roosevelt, 24 May 1898, in Henry Cabot Lodge and Charles F. Redmond, eds., *Selections from the Correspondence of Theodore Roosevelt and Henry Cabot Lodge, 1884-1918*, (New York, 1971 reprint edition), vol. 1. pp. 299–300; Roosevelt to Lodge, 25 May 1898, *ibid.*, 301. Lodge's statement is all too often mistakenly quoted to support the claim that McKinley had an imperialistic program in mind at this time, whereas it merely demonstrates Lodge's erroneous opinion.

49. For the first mention of the expedition, see Navy Department to Sampson, 20 May 1898, *BN 98*, 465. For the information of May 25 made available to Sampson, see Chadwick, *Spanish-American War*, vol. 1, p. 285. For Shafter's views, see Shafter to Corbin, 24 May 1898, *CWS*, vol. 1, pp. 14–15.

50. For accounts of the meeting of May 26, see Cosmas, *Army for Empire*, 180–181; Long Diary, 26 May 1898, in Mayo, ed., *America of Yesterday*, 196. Instructions to the forces at Tampa are in Miles to Shafter, 26 May 1898, quoted in Alger, *Spanish-American War*, 63. For Long's communication to the War Department, see Long to Alger, 27 May 1898, *CWS*, vol. 1, p. 16. Long's motivation is made clear in his diary for May 27: "Secretary Alger, who at the last Cabinet meeting announced that he had 75,000 men ready to put into Cuba, now says that they are not prepared and will not be for some two or three weeks. Alger is an enthusiastic, patriotic, and spirited man, but he does not seem to have things in hand. There is friction between him and his officers, from which the Navy is entirely free. He is apt to promise a great deal more than he can execute, simply because he is not thoroughly informed as to his own resources and preparations." (Long Diary, 27 May 1898, in Mayo, ed., *America of Yesterday*, 196–197.) Long's instructions to Sampson are in Long to Sampson, 27 May 1898, *CWS*, vol. 1, p. 17.

51. For this plan, see Miles to Alger, 27 May 1898, *ARWD 98*, 85–86. See also Cosmas, *Army for Empire*, 180.

52. Rowan told his story in "My Ride Across Cuba," *McClure's Magazine*, 11 (August, 1898): 372–379; and in *How I Carried the Message to Garcia* (San Francisco, 1922), a brief pamphlet. See also Philip Foner, *The Spanish-Cuban-American War and the Birth of American Imperialism, 1895-1902*, Volume 2: *1898-1902* (New York and London, 1972), 340–341. Some historians see in the Rowan mission not only an attempt to develop effective communication and cooperation with the insurgents but a plot to divide the Cuban leadership, but offer no evidence to support this view (see Herminio Portell Vilá, *Historia de Cuba en sus relaciones con los Estados Unidos y España*, Volume 3: *1878-1899* [Havana, 1939], 465). For a description of

Collazo's visit to Washington, see Gonzalo de Quesada to García, 30 May 1898, quoted in Cosme de la Torriente y Peraza, *Calixto García cooperó con las fuerzas armadas de los EE.U.U. in 1898, cumpliendo órdenes del gobierno Cubano* (Havana, 1952), 23–24. For the correspondence with the navy at Santiago de Cuba, working out arrangements with García, see Long to Schley, 29 May 1898, *RG 45*, NRC 371, vol. 1, p. 195 (reverse side); and Long to Sampson and Schley, 31 May 1898, quoted in Chadwick, *Spanish-American War*, vol. 1, p. 336. This message concluded, "Our Army wishes Garcia to close down on the land side of Santiago de Cuba, as previously telegraphed." For Miles's contact with García, see Cosmas, *Army for Empire*, 190; Foner, *Spanish-Cuban-American War*, vol. 2, p. 347; *ARWD 98*, 27–28; Miles to García, 2 June 1898, *ibid.*, 27; and García to Miles, 6 June 1898, *AF*, file 8, roll 231. For Sampson's report on García's letter of June 6, see Sampson to Long, 12 June 1898, *CWS*, vol. 1, p. 40; and Miles, *Serving the Republic*, 278.

53. For the President's plan and Alger's role, see Cosmas, *Army for Empire*, 180–181; and Alger, *Spanish-American War*, 52–53.

54. For the early orders, see Miles to Shafter, 29 May 1898, quoted in *ibid.*, 63; Long to Remey, 29 May 1898, *RG 45*, NRC 371, vol. 1, p. 196; and Miles to Shafter, 30 May 1898, *ARWD 98*, 57. For Edward J. McClernand's views, see his "The Santiago Campaign," in Society of the Army of Santiago de Cuba, *The Santiago Campaign: Reminiscences of the Operations for the Capture of Santiago de Cuba in the Spanish-American War, June and July, 1898* (Richmond, Va., 1927), 3. For the definitive order, see Corbin to Shafter, 31 May 1898, *CWS*, vol. 1, pp. 18–19.

55. For the Secretary of the Navy's letter, see Long to McKinley, 31 May 1898, *RG 45*, NRC 372, 63. A slightly variant text is given in *CWS*, vol. 1, pp. 19–20. For communication of these concerns to the Secretary of War, see Long to Alger, 31 May 1898, *RG 45*, NRC 372, 66. For Secretary Alger's response, see Alger to Long, 31 May 1898, quoted in Alger, *Spanish-American War*, 81.

56. For Lodge's letter, see Lodge to Roosevelt, 31 May 1898, *Selections From the Correspondence of Roosevelt to Lodge*, vol. 1, p. 302. Corbin's order and Shafter's response are Corbin to Shafter, 1 June 1898, *CWS*, vol. 1, p. 21; and Shafter to Corbin, 1 June 1898, *ibid.*, 21–22. The correspondence relating to the press boats is M. Sicard to Long, 3 June 1898, *ibid.*, 23; and Corbin to Shafter, 3 June 1898, *ibid.*, 23–24. For the Navy Department's order to hold press boats in port, putting a marine guard aboard them if necessary, see Allen to Remey, 3 June 1898, *RG 45*, Entry 19, no. 2, p. 6. For comments on the problems posed by the press boats, see George Kennan, *Campaigning in Cuba* (New York, 1899), 37.

CHAPTER 8

1. For these exchanges, see Shafter to Corbin, 4 June 1898, *CWS*, vol. 1, p. 24; Miles to Alger, 4 June 1898, in Record Group 108, Entry 119: "Letters and Telegrams Sent from Florida and Puerto Rico. May 31–Sept. 7, 1898," vi, 125, in the Records of the Headquarters of the Army, National Archives, Washington, D.C., (cited hereafter as *RG 108*, Entry 119); Miles to Alger, 4 June 1898, quoted in Russell A. Alger, *The Spanish-American War* (New York and London, 1901), 68; and Shafter to Alger, 4–5 June 1898, *ARWD 98*, 88.

2. For Miles's proposal, see Miles to Alger, 5 June 1898, quoted in Alger, *Spanish-American War*, 68–69. For Alger's malicious comment, see *ibid.*, 69. Edward Ranson comments on Miles's error in his "Nelson A. Miles as Commanding General, 1895–1903," *Military Affairs* 29 (Winter, 1965–1966): 185–186. For Alger's telegram of June 6, see Alger to Miles, 6 June 1898, quoted in *ARWD 98*, 24.

3. For the reports from Tampa, see Shafter to Corbin, 5 June 1898, *CWS*, vol. 1, p. 27; and Miles to Alger, 6 June 1898, *ibid.*, 28–29. Miles informed the President himself on June 7: "From the Commanding General down to the drummer boys, everyone is impatient to go, and annoyed at the delay" (Miles to McKinley, 7 June 1898, quoted in *ARWD 98*, 90). For pressure from the Navy Department, see Charles H. Allen (Acting Assistant Secretary of the Navy) to Alger (letter), 7 June 1898, *CWS*, vol. 1, p. 29. For the exchanges on the evening of June 7 between Washington and Tampa, see *ibid.*, 30–31.

4. Shafter is described in Virgil Carrington Jones, *Roosevelt's Rough Riders* (New York, 1971), 22. Cosmas makes his appraisal in his *An Army for Empire: The United States Army in the Spanish-American War* (Columbia, Mo., 1971), 194. For another negative comment, see Margaret Leech, *In the Days of McKinley* (New York, 1959), 202. George Kennan's observation is in *Campaigning in Cuba* (New York, 1899), 48.

5. For the quotation about the reception in Baltimore, see Frank E. Edwards, *The '98 Campaign of the 6th Massachusetts U.S.V.* (Boston, 1899), 23. Henry Cabot Lodge made a speech on this occasion; full information about the event is in *ibid.*, 11–24.

6. For Wood's views, see Jones, *Roosevelt's Rough Riders*, 48. Theodore Roosevelt's views are in his *Rough Riders* (New York, 1961 reprint edition), 40–41. For the report from the First Ohio, see Karl W. Heiser, *Hamilton [Ohio] in the War of '98* (Hamilton, Ohio, 1899), 20–21.

7. The poem by William Lightfoot Visscher is included in James Henry Brownlee, ed., *War-Time Echoes: Patriotic Poems Heroic and Pathetic, Humorous and Dialectic, of the Spanish-American War* (Akron, 1898), 73. For the chaplain's view, see Willard B. Gatewood, Jr., *"Smoked Yankees" and the Struggle for Empire: Letters from Negro Soldiers, 1898–1902* (Urbana, Ill., Chicago, and London, 1971), 26.

8. Bigelow is quoted in Charles H. Brown, *The Correspondents' War: Journalists in the Spanish-American War* (New York, 1967), 231.

9. For the reasons for the selection of Tampa and its inadequate rail connections, see Russell F. Weigley, *History of the United States Army* (New York, 1967), 301; Alger to Dodge, 6 October 1898, *IC*, vol. 1, p. 245 (Appendix H). Shafter's communications to Corbin are: Shafter to Corbin, 4–5 June 1898, *ARWD 98*, 88; Shafter to Corbin (letter), 7 June 1898, in Papers of General Henry Clark Corbin, box 1, Library of Congress, Manuscript Division, Washington, D.C. For Alger's views, see his *Spanish-American War*, 82.

10. For the description of Tampa, see Jones, *Roosevelt's Rough Riders*, 51. The hotel structure still survives at this writing as one of the buildings of the University of Tampa. For additional information about Tampa in 1898, see William J. Schellings, "The Rise of Florida in the Spanish-American War 1898," (Dissertation, University of Florida, 1958), 78–155. See also the same author's "The Advent of the Spanish-American War in Florida, 1898," *Florida Historical Quarterly* 29 (April, 1961): 311–329. For a comment on life at Plant's hotel, see Theodore Roosevelt to his children, 6 June 1898, quoted in Elting E. Morison et al., eds., *The Letters of Theodore Roosevelt*, Volume 2: *The Years of Preparation* (Cambridge, 1951), 834. For Wood's views, see Wood to Mrs. Wood, 9 April 1898, Papers of General Leonard Wood, box 190, Library of Congress, Manuscript Division, Washington, D.C.

11. For the comments of the New York soldier, see Charles Johnson Post, *The Little War of Private Post* (Boston and Toronto, 1960), 5, 53. For racial tension, see A. D. Webb, "Arizonans in Spanish-American War," *Arizona Historical Review* 1 (January, 1929): 50–68.

12. For the search for transports, see Weigley, *History of the United States Army*, 302–303; and Cosmas, *Army for Empire*, 183–185; *IC*, vol. 1, p. 134. For the com-

ments of Shafter's aide, see John D. Miley, *In Cuba With Shafter* (New York, 1899), 27–28. The views of Pope and Greenleaf are in *ARWD 98*, 738, 778.

13. For some details of the loading operation, see Walter Millis, *The Martial Spirit: A Study of Our War With Spain* (Boston and New York, 1931), 247.

14. For Roosevelt's exertions, see his *Rough Riders*, 45.

15. Walter W. Ward, *Springfield in the Spanish-American War* (Easthampton, Mass., 1899), 48–49.

16. For word that the transports were under way, see Shafter to Corbin, 8 June 1898, *CWS*, vol. 1, p. 33. He told the War Department, "The difficulties here have been almost insurmountable. Anything like quick loading is impossible, from the fact that wagons can not be driven within nearly a mile of the wharf, and the cars have to be run down, unloaded, and run back on the same track. Except when time is no object it should not be attempted to load more than 5,000 men at this place at one time." Perhaps Shafter reported more progress than he actually felt had occurred. One of Secretary Long's correspondents reported after the war that he had sent an officer to check on when the transports would be ready to depart: "Kline [the officer] found him [Shafter] at 6:30 A.M., sitting in a car and upon asking when the transports would be ready to sail he replied: 'My God, I don't know!!' returning on board he reported that the transfer was going on slowly among much confusion and that [he] could form no idea when embarkation would be completed" (John Hunker to Long, 13 March 1899, *AF*, file 8, roll 231). For the first word from Washington and Shafter's response, see Alger to Shafter, 8 June 1898, quoted in *ARWD 98*, 91; and Shafter to Alger, 8 June 1898, *ibid.*, 90. Miles also reported that the ships could be recalled (Miles to Alger, 8 June 1898, *CWS*, vol. 1, p. 32). For the orders to Sampson, see Allen to Sampson, 8 June 1898, *AF*, file 8, roll 321. The order to Commodore Remey stated, "The troops will not sail until further orders. Send some cruisers to scout straits and report movements of the Spanish. . . . The expedition to Santiago will be sent as soon as convoy is strengthened by two armored vessels from commander in chief, Atlantic Station" (Allen to Remey, 8 June 1898, *BN 98*, 668). See also John D. Long, *The New American Navy* (New York, 1903), vol. 2, pp. 12–13. For Miles's worries, see Miles to Alger (11:42 P.M.), 8 June 1898, *CWS*, vol. 1, p. 32.

17. For these events, see Sampson to Long, 3 August 1898, *BN 98*, 488–489. See also French Ensor Chadwick, *The Relations of the United States and Spain: The Spanish-American War* (New York, 1911), vol. 1, pp. 368–370. Sampson's explanation of the confusion arrived in Washington on June 12 (see Sampson to Long, 11 June 1898, *BN 98*, 490). For the action of the Naval War Board in this connection and Captain Alfred Thayer Mahan's reaction to it, see his "Narrative Account of the Work of the Naval War Board of 1898," 29 October 1906, in Record Group 7, Intelligence and Technological Archives, 1894–1945, Archives of the Naval War College, Newport, R.I., UNOpB, 17–18. Mahan praised Sampson for not obeying the order to send the armored vessels.

18. For the Navy Department's order to investigate the presence of Cervera, see Long to Sampson, 10 June 1898, *BN 98*, 491. For the activities of Lieutenant Victor Blue, described above in Chapter 6, see Long, *New Navy*, vol. 2, pp. 12–13. For Chadwick's views, see Chadwick to Long (letter), 10 June 1898, quoted in Gardner Weld Allen, ed., *Papers of John Davis Long, 1897–1904* (Boston, 1939), 137.

19. For correspondence relating to activities during the delay at Tampa, see Corbin to Shafter (4:10 P.M.), 8 June 1898, *CWS*, vol. 1, p. 32; Corbin to Shafter, 9 June 1898, *ibid.*, 35; Shafter to Corbin (6:05 P.M.), 9 June 1898, *ibid.*, 33; Shafter to Corbin (9:32 P.M.), 9 June 1898, *ibid.*, 35; and Shafter to Corbin, 10 June 1898, *ibid.* For Roosevelt's complaints, see Roosevelt to Lodge, 10 June 1898, quoted in Morison, ed., *Letters of Theodore Roosevelt*, vol. 2, pp. 837–838.

20. The two messages from the commanding general are Miles to Corbin (2:45 P.M.), 8

June 1898, *CWS*, vol. 1, p. 34; and Miles to Corbin (6:50 P.M.), 9 June 1898, *ARWD 98*, 91. The answer from the War Department is Alger to Miles, 9 June 1898, *ibid.*, 34.

21. McKinley's attitude is indicated in Cortelyou Diary, 8 June 1898, quoted in Charles S. Olcott, *The Life of William McKinley* (Boston and New York, 1916), vol. 2, p. 36.

22. For correspondence relating to the formation of the convoy, the role of the naval escort, and the route, see Allen to Alger, 11 June 1898, *CWS*, vol. 1, pp. 37–38; Corbin to Shafter, 11 June 1898, *ibid.*, 38; Allen to Alger, 12 June 1898, *ibid.*, 39; and Corbin to Shafter 12 June 1898, *ibid.*, 40. The exchange between Miles and Alger is in Miles to Alger, 12 June 1898, *ibid.*, 39; and Alger to Miles, 12 June 1898, *ibid.* For the final arrangements for departure, see Shafter to Corbin, 12 June 1898, *ibid.*, 41. See also Chadwick, *Spanish-American War*, vol. 2, p. 19.

23. For Miles's proposal, see Captain B. F. Montgomery (U.S.S. *Brady*) transmitting Miles to McKinley, 14 June 1898, in Chadwick, *Spanish-American War*, 44. Roosevelt's letters on departure are: Roosevelt to Corinne Roosevelt Robinson, 12 June 1898, in Morison, ed., *Letters of Theodore Roosevelt*, vol. 2, p. 839; and Roosevelt to Anna Roosevelt Cowles, 12 June 1898, *ibid.*

24. For the makeup of the convoy and its burden, see Weigley, *History of the United States Army*, 306; and Kennan, *Campaigning in Cuba*, 50–51. The only volunteer regiments in the original expedition were the First United States Volunteer Cavalry ("Rough Riders"), the Seventy-First New York, and the Second Massachusetts. For the information concerning animals and artillery, see Chadwick, *Spanish-American War*, vol. 2, pp. 19–20; and *IC*, vol. 1, p. 146. Other passengers included 30 civilian clerks, 272 teamsters and packers, 107 stevedores, 89 newspapermen, and 11 military attachés representing foreign nations. The expedition also had with it 112 six-mule wagons, 81 escort wagons, and only 7 ambulances. For information concerning naval escort, see Arthur L. Wagner, *Report of the Santiago Campaign, 1898* (Kansas City, Mo., 1908), 31. For a complete list of the transports and the units carried on each ship, see Chadwick, *Spanish-American War*, vol. 2, pp. 479–480. For the barge matter, see *ARWD 98*, 58.

25. For the views of the medical doctors, see J. Herbert Claiborne, Jr., *Three Months' Experience in Camp Thomas* (New York, 1899), 22, a pamphlet reprinted from the *Medical Record*, February 4, 1899. The anecdote about the guard is in Biederwolf, *History of the One Hundred and Sixty-first Indiana Volunteers*, 28. The witticism attributed to Bryan is recounted in Harry L. Harris and John T. Hilton, eds., *A History of the Second Regiment, N.G.N.J. Second N.J. Volunteers Spanish War Fifth New Jersey Infantry* (Paterson, N.J., 1908), 150–151. McKinley's orders to Alger to allow Bryan to serve as a colonel were issued on May 28, 1898. See W. S. Coursey, "McKinley as Commander in Chief," *National Magazine* 16 (May, 1902): 152. A commander of Louisiana Volunteers, Colonel Elmer E. Wood, spoke harshly of Bryan's leadership: "It [the Third Nebraska Volunteers] had a reputation in the common slang parlance of our regiment to be 'an aggregation of slobs' and it seemed so. They had a horrible camp. Their officers and men seemed to have received no military instruction and nothing seemed to run smoothly. There seemed to be friction everywhere. . . . Their dress parades were even better than a circus." Once Bryan resigned, however, the regiment improved in quality, according to this authority. (Walter Prichard, ed., "Louisiana in the Spanish-American War, 1898–1899, As Recorded by Colonel Elmer Ellsworth Wood, Commander of the Second Regiment of Louisiana Volunteer Infantry," *Louisiana Historical Quarterly* 26 [July, 1943]: 826.)

26. For this information, see Robert T. Kerlin, *The Camp Life of the Third [Missouri] Regiment* (Kansas City, Mo., 1898), 27; T. A. Turner, *Story of the Fifteenth Minnesota Volunteer Infantry* (Minneapolis, 1899), 78.

27. The song of Grigsby's Cowboys is quoted in Otto L. Sues, *Grigsby's Cowboys: Third United States Volunteer Cavalry, Spanish-American War* (Salem, S.D., 1900), 40. The poem of Torrey's regiment is quoted in Clifford Peter Westermeier, *Who Rush to Glory: The Cowboy Volunteers of 1898: Grisgby's Cowboys, Roosevelt's Rough Riders, Torrey's Rocky Mountain Riders* (Caldwell, Idaho, 1958), 232.

28. This theme has emerged with increasing clarity in recent studies of the war with Spain and of the Philippine insurrection (particularly in the exemplary work of Graham A. Cosmas). Wagner listed seven recommendations to be put into effect in future expeditions in order to avoid problems like those in Tampa: (1) Officers with full authority should be appointed to load transports; (2) materials should be loaded first, with loading of troops deferred until last; (3) supplies for each organization should be placed aboard with the troops; (4) a correct list of what was loaded in given transports should be maintained and distributed to proper authorities; (5) stores should be loaded so that one or two ships could be quickly unloaded to deal with emergencies; (6) railroad cars arriving at ports of embarkation should be clearly marked as to contents; and (7) private companies associated with embarkations should place military interests first. (Wagner, *Santiago Campaign,* 23–24.)

CHAPTER 9

1. For the Cuban officer's experience, see Anibal Escalante Beatón, *Calixto García: Su campaña en el 95* (Havana, 1946), 450.

2. For the poem, see Sidney A. Witherbee, *Spanish-American War Songs: A Complete Collection of Newspaper Verse During the Recent War With Spain* (Detroit, 1898), 27.

3. Both Roosevelt and Wood are quoted in Virgil Carrington Jones, *Roosevelt's Rough Riders* (New York, 1971), 81. For an interesting letter about the voyage, see Roosevelt to Corinne Roosevelt, 15 June 1898, in Elting E. Morison et al., eds., *The Letters of Theodore Roosevelt,* Volume 2: *The Years of Preparation* (Cambridge, 1951), 844.

4. For Webb's comments, see A. D. Webb, "Arizonans in Spanish-American War," *Arizona Historical Review* 1 (January, 1929): 57.

5. For the report of the naval officer in charge of the convoy from the Dry Tortugas to Santiago de Cuba, see H. C. Taylor to Sampson, 1 July 1898, *BN 98,* 676–678. For Mahan's views, see his "Narrative Account of the Work of the Naval War Board of 1898," 29 October 1906, in Record Group 7: Intelligence and Technological Archives, 1894 to 1945, Archives of the Naval War College, Naval War College, Newport, R.I., UNOpB. For the doctor's observations, see Report of Major Louis La Garde, 31 October 1898, in *ARWD 98,* 98. He was on the *Saratoga* from June 8 to June 26. For Pershing's views, see Frank E. Vandiver, *Black Jack: The Life and Times of John J. Pershing,* (College Station, Texas, and London), vol. 1, p. 186.

6. For the views of Richard Harding Davis, see his *The Cuban and Porto Rican Campaigns* (New York, 1898), 98–99. For Matthew A. Batson's report, see Batson Diary, 18 June 1898, in Records of the U.S. Army Military History Institute, Army War College, Carlisle Barracks, Penn. (hereafter cited as USAMHI). His letter to his wife is Batson to Mrs. Batson, 21 June 1898, USAMHI.

7. Cortelyou's diary is quoted in Charles S. Olcott, *The Life of William McKinley* (Boston and New York, 1916), vol. 2, pp. 55–56.

8. Early Spanish efforts to prepare the defense of Santiago de Cuba are recounted in Severo Gómez Núñez, *La guerra hispano-americana. Santiago de Cuba* (Madrid, 1901), 71. See also *ibid.,* 47–49. For exact figures of the strength of Spanish gar-

risons in eastern Cuba, both in the division of Santiago de Cuba and in the adjoining divisions of Holguín and Manzanillo, see Herbert H. Sargent, *The Campaign of Santiago de Cuba* (Chicago, 1907), vol. 3, pp. 158–159. For estimates of Spanish strength at Santiago de Cuba, see Miles to Alger, 1 June 1898, *CWS*, vol. 1, p. 21; Sampson to Long, 3 June 1898, *BN 98*, 483; and Shafter to Alger, 4 June 1898, *CWS*, vol. 1, p. 25. Sampson thought that about seven thousand men were entrenched outside the city at Juraguacito and Daiquirí, five thousand in the city, four hundred at the Morro, and a few others in locations around the bay. For the naval reinforcement, see Francisco Arderius, *La escuadra española en Santiago de Cuba* (Barcelona, 1903), 117–118. For additional information, see Graham A. Cosmas, *An Army for Empire: The United States Army in the Spanish-American War* (Columbia, Mo., 1971), 201; and José Müller y Tejeiro, *Combates y capitulación de Santiago de Cuba* (Madrid, 1898), 15.

9. For typical criticisms of Linares for not concentrating forces at Santiago de Cuba, see Sargent, *Campaign of Santiago de Cuba*, vol. 3, p. 93; U.S. Navy Department, *Sketches from the Spanish-American War by Commander J. . . .* (Washington, D.C., 1899), 17. For Müller's defense, see his *Combates y capitulación*, 275–276. See also in this regard Severo Gómez Núñez, *La guerra hispano-americana. La Habana: influencia de las plazas de guerra* (Madrid, 1900), 115–116. This authority mentions also the adverse political consequences of abandoning territory to the Cuban insurgents. Difficulties of moving by land are mentioned in Müller, *Combates y capitulatión*, 276–277. The troops at Santiago de Cuba were in miserable condition. Captain Víctor Concas y Palau describes them as follows: "The troops of the army at Santiago were completely exhausted by three years of warfare in that horrible climate, with arrears in pay amounting to thirteen months, and impossible food, the result of this lack of pay. They were more like specters than soldiers, and nothing but the steadfastness of the Spanish people could keep them at their posts." Víctor Concas y Palau, *The Squadron of Admiral Cervera* (Washington, 1900), 53.

10. This information is gathered from Cosmas, *Army for Empire*, 209; Gómez Núñez, *La guerra hispano-americana. Santiago de Cuba*, 46; Gabriel Maura Gamazo, *Historia crítica del reinado de don Alfonso XIII durante su menoridad bajo la regencia de su madre doña María Cristina de Austria* (Barcelona, 1925), vol. 2, p. 33; Gómez Núñez, *La guerra hispano-americana. La Habana*, 114–115; Russell A. Alger, *The Spanish-American War* (New York and London, 1901), 42; Tomas Alvarez Angulo, *Memorias de un hombre sin importancia* (Madrid, 1962), 203; and Felipe Martínez Arango, *Cronología crítica de la guerra hispano-americana*, 2nd ed., (Santiago de Cuba, 1960), 63.

11. For terrain analysis, see Arthur L. Wagner, *Report of the Santiago Campaign 1898* (Kansas City, Mo., 1808), 37–38; French Ensor Chadwick, *The Relations of the United States and Spain: The Spanish-American War*, (New York, 1911), vol. 2, pp. 26–29; and Müller, *Battles and Capitulation*, 9–11.

12. For the visit of the last ship, the *Mortera*, to Santiago de Cuba, see Gómez Núñez, *La guerra hispano-americana. Santiago de Cuba*, 52. For the supply of Santiago de Cuba, see also Chadwick, *Spanish-American War*, vol. 2, p. 41; and Müller, *Battles and Capitulation*, 32–33. The correspondent's view of Santiago de Cuba in 1898 is in George Kennan, *Campaigning in Cuba* (New York, 1899), 174–175. For additional information about the situation in Santiago de Cuba as the Americans arrived there, see Major General Joseph Wheeler, *The Santiago Campaign 1898* (New York, 1898), 245–257. Wheeler reports intelligence coming into his hands about the situation in the city.

13. Müller, *Battles and Capitulation*, 17–18. See also Chadwick, *Spanish-American War*, vol. 1, p. 318. Chadwick notes that a Spanish gunboat was sent out on April 23 to lay mines at Guantánamo.

14. Müller's comment is in *Battles and Capitulation*, 72. For information concerning the batteries, see *ibid.*, 19–20, 25; Wheeler, *Santiago Campaign*, 88; and Chadwick, *Spanish-American War*, vol. 1, pp. 319–320. For other information about the batteries, see Chapter 6 above. For Concas's comment, see his *Squadron of Admiral Cervera*, 53.

15. Müller points out: "Punta Gorda, owing to its admirable location and being high above the level of the sea, has entire control of the channel, and any ship trying to enter would necessarily be exposed to its fire and present her bow and port for at least twenty minutes. The very narrow entrance is well-adapted for laying lines of torpedoes which could be easily protected by rapid fire artillery erected on the western shore, preventing them from being dragged or blown up." (Müller, *Battles and Capitulation*, 11).

16. For Müller's views, see *ibid.*, 22, 71–72. For additional information, see Gómez Núñez, *La guerra hispano-americana. Santiago de Cuba*, 49–51, 54–55; Carlos Martínez de Campos y Serrano, Duque de la Torre, *España bélica: el siglo XIX* (Madrid, 1961), 354.

17. For the Governor-General's message, see Blanco to Correa, 20 June 1898, in Pascual Cervera y Topete, *The Spanish-American War: A Collection of Documents Relative to the Squadron Operations in the West Indies* (Washington, D.C., 1899), 106–107. See also Chadwick, *Spanish-American War*, vol. 1, pp. 54, 114–115. For the response from Madrid, see Alberto Risco, *Apuntes biográficos del Excmo. Sr. Almirante D. Pascual Cervera y Topete* (Toledo, 1920), 129; Auñón to Cervera, 24 June 1898, in Cervera, *Spanish-American War*, 110; and Arderius, *La escuadra española*, 118, 121. Santiago de Cuba, incidentally, maintained direct communications to Spain; one of the cables running south to Jamaica was never successfully grappled because of deep water (Chadwick, *Spanish-American War*, vol. 1, p. 387).

18. For developments in Spain, see Juan Nido y Segalerva, *Historia política y parlamentaria del Excmo. D. Práxedes Mateo Sagasta* (Madrid, 1915), 942–943; and Fernando Soldevilla, *Año político (1898)* (Madrid, 1899), 270, 273–275, 277–278. Auñón's remarks are in Ramón Auñón y Villalón, *Discursos pronunciados en el parlamento por el ministro del marina D. Ramon Auñón y Villalón durante la guerra con los Estados Unidos* (Madrid, 1912), 49–50.

19. Chadwick, *Spanish-American War*, vol. 1, p. 22. For the Secretary of the Navy's understanding of Sampson's views, see John D. Long, *The New American Navy* (New York, 1903), vol. 2, p. 23. See also Kennan, *Campaigning in Cuba*, 249. For Concas's view, see his *Squadron of Admiral Cervera*, 61.

20. For a typical defense of Sampson, see W. A. M. Goode, *With Sampson Through the War: Being an Account of the Naval Operations of the North Atlantic Squadron During the Spanish-American War of 1898* (New York, 1899), 146. For the views of Alfred Thayer Mahan, see his *Lessons of the War With Spain and Other Articles* (Freeport, N.Y., 1970 reprint edition), 186. For Sargent's view, see his *Campaign of Santiago*, vol. 3, pp. 54–60.

21. For the meeting at Aserraderos, see Escalante Beatón, *Calixto García*, 453; Davis, *Cuban and Porto Rican Campaigns*, 103; *ARWD 98*, 59; Sampson to Long, 22 June 1898, *BN 98*, 448–451; and Mariano Corona, *De la manigua (ecos de la epopeya)* (Santiago de Cuba, 1900), 93. The beach at Cabañas was not chosen for the landing because it could be reached by gunfire from Cervera's squadron inside the bay (Jack Cameron Dierks, *A Leap to Arms: The Cuban Campaign of 1898* [Philadelphia and New York, 1970], 79). Shafter was happy to accept García's offers of support, for which in return he was prepared to provide rations and munitions. The transfer of Cuban troops took place on schedule. However, Lieutenant John J. Pershing, Tenth Cavalry, reported that instead of three thousand men there were many fewer. His comment reflected growing anti-insurgent feeling among the American troops: "We brought back 1,000 and a miserable lot they are. In my opinion they will

prove of little service to the Americans." (Pershing Diary, 24 June 1898, quoted in Donald Smythe, "Pershing in the Spanish-American War," *Military Affairs* 29 [Spring, 1965–1966]: 25–33.)

22. Shafter's views are in Shafter to Corbin, 24 December 1898, quoted in Alger, *Spanish-American War*, 89–90. For the Secretary's overall account of these events, see *ibid.*, 85–91. Shafter gave this same version to a reporter after the war. See also Goode, *With Sampson Through the War*, 178. For Sampson's interpretation, see William T. Sampson, "The Atlantic Fleet in the Spanish War," *Century* 57 (April, 1898): 904–905. Sampson thought that it was Shafter's intention "to attack the shore batteries in the rear, and make it possible for the navy to clear the channel and get inside the harbor, it being his main object to assist the navy in destroying the Spanish fleet. Had the general followed this plan, we could have been of the greatest assistance to him, for we could have advanced within a few hundred yards of his left flank, and kept his front clear as if swept with a broom. However, another plan was followed, whether from force of circumstances, or for other good reasons for a change of view, I have never learned."

23. Chadwick's account is in his *Spanish-American War*, vol. 2, pp. 22–25. A somewhat simplistic rendition of the navy's viewpoints is in Goode, *With Sampson Through the War*, 178.

24. Shafter's view is in his "The Capture of Santiago de Cuba," *Century* 57 (February, 1899): 618.

25. For Shafter's reading about Lord Vernon, see Alger, *Spanish-American War*, 84. For Shafter's statement before the Dodge Commission, see *IC*, vol. 7, p. 3,200. For Wheeler's statement's, see *ibid.*, vol. 3. pp. 6, 16. For the views of Shafter's adjutant, see E. J. McClernand, "The Santiago Campaign," in Society of the Army of Santiago de Cuba, *The Santiago Campaign: Reminiscences of the Operations for the Capture of Santiago de Cuba in the Spanish-American War, June and July, 1898* (Richmond, Va., 1927), 9.

26. For information concerning the tactical difficulties associated with an attack on the Morro and the Socapa, see Wheeler, *Santiago Campaign*, 88; and Walter Millis, *The Martial Spirit: A Study of Our War With Spain* (Boston and New York, 1931), 260.

27. For the argument that Shafter did not comprehend the possibilities of joint operations, see Margaret Leech, *In the Days of McKinley* (New York, 1959), 243. For the view that he was jealous of the navy and wished to act in the interest of the army, see Millis, *Martial Spirit*, 260.

28. For Cosmas's views, see his *Army for Empire*, 196, 207–208.

29. For information about the Cuban insurgent forces, see Chadwick, *Spanish-American War*, vol. 1, p. 51; Herminio Portell Vilá, *Historia de Cuba en sus relaciones con los Estados Unidos y España*, Volume 3: *1876–1899* (Havana, 1939), 472–473; and Sargent, *Campaign of Santiago*, vol. 3, pp. 171–173. Portell Vilá points out the advantage to the Americans of a campaign at Santiago de Cuba rather than Havana (Portell Vilá, *Historia de Cuba*, vol. 3, p. 464). For the effect of Cuban operations on the Spanish army, see Enrique Collazo y Tejada, *La guerra en Cuba* (Havana, 1926), 437–438. For the effect of the blockade, see Philip Foner, *The Spanish-Cuban-American War and the Birth of American Imperialism 1895–1902*, Volume 2: *1898–1902* (New York and London, 1972), 377–378. Foner is at pains to criticize those historians who have failed to give due credit to the activities of the Cuban insurgent army. Some might argue, however, that in the service of this legitimate concern Foner has unduly minimized the role of the United States Army in the victory. See also David F. Healy, *The United States in Cuba 1898–1902: Generals, Politicians, and the Search for Policy* (Madison, Wis., 1963), 35.

30. For Estrada Palma's advice to García, see Cosme Torriente y Peraza, *Calixto García*

cooperó con las fuerzas armadas de los EE. UU. en 1898, cumpliendo órdenes del gobierno Cubano (Havana, 1952), 27–28. See also Portell Vilá, *Historia de Cuba*, vol. 3, p. 483. For Gómez'es reaction to the American intervention, see his letter to Georgio Billini, quoted in Emilio Rodríguez Demorizi, *Cartas de Máximo Gómez* (Ciudad Trujillo, 1936), 42–43. For Estrada Palma to Gómez, 27 May 1898, see Torriente y Peraza, *Calixto García cooperó*, 36–43. For García to Estrada Palma, 27 June 1898, see *ibid.*, 28–33. See also Foner, *Spanish-Cuban-American War*, vol. 2, p. 355. Gómez believed that the war would be decided at sea. He thought that once the Spanish squadron had been dealt with, little would be left for the American and Cuban forces to do (Gómez to Domingo Méndez Capote, 14 May 1898, in Emilio Rodríguez Rodríguez, *Algunos documentos políticos de Máximo Gómez* [Havana, 1962], 33). Another authority argues that Gómez would have preferred that the United States not intervene with armed forces but restrict itself to supplying him and blockading the Spanish squadron, for he, too, feared that United States intervention might lead to United States sovereignty (Charles F. Chapman, *A History of the Cuban Republic: A Study of Hispanic American Politics* [New York, 1927], 91–92). After war was declared between Spain and the United States, Blanco made an offer of alliance to the Cuban insurgents, but Gómez rejected it out of hand. For the exchange of correspondence, see Enrique Collazo, *Los americanos in Cuba* (Havana, 1905), 126–129. See also Emilio Roig de Leuchsenring, ed., *Ideario cubano*, Volume 2: *Máximo Gómez* (Havana, 1936), 99–100, and *idem, La guerra hispano-cubanoamericana fué ganade por el lugarteniente general del ejército libertador Calixto García Iñiguez* (Havana, 1955), 23–25. Another comment is in Portell Vilá, *Historia de Cuba*, vol. 3, pp. 187–192.

31. For information on the activities of the Cubans and their arrangements with Shafter, see Cosmas, *Army for Empire*, 209; and *ARWD 98*, 28. For the views of Concas, see his *Squadron of Admiral Cervera*, 60. The arrangements of June 19 and June 20 followed logically from earlier contacts made through the enterprise of General Miles. See Nelson A. Miles, *Serving the Republic: Memoirs of the Civil and Military Life of Nelson A. Miles Lieutenant-General, United States Army* (New York and London, 1911), 278, 280. See also Sampson to Long, 12 June 1898, in *CWS*, vol. 1, p. 40, reporting intelligence from García.

32. For a description of the June 19 meeting on the *New York*, see Chadwick, *Spanish-American War*, vol. 1, pp. 387–388. García became seasick on the American ship, one reason why the meeting of June 20 was held on land. For Sampson's favorable appraisal of the Cuban general, see Sampson to Long, 22 June 1898, in *BN 98*, 449: "My impressions of General Garcia are of a most pleasant character. He is a large, handsome man, of most frank and engaging manners and of most soldierly appearance. He remained some time on board, though unfortunately so seasick that he was obliged to lie down during the whole of his visit." For Wagner's views, see his *Santiago Campaign*, 32. Bennett's views are reported in Captain John Stronach, "The 34th Michigan Volunteer Infantry," *Michigan History* 30 (April–June, 1946): 301. For Parker's appraisal, see John H. Parker, *History of the Gatling Gun Detachment Fifth Army Corps at Santiago* (Kansas City, Mo., 1898), 78. For the views of Matthew A. Batson, see his letter to his wife, 26 June 1898, USAHMI. Foner says that Sampson and García disagreed over the proper landing place, García preferring a point west of the entrance, and the decision was postponed until Shafter could be consulted (Foner, *Spanish-Cuban-American War*, vol. 2, pp. 349–350).

33. For this information, see Leech, *In the Days of McKinley*, 273–274; and Healy, *United States in Cuba*, 35–37. Shafter's remark is quoted in *ibid.*, 36.

34. See Escario's comments on his expedition, made to General Joseph Wheeler on July 27, 1898, as reported in the latter's *Santiago Campaign*, 364. Escario had five battalions of regular infantry, one section of mountain artillery consisting of two eight-cm. pieces, and a small contingent of irregular cavalry. For full information con-

cerning Escario's remarkable march, see Müller, *Battles and Capitulation,* 116–125—the account on which other writers mostly rely. See, in this connection, Chadwick, *Spanish-American War,* vol. 2, p. 191; and Portell Vilá, *Historia de Cuba,* vol. 3, p. 483.

35. For information on this affair, see *ARWD 98,* 28; Portell Vilá, *Historia de Cuba,* vol. 3, p. 483—a slightly inaccurate version. The Cuban commander's message to the American commander is García to Shafter, 1 July 1898, in Record Group 165, Entry 310, box 479, folder 6-32.15, Records of the War Department General and Special Staffs, National Archives, Washington, D.C. (hereafter cited as *RG 165,* Entry 310). For Shafter to Wheeler, 4 July 1898, see Wheeler, *Santiago Campaign,* 297–298. For Shafter's report to the War Department on García's alleged error, see *CWS,* vol. 1, p. 87.

36. For information about Daiquirí, see Millis, *Martial Spirit,* 263. Alvarez Angulo's opinion is in his *Memorias de un hombre sin importancia,* 213. See also Cosmas, *Army for Empire,* 207. For criticism of Linares, see Dierks, *Leap to Arms,* 182. For a criticism of Linares for not resisting the landing at Daiquirí, see U.S. Navy Department, *Comments of Rear-Admiral Plüddemann, German Navy, on the Main Features of the War With Spain* (Washington, D.C., 1899), 14. See also *IC,* vol. 1, p. 135.

37. Millis used the term "moral inertia" in his *Martial Spirit,* 266. Wood is quoted in Jones, *Roosevelt's Rough Riders,* 91. For Sampson's order of June 21, 1898, see *BN 98,* 497–498.

38. Gómez Núñez reports that the Spanish forces at Daiquirí had orders to fall back as soon as the attack began, in order to avoid an envelopment (See his *La guerra hispano-americana. Santiago de Cuba,* 76). The ships assigned to various bombardments were: (1) Cabañas—*Scorpion, Vixen, Texas;* (2) Aguadores—*Eagle, Gloucester;* (3) Siboney—*Hornet, Helena, Bancroft;* and (4) Daiquirí—*Detroit, Castine, Wasp, New Orleans* (Wagner, *Santiago Campaign,* 43–44). Wagner argues that better reconnaissance and communications would have revealed the withdrawal of the Spanish. The Cuban General Demetrio Castillo actually controlled the situation, since the Spanish garrison had pulled out at 5:00 A.M., well before the bombardment began (*Ibid.,* 44). For additional information about the landing and its difficulties, see Goodrich to Sampson, 2 July 1898, *BN 98,* 685–688; and Cosmas, *Army for Empire,* 207. For an interesting comment on the problems of the transports, see Colonel C. F. Humphrey to Miles, 17 July 1898, in *RG 108,* Entry 119, vol. 2 of 2, p. 38. Humphrey, Shafter's quartermaster, noted, "Have informed Washington more than once of the absolute necessity for steam launches to be used as a means of communication between shore and vessels and that a great deal of time had been lost by not having them. It is impossible to keep vessels in shore. The Government does not take the marine risk; therefore Captains use their discretion as to where they will land."

39. For the landing, see Chadwick, *Spanish-American War,* vol. 2, pp. 36–37. For the army's early report on the landing, see Shafter to Corbin, 22 June 1898, *CWS,* vol. 1, p. 50. For the landing order, see Wagner, *Santiago Campaign,* 93. Matthew A. Batson to Mrs. Batson, 25 June 1898, is in USAMHI. For a first-hand account of the landing, see Jean Legrand, "The Landing at Daiquiri," *United States Naval Institute Proceedings* 26 (March, 1900): 117–126. He reported that only fifty-two boats were available to transfer men and material. James A. Huston notes that six thousand men landed the first day; the most effective method used was to tow boats with steam launches (see Huston's *The Sinews of War: Army Logistics 1775-1953* [Washington, 1956], 284).

40. For the death of the black troopers, see Jones, *Roosevelt's Rough Riders,* 4–5. Sargeant Bivins's letter is in Herschel V. Cashin et al., *Under Fire with the Tenth U.S. Cavalry* (New York, 1969 reprint edition), 74, 76.

41. Cervera to Auñón, 23 June 1898, in Cervera, *Spanish-American War*, 108. See also Spain, Ministry of the Marine, *Correspondencia oficial referente á las operaciones navales durante la guerra con los Estados Unidos en 1898* (Madrid, 1899), 150. Cervera's problems are listed in Cervera to Blanco, 25 June 1898, in Cervera, *Spanish-American War*, 110–111.

42. Sampson's message about Cervera to the blockading squadron, 21 June 1898, is quoted in Chadwick, *Spanish-American War*, vol. 2, p. 32. For the activity of the Secretary of the Navy, see Long to U.S.S. *Harvard*, 24 June 1898, in *RG 45*, Entry 19, no. 2, 60. For the activities of the Adjutant General, see Corbin to Shafter, 21 June 1898, *CWS*, vol. 1, p. 49.

43. For information concerning the problem of supply, see U.S. Navy Department, *Comments of Admiral Plüddemann*, 15. Each trooper supposedly carried three days' field rations and a hundred rounds of ammunition; another hundred rounds per man were available ashore (Wagner, *Santiago Campaign*, 43). For a good account of these problems, see Cosmas, *Army for Empire*, 209–212. He is more sympathetic to the army than most others: "The situation was not the fault of General Shafter or of the staff on the scene, all of whom struggled to surmount problems not of their own making. The attack on Santiago had been decided upon suddenly, in response to the Navy's plea for help. The War Department had neither the time nor the planning agency to work out in detail the strategy of the campaign, to study the terrain of the area, and to determine the transportation requirements of the army that was to fight under these conditions for the objective set" (*Ibid.*, 212). Shafter acknowledged the importance of naval assistance in thanking Sampson for the services of Captain Goodrich, who helped organize the landing (Shafter to Sampson, 30 July 1898, *AF*, file 8, roll 236): "I wish to invite your attention to the very efficient service rendered by Captain Goodrich of the Navy in debarking troops at Daiquiri and Siboney, and also his very courteous treatment of those with whom he was brought in contact."

44. Mahan to Long, 28 December 1898, in Gardner Weld Allen, ed., *Papers of John Davis Long 1897–1904* (Boston, 1939), 223.

45. Chadwick, *Spanish-American War*, vol. 2, pp. 77, 82, 101–102.

46. Cosmas, *Army for Empire*, 201.

47. *Ibid.*, 194.

48. For the message to the navy, see Shafter to Sampson, 22 June 1898, *AF*, file 8, roll 232. For the order to take Siboney, see McClernand to Lawton, 22 June 1898, in Alger, *Spanish-American War*, 102. See also Wagner, *Santiago Campaign*, 49–50; Dierks, *Leap to Arms*, 88; and Anastasio Mariano Azoy, *Charge! The Story of the Battle of San Juan Hill* (New York, 1961), 82. The completion of the operation is noted in John D. Miley, *In Cuba With Shafter*, (New York, 1899), 71; and Chadwick, *Spanish-American War*, vol. 2, p. 48.

49. Wells is quoted in Jones, *Roosevelt's Rough Riders*, 111–112.

50. For Wheeler's appointment and a characterization of him, see *ibid.*, 18. For his overall activities at Las Guásimas, see Joseph P. Dyer, *"Fightin' Joe" Wheeler* (University, La., 1941), 347–354.

51. For information on Wheeler's activities and preparations for the movement on Las Guásimas, see Alger, *Spanish-American War*, 103–104; *IC*, vol. 1, p. 225; Dierks, *Leap to Arms*, 88–89; Azoy, *Charge!* 82–83; Theodore Roosevelt, *The Rough Riders* (New York, 1961 reprint edition), 55; and Wagner, *Santiago Campaign*, 51–52, 55.

52. Davis, *Cuban and Porto Rican Campaigns*, 161–162.

53. For information on the Spanish defenders at Las Guásimas and Rubín's orders, see Gómez Núñez, *La guerra hispano-americana. Santiago de Cuba*, 108–114; and Müller, *Combates y capitulación*, 136, 139. The Spanish dispositions are noted in Wheeler, *Santiago Campaign*, 27; and Chadwick, *Spanish-American War*, vol. 2, p. 51. Young's report is quoted in *ibid.*, 52.

54. Hermann Hagedorn, *Leonard Wood: A Biography* (New York and London, 1931), vol. 1, pp. 163–164.

55. Young is quoted in Chadwick, *Spanish-American War*, vol. 2, p. 52.

56. Wood is quoted in Hagedorn, *Wood*, vol. 1, p. 170. See also Chadwick, *Spanish-American War*, vol. 2, pp. 53–54. General Wheeler, like Wood and Young, took special note of the Spanish practice of firing volleys. He told the Dodge Commission, which investigated the War Department after the war, "Thirty-three years ago we fought at short range. Here we commenced at 700 or 800 yards and could see no smoke or the enemy, and we could see the firing of our men was having its effect upon the enemy. The Spaniards fired in volleys, but when our men reached the foot of the hill upon which the Spanish were stationed, they retreated toward Santiago." (*IC*, vol. 3, p. 4.) Pershing is quoted in Cashin, *Under Fire With the Tenth Cavalry*, 202. See also the testimony of First Sergeant Peter McCown, Troop E, Tenth Cavalry, in *ibid.*, 218: "Our lines advanced very rapidly to the top of the hill. It was there that we broke the center of the Spanish lines which had been concentrating their fire on the Rough Riders, killing them at long range. Fearing that we might be mistaken we signalled the Rough Riders that we were the United States Tenth Cavalry. All this time the Spaniards kept up a heavy and terrific fire on our lines. But when we crossed the crest of the hill, the Spaniards were retreating toward Santiago." This account agrees with most others, but conflicts with that of Pershing in one respect—Pershing correctly stated that his troops fired on the Spanish right rather than their center, as McCown thought. (Battlefield reports often err in detail, given the stress of combat.)

57. Wood's remark about the flight of the Spanish is quoted in Hagedorn, *Wood*, vol. 1, p. 170. For his comment on the inability to pursue, see Chadwick, *Spanish-American War*, vol. 2, p. 54. See also, in this connection, Wheeler, *Santiago Campaign*, 19. Batson to Mrs. Batson, 25 June 1898, is in USAMHI. For the post-battle situation and casualties, see Dierks, *Leap to Arms*, 90–92. Gómez Núñez says that only seven Spaniards were killed and another seven wounded (*La guerra hispanoamericana. Santiago de Cuba*, 108–111). A later report given to Herbert H. Sargent mentioned nine Spanish dead and twenty-seven wounded (Sargent, *Campaign of Santiago*, vol. 3, p. 159). General Young claimed to have found forty-two dead Spaniards. (Wheeler, *Santiago Campaign*, 28). Roosevelt reported that he counted eleven Spanish dead, although he may have missed two or three bodies. "Indeed," he continued, "I doubt whether their loss was as heavy as ours, for they were under cover, while we advanced, often in the open, and their main lines fled long before we could get to close quarters." (*Rough Riders*, 70.) None of the American commanders seems to have realized at the time that the Spanish force had conducted a planned retreat. Shafter reported that 964 American troops had been engaged, including one squadron each from the First and Tenth Cavalry and two from the Rough Riders (*ARWD 98*, vol. 1, p. 61).

58. For Wood's denial, see Wood to Mrs. Wood, Papers of Leonard Wood, box 190, Library of Congress, Manuscript Division, Washington, D.C. For other refutations of the ambush theory, see Alger, *Spanish-American War*, 115; Wagner, *Santiago Campaign*, 55; and *IC*, vol. 1, pp. 225–226.

59. Shafter is quoted in *ARWD 98*, 61. The views of the Dodge Commission are in *IC*, vol. 1, pp. 225–226. For Alger's view, see his *Spanish-American War*, 112.

60. For criticism of Linares, see Kennan, *Campaigning in Cuba*, 94–96; Sargent, *Campaign of Santiago de Cuba*, vol. 3, p. 98; and Dierks, *Leap to Arms*, 182–183. Chadwick's counterargument is in his *Spanish-American War*, vol. 2, pp. 57–58. Lieutenant John J. Pershing, a participant in the attack, noted that a check at Las Guásimas "might have been disastrous." He thought that Linares gave up a strong position for a weaker one and "yielded the possiblity of bringing in any of his outlying troops. He lost an opportunity which an abler commander would have turned to his advantage." (Vandiver, *Black Jack*, vol. 1, p. 194.)

552   *Notes*

61. For comments on the problem of supply at Las Guásimas, see Wagner, *Santiago Campaign,* 58–59. Wagner thought that it might have been wise to await proper supply before moving on Las Guásimas. For Millis's views—reflected to some extent in this account—see his *Martial Spirit,* 275–276.
62. Roosevelt implied that Castillo had not fought at Las Guásimas because Spanish forces there had beaten him back the previous evening (*Rough Riders,* 58). For Portell Vilá's views, see his *Historia de Cuba,* vol. 3, pp. 479–481, 496. For Webb's letter, see his "Arizonans in Spanish-American War," 62.
63. Shafter to Wheeler, 24 June 1898, quoted in Alger, *Spanish-American War,* 118.

CHAPTER 10

1. For the communication to the naval commander, see Shafter to Sampson, 25 June 1898, *AF,* file 8, roll 232. Additional information is in French Ensor Chadwick, *The Relations of the United States and Spain: The Spanish-American War* (New York, 1911), vol. 2, p. 39; and Mariano Corona, *De la manigua (ecos de la epopeya)* (Santiago de Cuba, 1900), 95–100. Duffield's arrival is described in John D. Miley, *In Cuba With Shafter* (New York, 1899), 91. For activities in the War Department, see Corbin to Coppinger, 25 June 1898, and Coppinger to Corbin, 25 June 1898, *IC,* vol. 2, pp. 919–920. Corbin asked for a report on troops available for shipment at Tampa. General Coppinger replied that he had 629 officers and 12,680 men, but that he lacked transports. He knew of seven vessels at Port Tampa, but did not know who controlled them or how much capacity they had. This situation accounts for efforts of the War Department to get Shafter to return transports to Tampa as soon as possible. See Corbin to Shafter, 21 June 1898, *CWS,* vol. 1, p. 49, which reported the Department's intention to send Duffield's command to Santiago de Cuba on the *Yale* and *Harvard,* departing from Newport News, Virginia.
2. For Shafter's activities and orders to Wheeler, see Russell A. Alger, *The Spanish-American War* (New York and London, 1901), 126; and Joseph Wheeler, *The Santiago Campaign 1898* (New York, 1898), 253–254. For the description of Wheeler at this time, see Private St. Louis, *Forty Years After* (Boston, 1939), 33–34, a memoir by a soldier who began his service as a volunteer but also served later with the regulars in Cuba. (St. Louis is a pseudonym.)
3. Shafter to Sampson, 26 June 1898, *AF,* file 8, roll 232. See also Chadwick, *Spanish-American War,* vol. 2, pp. 61–62.
4. Frederick E. Pierce, *Reminiscences of the Experiences of Company L, Second Regiment Massachusetts Infantry, U.S.V., in the Spanish-American War* (Springfield, Mass., 1900), 30–31; and Roosevelt to Corinne Roosevelt Robinson, 27 June 1898, in Elting E. Morison, ed., *The Letters of Theodore Roosevelt,* Volume 2: *The Years of Preparation* (Cambridge, 1951), 845. See also Graham A. Cosmas, *An Army for Empire: The United States Army in the Spanish-American War* (Columbia, Mo., 1971), 209–211.
5. For Shafter's policy of delay until prepared, see Shafter to Alger, 28 June 1898, *IC,* vol. 2, p. 924; Wheeler, *Santiago Campaign,* 262; Alger to Shafter, 27 June 1898, reprinted in Alger, *Spanish-American War,* 125; and Cosmas, *Army for Empire,* 213.
6. For the Sergeant's view, see Merch Bradt Stewart, *The N'th Foot in War* (Kansas City, Mo., 1906), 90–91.
7. For communications, see Miley, *In Cuba With Shafter,* 94; and *CWS,* vol. 1, p. 50. For Shafter's statement, see *IC,* vol. 7, pp. 3, 197.
8. For Sampson's complaint, see Chadwick, *Spanish-American War,* vol. 2, pp. 217–218.
9. For the Long-Alger exchange, see Long Diary, 27 June 1898, quoted in Lawrence

Shaw Mayo, ed., *America of Yesterday: As Reflected in the Diary of John Davis Long* (Boston, 1923), 201. Shafter's admission is in *ARWD 98*, 61.

10. For this information concerning problems of supply, see Wagner, *Santiago Campaign*, 60; Cosmas, *Army for Empire*, 211; Miley, *In Cuba With Shafter*, 80–81, 87–88; Jack Cameron Dierks, *A Leap to Arms: The Cuban Campaign of 1898* (Philadelphia and New York, 1970), 87; and George Kennan, *Campaigning in Cuba* (New York, 1899), 153. Roosevelt's views are in his *The Rough Riders* (New York, 1961 reprint edition), 55.

11. For Shafter's report on artillery, see Shafter to Alger, 29 June 1898, *IC*, vol. 2, pp. 930–931. See also Cosmas, *Army for Empire*, 211–212. For War Department efforts to solve future problems, see Corbin to Shafter, 28 June 1898, *CWS*, vol. 1, p. 61; Shafter to Corbin, 30 June 1898, *ibid.*, 68; and Alger to Commissary-General of Subsistence, 2 July 1898, *ibid.*, 73.

12. For Linares's activities see Severo Gómez Núñez, *La guerra hispano-americana. Santiago de Cuba* (Madrid, 1901), 117. For the American reaction, see Richard Harding Davis, *The Cuban and Porto Rican Campaigns* (New York, 1898), 180. Chadwick's observation is in his *Spanish-American War*, vol. 2, p. 67.

13. Chadwick, *Spanish-American War*, vol. 2, pp. 71–72.

14. *Ibid.*, 72–73.

15. For Shafter's report of Escario's movements, see Shafter to Sampson, 28 June 1898, *AF*, file 8, roll 232; Shafter to Corbin, 29 June 1898, *CWS*, vol. 1, p. 64; Alger, *Spanish-American War*, 127; and Cosmas, *Army for Empire*, 213. For Shafter's orders to García, see Alger, *Spanish-American War*, 128. For information about El Caney and the San Juan Heights, see Chadwick, *Spanish-American War*, vol. 2, pp. 69–71; and Arthur L. Wagner, *Report of the Santiago Campaign 1898* (Kansas City, Mo., 1908), 107. For the fortifications and entrenchments, see also the brief comment of Major General J. C. Breckinridge (the Inspector General), in *ARWD 98*, 155.

16. Wagner's views are in his *Santiago Campaign*, 68. For additional information on the reconnaissance, see *ARWD 98*, 61–62; and Kennan, *Campaigning in Cuba*, 118–119.

17. Lawton was particularly influential in the decision to attack El Caney (Chadwick, *Spanish-American War*, vol. 2, pp. 68–69). See, for the plans, Wheeler, *Santiago Campaign*, 264; *ARWD 98*, 61–62; and Shafter, "Capture of Santiago de Cuba," 622. On June 30 Shafter sent the following to Sampson: "I expect to attack Santiago to-morrow morning. I wish you would bombard the works at Aguadores in support of a regiment of infantry which I shall send there early to-morrow, and also make such demonstration as you think proper at the mouth of the harbor, so as to keep as many of the enemy there as possible." (Quoted in Chadwick, *Spanish-American War*, vol. 2, p. 75). For Lawton's request to McClernand, see McClernand, "Santiago Campaign," 17.

18. *ARWD 98*, 64; Virgil Carrington Jones, *Roosevelt's Rough Riders* (New York, 1971), 172; Miley, *In Cuba with Shafter*, 107, 111; Wagner, *Santiago Campaign*, 97; and Margaret Leech, *In the Days of McKinley* (New York, 1959), 249.

19. For information on the demonstration at Aguadores, see Alger, *Spanish-American War*, 129–130; Chadwick, *Spanish-American War*, vol. 2, pp. 98–99; and Wagner, *Santiago Campaign*, 89–90. For reports of commanders of vessels taking part in the operations at Aguadores, see *AF*, file 8, roll 233.

20. For the dispositions around El Caney, see *IC*, vol. 1, p. 227; Alger, *Spanish-American War*, 132–133, 137; and *ARWD 98*, 52. For additional information concerning artillery activity, see Wagner, *Santiago Campaign*, 73–77; *ARWD 98*, 63; and Dierks, *Leap to Arms*, 99. When the light artillery under Grimes opened fire on the San Juan Heights at about 8:00 A.M., it was soon silenced because its black powder disclosed its location to opposing Spanish batteries. In a comment made

many years later Dwight E. Aultman scathingly criticized the use of the artillery on July 1, 1898: "The retention in reserve of half the pitiful quantity of artillery that accompanied the expedition seems amazing in the light of later training and experience, yet it is typical of the ignorance and ineptitude of our Army at the time and of the lack of study and training." (For this view see Society of the Army of Santiago de Cuba, *The Santiago Campaign: Reminiscences of the Operations for the Capture of Santiago de Cuba in Spanish-American War, June and July, 1898* [Richmond, Va., 1927], 188.) Aultman also noted that the 3.2-inch artillery gun was only a few years older than the famous French 75, yet it was "of the old non-recoil material, firing unfixed ammunition with black powder charges and unprovided with any of the laying apparatus for indirect fire" (*Ibid.*, 183). Wagner was also critical of the failure to bring up the artillery: "Guns can be taken to the front," he claimed, "if those who are in command of them are determined that they shall be." (Wagner, *Santiago Campaign*, 116.) Of course, the navy could have provided artillery support, but Shafter did not ask for it (Cosmas, *Army for Empire*, 214).

21. Kennan, *Campaigning in Cuba*, 121–122; Chadwick, *Spanish-American War*, vol. 2, p. 80; and *ARWD 98*, 62.

22. Gómez Núñez, *La guerra hispano-americana. Santiago de Cuba*, 120, 123; and Tomas Alvarez Angulo, *Memorias de un hombre sin importancia* (Madrid, 1962), 226–227. For the black powder problem, see Roosevelt, *Rough Riders*, 94. The Spanish troops were among those withdrawn from Las Guásimas on June 24.

23. McClernand's decision is recounted in Jones, *Roosevelt's Rough Riders*, 172. Shafter's recollections were given to the Dodge Commission after the war (See *IC*, vol. 7, p. 3,201). For the order to Lawton from Shafter, see Wagner, *Santiago Campaign*, 76–77. This authority criticized Shafter for having sent the order to disengage; he believed that the attack was necessary to protect the right flank of the troops before the San Juan heights. See also Chadwick, *Spanish-American War*, vol. 2, pp. 80–81. Shafter's order to Lawton was: "I would not bother with the little block-houses. They can't harm us. Bates's brigade and your division and García should move on the city and form the right of the line, going on the Sevilla road. Line [at the heights] is not hotly engaged." (*Ibid.*, 80.)

24. For the final attack see Kennan, *Campaigning in Cuba*, 121–123; and Chadwick, *Spanish-American War*, vol. 2, pp. 80–81. The praise of the Twenty-Fourth Infantry is in Alfred Seelye Roe, *Worcester in the Spanish War: Being the Stories of Companies A, C, and H, 2d Regiment and Company G, 9th Regiment M.V.M. during the War for the Liberation of Cuba May–November 1898* (Worcester, Mass., 1905), 46.

25. For the views of these authorities, see Chadwick, *Spanish-American War*, vol. 2, pp. 75, 81; Alger, *Spanish-American War*, 150; Wagner, *Santiago Campaign*, 69–70; and José Müller y Tejeiro, *Battles and Capitulation of Santiago de Cuba* (Washington, D.C., 1899), 90. Dierks agrees with Chadwick (*Leap to Arms*, 183–185). See also Hagedorn, *Wood*, vol. 1, pp. 173–174.

26. For information about the Spanish defenses, see Chadwick, *Spanish-American War*, vol. 2, p. 73—the most authoritative summary; Dierks, *Leap to Arms*, 95; Gómez Núñez, *La guerra hispano-americana. Santiago de Cuba*, 137–140; Müller, *Battles and Capitulation*, 83; Alberto Risco, *Apuntes biográficos del Excmo. Sr. Almirante D. Pascual Cervera y Topete* (Toledo, 1920), 139–141; Frank Freidel, *The Splendid Little War* (Boston, 1958), 120; and Alger, *Spanish-American War*, 152. The guns defending the San Juan Heights were mounted on June 13.

27. *Ibid.*, 152–153; *ARWD 98*, 63; Dierks, *Leap to Arms*, 103; Chadwick, *Spanish-American War*, vol. 2, p. 85; and Wagner, *Santiago Campaign*, 78. The illustrator Frederic Remington commented disgustedly on the failure of Grimes's battery, "Smokey powder belongs with arbalists and stone axes and the United States ord-

nance officers, which things all belong in museums with other dusty rust." (Quoted in Douglas Allen, *Frederic Remington and the Spanish-American War* [New York, 1971], 95.)

28. Wood's diary is quoted in Hagedorn, *Wood*, vol. 1, p. 174. Davis's views are in his *Cuban and Porto Rican Campaigns*, 212-213. For additional information concerning the balloon incident, see Wheeler, *Santiago Campaign*, 43; Alger, *Spanish-American War*, 155; *ARWD 98*, 63; Chadwick, *Spanish-American War*, vol. 2, pp. 86-87; and Kennan, *Campaigning in Cuba*, 124-125. The observation about the balloon is in U. G. McAlexander, *History of the Thirteenth Regiment United States Infantry* (Fort Mason, Calif., 1905), 102.

29. For terrain features, see Alger, *Spanish-American War*, 151; and Wagner, *Santiago Campaign*, 79-80. For the planned deployment prior to the attack, see Alger, *Spanish-American War*, 153.

30. For Sumner's movements, see Wagner, *Santiago Campaign*, 80; McAlexander, *Thirteenth Regiment*, 104-105; Walter Millis, *The Martial Spirit: A Study of Our War With Spain* (Boston and New York, 1971), 285-286; Davis, *Cuban and Porto Rican Campaigns*, 238-241; and Chadwick, *Spanish-American War*, vol. 2, p. 88. When Colonel Wikoff fell, Lieutenant Colonel Worth, Thirteenth Infantry, first assumed command. When Worth was then wounded, Lieutenant Colonel Liscum of the Twenty-Fourth Infantry took his place. Once again a Spanish bullet struck home, and then Lieutenant Colonel Ewers took command. (*ARWD 98*, 64.) For an acerbic but unconvincing defense of the Seventy-First New York, see Colonel Alexander Bacon, *The Seventy-first at San Juan*, 2d ed., (New York, n.d.). An eyewitness, Maurice O'Connor of the Ninth Infantry, offered this explanation: "The 71st Regiment N.Y. were badly handicapped as they were armed with the Springfield Rifle Cal. .45 and black powder was used for these arms, which was an open display whenever they fired on the enemy. Fortunately for the 71st Regiment N.Y. they did not advance as I believe they would be annihilated. There was a rumor that they did not act as they should under fire, but I was an eye witness and consider that the report was entirely erroneous. The existing circumstances did not permit them to participate in the battle, as they had intended to do. The troops armed with the modern rifle using smokeless powder had a hard proposition to face against what seemed to be tremendous odds. On that day it was thoroughly demonstrated that the use of black powder was to be forever discontinued. . . . " (USAMHI). The Ninth was in a different brigade than was the Seventy-First, and it is unlikely that O'Connor saw as much as he thought, but his testimony about the adverse consequences of the use of black powder is accurate.

31. For Shafter's comment, see *ARWD 98*, 64. For the reaction of the British correspondent, John Black Atkins, see Jones, *Roosevelt's Rough Riders*, 176.

32. Chadwick, *Spanish-American War*, vol. 2, p. 91.

33. For Parker's Gatling-gun employment at San Juan Hill, see Millis, *Martial Spirit*, 289; Wagner, *Santiago Campaign*, 87-88; Chadwick, *Spanish-American War*, vol. 2, pp. 92-93; Alger, *Spanish-American War*, 162; and Dierks, *Leap to Arms*, 105. For a detailed account of the Gatling-gun detachment see the book of its leader, John H. Parker, entitled *History of the Gatling Gun Detachment Fifth Army Corps at Santiago* (Kansas City, Mo., 1898). Allen's report of the charge is quoted in Chadwick, *Spanish-American War*, vol. 2, pp. 94-95. For another account see Alger, *Spanish-American War*, 163.

34. For the information about the military crest, see Charles Johnson Post, *The Little War of Private Post* (Boston and Toronto, 1960), 185.

35. For the charge on Kettle Hill and the movement on to the northern portion of San Juan Hill, see Millis, *Martial Spirit*, 290-291; and Roosevelt, *Rough Riders*, 86-88. Sergeant Berry's exploit is recounted in Chadwick, *Spanish-American War*, vol. 2, p. 92.

36. For Roosevelt's report of the trenches filled with Spaniards, see his *Rough Riders,* 91. For another description of the action, see Wheeler, *Santiago Campaign,* 45. For Bacon's refutation of T.R.'s account, see Bacon, *The Seventy-First at San Juan,* 43. See also St. Louis, *Forty Years After,* 66–67. Roosevelt's remark about the limited observation possible in combat is in his *Rough Riders,* 92.

37. Leech, *In the Days of McKinley,* 250–251.

38. Dierks, *Leap to Arms,* 108. For praise of the Spanish soldiers, see Roosevelt, *Rough Riders,* 103.

39. For Shafter's post-battle reactions and situation, see *ARWD 98,* 100; and Cosmas, *Army for Empire,* 214–215.

40. These casualty figures are derived from reports in Chadwick, *Spanish-American War,* vol. 2, pp. 82, 101–102; Dierks, *Leap to Arms,* 110; Müller, *Battles and Capitulation,* 90; and *ARWD 98,* 794. Portell Vilá claims that the insurgents endured some two hundred casualties, but this figure is open to serious question (Herminio Portell Vilá, *Historia de Cuba en sus relaciones con los Estados Unidos y España,* Volume 3: *1898-1899* [Havana, 1939], 486). For Rossevelt's view, see his *Rough Riders,* 104.

41. For a Spanish criticism of Linares's failure to concentrate his troops, see Efeele, *El desastre nacional y los vicios de nuestras instituciones nacionales* (Madrid, 1901), 58–59. "Efeele" appears to be a pseudonym made of the Spanish spellings of the letters "f" and "l." For a Spanish comment on Linares's failure to use available artillery support, see Domián Isern, *Del desastre nacional y sus causas* (Madrid, 1899), 508. For American criticisms of Linares, see Herbert H. Sargent, *The Campaign of Santiago de Cuba,* (Chicago, 1907), vol. 3, p. 93; and Dierks, *Leap to Arms,* 182–183. Dierks thinks that Linares could have had sixty-three hundred men at the Heights. He points out the possibility that, had Shafter been reversed at the San Juan Heights, the outcome might have been determined by a race between the American build-up for another effort and the arrival of tropical disease.

42. For some of these criticisms, particularly those relating to reconnaissance, El Caney, and the failure to concentrate all available troops at the San Juan Heights, see the views of Dierks in *Leap to Arms,* 183–185.

43. Roosevelt, *Rough Riders,* 81–83; *ARWD 98,* 65; Alger, *Spanish-American War,* 166–167, 170; and Wagner, *Santiago Campaign,* 96–98. For McClernand's account of Lawton's movements, see his "Santiago Campaign," 29–30.

44. Roosevelt, *Rough Riders,* 97. T.R. also commented on the Colt automatic machine guns that accompanied the expedition. These weapons proved less effective than the Gatlings. They were mounted on tripods and therefore less mobile than the Gatlings with their wheels. They became out of order easily, and did not use United States ammunition. T.R. positioned the Colts with the Gatlings. He was unstinting in praise of Parker, even stating, "I think Parker deserved rather more credit than any one man in the entire campaign" (*Ibid.,* 107–108). This praise of Parker probably reflected T.R.'s realization of the essential role that the Gatling fire had played in forcing the Spanish defenders off San Juan Hill. The army apparently never fully recognized the extent to which the Gatlings had turned the tide on July 1. Had it done so, perhaps the gun would have been more fully developed and more carefully integrated into the army prior to World War I. Parker became a great advocate of the machine gun in later years, to the extent that he became known as "Machine Gun" Parker and thought of as rather a nuisance.

45. Pershing is quoted in Herschel V. Cashin et al., *Under Fire With the Tenth U.S. Cavalry* (New York, 1969 reprint edition), 210. Roosevelt's views are in his *Rough Riders,* 95–96. For Kennan's observations, see his *Campaigning in Cuba,* 144.

46. For Whitney's observation, see Jones, *Roosevelt's Rough Riders,* 198. Havard's comment is in *ARWD 98,* 794. Frederic Remington, the artist, described the scene graphically: "All the broken spirits, bloody bodies, hopeless, helpless suffering

which drags its weary length to the rear, are so much more appalling than anything else in the world that words won't mean anything to one who has not seen it. Men half naked, men sitting down on the road-side utterly spent, men hopping on one foot with a rifle for a crutch, men out of their minds from sunstroke, men dead, and men dying.'' (Allen, *Remington*, 114.)

47. Müller, *Battles and Capitulation*, 91; and Leech, *In the Days of McKinley*, 251.

48. Cosmas summarizes the situation cogently in *Army for Empire*, 222–224. See also Julián Suárez Inclán, *Defensa del General Toral ante el Consejo Supremo de Guerra y Marina reunido y constituído en Sala de Justicia* (Madrid, 1899), 6–7. For Toral's new line of defense, see Gómez Núñez, *La guerra hispano-americana. Santiago de Cuba*, 216.

49. Dierks, *Leap to Arms*, 112; Wheeler, *Santiago Campaign*, 286–287; and Cosmas, *Army for Empire*, 216.

50. Shafter's statement is quoted in Jones, *Roosevelt's Rough Riders*, 200. Generals Wheeler, Lawton, Kent, and Bates were in attendance at Shafter's consultation. For information about proceedings, see Wheeler, *Santiago Campaign*, 46–47; Wheeler to Shafter, 2 July 1898, in *ibid.*, 277; Jones, *Roosevelt's Rough Riders*, 200–201; Chadwick, *Spanish-American War*, vol. 2, pp. 108–109; Cosmas, *Army for Empire*, 215; and McClernand, "Santiago Campaign," 31–32. Chadwick's disdainful view is in his *Spanish-American War*, vol. 2, p. 109. Toral did make some attempt to order General Pareja at Guantánamo to come to his aid, but his order never reached its destination, according to Suárez Inclán, *Defensa del General Toral*, 31.

51. For Roosevelt's postwar interpretation of events, see his *Rough Riders*, 97. See also Jones, *Roosevelt's Rough Riders*, 191. For his opinion at the time of the conference, see Roosevelt to Lodge, 3 July 1898, in Morison, ed., *Letters of Theodore Roosevelt*, vol. 2, p. 846. Davis is quoted in Jones, *Roosevelt's Rough Riders*, 204.

52. For Alger's wait with the President, see his *Spanish-American War*, 172. His message of 11:00 A.M. is Alger to Shafter, 3 July 1898, in *CWS*, vol. 1, p. 74.

53. For the message from Santiago de Cuba, see Shafter to Alger, 3 July 1898, *ARWD 98*, 29, 102. See also Chadwick, *Spanish-American War*, vol. 2, p. 109; and Leech, *In the Days of McKinley*, 254.

54. For the message to Cuba, see Alger to Shafter, 3 July 1898, quoted in *ARWD 98*, 103. See also Chadwick, *Spanish-American War*, vol. 2, p. 110. For the Adjutant General's message, see Corbin to Shafter, 3 July 1898, *CWS*, vol. 1, p. 77; and Cosmas, *Army for Empire*, 216. For the efforts of the War Department to send help to Shafter, see Alger, *Spanish-American War*, 177–178; and Cosmas, *Army for Empire*, 216. For an example of Long's efforts, see Long to Navy Yard (New York, N.Y.), 3 July 1898, in *RG 45*, Entry 19, no. 2, 84.

55. For the meetings that resulted in the message to Shafter and the despatch of Miles, see Leech, *In the Days of McKinley*, 263. These meetings apparently took place on July 3. For Miles's account of his orders, see his *Serving the Republic: Memoirs of the Civil and Military Life of Nelson H. Miles Lieutenant General United States Army* (New York and London, 1911), 282. Henry Cabot Lodge wrote an interesting account of the reaction to Shafter's pessimism in the War Department: "I was in the War Department on Sunday [July 3] when Shafter's disheartening despatch came in, and was alone there with the Secretary and his assistants. I was perfectly appalled by the utter lack of efficiency, organization, or plan there displayed by the head of the Department. I was a rank outsider and have no military education or experience, but I could have taken those problems up which they were muddling over and settled them in an hour. There is no plan in the War Department that I can see, and a great deal of time is spent asking why the Navy does not do this, that and the others. As it is, the Navy has taken its own warships to carry the troops, but Alger seemed to think that to blow up the *Iowa* in an attempt to enter Santiago would be a trivial incident, for, as he wisely said, 'what's

the loss of one ship after all.' How we get on as well as we do I cannot imagine, and I have been filled with anxiety about the Army in the last two or three days (owing to the state of things in the Department) which it is difficult to describe. However I hope and believe all will come out well.'' (Lodge to Roosevelt, 6 July 1898, quoted in Henry Cabot Lodge and Charles F. Redmond, eds., *Selections from the Correspondence of Theodore Roosevelt and Henry Cabot Lodge 1884-1918* [New York, 1971 reprint edition], vol. 1, p. 320.)

56. Chadwick, *Spanish-American War*, vol. 2, p. 58. See also Jones, *Roosevelt's Rough Riders*, 161, for a similar view, one frequently expressed. Just after the battles on July 1, Shafter requested that Sampson station a warship near Daiquirí and Siboney to protect the landing areas because troops there had to be ordered to the front. He also requested fire on the battery at Punta Gorda, which had proven troublesome; Sampson complied with this request. Later, Shafter also asked for fire on the waterfront at Santiago de Cuba, from which some six-inch guns had been firing on his lines. (For this information see two messages, Shafter to Sampson, 1 July 1898, *BN 98*, 617.) For reports of ships that fired on the Punta Gorda battery, see *AF*, file 8, roll 233.

57. Shafter to Sampson, 2 July 1898, *BN 98*, 504; Staunton to Shafter via telephone, 2 July 1898, *ibid.*, 504, 608; and Shafter to Sampson, 2 July 1898, *ibid.* For Chadwick's account of these exchanges, see his *Spanish-American War*, vol. 2, pp. 106–107.

58. Sampson to Shafter, 2 July 1898, *BN 98*, 504. See also Chadwick, *Spanish-American War*, vol. 2, p. 107. Captain Albert S. Barker, U.S.N., present at Santiago de Cuba, made a diary entry on July 2 dealing with these events: "It seems that General Shafter in command of the Army forces, is not having an easy time of it. He has lost five hundred men or so and he wants the ships to force a passage over the mines and into Santiago to assist him in the final assault. Lieutenant Staunton, Admiral Sampson's Aide, had been to see him and a remark had been made to the effect that the Navy as well as the Army should expose itself, but the view taken by the naval officers was that until the mines are removed or rendered useless, it would be foolhardy to rush over them with big ships and block up the channel. I think Sampson will pay some attention to destroying the mines but how the matter will end between the army and the navy we cannot say." (Quoted in Albert Smith Barker, *Everyday Life in the Navy: Autobiography of Rear Admiral Albert S. Barker* [Boston, 1928], 292.)

59. For Long's observation, see his *The New American Navy* (New York, 1903), vol. 2, p. 24.

60. Sampson to Long; 15 July 1898, *AF*, file 8, roll 234; *BN 98*, 618; and Shafter to Alger, 3 July 1898, *ARWD 98*, 29, 102.

61. McClernand's suggestion is recounted in his "Santiago Campaign," 34–35. See also Jones, *Roosevelt's Rough Riders*, 204. The exchange between the two commanders is Shafter to Toral, *CWS*, vol. 1, p. 79; Toral to Shafter, 3 July 1898, quoted in Chadwick, *Spanish-American War*, vol. 2, p. 111.

62. For the delay in the deadline for the bombardment, see *ARWD 98*, 66; *CWS*, vol. 1, p. 79. For Shafter's messages of July 3 to the War Department, see *ibid.*, 78; and *ARWD 98*, 103.

63. For Shafter's comment to Wheeler, see the latter's *Santiago Campaign*, 291. The commander's message of July 4 is quoted in Chadwick, *Spanish-American War*, vol. 2, p. 113. See also *CWS*, vol. 1, p. 79. For the reaction of the troops, see Shafter to Corbin, 4 July 1898, *ARWD 98*, 104–105.

64. For Escario's entry, see *ARWD 98*, 67; and Wheeler, *Santiago Campaign*, 292, 297–298. On July 3, 1898, García occupied San Vicente, Cuabitas, Bonato and Las Bocas (Felipe Martínez Arango, *Cronología crítica de la guerra hispano-americana*, 2nd ed., [Santiago de Cuba, 1966], 129). García's explanation is in García to

Gómez, 15 July 1898, quoted in Cosme Torriente y Peraza, *Calixto García cooperó con las fuerzas armadas de los EE.UU. en 1898, cumpliendo órdenes del gobierno Cubano* (Havana, 1952), 71; the full text of this interesting letter is in *ibid.*, 66–73. Foner gives his view in *Spanish-Cuban-American War*, vol. 2, pp. 362–364. George Kennan criticized Shafter for not reconnoitering to the west after first hearing of Escario's approach; the American General took no steps "either to ascertain the movements [of Escario] . . . or to prevent his junction with Linares" (Kennan, *Campaigning in Cuba*, 253). Müller's observation is in his *Battles and Capitulation*, 91. For the adverse consequences of Escario's entry, see, for example, Gabriel Maura Gamazo, *Historia crítica del reinado de don Alfonso XIII durante su menoridad bajo la regencia de su madre doña María Cristina de Austria* (Barcelona, 1925), vol. 2, p. 35. After the war Shafter commented on the Escario entry to General O. O. Howard, when Howard heard about García's failure to stop the Spanish column, "Really, General Howard, it didn't make any difference, and I said so at the time, because the more Spaniards that we could get in that pocket the larger would our capture become." (General Oliver Otis Howard, *Fighting for Humanity, or, Camp and Quarter-deck* [London and New York, 1898], 217.) Shafter's correspondence at the time, however, suggests that he was disturbed at the entry. He probably developed the rationale he gave Howard after the event.

65. Shafter to Corbin, Papers of General Henry Clark Corbin, box 1, Library of Congress, Manuscript Division, Washington, D.C., When, before the Dodge Commission after the war, Shafter was asked whether his health problem had affected the campaign in Cuba, he replied, "Not the slightest, sir. My conduct of the campaign was as I planned it, except that it took Lawton all day instead of two hours to settle the fight at El Caney," (*IC*, vol. 7, p. 3,204.) For the views of John E. Woodward see his Diary, 4 July 1898, USAMHI.

CHAPTER 11

1. For the report of the meeting of the captains on June 24, 1898, see Pascual Cervera y Topete, *The Spanish-American War: A Collection of Documents Relative to the Squadron Operations in the West Indies* (Washington, D.C., 1899), 107, 109. For the activities of Colonel Ordóñez, in charge of artillery, see Francisco Arderius, *La escuadra española en Santiago de Cuba: diario de un testigo* (Barcelona, 1903), 119. For the views of Villaamil, see *ibid.*, 120.

2. For Blanco's view, see Cervera, *Spanish-American War*, 111. For the Admiral's view, see Cervera to Linares, 25 June 1898, in *ibid.*, 111–112. The gist of this communication is in Cervera to Blanco, 25 June 1898, *ibid.*, 113. In this communication Cervera enumerated the deficiencies of his ships, discussed in Chapter 6 above. (See *ibid.*, 110–111.)

3. For Blanco's optimistic appraisal, see Blanco to Cervera, 26 June 1898, *ibid.*, 110–111. For Auñón's concurrence with Blanco, see Auñón to Cervera, 26 June 1898, in Spain, Ministry of the Marine, *Correspondencia oficial referente á las operaciones navales durante la guerra con los Estados Unidos* (Madrid, 1899), 154. The Admiral's answer to the Minister of the Marine is Cervera to Auñón, 27 June 1898, *ibid.* Cervera's orders to go out are in Blanco to Cervera, 28 June 1898, in Cervera, *Spanish-American War*, 115. This order apparently came in response to a message from Cervera to Blanco asking for clarification of the Governor-General's message of June 26 (Cervera to Blanco, 27 June 1898, *ibid.*, 114). Cervera later interpreted Blanco's order as meaning, "If favorable opportunity presents itself, to avail ourselves of it; if not, to go out at the last hour, even though loss of squadron be certain" (Cervera to Blanco, 29 June 1898, *ibid.*, 115). For Blanco's dealings with Auñón, see Blanco to Auñón, 30 June 1898, and Auñón to Manterola, 1 July

1898, in *ibid.*, 115–116. For the arrangements of June 30–July 1, see *ibid.*, 116–117.

4. For the minutes of the meeting of the captains on July 1, see *ibid.* For a general appraisal of how the Spanish commanders viewed the situation around Santiago de Cuba after the battles of July 1, see José Müller y Tejeiro, *Battles and Capitulation of Santiago de Cuba* (Washington, D.C., 1899), 90. For Cervera's proposal to Blanco see Cervera to Blanco, 1 July 1898, in Cervera, *Spanish-American War*, 117–118. The Governor-General's response is Blanco to Toral, 1 July 1898, *ibid.*, 118. For the view of Villaamil, see Arderius, *La escuadra española*, 113. For the Governor-General's last messages of July 1, see Blanco to Cervera (two messages), 1 July 1898, in Cervera, *Spanish-American War*, 118.

5. For the two messages, see Blanco to Toral, 2 July 1898, in Cervera, *Spanish-American War*, 120. Compare these reasons for attempting to preserve the squadron with those of a historian who argued that the Spanish government sent out Cervera "to justify in the eyes of all the armistice request and the peace negotiations" (F. Soldevilá, *Historia de España*, 2d ed. [Barcelona, 1964], vol. 8, p. 418). This view is a perversion of the valid argument that the Spanish government feared to seek an end to the war until it had been demonstrated that Spain's honor had been defended and that the armed forces had been defeated beyond reasonable doubt. For the final order, see Blanco to Cervera, 2 July 1898, in Cervera, *Spanish-American War*, 119.

6. For the plan of the sortie, see Víctor Concas y Palau, *The Squadron of Admiral Cervera* (Washington, D.C., 1900), 68–69; and Arderius, *La escuadra española*, 137. For Concas's comments on the effect of the narrow channel, see his *Squadron of Admiral Cervera*, 69–70.

7. For Jacobsen's views, see U.S. Navy Department, *Sketches from the Spanish-American War by Commander J . . .* (Washington, D.C., 1899), 17. For the Spanish Admiral's view, see Cervera to Blanco, 7 October 1898, in Cervera, *Spanish-American War*, 145–146. Cervera's son Angel, captured on July 3, told an American naval officer that the squadron had come out during the day because of the searchlights. (French Ensor Chadwick, *The Relations of the United States and Spain: The Spanish-American War* [New York, 1911], vol. 2, p. 170; see also Arderius, *La escuadra española*, 139–144.) Sampson's views are expressed in an essay entitled "Reasons for the Victory," in W. A. M. Goode, *With Sampson Through the War: Being an Account of the Naval Operations of the North Atlantic Squadron During the Spanish American War of 1898* (New York, 1899), 231–232.

8. Walter Millis, *The Martial Spirit: A Study of Our War With Spain* (Boston and New York, 1931), 305; and Arderius, *La escuadra española*, 152. On the previous evening, July 2, the contact mines were removed from the channel (Russell A. Alger, *The Spanish-American War* [New York, 1901], 232). Alger states that the electrical mines were largely disabled (See also Edwin Albert Falk, *Fighting Bob Evans* [New York, 1939, reprint edition], 319).

9. For the disposition of the squadron as the battle began, see Chadwick, *Spanish-American War*, vol. 2, pp. 129–131. For the comment on Sampson's misfortune, see Margaret Leech, *In the Days of McKinley* (New York, 1959), 257.

10. These data are derived from Robert Wilden Neeser, *Statistical and Chronological History of the United States Navy 1775–1907* (New York, 1909), vol. 2, pp. 262–263. It should be noted that six ten-inch guns supposedly available to the *Cristóbal Colón* were not actually aboard.

11. Philip is quoted in Edgar Stanton Maclay, *Life and Adventures of "Jack" Philip, Rear-Admiral United States Navy* (New York, 1903), 266. On the evening of July 2 an officer on the deck of the *Iowa* observed six columns of smoke rising near the channel; but since this phenomenon had occurred before, Captain Evans was unimpressed. However, Signal 250, "Enemy ships coming out," was bent on the

halyards and therefore ready to hoist the next morning when the Spanish ships emerged. (Robley Dunglison Evans, *A Sailor's Log: Recollections of Forty Years of Naval Life* [New York, 1908], 442.) Taylor's information is quoted in Chadwick, *Spanish-American War,* vol. 2, p. 133. The description of Captain Clark's response is in R. Cross, *The Voyage of the "Oregon" from San Francisco to Santiago in 1898 as Told by One of the Crew* (Boston, 1908), 30. This fascinating account was privately published in only 125 copies; one is now in the New York Public Library. Sampson's orders governing the response to be made in the type of situation that presented itself on the morning of July 3 were: "If the enemy tries to escape, the ships must close and engage as soon as possible, and endeavor to sink his vessels or force them to run ashore in the channel" (Quoted in Falk, *Fighting Bob Evans,* 323). In Squadron Order No. 9, 7 June 1898, Signal 250 is listed as "Enemy's ships escaping—number by numeral signal follows" (*AF,* file 8, roll 231).

12. For information about the exit of the *Infanta María Teresa* and its efforts to cripple the *Brooklyn,* see Cervera to Blanco, 9 July 1898, in Cervera, *Spanish-American War,* 123. See also Concas, *Squadron of Admiral Cervera,* 74. For the destruction of the Spanish flagship, see Cervera to Blanco, 9 July 1898, in Cervera, *Spanish-American War,* 124–126; and Chadwick, *Spanish-American War,* vol. 2, pp. 134–138.

13. Chadwick, *Spanish-American War,* vol. 2, pp. 142–147; Sampson to Long, 15 July 1898, *BN 98,* 506–507; and Long, *New Navy,* vol. 2, pp. 33–34. For the gunner's anecdote, see Cross, *Voyage of the "Oregon,"* 31.

14. For this phase of the battle, see Sampson to Long, 15 July 1898, *BN 98,* 506–507; Long, *New Navy,* vol. 2, pp. 33–34. For the recollection of the commander of the *Oregon,* see Rear Admiral Charles Edgar Clark, *My Fifty Years in the Navy* (Boston, 1917), 296.

15. Chadwick, *Spanish-American War,* vol. 2, pp. 151–157; and Sampson to Long, 15 July 1898, *BN 98,* 507–509. Reports of the commanders of American ships taking part in the sea battle are in *AF,* file 8, rolls 233 and 234. The *Brooklyn* and the *New York* pursued without the use of their forward engines (these had been decoupled to save fuel). Had the two ships stopped to couple these engines, they would have lost about fifteen minutes or approximately four miles. (Dierks, *Leap to Arms,* 136).

16. For American casualties, see Millis, *Martial Spirit,* 310; and Goode, *With Sampson Through the War,* 221. For damage to the American ships, see *ibid.,* 221–222. For Spanish casualties, see Concas, *Squadron of Admiral Cervera,* 83; Chadwick, *Spanish-American War,* vol. 2, pp. 176–177; Cervera, *Spanish-American War,* 128–130; and Dierks, *Leap to Arms,* 169. Maura Gamazo says that 253 Spaniards were killed and 1,670 taken prisoner (Gabriel Maura Gamazo, *Historia crítica del reinado de don Alfonso XIII durante su menoridad bajo la regencia de su madre doña María Cristina de Austria* [Barcelona, 1925], vol. 2, p. 38).

17. Maura Gamazo, *Historia crítica,* 176; Concas, *Squadron of Admiral Cervera,* 65–66; and Goode, *With Sampson through the War,* 228. See also Millis, *Martial Spirit,* 307.

18. Statistical information is given in Chadwick, *Spanish-American War,* vol. 2, p. 177.

19. Eulate's actions are detailed in *ibid.,* 175. For the heroism of José Casado, see Concas, *Squadron of Admiral Cervera,* 84. Arderius told his story in his *La escuadra española,* 188.

20. For the wait in Washington, see Long, *New Navy,* vol. 2, p. 149. For Sampson's message, see Sampson to Long, 3 July 1898, *BN 98,* 505. Margaret Leech drew attention to the reaction to this message in *In the Days of McKinley,* 259. See also Long, *New Navy,* vol. 2, p. 42–43. For the error of the aide to Sampson, see Long to unidentified correspondent, 27 July 1898, in Lawrence Shaw Mayo, ed., *America of Yesterday: As Reflected in the Journal of John Davis Long* (Boston, 1923), 207.

21. The first quotation by Long is from a letter to an unidentified correspondent, 27 July 1898, in Mayo, ed., *America of Yesterday*, 207. The second is from his *New Navy*, vol. 2, p. 46.
22. For Schley's explanation that he turned in order to be able to remain in good position for subsequent action, see U.S. Navy Department, *Record of Proceedings of a Court of Inquiry in the Case of Rear-Admiral Winfield S. Schley, U.S. Navy: Convened at the Navy-Yard, Washington, D.C., September 12, 1901* (Washington, D.C., 1902), vol. 2, 1,387–1,388. See also Winfield S. Schley, *Forty-Five Years Under the Flag* (New York, 1904), 302. For the crossfire explanation, see U.S. Navy Department, *Case of Schley*, vol. 2, 1,512. For the view that the Spanish ships might have been best advised to scatter, see Gregory Mason, *Remember the Maine* (New York, 1939), 203. Captain Philip of the *Texas* expressed a similar view: "For my part, I cannot help thinking that had Cervera been able to steam straight out, radiating the ships of his squadron from the Morro as a center, one or more of them, in the confusion that must have resulted, might have got safely away for the time. More especially would this have been the case had he sent his torpedo-boat destroyers in advance, under full head of steam, straight for our line of battle-ships." (John W. Philip, "The *Texas* at Santiago," *Century* 58 [May, 1898]: 94.)
23. For the recommendation of Sampson, see Sampson to Long, 10 July 1898, in Record Group 80, Entry E194: "Copies of messages received and sent by the Naval War Board," 266 1/2, General Records of the Department of the Navy, National Archives, Washington, D.C. (hereafter cited as *RG 80*, E194). Kohlsaat includes his recollection of McKinley's comment on Schley in his *From McKinley to Harding: Personal Recollections of the Presidents* (New York and London, 1923), 68. This source must be used with caution, and this reference is suspect because of Kohlsaat's misconception of Schley's movements in May; the commodore never approached Puerto Rico.
24. For messages of congratulation sent July 4, 1898, see Chadwick, *Spanish-American War*, vol. 2, p. 188. For Sampson's evaluation, see Sampson to Long, 16 July 1898, *AF*, file 8, roll 233.

CHAPTER 12

1. For Cámara's departure and the ships in his expedition, see French Ensor Chadwick, *The Relations of the United States and Spain: The Spanish-American War* (New York, 1911), vol. 2, p. 388; Spain, Ministry of the Marine, *Correspondencia oficial referente á las operaciones navales durante la guerra con los Estados Unidos* (Madrid, 1899), 289; Pablo de Azcárate, *La guerra del 98* (Madrid, 1968), 81; and Slocum (military attaché, Lisbon) to Corbin, 18 June 1898, *CWS*, vol. 2, p. 705. For the orders of the Spanish expedition, see Auñón to Cámara, *Correspondencia oficial*, 287–288. For Chadwick's calculations, see his *Spanish-American War*, vol. 2, p. 389.
2. For Auñón's statement in the Cortes, 10 September 1898, see Ramón Auñón y Villalón *Discursos pronunciados en el parlamento por el ministro de marina D. Ramón Auñón y Villalón durante la guerra con los Estados Unidos* (Madrid, 1912), 98. See also Azcárate, *La guerra del 98*, 81.
3. Reports began to come in from diplomatic officials and agents in Europe confirming that Cámara's initial destination was Suez (see Sprague to Day, 17 June 1898, and Carroll to Day, 17 June 1898, both transmitted to the Navy Department in Day to Long, 17 June 1898, in *AF*, file 4, roll 234), For the messages arranging the orders to Sampson to establish a special division for European service, see Sicard (for Naval War Board) to Long, 18 June 1898, in *RG 45*, NRC 371, vol. 2, p. 89. See also

Chadwick, *Spanish-American War*, vol. 2, p. 386. For the project to make plans for the Eastern Squadron known to the Spanish government through a leak in Paris, see John D. Long, *The New American Navy* (New York, 1903), vol. 2, p. 18. For the role of the Naval War Board, see Sicard (for the Naval War Board) to Long, 18 June 1898, *RG 45*, 371, vol. 2, p. 85. For the orders to Sims, see Long to Sims, *RG 38*, Entry 100. For doubt that Cámara could threaten Dewey, see A. S. Barker to Long, 17 June 1898, in Gardner Weld Allen, ed., *Papers of John Davis Long 1897–1904* (Boston, 1939), 141.

4. W. A. M. Goode, *With Sampson Through the War: Being an Account of the Naval Operations of the North Atlantic Squadron During the Spanish-American War of 1898* (New York, 1899), 184–185. For orders relating to the changes in the commands of Howell and Watson, see Long to Sampson, 27 June 1898, in *RG 45*, Entry 19, no. 2, 67. See also *BN 98*, 503.

5. For the President's wishes respecting the blockade and Sampson's response, see Long to Sampson, 19 June 1898, in *RG 45*, Entry 19, no. 2, 496; Sampson to Long, 19 June 1898, *AF*, file 8, roll 232. For Sampson's blockade order, see Navy Department General Order No. 492, in U.S. State Department, *Proclamations and Decrees During the War With Spain* (Washington, D.C., 1899), 85–89. For the Naval War Board's recommendation that the south side of Cuba be placed under blockade, see Sicard (for Naval War Board) to Long, 21 June 1898, *AF*, file 8, roll 232. For the activities of the *Terror*, see Goode, *With Sampson Through the War*, 186–187. See also the reports of the action by Captain Charles D. Sigsbee (28 June 1898) and Lieutenant Commander William P. Day (27 September 1898) in *BN 98*, 220–222, 223–224.

6. For information concerning Sampson's difficulties in fulfilling assigned responsibilities on the blockade, see Long to Sampson (two messages), 22 June 1898 and 24 June 1898, and Sampson to Long, 23 June 1898, in *BN 98*, 499, 501. For the order to extend the blockade, see Long to Sampson, 25 June 1898, *RG 45*, Entry 19, no. 2, 64. For Sampson's reply, see Sampson to Long, 27 June 1898, *AF*, file 8, roll 232. For the text of the proclamation of blockade issued June 28, 1898, see U.S. State Department, *Proclamations and Decrees*, 79–80. See also Goode, *With Sampson Through the War*, 242; and Long to Sampson, 28 June 1898, *AF*, file 8, roll 232. For a report of the action at Manzanillo, see Lieutenant Commander Adolph Marix to Sampson, 1 July 1898, *AF*, file 8, roll 233.

7. For reports on the movement of Cámara through the Mediterranean, see Sims to Navy Department, 18 June 1898, *RG 45*, Entry 100; Townsend to Day, 18 June 1898, transmitted to the Navy Department in Day to Long, 18 June 1898, *AF*, file 4, roll 34; Hay to Day, 18 June 1898, *AF*, file 4, roll 34; Sprague to Day, 19 June 1898, *AF*, file 4, roll 234, reporting difficulties of the Spanish ships with motors, electricity, and armaments; Townsend to Day, 22 June 1898, *AF*, file 4, roll 234, reporting that an agent had noted Cámara's presence at Cartagena and that "the movement was made to satisfy the people"; Sims to Navy Department, rec. 22 June 1898, *RG 38*, Entry 100, reporting that another agent at Madrid had reported that Cámara would shortly return westward but that this seemed improbable; and Sims to Navy Department, rec. 25 June 1898, *RG 38*, Entry 100, a further report about intelligence garnered in Madrid indicating that Cámara had orders to attack San Francisco as well as to operate in the Philippines. For the Secretary of the Navy's request to the State Department, see Long to Day, 20 June 1898, *RG 45*, NRC 372, 109. For Day's instructions of 22 June 1898 to the American vice-consul general at Cairo, to be transmitted also to consuls at stations such as Colombo and Singapore, see Day to Long, 25 June 1898, *AF*, file 4, roll 34. The vice-consul general, Ethelbert Watts, replied on June 24, 1898, "Instructions by cable received yesterday. This Government is favorably disposed." (*AF*, file 4, roll 34.) See also R. G. Neale, *Great Britain and United States Expansion: 1898–1900* (East Lansing,

Mich., 1966), 59–60. Dealings in Egypt were primarily with Lord Cromer, the British proconsul at the time.

8. For this highly interesting letter, see Sicard (for the Naval War Board) to Long, 20 June 1898, *RG 45*, NRC 372, 115–117. It seems entirely possible that Captain Mahan greatly influenced the contents of this communication. It was surely consistent with his general outlook.

9. Long to Sampson, 24 June 1898, *RG 45*, Entry 19, no. 2, 57; and Long to Sampson, 25 June 1898, *RG 45*, Entry 19, no. 2, 65. The Naval War Board recommended the addition of the *Brooklyn* (Sicard [for the Naval War Board] to Long, 25 June 1898, *RG 45*, NRC 371, vol. 2, p. 110). See also Chadwick, *Spanish-American War*, vol. 1, pp. 391–392.

10. For Sampson's protest, see Sampson to Long, 26 June 1898, *BN 98*, 502. See also *RG 80*, E194, 229–230. For the recommendation of the Naval War Board and subsequent changes, see Sicard (for the Naval War Board) to Long, 27 June 1898, *RG 45*, NRC 371, vol. 2, p. 115; and Long to Sampson, 27 June 1898, *RG 45*, Entry 19, no. 2, 69. This message is reprinted in *BN 98*, 502. See also Long, *New Navy*, vol. 2, p. 19; and Goode, *With Sampson Through the War*, 184. For the orders to Watson, see Sicard (for the Naval War Board) to Long, 27 June 1898, *RG 45*, NRC 371, vol. 2, p. 117; and Long to Watson (through Sampson), 27 June 1898, *RG 45*, Entry 19, no. 2, 70. See also Chadwick, *Spanish-American War*, vol. 2, p. 393.

11. For Long's message to Sampson encouraging the departure of Watson, see Long to Sampson, 28 June 1898, *RG 45*, Entry 19, no. 2, 71. For Long's concerns, see Long Diary, 28 June 1898, quoted in Lawrence Shaw Mayo, ed., *America of Yesterday: As Reflected in the Journal of John Davis Long* (Boston, 1923), 201. For Long's message of July 1 to Sampson, see *RG 45*, Entry 19, 82. See also Chadwick, *Spanish-American War*, vol. 2, pp. 393–395. It should be noted that in connection with the planning for the Eastern Squadron Secretary of State Day asked Ambassador Hay in London to make inquiries about the British attitude towards movement of American ships through the Suez Canal. (The British government largely controlled Egypt through Lord Cromer.) Hay reported that Salisbury "had no idea that any power would make any protest against our use of the canal, nor that any protest would hold if it were made. The attitude of the British Government is that we are unquestionably entitled to the use of the canal for war ships." A later message cited as authority for this view was the Convention of 1888 dealing with international use of the canal. Once again the London government manifested its friendly disposition toward the United States. (Day to Hay, 25 June 1898, *Foreign Relations, 1898*, 982. For Hay to Day [letter despatch], 25 June 1898, and Hay to Day [cablegram], 25 June 1898, see *ibid.*)

12. Cámara reported his arrival at Port Said in Cámara to Auñón, 26 June 1898, *Correspondencia oficial*, 290. Word of his arrival came to Washington in Sims to Navy Department, 26 June 1898, *RG 38*, Entry 100; and Ethelbert Watts to State Department, 26 June 1898, transmitted to the Navy Department in Adee to Long, 26 June 1898, *AF*, file 4, roll 34. Watts also reported that he was doing everything he could to prevent the Spanish squadron from coaling. His statement that he was succeeding in blocking Cámara is in Watts to State Department, 26 June 1898, transmitted to the Navy Department in Moore to Long, 27 June 1898, *AF*, file 4, roll 34. For Lord Cromer's role, see Neale, *Great Britain and United States Expansion: 1898-1900*, 64; and Donald A. Cameron to Salisbury, 5 July 1898, *FO 185*, box 866. For additional information on developments at Port Said, see Watts to State Department, 28 June 1898, transmitted to the Navy Department in Moore to Long, 29 June 1898, *AF*, file 10, roll 364; Hay to Day, 29 June 1898, in *AF*, file 4, roll 34, and also in *Foreign Relations, 1898*, p. 983; and Cameron to Salisbury, 5 July 1898, *FO 185*, box 866. For Cámara's initial reports of his problems with the

Egyptian authorities, see Alberto Risco, *Apuntes biográficos del Excmo. Sr. Almirante D. Pascual Cervera y Topete* (Toledo, 1920), 117–118; and Cámara to Auñón, 30 June 1898, *Correspondencia oficial*, 291, For the exchanges of July 1, see *ibid.*, 291–293. For American efforts to prevent Cámara from obtaining coal south and east of Suez, see Long to Day, 29 June 1898, *RG 45*, NRC 372, 139; Cridler to Cunningham (U.S. consul at Aden), 29 June 1898, *AF*, file 10, roll 364; and Day to Cunningham, 3 July 1898, transmitted to the Navy Department in Day to Long, 5 July 1898, *AF*, file 10, roll 364.

13. For the Auñón-Cámara exchange of July 3–4, 1898, see *Correspondencia oficial*, 294. Already the American naval attaché in London was reporting that plans were afoot to recall Cámara (see Colwell to Long, rec. 2 July 1898, *RG 38*, Entry 100). For the intelligence information from Paris, see Sims to Navy Department, rec. 4 July 1898, *RG 38*, Entry 100. For additional information, see Long, *New Navy*, vol. 2, p. 20; and Watts to State Department, 5 July 1898, transmitted to the Navy Department in Long to Day, 5 July 1898, *AF*, file 4, roll 34. For Auñón's activities on July 6, see Auñón to Camara (two messages), 6 July 1898, *Correspondencia oficial*, 295. For the recall, see Auñón to Cámara, 7 July 1898, *ibid.* On the next day Auñón reported to Cámara a rumor that supplies were being gathered for American use at Gibraltar in anticipation of the arrival of an American squadron there July 19. He did not credit this report, but thought it important for Cámara to hasten his return. (Auñón to Cámara, 8 July 1898, *ibid.*, 296.) For Auñón's statement to the Cortes, 10 September 1898, see Auñón, *Discursos*, 101. It is probably true that the ability of the American representatives in Egypt and elsewhere to preclude Cámara's coaling exercised some influence. This success was largely a result of the exercise of British influence on the Egyptian government. Also, the political resident of Great Britain at Aden assured Consul E. S. Cunningham that Cámara would not have been allowed to coal in that port had he approached the area. Cunningham concluded, "I am glad the fleet have gone back and I feel very grateful for my treatment by local authorities and their very great diligence in stopping proposed sale at Perim and Aden, of coal for Spanish" (Cunningham to Moore, 12 July 1898, *AF*, file 4, roll 34). For Cámara's instructions to show himself on the Spanish coast, dated July 23, 1898, see Chadwick, *Spanish-American War*, vol. 2, p. 390. One Spanish authority claimed that the squadron was recalled because, had it proceeded to the Philippines, it would have posed obstacles to negotiations with the United States toward an end to the war (F. Bonmatí y Codecido, *Alfonso XIII y su España*, Volume 1: *Libro Primero, 1886-1906*, (n.p., 1943), 123. This view is a plausible hypothesis, but evidence to support it is lacking.

14. For Mahan's fascinating analysis, see his "Narrative Account of the Work of the Naval War Board of 1898," 29 October 1906, in Record Group 7: Intelligence and Technological Archives, 1894 to 1945, 23–28, Archives of the Naval War College, Naval War College, Newport, R.I. The Naval War Board's role in the conduct of the war with Spain has been underestimated, as this episode reveals.

15. For Secretary Long's notice concerning the Eastern Squadron after Cervera's defeat, see Long to Sampson, 4 July 1898, *RG 80*, E194, 251. The same message is in *AF*, file 8, roll 233. His next message on this question is Long to Sampson, 7 July 1898, *RG 45*, Entry 19, no. 2, 92. The Naval War Board had recommended the dispatch of the two armored vessels (See Sicard [for the Naval War Board] to Long, 6 July 1898, *RG 45*, NRC 371, vol. 2, p. 152). For the admiral's response, see Sampson to Long (two messages), 7 July 1898, *RG 80*, E194, 257. Orders to concentrate the Eastern Squadron at Môle St. Nicolas are in Long to Sampson, 7 July 1898, *RG 45*, Entry 19, no. 2, 92. This order had been recommended by the Naval War Board in Sicard (for the Naval War Board) to Long, 7 July 1898, *RG 45*, NRC 371, vol. 2, p. 153. Meanwhile, efforts were being made to collect seven of the best available colliers for service with Watson (see Bureau of Equipment to Bureau of Navigation,

7 July 1898, *AF,* file 8, roll 234). Sampson's proposal to substitute the *Massachusetts* for the *Iowa* was approved the next day (Long to Sampson, 8 July 1898, *RG 45,* Entry 19, no. 2, 95). For information concerning the return of Cámara to Spain, see Watts to State Department, 8 July 1898, transmitted to the Navy Department in Day to Long, 8 July 1898, *AF,* file 4, roll 234; Long to Watson, 8 July 1898, *RG 45,* NRC 372, 161; Sims to Navy Department, rec. 8 July 1898, *RG 38,* Entry 100; Watts to State Department, transmitted to the Navy Department in Day to Long, 9 July 1898, *RG 38,* Entry 100; Watts to State Department, 9 July 1898, transmitted to the Navy Department in Moore to Long, 9 July 1898 (8:50 P.M.), *AF,* file 4, roll 34; Cameron to Salisbury, 11 July 1898, *FO 185,* 866; and Watts to State Department, 11 July 1898, transmitted to the Navy Department in Moore to Long, 11 July 1898, *AF,* file 4, foll 34. The report of Sims's agent is in Sims to Navy Department, rec. 9 July 1898, *RG 38,* Entry 100. Sampson's report that the Eastern Squadron could leave in two days is Sampson to Long, 19 July 1898, *RG 80,* E194, 266. He also reported that all but the *Yosemite* were in Cuban waters. The *Yosemite,* blockading San Juan, could be picked up on the outward voyage. The reorganization of Sampson's command is in Squadron General Order No. 13, 11 July 1898, *AF,* file 8, roll 234.

16. Orders to send all the armored vessels eastward came in Long to Sampson, 12 July 1898, *RG 45,* Entry 19, no. 2, 98. The Admiral's protest is in Sampson to Long, 14 July 1898, *RG 80,* Entry E194, 277–278. See also Chadwick, *Spanish-American War,* vol. 2, pp. 267–268.

17. Long to Sampson, 15 July 1898, *RG 45,* NRC 372, 184–190. This copy of the order has a crossed-out page that had Schley commanding the covering squadron and Watson in overall charge until separation. See also Chadwick, *Spanish-American War,* vol. 2, pp. 281–283. Captain Mahan described the intent of this arrangement as follows: "The determining factor in this proposed movement of the battle fleet as a whole was the necessity, or at least the advantage, of reinforcing Dewey, and of placing two battleships in the Pacific. It was not thought expedient now to send them by themselves, as at first proposed, for the reason already given; . . . that is, the impropriety of taking even a small risk, if unnecessary." (Alfred Thayer Mahan, *Lessons of the War With Spain and Other Articles* [Freeport, N.Y., 1970 reprint edition], 202.)

18. For this information, see Chadwick, *Spanish-American War,* vol. 2, p. 268; Sampson to Long, 17 July 1898, *AF,* file 8, roll 235; and Sampson to Long, 17 July 1898, *RG 80,* E194, 286–287. See also Chadwick, *Spanish-American War,* vol. 2, p. 268.

19. Sicard to Naval War Board, 18 July 1898, *AF,* file 8, roll 235.

20. Mahan to Naval War Board, 18 July 1898, *AF,* file 8, roll 235. Another copy is in *RG 45,* NRC 371, vol. 1, pp. 315–322.

21. For the Secretary of the Navy's request for advice, see Long to Naval War Board, 20 July 1898, *RG 80,* E194, 306. For the reply, see Sicard (for the Naval War Board) to Long, 21 July 1898, *RG 45,* NRC 371, vol. 1, pp. 312–314. This message is reprinted in Allen, ed., *Papers of John Davis Long,* 160–162.

22. Sampson's proposal—the solution opposed by Mahan—is in Sampson to Long, 20 July 1898, *RG 80,* Entry E194, 305. Sicard had offered it earlier. Watson's views are in Watson to Long, 21 July 1898, *RG 80,* E194, 308. For the Secretary of the Navy's search for information about Cámara's ships, see Long to Sims, 22 July 1898, *RG 38,* Entry 100. For the movements of Cámara, see Auñón to Cámara, 23 July 1898, in Cervera, *Spanish-American War,* 155–156. A diplomatic agent reported that Cámara might use Cartagena or Ceuta as a base for operations against Watson (Sprague to Day, 22 July 1898, transmitted to the Navy Department in Moore to Long, 22 July 1898, *AF,* file 4, roll 34). Clearly the Spanish naval authorities had been giving much thought to the prospect of Watson's arrival. See, for an example of this tendency, Sims's report from his spy in Madrid: "Spanish

Naval Authorities are discussing a plan to divide Camara's squadron, thus forcing division of United States squadron; definite decision will not be made until Camara's return" (Sims to Navy Department, rec. 16 July 1898, *RG 38,* Entry 100; see also Sprague to Day [cable], 20 July 1898, transmitted to the Navy Department in Day to Long, 20 July 1898, *AF,* file 4, roll 34). This message reported the arrival of three Spanish ocean liners at Gibraltar from Cádiz in order to obtain neutral protection against Watson. The American envoy in Brussels, Bellamy Storer, told his English counterpart there on July 17, 1898 that he expected "to see the American fleet arrive at the Canary Islands about Thursday week, with the view of them bringing the war more home to the Spanish public." (See E. Plunkett to Salisbury, 17 July 1898, *FO 185,* 866.) The Spanish government was certainly concerned about the Eastern Squadron. The Minister for the Colonies reported this concern to the Governor-General of Puerto Rico (Girón to Macías, 25 July 1898, in Sección de Ultramar (10), Puerto Rico, Government 1839–1899, bundle 5.143 (4), no. 41, National Historical Archives, Madrid. For the views of Gabriel Maura Gamazo, see his *Historia crítica del reinado de Don Alfonso XIII durante su menoridad bajo la regencia de su madre doña María Cristina de Austria* (Barcelona, 1925), vol. 2, p. 44. For Cámara's return to Cádiz, see Santalo to Auñón, 27 July 1898, *Correspondencia oficial,* 300; unsigned cable to State Department, 29 July 1898, transmitted to the Navy Department in Moore to Long, 29 July 1898, *AF,* file 10, roll 364. For the effect of the arrival of the Spanish peace note, see Long to Sampson, 26 July 1898, *RG 45,* Entry 19, no. 2, 122. In another message the Secretary of the Navy ordered Sampson to prepare orders assigning Commodore Howell to assume command of the blockade while Sampson was absent in the east: "Have a fast vessel ready to send him these papers the moment you are ordered to proceed on new duty assigned" (Long to Sampson, 26 July 1898, *RG 45,* Entry 19, no. 2, 124). This message indicates that the United States intended to maintain pressure on Spain while it dealt with the peace note.

23. Mahan to Long, 28 July 1898, in Allen, ed., *Papers of John Davis Long,* 166–167.
24. For the order to launch the expedition, see Long to Sampson, 2 August 1898, *RG 45,* Entry 19, no. 2, 135. This message developed from a recommendation in Sicard (for the Naval War Board) to Long, 2 August 1898, RG 45, NRC 371, vol. 2, p. 231. Once again the Naval War Board played a role not taken into account in later discussions of its activities in 1898. Orders for the components of the expedition are in Long to Sampson, 2 August 1898, *RG 45,* Entry 19, no. 2, 135. On the same day Sampson notified Shafter that he might soon depart for the Mediterranean Sea; he wanted to learn of the army's plans so that he could make a disposition of the Marine force encamped at Guantánamo (Sampson to Shafter, 2 August 1898, *AF,* file 8, roll 237). Sampson's proposal for further delay while he moved on San Juan is in Sampson to Long, 4 August 1898, *RG 80,* E194, 342. For the orders once again to delay departure, see Long to Sampson, 4 August 1898, *RG 45,* Entry 19, no. 2, 141. Once again the Naval War board played a role. The delay was recommended in Sicard (for the Naval War Board) to Long, 4 August 1898, *RG 45,* NRC 371, vol. 2, p. 237. On the same day the Secretary of the Navy delayed the sailing of the colliers intended to support the Eastern Squadron (Long to Commander Eugene W. Watson, 4 August 1898, *RG 80,* E194, 346).
25. For the admiral's inquiry, see Sampson to Long, 5 August 1898, *RG 80,* E194, 348. For the recommendation of the Naval War Board against this course and Long's message to Sampson, see Sicard (for Naval War Board) to Long, 6 August 1898, *RG 45,* NRC 371, vol. 2, 246; and Long to Sampson, 6 August 1898, *RG 80,* E194, 347.
26. For Miles's activity, see Millis, *Martial Spirit,* 321. For the proposal of Gómez, see report of Lieutenant Thomas W. Ryan (commanding the *Peoria*) in *RG 45,* NRC 372, 228–229.

CHAPTER 13

1. For Miles to Shafter, 3 July 1898, and Shafter to Miles, 4 July 1898, see Nelson A. Miles, *Serving the Republic: Memoirs of the Civil and Military Life of Nelson A. Miles Lieutenant General United States Army* (New York and London, 1911), 282–283.

2. For the exchange between Toral and Shafter, see Shafter to Commanding General Spanish Forces Santiago de Cuba, 4 July 1898, and Toral to Shafter, 4 July 1898, quoted in French Ensor Chadwick, *The Relations of the United States and Spain: The Spanish-American War* (New York, 1911), vol. 2, pp. 193–194.

3. Arthur L. Wagner's *Report of the Santiago Campaign 1898* (Kansas City, 1908) reports on the evacuation (see p. 100). For arrangements for the evacuation, see Shafter to Alger, 5 July 1898, *IC*, vol. 2, pp. 957–958. Pershing is quoted in Herschel V. Cashin et al., *Under Fire With the Tenth U.S. Cavalry* (New York, 1969 reprint edition), 213. For the observations of the Spanish officer, see Lieutenant José Müller y Tejeiro, *Battles and Capitulation of Santiago de Cuba* (Washington, D.C., 1899), 98–99. The British consul is quoted in Chadwick, *Spanish-American War*, vol. 2, p. 199.

4. For initial Spanish reactions in Santiago de Cuba, see Müller, *Battles and Capitulation*, 127; Jack Cameron Dierks, *A Leap to Arms: The Cuban Campaign of 1898* (Philadelphia and New York, 1970), 127. For the plan to sink the *Reina Mercedes*, see Toral to Blanco, 3 July 1898, in Spain, Ministry of the Marine, *Correspondencia oficial referente á las operaciones navales durante la guerra con Los Estados Unidos en 1898* (Madrid, 1899), 162. See also Pascual Cervera y Topete, *The Spanish-American War: A Collection of Documents Relative to the Squadron Operations in the West Indies* (Washington, D.C., 1899), 121. For the sinking of the *Reina Mercedes*, see Müller, *Battles and Capitulation*, 114; Chadwick, *Spanish-American War*, vol. 2, p. 197; Sampson to Long, rec. 6 July 1898, *AF*, file 8, roll 234; and Giles B. Harber to Long, 30 November 1900, *AF*, file 8, roll 233, a retrospective account by an observer. For a Spanish criticism of this decision, see J. Rodríguez Martínez, *Los desastres y la regeneración de España: relatos y impresiones* (La Coruña, 1899), 26–29.

5. For Spanish accounts of the incident on the *Harvard*, see Cervera, *Spanish-American War*, 157–159, and Víctor Concas y Palau, *The Squadron of Admiral Cervera* (Washington, D.C., 1900), 106. For American accounts, see Sampson to Long, 6 July 1898, *RG 45*, Entry 40, no. 2, 263; Chadwick, *Spanish-American War*, vol. 2, p. 189; W. A. M. Goode, *With Sampson Through the War: Being an Account of the Naval Operations of the North Atlantic Squadron During the Spanish American War of 1898* (New York, 1899), 256–257. Accounts differ slightly as to the time of the incident and the number of injuries. For the Spanish admiral's praise of his treatment, see Cervera to Blanco, 9 July 1898, in Cervera, *Spanish-American War*, 126. The wounded Spanish soldiers captured at El Caney received medical treatment from their American captors, much to their surprise. At this act the "prisoners showed signs of great amazement and gratitude, evidently as if they had expected harsh treatment." (See the report of Major Frank J. Ives, a surgeon of volunteers, in *ARWD 98*, 820.) For the confinement, see Cervera to Auñón, 20 September 1898, in Cervera, *Spanish-American War*, 141; and Chadwick, *Spanish-American War*, vol. 2, pp. 189–190. At Seavey's Island 20 officers and 1,661 enlisted men were held. Admiral Cervera, with seventy-eight officers and fourteen enlisted men, stayed at Annapolis.

6. For correspondence relating to Shafter's plans in regard to prisoners, see Shafter to Corbin (two messages), 5 July 1898, *ARWD 98*, 108; Shafter to Corbin, 6 July 1898, *CWS*, vol. 1, p. 95; and *ARWD 98*, 66. For the unilateral return of prisoners

on July 5, see Chadwick, *Spanish-American War*, vol. 2, pp. 193–194. For Hobson's return, see *ibid.*, 206–207. Stephen Crane described the reaction of the army when Hobson and his men approached the American lines: "Then the men of the regular army did a thing. They arose *en masse* and came to 'Attention.' Then the men of the regular army did another thing. They slowly lifted every weather-beaten hat and dropped it until it touched the knee. Then there was a magnificent silence, broken only by the measured hoofbeats of the little company's horses as they rode through the gap. It was solemn, funereal, this splendid silent welcome of a brave man by men who stood on a hill which they had earned out of blood and death." After this initial demonstration cheers and greetings rang out. (Stephen Crane, *Wounds in the Rain: War Stories* [Freeport, N.Y., 1972 reprint edition], 298.)

7. Washington's message to Shafter is Corbin to Shafter, 4 July 1898, *CWS*, vol. 1, p. 84. For the message concerning reinforcements, see Alger to Shafter, 4 July 1898, *IC*, vol. 2, p. 949. Shafter's inquiry about reinforcements is in Shafter to Corbin, 4 July 1898, *ARWD 98*, 107. His longer message dealing with the consequences of Escario's entry is Shafter to Corbin, 4 July 1898, *CWS*, vol. 1, p. 87. For the dispatch of Miles with reinforcements, see *ARWD 98*, 30; and Chadwick, *Spanish-American War*, vol. 2, p. 199.

8. For Shafter's messages to the War Department, see Shafter to Corbin, 4 July 1898, *ARWD 98*, 108; and Shafter to Corbin, 4 July 1898, *ibid.*, 29–30. For his message to Sampson, see Shafter to Sampson, 4 July 1898, *BN 98*, 609.

9. For the diary of John E. Woodward, 5 July 1898, see USAMHI. For Roosevelt's polemic, see Roosevelt to Lodge, 5 July 1898, in Elting E. Morison, ed., *The Letters of Theodore Roosevelt* (Cambridge, Mass., 1951), vol. 2, p. 849.

10. For the first message to Shafter ordering consultation with Sampson, see Corbin to Shafter, 5 July 1898, *ARWD 98*, 109. For an account of the Washington discussions at this time, see David F. Healy, "McKinley as Commander-in-Chief," in Paolo Coletta, ed., *Threshold to American Internationalism: Essays on the Foreign Policies of William McKinley* (New York, 1970), 96. For the exchange between Washington and Santiago de Cuba initiated by Shafter after his receipt of the order to consult with Sampson, see Shafter to Corbin, 5 July 1898, and Corbin to Shafter, 5 July 1898, *CWS*, vol. 1, p. 89.

11. For proposals to Sampson for a meeting, see Shafter to Sampson (2:13 P.M.), 5 July 1898, *BN 98*, 609; Shafter to Sampson (3:12 P.M.), 5 July 1898, *ibid.*, 610; and Shafter to Sampson (3:27 P.M.), 5 July 1898, *ibid.* For Alger's proposition, see Corbin to Shafter (4:30 P.M.), 5 July 1898, *CWS*, vol. 1, p. 91. Instructions to Sampson are in Long to Sampson, 5 July 1898, *RG 45*, Entry 19, no. 2, 86.

12. Sicard for the Naval War Board to Long, 5 July 1898, *RG 45*, NRC 371, vol. 2, 150; and Chadwick, *Spanish-American War*, vol. 2, pp. 202–203. Alger later argued that no danger of mines existed in the channel after July 3 because the contact mines had been removed to permit Cervera's ships to go out and the electrical mines were largely disabled (Russell A. Alger, *The Spanish-American War* [New York, 1901], 232). The Secretary of the Navy's letter to his colleague in the War Department on operations at Santiago de Cuba is Long to Alger, 5 July 1898, *RG 45*, NRC 372, 152.

13. Sampson's comment on Shafter's plan is in Sampson to Long, 15 July 1898, *BN 98*, 609. Chadwick's maxim is in his *Spanish-American War*, vol. 2, p. 202. Sampson remained convinced that Shafter should have adopted his proposal to move on the harbor entrance instead of proceeding by an interior route to the city proper. Note his statement of July 15: "I do not know why a change of plan occurred, unless it was that the troops on landing advanced themselves so far on the roads toward Santiago before any specific plan of operations had been decided upon that it was found inconvenient to divert them to other points. I believe that such

adherence would have resulted in a much quicker surrender of the Spanish troops, and with much less loss of life, excepting possibly to the Navy, which would have borne the brunt of the attack instead of the Army. The urgency, of course, was lessened by the destruction of the fleet on their sortie from the harbor, but the difficulty of the entrance remained much the same.'' (Sampson to Long, 15 July 1898, *BN 98,* 609.) Samspon's views were attractive, except that because of the removal of the contact mines and the inefficiency of the electrical mines his estimate of the dangers in the channel, once Cervera had departed, was probably in error.

14. Minutes of a conversation between Chadwick and Shafter, 6 July 1898, *BN 98,* 610. For accounts of the meeting, see Chadwick, *Spanish-American War,* vol. 2, pp. 205–206; and Margaret Leech, *In the Days of McKinley* (New York, 1959), 265.

15. The text of the letter and the circumstances of its drafting are described in Chadwick, *Spanish-American War,* vol. 2, pp. 204–205. For Shafter's later version, one that seems far less plausible than that of Chadwick, see Shafter to Corbin, 1 November 1899, in Papers of General Henry Clark Corbin, Manuscript Division, box 1, Library of Congress, Washington, D.C.

16. For Shafter's report to the War Department, see Shafter to Corbin, 7 July 1898, *ARWD 98,* 110. Corbin responded immediately in favorable terms: "Your long dispatch concerning second demand on city received and approved. We will be very glad if you can finish up that work without another assault." (Corbin to Shafter, 7 July 1898, *CWS,* vol. 1, p. 107.) Shafter's message to Sampson, 7 July 1898, is in *AF,* file 8, roll 234. Of the few authorities who take issue with the navy's views on forcing an entrance at Santiago de Cuba, Walter Millis is prehaps the most forthright. He did not think that the loss of one armored ship would have made any difference; if one was sunk in the entrance it would have accomplished the purpose associated with the attempt of the *Merrimac.* This line of thought ignores the question of whether the possible gain was commensurate with the risk. It also ignores the contingency that Spain might have received aid from a European power or that Germany might have created difficulties in the Pacific. These were indeed unlikely contingencies, but planning must often proceed on the basis of the "worst case." (Walter Millis, *The Martial Spirit: A Study of Our War With Spain* [Boston and New York, 1931], 296–297.) Millis was on sounder ground when he expressed the view that the navy might have attempted to drag the channel for mines. It made no attempt of this nature.

17. For explicit acknowledgement of the importance of the naval victory, see Wagner, *Santiago Campaign,* 151–152.

18. For George Kennan's observations, see his *Campaigning in Cuba* (New York, 1899), 148–149. For transport problems, see Chadwick, *Spanish-American War,* vol. 2, p. 105.

19. For the problems of the hospital, see Report of Colonel Charles R. Greenleaf, Chief Surgeon, 24 August 1898, *ARWD 98,* 73.

20. For Greenleaf's views, see *ibid.* For the report of Ives, see *ARWD 98,* 821.

21. For information concerning Shafter's supply problems and efforts to make improvements, see Grahan A. Cosmas, *An Army for Empire: The United States Army in the Spanish-American War* (Columbia, Mo., 1971), 217–218.

22. Shafter's comments on difficulties with transports are in Shafter to Corbin, 7 July 1898, *IC,* vol. 2, p. 971. Shafter got some assistance from the War Department. Corbin cabled back, "The President directs that you order transports to stand in by the shore and enforce demand. . . ." (Corbin to Shafter, 7 July 1898, in *CWS,* vol. 1, p. 107). For the report of Davis's charges, see Corbin to Shafter, 7 July 1898, in *ibid.,* 106. For Shafter's response to these charges, see Shafter to Corbin, 9 July 1898, in *ibid.,* 113.

23. Coleman is quoted in Virgil Carrington Jones, *Roosevelt's Rough Riders* (New

York, 1971), 226. For Roosevelt's attitude, see Roosevelt to Lodge, 7 July 1898, in Morison, ed., *Letters of Theodore Roosevelt*, vol. 2, p. 850.

24. Reported in Walter W. Ward, *Springfield in the Spanish-American War* (Easthampton, Mass., 1899), 104–105.

25. Miles's warning to Shafter about his uncovered right flank came in Miles to Shafter, 7 July 1898, in *RG 108*, Entry 118: "Letters sent from Florida, Cuba, and Puerto Rico, May–Sept. 1898," (hereafter cited as *RG 108*, Entry 118). Shafter's response is Shafter to Corbin, 7 July 1898, *CWS*, vol. 1, p. 106. His optimistic report on the strength of his position is Shafter to Corbin, 8 July 1898, *ARWD 98*, 114. Sergeant Bivins's letter is quoted in Willard B. Gatewood, Jr., *"Smoked Yankees" and the Struggle for Empire: Letters from Negro Soldiers, 1898-1902* (Urbana, Ill., Chicago, and London, 1971), 49.

26. For artillery dispositions, see Wagner, *Santiago Campaign*, 101–102; and Chadwick, *Spanish-American War*, vol. 2, p. 217.

27. Shafter's report of his intentions to Washington is in Shafter to Corbin, 8 July 1898, *ARWD 98*, 114.

28. For Toral's reply, see Chadwick, *Spanish-American War*, vol. 2, p. 214.

29. Shafter's message to Washington is Shafter to Alger, 8 July 1898, *ARWD 98*, 114. This development was reported to the American squadron (see Shafter to Sampson, 9 July 1898, in *BN 98*, 611). To this message Sampson responded with some suggestions regarding the arrangements for the Spanish surrender: "I think all batteries with guns, magazines, etc., and all fortifications and their materials should be surrendered intact, all contact mines taken up, and all observation mines destroyed so that ships can at once enter without danger" (Sampson to Shafter, 9 July 1898, in *ibid.*, 620).

30. Corbin to Shafter, 9 July 1898, *ARWD 98*, 114.

31. Shafter to Alger, 9 July 1898, *CWS*, vol. 1, pp. 117–118.

32. Corbin to Shafter, 9 July 1898, *ARWD 98*, 115.

33. For Shafter's communication to Toral, see Chadwick, *Spanish-American War*, vol. 2, p. 216. For the message to the War Department, see Shafter to Corbin, 10 July 1898, *ARWD 98*, 115.

34. For the extension of the American line, see *ARWD 98*, 67–68; and Chadwick, *Spanish-American War*, vol. 2, p. 210. For García's movements, see Felipe Martínez Arango, *Cronología crítica de la guerra hispanocubanoamericana*, 2d edition, (Santiago de Cuba, 1960), 129; and Shafter to Corbin, 11 July 1898, *CWS*, vol. 1, p. 125. For Shafter's comments on the right flank, see Shafter to Alger, 10 July 1898, *CWS*, vol. 1, p. 123.

35. Roosevelt to Lodge, 10 July 1898, in Morison, ed., *Letters of Theodore Roosevelt*, vol. 2, p. 850.

36. Toral's refusal to surrender is reported in Shafter to Corbin, 10 July 1898, *CWS*, vol. 1, p. 123. For the arrangements concerning the bombardment, see Shafter to Sampson, 10 July 1898, in *BN 98*, 611–612. For an order to begin the bombardment as planned, see Shafter to Sampson, 10 July 1898, in *ibid.*, 612. For the bombardment, see Chadwick, *Spanish-American War*, vol. 2, p. 220; and Shafter to Corbin, 11 July 1898, in *CWS*, vol. 1, p. 125. Shafter had no intention of attacking while the bombardment took place (Shafter to Alger, 11 July 1898, in *ibid.*). Shafter's instructions for resumption of the bombardment are in Shafter to Sampson, 11 July 1898, *BN 98*, 612.

37. For the report of the Board of Investigation to Sampson, 24 July 1898, see *AF*, file 8, roll 235. See also *Squadron Bulletin*, 11 July 1898, *AF*, file 8, roll 234. For Chadwick's response to criticism of the naval bombardment, see his *Spanish-American War*, vol. 2, 230–231. For the suspension of the bombardment, see *BN 98*, 613. Spanish casualties from the bombardment were seven killed and over fifty

wounded. In small-arms fire the Americans lost two killed and two wounded. (Cosmas, *Army for Empire*, 225.)

38. Goodrich to Long, 10 July 1898, quoted in Gardner Weld Allen, ed., *Papers of John Davis Long 1897-1904* (Boston, 1939), 154.

39. Alger's proposal is in Alger to Shafter, 10 July 1898, *CWS*, vol. 1, p. 125. For Alger's defense of this action, see his *Spanish-American War*, 198. The exchange between Shafter and Toral is printed in Chadwick, *Spanish-American War*, vol. 2, p. 223.

40. For the arrangements leading to Miles's movement to Santiago de Cuba, see Leech, *In the Days of McKinley*, 263. For notice to Shafter of Miles's role, see Corbin to Shafter, 8 July 1898, in *CWS*, vol. 1, p. 110. For Shafter's message to Washington about his health at this time, see Shafter to Corbin, 10 July 1898, in *ibid.*, 120. Alger gives his account of his role in the episode in his *Spanish-American War*, 204. See also Leech, *In the Days of McKinley*, 264.

41. For Miles's early planning, see his *Serving the Republic*, 285. He left Charleston, S.C., on July 8 with about thirty-five hundred troops loaded on the *Yale, Columbia*, and *Duchess*. For his message to Sampson on his plans, see Miles to Sampson, 11 July 1898, *RG 108*, Entry 118, 9. See also *BN 98*, 612. For Sampson's plans and preparations, see Hobson to Sampson, 18 July 1898, *AF*, file 8, roll 235. For additional correspondence on this plan, see Miles to Shafter, 12 July 1898, *RG 108*, Entry 118, 8–9; Miles to Sampson, 13 July 1898, *AF*, file 8, roll 234; Sampson to U.S.S. *Yale, Columbia*, and *Duchess*, 13 July 1898, *AF*, file 8, roll 234; and Miles to Alger, 14 July 1898, *RG 108*, Entry 118, 20–21. For other information, see Miles, *Serving the Republic*, 268; Society of the Army of Santiago de Cuba, *The Santiago Campaign: Reminiscences of the Operations for the Capture of Santiago de Cuba in the Spanish-American War, June and July 1898* (Richmond, Va., 1927), 265–266; and Nelson A. Miles, "The War with Spain—II," *North American Review* 168 (June, 1899): 755–757.

42. For Shafter's message, see Shafter to Alger, 12 July 1898, *CWS*, vol. 1, p. 132. His message to Miles is Shafter to Miles, *RG 108*, Entry 121, vol. 2 of 2, p. 8.

43. For the appeals to the War Department, see Shafter to Corbin, 12 July 1898, *ARWD 98*, 117; and Miles to War Department, 12 July 1898, in Chadwick, *Spanish-American War*, vol. 2, p. 231. See also Miles to Shafter, 12 July 1898, *RG 108*, Entry 118, 10–11.

44. For the letter to the Spanish commander, see Shafter to Toral, 12 July 1898, in Chadwick, *Spanish-American War*, vol. 2, p. 225. For the response, see Toral to Shafter, 12 July 1898, in *ibid.*, 225–226. Toral's reiteration of his earlier proposition, sent separately, stated in full, "I have the honor to insist upon my proposition to evacuate the Plaza and the territory of the division of Cuba under conditions hereinafter stated, for the [honor of the] Spanish arms, trusting that your chivalry and sentiment as a soldier will make you appreciate exactly the situation, and therefore must a solution be found that leaves the honor of my troops intact; otherwise you will comprehend that I shall see myself obliged to now make defense as far as my strength shall permit." (Toral to Shafter, 12 July 1898, in *ibid.*, 228.)

45. For this information, see *ibid.*, 233–234. The actions of Miles and Shafter were approved in Alger to Miles, 13 July 1898, *CWS*, vol. 1, pp. 134–135. For Miles's account, see his *Serving the Republic*, 287–288.

46. Mahan to Long, 17 June 1901, in Allen, ed., *Papers of John Davis Long*, 369–370. See also Mahan to Long, 21 August 1898, and Mahan to Long, 16 November 1898, in *ibid.*, 209–211, 267–268. Robert Seager notes that the navy had good reason for seeking to hasten Toral's surrender. The Navy Department was then preparing to counter the movements of Admiral Cámara and it was receiving disquieting reports about German activities in Manila. (Robert Seager, *Alfred Thayer Mahan: The Man and His Letters* [Annapolis, 1977], 386–387.)

47. For the reconfirmation, see Alger to Shafter, 13 July 1898, *ARWD 98*, 117. Permission to delay the attack is given in Alger to Miles, 13 July 1898, *RG 108*, Entry 121, vol. 2 of 2, p. 11.

48. For the Secretary of War's request, see Alger to Long, 13 July 1898, *AF*, file 8, roll 234. Long's acknowledgement is Long to Alger, 14 July 1898, *CWS*, vol. 1, p. 141. His message to his admiral at Santiago de Cuba is Long to Sampson, 13 July 1898, *AF*, file 8, roll 234. Sampson later included in a report a somewhat variant text of this message that does not differ in meaning (*BN 98*, 613).

49. For Long's feelings, see his diary entry of 13 July 1898, quoted in Lawrence Shaw Mayo, ed., *America of Yesterday: As Reflected in the Journal of John Davis Long* (Boston, 1923), 203.

50. For Sampson's views, see Sampson to Long, 14 July 1898, *BN 98*, 625. A day later he reiterated this argument, and also criticized Shafter's failure to prevent publication of information concerning army operations. This looseness he thought "too manifest for discussion." He urged that the Navy Department do something to counteract "such an invidious and false position before the country through the very unwise publication of Shafter's telegrams." (Sampson to Long, 15 July 1898, *AF*, file 8, roll 234.)

51. For Leech's view, see her *In the Days of McKinley*, 266. For the flare-up between Mahan and Alger, see Long Diary, 13 July 1898, quoted in Mayo, ed., *America of Yesterday*, 204. See also Long, *New Navy*, vol. 2, p. 152.

52. For correspondence concerning naval representation in the negotiations with Toral, see Sampson to Shafter, 13 July 1898, in *BN 98*, 624; and Shafter to Sampson, 13 July 1898, in *ibid.*

53. Alger to Miles, 13 July 1898, *ARWD 98*, 31; and Alger to Shafter, 13 July 1898, *CWS*, vol. 1, p. 138.

54. John D. Miley, *In Cuba With Shafter* (New York, 1899), 163. General Joseph Wheeler lent support to the views of Miley and Shafter in his *The Santiago Campaign 1898* (New York, 1898), 183.

55. For Müller's description of the situation in Santiago de Cuba, see his *Battles and Capitulation*, 46, 63. For the views of the Spanish army in Cuba, see Blanco to Correa, 9 July 1898, quoted in Juan Ortega Rubio, *Historia de la regencia de María Cristina Hapsbourg-Lorena* (Madrid, 1906), volume 4, p. 408. For the Prime Minister's response, see Sagasta to Blanco, 12 July 1898, quoted in Duque de Tetuán, *Apuntes del Ex-Ministro de Estado Duque de Tetuán para la defensa de la política internacional y gestión diplomática del gobierno liberal-conservador desde el 28 de Marzo de 1895 á 29 de Septiembre de 1897* (n.p., 1902), vol. 2, pp. 133–134.

56. For Linares's message, see Linares to Correa, 12 July 1898, quoted in Müller, *Battles and Capitulation*, 138–139. See also Wheeler, *Santiago Campaign*, 132–134. For the message of the Minister of War, see Correa to Blanco, 12 July 1898, quoted in Ortega Rubio, *Historia de la regencia*, vol. 4, pp. 408–409. Blanco responded with word that he would call his generals together for another conference (Blanco to Correa, 13 July 1898, in *ibid.*, 410). The decision in Havana is reported in Duque de Tetuán, *Apuntes de Tetuán*, 132–134. For additional information on this correspondence, see Jerónimo Bécker, *Historia de las relaciones exteriores de España durante el siglo XIX (apuntes para la historia diplomática)*, Volume 3: *1868-1900* (Madrid, 1926), 890. See also Severo Gómez Núñez, *La guerra hispano-americana. La Habana. Influencia de las plazas de guerra* (Madrid, 1900), 143–144. For the consultation and associated activities, see Juan de Arco, *Montero Ríos* (Madrid, 1947), 112; Gabriel Maura Gamazo, *Historia crítica del reinado de don Alfonso XIII durante su menoridad bajo la regencia de su madre doña María Cristina de Austria* (Barcelona, 1925), vol. 2, pp. 45–46.

57. For Toral's message agreeing to surrender, see Chadwick, *Spanish-American War*,

vol. 2, pp. 236–237. See also Wheeler, *Santiago Campaign*, 335–336. For Shafter's report of this action, see Shafter to Corbin, 14 July 1898, in *ARWD 98*, 119. The Adjutant General's response is Corbin to Shafter, 14 July 1898, in *ibid*. The commanding general's report is Miles to Alger, 14 July 1898, in *ibid.*, 120.

58. Miles's directive to Shafter is Miles to Shafter, 14 July 1898, *RG 108*, Entry 118, 9. For the relation of Sampson to these matters, see Chadwick, *Spanish-American War*, vol. 2, p. 237. See also Miles to Sampson, 14 July 1898 (9:25 A.M.), and Sampson to Miles, 14 July 1898 (10:45 A.M.), both in *BN 98*, 626. On the question of naval representation in discussions of the surrender, see messages from Shafter and Miles to Sampson, 14 July 1898, in *ibid.*, 613, 626. See also Sampson to Miles, *RG 108*, Entry 121, vol. 2 of 2, p. 15.

59. These events are chronicled in Chadwick, *Spanish-American War*, vol. 2, pp. 239–241. Toral did not delay in order to accomplish any military purposes. On July 15 he told Frederick Ramsden, the British consul, that he had made all the necessary arrangements for capitulation and only awaited formal authority from Madrid to surrender. If it did not arrive, he told Ramsden that he would capitulate anyway, even at the risk of a court-martial. (See *ibid.*, 241.) For another account, see Wheeler, *Santiago Campaign*, 122–125.

60. Sampson's inquiry is Sampson to Shafter, 15 July 1898, *BN 98*, 626. The response is Shafter to Sampson, 15 July 1898, *ibid*. Shafter's message to Miles, 15 July 1898, is in *RG 108*, Entry 121, vol. 2 of 2, p. 23. The inquiry from Washington is Corbin to Shafter, 15 July 1898, *CWS*, vol. 1, p. 145. The reply from Santiago de Cuba is Shafter to Corbin, 15 July 1898, *ARWD 98*, 120–121. See also Miles to Shafter, 15 July 1898, *RG 108*, Entry 118, 24. The Secretary of War's suspicions are expressed in Corbin to Shafter, 15 May 1898, in *IC*, vol. 2, p. 1,014. The reply is Shafter to Corbin, 15 July 1898, in *ibid.*, 1,015. Wheeler replied to inquiries from Shafter on the afternoon of July 15 with the soothing information that Mason and Toral had assured him Madrid would give consent (Wheeler, *Santiago Campaign*, 339).

61. Washington's consternation is expressed in Alger to Shafter, 15 July 1898, in *ARWD 98*, 121. Shafter's reply is Shafter to Corbin, 15 July 1898, in *ibid.*, 121. The views of Miles are in Miles to Shafter, 15 July 1898, *RG 108*, Entry 118, 24. The final word from Washington is in Corbin to Shafter, 15 July 1898, *CWS*, vol. 1, p. 148. Chadwick reported still another telegram from the War Department early on the morning of July 16 that stated, "The only concession is that the prisoners taken shall be paroled and sent to Spain." Shafter responded, "Surrender was made by Toral yesterday afternoon absolutely on conditions of returning troops to Spain. Delay was caused by the commissioners on his part insisting on approval of Madrid. I think they fear death when they get home. We may have to fight them yet." (Quoted in Chadwick, *Spanish-American War*, vol. 2, p. 243.)

62. For the discussion in Santiago de Cuba, see Müller, *Battles and Capitulation*, 140–143.

63. For the Spanish Commander's announcement, see Toral to Shafter, 15 July 1898, in Chadwick, *Spanish-American War*, vol. 2, pp. 243–244. For the message to the War Department, see Shafter to Corbin, 16 July 1898, *ARWD 98*, 122–123. Shafter reported even more briefly to Miles, "They surrender." Shafter to Miles, 16 July 1898, *RG 108*, Entry 121, vol. 2 of 2, 26.

64. The President's message is McKinley to Shafter, 16 July 1898, *ARWD 98*, 123. For the Dawes diary, 16 July 1898, see Bascom Timmons, ed., *A Journal of the McKinley Years by Charles G. Dawes* (Chicago, 1950), 164.

65. Wood to Mrs. Wood, in Papers of Leonard Wood, box 190, Manuscript Division, Library of Congress, Washington, D.C. See also Hermann Hagedorn, *Leonard Wood: A Biography* (New York and London, 1931), vol. 1, p. 180.

66. For the final actions of the commissioners, see Chadwick, *Spanish-American War*, vol. 2, pp. 243–245. For Wheeler's observations, see his *Santiago Campaign*,

128–130. See also Leech, *In the Days of McKinley*, 269. Toral was required to defend his actions at Santiago de Cuba before a judicial panel. For the text of his defense, see General de Brigada Julián Suárez Inclán, *Defensa del General Toral ante el Consejo Supremo de Guerra y Marina reunido y constituído en Sala de Justicia* (Madrid, 1899). He was acquitted. For the judgment, see Severo Gómez Núñez, *The Spanish-American War: Blockades and Coast Defense* (Washington, D.C., 1899), 111–120.

67. For the complete text of the articles of capitulation, see Chadwick, *Spanish-American War*, vol. 2, pp. 245–247. Wheeler also reprinted it in his *Santiago Campaign*, 135–137.

68. For Chadwick's activities, see Shafter to Sampson, 16 July 1898, *BN 98*, 627; and Chadwick, *Spanish-American War*, vol. 2, p. 245. For Sampson's comments, see his report, 1 August 1898, in *BN 98*, 627; and Chadwick, *Spanish-American War*, vol. 2, p. 247.

69. Shafter's comment is quoted in Millis, *Martial Spirit*, 324. For Toral's remark to Wheeler, see the latter's *Santiago Campaign*, 131–132. For Toral's reason for surrendering all the garrisons, see Suárez Inclán, *Defensa del General Toral*, 61–65. Gómez Núñez commented on this matter in his *La guerra hispano-americana. Santiago de Cuba.* 226–233. See also Millis, *Martial Spirit*, 324.

70. The Governor-General's quixotic views are in Blanco to Correa, 17 July 1898, quoted in Duque de Tetuán, *Apuntes del Tetuán*, vol. 2, pp. 134–135. When Blanco announced the capitulation of Santiago de Cuba, he was at pains to note that it had occurred "without any intervention of my authority" (Blanco to Correa, 17 July 1898, quoted in Alberto Risco, *Apuntes biográficos del Excmo. Sr. Almirante D. Pascual Cervera y Topete* [Toledo, 1920], 162).

71. For the surrender ceremonies, see Miley, *In Cuba With Shafter*, 185–186. This account is reprinted in Chadwick, *Spanish-American War*, vol. 2, p. 248. See also William R. Shafter, "The Capture of Santiago de Cuba," *Century*, 57 (February, 1899): 628–629. For Scovel's activities, see Shafter to Alger, 24 July 1898, *CWS*, vol. 1, p. 176; and Millis, *Martial Spirit*, 326. The order revoking Scovel's license, 26 July 1898, is in *CWS*, vol. 1, p. 179.

72. Davis became annoyed with Shafter at the time of the landing when the General would not let him go ashore in a small boat with the troops. When Shafter ruled that no reporters could board the small boats, Davis persisted, claiming to be a writer, not a reporter. Shafter angrily retorted, "I do not care a damn what you are. I'll treat you all alike." Colonel McClernand, who remembered this incident, believed that it may have influenced later reports on Shafter from Santiago de Cuba (E. J. McClernand, "The Santiago Campaign," in Society of the Army of Santiago de Cuba, *The Santiago Campaign: Reminiscences of the Operations for the Capture of Santiago de Cuba in the Spanish-American War, June and July, 1898* [Richmond, Va., 1927], 10–11). Shortly after the capitulation Shafter had some representatives of the New York *Journal* arrested for attempting to post signs in Santiago de Cuba reading "Remember the *Maine*." This act brought worried messages from the War Department, which looked more favorably upon the *Journal* than certain other New York newspapers. Shafter responded that he was not excluding all reporters, and he would happily accept "respectable" ones. (Alger to Shafter, 22 July 1898, in *CWS*, vol. 1, p. 172; Shafter to Alger, 23 July 1898, in *ibid.*, 174; and Alger to Shafter, 23 July 1898, in *ibid.*, 175.) For Shafter's rebuttal of charges made by Davis, see Shafter to Corbin, 23 July 1898, in *ibid.*, 172.

73. Chadwick, *Spanish-American War*, vol. 2, pp. 252–253; Sampson to Shafter (two messages), 18 July 1898, *AF*, file 8, roll 235. Before any ship could enter the channel, the mines had to be taken up. Seven contact mines were pulled out; two of the electrical mines opposite the Socapa firing station were exploded, but two others did not fire. It was reported to Sampson that apparently five mines controlled from

the Estrella firing station had been exploded when the *Merrimac* ran into the channel. (Louis J. Gulliver, "Sampson and Shafter at Santiago," *United States Naval Institute Proceedings*, 65 [June 1939]: 799–806.) See also Sampson to Shafter (two messages), 18 July 1898, *AF*, file 8, roll 235.

74. Wells is quoted in Jones, *Roosevelt's Rough Riders*, 245. Bennett is quoted in John Stronach, "The 34th Michigan Volunteer Infantry," *Michigan History*, 30 (April–June, 1946): 299.

CHAPTER 14

1. For Shafter's inquiry about the *Alvarado*, see Shafter to Alger, 16 July 1898, in *CWS*, vol. 1, p. 156. For the response, see Alger to Shafter, 17 July 1898, in *ibid*. For reiteration of orders to take the vessels, see Corbin to Shafter, 17 July 1898, in *ibid*. For Sampson's protest, see Sampson to Shafter, 17 July 1898, *AF*, file 8, roll 235. For the response, see Shafter to Sampson, 17 July 1898, *AF*, file 8, roll 235. For Shafter's version of events, see Shafter to Alger, 17 July 1898, *CWS*, vol. 1, p. 157. Sampson's referral to the Navy Department is in Sampson to Long, 17 July 1898, *RG 80*, E194, 286. Sampson conveyed his message to the Navy Department to Shafter, indicating that he would keep his men on the vessels in question until the President ruled (Sampson to Shafter [1:40 A.M.] 18 July 1898, *AF*, file 8, roll 235). Long's response is Long to Sampson, 18 July 1898, *RG 45*, NRC 371, vol. 2, p. 183. Shafter's conciliatory message to Sampson is Shafter to Sampson, 18 July 1898, *AF*, file 8, roll 235. For the Secretary of War's final views, see Alger to Shafter, 19 July 1898, *CWS*, vol. 1, p. 164. For arrangements regarding the ships, see Sampson to Shafter, 19 July 1898, *AF*, file 8, roll 235. For a full account of these events, see French Ensor Chadwick, *The Relations of the United States and Spain: The Spanish-American War*, (New York, 1911), vol. 2, pp. 249–252. For return of the ships to the army, see McKinley to Long, 23 July 1898, *AF*, file 8, roll 235; Alger to Shafter, 23 July 1898, *CWS*, vol. 1, p. 175; Sampson to Shafter, 24 July 1898, *AF*, file 8, roll 236; and Shafter to Sampson, 25 July 1898, *AF*, file 8, roll 235.

2. For the initial exchange on this question, see Sampson to Long, 17 July 1898, *RG 80*, E194, 286; and Long to Sampson, 18 July 1898, *RG 45*, NRC 371, vol. 2, p. 183. For Shafter's position, see Shafter to Alger, 19 July 1898, *CWS*, vol. 1, pp. 163–164. Sampson's effort to arrange the signature is in Sampson to Shafter, 31 July 1898, *AF*, file 8, roll 236. The refusal came in Shafter to Sampson, 1 August 1898, *AF*, file 8, roll 237. A slightly variant version of this message, not altered in substance, is in *BN 98*, 630. For Sampson's final comment, see Sampson to Long, 4 August 1898, *AF*, file 8, roll 237. See also Sampson to Shafter, 2 August 1898, *AF*, file 8, roll 237.

3. Long Diary, 22 July 1898, quoted in Lawrence Shaw Mayo, ed., *America of Yesterday, As Reflected in the Journal of John Davis Long* (Boston, 1923), 204–206.

4. For Margaret Leech's comment, see her *In the Days of McKinley* (New York, 1959), 273. For the War Department's statement, see Corbin to Lawton, 16 August 1898, *CWS*, vol. 1, p. 231.

5. For García's letter, see García to Shafter, 17 July 1898, quoted in Philip S. Foner, *The Spanish-Cuban-American War and the Birth of American Imperialism 1895–1902*, Volume 2: *1898–1902* (New York and London, 1972), 369–370. The Spanish text is in Cosme Torriente y Peraza, *Calixto García cooperó con las fuerzas de los EE.UU. en 1898, cumpliendo órdenes del gobierno Cubano* (Havana, 1952), 53–55. For García's resignation and letter on this matter to Gómez, see Foner,

Spanish-Cuban-American War, vol. 2, p. 369; and Torriente y Peraza, *Calixto García cooperó* . . . , 56–57.

6. Shafter's response to García is quoted in Virgil Carrington Jones, *Roosevelt's Rough Riders* (New York, 1971), 251–252.

7. Shafter's explanation of his dealings with García is in Shafter to Alger, 29 July 1898, *CWS,* vol. 1, p. 185. For the views of Emilio Roig de Leuchsenring, see his *1895 y 1898: dos guerras cubanos: ensayo de revaloración* (Havana, 1945), 195–196. For Shafter's lack of courtesy to García, see Leech, *In the Days of McKinley,* 274. For growing tension between the Americans and Cubans, see the exchange of correspondence between General Lawton and Corbin, 16 August 1898, *CWS,* vol. 1, pp. 230–231. Lawton noted disturbances he attributed to the threatening behavior of the insurgent troops. Corbin instructed him to inform the Cuban leaders that unruly behavior would not be tolerated. For the visit of García to Washington, see Enrique Piñeyro, *Comó acabó la dominación de España en América* (Paris, 1908), 262–264.

8. For Shafter's desire to get the prisoners away as soon as possible, see Shafter to Corbin, 17 July 1898, in *ARWD 98,* 124. See also an earlier request, Shafter to Corbin, 16 July 1898, in *ibid.* For Shafter's explanation of his reason for not asking for parole, see Shafter to Corbin, 16 July 1898, *CWS,* vol. 1, p. 154. For Miley's own account of his efforts to draw in the Spanish garrisons outside Santiago de Cuba, see his *In Cuba With Shafter* (New York, 1899), 190–214. See also Chadwick, *Spanish-American War,* vol. 2, pp. 261–262. The latter authority mentions the fact that the Spanish garrisons would not lay down their arms unless American guards were provided because of the menacing attitude of the Cuban insurgents. For information on the efforts of Shafter to collect and repatriate prisoners, see Shafter to Corbin (two messages), 19 July 1898, in *CWS,* vol. 1, pp. 164, 166; Shafter to Corbin, 22 July 1898, in *ibid.,* 171; Shafter to Alger, 24 July 1898, in *ibid.,* 167–177; and Shafter to Corbin, 17 August 1898, in *ibid.,* 234.

9. For the procedure and cost of repatriation, see the report of the Quartermaster General, 31 October 1898, *ARWD 98,* 163–164; *IC,* vol. 1, p. 135; Russell A. Alger, *The Spanish-American War* (New York, 1901), 279; Chadwick, *Spanish-American War,* vol. 2, p. 264; Pascual Cervera y Topete, *The Spanish-American War: A Collection of Documents Relative to the Squadron Operations in the West Indies* (Washington, D.C., 1899), 141; and Frank J. Hecker, *Recollections of My Services and Experiences in the Spanish-American War 1898–1899* (Detroit, 1913), 19–22. For information about the men imprisoned at Portsmouth, New Hampshire, see Tomás Benítez Francés, *El 3 de Julio desde el "Vizcaya." El manuscrito de un combate* (El Ferrol, 1898), 207–235. See also Francisco Arderius, *La escuadra española en Santiago de Cuba. Diario de un testigo* (Barcelona, 1903), 188–196.

10. For early concern about disease, see Chadwick, *Spanish-American War,* vol. 2, pp. 253–254. See also Theodore Roosevelt, *The Rough Riders* (New York, 1961), 431. For Greenleaf's recommendations, see "Memorandum for Sanitary Precautions in Moving the Army From Its Present Line to the Landing Near the Pier of the Jaragua Iron Works in Santiago Bay," 12 July 1898, *RG 108,* Entry 121, vol. 2 of 2, pp. 4–6.

11. The original plan of the War Department is in Corbin to Shafter, 13 July 1898, *CWS,* vol. 1, pp. 135–136. The exchange between Washington and Santiago de Cuba on this plan is Shafter to Corbin, 14 July 1898, *ibid.,* 139; and Corbin to Shafter, *ibid.,* 141. The views of the Secretary of War are in Alger to Miles, 14 July 1898, *IC,* vol. 2, p. 1,352.

12. The commanding general's recommendations are in Miles to Shafter, 14 July 1898, *RG 108,* Entry 118, 21; and Miles to Shafter, 16 July 1898, *RG 108,* Entry 118, 34. Colonel Greenleaf had been urging Miles to detail troops for provost duty in order

to enforce quarantine regulations (Greenleaf to Gilmore, 15 July 1898, *RG 108*, Entry 121, vol. 2 of 2, pp. 19–20). For the performance of the Twenty-Fourth Infantry, see Theophilus G. Steward, *The Colored Regulars in the United States Army* (New York, 1969 reprint edition), 222–225. Of the original unit only 11 officers and 229 men sailed to Montauk Point on the transport *Nueces*. Miles continued to believe that blacks were more immune than whites (see Miles to Alger, 11 August 1898, *IC*, vol. 2, p. 1,163).

13. The exchange between Washington and Santiago de Cuba on this question is Corbin to Shafter, 16 July 1898, in *CWS*, vol. 1, p. 156; and Shafter to Corbin, 18 July 1898, in *ibid.*, 158. For the continuing advice of the commanding general, see Miles to Shafter, 18 July 1898, *ibid.*

14. For Shafter's message, see Shafter to Miles, 18 July 1898, in *ARWD 98*, 36. For Miles's response, see Miles to Shafter, 18 July 1898, in *ibid*. When Miles later sent some orders to Shafter from Puerto Rico the commander of the Fifth Army Corps complained directly to the War Department: "I don't wish to be small about anything, and I don't care to be raising questions, but I am either in command here or I am not, and if my command can be interfered with by similar orders to this there is no extent to which it may not go." Shafter to Corbin, 10 August 1898, *CWS*, vol. 1, pp. 218–219.

15. The camp song is quoted in Gregory Mason, *Remember the Maine* (New York, 1939), 278. For a good description of the post-capitulation situation, particularly as affected by lack of proper food and the like, see John H. Parker, *History of the Gatling Gun Detachment Fifth Army Corps at Santiago* (Kansas City, 1898), 193–204. For Roosevelt's observations, see *Rough Riders*, 133. For the observations of Walter W. Ward, see his *Springfield in the Spanish-American War* (Easthampton, Mass., 1899), 121–122.

16. For Bennett's views, see John Stronach, "The 34th Michigan Volunteer Infantry," *Michigan History*, 30 (April–June, 1946): 302–303. To another correspondent Bennett described his own problems, particularly his lack of clothing, and concluded, "I live in hopes for better treatment soon—not so much for my sake as for the boys who lie sick all around me. Their groans keep me awake half the night. I can only say it is awful." (*Ibid.*, 300.) For Dick's views, see Leech, *In the Days of McKinley*, 271. For a particularly lurid description of affairs, see Theodore Roosevelt's letter to Henry Cabot Lodge, 19 July 1898, in Elting E. Morison, ed., *The Letters of Theodore Roosevelt*, Volume 2: *The Years of Preparation* (Cambridge, 1951), 851–852.

17. For Shafter's request for medical support, see Shafter to Corbin, 19 July 1898, in *CWS*, vol. 1, p. 164. For his request for immune regiments, see Shafter to Corbin (two messages), 19 July 1898, in *ibid.*, 166. The reaction of the War Department is in Corbin to Shafter, 19 July 1898, *ibid.* Shafter's report on the situation is in Shafter to Corbin, 22 July 1898, *IC*, vol. 2, p. 1,038. The last counsel of the commanding general is in Miles to Shafter, 21 July 1898, *ARWD, 98*, 126–127. For the request from the dismounted cavalry division to go to Puerto Rico, see Wheeler to Shafter, 21 July 1898, quoted in Joseph Wheeler, *The Santiago Campaign 1898* (New York, 1898), 354. He offered his services directly to Miles also (Wheeler to Miles, 24 July 1898, in *ibid.*, 357–358). For Roosevelt's proposal, see Roosevelt to Alger, 23 July 1898, in Morison, ed., *Letters of Theodore Roosevelt*, vol. 2, pp. 859–860.

18. For Shafter's recommendation, see Shafter to Corbin, 23 July 1898, in *CWS*, vol. 1, pp. 172–173. For his second message, minimizing his difficulties, see Shafter to Alger, 23 July 1898 in *ibid.*, 174–175. The War Department's responses are Corbin to Shafter, 23 July 1898, in *ibid.*, 173; and Alger to Shafter, 23 July 1898, in *ibid.*, 175.

19. For the sick reports, see Shafter to Corbin, 24 July 1898, in *ibid.*; Shafter to Corbin,

25 July 1898, in *ibid.*, 178; Shafter to Corbin, 27 July 1898, in *ibid.*, 183; Shafter to Corbin, 28 July 1898, in *ibid.*, 185; and Shafter to Corbin, 29 July 1898, in *ibid.*, 187. For the Secretary of War's suggestion, see Alger to Shafter, 28 July 1898, *IC*, vol. 2, p. 1,052.

20. For the affair of the *Seneca* and *Concho*, see Alger to Shafter, and Corbin to Shafter, 1 August 1898, *CWS*, vol. 1, p. 191. All this apparently aroused President McKinley. Margaret Leech reports him as developing "misgivings" about Alger because of this affair. (Leech, *In the Days of McKinley*, 293.) Shafter's bitter reaction to criticism stemming from the affair of the transports is in Shafter to Corbin, 3 August 1898, in *CWS*, vol. 1, pp. 197–198. Shafter's complaint about the Surgeon General is in Shafter to Corbin, 29 July 1898, in *ibid.*, 186. Corbin's irritated response is Corbin to Shafter, 30 July 1898, in *ibid.*, 187.

21. Shafter's urgent message is Shafter to Corbin, 2 August 1898, *IC*, vol. 2, p. 1,061. For the conference at the White House, see Leech, *In the Days of McKinley*, 274–275; and Alger, *Spanish-American War*, 262. For Alger's message to Shafter after the meeting, see Alger to Shafter, 2 August 1898, *IC*, vol. 2, p. 1,063.

22. For the question of the relations between malaria and a yellow fever epidemic, see Roosevelt to Lodge, 31 July 1898, in Morison, ed., *Letters of Theodore Roosevelt*, vol. 2, pp. 861–862. For Roosevelt's letter, see Roosevelt to Shafter, 3 August 1898, in *ibid.*, 864–865. T.R.'s account for these events is in his *Rough Riders*, 134–135.

23. For the text of the round robin letter, see Chadwick, *Spanish-American War*, vol. 2, pp. 257–258. See also *CWS*, vol. 1, p. 202. General Lawton signed the letter, but appended a statement that he did so only with the understanding that Shafter approved it and with reservations as to its language. The surgeons' letter is discussed in Alger, *Spanish-American War*, 268. A summary is in Shafter to Alger, 3 August 1898, *CWS*, vol. 1, p. 201.

24. Shafter to Corbin, 3 August 1898, in *CWS*, vol. 1, pp. 200–201. Shafter later explained his reasons for putting his views in such strong terms. Over 75 percent of his command had fallen victim to malaria, and this circumstance he thought made them subject to yellow fever. He did not realize that mosquitoes transmitted both malaria and yellow fever. He believed that new troops arriving at Santiago de Cuba would not experience as much difficulty as the Fifth Army Corps, because they would not have been exposed to the rigors of a campaign. (Shafter to Corbin, 8 August 1898, in *ibid.*, 213.)

25. For the accusation that Shafter abetted the leak, see Jones, *Roosevelt's Rough Riders*, 257, 261. Wood was aware as early as August 4 that the Associated Press had the documents (see Wood to Mrs. Wood, 4 August 1898, Wood Papers, box 190, Library of Congress). The President's reaction is chronicled in Charles S. Olcott, *The Life of President McKinley* (Boston, 1916), vol. 2, pp. 81–82. See also Long Diary, 7 August 1898, in Mayo, ed., *America of Yesterday*, 212. For Alger's condemnation of the leak, see his *Spanish-American War*, 270

26. The order to return home is Corbin to Shafter, 4 August 1898, in *CWS*, vol. 1, p. 203. See also Corbin to Shafter, 4 August 1898, in *ibid.*, 204. Miles, then in Puerto Rico, received word of the movement and was told to send all transports available to him to Santiago de Cuba in order to assist the evacuation of the Fifth Army Corps (Corbin to Miles, 5 August 1898, in *ibid.*, 360). For the reaction of the troops, see Shafter to Corbin, 4 August 1898, in *ibid.*, 204. For the sickness reports of August 1 and August 2, 1898, see *ibid.*, 197–202. For the views of A. D. Webb, see his "Arizona in the Spanish-American War," *Arizona Historical Review*, 1 (January, 1929): 66.

27. The War Department had actually begun to investigate possible sites for a camp to receive the returning troops as early as June. For early development of the Montauk camp, see the report of Colonel William H. Forwood, Chief Surgeon, Camp Wikoff, Montauk Point, Long Island, 18 October 1898, *ARWD 98*, 829; and

Graham A. Cosmas, *An Army for Empire: The United States Army in the Spanish-American War* (Columbia, Mo., 1971), 259–260.
28. Cosmas, *Army for Empire*, pp. 260–262. For the contributions of charitable organizations, see Colonel Forwood's report, 18 October 1898, *ARWD 98*, 831.
29. The critical comment is quoted in Dr. Nicholas Senn, *Medico-Surgical Aspects of the Spanish-American War* (Chicago, 1900), 178. For Powell's observations, see the report by Colonel Charles R. Greenleaf, 1 November 1898, in *ARWD 98*, 847.
30. For additional information concerning the development of Camp Wikoff, see the report of Surgeon General George Sternburg, "The Work of the Medical Department During the Spanish War," in *ARWD 98*, 706–708. See also Alger, *Spanish-American War*, 426; and Leech, *In the Days of McKinley*, 310.
31. Shafter's comment is in *ARWD 98*, 70.
32. The account of the return of the Second Massachusetts is in Ward, *Springfield in the Spanish-American War*, 145–146.

CHAPTER 15

1. Finley Peter Dunne, *Mr. Dooley in Peace and War* (Boston, 1899), 34.
2. For this information, see Julius W. Pratt, *America's Colonial Experiment: How the United States Gained, Governed, and In Part Gave Away a Colonial Empire* (New York, 1951), 18; *History of the First Regiment of Infantry [Kentucky], the Louisville Legion, and Other Military Organizations* (Louisville, 1907), 23; and Virginia Weisel Johnson, *The Unregimented General: A Biography of Nelson A. Miles* (Boston, 1962), 337. Rail lines connected the following cities: San Juan and Hatillo; Ponce and Yauco; Mayagüez and Aguadilla. These lines all paralleled the coast. (French Ensor Chadwick, *The Relations of the United States and Spain: The Spanish-American War* [New York, 1911], vol. 2, p. 299. For useful information on the history of both eastern Cuba and Puerto Rico prior to 1898, see Robert Bruce Hoernel, "A Comparison of Sugar and Social Change in Puerto Rico and Oriente, Cuba, 1898–1959" (Dissertation, John Hopkins University, 1977).
3. Edward J. Berbusse, *The United States in Puerto Rico* (Chapel Hill, N.C., 1946), 54–55; and Carmelo Rosario Natal, *Puerto Rico y la crisis de la guerra hispanoamericana (1895–1898)* (Hato Rey, Puerto Rico, 1975), 123–136.
4. For details of the autonomous government, see Maria M. Brau, *Island in the Crossroads: The History of Puerto Rico* (New York, 1968), 68–69; and Rosario Natal, *Puerto Rico (1895–1898)*, 151–152. For the election, see Berbusse, *United States in Puerto Rico*, 57–58, 64. Brau explains Muñoz's behavior in different terms. She claims that he believed it would be easier to deal with the Americans if Puerto Rico had a functioning government when the Spanish authority was eliminated. (Brau, *Island in the Crossroads*, 76.) Macías had relatively early warning of the American decision to move on Puerto Rico (see Correa to Macías, 25 June 1898, quoted in Angel Rivero Méndez, *Crónica de la guerra hispano americana en Puerto Rico* [Madrid, n.d.], 620). Macías's statement in April, 1898 is quoted in the U.S. Navy Department, *Sketches from the Spanish-American War by Commander J . . .* (Washington, D.C., 1899), 11.
5. For information concerning Macías's action, see Rivero, *Crónica de la guerra hispano americana*, 40.
6. For this summary, see *ibid.*, 44, 47–48; Julio Cervera Baviera, *La defensa militar de Puerto-Rico* (Puerto Rico, 1898), 8, 10, 19; Melchor Fernández Almagro, *Historia política de la España contemporánea*, Volume 2: *Regencia de doña María Cristina de Austria durante la menor edad su hijo don Alfonso XIII* (Madrid, 1959), 541; Severo Gómez Núñez, *La guerra hispano-americana. Puerto-Rico y Filipinas* (Madrid, 1902), 82–83; and Carlos Martínez de Campo y Serrano, Duque de la

Torre, *España bélica: el siglo XLX* (Madrid, 1961), 364. Despite pleas for reinforcements from Macías from before the declaration of war, the only response came on April 15, when 27 officers and 745 troops arrived along with two sections of mountain artillery (Cervera Baviera, *La defensa militar de Puerto-Rico*, 9; and Rivero, *Crónica de la guerra hispano americana*, 614–622).

7. For the correspondence relating to the commercial treaty—the one that Dupuy de Lôme had referred to in his ill-fated letter to Canalejas—see *Diplomatic Instructions, Spain*, roll 150, vol. 22, pp. 502–503.

8. For the activity of the joint army-navy board, see Graham A. Cosmas, *An Army for Empire: The United States Army in the Spanish-American War* (Columbia, Mo., 1971), 81. Two Puerto Ricans, Roberto Todd and Dr. José Julio Henna, contacted the Navy Department and provided it with certain maps and information. Theodore Roosevelt wrote to Todd in December, 1903, "I am going to confess more to you: until that moment we had not given any consideration to Puerto Rico in our plans in case of a war with Spain." (Roberto H. Todd, *La invasión americana: como surgió la idea de traer la guerra a Puerto Rico* (San Juan, 1938), 19.) For Schofield's activity, see Memorandum on the McKinley Administration, Papers of Major General John McAllister Schofield, Manuscript Division, Library of Congress, Washington, D.C. For the views of Mahan, see his *Lessons of the War With Spain and Other Articles* (Freeport, N.Y., 1970 reprint edition), 27. Mahan thought of Puerto Rico as an extraordinarily strategic location aside from its significance in a war with Spain. He considered it as important in relation to Cuba, a prospective isthmian canal, and the American west coast as was Malta in relation to Egypt, the Suez Canal, and beyond. (*Ibid.*, 29.) For the views of the Secretary of the Navy, see John D. Long, *The New American Navy* (New York, 1903), vol. 1, p. 205.

9. See General Miles's statement before the postwar investigating commission (*IC*, vol. 7, p. 3,249).

10. Hanna report from St. Thomas, 4 May 1898, *AF*, file 8, roll 229. See also Hanna to Day, 9 May 1898, *AF*, file 8, roll 229.

11. Nelson A. Miles, "The War with Spain.—III," *North American Review* 169 (July, 1899): 125. See also Chadwick, *Spanish-American War*, vol. 2, pp. 358–359. A Puerto Rican account of Whitney's activity is in Todd, *La invasión americana*, 14–16.

12. See Chapter 6 above for Sampson's operations at San Juan on May 12, 1898. For the exchange between Lodge and Roosevelt, see Lodge to Roosevelt, 24 May 1898, and Roosevelt to Lodge, 25 May 1898, in Henry Cabot Lodge and Charles F. Redmond, eds., *Selections from the Correspondence of Theodore Roosevelt and Henry Cabot Lodge, 1884–1918* (New York, 1971 reprint edition), vol. 1, pp. 299–300, 301.

13. For interest in Puerto Rico after Cervera was located, see Cosmas, *Army for Empire*, 179. The particular situation does not rule out the probability that more general considerations came to mind in connection with a campaign in Puerto Rico—that the island could function as a fine base for Spanish naval operations if left alone, and that it commanded the maritime approaches to the Central American isthmus. For the Miles plan, see two letters, Miles to Alger, 26 May and 27 May 1898, *CWS*, vol. 1, pp. 262–263. See also Russell A. Alger, *The Spanish-American War* (New York and London, 1901), 49–52; Walter Millis, *The Martial Spirit: A Study of Our War With Spain* (Boston and New York, 1931), 237–238; and Cosmas, *Army for Empire*, 180–181. For the Stone-Todd dealings, see Todd to Stone, 27 May 1898, and Stone to Todd, 29 May 1898, in Todd, *La invasión americana*, 11–12. For the mission assigned General Lee, see Cosmas, *Army for Empire*, 180. The order to Shafter is Corbin to Shafter, 31 May 1898, *CWS*, vol. 1, p. 19. For the Lodge comment, see Lodge to Roosevelt, 31 May 1898, in Lodge to Redmond, eds., *Selections*, vol. 1, p. 302.

14. For relevant correspondence, see Miles to Alger, 2 June 1898, *RG 108,* Entry 119, vol. 1, p. 15; and McKinley to Miles, 4 June 1898, *IC,* vol. 2, p. 1,343. For the interpretation that McKinley hoped to avoid the campaign against Havana, see Ernest R. May, "McKinley (1898)," in Ernest R. May, ed., *The Ultimate Decision: The President as Commander in Chief* (New York, 1960), 104.

15. See Chapter 19 for an account of the process leading to the demand for the cession of Puerto Rico.

16. The commanding general made his proposition in Miles to Alger, 6 June 1898, *CWS,* vol. 1, p. 264. See also Chadwick, *Spanish-American War,* vol. 2, p. 264. For the Secretary of War's rejection, see Alger to Miles, 6 June 1898, in *ibid,*. See also *ibid.,* 266; and Alger, *Spanish-American War,* 61.

17. For the War Department's orders to Miles to organize the Puerto Rican expedition, see Corbin to Miles, 7 June 1898, in *CWS,* vol. 1, p. 264. The proposal to consider a port of embarkation other than Tampa is in Alger to Miles, 8 June 1898, in *ibid.,* 32. The commanding general's counterproposal is in Miles to Alger, 8 June 1898, in *ibid.,* 32–33. Alger's reaction to the "ghost squadron" is in Miles to Alger, 9 June 1898, in *ibid.,* 34. The refusal is in Alger to Miles, 9 June 1898, in *ibid.*

18. For the correspondence relating to making up forces for the Puerto Rican expedition at this time, see Alger to Miles, and Miles to Alger, 10 June 1898, in *ibid.,* 34–35; Miles to Alger, and Alger to Miles, 12 June 1898, in *ibid.,* 38–39, 265–266; Alger to Miles, and Miles to Alger, 14 June 1898, in *ibid.,* 43–44, 45; and Alger to Miles, 14 June 1898, in *ibid.,* 267.

19. Alger to Miles (three messages), 15 June 1898, in *ibid.,* 47–48; 268; and Miles to Alger (two messages), 15 June 1898, in *ibid.,* 48.

20. For the meeting of June 18, see Long Diary, 19 June 1898, in Lawrence Shaw Mayo, ed., *America of Yesterday: As Reflected in the Journal of John Davis Long* (Boston, 1923), 200. On June 18 the commanding general recommended for the Puerto Rican campaign a comprehensive concentration of troops that reflected his earlier plans. He proposed that all troops at Jacksonville and certain units at Camp Thomas proceed to Fernandina; that troops at Mobile move to Mount Vernon, Alabama, for an early voyage to Cuba; that no troops be taken away from the camp at Miami, but that five thousand troops move immediately to Miami from Camp Thomas and an equal number make the trip again in two weeks; and that transports should proceed directly to Tampa to load troops for the expedition (Miles to Alger, 18 June 1898, *CWS,* vol. 1, pp. 48–49). For the revived plan to invade northern Cuba from Nuevitas, see Miles to Alger, 24 June 1898, quoted in Alger, *Spanish-American War,* 53–55. See also *ARWD 98,* 25–26.

21. For the Secretary of War's objections to Miles's plan, see his *Spanish-American War,* 55–56.

22. For the orders of June 26, see Alger to Miles, 26 June 1898, *ARWD 98,* 98. For preliminary orders arranging troop preparations and movements see Alger memorandum, 25 June 1898, in *CWS,* vol. 1, p. 57; Miles to Alger, 25 June 1898, in *ibid.,* 268; and Gilmore to Brooke, 25 June 1898, in *ibid.,* 53. Major General James F. Wade was to assume command at Camp Thomas. Sampson received notice on June 24 to provide an escort for twenty-five thousand troops to Puerto Rico (W. A. M. Goode, *With Sampson Through the War: Being an Account of the Naval Operations of the North Atlantic Squadron During the Spanish-American War of 1898* [New york, 1899], 183). For the two propositions of Miles, see Miles to Alger, 29 June 1898, in *CWS,* vol. 1, p. 67; and Miles to Alger, 1 July 1898, in *ibid.,* 101. Disapproval came in Alger to Miles, 1 July 1898, in *ibid.*

23. For the commanding general's views of July 5, see Miles to Alger, 5 July 1898, *CWS,* vol. 1, p. 271. See also Nelson A. Miles, "The War with Spain.—II," *North American Review* 168 (June, 1899): 753–754.

24. See Chapter 13 above for a discussion of the decision to send Miles to Santiago de

Cuba. For Miles's arrival at Santiago de Cuba, see Chadwick, *Spanish-American War*, vol. 2, pp. 216–217.

25. See Chapter 13 above for Miles's activities at Santiago de Cuba in connection with plans of campaign, and also for his role in the negotiations for the capitulation of that city. For the view that Miles thought himself the victim of a conspiracy, see Margaret Leech, *In the Days of McKinley* (New York, 1959), 279. A contributing factor in his thought was the arrangement that he was not to replace Shafter in command at Santiago de Cuba. Leech believed that Miles's haste to depart Cuba for Puerto Rico stemmed from this judgment. There is, however, no evidence that Alger intended to deprive Miles of the command. On July 19 Miles expressed to Shafter his reasons for not taking any of the troops there to Puerto Rico: "First, they have done enough; second, they might carry the fever." He had in mind, however, sending a brigade of "colored troops" from Santiago de Cuba to Puerto Rico, provided the fever could be controlled. He also retained the thought of sending a brigade to capture the Isle of Pines. (Miles to Shafter, 18 July 1898, *RG 108*, Entry 118, 61–62.) Shafter approved the dispatch of the black troops but refused to express his views on the Isle of Pines operation. What he really wished to do was send his troops back to the United States. (Shafter to Miles, 19 July 1898, *RG 108*, Entry 121, vol. 2 of 2, p. 59.) For the arrangements leading to Miles's concentration at Guantánamo Bay, see Miles to Alger, 14 July 1898, *CWS*, vol. 1, p. 273. Miles probably had something to do with an inquiry to Commander Bowman H. McCalla at Guantánamo made on July 4 as to the suitability of that bay as a rendezvous for the Puerto Rican expedition. McCalla reported favorably. (Long to McCalla, 4 July 1898, *RG 45*, Entry 19, no. 2, 85; and McCalla to Long, 5 July 1898, *RG 80*, E194, 251.) Miles at first planned to land troops at Guantánamo, but then decided against it, probably in response to a message from the War Department: "The Secretary of War says no troops will be landed at Guantanamo, as we are informed that there is much fever there. One of the islands immediately adjacent to Puerto Rico should be used instead" (Corbin to Miles, 15 July 1898, in *CWS*, vol. 1, p. 274). Miles then pointed out that the Marines were already encamped at Guantánamo Bay. He had also been considering Culebra Island or Crab Island, adjacent to Puerto Rico. (Miles to Alger, 15 July 1898, in *ibid.*, 150.) Another message from the War Department stated, "Secretary War wishes to know if, in your opinion and that of the medical experts about you, it would be safe to make use of the troops now at Santiago for the Porto Rico expedition. He does not wish any chances taken" (Corbin to Miles, 15 July 1898, in *ibid.*, 146). Miles ordered Shafter to separate healthy from unhealthy units. Every effort was to be made to assist the sickly units. Shafter was told "to improve their sanitary condition and to check the spread of the disease [yellow fever] by placing them in as healthy camps as possible." (Miles to Shafter, 14 July 1898, quoted in Joseph M. Wheeler, *The Santiago Campaign 1898* [New York, 1898], 341.) This step accorded with instructions in Alger to Miles, 14 July 1898, *RG 108*, Entry 121, vol. 2 of 2, p. 18. This communication also informed the commanding general that no more troops would be ordered to Santiago de Cuba. Shafter, however, did not wish to move very many units, with the exception of the cavalry division, until he had arranged the surrender of the Spanish garrison (Shafter to Miles, 16 July 1898, *RG 108*, Entry 121, vol. 2 of 2, p. 42). For Miles's activity in preparing to deal effectively with health problems in Puerto Rico, see Greenleaf to Gilmore, 23 July 1898, *RG 108*, Entry 121, vol. 2 of 2, pp. 93–94.

26. For the discussion of July 16, see Miles to Sampson, 16 July 1898, *RG 108*, Entry 118, 39. See also Chadwick, *Spanish-American War*, vol. 2, p. 266. For Sampson's reservations about the escort, see Sampson to Navy Department, 16 July 1898, enclosed with Sampson to Miles, 18 July 1898, *RG 108*, Entry 121, vol. 2 of 2, p. 75. For notification of activity to the War Department, see Miles to Alger, 16 July

1898, *CWS*, vol. 1, pp. 154–155. The Naval War Board concurred in the choice of Fajardo as a landing place (Sicard [for the Naval War Board] to Long, 19 July 1898, *RG 45*, NRC 371, vol. 2, p. 185).

27. For the correspondence of July 17, see Alger to Miles, 17 July 1898, in *CWS*, vol. 1, p. 279; Alger to Miles, 17 July 1898, in *ibid.*, 280; Miles to Alger, 17 July 1898 (rec. 6:45 P.M.), *ARWD 98*, 130; and Alger to Miles, 17 July 1898, *IC*, vol. 2, p. 1,361.

28. For the initial proposal of Nipe Bay, see Sicard (for the Naval War Board) to Long, 11 July 1898, *RG 45*, NRC 371, no. 2, 167–168. At this point the Navy planned to use three monitors to take Nipe Bay—the *Amphitrite, Puritan,* and *Terror.* They were to wait there and serve as naval escorts for the convoy to Puerto Rico. For the orders leading to the Nipe operation, see Long to Sampson, 17 July 1898, *RG 45*, Entry 19, no. 2, 107; Sampson to Long, 18 July 1898, *RG 80*, E194, 293; and Chadwick, *Spanish-American War*, vol. 2, pp. 355–356. For correspondence relating to actual operations, see Lt. Commander Cowles to Howell, 19 July 1898, *AF*, file 8, roll 235; and Commander Parker (U.S.S. *Annapolis*) to Sampson, 21 July 1898, *RG 45*, Entry 40, no. 2, 294. For the arrangements to use Guantánamo Bay, see Miles to Alger, 18 July 1898, *CWS*, vol. 1, pp. 283–284. See also a message authorizing Miles to decide the question of Nipe as against alternative locations (Alger to Miles, 18 July 1898, *IC*, vol. 2, p. 1,366). Miles made clear his opposition to the use of Nipe Bay in Miles to Sampson, 18 July 1898, *RG 108*, Entry 118, 71–72. Sampson, however, went ahead with the seizure because of his orders of July 17. He did not have time to recall the expedition before it attacked. (Sampson to Long, 21 July 1898, quoted in Alger, *Spanish-American War*, 253.)

29. For the order to go to Puerto Rico, see Corbin to Miles, 18 July 1898, *AF*, file 8, roll 235. Because of confusion arising from cables between Guantánamo Bay and Washington it took some time to clarify the actual decision (See Alger to Miles, 18 July 1898, in *ARWD 98*, 130; Miles to Alger, 18 July 1898, in *ibid.*; Corbin to Miles, 18 July 1898, in *ibid.*, 131; Miles to Alger, 19 July 1898 [rec. 2:05 P.M.], *CWS*, vol. 1, p. 288; and Alger to Miles, 19 July 1898, *IC*, vol. 2, p. 1,367). Miles's acknowledgement of the definitive order is Miles to Alger, 19 July 1898, *CWS*, vol. 1, p. 288.

30. The War Department's efforts to obtain transports for Miles included an order to Shafter at Santiago de Cuba to return all available transports to Newport News (Corbin to Shafter, 19 July 1898, in *CWS*, vol. 1, p. 167; and Corbin to Shafter, 21 July 1898, in *ibid.*, 169). For the Navy Department's order to Sampson regarding cooperation, see Long to Sampson, 18 July 1898, *AF*, file 8, roll 235. Sampson previously had requested orders on this question (Sampson to Long, 18 July 1898, *AF*, file 8, roll 235). The Naval War Board drafted the instructions (Sicard [for the Naval War Board] to Long, 18 July 1898, *RG 45*, NRC 371, vol. 2, p. 180). Sampson reported his intention to detail ships for the escort in Sampson to Miles, 18 July 1898, *AF*, file 8, roll 235. The Naval War Board was anxious to get the three monitors intended as escorts out to Guantánamo Bay from Key West (Sicard [for the Naval War Board] to Long, 18 July 1898, *RG 45*, NRC 371, vol. 2, p. 181). For correspondence about Miles's request for Schley, see Miles to Alger, 18 July 1898, *CWS*, vol. 1, p. 282; and Miles to Alger, 18 July 1898, *RG 108*, Entry 118, 58. The message from the Navy Department concerning the army's decision not to use Nipe Bay is in Long to Sampson, 19 July 1898, *RG 45*, NRC 371, vol. 2, p. 187. The commanding general's request to Sampson is Miles to Sampson, 19 July 1898, *AF*, file 8, roll 235.

31. Sampson's first message is in Sampson to Miles, 19 July 1898, *RG 108*, Entry 121, vol. 2 of 2, pp. 75–76. His proposal of July 20 is in Sampson to Miles, 20 July 1898, included in Miles to Alger, 21 July 1898, *ARWD 98*, 131. For Sampson's orders providing for the escort, see Sampson to Commander, U.S.S. *Columbia*, 20 July 1898, *AF*, file 8, roll 125; and Sampson to Commander, U.S.S. *Annapolis*, 20 July

1898, *AF*, file 8, roll 235. Miles's complaint is Miles to Alger, 20 July 1898, *RG 108*, Entry 118, 102–103. The Secretary of the Navy's message is Long to Sampson, 20 July 1898, *RG 45*, Entry 19, no. 2, 113. This response was recommended in Sicard (for the Naval War Board) to Long, 20 July 1898, *RG 45*, NRC, 371, vol. 2, p. 188.

32. For the President's action, see Corbin to Miles, 21 July 1898, transmitting text of McKinley to Long, 20 July 1898, *RG 108*, Entry 121, vol. 2 of 2, pp. 84–85. For interpretation of McKinley's motives, see David Healy, "McKinley as Commander-in-Chief," in Paolo Coletta, ed., *Threshold to American Internationalism: Essays on the Foreign Policies of William McKinley* (New York, 1970), 98.

33. For notice to Miles, see Alger to Miles, 21 July 1898, *CWS*, vol. 1, p. 299; and Alger to Miles, 21 July 1898, *ARWD 98*, 133. This latter message stated, "The Secretary of the Navy just informs me that he received an order from the President at 2 o'clock this morning to send the *Indiana* and *Newark*, or ships of that class, at once to convoy you and remain with you as long as needed. Don't go without them." For the orders to Sampson, see Long to Sampson, 21 July 1898, *RG 45*, Entry 19, no. 2, 115. For word of dispositions to fill out the escort, see Sampson to Miles, 21 July 1898, *RG 108*, Entry 121, vol. 2 of 2, pp. 83–84. Miles's response is Miles to Sampson, 21 July 1898, *RG 108*, Entry 118, 110. The General notified the War Department of Sampson's concession in Miles to Alger, 21 July 1898, *CWS*, vol. 1, pp. 299–300.

34. For the delay of the Eastern Squadron, see Cosmas, *Army for Empire*, 280. For Sampson's pained message to the Navy Department, see Sampson to Long, 22 July 1898, *RG 80*, E194, 308–309. For the response, see Long to Sampson, 22 July 1898, *RG 80*, E194, 315.

35. For some account of the attitude of troops waiting for the Puerto Rican campaign at Guantánamo, see R. S. Bunzey, *History of Companies I and E, Sixth Regiment, Illinois Volunteer Infantry from Whiteside County* (Morison, Ill., 1901), 206. For the makeup of the expedition, see *ARWD 98*, 38; and Chadwick, *Spanish-American War*, vol. 2, p. 284. Other vessels would join the escort as the expedition developed. The three monitors were en route, along with the *Cincinnati*, *Montgomery*, and three vessels that had attacked Nipe Bay—the *Annapolis*, *Wasp*, and *Leyden*. The *New Orleans* was off San Juan, blockading that port. For Miles's summary of his actions at Guantánamo Bay, see his "The War with Spain.—III," *North American Review* 167 (June, 1899): 126–127. Miles's request to take the Marines is Miles to Alger, 20 July 1898, *CWS*, vol. 1, p. 296. The refusal is Alger to Miles, 21 July 1898, *RG 108*, Entry 121, vol. 2 of 2, p. 3.

36. Miles's proposal for a change in strategy is in Miles to Higginson, 22 July 1898, *ARWD 98*, 39. See also John Black Atkins, *The War in Cuba: The Experiences of an Englishman With the United States Army* (London, 1899), 246–247. In all later statements on his change of plan Miles consistently cited the reasons he gave Higginson on July 22. (See Miles to Alger, 30 July 1898, *ARWD 98*, 133; Miles, "The War with Spain.—III," 128–129; and Nelson A. Miles, *Serving the Republic: Memoirs of the Civil and Military Life of Nelson A. Miles Lieutenant-General United States Army* [New York and London, 1911], 296–297. See also the comments of the postwar investigating commission in *IC*, vol. 1, p. 230.) In his report to Alger on July 30, 1898, Miles mentioned another consideration not touched upon elsewhere: "Ample time will be furnished here [Guánica-Ponce area] for thoroughly organizing the expedition before the march." For the views of Whitney, see his memorandum for Miles, 24 July 1898, *RG 108*, Entry 121, vol. 2 of 2, pp. 95–96.

37. Higginson to Sampson, 2 August 1898, *BN 98*, 636. See also Chadwick, *Spanish-American War*, vol. 2, pp. 285–287; and *ARWD 98*, 40.

38. For the views of Mahan, see Mahan to Long, 16 November 1898, in Gardner Weld Allen, ed., *Papers of John Davis Long 1897–1904* (Boston, 1939), 210. For Chad-

wick's views, see his *Spanish-American War*, vol. 2, pp. 286, 299–300. On August 7 a few sailors and marines easily seized the lighthouse at Cape San Juan (Goode, *With Sampson through the War*, 206). For the views of Walter Millis concerning Miles's desire to upstage the navy, see his *Martial Spirit*, 337. Concerning Miles's reasoning, Millis quotes Miles to Alger, 30 July 1898, *ARWD 98*, 133.

39. For Macías's advance warning, see Rivero, *Crónica*, 462. For the intelligence from Spain on Miles, see Girón to Macías, 25 July 1898, in *Ultramar Records*, bundle 5, 143 (4), no. 41. Macías's general instructions are mentioned in Rivero, *Crónica*, 576; Macías so informed Rivero in an interview on October 6, 1922. There is no reason to question this statement.

40. For strategic alternatives open to Macías, see Gómez Núñez, *La guerra hispano-americana. Puerto-Rico y Filipinas*, 91–96. This authority relies heavily on Efeele, *El desastre nacional y los vicios de nuestras instituciones militares* (Madrid, 1901).

41. For the landing operations, see Miles to Alger, 26 July 1898, *ARWD 98*, 132; Lt. Harry P. Huse to Higginson, 25 July 1898, *BN 98*, 642; and Higginson to Sampson, 2 August 1898, *BN 98*, 637. For Miles's praise of the navy, see *ARWD 98*, 40.

42. For Miles's views on the importance of Ponce, see Miles to Higginson, 25 July 1898, *RG 108*, Entry 118, 121. See also Miles to Alger, 26 July 1898, *ARWD 98*, 132. For the operation at Yauco, see Chadwick, *Spanish-American War*, vol. 2, p. 291; and Miles, "The War with Spain.—III," 131. Notice to Higginson of the success at Yauco is in Miles to Higginson, 27 July 1898, *AF*, file 8, roll 236. For the initial landing at the Port of Ponce, see Davis to Higginson, 27 July and 28 July 1898, in *BN 98*, 643–644; Higginson to Sampson, 2 August 1898, in *ibid.*, 637; and Chadwick, *Spanish-American War*, vol. 2, pp. 292–294. For orders to General Wilson to go to Ponce, see Miles, "The War with Spain.—III," 131; Chadwick, *Spanish-American War*, vol. 2, p. 296; and James Harrison Wilson, *Under the Old Flag: Recollections of Military Operations in the War for the Union, the Spanish War, the Boxer Rebellion, etc.* (New York and London, 1912), vol. 2, p. 440. The occupation of Ponce proper is recorded in Miles to Alger, 28 July 1898, *CWS*, vol. 1, p. 330; *ARWD 98*, 40; and Cervera Baviera, *La defensa militar de Puerto-Rico*, 21. San Martín was later arrested and court-martialed for failure to obey orders to resist the American landing. For Henry's views, see Henry to Gilmore, 26 July 1898, *RG 108*, Entry 121, vol. 2 of 2, pp. 122–123.

43. For this information, see Cosmas, *Army for Empire*, 233. For the text of the proclamation of July 28, 1898, see Chadwick, *Spanish-American War*, vol. 2, p. 297. The optimistic report is Miles to Alger, 28 July 1898, *ARWD 98*, 132. For Puerto Rican reception of the United States invasion, see Rosario Natal, *Puerto Rico (1895-1898)*, 221–257.

44. For information on reinforcements arriving in Puerto Rico, see Cosmas, *Army for Empire*, 231, 233; Alger, *Spanish-American War*, 305, 308; Gómez Núñez, *La guerra hispano-americana. Puerto-Rico y Filipinas*, 86, 88; and Miles, "The War with Spain.—III," 134. The addition of Wilson's Schwan's, and Brooke's troops brought the total available to 15,199 men. Later additions raised the figure to about seventeen thousand. Miles had a total of 106 mortars, howitzers, field guns, and siege guns. Schwan brought the Thirteenth and Nineteenth Infantry, a troop of the Second Cavalry, and two batteries of the Seventh Artillery. (Miles, "The War with Spain.—III," 133–134.)

45. For early comments on Miles's general plan, see Higginson to Sampson, 2 August 1898, *AF*, file 8, roll 235. Higginson commented that Miles at this point planned to advance on the military road from Ponce to San Juan. "There are many strong positions that can be occupied by the enemy but having command of the sea, these can all be flanked by making landings at ports on the right or left flanks, and the enemy made to evacuate any position by flanking rather than by direct assault." This comment captured the core of Miles's strategic design. See also Johnson, *Unregimented*

General, 337; Atkins, *War in Cuba,* 248; Frank E. Edwards, *The '98 Campaign of the 6th Massachusetts* (Boston, 1899), 135; *IC,* vol. 1, pp. 230–231; and Cosmas, *Army for Empire,* 234–235.

46. The message from Paris is Sims to Bureau of Navigation, rec. 29 July 1898, *RG 38,* Entry 100. Commander Jacobsen, a German officer who observed the war from the protected cruiser *Geier,* was typical of many critics who pointed up the inadequacy of Macías's strategy (U.S. Navy Department, *Sketches from the Spanish-American War by Commander J . . . ,* 23). Before General Brooke left Newport News, he received the following from Corbin: "I am instructed to say that the overtures for peace have not reached a stage that in any way warrants a hesitancy or absence of vigor on the part of our army operating against the enemy. You will give this information to General Miles, whom we may not be able to reach by cable before you report to him" (Corbin to Brooke, 28 July 1898, in *CWS,* vol. 1, p. 327). Brooke answered, "I understand about the conditions as related by you in the peace negotiations" (Brooke to Corbin, 28 July 1898, in *ibid.*). Miles was always prepared to support hard terms. On August 2 he proposed to Alger, "I respectfully suggest that in any peace negotiations all islands in the West Indies, such as Isle of Pines, Vieques, and others over which Spain has dominion, be ceded to the United States" (Miles to Alger, 2 August 1898, *CWS,* vol. 1, p. 351).

47. For the information from the field, see Stone to Miles, 29 July 1898, *RG 108,* Entry 121, vol. 2 of 2, pp. 130–131; Wilson to Miles, 30 July 1898, *RG 108,* Entry 121, vol. 2 of 2, p. 142; and Stone to Miles, 1 August 1898, *RG 108,* Entry 121, vol. 2 of 2, p. 151. For the movement on Guayama, see *ARWD 98,* 43; Miles, "War with Spain.—III," 134; and Chadwick, *Spanish-American War,* vol. 2, p. 296. Miles was encouraged when it appeared that his effort to win local favor had produced results. On August 2 he reported, "Some 300 volunteers have surrendered, and reports are received from different parts of the island that volunteers refuse to fight or march any longer and that in many places they are willing to surrender and receive their paroles and return to their homes" (Miles to Alger, 2 August 1898, in *CWS,* vol. 1, p. 351). The general's message concerning his troop requirements is Miles to Corbin, 8 August 1898, in *ibid.,* 368. Corbin had cabled earlier, "The Secretary of War desires an early report of how many more troops, if any, you require to prosecute the campaign in Puerto Rico. He wishes to hurry forward every man you require, but no more than you need" (Corbin to Miles, 6 August 1898, in *ibid.,* 364). The War Department then halted movements to Puerto Rico (see Corbin to Coppinger, 10 August 1898, in *IC,* vol. 2, p. 1,159). Coppinger was at Tampa with orders to go to Puerto Rico. He was informed that Miles had no need for him and that he would be sent north soon; any transports he had were to be sent to Santiago de Cuba. The War Department asked for all available transports for use at Santiago de Cuba in Corbin to Miles, 5 August 1898, in *ibid.,* 360. Miles replied, "Owing to the serious condition of General Shafter's command, I would not delay a single ship, notwithstanding our need of cavalry, and will order *Mohawk* and *Mobile* and every other vessel that can be spared to go with all speed to Santiago" (Miles to Alger, 6 August 1898, in *ibid.,* 366).

48. Macías to Correa, 5 August 1898, quoted in Rivero, *Crónica,* 624. Philip C. Hanna, former consul in Puerto Rico, summarized the situation accurately on August 3: "I am informed that General Macias will not now surrender the island. Some of the consuls [at St. Thomas] think he will make a 'show of a fight,' and after that surrender. I am of the opinion that when the time comes in which you demand his surrender he will very promptly comply. However, Spaniards dislike to surrender without first making a good showing. I am sure that if he did fight, it would be only to show his bravery, and not because he has any hope" (Hanna to unnamed correspondent [probably Miles], 3 August 1898, *RG 108,* Entry 121, vol. 2 of 2, p. 213).

49. For information on difficulties encountered by General Wilson at Ponce and General Brooke at Arroyo, see *IC*, vol. 1, p. 137; and Chadwick, *Spanish-American War*, vol. 2, p. 296. Chadwick quotes Wilson as follows: "Had our ultimate success depended on a prompt advance against the enemy, it would have been seriously endangered by the inadequate preparations to meet perfectly well-known conditions, such as shoal water which prevented transports coming within half a mile of the beach, lack of wharf and landing facilities, and especially of steam launches for towing lighters backward and forward between the transports and the shore." It should be remembered that Miles gave as one of the reasons for landing at Guánica rather than Fajardo the supposed availability of good port facilities on the southern shore of the island. For the proposal that the navy take San Juan, see C. H. Davis to Sampson, 2 August 1898, *AF*, file 8, roll 237. For Sampson's attempt to sell the project to the Secretary of the Navy, see Sampson to Long, 4 August 1898, *RG 80*, E194, 342. Mahan's observations are in Mahan to Long, 5 August 1898, in Allen, ed., *Papers of John Davis Long*, 176.

50. The messages about the plan from Miles to the War Department are Miles to Alger, 9 August 1898, *ARWD 98*, 137; and Miles to Alger, 10 August 1898, *IC*, vol. 2, p. 1,161. The General may have had some basis for his suspicions. Goode reported that on August 9 Sampson ordered Captain Rogers of the *Puritan*—one of the monitors at Puerto Rico—to give notice of bombardment to San Juan; Sampson indicated the general approach to the task, including an injunction not to bother with the batteries there (Goode, *With Sampson through the War*, 268). The Secretary of War's soothing message is Alger to Miles, 11 August 1898, *CWS*, vol. 1, p. 380.

51. For the left flank movement, see Miles to Schwan, 6 August 1898, *RG 108*, Entry 118, 242; and Miles, "War with Spain.—III," 134. For the observations of Gardner, see Constance Lodge Gardner, ed., *Some Letters of Augustus Peabody Gardner* (Boston and New York, 1920), 28. Gardner was Senator Henry Cabot Lodge's brother-in-law. The orders for the movement on the right flank are in Miles to Brooke, 8 August 1898, *RG 108*, Entry 118, 272–273. The activities relating to the engagement at Guayama on August 8, and preparations for further action in that vicinity, are in Miles, "War with Spain.—III," 134, 137; and Alger, *Spanish-American War*, 311.

52. For the engagement at Coamo, see *ARWD 98*, 44; Miles, "War with Spain.—III," 315; and Chadwick, *Spanish-American War*, vol. 2, pp. 301–304. For the first report of the engagement, see Miles to Alger, 9 August 1898, *CWS*, vol. 1, p. 372.

53. *ARWD 98*, 43; Chadwick, *Spanish-American War*, vol. 2, pp. 306–309; Miles, "War with Spain.—III," 136; and Alger, *Spanish-American War*, 314–316. Miles notes that in the period August 7–13 Schwan covered ninety-two miles and occupied nine towns. Chadwick reported that a Puerto Rican cavalry detachment under Lugo Viña provided the Americans with useful scouting. On August 13 an American detachment trapped some Spanish troops at the Prieto River near Las Marías and inflicted serious casualties at no loss to itself. Miles reported that seventeen Spanish soldiers were killed and fifty-six taken prisoners in this engagement.

54. *ARWD 98*, 43; and Miles, "War with Spain.—III," 134–136.

55. For word of the military road, see Miles to Wilson, 9 August 1898, *RG 108*, Entry 118, 301–302. For a letter reiterating previous instructions, see Miles to Brooke, Wilson, Henry, and Schwan, 11 August 1898, *RG 108*, Entry 118, 333–340. For Wilson's proposals for assistance, see Wilson to Gilmore, 11 August 1898, *RG 108*, Entry 121, vol. 2 of 2, pp. 377–378; Wilson to Gilmore, 13 August 1898, *RG 108*, Entry 121, vol. 2 of 2, p. 414; and Chadwick, *Spanish-American War*, vol. 2, pp. 304–307. For the Spanish strength at Aibonito, see Gómez Núñez, *La guerra hispano-americana. Puerto-Rico y Filipinas*, 97–98.

56. Announcement of the protocol is in Corbin to Miles, 12 August 1898, *ARWD 98*, 139. Word went to the field commanders in Miles to Brooke, Wilson, Henry, and

Schwan, 13 August 1898, *RG 108,* Entry 118, 369. Notice to the Spanish government was given in Miles to Macías, 13 August 1898, *RG 108,* Entry 118, 373.

57. Miles's statement about the situation at the cessation of hostilities is in Miles to Alger, 15 August 1898, *ARWD 98,* 138.

58. For the differences between the campaigns at Santiago de Cuba and Puerto Rico, see Cosmas, *Army for Empire,* 234. Only one serious breakdown occurred in the field: The commanding officer of the Sixth Massachusetts, the second-in-command, and two other officers were forced to resign from the service when they failed to report for duty in the face of the enemy. (For relevant information and correspondence see *ibid.,* 153; and *IC,* vol. 2, pp. 1,156–1,158.) For casualty figures, see Chadwick, *Spanish-American War,* vol. 2, p. 482; *ARWD 98,* 44; and Edward Ranson, "Nelson A. Miles as Commanding General, 1895–1903," *Military Affairs* 29 (Winter, 1965–1966): 179–200. The crime of Private de Haas is mentioned in Stone to Miles, 29 July 1898, *RG 108,* Entry 121, vol. 2 of 2, pp. 130–131; the report of the court-martial, 9 August 1898, is in *RG 108,* Entry 121, vol. 2 of 2, p. 243. A contract surgeon, Dr. Russell W. Chidsey, was convicted on similar charges; his penalty was to forfeit $100 and undergo solitary confinement at hard labor for eight months (in *ibid.,* 329–330). For Miles's interest in political prisoners, see Miles to Alger, 10 August 1898, *CWS,* vol. 1, p. 377.

59. The comment is in Karl Stephen Herman, *A Recent Campaign in Puerto Rico* (Boston, 1907), 34–35. For similar observations, see Charles E. Creager, *The Fourteenth Ohio National Guard—the Fourth Ohio Volunteer Infantry: A Complete Record of This Organization From Its Foundation to the Present Day* (Columbus, Ohio, 1899), 212. Creager complained of the "lowest type of Puerto Rican," whom he called "black, dirty, lazy, ignorant, immoral, naked and diseased."

60. For the return of the Spanish troops, see Miles to Alger, 17 August 1898, in *CWS,* vol. 1, p. 396; Corbin to Miles, 17 August 1898, in *ibid.,* 397; Corbin to Miles, 18 August 1898, in *ibid.,* 398; and Miles to Alger, 21 August 1898, *ibid.,* 399. In this latter message, in which Miles gave notice that preparations for the evacuation of the Spanish troops were well along, he also stated, "I expect very soon to return to Washington." The instructions for the commissioners, Generals Brooke and Gordon and Rear Admiral Schley, are in *Foreign Relations, 1898,* 909–911. See also Paolo E. Coletta, "The Peace Negotiations and the Treaty of Paris," in Coletta, ed., *Threshold to American Nationalism,* 132.

61. For the exchange between Corbin and Lodge, see Lodge to Corbin, 23 July 1898, in *CWS,* vol. 1, p. 308; and Corbin to Lodge, 23 July 1898, in *ibid.,* 311. For the case of the Indiana regiment, see Fairbanks to Alger, 26 July 1898, in *ibid.,* 320; and Corbin to Wade (Camp Thomas), 26 July 1898, in *ibid.* When Corbin substituted an Indiana regiment for one from Illinois, he encountered a stiff protest from Senator Shelby Cullom (Republican from Illinois). Corbin noted in reply that three Illinois regiments—the First, Third, and Sixth—had been ordered overseas, and he planned to hold back the Sixth Illinois so Indiana could have representation. He justified his decision in tactful but firm language: "This may be and doubtless is a hardship for the regiment. It had to be done, however, to give scant justice to the State of Indiana, and you will say it is but fair." (For this exchange, see Cullom to Alger, 30 July 1898, in *ibid.,* 335–336; and Corbin to Governor John R. Tanner and Cullom, 30 July 1898, in *ibid.,* 337.) Arthur Wallace Dunn a long time later recalled that Corbin said at the time, "We have to get these fellows afloat and on their way to Porto Rico before we get orders to halt hostilities. They've got to see service of some kind, or at least get a glimpse of foreign lands, and Porto Rico is our last chance. They have got to get off before we get notice of an armistice" (Arthur Wallace Dunn, *From Harrison to Harding: A Personal Narrative, Covering a Third of a Century 1888–1921* [New York and London, 1922], vol. 1, p. 245). Margaret Leech wrote that Secretary Alger, smarting under adverse publicity, thought he

might curry political favor by expediting the shipment of many volunteers to Ponce. When he made this suggestion to McKinley, the President said, "What do you think the people will say if they believe we unnecessarily and at great expense send these boys out of the country? Is it either necessary or expedient?" This remark ended the discussion. (Leech, *In the Days of McKinley*, 281.)

62. For the protest from Vermont, see Urban A. Woodbury to Alger, 31 July 1898, *CWS*, vol. 1, p. 340. The song is in Creager, *Fourteenth Ohio National Guard*, 217–218.

62. For the correspondence relating to Miles's desire to return his troops by thirds of units rather than whole regiments, see Miles to Alger, 23 August 1898, in *CWS*, vol. 1, p. 400; Corbin to Miles, 23 August 1898, in *ibid.*; Miles to Alger, 24 August 1898, in *ibid.*, 401; and Corbin to Miles, 24 August 1898, in *ibid.* The experience with the volunteer regiments in 1898 confirmed the long-standing antipathy of the regular army towards them. Difficulties encountered in mobilizing, training, assigning, and demobilizing the militia during the war with Spain were to be frequently cited in later years whenever efforts were made to reform the armed services.

64. For the views of Whitney T. Perkins, see his *Denial of Empire: The United States and Its Dependencies* (Leyden, 1962), 112. It is of interest that Puerto Ricans in touch with the Cuban *junta* in New York realized immediately that their island would probably not obtain independence (see, for example, two letters from Paris: Betances to Estrada Palma, 27 May 1898, and Betances to J. González Lanuza, 10 June 1898 in Cuban National Archives, *Correspondence diplomática de la delegación cubana en Nueva York durante la Guerra de Independencia de 1895 a 1898* (Havana, 1945), vol. 3, pp. 141–142.

CHAPTER 16

1. Admiral George Dewey's observation is in his *Autobiography of George Dewey: Admiral of the Navy* (New York, 1913), 234. For the movement to Cavite and the operation against Corregidor, see Dewey to Long, 4 May 1898, *BN 98*, 68; Nathan Sargent, *Dewey and the Manila Campaign* (Washington, D.C., 1947), 50; and Teodoro Agoncillo, *Malolos: The Crisis of the Republic* (Quezon City, 1960), 157. Dewey wrote later, "The machinery, docks, and workshops [of Cavite] were utilized for our ships, and, later, the many resources of the place were employed not only in keeping our squadron in good condition, but also in making repairs upon the other naval vessels and army transports which later arrived from home" (Dewey, *Autobiography*, 235). The Spanish consul in Hong Kong reported the cable-cutting of May 2 to Madrid (Navarro to Gullón, 3 May 1898, in *Spanish Diplomatic Documents*, Part 2, 180). Communications between Spain and the Philippines remained open through Iloilo, Cebu, because of a cable connection to Madrid. From Iloilo small ships could take messages to a cable station on the small island of Labuan off the north coast of Borneo that connected to Europe. On May 23, however, the Americans cut the cable to the Visayas. (Marinas [Spanish consul at Singapore] to Gullón, 29 May 1898, in *ibid.*, 181.) The garrison was still able to communicate thereafter with Madrid; the means are not clear. Perhaps messages were received and sent through the Belgian and German consuls in Manila; this is the belief of the journalist Oscar King Davis, as reported in *McClure's* of June, 1899, according to James A. Field, Jr. An American cable entrepreneur, James A. Scrymser, developed the erroneous view that Dewey had cut the cable between Manila and Cavite rather than the connection between Manila and Hong Kong. Scrymser's activities in Washington led to an official sealing of the cable end in Hong Kong, even though the line was inoperative. It also stimulated stillborn ef-

forts to lay an American cable from Manila to a point outside British jurisdiction near Hong Kong. (James A. Scrymser, *Personal Reminiscences of James A. Scrymser* [n.p., 1915], 97–100.) For comments on the importance of cables in 1898, see James A. Field, Jr., "American Imperialism: The 'Worst Chapter' in Almost Any Book," *American Historical Review*, 73 (June, 1978): 665–666. Dewey raised and spliced the cable on August 21, 1898, and communications resumed at that point (Dewey, *Autobiography*, 282). Admiral Montojo claimed that Governor-General Augustín could have arranged to preserve the cable by working through the British consul (Patricio Montojo, "El desastre de Cavite [1898]: Sus causas y sus efectos," MS 1326, 28–29, Library of the Spanish Naval Museum, Madrid, Spain). For the role of the *Zafiro* and the *McCulloch*, see Dewey, *Autobiography* 240–241. Dewey wrote as follows of the *Zafiro* and its activities at Hong Kong: "In the purchase of supplies . . . the officer in charge of the *Zafiro* had to exercise discretion, and particularly in their embarkation. The British authorities were personally so cordial and so inclined to be fair in their construction of the laws of neutrality that I thought we should be very careful, on our side, to commit no act that could be misconstrued. Both fresh meat and vegetables were bought by Chinese compradors from Chinese merchants, and were sent off to the *Zafiro* in small quantities under cover of night. Happily, we had the fact in our favor that the British part of Hong Kong harbor only extends to a certain limit; beyond this the Chinese authorities have control. Therefore the *Zafiro* could be anchored in the Chinese zone whenever she took on coal or provisions."

2. Dewey's initial report is Dewey to Long, 4 May 1898, in *BN 98*, 68. Long's query is in Long to Dewey, 7 May 1898, in *ibid.*, 69. For Dewey's answer, see Dewey to Long, 13 May 1898, in *ibid.*, 97–98. For Dewey's comments on the reason for requesting troops see his *Autobiography*, 240.

3. For the early attitude and communications to Spain, see Ignacio Salinas y Angulo, *Defensa del General Jáudenes* (Madrid, 1899), 43; and José Roca de Togores y Saravia, *Bloqueo y sitio de Manila en 1898* (Huesca, Spain, 1908), 189, 195–196. For the evacuation of the city, see *ibid.*, 101–103.

4. For the early efforts of Augustín to woo the Filipinos, see Gregorio Zaide, *The Philippine Revolution* (Manila, 1964), 178–179; and Agoncillo, *Malolos*, 118, 120. Agoncillo describes the Assembly as follows: "There is no record of the achievements of the Assembly—if indeed it had any—for it merely served as an advisory body without any powers. It was in essence an honorary body designed not as a co-equal power in the government, but as a decoration to flatter the vanity of the romantics among the intellectuals." For the activities of the Consultative Assembly and its decline, see John R. M. Taylor, *The Philippine Insurrection Against the United States* (Washington, D.C., 1906); 5 vols. of galley proof never published, galleys 10 AJ, 12 AJ; Zaide, *Philippine Revolution*, 179, 191; and Teodoro M. Kalaw, *The Philippine Revolution* (Quezon City, 1969), 97. For the militia, see Taylor, *Philippine Insurrection*, galley 10 AJ; and Agoncillo, *Malolos*, 118–119. On June 3 Augustín reported to Madrid, "I do not trust natives or militia, as many of them are deserting" (Taylor, *Philippine Insurrection*, 15 AJ). On June 8 he reported continuing difficulties of this nature (Spain, Ministry of the Marine. *Correspondencia oficial referente á las operaciones navales durante la guerra con los Estados Unidos en 1898* [Madrid, 1899], 282). See also his report of June 14 in Salinas, *Defensa del General Jáudenes*, 45. For Moret's comment on the Filipinos see Moret to Augustín, 15 May 1898, in *Ultramar Records*, Philippines, Government, bundles 5,302–5,303.

5. For statistics on troop strength, see Taylor, *Philippine Insurrection*, 8 AJ; Severo Gómez Núñez, *La guerra hispano-americana. Puerto-Rico y Filipinas* (Madrid, 1902), 193. For criticism of Augustín's failure to concentrate troops at Manila, see *ibid.*, 170; and Salinas, *Defensa del General Jáudenes*, 29–31. For the fate of the

Spanish troops, see Roca de Togores y Saravia, *Bloqueo y sitio de Manila*, 118–119; and Graham A. Cosmas, *An Army for Empire: The United States Army in the Spanish-American War* (Columbia, Mo., 1971), 237.

6. Zaide, *Philippine Revolution*, 242. For the leader's account, see Saturnino Martín Cerezo, *El sitio de Baler (notas y recuerdos)* (Guadalajara, Spain, 1904). When the garrison surrendered to the insurgents, it did so on condition that it be allowed to march out of the town and rejoin other Spanish forces (*Ibid.*, 194–195). Cerezo's work was translated by F. L. Dodds as *Under the Red and Gold: Being Notes and Recollections of the Siege of Baler* (Kansas City, 1909). For an account of the imprisonment, escape, and rescue of Gillmore and his men, see James C. Gillmore, "A Prisoner Among Filipinos," *McClure's Magazine*, two issues: 15 (August, 1900): 291–302 and 16 (September, 1900): 399–410. For an account by an enlisted man who had been taken prisoner and placed with the group—a member of the Signal Corps—see the account of Leland S. Smith, USAMHI.

7. For the defense of Manila, see Salinas, *Defensa del General Jáudenes*, 32–34, 37–39, 44; Carlos Ría-Baja, *El desastre filipino. Memorias de un prisonero* (Barcelona, 1899), 91; and Montojo, "El desastre de Cavite," 38.

8. Augustín's message of May 25 is quoted in Salinas, *Defensa del General Jáudenes*, 43. For messages during the next two weeks, see Augustín to Correa, 3 June 1898, in *Correspondencia oficial*, 281; Augustín to Correa, 8 June 1898, in *ibid.*, 282. For the Admiral's message, see Montojo to Auñón, 8 June 1898, in *ibid.*, 63. For Augustín to Correa, 13 June 1898, see *ibid.*, 263. See also mention of a message in similar language on June 14 in Salinas, *Defensa del General Jáudenes*, 45.

9. For the view of the Liberal ministry, see Correa to Auñón, n.d. but ca. 15 June 1898, in *Correspondencia oficial*, 284. For the diary entry, see Juan Toral and José Toral, *El sitio de Manila (1898). Memorias de un voluntario* (Manila, 1898), 204.

10. For Dewey's message, see Dewey to Long, 12 May 1898, in *BN 98*, 97. For Long's report, see Long to Dewey, 16 May 1898, in *ibid.*, 98. For the Senator's letter, see Chandler to Long, 19 May 1898, quoted in Gardner Weld Allen, ed., *Papers of John Davis Long 1897–1904* (Boston, 1939), 126. For Long's report of conflicting information, see Long to Dewey, 20 May 1898, *BN 98*, 99.

11. Sicard (for the Naval War Board) to Long, 20 May 1898, *AF*, file 10, roll 363. For the dispatch of the *Monterey*, see William Reynolds Braisted, *The United States Navy in the Pacific, 1897–1909* Austin, 1958), 29; and Long to Dewey, 27 May 1898, *BN 98*, 101. For the *Monadnock* decision, see Sicard (for the Naval War Board) to Long, 28 May 1898, *RG 45*, NRC 371, vol. 1, p. 193; and Sargent, *Dewey and the Manila Campaign*, 63. Robert Seager II believes that the *Monterey* was sent largely to balance the neutral foreign forces at Manila, but that the *Monadnock* was dispatched specifically to counter Cámara (Robert Seager II, *Alfred Thayer Mahan: The Man and His Letters* [Annapolis, 1977], 383).

12. Dewey's anxious message to Washington is Dewey to Long, 27 May 1898, *BN 98*, 101. His inquiry to Gibraltar is reported in Sprague to Moore, 29 May 1898, *AF*, file 4, roll 33. For the message, Dewey to Long, 12 June 1898, see *BN 98*, 106. Sargent's views are in his *Dewey and the Manila Campaign*, 63–65. A discussion of the difficulties with the German squadron is found later in this chapter. For Long's message about Cámara, see Long to Dewey, 29 May 1898, *BN 98*, 101. For the preparation of the monitors see C. H. Allen to Mare Island Navy Yard (two messages), 4 June 1898 and 8 June 1898, *RG 45*, Entry 19, no. 2, 7, 14; Long to Mare Island Navy Yard, 17 June 1898, *RG 45*, NRC 371, vol. 2, p. 82; and Sicard (for the Naval War Board) to Long, 18 June 1898, *RG 45*, NRC 371, vol. 2, p. 90.

13. For Mahan's views, see his "Narrative Account of the Work of the Naval War Board of 1898," 29 October 1906, in Record Group 7: Intelligence and Technological Archives, 1894 to 1945, Archives of the Naval War College, Newport, R.I., UNOpB, 22, 28.

14. For Mahan's views on the tardy dispatch of the monitors see *ibid.*, 22. The com-

parison of the two Spanish vessels with Dewey's fleet is in Dewey, *Autobiography*, 259. The Navy Department reported the departure of the *Monadnock* on June 25 in Long to Dewey, 27 June 1898, *BN 98,* 108. For Dewey's communications to Wildman, 11 June 1898, 27 June 1898, and 28 June 1898, see Edwin Wildman, "What Dewey Feared in Manila Bay," *Forum,* 59 (May, 1918): 521, 525, 525–526. For calculations about the arrival of the monitors and Cámara's squadron, see Mahan, "Narative Account of the Naval War Board," 22. On July 1 Dewey wrote once again to Wildman, "Hope that the Cadiz squadron has not yet reached Suez, in which case the 'Monterey' and possibly the 'Monadnock,' will get here before it can, in which case the Dons will be sorry they came" (Wildman, "What Dewey Feared in Manila Bay," 526).

15. For reports of the movements of Cámara sent to Dewey, see Long to Dewey, 18 June 1898, in *BN 98,* 107, reporting the passage off Ceuta; Long to Dewey, 22 June 1898, in *ibid.,* reporting the Spanish ships off Cartagena; Long to Dewey, 25 June 1898, *RG 45,* Entry 19, no. 2, 65, reporting them off Cape Bon; Long to Dewey, 27 June 1898, *BN 98,* 108, reporting them off Port Said; and Wildman to Day, transmitted to the Navy Department in Moore to Long, 27 June 1898, *AF,* file 4, role 34, reporting the consul's intention to notify Dewey of the sighting off Port Said. The exchange between Manila and Washington about a possible movement into Spanish waters is Dewey to Long, rec. 27 June 1898, in *BN 98,* 109; Long to Dewey, 29 June 1898, in *ibid.* See also Dewey, *Autobiography,* 258. For the message that Cámara had passed through the Suez Canal, see Long to Dewey, 5 July 1898, *BN 98,* 110.

16. The proposal of the Naval War Board is in Sicard (for the Naval War Board) to Long, 19 June 1898, *RG 45,* NRC 371, vol. 2, p. 91. The alternate landing place was Binangonam anchorage on the eastern coast of Luzon. From there troops could march on Manila. (Sicard [for Naval War Board] to Long, 1 July 1898, *RG 45,* NRC 371, vol. 2, p. 148.) For Dewey's notice to General Anderson regarding his decision to avoid battle with Cámara, see Anderson to Corbin (letter), 9 July 1898, in *CWS,* vol. 2, pp. 77–79. Anderson held his transports longer than had been anticipated, but he released them when it became likely that the monitors and additional troops would soon materialize. The possibility of making a defense in Subig Bay was reported to the War Department in Anderson to Corbin (letter), 14 July 1898, in *ibid.,* 779–780. The plan to move to the south and take Cámara by surprise is mentioned in Dewey, *Autobiography,* 261. This report came fifteen years after the event. The present author has found no documentary confirmation in the correspondence for 1898. Dewey's decision to steam east of Cape Engano and meet the *Monadnock* is reported in Dewey to Long, 17 July 1898, *BN 98,* 117. As late as July 18 Dewey was manifesting concern about Cámara; apparently he still had not learned that Cámara had turned back, although that event took place around July 7. To Wildman he wrote, "Without them [the monitors] I fear this squadron is not strong enough for even Spanish battleships. Please do not mention this matter to anyone, but I am quite anxious about it, as you may well imagine (Wildman, "What Dewey Feared in Manila Bay," 528).

17. For Mahan's analysis, see his "Narrative Account of the Naval War Board," 25. For the army's plan, see Thomas M. Anderson, "Our Rule in the Philippines," *North American Review* 170 (February, 1900): 274–275.

18. The quotation is from Toral and Toral, *El sitio de Manila,* 260. See, for similar interpretation of the reaction in Manila, Augustín's letter to María Cristina quoted in Duque de Tetuán, *Apuntes del ex-Ministro de Estado Duque de Tetuán para la defensa de la política internacional y gestión diplomática del gobierno liberal-conservador de 28 de Marzo de 1895 á 29 de Septiembre de 1897* (n.p., 1902), vol. 2, p. 128. See also Montojo, "El desastre de Cavite," 39.

19. For information concerning the arrival of various neutral ships, see Zaide, *Philippine Revolution,* 186; Donald William Mitchell, *History of the Modern American*

Navy: From 1883 Through Pearl Harbor (New York, 1946), 76–77; Braisted, *United States Navy in the Pacific, 1897-1909*, 35; Dewey, *Autobiography*, 256–257; Gómez Núñez, *La guerra hispano-americana. Puerto-Rico y Filipinas*, 196; Sargent, *Dewey and the Manila Campaign*, 68; Dewey to Long, rec. 27 June 1898, *BN 98*, 109; Moore to Long, 4 May 1898, *AF*, file 10, roll 363; Thomas A. Bailey, "Dewey and the Germans at Manila Bay," *American Historical Review* 45 (October, 1939): 60. Dewey claimed in 1913 that the *Raleigh* had fired across the bow of the *Cormoran*, but Braisted notes that the action was not recorded in Dewey's log.

20. Dewey, *Autobiography*, 251; Dewey to Long, 12 June 1898, *BN 98*, 106; and Sargent, *Dewey and the Manila Campaign*, 63–65.

21. This account is given in Alfred L. P. Dennis, *Adventures in American Diplomacy 1896-1906* (New York, 1969 reprint edition), 93–94.

22. For Bülow's actions, see Lester Burrell Shippee, "Germany and the Spanish-American War," *American Historical Review* 30 (July, 1925): 764–765. For his explanation to Tirpitz, see Bülow to Tirpitz, 18 May 1898, quoted in Leon María Guerrero, "The Kaiser and the Philippines," *Philippine Studies* 9 (October, 1961): 597. For Diederich's orders and activities, see Bailey, "Dewey and the Germans at Manila Bay," 61, 63–64. Braisted, however, notes that this order followed a German decision not to concur in the transfer of the Philippine Islands to another power unless Germany received compensation (Braisted, *United States Navy in the Pacific, 1897-1909*, 34). See, for the German posture, Ernest R. May, *Imperial Democracy: The Emergence of America as a Great Power* (New York, 1961), 228. Much later Diederichs replied to Dewey's anti-German version of events at Manila Bay. He claimed that his goal was "to avoid anything that could irritate the blockading party, so long, of course, as the honour of our flag was not menaced." He insisted that he had no political instructions. He had seen only one document, apparently a diplomatic communication to a German representative; it stated that Germany had no intention of setting up a protectorate for itself in the Philippines. His superior enjoined strict neutrality towards both the Americans and the Spanish. See the English edition of an article, originally in the *Marine Rundschau*, entitled "A Statement of Events in Manila Bay . . . ," *Journal of the Royal United Service Institution*, 59 (November, 1914): 424. For Brumby's encounter, see Synopsis by unidentified staff officer [Brumby] of conversation with Vice-Admiral von Diederichs, 7 July 1898, in *AF*, file 10, roll 364. See also Bailey, "Dewey and the Germans at Manila Bay," 67.

23. For these events see Sargent, *Dewey and the Manila Campaign*, 70. The claim that the *Irene* slipped her cable is in Zaide, *Philippine Revolution*, 187–188. See also Braisted, *United States Navy in the Pacific, 1897-1909*, 39. Dewey did not report this incident until July 13, and he did not indicate that the *Irene* had taken any hostile steps or violated any rules of neutrality (Dewey to Long, 13 July 1898, *BN 98*, 110–111).

24. See Butler's report of the conversation of 15 November 1930, *AF*, file 10, roll 364. Diederichs himself provided an account of this conversation in "A Statement of Events in Manila Bay," 437–438. See also Bailey, "Dewey and the Germans at Manila Bay," 67–68; and Holger H. Herwig, *Politics of Frustration: The United States in German Naval Planning, 1889-1941* (Boston and Toronto, 1976), 30–31.

25. Dewey to von Diederichs, 11 July 1898, in Papers of Admiral George Dewey, box 5, Manuscript Division, Library of Congress, Washington, D.C.; von Diederichs to Dewey, n.d. but ca. 12 July 1898, in Dewey Papers, box 5; Dewey to von Diederichs, 12 July 1898, in Dewey Papers, box 5; and von Diederichs to Dewey, n.d. but ca. 13 July 1898, in Dewey Papers, box 5.

26. For the views of Bailey, see "Dewey and the Germans at Manila Bay," 81.

Diederichs is quoted in J. Fred Rippy, "The European Powers and the Spanish-American War," *James Sprunt Historical Studies*, 19, no. 2 (Chapel Hill, 1927): 35. For Spring Rice to Hay, 16 July 1898, see Stephen Gwynn, ed., *The Letters and Friendships of Sir Cecil Spring Rice: A Record* (Freeport, N.Y., 1972 reprint edition), vol. 1, p. 251. Dewey's concern reached to Washington, and the Navy Department made inquiries about whether any German armored vessels were preparing for sea. The attaché in Berlin reported no such activity at Kiel and Wilhelmshaven. (Long to Barber, 22 July 1898, *RG 38,* Entry 100; Barber to Long, rec. 1 August 1898, *RG 38,* Entry 100.) A recent authority offers the view that Diederich's purpose was "to be at hand should the Americans decide not to take the Philippines" (Paul M. Kennedy, *The Samoan Tangle: A Study of Anglo-American Relations 1878-1900* [Dublin, 1974], 139).

27. For the commanding general's recommendations, see Miles to Alger, 3 May 1898, *CWS,* vol. 2, p. 635. For McKinley's memorandum regarding the expedition, see McKinley to Alger, 4 May 1898, *IC,* vol. 2, p. 1,191. For Long's orders regarding a transport, the *City of Pekin,* see Long to Navy Yard (Mare Island, Calif.), 4 May 1898, in *BN 98,* 136. For the orders concerning Guam, see Long to Commanding Officer, U.S.S. *Charleston,* 10 May 1898, in *ibid.,* 151.

28. For the views of the secretaries, see Russell A. Alger, *The Spanish-American War* (New York and London, 1901), 326; Long to unidentified neighbor (Hingham, Mass.), 1 November 1898, in Lawrence Shaw Mayo, ed., *America of Yesterday: As Reflected in the Diary of John Davis Long* (Boston, 1923), 213-214. Captain Chadwick argued that the delay in the dispatch of the *Monterey* and *Monadnock* supports the view that the United States government did not contemplate territorial acquisitions in the Philippine Islands at the outset of the war (French Ensor Chadwick, *The Relations of The United States and Spain: The Spanish-American War* [New York, 1911], vol. 1, p. 154). Paolo E. Coletta maintains that although the attack on the Philippines led ultimately to annexation, this outcome is without prejudice to the motives entertained at the outset (see his "The Peace Negotiations and the Treaty of Paris," in Paolo E. Coletta, ed., *Threshold to American Internationalism: Essays in the Foreign Policies of William McKinley* [New York, 1970], 145). Ernest R. May advances the thesis that the McKinley Administration had in mind hastening the peace settlement with its follow-up campaign in the Philippines. The President acted in the Pacific simply because he could not hope to launch a really large expedition in the Caribbean for some time; the army was not prepared for an early campaign there of the first magnitude. The motive of impressing Spain played a role in enlarging the expedition beyond early plans. "The President obviously hoped that it would be possible to win the Cuban war by pressure on the Philippine Islands" (May, *Imperial Republic,* 99).

29. For Merritt's orders, 12 May 1898, see *CWS,* vol. 2, p. 637. Merritt, the senior Major General, had the choice of a command elsewhere (Alger, *Spanish-American War,* 327). Brigadier General Elwell S. Otis, destined later to play a most important role in the Philippine Insurrection, was assigned as second-in-command (Corbin to Otis, 11 May 1898, *ibid.,* 636; Otis to Corbin, 11 May 1898, *ibid.*; and Corbin to Otis, 12 May 1898, *ibid.,* 637). Merritt's letter requesting a larger force than was earlier contemplated is Merritt to McKinley, 13 May 1898, *IC,* vol. 2, pp. 1,199-1,200. On the same day Merritt asked to have the orders relieving him from his present assignment held up until he could communicate with the Secretary of War. Was this a covert form of pressure? (Merritt to Corbin, 13 May 1898, in *CWS,* II, 649.) The question of the mission and the problem of the insurgents are posed in Merritt to McKinley, 15 May 1898, in *ibid.,* 645-646. In this communication Merritt asked for a siege battery and an ordnance detachment in addition to his requests of May 13. He also proposed that an inquiry be dispatched to Dewey asking about the situation in the Philippine Islands. This inquiry went out in Long to

Dewey, 16 May 1898, *BN 98,* 99. Merritt's request for information stimulated responses from various quarters (see memorandum on the Merritt inquiry, 17 May 1898, *CWS,* vol. 2, pp. 654–656; Wildman to Day, 17 May 1898, *AF,* file 10, roll 363, also forwarded to the War Department in Adee to Alger, 21 May 1898, in *CWS,* vol. 2, p. 665; and Dewey to Long, 27 May 1898, in *ibid.,* 675–676).

30. The immediate reaction of the War Department is reflected in Corbin to Merriam, 13 May 1898, in *CWS,* vol. 2, p. 39. The recommendation of the commanding general is Miles to Alger, 16 May 1898, in *ibid.,* 647–648. The states expected to supply volunteers were California, Colorado, Kansas, Montana, Nebraska, Oregon, Utah, Washington, North Dakota, South Dakota, Idaho, Wyoming, and Minnesota. This recommendation made logistical sense, given the proximity of these states to the probable training camps and ports of embarkation. Troops from more easterly states would presumably be utilized in operations against Cuba and Puerto Rico. Merritt's public statement is mentioned in Margaret Leech, *In the Days of McKinley* (New York, 1959), 211. Merritt's endorsement to Miles's letter is 17 May 1898, in *CWS,* vol. 2, p. 648. Miles's endorsement of the Merritt endorsement is 18 May 1898, in *ibid.,* 648–649.

31. For Merritt's explanation, see Merritt to J. Addison Porter, 17 May 1898, in Papers of William McKinley, Presidential Papers Microfilm, Library of Congress (Washington, 1961), series 1, roll 3. For the expansion of Merritt's forces, see Leech, *In the Days of McKinley,* 211. For the instructions, see Alger to Merritt, conveying instructions, and McKinley to Alger for Merritt, both 19 May 1898, *CWS,* vol. 2, pp. 676–678.

32. Cosmas, *Army for Empire,* 121. Margaret Leech notes that the situation was unprecedented. John Bassett Moore, a Democrat who was Professor of International Law at Columbia University, had been called to the State Department; he was consulted regarding the question of how to administer a conquered territory. (Leech, *In the Days of McKinley,* 211.) McKinley gave no authority to recognize the insurgent government of Emilio Aguinaldo, but included no language that would preclude this step in the future. (Taylor, *Philippine Insurrection,* galley 36 AJ.) Merritt's assignment to command the "Department of the Pacific," comprised of the Philippine Islands only, was conveyed to him in Schwan to Merritt, 16 May 1898, *CWS,* vol. 2, p. 649.

33. For information regarding the departure of Anderson, see Taylor, *Philippine Insurrection,* galley 34 AJ; *IC,* vol. 1, p. 138; and Douglas White, *On to Manila: A True and Concise History of the Philippine Campaigns, Secured While Afloat With Admiral Dewey's Fleet, and in the Field With the 8th U.S. Army Corps* (San Francisco, 1899). Correspondence concerning the departure includes: Corbin to Otis, 14 May 1898, *CWS,* vol. 2, pp. 639–640; Long to Dewey, 16 May 1898, *BN 98,* 98; Corbin to Otis, 19 May 1898, *CWS,* vol. 2, p. 661; Long to Dewey, 20 May 1898, in *BN 98,* 99; Long to Dewey, 21 May 1898, in *ibid.,* 100; and Long to Dewey, 29 May 1898, in *ibid.,* 101. For the orders to Anderson see Corbin to Otis, 23 May 1898, *CWS,* vol. 2, pp. 668–669.

34. For some comment on the strategic location of Guam, see Harold and Margaret Sprout, *Toward a New Order of Sea Power: American Naval Power and the World Scene, 1918-1922* (Princeton, 1940), 29. For the recollections of the warrant officer of the Second Oregon, see George A. Courtright to Professor W. Reed West, 18 February 1941, *AF,* file 10, roll 364. For the seizure of Guam, see Report of Captain Henry Glass, 24 June 1898, *BN 98,* 151–152; and Lt. W. Braunersreuther (commander of landing party) to Glass, 21 June 1898, *AF,* file 10, roll 364. See also Cosmas, *Army for Empire,* 236; Chadwick, *Spanish-American War,* vol. 2, pp. 373–374; and John R. Spears, *Our Navy in the War With Spain* (New York, 1898), 345. For personal recollections of the capture, see the account of a member of the Second Oregon, H. C. Thompson—"War Without Medals," *Oregon Historical*

Quarterly 59 (December, 1898): 293–325. Frank Portusach, the naturalized American who visited the *Charleston* on June 20, 1898, gives his account in "History of the Capture of Guam by the United States Man-of-War *Charleston* and Its Transports," *United States Naval Institute Proceedings* 43 (April, 1917): 707–718.

35. For correspondence leading to the designation of Merritt's command as the Eighth Army Corps, see Merritt to Corbin, 11 June 1898, in *CWS*, vol. 2, pp. 705–706; Corbin to Merritt, 21 June 1898, in *ibid.*, 707–708. For the views of Cosmas concerning differences in efficiency between the expeditions to Cuba and Manila, see his *Army for Empire*, 193. For Merritt's activity in preparing the expeditions, see *ibid.*, 199–201; Corbin to Merritt, 29 May 1898, in *CWS*, vol. 2, p. 680; Merritt to Corbin, 29 May 1898, in *ibid.*; Merritt to Corbin, 6 June 1898, in *ibid.*, 691–692; and Merritt to Corbin, 22 June 1898, *IC*, vol. 2, p. 1,266.

36. For the departure of the Eighth Army Corps, see *IC*, vol. 1, p. 138; Taylor, *Philippine Insurrection*, galleys 34, 35 and 36 AJ; and Cosmas, *Army for Empire*, 201. Dewey received frequent information concerning the progress of the Eighth Army Corps (see, for example, Long to Dewey, 18 June 1898, in *BN 98*, 107; Long to Dewey, 24 June 1898, in *ibid.*; Long to Dewey, 25 June 1898, in *ibid.*, 108; and Long to Dewey, 29 June 1898, in *ibid.*, 109). Dewey reported the arrival of various contingents in Dewey to Long, 4 July 1898, in *ibid.*, 110; Dewey to Long, 17 July 1898, in *ibid.*, 117; and Dewey to Long, 26 July 1898, in *ibid.*, 118.

37. For the recollection of the voyage, see George A. Courtright to Professor W. Reed West, 18 February 1941, *AF*, file 10, roll 364. The delay experienced because of the slow speed of the *Charleston* did not affect later passages because escorts were deemed unnecessary (Corbin to Merritt, 26 June 1898, *CWS*, vol. 2, p. 714). For the observations of the naval officer, see Lieutenant Ralph H. Miner to Chief of the Bureau of Navigation, 19 October 1898, *BN 98*, 138. General Anderson pointed out problems on board his transports and made recommendations to correct them; he mentioned inadequate cooking facilities, poor refrigeration, lack of sufficient fresh water, and slow speed of the convoy (Anderson to Corbin, 11 July 1898, *CWS*, vol. 2, p. 676).

38. For background on the treaty of annexation, see Sylvester K. Stevens, *American Expansion in Hawaii 1842–1898* (New York, 1968 reprint edition), 284–285. He reports that the Hawaiian legislature voted in favor of the treaty on May 27, 1896. For the American response to the Hawaiian proposal, see William Adam Russ, Jr., *The Hawaiian Republic (1894–1898) and Its Struggle to Win Annexation* (Selinsgrove, Pa., 1961), 192–194. For the Japanese protest, see Merze Tate, *The United States and the Hawaiian Kingdom: A Political History* (New Haven and London, 1965), 283. For Toru Hoshi's statement, see Payson J. Treat, *Diplomatic Relations Between the United States and Japan 1895–1905* (Gloucester, Mass., 1963), 32. For Sherman's reaction, see Thomas A. Bailey, "Japan's Protest Against the Annexation of Hawaii," *Journal of Modern History* 3 (March, 1931): 52. For additional information, see Treat, *Diplomatic Relations Between the United States and Japan*, 43–44; and Julius W. Pratt, *America's Colonial Experiment: How the United States Gained, Governed, and In Part Gave Away a Colonial Empire* (New York, 1951), 38–39. For the motives of the Japanese government, see Bailey, "Japan's Protest Against the Annexation of Hawaii," 60–61.

39. McKinley's comments to the Senator from Massachusetts are in George F. Hoar, *Autobiography of Seventy Years* (London, 1904), vol. 2, pp. 307–308.

40. For the joint resolution, see Pratt, *America's Colonial Experiment*, 75; and May, *Imperial Democracy*, 243. For McKinley's statement to Cortelyou, see Leech, *In the Days of McKinley*, 213. For a detailed analysis of the debates in Congress during June–July, 1898, see Russ, *Hawaiian Republic*, 193–356. Thomas A. Bailey summarizes the reasons offered for Hawaiian annexation: (1) Present policy was morally

unsound; (2) annexation was an imperative war measure; and (3) annexation was necessary to ensure defense of the Pacific coast and the Philippine Islands (Thomas A. Bailey, "The United States and Hawaii During the Spanish-American War," *American Historical Review* 36 [April, 1931]: 559–560). He notes also that during the emergency of 1898 prior to annexation Hawaii chose to cooperate actively with the United States rather than adopt strict neutrality or follow a policy of silence and passivity (*ibid.*, 533). For the role of the Chairman of the Senate Foreign Committee, see Dwight Richard Coy, "Cushman K. Davis and American Foreign Policy, 1887–1900" (Dissertation, University of Minnesota, 1965), 216–264.

41. For the transfer of power in Hawaii, see Tate, *The United States and the Hawaiian Kingdom*, 301–306; Ellis Paxson Oberholzer, *A History of the United States Since the Civil War* (New York, 1937), vol. 5, pp. 547–548. On July 10, 1898, President McKinley and Secretary Alger decided that the First New York Volunteers should be assigned occupation duty in Hawaii rather than service with the Eighth Army Corps as originally planned (Corbin to Otis, 10 July 1898, *IC,* vol. 2, p. 1,282). The quotation is in Marilyn B. Young, *The Rhetoric of Empire: America's China Policy 1895–1901* (Cambridge, Mass., 1968), 220.

CHAPTER 17

1. For the initial activities of the expedition, see John R. M. Taylor, *The Philippine Insurrection Against the United States* (Washington, D.C., 1906; 5 vols. of galley proof never published), galley 35 AJ; Walter Millis, *The Martial Spirit: A Study of Our War With Spain* (Boston and New York, 1931), 333–334; French Ensor Chadwick, *The Relations of the United States and Spain: The Spanish-American War* (New York, 1911), vol. 2, pp. 391–393. For Merritt's observations upon arrival, see Merritt to Corbin, 25 July 1898, *CWS,* vol. 2, pp. 781–782.

2. Taylor, *Philippine Insurrection,* galleys 18, 19, 20, and 22 FZ H; Teodoro A. Agoncillo, *The Revolt of the Masses: The Story of Bonifacio and the Katipunan* (Quezon City, 1906), 15; Leon Wolff, *Little Brown Brother: How the United States Purchased and Pacified the Philippine Islands at the Century's Turn* (New York, 1961), 17–18; and Bonifacio S. Salamanca. *The Filipino Reaction to American Rule 1901–1913* (Hamden, Conn., 1968), 9–11.

3. Agoncillo, *Revolt of the Masses,* 22–26; Salamanca, *Filipino Reaction to American Rule,* 11–16; and Gregorio Zaide, *The Philippine Revolution* (Manila, 1962), 42. Zaide lists the aims of the *Liga filipina*: (1) uniting the whole archipelago into a compact body; (2) providing mutual protection in every want and necessity; (3) ensuring defense against all violence and injustice; (4) encouraging instruction, agriculture, and commerce; (5) studying and applying reforms. For the early nationalist movement, see John N. Schumacher, *The Propaganda Movement: 1880–1895* (Manila, 1973).

4. Agoncillo described the Masonic basis of the *Katipunan (Revolt of the Masses,* 46). For the origins and purposes of the *Katipunan,* see *ibid.*, 40–59. See also Zaide, *Philippine Revolution,* 78–79. The full name of the organization in the Malayan language is *Kataastaasan Kagalanggalang Na Katipunan Ng Mga Anak Ng Bayan*— "Highest and Most Respectable Society of the Sons of the People." See also Eufronio M. Alip, *Political and Cultural History of the Philippines* (Manila, 1949), 103–104. For Mabini's views, see Apolinario Mabini, *The Philippine Revolution* (n.p., 1969), 42. For Taylor's views, see *Philippine Insurrection,* galley 27 FZ H.

5. Zaide, *Philippine Revolution,* 107–109; Taylor, *Philippine Insurrection,* galleys 27 and 28 FZ H; and Wolff, *Little Brown Brother,* 27–28. It is said that Aguinaldo's name means "Christmas box" (Lázaro Segovia, *The Full Story of Aguinaldo's Capture* [Manila, 1902], 172).

6. Major John S. Mallory, "The Philippine Insurrection, 1896–1898," in U.S. War Department, *Annual Reports of the War Department for the Fiscal Year Ended June 30, 1903*, Volume 3: *Reports of Department and Division Commanders* (Washington, D.C., 1903), 399–405 (hereafter cited as *ARWD 03*). See also Zaide, *Philippine Revolution*, 117.

7. Polavieja's statement is quoted in Zaide, *Philippine Insurrection*, 127. For Rizal's execution, see Taylor, *Philippine Insurrection*, galley 32 FZ H; Melchor Fernández Almagro, *Historia política de la España contemporánea*, Volume 2: *Regencia de doña María Cristina durante la menor edad de su hijo don Alfonso XIII* (Madrid, 1959), 350–351; and Austin Coates, *Rizal: Philippine Nationalist and Martyr* (Hong Kong, 1968), 327–331. Coates denies the allegation that Rizal recanted before his execution and married Josephine Bracken, his mistress. For military operations early in 1897, see Taylor, *Philippine Insurrection*, galleys 31 and 32 FZ H; Zaide, *Philippine Insurrection*, 139–141; and Mallory, "Philippine Insurrection," *ARWD 03*, 405–423. During this period the insurgents made their first efforts to attract international support. José Alejandrino attempted without much success to purchase arms in Japan during February–March, 1897. (José Alejandrino, *The Price of Freedom (La Senda del Sacrificio): Episodes and Anecdotes of Our Struggles for Freedom* [Manila, 1949], 59–74.)

8. For the execution of Bonifacio, see Zaide, *Philippine Revolution*, 147–149; and Teodoro M. Kalaw, *The Philippine Revolution* (Quezon City, 1969 reprint edition), 58. Aguinaldo's version of this episode is that he commuted Bonifacio's sentence but withdrew the commutation at the urging of Noriel and del Pilar. The official order to execute the Bonifacio brothers came from Noriel; Aguinaldo said that he did not know of the order. (Emilio Aguinaldo and Vicente Pacis, *A Second Look at America* [New York, 1957], 24–25). For the retreat of Aguinaldo to Biyakna-Bató, see Taylor, *Philippine Insurrection*, galleys 32, 33, and 36 FZ H.

9. For an English translation of the insurgent proclamation, see Charles S. Olcott, *The Life of William McKinley* (Boston and New York, 1916), vol. 2, pp. 158–159.

10. For the negotiation and terms of the Pact of Biyak-na-Bató, see John Morgan Gates, *Schoolbooks and Krags: The United States Army in the Philippines, 1898-1902* (Westport, Conn., and London, 1973), 14; Teodoro A. Agoncillo, *Malolos: The Crisis of the Republic* (Quezon City, 1960), 25–44; Olcott, *McKinley*, vol. 2, pp. 160–161; Taylor, *Philippine Insurrection*, galleys 36 and 38 FZ H; and Chadwick, *Spanish-American War*, vol. 2, p. 344. For Alejandrino to Blumentritt, 4 November 1897, see Alejandrino, *Price of Freedom*, 78. (This work, however, must be used with caution.) For Moret to Primo de Rivera, 4 December 1897, see Patricio Montojo, "El desastre de Cavite (1898): Sus causas y sus efectos," MS 1326, Library of the Spanish Naval Museum, Madrid, Spain.

11. For the outcome of the Pact of Biyak-na-Bató see Taylor, *Philippine Insurrection*, galley 41 FZ H; Agoncillo, *Malolos*, 55–56; and Kalaw, *Philippine Revolution*, 75. For Alejandrino to Blumentritt, 21 February 1898, see Alejandrino, *Price of Freedom*, 79–80. Agoncillo comments on the differences of opinion within the insurgent movement between the dissidents with European backgrounds and those in Hong Kong. These differences had considerable effects on the course of later events. "The former wanted reforms and administration within the framework of the Spanish monarchy; the latter wanted independence and freedom under an American protectorate. The former, because of their financial status, wanted to protect their interests by eschewing radical changes in the political set-up which might ultimately affect their finances. The latter, however, though with some means, had been deprived of these means by the Spanish Government and, therefore, had practically nothing to lose in advocating independence." (Agoncillo, *Malolos*, 115.) For a parallel view, see Taylor, *Philippine Insurrection*, galley 7 AJ. This formulation might be an oversimplification, but no reasonable doubt exists that such con-

siderations constituted at least one of the elements dividing various insurgent factions.

12. For the activity in Zambales and outbreaks elsewhere, see Taylor, *Philippine Insurrection*, galley 4 AJ. For information from the consulate in Manila, see Williams to Thomas F. Cridler, 22 February 1898, in *CWS*, vol. 2, p. 650; and Williams to Cridler, 19 March 1898, in *ibid.*, 651. For a dramatic account of barbarities associated with violence in the Philippines, see Williams to Cridler, 27 March 1898, in *ibid.*, 651-652. The British consul in Manila reported similar views to the Foreign Office: "I am extremely afraid that there will soon be a general rising throughout these islands, as there is great disinterest and none of the reforms promised to the natives have as yet been carried out" (E. H. Rawson Walker to Salisbury, 15 April 1898, *FO 185*, box 865).

13. For the initial notice of the insurgent proposal, see Wildman to Day, 3 November 1897, quoted in Olcott, *William McKinley*, vol. 2, pp. 42-43. See also William J. Pomeroy, *American Neo-Colonialism: Its Emergence in the Philippines and Asia* (New York, 1970), 38-39. The reply is Cridler to Wildman, 15 December 1897, quoted in Olcott, *McKinley*, vol. 2, p. 144. Pomeroy advances the highly implausible view that, because some six weeks intervened between Wildman's cable of November 3 and Cridler's response of December 15, the cable must have received serious consideration in Washington (Pomeroy, *American Neo-Colonialism*, 39). An infinitely more plausible view is that the item was of low priority because of the press of other business considered vastly more important than Wildman's message.

14. See Zaide, *Philippine Revolution*, 173; and Henry F. Graff, ed., *American Imperialism and the Philippine Insurrection: Testimony Taken From Hearings on Affairs in the Philippine Islands Before the Senate Committee on the Philippines—1902* (Boston, 1969), x-xi.

15. Taylor, *Philippine Insurrection*, galley 42 FZ H. See also William Reynolds Braisted, *The United States Navy in the Pacific, 1897-1909* (Austin, 1958), 43.

16. This account is taken from Millis, *Martial Spirit*, 181; Rhoda E. A. Hackler, "Discoverer of Aguinaldo?" *Foreign Service Journal* 47 (January, 1970): 32-34, 44; Agoncillo, *Malolos*, 123-125; Emilio Aguinaldo y Famy, *True Version of the Philippine Revolution* (Tarlac, P.I., 1899), 10-12; and Taylor, *Philippine Insurrection*, galley 43 FZ H.

17. Kalaw, *Philippine Revolution*, 91-92; and Agoncillo, *Malolos*, 149.

18. For Dewey's testimony, see Graff, ed., *American Imperialism and the Philippine Insurrection*, 6-8. For Dewey's explanation of 1913, see Dewey, *Autobiography*, 245. The story of the visit of the Filipinos to the *Olympia* is in Alejandrino, *The Price of Freedom*, 91.

19. Dewey's comment on the influence of the consuls is in Graff, ed., *American Imperialism and the Philippine Insurrection*, 23-24. For Dewey's views on what might have happened if he had been able to capture Manila immediately, see *ibid.*, 19.

20. For the meeting of May 4, 1898, see Zaide, *Philippine Revolution*, 173-174; Kalaw, *Philippine Revolution*, 92-94; Agoncillo, *Malolos*, 129-133; and Millis, *Martial Spirit*, 223. Braisted argues plausibly that Aguinaldo's hesitancy to return at this time undercuts the argument that he had been promised independence, even though Pratt had obviously made or implied unauthorized commitments (Braisted, *United States Navy in the Pacific, 1897-1909*, 44-45). For arrangements leading to the return of Aguinaldo, see Nathan Sargent, *Dewey and the Manila Campaign* (Washington, D.C., 1957), 57; and U.S. Revenue Cutter Service, *The United States Revenue Cutter Service in the War With Spain, 1898* (Washington, D.C., 1899), 16.

21. For Dewey's first explanation of his reason for letting Aguinaldo come to Cavite, see Graff, ed., *American Imperialism and the Philippine Insurrection*, 9. For the second explanation, see Dewey, *Autobiography*, 246. There is no proof to support

the allegation that Dewey acted to fulfill his side of a bargain made with Aguinaldo—he to further Filipino independence in return for military assistance against Spain. In testimony before the Schurman Commission, which investigated affairs in the Philippines in 1899 shortly after the outbreak of the Philippine Insurrection, Dewey testified that Consul Oscar F. Williams had told him of a camp of five thousand insurgents who presumably would rise up on his appearance at Manila. Nothing happened after May 1, so Dewey permitted Aguinaldo to come to Manila. "This was done with the purpose of strengthening the United States forces and weakening those of the enemy. No alliance of any kind was entered into with Aguinaldo, nor was any promise of independence made to him then or at any other time." (U.S. Senate, *Report of the Philippine Commission to the President, January 31, 1900*, 56th Cong., 1 st Sess., Sen Doc. No. 138, Part 2, p. 172.)

22. This interpretation of the talks follows that of Agoncillo, *Malolos*, 148–149, 152–153. For Braisted's view, see his *United States Navy in the Pacific, 1897–1909*, 43.

23. For the Dewey-Aguinaldo interview and its outcome, see Taylor, *Philippine Insurrection*, galleys 18 AJ and 19 AJ; Aguinaldo, *True Version*, 16–19; and Sargent, *Dewey and the Manila Campaign*, 57. For the first mention of Aguinaldo in reports, see Dewey to Long, 20 May 1898, *BN 98*, 100.

24. Alejandrino to Blumentritt, 19 May 1898, quoted in Alejandrino, *Price of Freedom*, 94.

25. Dewey's remarks are in Graff, ed., *American Imperialism and the Philippine Insurrection*, 3, 12, 15. After the war Dewey was asked why, if he had not realized early in his dealings with Aguinaldo that the Filipino sought independence, he had expressed himself at the time as of the opinion that the Filipinos were capable of self-government. He answered, "Because I saw in the newspapers that Congress contemplated giving the Cubans independence, and I knew that our people did not know very much about the Filipinos at that time. I knew that because before going there I had great difficulty in finding out anything about them. Therefore I gave this information as something which was not generally known." (*Ibid.*, 9.)

26. Long to Dewey, 26 May 1898, in *BN 98*, 101.

27. Dewey to Long, 3 June 1898, in *ibid.*, 102. Dewey described his approach to Aguinaldo with fair accuracy in his *Autobiography:* "From observation of Aguinaldo and his advisers I decided that it would be unwise to co-operate with him or his adherents in an official manner. . . . In short, my policy was to avoid any entangling alliance with the insurgents, while I appreciated that, pending the arrival of our troops, they might be of service in clearing the long neck of land that stretches out from Cavite Peninsula to the environs of Manila." (Dewey, *Autobiography*, 247.)

28. Agoncillo, *Malolos*, 217–221; Taylor, *Philippine Insurrection*, galley 27 AJ; and Dewey, *Autobiography*, 312–313.

29. For arms purchases in China, see Zaide, *Philippine Revolution*, 181; Agoncillo, *Malolos*, 127–128; Eufronio Melo Alip, *In the Days of General Emilio Aguinaldo: A Study of the Life and Times of a Great Military Leader, Statesman, and Patriot Who Founded the First Republic of Asia* (Manila, 1969), 55–56; and Taylor, *Philippine Insurrection*, galley 14 AJ. For the sinking of the *Nunobiki Maru*, see Zaide, *Philippine Revolution*, 285; Payson J. Treat, *Diplomatic Relations Between the United States and Japan 1895–1905* (Gloucester, Mass., 1963 reprint edition), 67–68; and Gates, *Schoolbooks and Krags*, 100–101. The ship carried ten thousand rifles, six million rounds of ammunition, and other supplies. For the activities of Filipinos in Japan, especially José Alejandrino, Faustino Lichauco, and Mariano Ponce, see Josefa Saniel, "Japan and the Philippines," (Dissertation, University of Michigan, 1962), 307–322.

30. For Aguinaldo's compaigns, see Major John S. Mallory, "The Philippine Insurrec-

tion," in *ARWD 03*, vol. 3, pp. 423–433; Graham A. Cosmas, *An Army for Empire: The United States Army in the War With Spain* (Columbia, Mo., 1971), 191; Alip, *In the Days of Aguinaldo*, 56–57; Kalaw, *Philippine Revolution*, 113; and Taylor, *Philippine Insurrection*, galley 14 AJ. Dewey reported briefly on Aguinaldo's operations, indicating the Filipino successes but reflecting confidence that Aguinaldo could not take Manila by himself (Dewey to Long, 30 May 1898, in *BN 98*, 102; Dewey to Long, 6 June 1898, in *ibid.*, 102–103; and Dewey to Long, 12 June 1898, in *ibid.*, 106). For Dewey's views on his relations with Aguinaldo, see Graff, ed., *American Imperialism and the Philippine Insurrection*, 3–4. Taylor believed that Aguinaldo went out of his way to cultivate Dewey because the insurgent leader "had to maintain such relations with the Americans as would induce the Spaniards to believe that their fleet was at his disposal, and also such apparent harmony and cooperation with them in the execution of their plans that the recalcitrant among the Filipinos would be forced to believe that the Americans would in all ways use their forces to support Aguinaldo in the attainment of his desires." (Taylor, *Philippine Insurrection*, galley 14 AJ.)

31. For the quotation, see Taylor, *Philippine Insurrection*, galleys 22 AJ. For additional information, see Alip, *In the Days of Aguinaldo*, 57–58.

32. For Taylor's observation on the lack of Filipino consensus, see his *Philippine Insurrection*, galley 31 AJ. For his view of the inner nature of the Aguinaldo regime, see *ibid.*, galley 27 AJ. Taylor insisted throughout his work that while the insurgent government spoke much of democracy and republicanism, its real intentions were consistently authoritarian. See also Agoncillo, *Malolos*, 227–231; and Alip, *In the Days of Aguinaldo*, 54. For additional information, see Zaide, *Philippine Revolution*, 201–203; and Kalaw, *Philippine Revolution*, 106, 109–110.

33. Apolinario Mabini, *The Philippine Revolution* (n.p., 1969), 52; and Agoncillo, *Malolos*, 223–226. For Taylor's view, see *Philippine Insurrection*, galley 24 AJ.

34. Long to Dewey, 14 June 1898, *BN 98*, 103; Day to Pratt, 16 June 1898, quoted in Gates, *Schoolbooks and Krags*, 18. E. Spencer Pratt later informed the Secretary of State that he had made no commitments to Aguinaldo: "I know," he wrote, "from the observations made upon it [a speech] at the time and since, that it was not construed by the Philippinos [*sic*] or others present as in any way implying an endorsement of the insurgents' political programme, but on the contrary as being especially non-commital in that particular." (Pratt to Day, 31 August 1898, in National Archives Microfilm Publications, *Records of the Department of State Relating to the Paris Peace Commission, 1898* (Washington, D.C., 1965), Microcopy TP954, (hereafter cited as *PPC*).

35. Dewey to Long, 27 June 1898, *BN 98*, 103. On June 16 Consul Oscar F. Williams, who remained with Dewey, reported on his activities to the Secretary of State: "For future advantage I am maintaining cordial relations with Gen. Aguinaldo having stipulated submissiveness to our forces when treating for their return here. Last Sun. 12, they held a council to form provisional Government, I was invited to attend but thought it best to decline. A form of Govt. was adopted, but Gen. Aguinaldo told me today that his friends all hoped that the Philippines would be held as a Colony of U.S.A." Williams explained his motives in maintaining friendly unofficial contact: "It has been my effort to maintain harmony with insurgents in order to exercise greater influence hereafter when we reorganize government." (Williams to Day, 16 June 1898, *AF*, file 10, roll 364).

36. Williams is quoted in Hackler, "Discoverer of Aguinaldo?" 34.

37. Anderson's initial dealings with Aguinaldo are discussed in Chadwick, *Spanish-American War*, vol. 2, p. 375. For early communications to Aguinaldo from Anderson regarding efforts to cooperate and avoid conflicts of authority, see Anderson to Aguinaldo, 4 July 1898, in *CWS*, vol. 2, p. 805; and Anderson to Aguinaldo, 6 July 1898, in *ibid.*, 806. For Anderson's suspicions of Aguinaldo, see Anderson to Cor-

bin, 9 July 1898, in *ibid.*, vol. 1, p. 778. Dealings with the Filipino leader during the middle of July may be traced in Anderson to Corbin (letter), 14 July 1898, *IC*, vol. 2, pp. 1,335–1,336; S. R. Jones to Aguinaldo, 17 July 1898, in *CWS*, vol. 2, p. 807; Aguinaldo letter (brief), 18 July 1898, in *ibid.*, 809; Anderson to Aguinaldo, 18 July 1898, in *ibid.*; and Aguinaldo letter (brief), rec. 20 July 1898, in *ibid.*, 807. For Anderson to Corbin (letter), 18 July 1898, see *ibid.*, 781. For Anderson's views on the abilities of the Filipinos, see Anderson to Corbin (letter), 21 July 1898, in *ibid.*, 809. For additional information about the American dealings with Aguinaldo, see Anderson to Aguinaldo, 22 July 1898, in *ibid.*, 810; unsigned (but probably Anderson) to Aguinaldo, 23 July 1898, in *ibid.*, 811; Aguinaldo letter (brief), 24 July 1898, in *ibid.*; and Anderson to Aguinaldo, 24 July 1898, in *ibid.*

38. Merritt report, ARWD 98, 48; Cosmas, *Army for Empire*, 192.

CHAPTER 18

1. For Dewey's views of the situation in the city, see Dewey to Long, 26 July 1898, *BN 98*, 118. On the same date he wrote to Wildman, "Affairs are most critical in Manila, and I would not be surprised to have them offer to capitulate at any moment, now they know that relief cannot possible [*sic*] reach them" (Edwin Wildman, "What Dewey Feared in Manila Bay," *Forum* 59 [May, 1918]: 529). Augustín kept up a continuous lament in messages to Madrid indicating the hopelessness of his situation in the absence of reinforcements. See his messages of 23 June 1898 and 18 July 1898, quoted in Ignacio Salinas y Angulo, *Defensa del general Jáudenes* (Madrid, 1899), 45–46. For his announcement of Merritt's arrival, see Augustín to Correa, 25 July 1898, quoted in Duque de Tetuán, *Apuntes del Ex-Ministro del Estado Duque de Tetuán para la defensa de la política internacional y gestión diplomática del gobierno liberal-conservador desde el 28 de Mayo de 1895 á 29 de Septiembre de 1897* (n.p., 1902), vol. 2, pp. 119–120. The mood of the city is described in Juan Toral and José Toral, *El sitio de Manila (1898). Memorias de un voluntario* (Manila, 1898), 265. For information about the food shortage, see José Roca de Togores y Saravia, *Bloqueo y sitio de Manila en 1898* (Huesca, Spain, 1908), 208–210. He reports, however, that spirits were high among the Spanish soldiers mounting fortifications outside the city: "In the trenches the soldiers continued singing and firing, and if someone had pronounced the word *surrender* they would have lynched him" (*ibid.*, 210).

2. Dewey to Long, 26 July 1898, *BN 98*, 118; and Dewey to Wildman, 26 July 1898, in Wildman, "What Dewey Feared in Manila Bay," 529.

3. For McKinley's statement, see *Foreign Relations, 1898*, lvix.

4. The American movement into the line below Manila is recounted in John R. M. Taylor, *The Philippine Insurrection Against the United States* (Washington, D.C., 1906; 5 vols. of galley proofs never published), galley 37 AJ; French Ensor Chadwick, *The Relations of the United States and Spain: The Spanish-American War* (New York, 1911), vol. 2, pp. 398–401; ARWD 98, 47–49; and Russell H. Alger, *The Spanish-American War* (New York and London, 1901), 333–334.

5. For Dewey's actions, see his *Autobiography of George Dewey: Admiral of the Navy* (New York, 1913), 272–273; Alger, *Spanish-American War*, 334; and Nathan Sargent, *Dewey and the Manila Campaign* (Washington, D.C., 1947), 77. For Dewey's word to the Navy Department, see Dewey to Long, 29 July 1898, *BN 98*, 118. For Merritt's report to the War Department, see Merritt to Corbin, rec. 1 August 1898, in *CWS*, vol. 2, p. 743. The War Department responded by informing General Merriam at San Francisco that he might have to send out forces "at the earliest possible day" (Corbin to Merriam, 9 August 1898, in *ibid.*, 749). Dewey's general tendency to seek a political rather than military solution to the Spanish

resistance at Manila may have been influenced to some extent by the course of events at Santiago de Cuba. He wrote Wildman on July 9, "Manila is ready to fall into our hands, but I doubt very much if any movement is made before the arrival of more troops. We don't want too many 'drawn' battles like that in Santiago the other day." (Quoted in Wildman, "What Dewey Feared in Manila Bay," 527).

6. For the arrival of the *Monterey* and the Dewey-Merritt differences, see Chadwick, *Spanish-American War*, vol. 2, p. 403; John R. Spears, *Our Navy in the War With Spain* (New York, 1898), 348; Sargent, *Dewey and the Manila Campaign*, 79; and Dewey, *Autobiography*, 272. For the replacement of Augustín, see Taylor, *Philippine Insurrection*, galley 15 AJ. Montojo reports the motives of the Sagasta ministry in his "El desastre de Cavite (1898): Sus causas y sus efectos," MS 1326, Library of the Spanish Naval Museum, Madrid, Spain, 40.

7. For the first surrender demand, see Merritt and Dewey to Jáudenes, 7 August 1898, *ARWD 98*, 54. For the situation in the city, see Salinas, *Defensa del Jáudenes*, 54; and Severo Gómez Núñez, *La guerra hispano-americana. Puerto-Rico y Filipinas* (Madrid, 1902), 219. The latter gives locations of troops stationed in and around the walled city. The Spanish response is Jáudenes to Merritt and Dewey, 7 August 1898, in *ARWD 98*, 54. The second demand is Merritt and Dewey to Jáudenes, 9 August 1898, in *ibid*. The reply is Jáudenes to Merritt and Dewey, 9 August 1898, in *ibid.*, 55. See also Salinas, *Defensa del General Jáudenes*, 57–58; and Gregorio Zaide, *The Philippine Revolution* (Manila, 1964), 210. For the rejection of Jáudenes's request, see Merritt and Dewey to Jáudenes, 10 August 1898, *ARWD 98*, 55.

8. André replaced the original go-between, the English Consul General Rawson-Walker, who died during the siege. For the role of André, see Zaide, *Philippine Revolution*, 209–210; and Teodoro Agoncillo, *Malolos: The Crisis of the Republic* (Quezon City, P.I., 1960), 187–188. For André's method of negotiation, see Thomas M. Anderson, "Our Rule in the Philippines," *North American Review*, 170 (February, 1900): 278. For the conversation between McKinnon and Nozaleda, see B. Edmund McDevitt, *The First California's Chaplain* (Fresno, Calif., 1956), 94–95.

9. Dewey's testimony of 1902 is quoted in Henry F. Graff, ed., *American Imperialism and the Philippine Insurrection: Testimony Taken From Hearings on Affairs in the Philippine Islands Before the Senate Committee on the Philippines—1902* (Boston, 1969), 4–5, 19. The message to the Secretary of the Navy is Dewey to Long, 17 August 1898, *BN 98*, 125–126. Dewey's comment of 1913 is in his *Autobiography*, 275.

10. Anderson's comment on the deal is in his "Our Rule in the Philippines," 278. For discussions of the informal agreement with Jáudenes, see Leon Wolff, *Little Brown Brother: How the United States Purchased and Pacified the Philippine Islands at the Century's Turn* (New York, 1961), 117–119; Dewey, *Autobiography*, 272–275; Sargent, *Dewey and the Manila Campaign*, 81; Graham A. Cosmas, *An Army for Empire: The United States Navy in the War with Spain* (Columbia, Mo., 1971), 240–241; and William Reynolds Braisted, *The United States Navy in the Pacific, 1897–1909* (Austin, 1958), 48–49.

11. Merritt's instructions (10 August 1898) dealing with the insurgents are in *CWS*, vol. 2, p. 812. For Anderson's arrangements to occupy positions in front of Blockhouse No. 14, see Anderson to Aguinaldo, 10 August 1898, in *ibid.*; and Aguinaldo to Anderson, 10 August 1898, in *ibid.*, 813. Merritt's plan of attack is given in *ARWD 98*, 50. The units of MacArthur's brigade included three battalions in the advance from the Thirteenth Minnesota and eight battalions in reserve from the Twenty-Third Infantry, the First North Dakota, the Fourteenth Infantry, and the Astor Battery. Greene had seven battalions in advance from the First Colorado, the Eighteenth Infantry, and the Third Artillery. Eight battalions in support came from the First California, the First Nebraska, and the Tenth Pennsylvania.

12. For this information, see Chadwick, *Spanish-American War*, vol. 2, pp. 409–410; *ARWD 98*, 50; and Cosmas, *Army for Empire*, 241.
13. For the naval activity, see Sargent, *Dewey and the Manila Campaign*, 84; Chadwick, *Spanish-American War*, vol. 2, p. 410; and Dewey, *Autobiography*, 277–278. For official reports of commanders involved in the action, see *AF*, file 10, roll 364. For Bradley Allen Fiske's recollection, see his *From Midshipman to Rear-Admiral* (New York, 1919), 279. Dewey later stated to a Congressional committee, "They did not fire a shot; although they had probably 15,000 troops in the city and forty-seven rifled guns on the city front, they did not fire a shot at my squadron" (Quoted in Graff, ed., *American Imperialism and the Philippine Insurrection*, 5).
14. For the land actions, see Taylor, *Philippine Insurrection*, galley 39 AJ; Chadwick, *Spanish-American War*, vol. 2, pp. 412–418; and *ARWD 98*, 50–51.
15. For Dewey's recollection, see Graff, ed., *American Imperialism and the Philippine Insurrection*, 19. For the surrender, see Dewey, *Autobiography*, 280; Sargent, *Dewey and the Manila Campaign*, 85–86; and Braisted, *United States Navy in the Pacific, 1897–1909*, 49. An eyewitness at Manila, Oscar King Davis, summarized Dewey's views of the situation accurately: "Dewey's negotiations with the Spanish Captain-General had proceeded so successfully that he was confident there would be no real action, and that a little demonstration of force was all that would be necessary" (Oscar King Davis, *Released for Publication: Some Inside Political History of Theodore Roosevelt and His Times 1898-1918* [Boston and New York, 1925], 15).
16. See Thomas A. Bailey, "Dewey and the Germans at Manila Bay," *American Historical Review* 45 (October, 1939): 74–78. See also Bradford Perkins, *The Great Rapprochement: England and the United States, 1895-1914* (New York, 1968), 47; and Braisted, *United States Navy in the Pacific, 1897-1909*, 49.
17. For Anderson's message to Aguinaldo and the response, see Agoncillo, *Malolos*, 188–189; Taylor, *Philippine Insurrection*, galley 34 AJ. See also William T. Sexton, *Soldiers in the Sun: An Adventure in Imperialism* (Harrisburg, Pa., 1939), 46.
18. Juan Ortega Rubio states that Jáudenes did not know of the course of events in Washington in his *Historia de la regencia de María Cristina Hapsbourg-Lorena* (Madrid, 1906), vol. 4, p. 137. For Taylor's summary of the reasons for Jáudenes's surrender, see his *Philippine Insurrection*, galley 17 AJ. Merritt later wrote rather boastfully but accurately in his report, "I submit that for troops to enter under fire a town covering a wide area, to rapidly deploy and guard all principal points in the extensive suburbs, to keep out the insurgent forces pressing for admission, to quietly disarm an army of Spaniards more than equal in numbers to the American troops, and finally by all this to prevent entirely all rapine, pillage, and disorder, and gain entire and complete possession of a city of 300,000 people filled with natives hostile to the European interest, and stirred up by the knowledge that their own people were fighting in the outside trenches, was an act that only the law-abiding, temperate, resolute American soldier, well and skillfully handled by his regimental and brigade commanders, could accomplish" (*ARWD 98*, 51). Merritt conveniently neglected to mention the fact that for the most part the battle was a sham affair, even if most of the troops ashore had not been informed of this fact.
19. For the agreement, see Dewey, *Autobiography*, 321–323. Those who signed for the American forces were Brigadier General Francis V. Greene, Captain B. P. Lamberton, Lieutenant Colonel Charles A. Whittier, and Lieutenant Colonel Enoch H. Crowder. Those who signed for the Spanish forces were Lieutenant Colonel Nicolas de la Peña, Colonel Carlos Reyes, and Colonel José María Olaquén Felia. See also Taylor, *Philippine Insurrection*, galley 40 AJ; and Chadwick, *Spanish-American War*, vol. 2, pp. 421–422.
20. Dewey records the arrival of news of the protocol in his *Autobiography*, 282. Jáudenes's protest is discussed in *ARWD 98*, 52.
21. For the President's message of congratulations, see McKinley to Merritt, 21 August

1898, *IC,* vol. 2, p. 1,315. It stated, "In my own behalf and for the nation I extend to you and the officers and men of your command sincere thanks and congratulations for the conspicuously gallant conduct displayed in your campaign." Dewey sensed that the situation might well deteriorate after the Spanish surrender; on August 4 he had written Wildman, "I think they will surrender as soon as they see we mean business. Then Merritt's troubles will begin. Aguinaldo is not behaving well. It will take some time, I should think, for the two countries to get together on the peace question" (Wildman, "What Dewey Feared in Manila Bay," 529). The only interservice difficulty at Manila related to Dewey's tendency to delay the attack on Manila. Merritt considered Dewey a friend, and had cordial relations with him at Manila. He later told Whitelaw Reid, "The Admiral had been a little stiff sometimes as to what the navy would or would not do in the matter of cooperating in attack. [Dewey] had been careful to keep his ships and himself out of the range of fire, and was evidently resolved not to injure ships or risk the loss of any life in bombarding Manila in order to aid the army in capturing it. He [Merritt] said that at no time during the bombardment did the Admiral or any of the important ships of his squadron get closer than two miles to the shore. He said some of his vessels commanded by younger and more impetuous officers worked their way further in." (Diary of Whitelaw Reid, 4 October 1898, quoted in Howard Wayne Morgan, ed., *Making Peace With Spain: The Diary of Whitelaw Reid September-December 1898* [Austin, 1965], 58).

CHAPTER 19

1. Adams to Hay, 5 May 1898, quoted in Worthington Chauncey Ford, ed., *Letters of Henry Adams (1892-1916)* (Boston and New York, 1938), vol. 2, pp. 175-176.
2. The message from London is Hay to Day, 8 May 1898, Papers of John Hay, box 3, Manuscript Division, Library of Congress, Washington, D.C. For the White House meeting on peace terms, see Diary of John Davis Long, 9 May 1898, quoted in Lawrence Shaw Mayo, ed., *America of Yesterday: As Reflected in the Diary of John Davis Long* (Boston, 1923), 191. The Secretary of State's request to Hay is Day to Hay, 9 May 1898, Hay Papers, box 16. The reply is Hay to Day, 10 May 1898, Hay Papers, box 3.
3. For Chamberlain's speech, see William Roscoe Thayer, *The Life and Letters of John Hay* (Boston and New York, 1908), vol. 2, p. 169. See also James Lewis Garvin, *The Life of Joseph Chamberlain,* Volume 3: *1895-1900: Empire and World Policy* (London, 1934), 301-304; Charles S. Campbell, Jr., "Anglo-American Relations, 1897-1901," in Paolo E. Coletta, ed., *Threshold to American Internationalism: Essays on the Foreign Policies of William McKinley* (New York, 1970), 225-226. For Chamberlain's comments in Parliament and the interpretation offered above, see Ernest R. May, *Imperial Democracy: The Emergence of America as a Great Power* (New York, 1961), 222-223. Hay continued to report favorable signs and portents. To Henry Cabot Lodge he wrote, "The state of feeling here is the best I have ever known. From every quarter, the evidences of it come to me. The royal family, by habit and tradition, are most careful not to break the rules of strict neutrality, but even among them I find nothing but hearty kindness, and, so far as is consistent with propriety—sympathy. Among the political leaders on both sides, I find not only sympathy but a somewhat eager desire that 'the other fellows' will not seem the more friendly. C——'s [Chamberlain's] startling speech was partly due to a conversation I had with him in which I hoped he would not let the opposition have a monopoly of expressions of good-will to America. He is greatly pleased with the reception his speech met with on our side, and said 'He don't care a hang what they say about it on the Continent.'" (Hay to Lodge, 25 may 1898, quoted in Thayer, ed., *Letters of John Hay,* vol. 3, pp. 124-125.)

4. For the war aims message, see Day to Hay, 3 June 1898, quoted in Tyler Dennett, *John Hay: From Poetry to Politics* (New York, 1933), 190. For the modification, see Day to Hay, 14 June 1898, quoted in *ibid.*, 191.
5. For Hay's notice that Salisbury would forward the terms, see Hay to Day, 5 June 1898, Hay Papers, box 3. For the Secretary of State's response see Day to Hay, 7 June 1898, Hay Papers, box 16. Hay's report of the word from Goluchowski is in Hay to Day, 8 June 1898, Hay Papers, box 3.
6. For the report of the British Foreign Office, see Horace Rumbold to Salisbury, 11 June 1898, *FO 185*, box 865. For Hay's summary of the outcome, see Hay to McKinley, 10 June 1898, quoted in Charles S. Olcott, *The Life of William McKinley* (Boston and New York, 1916), vol. 2, pp. 131–132. Day later praised Hay for his handling of what he called "this most delicate matter" (Day to Hay, 23 June, 1898, Hay Papers, box 16). Obviously, given the Spanish attitude, the United States had no alternative but to drop the idea of stimulating early peace negotiations; but there may have been other reasons for following this course. Ernest R. May speculates that McKinley may have decided to delay the matter because of the emergence of Aguinaldo in the Philippines or perhaps because of the navy's success in blockading Cervera at Santiago de Cuba—an achievement that seemed almost to guarantee the success of the army expedition there—but he suspects that most probably McKinley's change of course reflected more than anything else the growing interest manifest across the United States in the annexation of the Philippine Islands (Ernest R. May, "McKinley [1898]," in Ernest R. May, ed., *The Ultimate Decision: The President as Commander in Chief* [New York, 1960], 100–101). It seems likely, however, that McKinley would have jumped at an indication that Spain was prepared to negotiate on his terms. He could not do so simply because no word came from Madrid.
7. For the Spanish proposal, see a memorandum by Salisbury, 13 June 1898, in *FO 185*, box 865. A similar feeler put out in Rome and Vienna did not lead to anything (see British Ambassador in Austria to Salisbury, 14 June 1898, *FO 185*, box 865; and Paris Embassy of Great Britain to Salisbury, 14–15 June 1898, *FO 185*, box 865). For Salisbury's report to Hay, see Hay to Day, 15 June 1898, Hay Papers, box 3. See also May, *Imperial Democracy*, 223. Honesto A. Villanueva notes the failure of the Spanish initiative in his "Diplomacy of the Spanish-American War," *Philippine Social Sciences and Humanities Review* 14 (March, 1949): 449. For the remaining information in this paragraph, see May, *Imperial Democracy*, 226–236. On June 2 a British representative in St. Petersburg informed Salisbury of a comment made by Count Muraviev to a colleague in response to possible American annexation of the Philippines: "Count Muraviev replied that the possession of the Philippines was not a matter of much interest to Russia. At the same time he gave him to understand that any interest they might ultimately be compelled to take in the question would be due to friendly feeling towards another Power" (N. R. O'Conor to Salisbury, 2 June 1898, *FO 185*, box 865). On June 16 the American ambassador in St. Petersburg, Ethan Hitchcock, asked Muraviev whether there was any truth to reports that a European congress might be called to deal with the Philippine question. Muraviev denied knowledge of any such project. Hitchcock informed him that any such development would be considered an "unfriendly act." (Edward H. Zabriskie, *American-Russian Rivalry in the Far East: A Study in Diplomacy and Power Politics 1895–1914* [Philadelphia, 1946], 50.) For information concerning dealings with Germany, see Lester Burrell Shippee, "Germany and the Spanish-American War," *American Historical Review*, 30 (July, 1925): 766–767. When Kaiser Wilhelm learned of a possible peace move by the powers early in June he expressed himself as against any such project: "Until one or the other of the belligerents has had its fill of fighting mediation is folly" (*ibid.*, 763). Once the American attitude towards the Philippines began to become evident, the Germans interested themselves in other Spanish possessions in the Pacific, notably

the Carolines, the Samoas, and the Ladrones. A well-placed friend of John Hay, Cecil Spring Rice, reported a conversation with Prince Metternich indicating that Germany had no wish to antagonize the United States. (Spring Rice to Hay, 16 July 1898, quoted in Stephen Gwynn, ed., *Letters and Friendships of Sir Cecil Spring Rice: A Record* [Freeport, N.Y., 1972 edition], vol. 1, p. 251.) When Théophile Delcassé succeeded Gabriel Hanotaux as Foreign Minister of France late in June, 1898, he adopted the hands-off policy of his predecessor (Tom Tandy Lewis, "Franco-American Relations, 1898–1907," [Dissertation, University of Oklahoma, 1970], 47–48). The principal consequence of diplomacy during 1898 was to harden continental European attitudes towards the United States, however deferential they may have appeared. A comment of the German Hohenlohe-Schillingfurst to Philip Eulenberg illustrates the point: Referring to the Americans, he wrote, "when they have built up a strong fleet and a respectable army as a result of the war, the Americans will make themselves very disagreeable in Europe. This prospect will hopefully convince our narrow-minded bourgeois that we need a strong fleet." (Hohenlohe to Eulenberg, 22 July 1898, quoted in Paul M. Kennedy, *The Samoan Tangle: A Study of Anglo-American Relations 1878–1900* [Dublin, 1974], 141.)

8. Spain's attitude clearly shifted after the outcome at Santiago de Cuba. Before the defeats in Cuba on land and sea Lieutenant Sims reported on June 15 that one of his secret agents had learned of considerable confidence among Spanish leaders in Madrid, that they thought time was on their side, and that they would open negotiations for peace through Paris when their forces had achieved a victory at Santiago de Cuba. (Sims to Bureau of Navigation, rec. 15 June 1898, *RG 38*, Entry 100). Hay's letter is Hay to McKinley, 6 July 1898, quoted in Olcott, *McKinley*, vol. 2, pp. 132–133. Reports from the naval attaché in London include Colwell to Long, rec. 7 July 1898, a telegram that somehow leaked to the London press; Colwell to Long, rec. 8 July 1898; Colwell to Long, rec. 11 July 1898; Colwell to Long, 12 July 1898; and Colwell to Long, rec. 14 July 1898—all in *RG 38*, Entry 100. Much that Colwell learned from his agents, particularly the information that Spain sought to negotiate, proved to be correct. Other capitals also heard of Spanish dejection and interest in peace. See, for example, a report from Vienna in Horace Rumbold to Salisbury, 8 July 1898, *FO 185*, box 866.

9. Almodóvar's message is Almodóvar to León y Castillo, 18 July 1898, *Spanish Diplomatic Documents*, 200. For additional information, see Olcott, *McKinley*, vol. 2, p. 58. See also Pablo de Azcárate, *La guerra del 98* (Madrid, 1968), 149; and Margaret Leech, *In the Days of McKinley* (New York, 1959), 281–282. Sagasta consulted a number of major political figures representing various opinions in Spain, a customary procedure. Silvela and Moret thought it proper to proceed, provided a settlement involved only Cuba and Puerto Rico. Everyone agreed that it was necessary to seek peace. (Conde de Romanones, *Sagasta, o el político* [Madrid y Barcelona, 1930], 200–201.) The Liberal ministry hoped that an early armistice might help its efforts to retain the Philippines.

10. Queen Regent to McKinley, 22 July 1898, *Foreign Relations, 1898*, 819–820. The message transmitting the letter is Almodóvar to Cambon, included in Almodóvar to León y Castillo, 22 July 1898, *Spanish Diplomatic Documents*, 203. The story of the delay is in Chadwick, *Spanish-American War*, vol. 2, p. 429; and Walter Millis, *The Martial Spirit: A Study of Our War With Spain* (Boston and New York, 1931), 338.

11. For Hay's mention of "the splendid little war" in a letter of July 27, 1898, see Millis, *The Martial Spirit*, 340. For information from London and Paris about Spain's views, see Sims to Bureau of Navigation, rec. 24 July 1898; Sims to Bureau of Navigation, rec. 26 July 1898; Colwell to Long, rec. 30 July 1898; and Sims to Bureau of Navigation, 2 August 1898—all in *RG 38*, Entry 100. For Cabinet views, see Long Diary, 27 July 1898, quoted in Mayo, ed., *America of Yesterday*,

210–211. Long thought that the outcome on the Philippines question would be a decision to retain a port in Luzon. Secretary Day asked Hay in London whether he had reason to think differently of the terms mentioned on June 3. Hay replied that he continued to favor independence for Cuba and annexation of Puerto Rico, but that he now believed a settlement should ensure fair treatment of the Filipinos and include a provision prohibiting Spain from leasing or alienating territory in the Philippines without American consent. Was this latter statement a reaction to rumors of German interest in the archipelago? Hay noted the British desire that the Americans annex the islands, or, alternatively, that London obtain an option to purchase them in the future. (See Dennett, *Hay*, 191.) For additional information about the Cabinet's views, see Paolo E. Coletta, "The Peace Negotiations and the Treaty of Paris," in Paolo E. Coletta, ed., *Threshold to American Internationalism: Essays on the Foreign Policies of William McKinley* (New York, 1970), 124.

12. For the White House interest in the public's views on war aims, see the Cortelyou Diary, 30 July 1898: President McKinley "made frequent comments upon the suggestions for peace brought to his attention. These suggestions have been coming in from all over the country, by mail and by telegraph, from the highest to the lowest citizen, and altogether with the comments, editorial and otherwise, in the public press, formed a not unimportant guide to public sentiment." (Cortelyou Diary, 30 July 1898, quoted in Olcott, *McKinley*, vol. 2, pp. 66–67.) For Borden's comments, see Borden to McKinley, 27 July 1898, quoted in Coletta, "The Peace Negotiations and the Treaty of Paris," 173. For the views of Storey, see Storey to Long, 28 July 1898, quoted in Gardner Weld Allen, ed., *Papers of John Davis Long 1897-1904* (Boston, 1939), 165.

13. Almodóvar to León y Castillo, 27 July 1898, in *Spanish Diplomatic Documents*, 206; and Almodóvar to León y Castillo for Cambon, 28 July 1898, in *ibid.*, 209.

14. For Cambon's letter to Hanotaux, 28 July 1898, see Geneviève R. Tabouis, *The Life of Jules Cambon* (London, 1938), 103. For the question of empowering Cambon, see León y Castillo to Almodóvar, 28 July 1898, *Spanish Diplomatic Documents*, 210.

15. León y Castillo to Almodóvar, 31 July 1898, in *Spanish Diplomatic Documents*, 211–212.

16. This conversation is reported in León y Castillo to Almodóvar, 1 August 1898, in *ibid.*, 214. The official notice of American terms is Day to Almodóvar, 30 July 1898, *Foreign Relations, 1898*, 820–821.

17. For the views of Dawes, see his journal, 30 July 1898, quoted in Bascom Timmons, ed., *A Journal of the McKinley Years by Charles G. Dawes* (Chicago, 1950), 166. On July 29 George Cortelyou noted, "The Cabinet appears to be nearly if not quite unanimous on the main points which will form the basis of this Government's response. Naturally the disposition made of the Philippines consumed most time and elicited the greatest amount of discussion" (Cortelyou Diary, 29 July 1898, quoted in Olcott, *McKinley*, vol. 2, p. 64). For the incident of the terms, see Cortelyou Diary, 31 July 1898, quoted in *ibid.*, 67. For additional evidence to support the view that McKinley kept control of the debate on the terms to be demanded, see Leech, *In the Days of McKinley*, 285–286.

18. For the Spanish Foreign Minister's desires, see Almodóvar to León y Castillo, 1 August 1898, in *Spanish Diplomatic Documents*, 214–215.

19. For the report of the President's views, see León y Castillo to Almodóvar, 4 August 1898, in *ibid.*, 216–217. Apparently American officials did not make a great effort to conceal their terms from diplomatic representatives of other powers in Washington. Sir Julian Pauncefote reported the terms to Salisbury on August 2, 1898, and also the fact that Cambon was urging Spain to accept them on the grounds that the United States would take nothing less. (Pauncefote to Salisbury, 2 August 1898, *FO 185*, box 866.)

20. For an account of McKinley's reaction, see Leech, *In the Days of McKinley*, 276–277. Cambon is quoted in Tabouis, *Cambon*, 105.
21. León y Castillo to Almodóvar, 5 August 1898, in *Spanish Diplomatic Documents*, 217.
22. Almodóvar to León y Castillo for Cambon, 7 August 1898, in *ibid.*, 218–219; and Almodóvar to Day through Cambon, 7 August 1898, *Foreign Relations, 1898,* 823.
23. Mahan to Long, 7 August 1898, quoted in Allen, ed., *Papers of John Davis Long*, 180.
24. León y Castillo to Almodóvar, 11 August 1898, forwarding Cambon to Almodóvar, 10 August 1898, *Spanish Diplomatic Documents,* 219–220; and Leech, *In the Days of McKinley,* 288.
25. See *Foreign Relations, 1898,* lxiv; and Day to Cambon, 10 August 1898, in *ibid.,* 823–825. For Cambon's advice to Madrid to accept the protocol, see León y Castillo to Almodóvar, 11 August 1898, forwarding Cambon to Almodóvar, 10 August 1898, *Spanish Diplomatic Documents,* 219–220. For his efforts to distinguish between the demands of July 30 and the provisions of August 10, see Cambon to Almodóvar, 11 August 1899, transmitted in León y Castillo to Almodóvar, 11 August 1898, in *ibid.,* 221–222.
26. For the meeting of the Sagasta ministry, see Melchor Fernández Almagro, *Historia política de la España contemporánea,* Volume 2: *Regencia de doña María Cristina de Austria durante la menor edad de su hijo don Alfonso XIII* (Madrid, 1959), 568. For Cambon's authority, see Almodóvar to Cambon, enclosed in Almodóvar to León y Castillo, 11 August 1898, *Spanish Diplomatic Documents,* 222–223. This message included the statement: "The Government of His Majesty has resolved to accept in all its parts the text as drawn up by the Federal Government. In consequence of the acceptance of the protocol, which implies the suspension of hostilities between the two belligerents, this Government desires to make known its expectation that the United States will use all means to prevent the separatist forces in Cuba undertaking any aggressive acts." For an assessment of the reasons for the Spanish acceptance similar to the one given above, see Cosmas, *Army for Empire,* 243.
27. For the signing, see Chadwick, *Spanish-American War,* vol. 2, p. 441. The proclamation announcing the end of hostilities, issued by President McKinley on August 12, 1898, is in U.S. Department of State, *Proclamations and Decrees During the War With Spain* (Washington, D.C., 1899), 80. Cambon reported the signature ceremony in Cambon to Almodóvar, 12 August 1898, transmitted in León y Castillo to Almodóvar, 13 August 1898, *Spanish Diplomatic Documents,* 223–224. For the views of Eugenio Montero Ríos, see his *El tratado de París. Conferencias pronunciadas en el círculo de la Unión Mercantil en los días 22, 24 y 27 Febrero de 1904* (Madrid, 1904), 37.
28. For the appointment of Day, and also that of Hay, see Leech, *In the Days of McKinley,* 328–329. Late in September, 1898, as Hay took up his responsibilities in Washington, he wrote to his wife, "He [McKinley] scared me by saying he would not worry any more about the State Department. He has evidently been Secr. of State for the past year." (Hay to Mrs. Hay, 29 September 1898, quoted in Dennett, *Hay,* 197.) Senator Wiliam E. Chandler maintained that appointment of senators to the commission violated the principle of separation of powers. McKinley had sought to name two Supreme Court justices, both with backgrounds in the Democratic Party—Chief Justice Melville Fuller and Associate Justice Edward D. White—but each refused on the grounds of public duties as jurists. (Leech, *In the Days of McKinley,* 329–330; Coletta, "The Peace Negotiations and the Treaty of Paris," 132–133; and H. Wayne Morgan, *William McKinley and His America,* [Syracuse, 1963], 401.)
29. For Silvela's statement, see Melchor Fernández Almagro, *En torno al 98. Política y*

literatura (Madrid, 1948), 44–47. For the full text, see Fernández Almagro, *Historia política*, vol. 2, pp. 866–869. For Silvela's statement of September 16, 1898, see Helene Tzitsikas, compiler, *El pensamiento español (1898-1899)* (Mexico City, 1967), 26. See also Enrique de Tapia, *Francisco Silvela. Gobernante austero* (Madrid, 1968). 230. For the refusal of the Conservative Party to participate, see Gabriel Maura Gamazo, *Historia crítica del reinado de Don Alfonso XIII durante su menoridad bajo la regencia de su madre Doña María Cristina de Austria* (Barcelona, 1925), vol. 2, p. 53. For the composition of the Spanish commission, see Juan del Arco, *Montero Ríos* (Madrid, 1947), 117–118; Marqués de Villa-Urrutia (Wenceslao Ramírez de Villaurrutia y Villaurrutia), *Palique diplomático. Recuerdos de un embajador* (Madrid, 1923), 111; and James Thomas Murphy, Jr., "A History of American Diplomacy at the Paris Peace Conference of 1898," (Dissertation, American University, 1965), 30–31. Before Sagasta could negotiate with the United States he had to obtain formal approval from the Cortes. On September 5, 1898, he proposed a law authorizing him to treat, which provoked heated debate. The law was approved on September 13, 1898, by a vote of 161 to 48, with many deputies choosing to abstain. Another manifestation of discontent at this time was an act of the popular conservative General Camilio G. de Polavieja, who issued a manifesto on September 1, 1898, calling for a nonpartisan movement to restore the country. (Fernández Almagro, *Historia política*, vol. 2, pp. 869–877.) The quintrain of Manuel del Palacio—as quoted by the Marqués de Lema in his *Mis recuerdos (1880-1901)* (Madrid, Barcelona and Buenos Aires, 1930), 247—is as follows:

> Parece grande y es chico;
> fué ministro porque sí
> Y en siete meses y pico
> perdió á Cuba, á Puerto Rico
> á Filipinas y á mi!

A slightly variant version appears in Emilio Gutiérrez-Gamero, *Mis primeras ochenta años (memorias)*, (Madrid, 1948), vol. 3, p. 321. For the comment of Augusto Conte see his *Recuerdos de un diplomático* (n.p., 1903), vol. 3, pp. 586–587.

30. The initial notice is Almodóvar to *chargé* of France in Spain, 7 September 1898, in *Spanish Diplomatic Documents*, 238. For the American answer, see Cambon transmission of United States response to note of September 7, 1898, dated 22 September 1898, in *ibid.*, 245. Almodóvar's rejoinder is Almodóvar to French *chargé* in *ibid.*, 246–249.
31. For a comparable analysis, see Richard Hofstadter, "Manifest Destiny in the Philippines," in Daniel Aaron, ed., *America in Crisis: Fourteen Crucial Episodes in American History* (New York, 1952), 185.
32. Fisher to Long, 9 May 1898, in Allen, ed., *Papers of John Davis Long*, 116–119.
33. Jones to Long, 14 May 1898, quoted in *ibid.*, 33. When expansionists sensed that President McKinley might drag his heels, they had recourse among other things to scathing doggerel. One unidentified versifier offered a poem entitled *Hold the Philippines:*

> Why doth President McKinley, in the protocol he signs,
> Leave us undetermined still the future of the Philippines?
> We have brought the haughty Spaniard to his knees to sue for peace;
> Are we only wise in battle? Are we fools when fightings cease?
> Shall we with a child's abandon throw what we have won away?
> Counting as of no advantage, this, our gateway to Cathay?
> Yield again unto the foeman land wherever our boys have trod;
> Land he could not hold against us? Never, in the name of God!

34. Endicott, Jr., to Long, 30 May 1898, quoted in *ibid.*, 132.
35. Mr. Dooley's view is in Dunne, *Mr. Dooley in Peace and War*, 9. Lodge's letters are Lodge to Roosevelt, 24 May 1898, in Henry Cabot Lodge and Charles F. Redmond, eds., *Selections From the Correspondence of Theodore Roosevelt and Henry Cabot Lodge 1884-1918* (New York, 1971 reprint edition), vol. 1, 300; Lodge to Roosevelt, 15 June 1898, in *ibid.*, 311; Lodge to Roosevelt, 24 June 1898, in *ibid.*, 313; Lodge to Roosevelt, 12 July 1898, in *ibid.*, 232-234; and Lodge to Roosevelt, 22 July 1898, in *ibid.*, 330.
36. For McKinley's opinions in July, see William M. Laffin to Lodge, 14 July 1898, quoted in John A. S. Grenville and George Berkeley Young, *Politics, Strategy, and American Diplomacy: Studies in Foreign Policy, 1873-1917* (New Haven and London, 1966), 286. For Hay's views, see Hay to McKinley, 2 August 1898, quoted in Olcott, *McKinley*, vol. 2, pp. 135-136.
37. For Lodge's views on public opinion, see Lodge to White, 12 August 1898, quoted in Allan Nevins, *Henry White: Thirty Years of American Diplomacy* (New York and London, 1930), 136. For the views of Platt, see Platt to McKinley, 15 August 1898, quoted in Louis A. Coolidge, *An Old Fashioned Senator: Orville H. Platt of Connecticut* (New York and London, 1910), 287-288.
38. For correspondence concerning McKinley's search for information about the Philippines and his desire to secure it, see Allen to Dewey, 13 August 1898, in *BN 98*, 122-123; Dewey to Long, 20 August 1898, in *ibid.*, 123; Corbin to Merritt, 25 August 1898, *CWS*, vol. 2, p. 764; Merritt to Corbin, 26 August 1898, in *ibid.*; Corbin to Merritt, 26 August 1898, in *ibid.*, 765; Allen to Dewey, 27 August 1898, *BN 98*, 123. See also *ARWD 98*, 52. For Hay's observations, see Hay to Bigelow, 5 September 1898, quoted in *Letters of John Hay and Extracts from Diary* (New York, 1969 reprint edition), vol. 3, p. 134.
39. The views of the commissioners are reviewed in Reid Diary, quoted in Howard Wayne Morgan, ed., *Making Peace with Spain: The Diary of Whitelaw Reid September-December 1898* (Austin, 1965), 26-30. McKinley's observations are in *ibid.*, 30-31. The night before his meeting with the commissioners, the President went riding with Reid, and expressed his view that agitation on the part of troops then in the Philippines to return home might reflect a general national desire to avoid further warfare in the interest of expansion. Reid did not agree but made no argument. (Coletta, "The Peace Negotiations and the Treaty of Paris," 133.)
40. "Instructions to Peace Commissioners," 16 September 1898, in *Foreign Relations, 1898*, 907.
41. The full text of the instructions is in *ibid.*, 904-908.
42. For the conversation with Delcassé, see Reid Diary, 28 September 1898, quoted in Morgan, ed., *Making Peace With Spain*, 37. For the talk with León y Castillo, see Reid Diary, 29 September 1898, *ibid.*, 38-39. For a report to the President conveying the same information, see Reid to McKinley, 4 October 1898, quoted in Olcott, *McKinley*, vol. 2, pp. 123-124.
43. Felipe Agoncillo, a lawyer by vocation, came from Taal, a town in Batangas Province, Luzon. He belonged to a distinquished family and was well educated. For information concerning his fruitless mission, see Coletta, "The Peace Negotiations and the Treaty of Paris," 138; Howard Wayne Morgan, *America's Road to Empire: The War With Spain and Overseas Expansion* (New York, London, and Sydney, 1965), 90; and Wolff, *Little Brown Brother*, 161, 211-212. Information was conveyed to the Spanish government that Agoncillo's visit to Paris was in no way at the instance of the United States government or in cooperation with it (Hay to Day, 4 October 1898, in *PPC*, roll 2; and Delcassé to Almodóvar, 14 October 1898, *Spanish Diplomatic Documents*, 253). For additional information concerning the abortive Agoncillo mission, see Teodoro M. Kalaw, *The Philippine Revolution* (Quezon City, 1969 reprint edition), 119, 123-124, 160-163.

CHAPTER 20

1. For the American decision to postpone the Philippine question, see Reid Diary, 29–30 September 1898, in Howard Wayne Morgan, ed., *Making Peace With Spain: The Diary of Whitelaw Reid September-December 1898* (Austin, 1965), 40–41. For the Spanish procedure, see Almodóvar to Montero Ríos, 29 September 1898, in *Spanish Diplomatic Documents*, 270–271; Almodóvar to Montero Ríos, 1 October 1898, in *ibid.*, 273–274; Reid Diary, 1 October 1898, in Morgan, ed., *Making Peace with Spain*, 46–48. Reid thought the Spanish argument that the capitulation was invalid might be sound, but Day did not agree. It is of interest that the American delegation had information, received before its arrival in Paris, that Spain would resist the cession of the Philippine Islands, hoping that this effort would lead to a sale (Paolo E. Coletta, "The Peace Negotiations and the Treaty of Paris," in Paolo E. Coletta, ed., *Threshold to American Internationalism: Essays on the Foreign Policies of William McKinley* [New York, 1970], 136). On October 4 The Spanish government communicated to the United States through a French intermediary its views on the issue of the capitulation versus the protocol. It refuted the argument that the protocol did not take effect until notification came to commanders in the field, insisting that "the United States can not exercise, in the city, port, and bay of Manila, over which the sovereignty of Spain has not been relinquished, anything more than the jurisdiction which is indispensable to secure public order until the conclusion of the treaty of peace." (Thiebaut to Hay, 4 October 1898, *Foreign Relations, 1898*, 816.) For Protocol No. 1, reporting the meeting of 1 October 1898, see *PPC*, roll 1. For the description of the second session, see Reid Diary, 3 October 1898, in Morgan, ed., *Making Peace With Spain*, 53. For Protocol No. 2, 3 October 1898, reporting this meeting, see *PPC*, roll 1.

2. For Reid to McKinley, 4 October 1898, see Charles S. Olcott, *The Life of William McKinley* (Boston and New York, 1916), vol. 2, pp. 123–134. Reid explained the Spanish strategy of delay in his diary, 3 October 1898, in Morgan, ed., *Making Peace With Spain*, 50, 52–53. One of the Spanish delegates, the Marqués de Villa-Urrutia, later confirmed that Montero Ríos sought to encourage European intervention and possibly also arbitration through delaying methods (see Marqués de Villa-Urrutia, *Palique diplomático. Recuerdos de un embajador* [Madrid, 1923], 113). For Coletta's views, see his "The Peace Negotiations and the Treaty of Paris," 139, 142.

3. For the concerns of the commission dealing with the evacuation of Cuba, see Hay to Day, 6 October 1898, in *Foreign Relations, 1898*, 918. For the exchange on this matter, see Day to Hay, 7 October 1898, in *ibid.*, 922; and Hay to Day, 9 October 1898, in *ibid.*, 922–923. The American group in Havana rejected all the Spanish claims and insisted upon their views (see Blanco to Girón, 7 October 1898, *Spanish Diplomatic Documents*, 250–251). For the exchange on the Puerto Rican matter, see McKinley to Day, 7 October 1898, in *Foreign Relations, 1898*, 923; and Day to McKinley, 7 October 1898, in *ibid*. For the procedure for protests, see Montero Ríos to Almodóvar (letter), 7 October 1898, *Spanish Diplomatic Documents*, 285–286; and Reid Diary, 7 October 1898, Morgan, ed., in *Making Peace With Spain*, 61.

4. For the debt issue, see Montero Ríos to Almodóvar, 5 October 1898, *Spanish Diplomatic Documents*, 281–282. The American delegation had information that Spain would attempt to saddle the $400 million on either Cuba or the United States (Coletta, "The Peace Negotiations and the Treaty of Paris," 136). For the Foreign Minister's reply, see Almodóvar to Montero Ríos, 6 October 1898, *ibid.*, 283. The Marqués de Villa-Urrutia claimed later that Montero Ríos thought the debt question exaggerated in importance (Marqués de Villa-Urrutia, *Palique diplomático*, 114).

5. For the formal session of 3 October 1898, see Protocol No. 3, *PPC*, roll 1. For Day's

statement to Washington of his intentions, see Day to Hay (No. 7), 8 October 1898, in *Foreign Relations, 1898*, 924. Approval came in Hay to Day, 8 October 1898, in *ibid.*, 925. Senator Gray's views are discussed in Day to Hay (No. 9), in *ibid.*, 927. Support for Day's position on relinquishment came in Hay to Day, 13 October 1898, in *ibid.* For the discussion of October 14 see Montero Ríos to Almodóvar, 15 October 1898, *Spanish Diplomatic Documents*, 290–291. Hay's proposal to utilize the wording of the protocol in the treaty is mentioned in Day to Hay (No. 10), 17 October 1898, *Foreign Relations, 1898*, 928. Spanish opposition is evident in Montero Ríos to Almodóvar, 17 October 1898, *Spanish Diplomatic Documents*, 291.

6. Reid Diary, 18 October 1898, in Morgan, ed., *Making Peace With Spain*, 87–88. Reid was the only American who spoke French and could communicate with the French-speaking Spaniards without an interpreter. (Bingham Duncan, *Whitelaw Reid: Journalist, Politician, Diplomat* [Athens, Ga., 1975], 187).

7. For the plan to concede the American demands under protest, see Montero Ríos to Almodóvar, 18 October 1898, in *Spanish Diplomatic Documents*, 293–294. For the Foreign Minister's alternative, see Almodóvar to Montero Ríos, 21 October 1898, in *ibid.*, 293.

8. For the account of the intimate dinner, see Reid Diary, 20 October 1898, in Morgan, ed., *Making Peace With Spain*, 94–96. For the formal session of the negotiators, see Protocol No. 7, 21 October 1898, and No. 8, 24 October 1898, in *PPC*, roll 1. A new Spanish proposal, substantively unchanged from prior proposals, is discussed in Montero Ríos to Almodóvar, 21 October 1898, in *Spanish Diplomatic Documents*, 292; and Montero Ríos to Almodóvar, 22 October 1898, in *ibid.*, 295–296. The American scheme is discussed in Day to Hay (No. 13), 22 October 1898, *Foreign Relations, 1898*, 930. Day later proposed a minor alteration: "Under the circumstances," he cabled to Hay, "we deem it important, while refusing to assume Cuban debt, to express readiness to incorporate in treaty properly guarded stipulations, acknowledging and assuming any legal responsibility to which we are by our own declaration and course of conduct committed." (Day to Hay [No. 14], 22 October 1898, in *ibid.*) For a report of the meeting on October 24, see Montero Ríos to Almodóvar, 24 October 1898, *Spanish Diplomatic Documents*, 296.

9. Day's proposition is in Day to Hay (No. 15), 25 October 1898, in *Foreign Relations, 1898*, 931. The President's decision is in Hay to Day, 25 October 1898, in *ibid.*, 932.

10. For the Spanish scheme, see Montero Ríos to Almodóvar, 25 October 1898, in *Spanish Diplomatic Documents*, 297–299. For various reports of León y Castillo's conversations, see León y Castillo to Almodóvar, 25 October 1898, in *ibid.*, 299; Reid Diary, 25 October 1898, in Morgan, ed., *Making Peace With Spain*, 114–117; Day to Hay (Special No. 17A), 27 October 1898, *Foreign Relations, 1898*, 936; and León y Castillo to Almodóvar, 27 October 1898, *Spanish Diplomatic Documents*, 301–302.

11. For the Spanish action, see Day to Hay (No. 18), *Foreign Relations, 1898*, 937; and Montero Ríos to Almodóvar, 27 October 1898, *Spanish Diplomatic Documents*, 304–305. For Day's report of the enterprise, see Day to Hay (No. 17A), 27 October 1898, *Foreign Relations, 1898*, 936–937. See also Montero Ríos to Almodóvar, 28 October 1898, *Spanish Diplomatic Documents*, 305–307. Senator Gray shared Day's view that Reid's hints to León y Castillo had influenced the Spanish delegation (Reid Diary, 26 October 1898, in Morgan, ed., *Making Peace With Spain*, 120. The entry reads, "Senator Gray pressed my elbow as the meaning of the document finally was disclosed and whispered: 'There is the result of your conversation with the Spanish Ambassador.'") For Montero Ríos's views on proper procedure, see Montero Ríos to Almodóvar, 27 October 1898, *Spanish Diplomatic Documents*,

303–304. See also Eugenio Montero Ríos, *El tratado de París. Conferencias pronunciadas en al círculo de la Unión Mercantil en los días 22, 24 y 27 Febrero 1904* (Madrid, 1904), 59–60. For meetings of the conference at this time, see Protocols No. 9, 26 October 1898, and No. 10, 27 October 1898, in *PPC,* roll 1.

12. For a general summary of the hearings, see Margaret Leech, *In the Days of McKinley* (New York, 1959), 339–341. See also Reid Diary, 4 October 1898, in Morgan, ed., *Making Peace With Spain,* 55, 58; Day to Hay (No. 2), 4 October 1898, in *Foreign Relations, 1898,* 917; Hay to Day, 5 October 1898, in *ibid.*; Day to Hay (No. 3), 6 October 1898, in *ibid.,* 918–922; Reid Diary, 8 October 1898, in Morgan, ed., *Making Peace With Spain,* 64–65; Hay to Day (No. 8), 9 October 1898, *Foreign Relations, 1898,* 925–927; Reid Diary, 14 October 1898, in Morgan, ed., *Making Peace With Spain,* 73–74; and William Reynolds Braisted, *The United States Navy in the Pacific, 1897-1909* (Austin, 1958), 53–54.

13. The views of commission members were summarized in Day to Hay (No. 16), 25 October 1898, *Foreign Relations, 1898,* 932–935. See also Leech, *In the Days of McKinley,* 341. Reid had earlier observed some alteration in Day's initial position (Reid diary, 1 October 1898, in Morgan, ed., *Making Peace With Spain,* 44). For the expansionist views of Cushman K. Davis, see Dwight Richard Coy, "Cushman K. Davis and American Foreign Policy, 1887-1900" (Dissertation, University of Minnesota, 1965), 269–276.

14. Leech, *In the Days of McKinley,* 334–336.

15. The quotation concerning the contradiction between American expansion and reduction of military power, is in *ibid.,* 334. The speech at Tama, Iowa is in *Speeches and Addresses of William McKinley: From March 1, 1897, to May 30, 1900* (New York, 1900), 90–91. The speech at Boone, Iowa is in *ibid.,* 95.

16. For the talk at Omaha, see *ibid.,* 105. See also Morgan, *William McKinley and His America,* 407. The Ottumwa speech is in *Speeches and Adresses of William McKinley,* 115. For the speech at Springfield, see *ibid.,* 127–128. For the speech at Chicago, see *ibid.,* 131.

17. For the speech at Chicago, see *ibid.,* 134.

18. The conversation with Schurman is in Leech, *In the Days of McKinley,* 344. For a discussion of alternatives to annexation of all the Philippines and their probable consequences, see *ibid.,* 327–328. See also Richard Hofstadter, "Manifest Destiny in the Philippines," in Daniel Aaron, ed., *America in Crisis: Fourteen Crucial Episodes in American History* (New York, 1952), 187. Because McKinley held his decision so close, revealing his inner thoughts to no one, it is impossible to completely rule out other interpretations of his course. Scholars of radical persuasion, whether Marxist-oriented or not, generally hold that McKinley intended from the first to use the war situation to acquire an overseas empire. The para-Marxist "New Left" school of historians argues that McKinley sought access to overseas markets in order to solve domestic economic problems of overproduction, and that an empire would resolve burgeoning class conflict at home. Some historians of moderate outlook, such as H. Wayne Morgan, agree with radicals that McKinley had annexation in mind at least from the time of Dewey's victory at Manila Bay: "He was . . . creating support for this policy through his tour, his careful public attitude, his instructions to the Peace Commission, and within his own party and Administration." John A. S. Grenville and George Berkeley Young come to essentially the same conclusion: McKinley "waited for the annexationist sentiment to win overwhelming support in the country so that the American people and the Senate might support his own firm policy." Ernest R. May argues a different position, one close to that expressed in this work. He believes that concern about the Filipino insurgents—but more especially fear of coming into conflict with public sentiment as he had done just prior to the outbreak of the war—moved McKinley to his decision: "Earlier, when dealing with the Cuban issue, he had sought to escape

public clamor and pursue safe, cautious courses defined by himself and conservative statesmen and businessmen around him. After the crisis that brought on the war, he wanted only to hear the people's wishes and obey.'' If the President hoped during the spring and early summer of 1898 for a quick victory to head off demands for expansion, or if he thought that the annexation of Puerto Rico might satiate the desire for territory, he soon learned his error. By August, 1898, a poll published in the magazine *Public Opinion* showed that 43 percent of the respondents favored retention of the Philippines whereas only 24.5 percent were opposed to this policy. At this point 34.4 percent were "wavering," a term that indicated leaning towards retention. Whatever other disagreements, no historian disputes the judgment that popular expansionist sentiment grew by leaps and bounds during the latter months of 1898 and early weeks of 1899, when the treaty was being negotiated and then taken up in the Senate. The enduring question is the motivation of this public enthusiasm. Expansion had aroused no public response for a generation and more prior to 1898, despite the dedicated efforts of a most talented group of imperialist publicists—Alfred Thayer Mahan, Josiah Strong, John W. Burgess, Henry Cabot Lodge among them. For Morgan's views, see his *Making Peace With Spain*, 102. He develops this thesis in other places, notably in *William McKinley and His America* (Syracuse, 1963), 398–399; and *America's Road to Empire: The War With Spain and Overseas Expansion* (New York, London, and Sydney, 1965), 75–76. For the views of John A. S. Grenville and George Berkeley Young, see their *Politics, Strategy, and American Diplomacy: Studies in Foreign Policy, 1873-1917* (New Haven and London, 1966), 287–288. For the views of May, see his *Imperial Democracy: The Emergence of America as a Great Power* (New York, 1961), 259–260. The public opinion poll is described in Hofstadter, "Manifest Destiny in the Philippines," 187–188.

19. Henry S. Pritchett, "Some Recollections of President McKinley and the Cuban Intervention," *North American Review* 189 (March, 1909): 400–401.

20. Long to unidentified neighbor, 1 November 1898, quoted in Lawrence Shaw Mayo, ed., *America of Yesterday: As Reflected in the Diary of John Davis Long* (Boston, 1923), 213–215. Students of McKinley's eventual decision to annex the entire Philippine archipelago should consider the importance of his accomplishment during the war in gaining national trust. The war made him a popular and even revered leader; he did not wish to sacrifice that position. As Margaret Leech wrote, "Millions of Americans who did not endorse McKinley's policies and would never cast a vote for him had come to trust his intention to shape the government's course for the benefit of all the people, without partisan bias or sectional prejudice." In this connection she noted the effect of McKinley's policy of appointing two Confederate generals to major commands during the war. (Leech, *In the Days of McKinley*, 229.)

21. For the President's decision, see Hay to Day, 26 October 1898, in *Foreign Relations, 1898*, 935. For the Secretary of State's emendations, see Hay to Day, 28 October 1898, in *ibid.*, 937–938. Hay's reasons for not opposing McKinley's decision to annex the Philippines are given in Kenton J. Clymer, *John Hay: The Gentleman as Diplomat* (Ann Arbor, Mich., 1975), 133.

22. For Gray's feelings, see Reid Diary, 26 October 1898, in Morgan, ed., *Making Peace With Spain*, 119. Hay notified Day that the instruction of October 28 had been approved by all Cabinet members except Secretary Long, who was in Massachusetts. He had a kind word for the commission: "Let me add your course has the warm approval of us all." (Hay to Day, 28 October 1898, *Foreign Relations, 1898*, 938.) For Gray's decision to support the President in Paris, see Reid Diary, 29 October 1898, in Morgan, ed., *Making Peace With Spain*, 128.

23. For the American announcement that the United States wished to annex the entire Philippine Islands, see Day to Hay (No. 19), 29 October 1898, in *Foreign Relations*,

1898, 938; Hay to Day, 30 October 1898, in *ibid.*; and Montero Ríos to Almodóvar, 31 October 1898, in *Spanish Diplomatic Documents*, 307. For the reactions of the leader of the Spanish delegation, see Montero Ríos to Almodóvar, 1 November 1898, in *ibid.*, 310. See also Montero Ríos to Almodóvar, 2 November 1898, in *ibid.* For the instructions to the Spanish delegation, see Almodóvar to Montero Ríos, 3 November 1898, in *ibid.*, 311–312. The message to the Spanish ambassador is Almodóvar to León y Castillo, 3 November 1898, in *ibid.*, 313.

24. For Gray's views, see Reid Diary, 1 November 1898, in Morgan, ed., *Making Peace With Spain*, 132. For Frye's cable, see Frye to Adee for McKinley, 30 October 1898, *Foreign Relations, 1898*, 939.

25. For the President's response, see Hay to Frye, 1 November 1898, in *Foreign Relations, 1898*, pp. 939–940.

26. For the commission's decision that it could not pursue a claim based on conquest, see Day to Adee for McKinley, 3 November 1898, in *ibid.*, 940. See also Reid Diary, 31 October 1898, in Morgan, ed., *Making Peace With Spain*, 129.

27. For McKinley's views, see Hay to Day, 3 November 1898, in *Foreign Relations, 1898*, 940. Day's response and the President's reply are in Day to Adee for McKinley, 4 November 1898, in *ibid.*, 941; and Hay to Day, 5 November 1898, in *ibid.*

28. For the peace commission's meeting, see Protocol No. 12, 4 November 1898, in *PPC*, roll 1. The Spanish case against the claim by right of conquest is mentioned in Day to Hay (No. 20), 5 November 1898, in *Foreign Relations, 1898*, 942–943; and Montero Ríos to Almodóvar, 4 November 1898, in *Spanish Diplomatic Documents*, 313. Montero Ríos's arguments against the idea of a development company are in Montero Ríos to Almodóvar, 5 November 1898, in *ibid.*, 313–316. The Foreign Minister's response is in Almodóvar to Montero Ríos, 7 November 1898, in *ibid.*, 316.

29. For the meeting of the commissions, see Protocol No. 13, 9 November 1898, in *PPC*, roll 1. The American rejection of the Spanish arguments is noted in Day to Hay (No. 21), 9 November 1898, *Foreign Relations, 1898*, 943–944; Montero Ríos to Almodóvar, 9 November 1898, in *Spanish Diplomatic Documents*, 318. The Spanish Foreign Minister's instructions are in Almodóvar to Montero Ríos, 10 November 1898, in *ibid.*, 319. The exchange concerning a proposal of arbitration is in Montero Ríos to Almodóvar (letter), 10 November 1898, in *ibid.*, 321–322; Montero Ríos to Almodóvar, 11 November 1898, in *ibid.*, 319–320; and Almodóvar to Montero Ríos, 11 November 1898, in *ibid.*, 320. See also Almodóvar to Montero Ríos, 12 November 1898, in *ibid.*, 322–323.

30. American Peace Commission to Hay (No. 23 special), 11 November 1898 in *Foreign Relations, 1898*, 945–948.

31. Hay to Day, 13 November 1898, in *ibid.*, 948–949.

32. For activity prior to November 21, 1898, see Montero Ríos to Almodóvar, 16 November 1898, *Spanish Diplomatic Documents*, 323–324; Moore to Hay (No. 25), 18 November 1898, in *Foreign Relations, 1898*, 951–954; Day to McKinley (special), 18 November 1898, in *ibid.*, 955–957; and Hay to Day, 19 November 1898, in *ibid.*, 957. Reid's views are in Reid to McKinley, 15 November 1898, quoted in Olcott, *McKinley*, vol. 2, p. 126. Day's views are in Day to Adee for McKinley, 15 November 1898, in *Foreign Relations, 1898*, 949. McKinley's firm position is evident in Hay to Day, 15 November 1898, in *ibid.* For the text of the American proposition and approval of it see Moore to Day (No. 24 special), 15 November 1898, in *ibid.*, 950–951; and Hay to Day, 16 November 1898, in *ibid.*, 951. For the meeting of the peace commissions on 21 November 1898, see Protocol No. 15 in *PPC*, roll 1. It should be remembered that the congressional elections had taken place early in November and that the Republican Party had achieved a clear victory. Spanish hopes that McKinley would suffer a political rebuff at home came

to naught. The Spanish report of the American proposition is in Montero Ríos to Almodóvar, 21 November 1898, in *Spanish Diplomatic Documents*, 325–326. See also Montero Ríos to Almodóvar, 22 November 1898, in *ibid.*, 328; Day to Hay (No. 26), 21 November 1898, *Foreign Relations, 1898*, 958; and Montero Ríos to Almodóvar (letter), 23 November 1898, *Spanish Diplomatic Documents*, 330. Day's notice of what lay ahead if the Spanish delegation refused the American proposition is in Day to Adee for McKinley, 22 November 1898, in *Foreign Relations, 1898*, 958. Approval of the delegation's position came in Hay to Day, 22 November 1898, in *ibid.* Reid made a special visit to León y Castillo to inform him of the ultimatum and emphasize its significance. In his report of the visit the Spanish ambassador wrote, "He [Reid] added that the instructions which had been received from the Washington government were such that what to his great regret was proposed to-day were their final words. I thanked him for the information, but answered nothing, all discussion being now unprofitable and useless, under the circumstances." (León y Castillo to Almodóvar, 22 November 1898, *Spanish Diplomatic Documents*, 326.)

33. For Bradford's testimony, see Braisted, *United States Navy in the Pacific, 1897–1909*, 53–54. When the war was still on the question of the Carolines had arisen on occasion. Early in May Admiral Stephen B. Luce and Henry Cabot Lodge exchanged letters in which they agreed upon the wisdom of occupying both the Carolines and the Ladrones. McKinley authorized the occupation of Guam, southernmost of the Ladrones, and it was duly seized on June 20, 1898. During the earlier phase of the war the Naval War Board inquired into the possibility of acquiring a coaling station in the Pacific halfway between Honolulu and Manila. In this connection the possibility of there being a supply of coal at Yap, one of the principal islands in the Carolines, came to the attention of the Board. For the most part, however, the question of the Carolines remained secondary; Guam provided the necessary wartime communications. For the exchange between Luce and Lodge, see Luce to Lodge, 10 May 1898, and Lodge to Luce, 12 May 1898, quoted in Albert Gleaves, *Life and Letters of Stephen B. Luce, U.S. Navy, Founder of the Naval War College* (New York and London, 1925), 279–280. For the interest in a coaling station, see Sicard to Long (for the Naval War Board), 3 June 1898, *RG 38*, NRC 371; Sicard to Bradford, 4 June 1898, *RG 38*, NRC 371, vol. 1, p. 238. Cable companies desirous of landing rights on Kusaie were effective in interesting McKinley in the matter. Hay informed Day on November 1, 1898, "The President thinks that the possession of this island [Kusaie] is desirable to us for cable purposes and is inclined to recommend that you try to acquire it by purchase. . . ." (*PPC*, roll 2). For information on the Carolines question, see James Thomas Murphy, Jr., "A History of American Diplomacy at the Paris Peace Conference of 1898" (Dissertation, American University, 1965), 86–100.

34. For early German interest in Pacific islands, see Braisted, *United States Navy in the Pacific, 1897–1909*, 34. For the Hay-Hatzfelt conversation, see Alfred L. P. Dennis, *Adventures in American Diplomacy 1896–1906* (New York, 1969 reprint edition), 93–94. Hay then talked with the British ambassador to Germany, Lascelles, who claimed that Germany would not take any steps to cause a disagreement with the United States. See, for another such view Hay to McKinley, 14 July 1898, quoted in Olcott, *McKinley*, vol. 2, pp. 133–135.

35. For the message from the attaché, see Barber to Long, rec. 12 July 1898, *RG 38*, Entry 100. See also Braisted, *United States Navy in the Pacific, 1897–1909*, 39. The rebuke came in Long to Barber, 13 July 1898, *RG 38*, Entry 100. For the message to Dewey, see Long to Dewey, 19 July 1898, RG 80, E194.

36. For White's suggestion to Richthofen, see White to Day, 30 July 1898, quoted in Dennis, *Adventures in Diplomacy*, 94–96. The implied reprimand to White is in Day to White, 15 August 1898, quoted in *ibid.*, 96–98.

37. For the original German inquiry, see J. Fred Rippy, *Latin America in World Politics: An Outline Survey*, 3d edition (New York, 1942), 172–173. For the inquiry leading to the secret understanding, see Richthofen to Radowitz, 13 August 1898, quoted in Leon María Guerrero, "The Kaiser and the Philippines," *Philippine Studies* (October, 1961), vol. 1, p. 600. For the understanding itself, see Pearl E. Quinn, "The Diplomatic Struggle for the Carolines, 1898," *Pacific Historical Review* 14 (September, 1945): 295–296. Even Belgium manifested interest in capitalizing on the demise of Spanish influence in the Pacific (see Arnold Blumberg, "Belgium and a Philippine Protectorate: A Stillborn Plan," *Asian Studies* 10 [December, 1972]: 336–343).

38. The contacts with Reid are mentioned in the Reid Diary, 8 November 1898, and 13 November 1898, in Morgan, ed., *Making Peace With Spain*, 141–142, 148–149. For the request from Münster to Reid regarding use of his name, see Reid Diary, 25 November 1898, in *ibid.*, 163–164. Word of German interest in the Carolines at this time also came from Berlin (Coletta, "The Peace Negotiations and the Treaty of Paris," 156–157).

39. For views within the Spanish delegation, see Montero Ríos to Almodóvar, 21 November 1898, in *Spanish Diplomatic Documents*, 326. See also Montero Ríos to Almodóvar (letter), 21 November 1898, in *ibid.*, 328–329; Marqués de Villa-Urrutia, *Palique diplomático*, 116; and Montero Ríos, *El tratado de París*, 65–66. For Almodóvar's concerns, see Almodóvar to Montero Ríos, 22 November 1898, in *Spanish Diplomatic Documents*, 327. Montero Ríos's suggestions of November 24 included (1) cession of the entire archipelago, including Mindanao and Joló, for $100 million in compensation for public works in the Philippines and Antilles; (2) cession of Kusaie in the Carolines, the right to land cables in the Carolines or Marianas, and cession of the Philippines with the exception of Mindanao and Joló for compensation of $50 million; (3) gratuitous cession of the archipelago including Mindanao and Joló with submission of the debt question to arbitration (Montero Ríos to Almodóvar, 24 November 1898, in *ibid.*, 331). For permission to submit the propositions to the Americans and the response from Paris, see Almodóvar to Montero Ríos, 24 November 1898, in *ibid.*, 332; and Montero Ríos to Almodóvar, 25 November 1898, in *ibid.*, 332–333.

40. For expressions of views, see Moore to Hay (No. 27), 25 November 1898, in *Foreign Relations, 1898*, 958–959; Davis to Hay (No. 28), 25 November 1898, in *ibid.*, 958–959; and Gray to Hay (No. 29), 25 November 1898, in *ibid.*, 959–960. For the President's reaction, see Hay to Day, 25 November 1898, in *ibid.*, 960. Montero Ríos reported the American rejection of his propositions in Montero Ríos to Almodóvar, 26 November 1898, *Spanish Diplomatic Documents*, 335.

41. Orders to sign are in Almodovar to Montero Ríos, 25 November 1898, in *Spanish Diplomatic Documents*, 333–334. See also Montero Ríos, *El tratado de París*, 66. For the exchange between Paris and Madrid, see Montero Ríos to Almodóvar, 26 November 1898, in *Spanish Diplomatic Documents*, 334–335; and Almodóvar to Montero Ríos, 27 November 1898, in *ibid.*, 336. The Sagasta Ministry held to its final decision when Montero Ríos sought clarification about what he was to accept. Almodóvar informed him that he was to accept only what the United States demanded, not whatever additional provisions it might desire that were not covered by the ultimatum. He had in mind the question of the Carolines and other matters. (Montero Ríos to Almodóvar, 27 November 1898, in *ibid.*, 337; Almodóvar to Montero Ríos, 27 November 1898, in *ibid.*; Montero Ríos to Almodóvar, 28 November 1898, in *ibid.*, 338–339; and Almodóvar to Montero Ríos, 28 November 1898, in *ibid.*) When Montero Ríos received orders to sign, he requested that secrecy be maintained in Madrid. He obviously did not want word of the Ministry's decision to prejudice any last-minute opportunities. (Montero Ríos to Almodóvar, 25 November 1898, in *ibid.*, 334.) Almodóvar replied, "But your excellency knows

how difficult it is for our press to judge what is due to public utility, as also the deficiencies of censorship. Therefore I had recourse to the remedy of contradictory notice, in order to disguise the plans of the Government and to give occasion for various interpretations'' (Almodóvar to Montero Ríos, 27 November 1898, in *ibid.*, 336).

42. For the Spanish concession see Montero Ríos to Almodóvar, 28 November 1898, in *Spanish Diplomatic Documents*, 339; Montero Ríos to Almodóvar, 28 November 1898, in *ibid.*, 339–341; and Day to Hay (No. 31), 29 November 1898, *Foreign Relations, 1898*, 961. For Reid's description, see Reid to McKinley, 29 November 1898, quoted in Olcott, *McKinley*, vol. 2, p. 128. Montero Ríos's effort to leave Paris is mentioned in the statesman's *El tratado de París*, 67.

43. For the lengthy correspondence dealing with Kusaie, see Almodóvar to Montero Ríos, 29 November 1898, *Spanish Diplomatic Documents*, 341–342; Moore to Day (No. 32), 29 November 1898, *Foreign Relations, 1898*, 962; Coletta, "The Peace Negotiations and the Treaty of Paris," 157; Montero Ríos to Almodóvar, 30 November 1898, *Spanish Diplomatic Documents*, 342–343; Moore to Day (No. 33), 30 November 1898, in *Foreign Relations, 1898*, 962–963; Hay to Day, 1 December 1898, in *ibid.*, 963; Montero Ríos to Almodóvar, 2 December 1898, in *Spanish Diplomatic Documents*, 348; Montero Ríos to Almodóvar, 2 December 1898, in *ibid.*, 349; Almodóvar to Montero Ríos, 2 December 1898, in *ibid.*, 350; Day to Hay, (No. 36), 3 December 1898, in *Foreign Relations, 1898*, 964; Hay to Day, 3 December 1898, in *ibid.*, which definitively rejected a *quid pro quo*, the commercial concessions for Kusaie, cable landing rights, religious freedom in the Carolines, release of political prisoners, and revival of treaties in force prior to the war; Almodóvar to Montero Ríos, 4 December 1898, in *Spanish Diplomatic Documents*, 353–354; Montero Ríos to Almodóvar, 5 December 1898, in *ibid.*, 354–355; Day to Hay (No. 37), 8 December 1898, *Foreign Relations, 1898*, 964; and Montero Ríos to Almodóvar, in *Spanish Diplomatic Documents*, 359–360. For return of troops at American expense and prisoner exchanges, see Montero Ríos to Almodóvar, 29 November 1898, in *ibid.*, 341; Almodóvar to Montero Ríos, 30 November 1898, in *ibid.*, 343; Montero Ríos to Almodóvar, 2 December 1898, in *ibid.*, 348–349; Almodóvar to Montero Ríos, 2 December 1898, in *ibid.*, 350; and Montero Ríos to Almodóvar, 6 December 1898, in *ibid.*, 355–356. For the rejection of the proposition regarding preservation of public order, see Montero Ríos to Almodóvar, 30 November 1898, in *ibid.*, 345; Almodóvar to Montero Ríos, 1 December 1898, in *ibid.*, 346; Montero Ríos to Almodóvar, 3 December 1898, in *ibid.*, 351; and Montero Ríos to Almodóvar, 5 December 1898, in *ibid.*, 355. For correspondence regarding the attempt to arrange arbitration of the dispute over the *Maine*, see Almodóvar to Montero Ríos, 7 December 1898, in *ibid.*, 358; Montero Ríos to Almodóvar, 7 December 1898, in *ibid.*, 359; and Montero Ríos to Almodóvar, 10 December 1898, in *ibid.*, 361–362.

44. For the final session of the conference, see Protocol No. 22, 10 December 1898, *PPC*, roll 1. For the formal agreement, see Moore to Hay, 10 December 1898, in *Foreign Relations, 1898*, 965; Day to Hay, 10 December 1898, in *ibid.*; Montero Ríos to Almodóvar, 10 December 1898, *Spanish Diplomatic Documents*, 361–362. Count Herbert Münster, the German ambassador in Paris, assured Reid on December 9, 1898 that the Spanish delegation would sign the treaty. He had word to this effect from Madrid. (Reid Diary, 9 December 1898, in Morgan, ed., *Making Peace with Spain*, 223.) Obviously the Germans had an interest in an early settlement; otherwise their desire for the Carolines, the Palaus, and the Marianas might be frustrated. The treaty clauses were: (1) Spain to relinquish sovereignty in Cuba with the United States to discharge obligations under international law for the protection of life and property as long as it occupied the island; (2) Spain to cede Puerto Rico and Guam; (3) Spain to cede the Philippine Islands, the United States to

pay $20 million within three months of the exchange of ratifications; (4) Spain to receive ten years of equal commercial treatment in the Philippine Islands from date of exchange of ratifications; (5) the United States to return Spanish troops from the Philippine Islands at its own expense, with soldiers to retain arms, evacuation to take place as prescribed for Cuba and Puerto Rico with completion date to be arranged by the two governments and with arrangements for negotiations to allow the United States to purchase certain military materials that remain in Spanish hands; (6) Spain to release prisoners of war and certain political prisoners, with the United States to release its prisoners of war and seek release of those held by the Filipino insurgents, the United States paying costs of return; (7) each power to renounce reciprocally indemnity claims; (8) Spain to receive public records and archives; (9) Spanish citizens to have freedom to remain in ceded or relinquished areas with provision for declaring permanent citizenship within a year, the United States to make arrangements for civil rights and political status of those in territories ceded to it; (10) freedom of religion guaranteed in areas ceded or relinquished; (11) Spanish citizens remaining in ceded or relinquished regions to be subject to local laws; (12) court proceedings pending at time of exchange of ratifications to be completed; (13) Spanish copyrights and patents to be protected; (14) Spain to have the right to establish consular offices in lost territories; (15) each country to assess the same amounts of port charges, subject to termination on six months' notice by either side; (16) the United States to assume obligations in Cuba only for the period of occupation, but to advise a Cuban government to continue these obligations; (17) specification of ratification procedure. (Treaty text, 10 December 1898, *Foreign Relations, 1898*, 831–840.) For the observations of Dawes, see his Diary, 10 December 1898, quoted in Bascom Timmons, ed., *Journal of the McKinley Years, by Charles G. Dawes* (Chicago, 1950), 176. For the observation of the Secretary of the Navy, see Long to Mrs. Long, quoted in Margaret Long, ed., *The Journal of John D. Long* (Rindge, N.H., 1956), 231.

45. For the German acquisition of the islands, see J. Fred Rippy, "The European Powers and the Spanish-American War," *James Sprunt Historical Studies*, 19 (Chapel Hill, N.C., 1927), 47; and Quinn, "Diplomatic Struggle for the Carolines," 301–302. See also Braisted, *United States Navy in the Pacific, 1897–1909*, 55–56; Jerónimo Bécker, *Historia de las relaciones exteriores de España durante el siglo XIX (Apuntes para una historia diplomática)*, Volume 3: *(1868-1900)* (Madrid, 1926), 947–948. For the views of Bülow, see Bernhard, Prince Von Bülow, *Memoirs of Prince Bülow*, Volume 1: *From Secretary of State to Imperial Chancellor 1897-1903* (Boston, 1931), 336. See also Jeannette Keim, *Forty Years of German-American Political Relations* (Philadelphia, 1919), 232–233.

46. For the views of Harold and Margaret Sprout, see *Toward a New Order of Sea Power: American Naval Policy and the World Scene, 1918-1922* (New York, 1969 reprint edition), 31. Earl S. Pomeroy attributes the failure of the United States to press for annexation of the Carolines to indifference at bottom. See his *Pacific Outpost: American Strategy in Guam and Micronesia* (Stanford, 1951), 16. For the Samoan arrangements—agreed to in April, 1899 and completed on December 2, 1899, with exchange of ratifications between the three parties on February 16, 1900—see George Herbert Ryden, *The Foreign Policy of the United States in Relation to Samoa* (New Haven, 1928), 62, 571–572; Dennis, *Adventures in American Diplomacy*, 110–111; and Julius Pratt, *America's Colonial Experiment: How the United States Gained, Governed, and In Part Gave Away a Colonial Empire* (New York, 1951), 77–79.

47. For the view of Hay, see Hay to McKinley, 9 September 1898, quoted in Olcott, *McKinley*, vol. 2, p. 135. For the Spanish initiative regarding Gibraltar, see May, *Imperial Democracy*, 224–225. R. G. Neale's view is in his *Great Britain and United States Expansion: 1898-1900* (East Lansing, Mich., 1966), 132.

48. For the acquisition of Wake Island, see Rippy, "The European Powers and the Spanish-American War," 50; Pratt, *America's Colonial Experiment*, 76–77; and Braisted, *United States Navy in the Pacific, 1897–1909*, 56–57.

49. Reid to McKinley, 15 November 1898, quoted in Olcott, *McKinley*, vol. 2, p. 127.

50. The poll is discussed in Hofstadter, "Manifest Destiny in the Philippines," 188. For the anecdote about McKinley, see George F. Hoar, *Autobiography of Seventy Years* (London, 1904), vol. 1, p. 315.

51. For the Vest resolution, see William J. Pomeroy, *American Neo-Colonialism: Its Emergence in the Philippines and Asia* (New York, 1970), 58–59. This view reflected one interpretation of the provision in the Constitution that "Congress shall have power to dispose of and make rules and regulations respecting the territory and other property belonging to the United States." For the Mason resolution, see *ibid.*, 59. For the Bacon resolution, see Coletta, "The Peace Negotiations and the Treaty of Paris," 161–162. Senator Gorman's activities are mentioned in Morgan, *William McKinley and His America*, 418–419.

52. For some discussion of these matters, see Morgan, *America's Road to Empire*, 101. Paolo E. Coletta has made an exhaustive study of Bryan's position on the treaty. He disagrees with those who believe that Bryan's actions reflected a desire to make expansion the issue in the presidential campaign of 1900. See his *William Jennings Bryan*, Volume 1: *Political Evangelist 1860–1908* (Lincoln, Nebr. 1964), 237. He summarizes his views conveniently in "The Peace Negotiations and the Treaty of Paris." See also a number of Coletta's articles: "Bryan, McKinley, and the Treaty of Paris," *Pacific Historical Review* 26 (May, 1957): 131–146; "McKinley, the Peace Negotiations, and the Acquisition of the Philippines," *Pacific Historical Review* 30 (November, 1961): 341–350; and "Bryan, Anti-Imperialism and Missionary Diplomacy," *Nebraska History* 44 (September, 1963): 166–187. Senator Hoar stated as well as anyone the interpretation that Coletta is at pains to refute. In his autobiography he noted that Bryan came to Washington during the treaty debate to drum up support for the treaty because he thought "the Democratic Party could not hope to win a victory on the financial questions at stake after they had been beaten on them in a time of adversity; and . . . they must have this issue for the coming campaign." (Hoar, *Autobiography*, vol. 2, p. 322.)

53. McKinley is quoted in Leech, *In the Days of McKinley*, 358. For the reasons for the outcome of February 6, see Coletta, "The Peace Negotiations and the Treaty of Paris," 161–162. The Bacon amendment met defeat by a vote of thirty to twenty-nine on February 14, with Vice-President Garrett Hobart breaking a tie vote. The McEnery resolution passed the Senate by a vote of twenty-six to twenty-two, but never came up in the House of Representatives. (Pomeroy, *American Neo-Colonialism*, 61–62.)

54. For events in Spain, see Juan del Arco, *Montero Ríos* (Madrid, 1947), 127; Coletta, "The Peace Negotiations and the Treaty of Paris," 164–165; Bécker, *Historia de las relaciones exteriores de España*, vol. 3, pp. 937–938.

55. For these developments, see Melchor Fernández Almagro, *Historia política de la España contemporánea*, Volume 2: *La regencia de doña María Cristina de Austria durante la menor edad de su hijo don Alfonso XIII* (Madrid, 1959), 897–900; and Frederick P. Pike, *Hispanismo, 1898–1936: Spanish Conservatives and Liberals and Their Relations With Spanish America* (Notre Dame and London, 1971), 49–55. Pío Rioja's remark is quoted in Rita Maria Cancio, *The Function of Maria Cristina of Austria's Regency (1885–1902), in Preserving the Spanish Monarchy* (Mexico City, 1957), 68. Salisbury's comment is quoted in Fernando León y Castillo, *Mis tiempos* (Madrid, 1921), vol. 2, p. 118. The ancient military code of Spain led to punishment for some of the war leaders and absolution for others. The leaders in the Philippines at the time of the capitulation, Admiral Montojo and General Jáudenes, were convicted by court-martial of negligence and separated from the ser-

vice. The leaders in Cuba at the time of the capitulation, Admiral Cervera and General Toral, fared better, both managing to gain acquittal. (Gabriel Maura Gamazo, *Historia crítica del reinado de don Alfonso XIII durante su menoridad bajo la regencia de su madre doña María Cristina de Austria* (Barcelona, 1925), vol. 2, p. 51.

56. For the comment before the Home Market Club, see *Speeches and Addresses of William McKinley,* 192. The analysis in this paragraph follows that of Coletta in "The Peace Negotiations and the Treaty of Paris," 164. For the comment to the Massachusetts legislature, see *ibid.,* 196–197. The interpretation of McKinley's motives accords with that of Ernest R. May, expressed in various of his writings.

57. Quoted in Whitelaw Reid, *The Treaty of Paris: Some Speeches on Its Policy and Scope* (New York, 1899), 11.

CONCLUSION

1. For a summary statement of this view, see David F. Trask, "President William McKinley as Strategist in 1898," in *Proceedings of The Citadel Conference on War and Diplomacy 1977* (n.p., 1979), 111–116.

2. Note the authoritative judgment of the historian James A. Huston: "Fraught with confusion, wasted motion, and lack of co-ordination as it was, the mobilization of men and material was little short of remarkable. Starting almost from scratch the Army had under arms more than a quarter of a million men within four months. Less than five weeks after the first call for troops an expeditionary force sailed from San Francisco for the Philippines, and less than two weeks later a force set out for the invasion of Cuba. It should be recalled that at the beginning of the Civil War, after the Preisdent's call for militia on 15 April and the call for volunteers on 3 May 1861, only 16,161 enlisted men had been mustered into service by the end of May; in 1898, with the first call for volunteers on 23 April and the second on 25 May, 163,626 enlisted men had been mustered into service by the end of May. The total strength of 274,717 officers and men that the Army reached in August 1898 was not attained in the Civil War until November." *The Sinews of War: Army Logistics 1775–1953* (Washington, D.C., 1966), 280.

3. For the announcement of the Dodge Commission, see *Speeches and Addresses of William McKinley: From March 1, 1897 to May 30, 1900* (New York, 1900), 83. For McKinley's political motives, see a memorandum written by Major General John M. Schofield entitled "Some of My Experiences With the Administration of President McKinley," 16 September 1898, Papers of General John M. Schofield, box 93, p. 34, Manuscript Division, Library of Congress, Washington, D.C. Members of the Dodge Commission were General Grenville M. Dodge (presiding), Iowa; Colonel James A. Sexton, Illinois, Captain Evan P. Howell, Georgia; Urban A. Woodbury, Vermont; Brigadier General John M. Wilson, Chief of Engineers; General James A. Beaver, Pennsylvania; Major General Alexander McD. McCook; and Dr. Phineas S. Conner, Ohio (*IC,* vol. 1, pp. 107–111). Its conclusions are in *ibid.,* 111–116.

4. For the rejection of Miles's charges by the Dodge Commission, see *ibid.,* 153–168. For the report of the investigation into "embalmed beef," see U.S. Senate, *Food Furnished by Subsistence Department to Troops in the Field; Letter From the Secretary of War, Transmitting, in Response to Resolution of the Senate of March 30, 1900, the Original Record of the Court of Inquiry Relative to the Unfitness for Issue of Certain Articles of Food Furnished by the Subsistence Department to Troops in the Field During the Recent Operations in Cuba and Porto Rico* (3 Volumes), 56th Cong., 1st Sess., Sen. Doc. No. 270 (Washington, D.C., 1900). For its conclusion, see vol. 2, pp. 1,892–1,893.

5. For the Root reforms, see Marvin A. Kreidberg and Merton G. Henry, *History of*

Military Mobilization in the United States Army 1775-1945 (Washington, D.C., 1955), 173, 176–179; Richard W. Leopold, *Elihu Root and the Conservative Tradition* (Boston, 1954), 38–42; Russell F. Weigley, *History of the United States Army* (New York, 1967), 314–318; Robert Bacon and James Brown Scott, eds., *The Military and Colonial Policy of the United States: Addresses and Reports by Elihu Root* (Cambridge, Mass., 1916), 4, 401–410, 411–415, 417–420; Major General William Harding Carter, *Creation of the American General Staff; Personal Narrative of the General Staff System of the American Army* (Washington, D.C., 1924); and James A. Hewes, Jr., *From Root to McNamara: Army Organization and Administration, 1900-1963* (Washington, D.C., 1975).

6. For the court of inquiry that investigated the behavior of Admiral Schley during the war with Spain, see U.S. Navy Department, *Record of Proceedings of a Court of Inquiry in the Case of Rear-Admiral Winfield S. Schley, U.S. Navy: Convened at the Navy-Yard, Washington, D.C., September 12, 1901*, 2 volumes (Washington, D.C., 1902). For the conclusions of the court, including a dissent from the majority by Admiral George Dewey, see *ibid.*, vol. 2, pp. 1,829–1,830. For modern summaries of developments in the U.S. Navy between the war with Spain and the onset of the Office of the Chief of Naval Operations, see three essays in Kenneth J. Hagan, ed., *In Peace and War: Interpretations of American Naval History, 1775-1978* (Westport, Conn., and London, 1978): Ronald Spector, "The Triumph of Professional Ideology: The U.S. Navy in the 1890s," 174–185; Richard W. Turk, "Defending the 'New Empire, 1900–1914," 186–204; and David F. Trask, "The American Navy in a World at War, 1914–1919," 205–220.

7. For an early expression of the consequences of the war with Spain, see Brooks Adams, "The Spanish War and the Equilibrium of the World," *Forum* 25 (1898): 641–651. A cogent critique of careless generalizations about American imperialism at the turn of the century is in James A. Field, Jr., "American Imperialism: The 'Worst Chapter' in Almost Any Book," *American Historical Review* 83 (June, 1978): 644–668. Richard G. Challener judiciously surveys the consequences of the war with Spain in terms of relations between force and diplomacy in *Admirals, Generals, and American Foreign Policy 1898-1914* (Princeton, 1973).

Index